Dear reader,

thank you for your trust and for buying this book. I'm always greatly moved when I see someone with a desire to get closer to God, to accept Him as their Lord and Saviour and invite Him into their everyday life, to each and every part of it.

By studying His Word systematically, each and every day is a day we live with Him, we let Him illuminate the path of our lives.

I am glad that together we can walk this wonderful path. I ask each of you to pray for me, and I, for my part, promise to remember each and every one of you in my prayers.

Before every encounter with the Lord in His Word, let us pray to the Holy Spirit, may He guide us, for He is the true author of this Word and, at the same time, He knows us better than anyone else, better even than we know ourselves. May He speak directly to our hearts, our minds. May He enter with His Word into our lives, into all our affairs - the pleasant ones as well as the difficult ones

After praying to the Holy Spirit, let us read a given passage of the Scripture. Let's do this slowly, we may even repeat it several times. The Lord will speak to us sometimes through a whole passage, sometimes through a single sentence or word. Sometimes He speaks immediately, sometimes He speaks subtly, after a long time.

Let's write down what the Lord wants to say through the given passage. His Word will sustain us as we remember it throughout the day, act and live with it, with HIM.

May The Lord in Heaven bless you, dear reader. Amen.

CONTENTS

PRINCIPAL CELEBRATIONS OF THE LITURGICAL YEAR 2024

First Sunday of Advent	December 3, 2023
Ash Wednesday	February 14, 2024
Easter Sunday	March 31, 2024
The Ascension of the Lord [Thursday]	May 9, 2024
Pentecost Sunday	May 19, 2024
The Most Holy Body and Blood of Christ	June 2, 2024
First Sunday of Advent	December 1, 2024

CYCLES — LECTIONARY FOR MASS

Sunday Cycle	YEAR B	December 3, 2023 to November 24, 2024
Weekday Cycle	CYCLE II	January 9 to February 13, 2024 May 20 to November 30, 2024
Sunday Cycle	YEAR C	December 1, 2024 to November 23, 2025

Monday, January 1, 2024
SOLEMNITY OF MARY, THE HOLY MOTHER OF GOD

First Reading: Numbers 6: 22-27

22 Yahweh spoke to Moses, saying, 23 "Speak to Aaron and to his sons, saying, 'This is how you shall bless the children of Israel.' You shall tell them, 24 'Yahweh bless you, and keep you. 25 Yahweh make his face to shine on you, and be gracious to you. 26 Yahweh lift up his face toward you, and give you peace.' 27 "So they shall put my name on the children of Israel; and I will bless them."

Responsorial Psalm: Psalms 67: 2-3, 5, 6, 8

2 That your way may be known on earth,
and your salvation among all nations,
3 let the peoples praise you, God.
Let all the peoples praise you.
5 Let the peoples praise you, God.
Let all the peoples praise you.
6 The earth has yielded its increase.
God, even our own God, will bless us.
8 God will bless us.
All the ends of the earth shall fear him.

Second Reading: Galatians 4: 4-7

4 But when the fullness of the time came, God sent out his Son, born to a woman, born under the law, 5 that he might redeem those who were under the law, that we might receive the adoption as children. 6 And because you are children, God sent out the Spirit of his Son into your hearts, crying, "Abba,† Father!" 7 So you are no longer a bondservant, but a son; and if a son, then an heir of God through Christ.

Gospel: Luke 2: 16-21

16 They came with haste and found both Mary and Joseph, and the baby was lying in the feeding trough. 17 When they saw it, they publicized widely the saying which was spoken to them about this child. 18 All who heard it wondered at the things which were spoken to them by the shepherds. 19 But Mary kept all these sayings, pondering them in her heart. 20 The shepherds returned, glorifying and praising God for all the things that they had heard and seen, just as it was told them. 21 When eight days were fulfilled for the

circumcision of the child, his name was called Jesus, which was given by the angel before he was conceived in the womb.

Thuesday, January 2, 2024
Saints Basil the Great and Gregory Nazianzen, Bishops and Doctors of the Church

First Reading: First John 2:22-28

22 Who is the liar but he who denies that Jesus is the Christ? This is the Antichrist, he who denies the Father and the Son. 23 Whoever denies the Son doesn't have the Father. He who confesses the Son has the Father also. 24 Therefore, as for you, let that remain in you which you heard from the beginning. If that which you heard from the beginning remains in you, you also will remain in the Son, and in the Father. 25 This is the promise which he promised us, the eternal life.
26 These things I have written to you concerning those who would lead you astray. 27 As for you, the anointing which you received from him remains in you, and you don't need for anyone to teach you. But as his anointing teaches you concerning all things, and is true, and is no lie, and even as it taught you, you will remain in him.
28 Now, little children, remain in him, that when he appears, we may have boldness and not be ashamed before him at his coming.

Responsorial Psalm: Psalms 98: 1-4

1 Sing to Yahweh a new song,
for he has done marvelous things!
His right hand and his holy arm have worked salvation for him.
2 Yahweh has made known his salvation.
He has openly shown his righteousness in the sight of the nations.

3 He has remembered his loving kindness and his faithfulness toward the house of Israel. All the ends of the earth have seen the salvation of our God.
4 Make a joyful noise to Yahweh, all the earth! Burst out and sing for joy, yes, sing praises!

Gospel: John 1: 19-28

19 This is John's testimony, when the Jews sent priests and Levites from Jerusalem to ask him, "Who are you?"
20 He declared, and didn't deny, but he declared, "I am not the Christ."
21 They asked him, "What then? Are you Elijah?" He said, "I am not." "Are you the prophet?" He answered, "No."
22 They said therefore to him, "Who are you? Give us an answer to take back to those who sent us. What do you say about yourself?"
23 He said, "I am the voice of one crying in the wilderness, 'Make straight the way of the Lord,'* as Isaiah the prophet said."
24 The ones who had been sent were from the Pharisees. 25 They asked him, "Why then do you baptize if you are not the Christ, nor Elijah, nor the prophet?"
26 John answered them, "I baptize in water, but among you stands one whom you don't know. 27 He is the one who comes after me, who is preferred before me, whose sandal strap I'm not worthy to loosen." 28 These things were done in Bethany beyond the Jordan, where John was baptizing.

1. Invite the Holy Spirit into this reading, asking the Author of Scripture to speak to you through His Word
2. Read today's passage as many times as you need, take your time
3. Write down (below) what the Lord is saying to you today
4. Live with this Word in your heart through the day

Wednesday, January 3, 2024
Christmas Weekday/ Holy Name of Jesus

First Reading: First John 2: 29 – 3: 6

29 If you know that he is righteous, you know that everyone who practices righteousness has been born of him.

1 See how great a love the Father has given to us, that we should be called children of God! For this cause the world doesn't know us, because it didn't know him. 2 Beloved, now we are children of God. It is not yet revealed what we will be; but we know that when he is revealed, we will be like him, for we will see him just as he is. 3 Everyone who has this hope set on him purifies himself, even as he is pure.

4 Everyone who sins also commits lawlessness. Sin is lawlessness. 5 You know that he was revealed to take away our sins, and no sin is in him. 6 Whoever remains in him doesn't sin. Whoever sins hasn't seen him and doesn't know him.

Responsorial Psalm: Psalms 98: 1, 3-6

1 Sing to Yahweh a new song,
for he has done marvelous things!
His right hand and his holy arm have worked salvation for him.
3 He has remembered his loving kindness and his faithfulness toward the house of Israel.
All the ends of the earth have seen the salvation of our God.
4 Make a joyful noise to Yahweh, all the earth!
Burst out and sing for joy, yes, sing praises!
5 Sing praises to Yahweh with the harp,
with the harp and the voice of melody.
6 With trumpets and sound of the ram's horn,
make a joyful noise before the King, Yahweh.

Gospel: John 1: 29-34

29 The next day, he saw Jesus coming to him, and said, "Behold,§ the Lamb of God, who takes away the sin of the world! 30 This is he of whom I said, 'After me comes a man who is preferred before me, for he was before me.' 31 I didn't know him, but for this reason I came baptizing in water, that he would be revealed to Israel." 32 John testified, saying, "I have seen the Spirit descending like a dove out of heaven, and it remained on him. 33 I didn't recognize him, but he who sent me to baptize in water said to me, 'On whomever you will see the Spirit descending and remaining on him is he who baptizes in the Holy Spirit.' 34 I have seen and have testified that this is the Son of God."

1. Invite the Holy Spirit into this reading, asking the Author of Scripture to speak to you through His Word
2. Read today's passage as many times as you need, take your time
3. Write down (below) what the Lord is saying to you today
4. Live with this Word in your heart through the day

_____

_____

Thursday, January 4, 2024
Elizabeth Ann Seton, Religious Obligatory Memorial

First Reading: First John 3: 7-10

7 Little children, let no one lead you astray. He who does righteousness is righteous, even as he is righteous. 8 He who sins is of the devil, for the devil has been sinning from the beginning. To this end the Son of God was revealed: that he might destroy the works of the devil. 9 Whoever is born of God doesn't commit sin, because his seed remains in him, and he can't sin, because he is born of God. 10 In this the children of God are revealed, and the children of the devil. Whoever doesn't do righteousness is not of God, neither is he who doesn't love his brother.

Responsorial Psalm: 98: 1, 7-8, 9

1 Sing to Yahweh a new song,
for he has done marvelous things!
His right hand and his holy arm have worked salvation for him.
7 Let the sea roar with its fullness;
the world, and those who dwell therein.
8 Let the rivers clap their hands.
Let the mountains sing for joy together.
9 Let them sing before Yahweh,
for he comes to judge the earth.
He will judge the world with righteousness,
and the peoples with equity.

Gospel: John 1: 35-42

35 Again, the next day, John was standing with two of his disciples, 36 and he looked at Jesus as he walked, and said, "Behold, the Lamb of God!" 37 The two disciples heard him speak, and they followed Jesus. 38 Jesus turned and saw them following, and said to them, "What are you looking for?"
They said to him, "Rabbi" (which is to say, being interpreted, Teacher), "where are you staying?"
39 He said to them, "Come and see."
They came and saw where he was staying, and they stayed with him that day. It was about the tenth hour.† 40 One of the two who heard John and followed him was Andrew, Simon Peter's brother. 41 He first found his own brother, Simon, and said to him, "We have found the Messiah!" (which is, being interpreted, Christ‡). 42 He brought him to Jesus. Jesus

looked at him and said, "You are Simon the son of Jonah. You shall be called Cephas" (which is by interpretation, Peter).

Friday, January 5, 2024
John Neumann, Bishop Obligatory Memorial

First Reading: First John 3: 11-21

11 For this is the message which you heard from the beginning, that we should love one another— 12 unlike Cain, who was of the evil one and killed his brother. Why did he kill him? Because his deeds were evil, and his brother's righteous.
13 Don't be surprised, my brothers, if the world hates you. 14 We know that we have passed out of death into life, because we love the brothers. He who doesn't love his brother remains in death. 15 Whoever hates his brother is a murderer, and you know that no murderer has eternal life remaining in him.
16 By this we know love, because he laid down his life for us. And we ought to lay down our lives for the brothers. 17 But whoever has the world's goods and sees his brother in need, then closes his heart of compassion against him, how does God's love remain in him?
18 My little children, let's not love in word only, or with the tongue only, but in deed and truth. 19 And by this we know that we are of the truth and persuade our hearts before him, 20 because if our heart condemns us, God is greater than our heart, and knows all things. 21 Beloved, if our hearts don't condemn us, we have boldness toward God

Responsorial Psalm: 100: 1b-2, 3, 4, 5

1 Shout for joy to Yahweh, all you lands!
2 Serve Yahweh with gladness.
Come before his presence with singing.
3 Know that Yahweh, he is God.

It is he who has made us, and we are his.
We are his people, and the sheep of his pasture.
4 Enter into his gates with thanksgiving,
and into his courts with praise.
Give thanks to him, and bless his name.
5 For Yahweh is good.
His loving kindness endures forever,
his faithfulness to all generations.

Gospel: John 1: 43-51

43 On the next day, he was determined to go out into Galilee, and he found Philip. Jesus said to him, "Follow me." 44 Now Philip was from Bethsaida, the city of Andrew and Peter.
45 Philip found Nathanael, and said to him, "We have found him of whom Moses in the law and also the prophets, wrote: Jesus of Nazareth, the son of Joseph."
46 Nathanael said to him, "Can any good thing come out of Nazareth?"
Philip said to him, "Come and see."
47 Jesus saw Nathanael coming to him, and said about him, "Behold, an Israelite indeed, in whom is no deceit!"
48 Nathanael said to him, "How do you know me?"
Jesus answered him, "Before Philip called you, when you were under the fig tree, I saw you."
49 Nathanael answered him, "Rabbi, you are the Son of God! You are King of Israel!"
50 Jesus answered him, "Because I told you, 'I saw you underneath the fig tree,' do you believe? You will see greater things than these!" 51 He said to him, "Most certainly, I tell you all, hereafter you will see heaven opened, and the angels of God ascending and descending on the Son of Man."

1. Invite the Holy Spirit into this reading, asking the Author of Scripture to speak to you through His Word
2. Read today's passage as many times as you need, take your time
3. Write down (below) what the Lord is saying to you today
4. Live with this Word in your heart through the day

_____

_____

Saturday, January 6, 2024
Saint André Bessette, Religious

First Reading: First John 5: 5-13

5 Who is he who overcomes the world, but he who believes that Jesus is the Son of God? 6 This is he who came by water and blood, Jesus Christ; not with the water only, but with the water and the blood. It is the Spirit who testifies, because the Spirit is the truth. 7 For there are three who testify:† 8 the Spirit, the water, and the blood; and the three agree as one. 9 If we receive the witness of men, the witness of God is greater; for this is God's testimony which he has testified concerning his Son. 10 He who believes in the Son of God has the testimony in himself. He who doesn't believe God has made him a liar, because he has not believed in the testimony that God has given concerning his Son. 11 The testimony is this: that God gave to us eternal life, and this life is in his Son. 12 He who has the Son has the life. He who doesn't have God's Son doesn't have the life.
13 These things I have written to you who believe in the name of the Son of God, that you may know that you have eternal life, and that you may continue to believe in the name of the Son of God.

Responsorial Psalm: 147: 12-15, 19-20

12 Praise Yahweh, Jerusalem!
Praise your God, Zion!
13 For he has strengthened the bars of your gates.
He has blessed your children within you.
14 He makes peace in your borders.
He fills you with the finest of the wheat.
15 He sends out his commandment to the earth.
19 He shows his word to Jacob,
his statutes and his ordinances to Israel.
20 He has not done this for just any nation.
They don't know his ordinances.
Praise Yah!

Gospel: Mark 1: 7-11

7 He preached, saying, "After me comes he who is mightier than I, the thong of whose sandals I am not worthy to stoop down and loosen. 8 I baptized you in§ water, but he will baptize you in the Holy Spirit."
9 In those days, Jesus came from Nazareth of Galilee, and was baptized by John in the Jordan. 10 Immediately coming up from the water, he saw the heavens parting and the Spirit descending on him like a dove. 11 A voice came out of the sky, "You are my beloved Son, in whom I am well pleased."

1. Invite the Holy Spirit into this reading, asking the Author of Scripture to speak to you through His Word
2. Read today's passage as many times as you need, take your time
3. Write down (below) what the Lord is saying to you today
4. Live with this Word in your heart through the day

_____

_____

Sunday, January 7, 2024
Epiphany of the Lord Solemnity

First Reading: Isaiah 60: 1-6

1 "Arise, shine; for your light has come, and Yahweh's glory has risen on you!
2 For behold, darkness will cover the earth, and thick darkness the peoples;
but Yahweh will arise on you, and his glory shall be seen on you.
3 Nations will come to your light, and kings to the brightness of your rising.
4 "Lift up your eyes all around, and see: they all gather themselves together.
They come to you. Your sons will come from far away, and your daughters will be carried in arms.
5 Then you shall see and be radiant, and your heart will thrill and be enlarged;
because the abundance of the sea will be turned to you. The wealth of the nations will come to you.
6 A multitude of camels will cover you, the dromedaries of Midian and Ephah.
All from Sheba will come. They will bring gold and frankincense,
and will proclaim the praises of Yahweh.

Responsorial Psalm: Psalms 72: 1-2, 7-8, 10-13

1 God, give the king your justice;
your righteousness to the royal son.
2 He will judge your people with righteousness,
and your poor with justice.
7 In his days, the righteous shall flourish,
and abundance of peace, until the moon is no more.
8 He shall have dominion also from sea to sea,
from the River to the ends of the earth.

10 The kings of Tarshish and of the islands will bring tribute.

The kings of Sheba and Seba shall offer gifts.

11 Yes, all kings shall fall down before him.

All nations shall serve him.

12 For he will deliver the needy when he cries;

the poor, who has no helper.

13 He will have pity on the poor and needy.

He will save the souls of the needy.

Second Reading: Ephesians 3: 2-3a, 5-6

2 if it is so that you have heard of the administration of that grace of God which was given me toward you, 3 how that by revelation the mystery was made known to me, 5 which in other generations was not made known to the children of men, as it has now been revealed to his holy apostles and prophets in the Spirit, 6 that the Gentiles are fellow heirs and fellow members of the body, and fellow partakers of his promise in Christ Jesus through the Good News

Gospel: Matthew 2: 1-12

1 Now when Jesus was born in Bethlehem of Judea in the days of King Herod, behold, wise men† from the east came to Jerusalem, saying, 2 "Where is he who is born King of the Jews? For we saw his star in the east, and have come to worship him." 3 When King Herod heard it, he was troubled, and all Jerusalem with him. 4 Gathering together all the chief priests and scribes of the people, he asked them where the Christ would be born. 5 They said to him, "In Bethlehem of Judea, for this is written through the prophet,

6 'You Bethlehem, land of Judah,

are in no way least among the princes of Judah;

for out of you shall come a governor

who shall shepherd my people, Israel.' "*

7 Then Herod secretly called the wise men, and learned from them exactly what time the star appeared. 8 He sent them to Bethlehem, and said, "Go and search diligently for the young child. When you have found him, bring me word, so that I also may come and worship him."

9 They, having heard the king, went their way; and behold, the star, which they saw in the east, went before them until it came and stood over where the young child was. 10 When they saw the star, they rejoiced with exceedingly great joy. 11 They came into the house and saw the young child with Mary, his mother, and they fell down and worshiped him. Opening their treasures, they offered to him gifts: gold, frankincense, and myrrh. 12 Being warned in a dream not to return to Herod, they went back to their own country another way.

1. Invite the Holy Spirit into this reading, asking the Author of Scripture to speak to you through His Word
2. Read today's passage as many times as you need, take your time
3. Write down (below) what the Lord is saying to you today
4. Live with this Word in your heart through the day

_____

_____

Monday, January 8, 2024
Baptism of the Lord Feast

First Reading: Isaiah 55: 1-11

1 "Hey! Come, everyone who thirsts, to the waters!
Come, he who has no money, buy, and eat!
Yes, come, buy wine and milk without money and without price.
2 Why do you spend money for that which is not bread,
and your labor for that which doesn't satisfy?
Listen diligently to me, and eat that which is good,
and let your soul delight itself in richness.
3 Turn your ear, and come to me.
Hear, and your soul will live.
I will make an everlasting covenant with you, even the sure mercies of David.
4 Behold, I have given him for a witness to the peoples,
a leader and commander to the peoples.
5 Behold, you shall call a nation that you don't know;
and a nation that didn't know you shall run to you,
because of Yahweh your God,
and for the Holy One of Israel;
for he has glorified you."
 6 Seek Yahweh while he may be found.
Call on him while he is near.
7 Let the wicked forsake his way,
and the unrighteous man his thoughts.
Let him return to Yahweh, and he will have mercy on him,
to our God, for he will freely pardon.

8 "For my thoughts are not your thoughts,
and your ways are not my ways," says Yahweh.
9 "For as the heavens are higher than the earth,
so are my ways higher than your ways,
and my thoughts than your thoughts.
10 For as the rain comes down and the snow from the sky,
and doesn't return there, but waters the earth,
and makes it grow and bud,
and gives seed to the sower and bread to the eater;
11 so is my word that goes out of my mouth:
it will not return to me void,
but it will accomplish that which I please,
and it will prosper in the thing I sent it to do.

Responsorial Psalm: Isaiah 12: 2-6

2 Behold, God is my salvation. I will trust, and will not be afraid; for Yah, Yahweh, is my strength and song; and he has become my salvation." 3 Therefore with joy you will draw water out of the wells of salvation.
4 In that day you will say, "Give thanks to Yahweh! Call on his name! Declare his doings among the peoples! Proclaim that his name is exalted!
5 Sing to Yahweh, for he has done excellent things! Let this be known in all the earth! 6 Cry aloud and shout, you inhabitant of Zion, for the Holy One of Israel is great among you!"

Second Reading: First John 5: 1-9

1 Whoever believes that Jesus is the Christ has been born of God. Whoever loves the Father also loves the child who is born of him. 2 By this we know that we love the children of God, when we love God and keep his commandments. 3 For this is loving God, that we keep his commandments. His commandments are not grievous. 4 For whatever is born of God overcomes the world. This is the victory that has overcome the world: your faith. 5 Who is he who overcomes the world, but he who believes that Jesus is the Son of God?
6 This is he who came by water and blood, Jesus Christ; not with the water only, but with the water and the blood. It is the Spirit who testifies, because the Spirit is the truth. 7 For there are three who testify:† 8 the Spirit, the water, and the blood; and the three agree as one. 9 If we receive the witness of men, the witness of God is greater; for this is God's testimony which he has testified concerning his Son.

Gospel: Mark 1: 7-11

7 He preached, saying, "After me comes he who is mightier than I, the thong of whose sandals I am not worthy to stoop down and loosen. 8 I baptized you in§ water, but he will baptize you in the Holy Spirit."

9 In those days, Jesus came from Nazareth of Galilee, and was baptized by John in the Jordan. 10 Immediately coming up from the water, he saw the heavens parting and the Spirit descending on him like a dove. 11 A voice came out of the sky, "You are my beloved Son, in whom I am well pleased."

1. Invite the Holy Spirit into this reading, asking the Author of Scripture to speak to you through His Word
2. Read today's passage as many times as you need, take your time
3. Write down (below) what the Lord is saying to you today
4. Live with this Word in your heart through the day

_____

_____

Tuesday, January 9, 2024

First Reading: First Samuel 1: 9-20

9 So Hannah rose up after they had finished eating and drinking in Shiloh. Now Eli the priest was sitting on his seat by the doorpost of Yahweh's temple. 10 She was in bitterness of soul, and prayed to Yahweh, weeping bitterly. 11 She vowed a vow, and said, "Yahweh of Armies, if you will indeed look at the affliction of your servant and remember me, and not forget your servant, but will give to your servant a boy, then I will give him to Yahweh all the days of his life, and no razor shall come on his head."

12 As she continued praying before Yahweh, Eli saw her mouth. 13 Now Hannah spoke in her heart. Only her lips moved, but her voice was not heard. Therefore Eli thought she was drunk. 14 Eli said to her, "How long will you be drunk? Get rid of your wine!"

15 Hannah answered, "No, my lord, I am a woman of a sorrowful spirit. I have not been drinking wine or strong drink, but I poured out my soul before Yahweh. 16 Don't consider your servant a wicked woman; for I have been speaking out of the abundance of my complaint and my provocation."

17 Then Eli answered, "Go in peace; and may the God‡ of Israel grant your petition that you have asked of him."

18 She said, "Let your servant find favor in your sight." So the woman went her way and ate; and her facial expression wasn't sad any more.

19 They rose up in the morning early and worshiped Yahweh, then returned and came to their house to Ramah. Then Elkanah knew Hannah his wife; and Yahweh remembered her.

20 When the time had come, Hannah conceived, and bore a son; and she named him Samuel,§ saying, "Because I have asked him of Yahweh."

Responsorial Psalm: First Samuel 2: 1, 4-8

1 Hannah prayed, and said,
"My heart exults in Yahweh!
My horn is exalted in Yahweh.
My mouth is enlarged over my enemies,
because I rejoice in your salvation.
4 "The bows of the mighty men are broken.
Those who stumbled are armed with strength.
5 Those who were full have hired themselves out for bread.
Those who were hungry are satisfied.
Yes, the barren has borne seven.
She who has many children languishes.
6 "Yahweh kills and makes alive.
He brings down to Sheol† and brings up.
7 Yahweh makes poor and makes rich.
He brings low, he also lifts up.
8 He raises up the poor out of the dust.
He lifts up the needy from the dunghill
to make them sit with princes
and inherit the throne of glory.
For the pillars of the earth are Yahweh's.
He has set the world on them.

Gospel: Mark 1: 21-28

21 They went into Capernaum, and immediately on the Sabbath day he entered into the synagogue and taught. 22 They were astonished at his teaching, for he taught them as having authority, and not as the scribes. 23 Immediately there was in their synagogue a man with an unclean spirit, and he cried out, 24 saying, "Ha! What do we have to do with you, Jesus, you Nazarene? Have you come to destroy us? I know who you are: the Holy One of God!"
25 Jesus rebuked him, saying, "Be quiet, and come out of him!"
26 The unclean spirit, convulsing him and crying with a loud voice, came out of him. 27 They were all amazed, so that they questioned among themselves, saying, "What is this?

A new teaching? For with authority he commands even the unclean spirits, and they obey him!" 28 The report of him went out immediately everywhere into all the region of Galilee and its surrounding area.

1. Invite the Holy Spirit into this reading, asking the Author of Scripture to speak to you through His Word
2. Read today's passage as many times as you need, take your time
3. Write down (below) what the Lord is saying to you today
4. Live with this Word in your heart through the day

Wednesday, January 10, 2024

First Reading: First Samuel 3: 1-10, 19-20

1 The child Samuel ministered to Yahweh before Eli. Yahweh's word was rare in those days. There were not many visions, then. 2 At that time, when Eli was laid down in his place (now his eyes had begun to grow dim, so that he could not see), 3 and God's lamp hadn't yet gone out, and Samuel had laid down in Yahweh's temple where God's ark was, 4 Yahweh called Samuel. He said, "Here I am."
5 He ran to Eli and said, "Here I am; for you called me."
He said, "I didn't call. Lie down again."
He went and lay down. 6 Yahweh called yet again, "Samuel!"
Samuel arose and went to Eli and said, "Here I am; for you called me."
He answered, "I didn't call, my son. Lie down again." 7 Now Samuel didn't yet know Yahweh, neither was Yahweh's word yet revealed to him. 8 Yahweh called Samuel again the third time. He arose and went to Eli and said, "Here I am; for you called me."
Eli perceived that Yahweh had called the child. 9 Therefore Eli said to Samuel, "Go, lie down. It shall be, if he calls you, that you shall say, 'Speak, Yahweh; for your servant hears.' " So Samuel went and lay down in his place. 10 Yahweh came, and stood, and called as at other times, "Samuel! Samuel!"
Then Samuel said, "Speak; for your servant hears."
19 Samuel grew, and Yahweh was with him and let none of his words fall to the ground. 20 All Israel from Dan even to Beersheba knew that Samuel was established to be a prophet of Yahweh.

Responsorial Psalm: Psalms 40: 2, 5, 7-10

2 He brought me up also out of a horrible pit,
out of the miry clay.
He set my feet on a rock,
and gave me a firm place to stand.
5 Many, Yahweh, my God, are the wonderful works which you have done,
and your thoughts which are toward us.
They can't be declared back to you.
If I would declare and speak of them, they are more than can be counted.
7 Then I said, "Behold, I have come.
It is written about me in the book in the scroll.
8 I delight to do your will, my God.
Yes, your law is within my heart."
9 I have proclaimed glad news of righteousness in the great assembly.
Behold, I will not seal my lips, Yahweh, you know.
10 I have not hidden your righteousness within my heart.
I have declared your faithfulness and your salvation.
I have not concealed your loving kindness and your truth from the great assembly.

Gospel: Mark 1: 29-39

29 Immediately, when they had come out of the synagogue, they came into the house of Simon and Andrew, with James and John. 30 Now Simon's wife's mother lay sick with a fever, and immediately they told him about her. 31 He came and took her by the hand and raised her up. The fever left her immediately,† and she served them.
32 At evening, when the sun had set, they brought to him all who were sick and those who were possessed by demons. 33 All the city was gathered together at the door. 34 He healed many who were sick with various diseases and cast out many demons. He didn't allow the demons to speak, because they knew him.
35 Early in the morning, while it was still dark, he rose up and went out, and departed into a deserted place, and prayed there. 36 Simon and those who were with him searched for him. 37 They found him and told him, "Everyone is looking for you."
38 He said to them, "Let's go elsewhere into the next towns, that I may preach there also, because I came out for this reason." 39 He went into their synagogues throughout all Galilee, preaching and casting out demons.

1. Invite the Holy Spirit into this reading, asking the Author of Scripture to speak to you through His Word
2. Read today's passage as many times as you need, take your time
3. Write down (below) what the Lord is saying to you today

Thursday, January 11, 2024

First Reading: First Samuel 4: 1-11

1 The word of Samuel came to all Israel.
Now Israel went out against the Philistines to battle, and encamped beside Ebenezer; and the Philistines encamped in Aphek. 2 The Philistines put themselves in array against Israel. When they joined battle, Israel was defeated by the Philistines, who killed about four thousand men of the army in the field. 3 When the people had come into the camp, the elders of Israel said, "Why has Yahweh defeated us today before the Philistines? Let's get the ark of Yahweh's covenant out of Shiloh and bring it to us, that it may come among us and save us out of the hand of our enemies."
4 So the people sent to Shiloh, and they brought from there the ark of the covenant of Yahweh of Armies, who sits above the cherubim; and the two sons of Eli, Hophni and Phinehas, were there with the ark of the covenant of God. 5 When the ark of Yahweh's covenant came into the camp, all Israel shouted with a great shout, so that the earth resounded. 6 When the Philistines heard the noise of the shout, they said, "What does the noise of this great shout in the camp of the Hebrews mean?" They understood that Yahweh's ark had come into the camp. 7 The Philistines were afraid, for they said, "God has come into the camp." They said, "Woe to us! For there has not been such a thing before. 8 Woe to us! Who shall deliver us out of the hand of these mighty gods? These are the gods that struck the Egyptians with all kinds of plagues in the wilderness. 9 Be strong and behave like men, O you Philistines, that you not be servants to the Hebrews, as they have been to you. Strengthen yourselves like men, and fight!" 10 The Philistines fought, and Israel was defeated, and each man fled to his tent. There was a very great slaughter; for thirty thousand footmen of Israel fell. 11 God's ark was taken; and the two sons of Eli, Hophni and Phinehas, were slain.

Responsorial Psalm: Psalms 44: 10-11, 14-15, 24-25

10 You make us turn back from the adversary.
Those who hate us take plunder for themselves.
11 You have made us like sheep for food,

and have scattered us among the nations.
14 You make us a byword among the nations,
a shaking of the head among the peoples.
15 All day long my dishonor is before me,
and shame covers my face,
24 Why do you hide your face,
and forget our affliction and our oppression?
25 For our soul is bowed down to the dust.
Our body clings to the earth.

Gospel: Mark 1: 40-45

40 A leper came to him, begging him, kneeling down to him, and saying to him, "If you want to, you can make me clean."
41 Being moved with compassion, he stretched out his hand, and touched him, and said to him, "I want to. Be made clean." 42 When he had said this, immediately the leprosy departed from him and he was made clean. 43 He strictly warned him and immediately sent him out, 44 and said to him, "See that you say nothing to anybody, but go show yourself to the priest and offer for your cleansing the things which Moses commanded, for a testimony to them."
45 But he went out, and began to proclaim it much, and to spread about the matter, so that Jesus could no more openly enter into a city, but was outside in desert places. People came to him from everywhere.

1. Invite the Holy Spirit into this reading, asking the Author of Scripture to speak to you through His Word
2. Read today's passage as many times as you need, take your time
3. Write down (below) what the Lord is saying to you today
4. Live with this Word in your heart through the day

_____

_____

Friday, January 12, 2024

First Reading: First Samuel 8: 4-7, 10-22a

4 Then all the elders of Israel gathered themselves together and came to Samuel to Ramah. 5 They said to him, "Behold, you are old, and your sons don't walk in your ways. Now make us a king to judge us like all the nations." 6 But the thing displeased Samuel when they said, "Give us a king to judge us."

Samuel prayed to Yahweh. 7 Yahweh said to Samuel, "Listen to the voice of the people in all that they tell you; for they have not rejected you, but they have rejected me as the king over them.

10 Samuel told all Yahweh's words to the people who asked him for a king. 11 He said, "This will be the way of the king who shall reign over you: he will take your sons and appoint them as his servants, for his chariots and to be his horsemen; and they will run before his chariots. 12 He will appoint them to him for captains of thousands and captains of fifties; and he will assign some to plow his ground and to reap his harvest; and to make his instruments of war and the instruments of his chariots. 13 He will take your daughters to be perfumers, to be cooks, and to be bakers. 14 He will take your fields, your vineyards, and your olive groves, even your best, and give them to his servants. 15 He will take one tenth of your seed and of your vineyards, and give it to his officers and to his servants. 16 He will take your male servants, your female servants, your best young men, and your donkeys, and assign them to his own work. 17 He will take one tenth of your flocks; and you will be his servants. 18 You will cry out in that day because of your king whom you will have chosen for yourselves; and Yahweh will not answer you in that day."

19 But the people refused to listen to the voice of Samuel; and they said, "No, but we will have a king over us, 20 that we also may be like all the nations; and that our king may judge us, and go out before us, and fight our battles."

21 Samuel heard all the words of the people, and he rehearsed them in the ears of Yahweh. 22 Yahweh said to Samuel, "Listen to their voice, and make them a king."

Responsorial Psalm: Psalms 89: 16-19

16 In your name they rejoice all day.
In your righteousness, they are exalted.
17 For you are the glory of their strength.
In your favor, our horn will be exalted.
18 For our shield belongs to Yahweh,
our king to the Holy One of Israel.
19 Then you spoke in vision to your saints,
and said, "I have given strength to the warrior.
I have exalted a young man from the people.

Gospel: Mark 2: 1-12

1 When he entered again into Capernaum after some days, it was heard that he was at home. 2 Immediately many were gathered together, so that there was no more room, not even around the door; and he spoke the word to them. 3 Four people came, carrying a paralytic to him. 4 When they could not come near to him for the crowd, they removed the roof where he was. When they had broken it up, they let down the mat that the paralytic was lying on. 5 Jesus, seeing their faith, said to the paralytic, "Son, your sins are forgiven you."

6 But there were some of the scribes sitting there and reasoning in their hearts, 7 "Why does this man speak blasphemies like that? Who can forgive sins but God alone?"

8 Immediately Jesus, perceiving in his spirit that they so reasoned within themselves, said to them, "Why do you reason these things in your hearts? 9 Which is easier, to tell the paralytic, 'Your sins are forgiven;' or to say, 'Arise, and take up your bed, and walk'? 10 But that you may know that the Son of Man has authority on earth to forgive sins"—he said to the paralytic— 11 "I tell you, arise, take up your mat, and go to your house."

12 He arose, and immediately took up the mat and went out in front of them all, so that they were all amazed and glorified God, saying, "We never saw anything like this!"

1. Invite the Holy Spirit into this reading, asking the Author of Scripture to speak to you through His Word
2. Read today's passage as many times as you need, take your time
3. Write down (below) what the Lord is saying to you today
4. Live with this Word in your heart through the day

_____

_____

Saturday, January 13, 2024

First Reading: First Samuel 9: 1-4, 17-19; 10: 1

1 Now there was a man of Benjamin, whose name was Kish the son of Abiel, the son of Zeror, the son of Becorath, the son of Aphiah, the son of a Benjamite, a mighty man of valor. 2 He had a son whose name was Saul, an impressive young man; and there was not among the children of Israel a more handsome person than he. From his shoulders and upward he was taller than any of the people.

3 The donkeys of Kish, Saul's father, were lost. Kish said to Saul his son, "Now take one of the servants with you, and arise, go look for the donkeys." 4 He passed through the hill country of Ephraim, and passed through the land of Shalishah, but they didn't find them.

Then they passed through the land of Shaalim, and they weren't there. Then he passed through the land of the Benjamites, but they didn't find them.

17 When Samuel saw Saul, Yahweh said to him, "Behold, the man of whom I spoke to you! He will have authority over my people."

18 Then Saul approached Samuel in the gateway, and said, "Please tell me where the seer's house is."

19 Samuel answered Saul and said, "I am the seer. Go up before me to the high place, for you are to eat with me today. In the morning I will let you go and will tell you all that is in your heart.

1 Then Samuel took the vial of oil and poured it on his head, then kissed him and said, "Hasn't Yahweh anointed you to be prince over his inheritance?

Responsorial Psalm: Psalms 21: 2-7

2 You have given him his heart's desire,
and have not withheld the request of his lips.
3 For you meet him with the blessings of goodness.
You set a crown of fine gold on his head.
4 He asked life of you and you gave it to him,
even length of days forever and ever.
5 His glory is great in your salvation.
You lay honor and majesty on him.
6 For you make him most blessed forever.
You make him glad with joy in your presence.
7 For the king trusts in Yahweh.
Through the loving kindness of the Most High, he shall not be moved.

Gospel: Mark 2: 13-17

13 He went out again by the seaside. All the multitude came to him, and he taught them.
14 As he passed by, he saw Levi the son of Alphaeus sitting at the tax office. He said to him, "Follow me." And he arose and followed him.

15 He was reclining at the table in his house, and many tax collectors and sinners sat down with Jesus and his disciples, for there were many, and they followed him. 16 The scribes and the Pharisees, when they saw that he was eating with the sinners and tax collectors, said to his disciples, "Why is it that he eats and drinks with tax collectors and sinners?"

17 When Jesus heard it, he said to them, "Those who are healthy have no need for a physician, but those who are sick. I came not to call the righteous, but sinners to repentance."

1. Invite the Holy Spirit into this reading, asking the Author of Scripture to speak to you through His Word
2. Read today's passage as many times as you need, take your time
3. Write down (below) what the Lord is saying to you today
4. Live with this Word in your heart through the day

_____

_____

Sunday, January 14, 2024
Second Sunday in Ordinary Time

First Reading: First Samuel 3: 3b-10, 19

3 and God's lamp hadn't yet gone out, and Samuel had laid down in Yahweh's temple where God's ark was, 4 Yahweh called Samuel. He said, "Here I am."
5 He ran to Eli and said, "Here I am; for you called me."
He said, "I didn't call. Lie down again."
He went and lay down. 6 Yahweh called yet again, "Samuel!"
Samuel arose and went to Eli and said, "Here I am; for you called me."
He answered, "I didn't call, my son. Lie down again." 7 Now Samuel didn't yet know Yahweh, neither was Yahweh's word yet revealed to him. 8 Yahweh called Samuel again the third time. He arose and went to Eli and said, "Here I am; for you called me."
Eli perceived that Yahweh had called the child. 9 Therefore Eli said to Samuel, "Go, lie down. It shall be, if he calls you, that you shall say, 'Speak, Yahweh; for your servant hears.' " So Samuel went and lay down in his place. 10 Yahweh came, and stood, and called as at other times, "Samuel! Samuel!"
Then Samuel said, "Speak; for your servant hears."
19 Samuel grew, and Yahweh was with him and let none of his words fall to the ground.

Responsorial Psalm: Psalms 40: 2, 4ab, 7-10

2 He brought me up also out of a horrible pit,
out of the miry clay.
He set my feet on a rock,
and gave me a firm place to stand.
3 He has put a new song in my mouth, even praise to our God.
Many shall see it, and fear, and shall trust in Yahweh.

4 Blessed is the man who makes Yahweh his trust,

and doesn't respect the proud, nor such as turn away to lies.

7 Then I said, "Behold, I have come.

It is written about me in the book in the scroll.

8 I delight to do your will, my God.

Yes, your law is within my heart."

9 I have proclaimed glad news of righteousness in the great assembly.

Behold, I will not seal my lips, Yahweh, you know.

10 I have not hidden your righteousness within my heart.

I have declared your faithfulness and your salvation.

I have not concealed your loving kindness and your truth from the great assembly.

Second Reading: First Corinthians 6: 13c-15a, 17-20

13 But the body is not for sexual immorality, but for the Lord, and the Lord for the body. 14 Now God raised up the Lord, and will also raise us up by his power. 15 Don't you know that your bodies are members of Christ?

17 But he who is joined to the Lord is one spirit. 18 Flee sexual immorality! "Every sin that a man does is outside the body," but he who commits sexual immorality sins against his own body. 19 Or don't you know that your body is a temple of the Holy Spirit who is in you, whom you have from God? You are not your own, 20 for you were bought with a price. Therefore glorify God in your body and in your spirit, which are God's.

Gospel: John 1: 35-42

35 Again, the next day, John was standing with two of his disciples, 36 and he looked at Jesus as he walked, and said, "Behold, the Lamb of God!" 37 The two disciples heard him speak, and they followed Jesus. 38 Jesus turned and saw them following, and said to them, "What are you looking for?"

They said to him, "Rabbi" (which is to say, being interpreted, Teacher), "where are you staying?"

39 He said to them, "Come and see."

They came and saw where he was staying, and they stayed with him that day. It was about the tenth hour.† 40 One of the two who heard John and followed him was Andrew, Simon Peter's brother. 41 He first found his own brother, Simon, and said to him, "We have found the Messiah!" (which is, being interpreted, Christ‡). 42 He brought him to Jesus. Jesus looked at him and said, "You are Simon the son of Jonah. You shall be called Cephas" (which is by interpretation, Peter).

1. Invite the Holy Spirit into this reading, asking the Author of Scripture to speak to you through His Word

2. Read today's passage as many times as you need, take your time
3. Write down (below) what the Lord is saying to you today
4. Live with this Word in your heart through the day

Monday, January 15, 2024

First Reading: First Samuel 15: 16-23

16 Then Samuel said to Saul, "Stay, and I will tell you what Yahweh said to me last night." He said to him, "Say on."
17 Samuel said, "Though you were little in your own sight, weren't you made the head of the tribes of Israel? Yahweh anointed you king over Israel; 18 and Yahweh sent you on a journey, and said, 'Go, and utterly destroy the sinners the Amalekites, and fight against them until they are consumed.' 19 Why then didn't you obey Yahweh's voice, but took the plunder, and did that which was evil in Yahweh's sight?"
20 Saul said to Samuel, "But I have obeyed Yahweh's voice, and have gone the way which Yahweh sent me, and have brought Agag the king of Amalek, and have utterly destroyed the Amalekites. 21 But the people took of the plunder, sheep and cattle, the best of the devoted things, to sacrifice to Yahweh your God in Gilgal."
22 Samuel said, "Has Yahweh as great delight in burnt offerings and sacrifices, as in obeying Yahweh's voice? Behold, to obey is better than sacrifice, and to listen than the fat of rams. 23 For rebellion is as the sin of witchcraft, and stubbornness is as idolatry and teraphim.† Because you have rejected Yahweh's word, he has also rejected you from being king."

Responsorial Psalm: Psalms 50: 8-9, 16bc-17, 21 and 23

8 I don't rebuke you for your sacrifices.
Your burnt offerings are continually before me.
9 I have no need for a bull from your stall,
nor male goats from your pens.
16 "What right do you have to declare my statutes,
that you have taken my covenant on your lips,
17 since you hate instruction,
and throw my words behind you?

21 You have done these things, and I kept silent.
You thought that I was just like you.
I will rebuke you, and accuse you in front of your eyes.
23 Whoever offers the sacrifice of thanksgiving glorifies me,
and prepares his way so that I will show God's salvation to him."

Gospel: Mark 2: 18-22

18 John's disciples and the Pharisees were fasting, and they came and asked him, "Why do John's disciples and the disciples of the Pharisees fast, but your disciples don't fast?" 19 Jesus said to them, "Can the groomsmen fast while the bridegroom is with them? As long as they have the bridegroom with them, they can't fast. 20 But the days will come when the bridegroom will be taken away from them, and then they will fast in that day. 21 No one sews a piece of unshrunk cloth on an old garment, or else the patch shrinks and the new tears away from the old, and a worse hole is made. 22 No one puts new wine into old wineskins; or else the new wine will burst the skins, and the wine pours out, and the skins will be destroyed; but they put new wine into fresh wineskins."

1. Invite the Holy Spirit into this reading, asking the Author of Scripture to speak to you through His Word
2. Read today's passage as many times as you need, take your time
3. Write down (below) what the Lord is saying to you today
4. Live with this Word in your heart through the day

_____

_____

Tuesday, January 16, 2024

First Reading: First Samuel 16: 1-13

1 Yahweh said to Samuel, "How long will you mourn for Saul, since I have rejected him from being king over Israel? Fill your horn with oil, and go. I will send you to Jesse the Bethlehemite, for I have provided a king for myself among his sons."
2 Samuel said, "How can I go? If Saul hears it, he will kill me."
Yahweh said, "Take a heifer with you, and say, 'I have come to sacrifice to Yahweh.' 3 Call Jesse to the sacrifice, and I will show you what you shall do. You shall anoint to me him whom I name to you."

4 Samuel did that which Yahweh spoke, and came to Bethlehem. The elders of the city came to meet him trembling, and said, "Do you come peaceably?"

5 He said, "Peaceably; I have come to sacrifice to Yahweh. Sanctify yourselves, and come with me to the sacrifice." He sanctified Jesse and his sons, and called them to the sacrifice.

6 When they had come, he looked at Eliab, and said, "Surely Yahweh's anointed is before him."

7 But Yahweh said to Samuel, "Don't look on his face, or on the height of his stature, because I have rejected him; for I don't see as man sees. For man looks at the outward appearance, but Yahweh looks at the heart."

8 Then Jesse called Abinadab, and made him pass before Samuel. He said, "Yahweh has not chosen this one, either." 9 Then Jesse made Shammah to pass by. He said, "Yahweh has not chosen this one, either." 10 Jesse made seven of his sons to pass before Samuel. Samuel said to Jesse, "Yahweh has not chosen these." 11 Samuel said to Jesse, "Are all your children here?"

He said, "There remains yet the youngest. Behold, he is keeping the sheep."

Samuel said to Jesse, "Send and get him, for we will not sit down until he comes here."

12 He sent, and brought him in. Now he was ruddy, with a handsome face and good appearance. Yahweh said, "Arise! Anoint him, for this is he."

13 Then Samuel took the horn of oil and anointed him in the middle of his brothers. Then Yahweh's Spirit came mightily on David from that day forward. So Samuel rose up and went to Ramah.

Responsorial Psalm: Psalms 89: 20-22, 27-28

20 I have found David, my servant.
I have anointed him with my holy oil,
21 with whom my hand shall be established.
My arm will also strengthen him.
22 No enemy will tax him.
No wicked man will oppress him.
27 I will also appoint him my firstborn,
the highest of the kings of the earth.
28 I will keep my loving kindness for him forever more.
My covenant will stand firm with him.

Gospel: Mark 2: 23-28

23 He was going on the Sabbath day through the grain fields; and his disciples began, as they went, to pluck the ears of grain. 24 The Pharisees said to him, "Behold, why do they do that which is not lawful on the Sabbath day?"

25 He said to them, "Did you never read what David did when he had need and was hungry—he, and those who were with him? 26 How he entered into God's house at the time of Abiathar the high priest, and ate the show bread, which is not lawful to eat except for the priests, and gave also to those who were with him?"

27 He said to them, "The Sabbath was made for man, not man for the Sabbath. 28 Therefore the Son of Man is lord even of the Sabbath."

1. Invite the Holy Spirit into this reading, asking the Author of Scripture to speak to you through His Word
2. Read today's passage as many times as you need, take your time
3. Write down (below) what the Lord is saying to you today
4. Live with this Word in your heart through the day

Wednesday, January 17, 2024
Saint Anthony, Abbot

First Reading: First Samuel 17: 32-33, 37, 40-51

32 David said to Saul, "Let no man's heart fail because of him. Your servant will go and fight with this Philistine."

33 Saul said to David, "You are not able to go against this Philistine to fight with him; for you are but a youth, and he a man of war from his youth."

37 David said, "Yahweh, who delivered me out of the paw of the lion and out of the paw of the bear, will deliver me out of the hand of this Philistine."
Saul said to David, "Go! Yahweh will be with you."

40 He took his staff in his hand, and chose for himself five smooth stones out of the brook, and put them in the pouch of his shepherd's bag which he had. His sling was in his hand; and he came near to the Philistine. 41 The Philistine walked and came near to David; and the man who bore the shield went before him. 42 When the Philistine looked around and saw David, he disdained him; for he was but a youth, and ruddy, and had a good looking face. 43 The Philistine said to David, "Am I a dog, that you come to me with sticks?" The Philistine cursed David by his gods. 44 The Philistine said to David, "Come to me, and I will give your flesh to the birds of the sky and to the animals of the field."

45 Then David said to the Philistine, "You come to me with a sword, with a spear, and with a javelin; but I come to you in the name of Yahweh of Armies, the God of the armies of Israel, whom you have defied. 46 Today, Yahweh will deliver you into my hand. I will strike

you and take your head from off you. I will give the dead bodies of the army of the Philistines today to the birds of the sky and to the wild animals of the earth, that all the earth may know that there is a God in Israel, 47 and that all this assembly may know that Yahweh doesn't save with sword and spear; for the battle is Yahweh's, and he will give you into our hand."

48 When the Philistine arose, and walked and came near to meet David, David hurried and ran toward the army to meet the Philistine. 49 David put his hand in his bag, took a stone and slung it, and struck the Philistine in his forehead. The stone sank into his forehead, and he fell on his face to the earth. 50 So David prevailed over the Philistine with a sling and with a stone, and struck the Philistine and killed him; but there was no sword in David's hand. 51 Then David ran, stood over the Philistine, took his sword, drew it out of its sheath, killed him, and cut off his head with it.

When the Philistines saw that their champion was dead, they fled.

Responsorial Psalm: Psalms 144: 1b, 2, 9-10

1 Blessed be Yahweh, my rock,
who trains my hands to war,
and my fingers to battle—
2 my loving kindness, my fortress,
my high tower, my deliverer,
my shield, and he in whom I take refuge,
who subdues my people under me.
9 I will sing a new song to you, God.
On a ten-stringed lyre, I will sing praises to you.
10 You are he who gives salvation to kings,
who rescues David, his servant, from the deadly sword.

Gospel: Mark 3: 1-6

1 He entered again into the synagogue, and there was a man there whose hand was withered. 2 They watched him, whether he would heal him on the Sabbath day, that they might accuse him. 3 He said to the man whose hand was withered, "Stand up." 4 He said to them, "Is it lawful on the Sabbath day to do good or to do harm? To save a life or to kill?" But they were silent. 5 When he had looked around at them with anger, being grieved at the hardening of their hearts, he said to the man, "Stretch out your hand." He stretched it out, and his hand was restored as healthy as the other. 6 The Pharisees went out, and immediately conspired with the Herodians against him, how they might destroy him.

1. Invite the Holy Spirit into this reading, asking the Author of Scripture to speak to you through His Word

2. Read today's passage as many times as you need, take your time
3. Write down (below) what the Lord is saying to you today
4. Live with this Word in your heart through the day

Thursday, January 18, 2024

First Reading: First Samuel 18: 6-9; 19: 1-7

6 As they came, when David returned from the slaughter of the Philistine, the women came out of all the cities of Israel, singing and dancing, to meet King Saul with tambourines, with joy, and with instruments of music. 7 The women sang to one another as they played, and said,
"Saul has slain his thousands,
and David his ten thousands."
8 Saul was very angry, and this saying displeased him. He said, "They have credited David with ten thousands, and they have only credited me with thousands. What can he have more but the kingdom?" 9 Saul watched David from that day and forward.
1 Saul spoke to Jonathan his son and to all his servants, that they should kill David. But Jonathan, Saul's son, greatly delighted in David. 2 Jonathan told David, saying, "Saul my father seeks to kill you. Now therefore, please take care of yourself in the morning, live in a secret place, and hide yourself. 3 I will go out and stand beside my father in the field where you are, and I will talk with my father about you; and if I see anything, I will tell you."
4 Jonathan spoke good of David to Saul his father, and said to him, "Don't let the king sin against his servant, against David; because he has not sinned against you, and because his works have been very good toward you; 5 for he put his life in his hand and struck the Philistine, and Yahweh worked a great victory for all Israel. You saw it and rejoiced. Why then will you sin against innocent blood, to kill David without a cause?"
6 Saul listened to the voice of Jonathan; and Saul swore, "As Yahweh lives, he shall not be put to death."
7 Jonathan called David, and Jonathan showed him all those things. Then Jonathan brought David to Saul, and he was in his presence as before.

Responsorial Psalm: Psalms 56: 2-3, 9-13

2 My enemies want to swallow me up all day long,
for they are many who fight proudly against me.
3 When I am afraid,
I will put my trust in you.
9 Then my enemies shall turn back in the day that I call.
I know this: that God is for me.
10 In God, I will praise his word.
In Yahweh, I will praise his word.
11 I have put my trust in God.
I will not be afraid.
What can man do to me?
12 Your vows are on me, God.
I will give thank offerings to you.
13 For you have delivered my soul from death,
and prevented my feet from falling,
that I may walk before God in the light of the living.

Gospel: Mark 3: 7-12

7 Jesus withdrew to the sea with his disciples; and a great multitude followed him from Galilee, from Judea, 8 from Jerusalem, from Idumaea, beyond the Jordan, and those from around Tyre and Sidon. A great multitude, hearing what great things he did, came to him. 9 He spoke to his disciples that a little boat should stay near him because of the crowd, so that they wouldn't press on him. 10 For he had healed many, so that as many as had diseases pressed on him that they might touch him. 11 The unclean spirits, whenever they saw him, fell down before him and cried, "You are the Son of God!" 12 He sternly warned them that they should not make him known.

1. Invite the Holy Spirit into this reading, asking the Author of Scripture to speak to you through His Word
2. Read today's passage as many times as you need, take your time
3. Write down (below) what the Lord is saying to you today
4. Live with this Word in your heart through the day

_____

_____

Friday, January 19, 2024

First Reading: First Samuel 24: 3-21

3 He came to the sheep pens by the way, where there was a cave; and Saul went in to relieve himself. Now David and his men were staying in the innermost parts of the cave. 4 David's men said to him, "Behold, the day of which Yahweh said to you, 'Behold, I will deliver your enemy into your hand, and you shall do to him as it shall seem good to you.' " Then David arose and cut off the skirt of Saul's robe secretly. 5 Afterward, David's heart struck him because he had cut off Saul's skirt. 6 He said to his men, "Yahweh forbid that I should do this thing to my lord, Yahweh's anointed, to stretch out my hand against him, since he is Yahweh's anointed." 7 So David checked his men with these words, and didn't allow them to rise against Saul. Saul rose up out of the cave, and went on his way. 8 David also arose afterward, and went out of the cave and cried after Saul, saying, "My lord the king!"

When Saul looked behind him, David bowed with his face to the earth, and showed respect. 9 David said to Saul, "Why do you listen to men's words, saying, 'Behold, David seeks to harm you'? 10 Behold, today your eyes have seen how Yahweh had delivered you today into my hand in the cave. Some urged me to kill you, but I spared you. I said, 'I will not stretch out my hand against my lord, for he is Yahweh's anointed.' 11 Moreover, my father, behold, yes, see the skirt of your robe in my hand; for in that I cut off the skirt of your robe and didn't kill you, know and see that there is neither evil nor disobedience in my hand. I have not sinned against you, though you hunt for my life to take it. 12 May Yahweh judge between me and you, and may Yahweh avenge me of you; but my hand will not be on you. 13 As the proverb of the ancients says, 'Out of the wicked comes wickedness;' but my hand will not be on you. 14 Against whom has the king of Israel come out? Whom do you pursue? A dead dog? A flea? 15 May Yahweh therefore be judge, and give sentence between me and you, and see, and plead my cause, and deliver me out of your hand."

16 It came to pass, when David had finished speaking these words to Saul, that Saul said, "Is that your voice, my son David?" Saul lifted up his voice and wept. 17 He said to David, "You are more righteous than I; for you have done good to me, whereas I have done evil to you. 18 You have declared today how you have dealt well with me, because when Yahweh had delivered me up into your hand, you didn't kill me. 19 For if a man finds his enemy, will he let him go away unharmed? Therefore may Yahweh reward you good for that which you have done to me today. 20 Now, behold, I know that you will surely be king, and that the kingdom of Israel will be established in your hand. 21 Swear now therefore to me by Yahweh that you will not cut off my offspring after me, and that you will not destroy my name out of my father's house."

Responsorial Psalm: 57: 2-4, 6 and 11

2 I cry out to God Most High,
to God who accomplishes my requests for me.

3 He will send from heaven, and save me,
he rebukes the one who is pursuing me.
God will send out his loving kindness and his truth.
4 My soul is among lions.
I lie among those who are set on fire,
even the sons of men, whose teeth are spears and arrows,
and their tongue a sharp sword.
6 They have prepared a net for my steps.
My soul is bowed down.
They dig a pit before me.
They fall into the middle of it themselves.
11 Be exalted, God, above the heavens.
Let your glory be over all the earth.

Gospel: Mark 3: 13-19

13 He went up into the mountain and called to himself those whom he wanted, and they went to him. 14 He appointed twelve, that they might be with him, and that he might send them out to preach 15 and to have authority to heal sicknesses and to cast out demons: 16 Simon (to whom he gave the name Peter); 17 James the son of Zebedee; and John, the brother of James, (whom he called Boanerges, which means, Sons of Thunder); 18 Andrew; Philip; Bartholomew; Matthew; Thomas; James, the son of Alphaeus; Thaddaeus; Simon the Zealot; 19 and Judas Iscariot, who also betrayed him.
Then he came into a house.

1. Invite the Holy Spirit into this reading, asking the Author of Scripture to speak to you through His Word
2. Read today's passage as many times as you need, take your time
3. Write down (below) what the Lord is saying to you today
4. Live with this Word in your heart through the day

_____

_____

Saturday, January 20, 2024

First Reading: Second Samuel 1: 1-4, 11-12, 19, 23-27

1 After the death of Saul, when David had returned from the slaughter of the Amalekites, and David had stayed two days in Ziklag, 2 on the third day, behold,† a man came out of the camp from Saul, with his clothes torn and earth on his head. When he came to David, he fell to the earth and showed respect.

3 David said to him, "Where do you come from?"

He said to him, "I have escaped out of the camp of Israel."

4 David said to him, "How did it go? Please tell me."

He answered, "The people have fled from the battle, and many of the people also have fallen and are dead. Saul and Jonathan his son are dead also."

11 Then David took hold on his clothes and tore them; and all the men who were with him did likewise. 12 They mourned, wept, and fasted until evening for Saul and for Jonathan his son, and for the people of Yahweh,‡ and for the house of Israel, because they had fallen by the sword.

19 "Your glory, Israel, was slain on your high places!

How the mighty have fallen!

23 Saul and Jonathan were lovely and pleasant in their lives.

In their death, they were not divided.

They were swifter than eagles.

They were stronger than lions.

24 You daughters of Israel, weep over Saul,

who clothed you delicately in scarlet,

who put ornaments of gold on your clothing.

25 How the mighty have fallen in the middle of the battle!

Jonathan was slain on your high places.

26 I am distressed for you, my brother Jonathan.

You have been very pleasant to me.

Your love to me was wonderful,

surpassing the love of women.

27 How the mighty have fallen,

and the weapons of war have perished!"

Responsorial Psalm: Psalms 80: 2-3, 5-7

2 Before Ephraim, Benjamin, and Manasseh, stir up your might!

Come to save us!

3 Turn us again, God.

Cause your face to shine,

and we will be saved.

5 You have fed them with the bread of tears,

and given them tears to drink in large measure.

6 You make us a source of contention to our neighbors.

Our enemies laugh among themselves.
7 Turn us again, God of Armies.
Cause your face to shine,
and we will be saved.

Gospel: Mark 3: 20-21

20 The multitude came together again, so that they could not so much as eat bread. 21 When his friends heard it, they went out to seize him; for they said, "He is insane."

1. Invite the Holy Spirit into this reading, asking the Author of Scripture to speak to you through His Word
2. Read today's passage as many times as you need, take your time
3. Write down (below) what the Lord is saying to you today
4. Live with this Word in your heart through the day

Sunday, January 21, 2024
Third Sunday in Ordinary Time

First Reading: Jonah 3: 1-5, 10

1 Yahweh's word came to Jonah the second time, saying, 2 "Arise, go to Nineveh, that great city, and preach to it the message that I give you."
3 So Jonah arose, and went to Nineveh, according to Yahweh's word. Now Nineveh was an exceedingly great city, three days' journey across. 4 Jonah began to enter into the city a day's journey, and he cried out, and said, "In forty days, Nineveh will be overthrown!"
5 The people of Nineveh believed God; and they proclaimed a fast and put on sackcloth, from their greatest even to their least.
10 God saw their works, that they turned from their evil way. God relented of the disaster which he said he would do to them, and he didn't do it.

Responsorial Psalm: Psalms 25: 4-9

4 Show me your ways, Yahweh.
Teach me your paths.

5 Guide me in your truth, and teach me,

for you are the God of my salvation.

I wait for you all day long.

6 Yahweh, remember your tender mercies and your loving kindness,

for they are from old times.

7 Don't remember the sins of my youth, nor my transgressions.

Remember me according to your loving kindness,

for your goodness' sake, Yahweh.

8 Good and upright is Yahweh,

therefore he will instruct sinners in the way.

9 He will guide the humble in justice.

He will teach the humble his way.

Second Reading: First Corinthians 7: 29-31

29 But I say this, brothers: the time is short. From now on, both those who have wives may be as though they had none; 30 and those who weep, as though they didn't weep; and those who rejoice, as though they didn't rejoice; and those who buy, as though they didn't possess; 31 and those who use the world, as not using it to the fullest. For the mode of this world passes away.

Gospel: Mark 1: 14-20

14 Now after John was taken into custody, Jesus came into Galilee, preaching the Good News of God's Kingdom, 15 and saying, "The time is fulfilled, and God's Kingdom is at hand! Repent, and believe in the Good News."

16 Passing along by the sea of Galilee, he saw Simon and Andrew, the brother of Simon, casting a net into the sea, for they were fishermen. 17 Jesus said to them, "Come after me, and I will make you into fishers for men."

18 Immediately they left their nets, and followed him.

19 Going on a little further from there, he saw James the son of Zebedee, and John his brother, who were also in the boat mending the nets. 20 Immediately he called them, and they left their father, Zebedee, in the boat with the hired servants, and went after him.

1. Invite the Holy Spirit into this reading, asking the Author of Scripture to speak to you through His Word

2. Read today's passage as many times as you need, take your time

3. Write down (below) what the Lord is saying to you today

4. Live with this Word in your heart through the day

First Reading: Second Samuel 5: 1-7, 10

1 Then all the tribes of Israel came to David at Hebron and spoke, saying, "Behold, we are your bone and your flesh. 2 In times past, when Saul was king over us, it was you who led Israel out and in. Yahweh said to you, 'You will be shepherd of my people Israel, and you will be prince over Israel.' " 3 So all the elders of Israel came to the king to Hebron, and King David made a covenant with them in Hebron before Yahweh; and they anointed David king over Israel.

4 David was thirty years old when he began to reign, and he reigned forty years. 5 In Hebron he reigned over Judah seven years and six months, and in Jerusalem he reigned thirty-three years over all Israel and Judah.

6 The king and his men went to Jerusalem against the Jebusites, the inhabitants of the land, who spoke to David, saying, "The blind and the lame will keep you out of here," thinking, "David can't come in here." 7 Nevertheless David took the stronghold of Zion. This is David's city.

10 David grew greater and greater, for Yahweh, the God of Armies, was with him.

Responsorial Psalm: Psalms 89: 20-22, 25-26

20 I have found David, my servant.
I have anointed him with my holy oil,
21 with whom my hand shall be established.
My arm will also strengthen him.
22 No enemy will tax him.
No wicked man will oppress him.
25 I will set his hand also on the sea,
and his right hand on the rivers.
26 He will call to me, 'You are my Father,
my God, and the rock of my salvation!'

Gospel: Mark 3: 22-30

22 The scribes who came down from Jerusalem said, "He has Beelzebul," and, "By the prince of the demons he casts out the demons."

23 He summoned them and said to them in parables, "How can Satan cast out Satan? 24 If a kingdom is divided against itself, that kingdom cannot stand. 25 If a house is divided against itself, that house cannot stand. 26 If Satan has risen up against himself, and is

divided, he can't stand, but has an end. 27 But no one can enter into the house of the strong man to plunder unless he first binds the strong man; then he will plunder his house. 28 "Most certainly I tell you, all sins of the descendants of man will be forgiven, including their blasphemies with which they may blaspheme; 29 but whoever may blaspheme against the Holy Spirit never has forgiveness, but is subject to eternal condemnation."† 30 —because they said, "He has an unclean spirit."

1. Invite the Holy Spirit into this reading, asking the Author of Scripture to speak to you through His Word
2. Read today's passage as many times as you need, take your time
3. Write down (below) what the Lord is saying to you today
4. Live with this Word in your heart through the day

_____

_____

Tuesday, January 23, 2024

First Reading: Second Samuel 6: 12b-15, 17-19

12 King David was told, "Yahweh has blessed the house of Obed-Edom, and all that belongs to him, because of God's ark."
So David went and brought up God's ark from the house of Obed-Edom into David's city with joy. 13 When those who bore Yahweh's ark had gone six paces, he sacrificed an ox and a fattened calf. 14 David danced before Yahweh with all his might; and David was clothed in a linen ephod. 15 So David and all the house of Israel brought up Yahweh's ark with shouting and with the sound of the trumpet.
17 They brought in Yahweh's ark, and set it in its place in the middle of the tent that David had pitched for it; and David offered burnt offerings and peace offerings before Yahweh. 18 When David had finished offering the burnt offering and the peace offerings, he blessed the people in the name of Yahweh of Armies. 19 He gave to all the people, even among the whole multitude of Israel, both to men and women, to everyone a portion of bread, dates, and raisins. So all the people departed, each to his own house.

Responsorial Psalm: Psalms 24: 7-10

7 Lift up your heads, you gates!
Be lifted up, you everlasting doors,

and the King of glory will come in.
8 Who is the King of glory?
Yahweh strong and mighty,
Yahweh mighty in battle.
9 Lift up your heads, you gates;
yes, lift them up, you everlasting doors,
and the King of glory will come in.
10 Who is this King of glory?
Yahweh of Armies is the King of glory!

Gospel: Mark 3: 31-35

31 His mother and his brothers came, and standing outside, they sent to him, calling him. 32 A multitude was sitting around him, and they told him, "Behold, your mother, your brothers, and your sisters‡ are outside looking for you."
33 He answered them, "Who are my mother and my brothers?" 34 Looking around at those who sat around him, he said, "Behold, my mother and my brothers! 35 For whoever does the will of God is my brother, my sister, and mother."

1. Invite the Holy Spirit into this reading, asking the Author of Scripture to speak to you through His Word
2. Read today's passage as many times as you need, take your time
3. Write down (below) what the Lord is saying to you today
4. Live with this Word in your heart through the day

―――

―――

Wednesday, January 24, 2024
Saint Francis de Sales, Bishop and Doctor of the Church

First Reading: Second Samuel 7: 4-17

14 I will be his father, and he will be my son. If he commits iniquity, I will chasten him with the rod of men and with the stripes of the children of men; 15 but my loving kindness will not depart from him, as I took it from Saul, whom I put away before you. 16 Your house and your kingdom will be made sure forever before you. Your throne will be

established forever.' " " 17 Nathan spoke to David all these words, and according to all this vision.

Responsorial Psalm: Psalms 89: 4-5, 27-30

4 'I will establish your offspring forever,
and build up your throne to all generations.' "
5 The heavens will praise your wonders, Yahweh,
your faithfulness also in the assembly of the holy ones.
27 I will also appoint him my firstborn,
the highest of the kings of the earth.
28 I will keep my loving kindness for him forever more.
My covenant will stand firm with him.
29 I will also make his offspring endure forever,
and his throne as the days of heaven.
30 If his children forsake my law,
and don't walk in my ordinances;

Gospel: Mark 4: 1-20

1 Again he began to teach by the seaside. A great multitude was gathered to him, so that he entered into a boat in the sea and sat down. All the multitude were on the land by the sea. 2 He taught them many things in parables, and told them in his teaching, 3 "Listen! Behold, the farmer went out to sow. 4 As he sowed, some seed fell by the road, and the birds† came and devoured it. 5 Others fell on the rocky ground, where it had little soil, and immediately it sprang up, because it had no depth of soil. 6 When the sun had risen, it was scorched; and because it had no root, it withered away. 7 Others fell among the thorns, and the thorns grew up and choked it, and it yielded no fruit. 8 Others fell into the good ground and yielded fruit, growing up and increasing. Some produced thirty times, some sixty times, and some one hundred times as much." 9 He said, "Whoever has ears to hear, let him hear."
10 When he was alone, those who were around him with the twelve asked him about the parables. 11 He said to them, "To you is given the mystery of God's Kingdom, but to those who are outside, all things are done in parables, 12 that 'seeing they may see and not perceive, and hearing they may hear and not understand, lest perhaps they should turn again, and their sins should be forgiven them.' "*
13 He said to them, "Don't you understand this parable? How will you understand all of the parables? 14 The farmer sows the word. 15 The ones by the road are the ones where the word is sown; and when they have heard, immediately Satan comes and takes away the word which has been sown in them. 16 These in the same way are those who are sown on the rocky places, who, when they have heard the word, immediately receive it with joy.

17 They have no root in themselves, but are short-lived. When oppression or persecution arises because of the word, immediately they stumble. 18 Others are those who are sown among the thorns. These are those who have heard the word, 19 and the cares of this age, and the deceitfulness of riches, and the lusts of other things entering in choke the word, and it becomes unfruitful. 20 Those which were sown on the good ground are those who hear the word, accept it, and bear fruit, some thirty times, some sixty times, and some one hundred times."

1. Invite the Holy Spirit into this reading, asking the Author of Scripture to speak to you through His Word
2. Read today's passage as many times as you need, take your time
3. Write down (below) what the Lord is saying to you today
4. Live with this Word in your heart through the day

Thursday, January 25, 2024
The Conversion of Saint Paul the Apostle

First Reading: Acts 22: 3-16

3 "I am indeed a Jew, born in Tarsus of Cilicia, but brought up in this city at the feet of Gamaliel, instructed according to the strict tradition of the law of our fathers, being zealous for God, even as you all are today. 4 I persecuted this Way to the death, binding and delivering into prisons both men and women, 5 as also the high priest and all the council of the elders testify, from whom also I received letters to the brothers, and traveled to Damascus to bring them also who were there to Jerusalem in bonds to be punished.

6 "As I made my journey and came close to Damascus, about noon suddenly a great light shone around me from the sky. 7 I fell to the ground and heard a voice saying to me, 'Saul, Saul, why are you persecuting me?' 8 I answered, 'Who are you, Lord?' He said to me, 'I am Jesus of Nazareth, whom you persecute.'

9 "Those who were with me indeed saw the light and were afraid, but they didn't understand the voice of him who spoke to me. 10 I said, 'What shall I do, Lord?' The Lord said to me, 'Arise, and go into Damascus. There you will be told about all things which are appointed for you to do.' 11 When I couldn't see for the glory of that light, being led by the hand of those who were with me, I came into Damascus.

12 "One Ananias, a devout man according to the law, well reported of by all the Jews who lived in Damascus, 13 came to me, and standing by me said to me, 'Brother Saul, receive your sight!' In that very hour I looked up at him. 14 He said, 'The God of our fathers has appointed you to know his will, and to see the Righteous One, and to hear a voice from his mouth. 15 For you will be a witness for him to all men of what you have seen and heard. 16 Now why do you wait? Arise, be baptized, and wash away your sins, calling on the name of the Lord.'

Responsorial Psalm: Psalms 117: 1-2

1 Praise Yahweh, all you nations!
Extol him, all you peoples!
2 For his loving kindness is great toward us.
Yahweh's faithfulness endures forever.
Praise Yah!

Gospel: Mark 16: 15-18

15 He said to them, "Go into all the world and preach the Good News to the whole creation. 16 He who believes and is baptized will be saved; but he who disbelieves will be condemned. 17 These signs will accompany those who believe: in my name they will cast out demons; they will speak with new languages; 18 they will take up serpents; and if they drink any deadly thing, it will in no way hurt them; they will lay hands on the sick, and they will recover."

1. Invite the Holy Spirit into this reading, asking the Author of Scripture to speak to you through His Word
2. Read today's passage as many times as you need, take your time
3. Write down (below) what the Lord is saying to you today
4. Live with this Word in your heart through the day

_____

_____

Friday, January 26, 2024
Saints Timothy and Titus, Bishops

First Reading: Second Timothy 1: 1-8

1 Paul, an apostle of Jesus Christ† through the will of God, according to the promise of the life which is in Christ Jesus, 2 to Timothy, my beloved child: Grace, mercy, and peace, from God the Father and Christ Jesus our Lord.

3 I thank God, whom I serve as my forefathers did, with a pure conscience. How unceasing is my memory of you in my petitions, night and day 4 longing to see you, remembering your tears, that I may be filled with joy; 5 having been reminded of the sincere faith that is in you, which lived first in your grandmother Lois and your mother Eunice and, I am persuaded, in you also.

6 For this cause, I remind you that you should stir up the gift of God which is in you through the laying on of my hands. 7 For God didn't give us a spirit of fear, but of power, love, and self-control. 8 Therefore don't be ashamed of the testimony of our Lord, nor of me his prisoner; but endure hardship for the Good News according to the power of God,

Responsorial Psalm: Psalms 96: 1-3, 7-8a, 10

1 Sing to Yahweh a new song!
Sing to Yahweh, all the earth.
2 Sing to Yahweh!
Bless his name!
Proclaim his salvation from day to day!
3 Declare his glory among the nations,
his marvelous works among all the peoples.
7 Ascribe to Yahweh, you families of nations,
ascribe to Yahweh glory and strength.
8 Ascribe to Yahweh the glory due to his name.
Bring an offering, and come into his courts.
10 Say among the nations, "Yahweh reigns."
The world is also established.
It can't be moved.
He will judge the peoples with equity.

Gospel: Mark 4: 26-34

26 He said, "God's Kingdom is as if a man should cast seed on the earth, 27 and should sleep and rise night and day, and the seed should spring up and grow, though he doesn't know how. 28 For the earth bears fruit by itself: first the blade, then the ear, then the full grain in the ear. 29 But when the fruit is ripe, immediately he puts in the sickle, because the harvest has come."

30 He said, "How will we liken God's Kingdom? Or with what parable will we illustrate it? 31 It's like a grain of mustard seed, which, when it is sown in the earth, though it is less

than all the seeds that are on the earth, 32 yet when it is sown, grows up and becomes greater than all the herbs, and puts out great branches, so that the birds of the sky can lodge under its shadow."

33 With many such parables he spoke the word to them, as they were able to hear it. 34 Without a parable he didn't speak to them; but privately to his own disciples he explained everything.

1. Invite the Holy Spirit into this reading, asking the Author of Scripture to speak to you through His Word
2. Read today's passage as many times as you need, take your time
3. Write down (below) what the Lord is saying to you today
4. Live with this Word in your heart through the day

_____

_____

Saturday, January 27, 2024
Saint Angela Merici, Virgin

First Reading: Second Samuel 12: 1-7a, 10-17

1 Yahweh sent Nathan to David. He came to him, and said to him, "There were two men in one city: the one rich, and the other poor. 2 The rich man had very many flocks and herds, 3 but the poor man had nothing, except one little ewe lamb, which he had bought and raised. It grew up together with him and with his children. It ate of his own food, drank of his own cup, and lay in his bosom, and was like a daughter to him. 4 A traveler came to the rich man, and he didn't want to take of his own flock and of his own herd to prepare for the wayfaring man who had come to him, but took the poor man's lamb and prepared it for the man who had come to him."

5 David's anger burned hot against the man, and he said to Nathan, "As Yahweh lives, the man who has done this deserves to die! 6 He must restore the lamb fourfold, because he did this thing and because he had no pity!"

7 Nathan said to David, "You are the man! This is what Yahweh, the God of Israel, says: 'I anointed you king over Israel, and I delivered you out of the hand of Saul.

10 Now therefore the sword will never depart from your house, because you have despised me and have taken Uriah the Hittite's wife to be your wife.'

11 "This is what Yahweh says: 'Behold, I will raise up evil against you out of your own house; and I will take your wives before your eyes and give them to your neighbor, and he

will lie with your wives in the sight of this sun. 12 For you did this secretly, but I will do this thing before all Israel, and before the sun.' "

13 David said to Nathan, "I have sinned against Yahweh."

Nathan said to David, "Yahweh also has put away your sin. You will not die. 14 However, because by this deed you have given great occasion to Yahweh's enemies to blaspheme, the child also who is born to you will surely die." 15 Then Nathan departed to his house.

Yahweh struck the child that Uriah's wife bore to David, and he was very sick. 16 David therefore begged God for the child; and David fasted, and went in and lay all night on the ground. 17 The elders of his house arose beside him, to raise him up from the earth; but he would not, and he didn't eat bread with them.

Responsorial Psalm: Psalms 51: 12-17

12 Restore to me the joy of your salvation.
Uphold me with a willing spirit.
13 Then I will teach transgressors your ways.
Sinners will be converted to you.
14 Deliver me from the guilt of bloodshed, O God, the God of my salvation.
My tongue will sing aloud of your righteousness.
15 Lord, open my lips.
My mouth will declare your praise.
16 For you don't delight in sacrifice, or else I would give it.
You have no pleasure in burnt offering.
17 The sacrifices of God are a broken spirit.
O God, you will not despise a broken and contrite heart.

Gospel: Mark 4: 35-41

35 On that day, when evening had come, he said to them, "Let's go over to the other side." 36 Leaving the multitude, they took him with them, even as he was, in the boat. Other small boats were also with him. 37 A big wind storm arose, and the waves beat into the boat, so much that the boat was already filled. 38 He himself was in the stern, asleep on the cushion; and they woke him up and asked him, "Teacher, don't you care that we are dying?"

39 He awoke and rebuked the wind, and said to the sea, "Peace! Be still!" The wind ceased and there was a great calm. 40 He said to them, "Why are you so afraid? How is it that you have no faith?"

41 They were greatly afraid and said to one another, "Who then is this, that even the wind and the sea obey him?"

1. Invite the Holy Spirit into this reading, asking the Author of Scripture to speak to you through His Word
2. Read today's passage as many times as you need, take your time
3. Write down (below) what the Lord is saying to you today
4. Live with this Word in your heart through the day

_____

_____

Sunday, January 28, 2024
Fourth Sunday in Ordinary Time

First Reading: Deuteronomy 18: 15-20

15 Yahweh your God will raise up to you a prophet from among you, of your brothers, like me. You shall listen to him. 16 This is according to all that you desired of Yahweh your God in Horeb in the day of the assembly, saying, "Let me not hear again Yahweh my God's voice, neither let me see this great fire any more, that I not die."
17 Yahweh said to me, "They have well said that which they have spoken. 18 I will raise them up a prophet from among their brothers, like you. I will put my words in his mouth, and he shall speak to them all that I shall command him. 19 It shall happen, that whoever will not listen to my words which he shall speak in my name, I will require it of him. 20 But the prophet who speaks a word presumptuously in my name, which I have not commanded him to speak, or who speaks in the name of other gods, that same prophet shall die."

Responsorial Psalm: Psalms 95: 1-2, 6-9

1 Oh come, let's sing to Yahweh.
Let's shout aloud to the rock of our salvation!
2 Let's come before his presence with thanksgiving.
Let's extol him with songs!
6 Oh come, let's worship and bow down.
Let's kneel before Yahweh, our Maker,
7 for he is our God.
We are the people of his pasture,
and the sheep in his care.
Today, oh that you would hear his voice!

8 Don't harden your heart, as at Meribah,
as in the day of Massah in the wilderness,
9 when your fathers tempted me,
tested me, and saw my work.

Second Reading: First Corinthians 7: 32-35

32 But I desire to have you to be free from cares. He who is unmarried is concerned for the things of the Lord, how he may please the Lord; 33 but he who is married is concerned about the things of the world, how he may please his wife. 34 There is also a difference between a wife and a virgin. The unmarried woman cares about the things of the Lord, that she may be holy both in body and in spirit. But she who is married cares about the things of the world—how she may please her husband. 35 This I say for your own benefit, not that I may ensnare you, but for that which is appropriate, and that you may attend to the Lord without distraction.

Gospel: Mark 1: 21-28

21 They went into Capernaum, and immediately on the Sabbath day he entered into the synagogue and taught. 22 They were astonished at his teaching, for he taught them as having authority, and not as the scribes. 23 Immediately there was in their synagogue a man with an unclean spirit, and he cried out, 24 saying, "Ha! What do we have to do with you, Jesus, you Nazarene? Have you come to destroy us? I know who you are: the Holy One of God!"
25 Jesus rebuked him, saying, "Be quiet, and come out of him!"
26 The unclean spirit, convulsing him and crying with a loud voice, came out of him. 27 They were all amazed, so that they questioned among themselves, saying, "What is this? A new teaching? For with authority he commands even the unclean spirits, and they obey him!" 28 The report of him went out immediately everywhere into all the region of Galilee and its surrounding area.

1. Invite the Holy Spirit into this reading, asking the Author of Scripture to speak to you through His Word
2. Read today's passage as many times as you need, take your time
3. Write down (below) what the Lord is saying to you today
4. Live with this Word in your heart through the day

_____

_____

Monday, January 29, 2024

First Reading: Second Samuel 15: 13-14, 30; 16: 5-13

13 A messenger came to David, saying, "The hearts of the men of Israel are after Absalom." 14 David said to all his servants who were with him at Jerusalem, "Arise! Let's flee, or else none of us will escape from Absalom. Hurry to depart, lest he overtake us quickly and bring down evil on us, and strike the city with the edge of the sword."

30 David went up by the ascent of the Mount of Olives, and wept as he went up; and he had his head covered and went barefoot. All the people who were with him each covered his head, and they went up, weeping as they went up.

5 When King David came to Bahurim, behold, a man of the family of Saul's house came out, whose name was Shimei, the son of Gera. He came out and cursed as he came. 6 He cast stones at David and at all the servants of King David, and all the people and all the mighty men were on his right hand and on his left. 7 Shimei said when he cursed, "Be gone, be gone, you man of blood, and wicked fellow! 8 Yahweh has returned on you all the blood of Saul's house, in whose place you have reigned! Yahweh has delivered the kingdom into the hand of Absalom your son! Behold, you are caught by your own mischief, because you are a man of blood!"

9 Then Abishai the son of Zeruiah said to the king, "Why should this dead dog curse my lord the king? Please let me go over and take off his head." 10 The king said, "What have I to do with you, you sons of Zeruiah? Because he curses, and because Yahweh has said to him, 'Curse David,' who then shall say, 'Why have you done so?' "

11 David said to Abishai and to all his servants, "Behold, my son, who came out of my bowels, seeks my life. How much more this Benjamite, now? Leave him alone, and let him curse; for Yahweh has invited him. 12 It may be that Yahweh will look on the wrong done to me, and that Yahweh will repay me good for the cursing of me today." 13 So David and his men went by the way; and Shimei went along on the hillside opposite him and cursed as he went, threw stones at him, and threw dust.

Responsorial Psalm: Psalms 3: 2-7

2 Many there are who say of my soul,
"There is no help for him in God."†
3 But you, Yahweh, are a shield around me,
my glory, and the one who lifts up my head.
4 I cry to Yahweh with my voice,
and he answers me out of his holy hill.
5 I laid myself down and slept.
I awakened, for Yahweh sustains me.

6 I will not be afraid of tens of thousands of people
who have set themselves against me on every side.
7 Arise, Yahweh!
Save me, my God!
For you have struck all of my enemies on the cheek bone.
You have broken the teeth of the wicked.

Gospel: Mark 5: 1-20

1 They came to the other side of the sea, into the country of the Gadarenes. 2 When he had come out of the boat, immediately a man with an unclean spirit met him out of the tombs. 3 He lived in the tombs. Nobody could bind him any more, not even with chains, 4 because he had been often bound with fetters and chains, and the chains had been torn apart by him, and the fetters broken in pieces. Nobody had the strength to tame him. 5 Always, night and day, in the tombs and in the mountains, he was crying out, and cutting himself with stones. 6 When he saw Jesus from afar, he ran and bowed down to him, 7 and crying out with a loud voice, he said, "What have I to do with you, Jesus, you Son of the Most High God? I adjure you by God, don't torment me." 8 For he said to him, "Come out of the man, you unclean spirit!"
9 He asked him, "What is your name?"
He said to him, "My name is Legion, for we are many." 10 He begged him much that he would not send them away out of the country. 11 Now on the mountainside there was a great herd of pigs feeding. 12 All the demons begged him, saying, "Send us into the pigs, that we may enter into them."
13 At once Jesus gave them permission. The unclean spirits came out and entered into the pigs. The herd of about two thousand rushed down the steep bank into the sea, and they were drowned in the sea. 14 Those who fed the pigs fled, and told it in the city and in the country.
The people came to see what it was that had happened. 15 They came to Jesus, and saw him who had been possessed by demons sitting, clothed, and in his right mind, even him who had the legion; and they were afraid. 16 Those who saw it declared to them what happened to him who was possessed by demons, and about the pigs. 17 They began to beg him to depart from their region.
18 As he was entering into the boat, he who had been possessed by demons begged him that he might be with him. 19 He didn't allow him, but said to him, "Go to your house, to your friends, and tell them what great things the Lord has done for you and how he had mercy on you."
20 He went his way, and began to proclaim in Decapolis how Jesus had done great things for him, and everyone marveled.

Tuesday, January 30, 2024

First Reading: Second Samuel 18: 9-10, 14, 24-25a, 30 – 19: 3

9 Absalom happened to meet David's servants. Absalom was riding on his mule, and the mule went under the thick boughs of a great oak; and his head caught hold of the oak, and he was hanging between the sky and earth; and the mule that was under him went on. 10 A certain man saw it, and told Joab, and said, "Behold, I saw Absalom hanging in an oak."

14 Then Joab said, "I'm not going to wait like this with you." He took three darts in his hand and thrust them through Absalom's heart while he was still alive in the middle of the oak.

24 Now David was sitting between the two gates; and the watchman went up to the roof of the gate to the wall, and lifted up his eyes and looked, and, behold, a man running alone. 25 The watchman shouted and told the king.

30 The king said, "Come and stand here." He came and stood still.

31 Behold, the Cushite came. The Cushite said, "Good news for my lord the king, for Yahweh has avenged you today of all those who rose up against you."

32 The king said to the Cushite, "Is it well with the young man Absalom?"

The Cushite answered, "May the enemies of my lord the king, and all who rise up against you to do you harm, be as that young man is."

33 The king was much moved, and went up to the room over the gate and wept. As he went, he said, "My son Absalom! My son, my son Absalom! I wish I had died instead of you, Absalom, my son, my son!"

1 Joab was told, "Behold, the king weeps and mourns for Absalom." 2 The victory that day was turned into mourning among all the people, for the people heard it said that day, "The king grieves for his son."

3 The people sneaked into the city that day, as people who are ashamed steal away when they flee in battle.

Responsorial Psalm: Psalms 86: 1-6

1 Hear, Yahweh, and answer me,
for I am poor and needy.
2 Preserve my soul, for I am godly.
You, my God, save your servant who trusts in you.
3 Be merciful to me, Lord,
for I call to you all day long.
4 Bring joy to the soul of your servant,
for to you, Lord, do I lift up my soul.
5 For you, Lord, are good, and ready to forgive,
abundant in loving kindness to all those who call on you.
6 Hear, Yahweh, my prayer.
Listen to the voice of my petitions.

Gospel: Mark 5: 21-43

21 When Jesus had crossed back over in the boat to the other side, a great multitude was gathered to him; and he was by the sea. 22 Behold, one of the rulers of the synagogue, Jairus by name, came; and seeing him, he fell at his feet 23 and begged him much, saying, "My little daughter is at the point of death. Please come and lay your hands on her, that she may be made healthy, and live."

24 He went with him, and a great multitude followed him, and they pressed upon him on all sides. 25 A certain woman who had a discharge of blood for twelve years, 26 and had suffered many things by many physicians, and had spent all that she had, and was no better, but rather grew worse, 27 having heard the things concerning Jesus, came up behind him in the crowd and touched his clothes. 28 For she said, "If I just touch his clothes, I will be made well." 29 Immediately the flow of her blood was dried up, and she felt in her body that she was healed of her affliction.

30 Immediately Jesus, perceiving in himself that the power had gone out from him, turned around in the crowd and asked, "Who touched my clothes?"

31 His disciples said to him, "You see the multitude pressing against you, and you say, 'Who touched me?' "

32 He looked around to see her who had done this thing. 33 But the woman, fearing and trembling, knowing what had been done to her, came and fell down before him, and told him all the truth.

34 He said to her, "Daughter, your faith has made you well. Go in peace, and be cured of your disease."

35 While he was still speaking, people came from the synagogue ruler's house, saying, "Your daughter is dead. Why bother the Teacher any more?"

36 But Jesus, when he heard the message spoken, immediately said to the ruler of the synagogue, "Don't be afraid, only believe." 37 He allowed no one to follow him except Peter, James, and John the brother of James. 38 He came to the synagogue ruler's house, and he saw an uproar, weeping, and great wailing. 39 When he had entered in, he said to them, "Why do you make an uproar and weep? The child is not dead, but is asleep."
40 They ridiculed him. But he, having put them all out, took the father of the child, her mother, and those who were with him, and went in where the child was lying. 41 Taking the child by the hand, he said to her, "Talitha cumi!" which means, being interpreted, "Girl, I tell you, get up!" 42 Immediately the girl rose up and walked, for she was twelve years old. They were amazed with great amazement. 43 He strictly ordered them that no one should know this, and commanded that something should be given to her to eat.

1. Invite the Holy Spirit into this reading, asking the Author of Scripture to speak to you through His Word
2. Read today's passage as many times as you need, take your time
3. Write down (below) what the Lord is saying to you today
4. Live with this Word in your heart through the day

Wednesday, January 31, 2024
Saint John Bosco, Priest

First Reading: Second Samuel 24: 2, 9-17

2 The king said to Joab the captain of the army, who was with him, "Now go back and forth through all the tribes of Israel, from Dan even to Beersheba, and count the people, that I may know the sum of the people."
9 Joab gave up the sum of the counting of the people to the king; and there were in Israel eight hundred thousand valiant men who drew the sword, and the men of Judah were five hundred thousand men.
10 David's heart struck him after he had counted the people. David said to Yahweh, "I have sinned greatly in that which I have done. But now, Yahweh, put away, I beg you, the iniquity of your servant; for I have done very foolishly."
11 When David rose up in the morning, Yahweh's word came to the prophet Gad, David's seer, saying, 12 "Go and speak to David, 'Yahweh says, "I offer you three things. Choose one of them, that I may do it to you." ' "

13 So Gad came to David, and told him, saying, "Shall seven years of famine come to you in your land? Or will you flee three months before your foes while they pursue you? Or shall there be three days' pestilence in your land? Now answer, and consider what answer I shall return to him who sent me."

14 David said to Gad, "I am in distress. Let us fall now into Yahweh's hand, for his mercies are great. Let me not fall into man's hand."

15 So Yahweh sent a pestilence on Israel from the morning even to the appointed time; and seventy thousand men died of the people from Dan even to Beersheba. 16 When the angel stretched out his hand toward Jerusalem to destroy it, Yahweh relented of the disaster, and said to the angel who destroyed the people, "It is enough. Now withdraw your hand." Yahweh's angel was by the threshing floor of Araunah the Jebusite.

17 David spoke to Yahweh when he saw the angel who struck the people, and said, "Behold, I have sinned, and I have done perversely; but these sheep, what have they done? Please let your hand be against me, and against my father's house."

Responsorial Psalm: Psalms 32: 1-2, 5- 7

1 Blessed is he whose disobedience is forgiven,
whose sin is covered.
2 Blessed is the man to whom Yahweh doesn't impute iniquity,
in whose spirit there is no deceit.
5 I acknowledged my sin to you.
I didn't hide my iniquity.
I said, I will confess my transgressions to Yahweh,
and you forgave the iniquity of my sin.
6 For this, let everyone who is godly pray to you in a time when you may be found.
Surely when the great waters overflow, they shall not reach to him.
7 You are my hiding place.
You will preserve me from trouble.
You will surround me with songs of deliverance.

Gospel: Mark 6: 1-6

1 He went out from there. He came into his own country, and his disciples followed him. 2 When the Sabbath had come, he began to teach in the synagogue, and many hearing him were astonished, saying, "Where did this man get these things?" and, "What is the wisdom that is given to this man, that such mighty works come about by his hands? 3 Isn't this the carpenter, the son of Mary and brother of James, Joses, Judah, and Simon? Aren't his sisters here with us?" So they were offended at him.

4 Jesus said to them, "A prophet is not without honor, except in his own country, and among his own relatives, and in his own house." 5 He could do no mighty work there,

except that he laid his hands on a few sick people and healed them. 6 He marveled because of their unbelief.

He went around the villages teaching.

Thursday, February 1, 2024

First Reading: First Kings 2: 1-4, 10-12

1 Now the days of David came near that he should die; and he commanded Solomon his son, saying, 2 "I am going the way of all the earth. You be strong therefore, and show yourself a man; 3 and keep the instruction of Yahweh your God, to walk in his ways, to keep his statutes, his commandments, his ordinances, and his testimonies, according to that which is written in the law of Moses, that you may prosper in all that you do and wherever you turn yourself. 4 Then Yahweh may establish his word which he spoke concerning me, saying, 'If your children are careful of their way, to walk before me in truth with all their heart and with all their soul, there shall not fail you,' he said, 'a man on the throne of Israel.'

10 David slept with his fathers, and was buried in David's city. 11 The days that David reigned over Israel were forty years; he reigned seven years in Hebron, and he reigned thirty-three years in Jerusalem. 12 Solomon sat on David his father's throne; and his kingdom was firmly established.

Responsorial Psalm: First Chronicles 29: 10-12

10 Therefore David blessed Yahweh before all the assembly; and David said, "You are blessed, Yahweh, the God of Israel our father, forever and ever. 11 Yours, Yahweh, is the greatness, the power, the glory, the victory, and the majesty! For all that is in the heavens and in the earth is yours. Yours is the kingdom, Yahweh, and you are exalted as head above all. 12 Both riches and honor come from you, and you rule over all! In your hand is power and might! It is in your hand to make great, and to give strength to all!

Gospel: Mark 6: 7-13

7 He called to himself the twelve, and began to send them out two by two; and he gave them authority over the unclean spirits. 8 He commanded them that they should take nothing for their journey, except a staff only: no bread, no wallet, no money in their purse, 9 but to wear sandals, and not put on two tunics. 10 He said to them, "Wherever you enter into a house, stay there until you depart from there. 11 Whoever will not receive you nor hear you, as you depart from there, shake off the dust that is under your feet for a testimony against them. Assuredly, I tell you, it will be more tolerable for Sodom and Gomorrah in the day of judgment than for that city!"
12 They went out and preached that people should repent. 13 They cast out many demons, and anointed many with oil who were sick and healed them.

1. Invite the Holy Spirit into this reading, asking the Author of Scripture to speak to you through His Word
2. Read today's passage as many times as you need, take your time
3. Write down (below) what the Lord is saying to you today
4. Live with this Word in your heart through the day

_____

_____

Friday, February 2, 2024
The Presentation of the Lord

First Reading: Malachi 3: 1-4

1 "Behold, I send my messenger, and he will prepare the way before me! The Lord, whom you seek, will suddenly come to his temple. Behold, the messenger of the covenant, whom you desire, is coming!" says Yahweh of Armies. 2 "But who can endure the day of his coming? And who will stand when he appears? For he is like a refiner's fire, and like launderers' soap; 3 and he will sit as a refiner and purifier of silver, and he will purify the sons of Levi, and refine them as gold and silver; and they shall offer to Yahweh offerings in righteousness. 4 Then the offering of Judah and Jerusalem will be pleasant to Yahweh as in the days of old and as in ancient years.

Responsorial Psalm: Psalms 24: 7- 10

7 Lift up your heads, you gates!
Be lifted up, you everlasting doors,
and the King of glory will come in.
8 Who is the King of glory?
Yahweh strong and mighty,
Yahweh mighty in battle.
9 Lift up your heads, you gates;
yes, lift them up, you everlasting doors,
and the King of glory will come in.
10 Who is this King of glory?
Yahweh of Armies is the King of glory!

Second Reading: Hebrews 2: 14-18

14 Since then the children have shared in flesh and blood, he also himself in the same way partook of the same, that through death he might bring to nothing him who had the power of death, that is, the devil, 15 and might deliver all of them who through fear of death were all their lifetime subject to bondage. 16 For most certainly, he doesn't give help to angels, but he gives help to the offspring§ of Abraham. 17 Therefore he was obligated in all things to be made like his brothers, that he might become a merciful and faithful high priest in things pertaining to God, to make atonement for the sins of the people. 18 For in that he himself has suffered being tempted, he is able to help those who are tempted.

Gospel: Luke 2: 22-32

22 When the days of their purification according to the law of Moses were fulfilled, they brought him up to Jerusalem to present him to the Lord 23 (as it is written in the law of the Lord, "Every male who opens the womb shall be called holy to the Lord"),* 24 and to offer a sacrifice according to that which is said in the law of the Lord, "A pair of turtledoves, or two young pigeons."*
25 Behold, there was a man in Jerusalem whose name was Simeon. This man was righteous and devout, looking for the consolation of Israel, and the Holy Spirit was on him. 26 It had been revealed to him by the Holy Spirit that he should not see death before he had seen the Lord's Christ.‡ 27 He came in the Spirit into the temple. When the parents brought in the child, Jesus, that they might do concerning him according to the custom of the law, 28 then he received him into his arms and blessed God, and said,
29 "Now you are releasing your servant, Master,
according to your word, in peace;
30 for my eyes have seen your salvation,
31 which you have prepared before the face of all peoples;
32 a light for revelation to the nations,

and the glory of your people Israel."

_____

_____

Saturday, February 3, 2024
Saint Blaise, Bishop and Martyr; Saint Ansgar, Bishop

First Reading: First Kings 3: 4-13

4 The king went to Gibeon to sacrifice there, for that was the great high place. Solomon offered a thousand burnt offerings on that altar. 5 In Gibeon, Yahweh appeared to Solomon in a dream by night; and God said, "Ask for what I should give you."
6 Solomon said, "You have shown to your servant David my father great loving kindness, because he walked before you in truth, in righteousness, and in uprightness of heart with you. You have kept for him this great loving kindness, that you have given him a son to sit on his throne, as it is today. 7 Now, Yahweh my God, you have made your servant king instead of David my father. I am just a little child. I don't know how to go out or come in. 8 Your servant is among your people which you have chosen, a great people, that can't be numbered or counted for multitude. 9 Give your servant therefore an understanding heart to judge your people, that I may discern between good and evil; for who is able to judge this great people of yours?"
10 This request pleased the Lord, that Solomon had asked this thing. 11 God said to him, "Because you have asked this thing, and have not asked for yourself long life, nor have you asked for riches for yourself, nor have you asked for the life of your enemies, but have asked for yourself understanding to discern justice, 12 behold, I have done according to your word. Behold, I have given you a wise and understanding heart, so that there has been no one like you before you, and after you none will arise like you. 13 I have also given you that which you have not asked, both riches and honor, so that there will not be any among the kings like you for all your days.

Responsorial Psalm: Psalms 119: 9- 14

9 How can a young man keep his way pure?
By living according to your word.
10 With my whole heart I have sought you.
Don't let me wander from your commandments.
11 I have hidden your word in my heart,
that I might not sin against you.
12 Blessed are you, Yahweh.
Teach me your statutes.
13 With my lips,
I have declared all the ordinances of your mouth.
14 I have rejoiced in the way of your testimonies,
as much as in all riches.

Gospel: Mark 6: 30-34

30 The apostles gathered themselves together to Jesus, and they told him all things, whatever they had done, and whatever they had taught. 31 He said to them, "Come away into a deserted place, and rest awhile." For there were many coming and going, and they had no leisure so much as to eat. 32 They went away in the boat to a deserted place by themselves. 33 They† saw them going, and many recognized him and ran there on foot from all the cities. They arrived before them and came together to him. 34 Jesus came out, saw a great multitude, and he had compassion on them because they were like sheep without a shepherd; and he began to teach them many things.

1. Invite the Holy Spirit into this reading, asking the Author of Scripture to speak to you through His Word
2. Read today's passage as many times as you need, take your time
3. Write down (below) what the Lord is saying to you today
4. Live with this Word in your heart through the day

_____

_____

Sunday, February 4, 2024
Fifth Sunday in Ordinary Time

First Reading: Job 7: 1-4, 6-7

1 "Isn't a man forced to labor on earth?
Aren't his days like the days of a hired hand?
2 As a servant who earnestly desires the shadow,
as a hireling who looks for his wages,
3 so I am made to possess months of misery,
wearisome nights are appointed to me.
4 When I lie down, I say,
'When will I arise, and the night be gone?'
I toss and turn until the dawning of the day.
6 My days are swifter than a weaver's shuttle,
and are spent without hope.
7 Oh remember that my life is a breath.
My eye will no more see good.

Responsorial Psalm: Psalms 147: 1-6

1 Praise Yah,
for it is good to sing praises to our God;
for it is pleasant and fitting to praise him.
2 Yahweh builds up Jerusalem.
He gathers together the outcasts of Israel.
3 He heals the broken in heart,
and binds up their wounds.
4 He counts the number of the stars.
He calls them all by their names.
5 Great is our Lord, and mighty in power.
His understanding is infinite.
6 Yahweh upholds the humble.
He brings the wicked down to the ground.

Second Reading: First Corinthians 9: 16-19, 22-23

16 For if I preach the Good News, I have nothing to boast about, for necessity is laid on me; but woe is to me if I don't preach the Good News. 17 For if I do this of my own will, I have a reward. But if not of my own will, I have a stewardship entrusted to me. 18 What then is my reward? That when I preach the Good News, I may present the Good News of Christ without charge, so as not to abuse my authority in the Good News.
19 For though I was free from all, I brought myself under bondage to all, that I might gain the more.

22 To the weak I became as weak, that I might gain the weak. I have become all things to all men, that I may by all means save some. 23 Now I do this for the sake of the Good News, that I may be a joint partaker of it.

Gospel: Mark 1: 29-39

29 Immediately, when they had come out of the synagogue, they came into the house of Simon and Andrew, with James and John. 30 Now Simon's wife's mother lay sick with a fever, and immediately they told him about her. 31 He came and took her by the hand and raised her up. The fever left her immediately,† and she served them.

32 At evening, when the sun had set, they brought to him all who were sick and those who were possessed by demons. 33 All the city was gathered together at the door. 34 He healed many who were sick with various diseases and cast out many demons. He didn't allow the demons to speak, because they knew him.

35 Early in the morning, while it was still dark, he rose up and went out, and departed into a deserted place, and prayed there. 36 Simon and those who were with him searched for him. 37 They found him and told him, "Everyone is looking for you."

38 He said to them, "Let's go elsewhere into the next towns, that I may preach there also, because I came out for this reason." 39 He went into their synagogues throughout all Galilee, preaching and casting out demons.

1. Invite the Holy Spirit into this reading, asking the Author of Scripture to speak to you through His Word
2. Read today's passage as many times as you need, take your time
3. Write down (below) what the Lord is saying to you today
4. Live with this Word in your heart through the day

_____

_____

Monday, February 5, 2024
Saint Agatha, Virgin and Martyr

First Reading: First Kings 8: 1-7, 9-13

1 Then Solomon assembled the elders of Israel with all the heads of the tribes, the princes of the fathers' households of the children of Israel, to King Solomon in Jerusalem, to bring up the ark of Yahweh's covenant out of David's city, which is Zion. 2 All the men of Israel

assembled themselves to King Solomon at the feast in the month Ethanim, which is the seventh month. 3 All the elders of Israel came, and the priests picked up the ark. 4 They brought up Yahwch's ark, the Tent of Meeting, and all the holy vessels that were in the Tent. The priests and the Levites brought these up. 5 King Solomon and all the congregation of Israel, who were assembled to him, were with him before the ark, sacrificing sheep and cattle that could not be counted or numbered for multitude. 6 The priests brought in the ark of Yahweh's covenant to its place, into the inner sanctuary of the house, to the most holy place, even under the cherubim's wings. 7 For the cherubim spread their wings out over the place of the ark, and the cherubim covered the ark and its poles above. 9 There was nothing in the ark except the two stone tablets which Moses put there at Horeb, when Yahweh made a covenant with the children of Israel, when they came out of the land of Egypt. 10 It came to pass, when the priests had come out of the holy place, that the cloud filled Yahweh's house, 11 so that the priests could not stand to minister by reason of the cloud; for Yahweh's glory filled Yahweh's house.
12 Then Solomon said, "Yahweh has said that he would dwell in the thick darkness. 13 I have surely built you a house of habitation, a place for you to dwell in forever."

Responsorial Psalm: Psalms 132: 6-10

6 Behold, we heard of it in Ephrathah.
We found it in the field of Jaar.
7 "We will go into his dwelling place.
We will worship at his footstool."
8 Arise, Yahweh, into your resting place,
you, and the ark of your strength.
9 Let your priests be clothed with righteousness.
Let your saints shout for joy!
10 For your servant David's sake,
don't turn away the face of your anointed one.

Gospel: Mark 6: 53-56

53 When they had crossed over, they came to land at Gennesaret and moored to the shore. 54 When they had come out of the boat, immediately the people recognized him, 55 and ran around that whole region, and began to bring those who were sick on their mats to where they heard he was. 56 Wherever he entered—into villages, or into cities, or into the country—they laid the sick in the marketplaces and begged him that they might just touch the fringe‡ of his garment; and as many as touched him were made well.

1. Invite the Holy Spirit into this reading, asking the Author of Scripture to speak to you through His Word

2. Read today's passage as many times as you need, take your time
3. Write down (below) what the Lord is saying to you today
4. Live with this Word in your heart through the day

Tuesday, February 6, 2024
Saint Paul Miki and Companions, Martyrs

First Reading: First Kings 8: 22-23, 27-30

22 Solomon stood before Yahweh's altar in the presence of all the assembly of Israel, and spread out his hands toward heaven; 23 and he said, "Yahweh, the God of Israel, there is no God like you, in heaven above, or on earth beneath; who keeps covenant and loving kindness with your servants who walk before you with all their heart;
27 But will God in very deed dwell on the earth? Behold, heaven and the heaven of heavens can't contain you; how much less this house that I have built! 28 Yet have respect for the prayer of your servant and for his supplication, Yahweh my God, to listen to the cry and to the prayer which your servant prays before you today; 29 that your eyes may be open toward this house night and day, even toward the place of which you have said, 'My name shall be there;' to listen to the prayer which your servant prays toward this place. 30 Listen to the supplication of your servant, and of your people Israel, when they pray toward this place. Yes, hear in heaven, your dwelling place; and when you hear, forgive.

Responsorial Psalm: Psalms 84: 3- 5 and 10-11

3 Yes, the sparrow has found a home,
and the swallow a nest for herself, where she may have her young,
near your altars, Yahweh of Armies, my King, and my God.
4 Blessed are those who dwell in your house.
They are always praising you.
5 Blessed are those whose strength is in you,
who have set their hearts on a pilgrimage.
10 For a day in your courts is better than a thousand.
I would rather be a doorkeeper in the house of my God,
than to dwell in the tents of wickedness.
11 For Yahweh God is a sun and a shield.

Yahweh will give grace and glory.
He withholds no good thing from those who walk blamelessly.

Gospel: Mark 7: 1-13

1 Then the Pharisees and some of the scribes gathered together to him, having come from Jerusalem. 2 Now when they saw some of his disciples eating bread with defiled, that is unwashed, hands, they found fault. 3 (For the Pharisees and all the Jews don't eat unless they wash their hands and forearms, holding to the tradition of the elders. 4 They don't eat when they come from the marketplace unless they bathe themselves, and there are many other things which they have received to hold to: washings of cups, pitchers, bronze vessels, and couches.) 5 The Pharisees and the scribes asked him, "Why don't your disciples walk according to the tradition of the elders, but eat their bread with unwashed hands?"
6 He answered them, "Well did Isaiah prophesy of you hypocrites, as it is written,
'This people honors me with their lips,
but their heart is far from me.
7 They worship me in vain,
teaching as doctrines the commandments of men.'*
8 "For you set aside the commandment of God, and hold tightly to the tradition of men— the washing of pitchers and cups, and you do many other such things." 9 He said to them, "Full well do you reject the commandment of God, that you may keep your tradition. 10 For Moses said, 'Honor your father and your mother;'* and, 'He who speaks evil of father or mother, let him be put to death.'* 11 But you say, 'If a man tells his father or his mother, "Whatever profit you might have received from me is Corban," ' "† that is to say, given to God, 12 "then you no longer allow him to do anything for his father or his mother, 13 making void the word of God by your tradition which you have handed down. You do many things like this."

1. Invite the Holy Spirit into this reading, asking the Author of Scripture to speak to you through His Word
2. Read today's passage as many times as you need, take your time
3. Write down (below) what the Lord is saying to you today
4. Live with this Word in your heart through the day

———————————————————————————————————————

———————————————————————————————————————

Wednesday, February 7, 2024

First Reading: First Kings 10: 1-10

1 When the queen of Sheba heard of the fame of Solomon concerning Yahweh's name, she came to test him with hard questions. 2 She came to Jerusalem with a very great caravan, with camels that bore spices, very much gold, and precious stones; and when she had come to Solomon, she talked with him about all that was in her heart. 3 Solomon answered all her questions. There wasn't anything hidden from the king which he didn't tell her. 4 When the queen of Sheba had seen all the wisdom of Solomon, the house that he had built, 5 the food of his table, the sitting of his servants, the attendance of his officials, their clothing, his cup bearers, and his ascent by which he went up to Yahweh's house, there was no more spirit in her. 6 She said to the king, "It was a true report that I heard in my own land of your acts and of your wisdom. 7 However, I didn't believe the words until I came and my eyes had seen it. Behold, not even half was told me! Your wisdom and prosperity exceed the fame which I heard. 8 Happy are your men, happy are these your servants who stand continually before you, who hear your wisdom. 9 Blessed is Yahweh your God, who delighted in you, to set you on the throne of Israel. Because Yahweh loved Israel forever, therefore he made you king, to do justice and righteousness." 10 She gave the king one hundred twenty talents of gold, and a very great quantity of spices, and precious stones. Never again was there such an abundance of spices as these which the queen of Sheba gave to King Solomon.

Responsorial Psalm: Psalms 37: 5-6, 30-31, 39-40

5 Commit your way to Yahweh.
Trust also in him, and he will do this:
6 he will make your righteousness shine out like light,
and your justice as the noon day sun.
30 The mouth of the righteous talks of wisdom.
His tongue speaks justice.
31 The law of his God is in his heart.
None of his steps shall slide.
39 But the salvation of the righteous is from Yahweh.
He is their stronghold in the time of trouble.
40 Yahweh helps them and rescues them.
He rescues them from the wicked and saves them,
because they have taken refuge in him.

Gospel: Mark 7: 14-23

14 He called all the multitude to himself and said to them, "Hear me, all of you, and understand. 15 There is nothing from outside of the man that going into him can defile

him; but the things which proceed out of the man are those that defile the man. 16 If anyone has ears to hear, let him hear!"‡

17 When he had entered into a house away from the multitude, his disciples asked him about the parable. 18 He said to them, "Are you also without understanding? Don't you perceive that whatever goes into the man from outside can't defile him, 19 because it doesn't go into his heart, but into his stomach, then into the latrine, making all foods clean?"§ 20 He said, "That which proceeds out of the man, that defiles the man. 21 For from within, out of the hearts of men, proceed evil thoughts, adulteries, sexual sins, murders, thefts, 22 covetings, wickedness, deceit, lustful desires, an evil eye, blasphemy, pride, and foolishness. 23 All these evil things come from within and defile the man."

1. Invite the Holy Spirit into this reading, asking the Author of Scripture to speak to you through His Word
2. Read today's passage as many times as you need, take your time
3. Write down (below) what the Lord is saying to you today
4. Live with this Word in your heart through the day

_____

_____

Thursday, February 8, 2024
Saint Jerome Emiliani; Saint Josephine Bakhita, Virgin

First Reading: First Kings 11: 4-13

4 When Solomon was old, his wives turned away his heart after other gods; and his heart was not perfect with Yahweh his God, as the heart of David his father was. 5 For Solomon went after Ashtoreth the goddess of the Sidonians, and after Milcom the abomination of the Ammonites. 6 Solomon did that which was evil in Yahweh's sight, and didn't go fully after Yahweh, as David his father did. 7 Then Solomon built a high place for Chemosh the abomination of Moab, on the mountain that is before Jerusalem, and for Molech the abomination of the children of Ammon. 8 So he did for all his foreign wives, who burned incense and sacrificed to their gods. 9 Yahweh was angry with Solomon, because his heart was turned away from Yahweh, the God of Israel, who had appeared to him twice, 10 and had commanded him concerning this thing, that he should not go after other gods; but he didn't keep that which Yahweh commanded. 11 Therefore Yahweh said to Solomon, "Because this is done by you, and you have not kept my covenant and my statutes, which I have commanded you, I will surely tear the kingdom from you, and will give it to your

servant. 12 Nevertheless, I will not do it in your days, for David your father's sake; but I will tear it out of your son's hand. 13 However, I will not tear away all the kingdom; but I will give one tribe to your son, for David my servant's sake, and for Jerusalem's sake which I have chosen."

Responsorial Psalm: Psalms 106: 3-4, 35-36, 37 and 40

3 Blessed are those who keep justice.
Blessed is one who does what is right at all times.
4 Remember me, Yahweh, with the favor that you show to your people.
Visit me with your salvation,
35 but mixed themselves with the nations,
and learned their works.
36 They served their idols,
which became a snare to them.
37 Yes, they sacrificed their sons and their daughters to demons.
40 Therefore Yahweh burned with anger against his people.
He abhorred his inheritance.

Gospel: Mark 7: 24-30

24 From there he arose and went away into the borders of Tyre and Sidon. He entered into a house and didn't want anyone to know it, but he couldn't escape notice. 25 For a woman whose little daughter had an unclean spirit, having heard of him, came and fell down at his feet. 26 Now the woman was a Greek, a Syrophoenician by race. She begged him that he would cast the demon out of her daughter. 27 But Jesus said to her, "Let the children be filled first, for it is not appropriate to take the children's bread and throw it to the dogs." 28 But she answered him, "Yes, Lord. Yet even the dogs under the table eat the children's crumbs."
29 He said to her, "For this saying, go your way. The demon has gone out of your daughter."
30 She went away to her house, and found the child having been laid on the bed, with the demon gone out.

1. Invite the Holy Spirit into this reading, asking the Author of Scripture to speak to you through His Word
2. Read today's passage as many times as you need, take your time
3. Write down (below) what the Lord is saying to you today
4. Live with this Word in your heart through the day

_____

_____

Friday, February 9, 2024

First Reading: First Kings 11: 29-32; 12: 19

29 At that time, when Jeroboam went out of Jerusalem, the prophet Ahijah the Shilonite found him on the way. Now Ahijah had clad himself with a new garment; and the two of them were alone in the field. 30 Ahijah took the new garment that was on him, and tore it in twelve pieces. 31 He said to Jeroboam, "Take ten pieces; for Yahweh, the God of Israel, says, 'Behold, I will tear the kingdom out of the hand of Solomon and will give ten tribes to you 32 (but he shall have one tribe, for my servant David's sake and for Jerusalem's sake, the city which I have chosen out of all the tribes of Israel),
19 So Israel rebelled against David's house to this day.

Responsorial Psalm: Psalms 81: 10-15

10 I am Yahweh, your God,
who brought you up out of the land of Egypt.
Open your mouth wide, and I will fill it.
11 But my people didn't listen to my voice.
Israel desired none of me.
12 So I let them go after the stubbornness of their hearts,
that they might walk in their own counsels.
13 Oh that my people would listen to me,
that Israel would walk in my ways!
14 I would soon subdue their enemies,
and turn my hand against their adversaries.
15 The haters of Yahweh would cringe before him,
and their punishment would last forever.

Gospel: Mark 7: 31-37

31 Again he departed from the borders of Tyre and Sidon, and came to the sea of Galilee through the middle of the region of Decapolis. 32 They brought to him one who was deaf and had an impediment in his speech. They begged him to lay his hand on him. 33 He took him aside from the multitude privately and put his fingers into his ears; and he spat and touched his tongue. 34 Looking up to heaven, he sighed, and said to him, "Ephphatha!" that is, "Be opened!" 35 Immediately his ears were opened, and the impediment of his tongue was released, and he spoke clearly. 36 He commanded them that they should tell no one, but the more he commanded them, so much the more widely they proclaimed it.

37 They were astonished beyond measure, saying, "He has done all things well. He makes even the deaf hear and the mute speak!"

Saturday, February 10, 2024
Saint Scholastica, Virgin

First Reading: First Kings 12: 26-32; 13: 33-34

26 Jeroboam said in his heart, "Now the kingdom will return to David's house. 27 If this people goes up to offer sacrifices in Yahweh's house at Jerusalem, then the heart of this people will turn again to their lord, even to Rehoboam king of Judah; and they will kill me, and return to Rehoboam king of Judah." 28 So the king took counsel, and made two calves of gold; and he said to them, "It is too much for you to go up to Jerusalem. Look and behold your gods, Israel, which brought you up out of the land of Egypt!" 29 He set the one in Bethel, and the other he put in Dan. 30 This thing became a sin, for the people went even as far as Dan to worship before the one there. 31 He made houses of high places, and made priests from among all the people, who were not of the sons of Levi. 32 Jeroboam ordained a feast in the eighth month, on the fifteenth day of the month, like the feast that is in Judah, and he went up to the altar. He did so in Bethel, sacrificing to the calves that he had made, and he placed in Bethel the priests of the high places that he had made.
33 After this thing, Jeroboam didn't turn from his evil way, but again made priests of the high places from among all the people. Whoever wanted to, he consecrated him, that there might be priests of the high places. 34 This thing became sin to the house of Jeroboam, even to cut it off and to destroy it from off the surface of the earth.

Responsorial Psalm: Psalms 106: 6-7, 19-22

6 We have sinned with our fathers.
We have committed iniquity.

We have done wickedly.

7 Our fathers didn't understand your wonders in Egypt.

They didn't remember the multitude of your loving kindnesses,

but were rebellious at the sea, even at the Red Sea.

19 They made a calf in Horeb,

and worshiped a molten image.

20 Thus they exchanged their glory

for an image of a bull that eats grass.

21 They forgot God, their Savior,

who had done great things in Egypt,

22 wondrous works in the land of Ham,

and awesome things by the Red Sea.

Gospel: Mark 8: 1-10

1 In those days, when there was a very great multitude, and they had nothing to eat, Jesus called his disciples to himself and said to them, 2 "I have compassion on the multitude, because they have stayed with me now three days and have nothing to eat. 3 If I send them away fasting to their home, they will faint on the way, for some of them have come a long way."

4 His disciples answered him, "From where could one satisfy these people with bread here in a deserted place?"

5 He asked them, "How many loaves do you have?"

They said, "Seven."

6 He commanded the multitude to sit down on the ground, and he took the seven loaves. Having given thanks, he broke them and gave them to his disciples to serve, and they served the multitude. 7 They also had a few small fish. Having blessed them, he said to serve these also. 8 They ate and were filled. They took up seven baskets of broken pieces that were left over. 9 Those who had eaten were about four thousand. Then he sent them away.

10 Immediately he entered into the boat with his disciples and came into the region of Dalmanutha.

1. Invite the Holy Spirit into this reading, asking the Author of Scripture to speak to you through His Word
2. Read today's passage as many times as you need, take your time
3. Write down (below) what the Lord is saying to you today
4. Live with this Word in your heart through the day

_____

_____

First Reading: Leviticus 13: 1-2, 44-46

1 Yahweh spoke to Moses and to Aaron, saying, 2 "When a man shall have a swelling in his body's skin, or a scab, or a bright spot, and it becomes in the skin of his body the plague of leprosy, then he shall be brought to Aaron the priest or to one of his sons, the priests. 44 he is a leprous man. He is unclean. The priest shall surely pronounce him unclean. His plague is on his head.
45 "The leper in whom the plague is shall wear torn clothes, and the hair of his head shall hang loose. He shall cover his upper lip, and shall cry, 'Unclean! Unclean!' 46 All the days in which the plague is in him he shall be unclean. He is unclean. He shall dwell alone. His dwelling shall be outside of the camp.

Responsorial Psalm: Psalms 32: 1-2, 5, 11

1 Blessed is he whose disobedience is forgiven,
whose sin is covered.
2 Blessed is the man to whom Yahweh doesn't impute iniquity,
in whose spirit there is no deceit.
5 I acknowledged my sin to you.
I didn't hide my iniquity.
I said, I will confess my transgressions to Yahweh,
and you forgave the iniquity of my sin.
11 Be glad in Yahweh, and rejoice, you righteous!
Shout for joy, all you who are upright in heart!

Second Reading: First Corinthians 10: 31 – 11: 1

31 Whether therefore you eat or drink, or whatever you do, do all to the glory of God. 32 Give no occasion for stumbling, whether to Jews, to Greeks, or to the assembly of God; 33 even as I also please all men in all things, not seeking my own profit, but the profit of the many, that they may be saved.
1 Be imitators of me, even as I also am of Christ.

Gospel: Mark 1: 40-45

40 A leper came to him, begging him, kneeling down to him, and saying to him, "If you want to, you can make me clean."

41 Being moved with compassion, he stretched out his hand, and touched him, and said to him, "I want to. Be made clean." 42 When he had said this, immediately the leprosy departed from him and he was made clean. 43 He strictly warned him and immediately sent him out, 44 and said to him, "See that you say nothing to anybody, but go show yourself to the priest and offer for your cleansing the things which Moses commanded, for a testimony to them."

45 But he went out, and began to proclaim it much, and to spread about the matter, so that Jesus could no more openly enter into a city, but was outside in desert places. People came to him from everywhere.

1. Invite the Holy Spirit into this reading, asking the Author of Scripture to speak to you through His Word
2. Read today's passage as many times as you need, take your time
3. Write down (below) what the Lord is saying to you today
4. Live with this Word in your heart through the day

_____

_____

Monday, February 12, 2024

First Reading: James 1: 1-11

1 James, a servant of God and of the Lord Jesus Christ,† to the twelve tribes which are in the Dispersion: Greetings.

2 Count it all joy, my brothers,‡ when you fall into various temptations, 3 knowing that the testing of your faith produces endurance. 4 Let endurance have its perfect work, that you may be perfect and complete, lacking in nothing.

5 But if any of you lacks wisdom, let him ask of God, who gives to all liberally and without reproach, and it will be given to him. 6 But let him ask in faith, without any doubting, for he who doubts is like a wave of the sea, driven by the wind and tossed. 7 For that man shouldn't think that he will receive anything from the Lord. 8 He is a double-minded man, unstable in all his ways.

9 Let the brother in humble circumstances glory in his high position; 10 and the rich, in that he is made humble, because like the flower in the grass, he will pass away. 11 For the sun arises with the scorching wind and withers the grass; and the flower in it falls, and the beauty of its appearance perishes. So the rich man will also fade away in his pursuits.

Responsorial Psalm: Psalms 119: 67, 68, 71, 72, 75, 76

67 Before I was afflicted, I went astray;
but now I observe your word.
68 You are good, and do good.
Teach me your statutes.
71 It is good for me that I have been afflicted,
that I may learn your statutes.
72 The law of your mouth is better to me than thousands of pieces of gold and silver.
75 Yahweh, I know that your judgments are righteous,
that in faithfulness you have afflicted me.
76 Please let your loving kindness be for my comfort,
according to your word to your servant.

Gospel: Mark 8: 11-13

11 The Pharisees came out and began to question him, seeking from him a sign from heaven and testing him. 12 He sighed deeply in his spirit and said, "Why does this generation† seek a sign? Most certainly I tell you, no sign will be given to this generation." 13 He left them, and again entering into the boat, departed to the other side.

1. Invite the Holy Spirit into this reading, asking the Author of Scripture to speak to you through His Word
2. Read today's passage as many times as you need, take your time
3. Write down (below) what the Lord is saying to you today
4. Live with this Word in your heart through the day

_____

_____

Tuesday, February 13, 2024

First Reading: James 1: 12-18

12 Blessed is a person who endures temptation, for when he has been approved, he will receive the crown of life which the Lord promised to those who love him.
13 Let no man say when he is tempted, "I am tempted by God," for God can't be tempted by evil, and he himself tempts no one. 14 But each one is tempted when he is drawn away

by his own lust and enticed. 15 Then the lust, when it has conceived, bears sin. The sin, when it is full grown, produces death. 16 Don't be deceived, my beloved brothers. 17 Every good gift and every perfect gift is from above, coming down from the Father of lights, with whom can be no variation nor turning shadow. 18 Of his own will he gave birth to us by the word of truth, that we should be a kind of first fruits of his creatures.

Responsorial Psalm: Psalms 94: 12-15, 18-19

12 Blessed is the man whom you discipline, Yah,
and teach out of your law,
13 that you may give him rest from the days of adversity,
until the pit is dug for the wicked.
14 For Yahweh won't reject his people,
neither will he forsake his inheritance.
15 For judgment will return to righteousness.
All the upright in heart shall follow it.
18 When I said, "My foot is slipping!"
Your loving kindness, Yahweh, held me up.
19 In the multitude of my thoughts within me,
your comforts delight my soul.

Gospel: Mark 8: 14-21

14 They forgot to take bread; and they didn't have more than one loaf in the boat with them. 15 He warned them, saying, "Take heed: beware of the yeast of the Pharisees and the yeast of Herod."
16 They reasoned with one another, saying, "It's because we have no bread."
17 Jesus, perceiving it, said to them, "Why do you reason that it's because you have no bread? Don't you perceive yet or understand? Is your heart still hardened? 18 Having eyes, don't you see? Having ears, don't you hear? Don't you remember? 19 When I broke the five loaves among the five thousand, how many baskets full of broken pieces did you take up?"
They told him, "Twelve."
20 "When the seven loaves fed the four thousand, how many baskets full of broken pieces did you take up?"
They told him, "Seven."
21 He asked them, "Don't you understand yet?"

1. Invite the Holy Spirit into this reading, asking the Author of Scripture to speak to you through His Word
2. Read today's passage as many times as you need, take your time

3. Write down (below) what the Lord is saying to you today
4. Live with this Word in your heart through the day

Wednesday, February 14, 2024
Ash Wednesday

First Reading: Joel 2: 12-18

12 "Yet even now," says Yahweh, "turn to me with all your heart,
and with fasting, and with weeping, and with mourning."
13 Tear your heart and not your garments,
and turn to Yahweh, your God;
for he is gracious and merciful,
slow to anger, and abundant in loving kindness,
and relents from sending calamity.
14 Who knows? He may turn and relent,
and leave a blessing behind him,
even a meal offering and a drink offering to Yahweh, your God.
15 Blow the trumpet in Zion!
Sanctify a fast.
Call a solemn assembly.
16 Gather the people.
Sanctify the assembly.
Assemble the elders.
Gather the children, and those who nurse from breasts.
Let the bridegroom go out of his room,
and the bride out of her chamber.
17 Let the priests, the ministers of Yahweh, weep between the porch and the altar,
and let them say, "Spare your people, Yahweh,
and don't give your heritage to reproach,
that the nations should rule over them.
Why should they say among the peoples,
'Where is their God?' "
18 Then Yahweh was jealous for his land,
and had pity on his people.

Responsorial Psalm: Psalms 51: 3-6, 12-14 and 17

3 For I know my transgressions.
My sin is constantly before me.
4 Against you, and you only, I have sinned,
and done that which is evil in your sight,
so you may be proved right when you speak,
and justified when you judge.
5 Behold, I was born in iniquity.
My mother conceived me in sin.
6 Behold, you desire truth in the inward parts.
You teach me wisdom in the inmost place.
12 Restore to me the joy of your salvation.
Uphold me with a willing spirit.
13 Then I will teach transgressors your ways.
Sinners will be converted to you.
14 Deliver me from the guilt of bloodshed, O God, the God of my salvation.
My tongue will sing aloud of your righteousness.
17 The sacrifices of God are a broken spirit.
O God, you will not despise a broken and contrite heart.

Second Reading: Second Corinthians 5: 20 – 6:2

20 We are therefore ambassadors on behalf of Christ, as though God were entreating by us: we beg you on behalf of Christ, be reconciled to God. 21 For him who knew no sin he made to be sin on our behalf, so that in him we might become the righteousness of God.
1 Working together, we entreat also that you do not receive the grace of God in vain. 2 For he says,
"At an acceptable time I listened to you.
In a day of salvation I helped you."*
Behold, now is the acceptable time. Behold, now is the day of salvation.

Gospel: Matthew 6: 1-6, 16-18

1 "Be careful that you don't do your charitable giving† before men, to be seen by them, or else you have no reward from your Father who is in heaven. 2 Therefore, when you do merciful deeds, don't sound a trumpet before yourself, as the hypocrites do in the synagogues and in the streets, that they may get glory from men. Most certainly I tell you, they have received their reward. 3 But when you do merciful deeds, don't let your left hand know what your right hand does, 4 so that your merciful deeds may be in secret, then your Father who sees in secret will reward you openly.

5 "When you pray, you shall not be as the hypocrites, for they love to stand and pray in the synagogues and in the corners of the streets, that they may be seen by men. Most certainly, I tell you, they have received their reward. 6 But you, when you pray, enter into your inner room, and having shut your door, pray to your Father who is in secret; and your Father who sees in secret will reward you openly.

16 "Moreover when you fast, don't be like the hypocrites, with sad faces. For they disfigure their faces that they may be seen by men to be fasting. Most certainly I tell you, they have received their reward. 17 But you, when you fast, anoint your head and wash your face, 18 so that you are not seen by men to be fasting, but by your Father who is in secret; and your Father, who sees in secret, will reward you.

1. Invite the Holy Spirit into this reading, asking the Author of Scripture to speak to you through His Word
2. Read today's passage as many times as you need, take your time
3. Write down (below) what the Lord is saying to you today
4. Live with this Word in your heart through the day

_____

_____

Thursday, February 15, 2024
Thursday after Ash Wednesday

First Reading: Deuteronomy 30: 15-20

15 Behold, I have set before you today life and prosperity, and death and evil. 16 For I command you today to love Yahweh your God, to walk in his ways and to keep his commandments, his statutes, and his ordinances, that you may live and multiply, and that Yahweh your God may bless you in the land where you go in to possess it. 17 But if your heart turns away, and you will not hear, but are drawn away and worship other gods, and serve them, 18 I declare to you today that you will surely perish. You will not prolong your days in the land where you pass over the Jordan to go in to possess it. 19 I call heaven and earth to witness against you today that I have set before you life and death, the blessing and the curse. Therefore choose life, that you may live, you and your descendants, 20 to love Yahweh your God, to obey his voice, and to cling to him; for he is your life, and the length of your days, that you may dwell in the land which Yahweh swore to your fathers, to Abraham, to Isaac, and to Jacob, to give them.

Responsorial Psalm: Psalms 1: 1-2, 3, 4 and 6

1 Blessed is the man who doesn't walk in the counsel of the wicked,
nor stand on the path of sinners,
nor sit in the seat of scoffers;
2 but his delight is in Yahweh's† law.
On his law he meditates day and night.
3 He will be like a tree planted by the streams of water,
that produces its fruit in its season,
whose leaf also does not wither.
Whatever he does shall prosper.
4 The wicked are not so,
but are like the chaff which the wind drives away.
6 For Yahweh knows the way of the righteous,
but the way of the wicked shall perish.

Gospel: Luke 9: 22-25

"The Son of Man must suffer many things, and be rejected by the elders, chief priests, and scribes, and be killed, and the third day be raised up."
23 He said to all, "If anyone desires to come after me, let him deny himself, take up his cross,§ and follow me. 24 For whoever desires to save his life will lose it, but whoever will lose his life for my sake will save it. 25 For what does it profit a man if he gains the whole world, and loses or forfeits his own self?

1. Invite the Holy Spirit into this reading, asking the Author of Scripture to speak to you through His Word
2. Read today's passage as many times as you need, take your time
3. Write down (below) what the Lord is saying to you today
4. Live with this Word in your heart through the day

_____

_____

Friday, February 16, 2024
Friday after Ash Wednesday

First Reading: Isaiah 58: 1-9a

1 "Cry aloud! Don't spare!
Lift up your voice like a trumpet!
Declare to my people their disobedience,
and to the house of Jacob their sins.
2 Yet they seek me daily,
and delight to know my ways.
As a nation that did righteousness,
and didn't forsake the ordinance of their God,
they ask of me righteous judgments.
They delight to draw near to God.
3 'Why have we fasted,' they say, 'and you don't see?
Why have we afflicted our soul, and you don't notice?'
 "Behold, in the day of your fast you find pleasure,
and oppress all your laborers.
4 Behold, you fast for strife and contention,
and to strike with the fist of wickedness.
You don't fast today so as to make your voice to be heard on high.
5 Is this the fast that I have chosen?
A day for a man to humble his soul?
Is it to bow down his head like a reed,
and to spread sackcloth and ashes under himself?
Will you call this a fast,
and an acceptable day to Yahweh?
6 "Isn't this the fast that I have chosen:
to release the bonds of wickedness,
to undo the straps of the yoke,
to let the oppressed go free,
and that you break every yoke?
7 Isn't it to distribute your bread to the hungry,
and that you bring the poor who are cast out to your house?
When you see the naked,
that you cover him;
and that you not hide yourself from your own flesh?
8 Then your light will break out as the morning,
and your healing will appear quickly;
then your righteousness shall go before you,
and Yahweh's glory will be your rear guard.
9 Then you will call, and Yahweh will answer.
You will cry for help, and he will say, 'Here I am.'

Responsorial Psalm: Psalms 51: 3-6, 18-19

3 For I know my transgressions.
My sin is constantly before me.
4 Against you, and you only, I have sinned,
and done that which is evil in your sight,
so you may be proved right when you speak,
and justified when you judge.
5 Behold, I was born in iniquity.
My mother conceived me in sin.
6 Behold, you desire truth in the inward parts.
You teach me wisdom in the inmost place.
18 Do well in your good pleasure to Zion.
Build the walls of Jerusalem.
19 Then you will delight in the sacrifices of righteousness,
in burnt offerings and in whole burnt offerings.
Then they will offer bulls on your altar.

Gospel: Matthew 9: 14-15

14 Then John's disciples came to him, saying, "Why do we and the Pharisees fast often, but your disciples don't fast?"
15 Jesus said to them, "Can the friends of the bridegroom mourn as long as the bridegroom is with them? But the days will come when the bridegroom will be taken away from them, and then they will fast.

1. Invite the Holy Spirit into this reading, asking the Author of Scripture to speak to you through His Word
2. Read today's passage as many times as you need, take your time
3. Write down (below) what the Lord is saying to you today
4. Live with this Word in your heart through the day

_____

_____

Saturday, February 17, 2024
Saturday after Ash Wednesday
The Seven Holy Founders of the Servite Order

First Reading: Isaiah 58: 9b-14

9b "If you take away from among you the yoke,
finger pointing,
and speaking wickedly;
10 and if you pour out your soul to the hungry,
and satisfy the afflicted soul,
then your light will rise in darkness,
and your obscurity will be as the noonday;
11 and Yahweh will guide you continually,
satisfy your soul in dry places,
and make your bones strong.
You will be like a watered garden,
and like a spring of water
whose waters don't fail.
12 Those who will be of you will build the old waste places.
You will raise up the foundations of many generations.
You will be called Repairer of the Breach,
Restorer of Paths with Dwellings.
13 "If you turn away your foot from the Sabbath,
from doing your pleasure on my holy day,
and call the Sabbath a delight,
and the holy of Yahweh honorable,
and honor it,
not doing your own ways,
nor finding your own pleasure,
nor speaking your own words,
14 then you will delight yourself in Yahweh,
and I will make you to ride on the high places of the earth,
and I will feed you with the heritage of Jacob your father;"
for Yahweh's mouth has spoken it.

Responsorial Psalm: Psalms 86: 1-6

1 Hear, Yahweh, and answer me,
for I am poor and needy.
2 Preserve my soul, for I am godly.
You, my God, save your servant who trusts in you.
3 Be merciful to me, Lord,
for I call to you all day long.
4 Bring joy to the soul of your servant,

for to you, Lord, do I lift up my soul.
5 For you, Lord, are good, and ready to forgive,
abundant in loving kindness to all those who call on you.
6 Hear, Yahweh, my prayer.
Listen to the voice of my petitions.

Gospel: Luke 5: 27-32

27 After these things he went out and saw a tax collector named Levi sitting at the tax office, and said to him, "Follow me!"
28 He left everything, and rose up and followed him. 29 Levi made a great feast for him in his house. There was a great crowd of tax collectors and others who were reclining with them. 30 Their scribes and the Pharisees murmured against his disciples, saying, "Why do you eat and drink with the tax collectors and sinners?"
31 Jesus answered them, "Those who are healthy have no need for a physician, but those who are sick do. 32 I have not come to call the righteous, but sinners, to repentance."

1. Invite the Holy Spirit into this reading, asking the Author of Scripture to speak to you through His Word
2. Read today's passage as many times as you need, take your time
3. Write down (below) what the Lord is saying to you today
4. Live with this Word in your heart through the day

_____

_____

Sunday, February 18, 2024
FIRST SUNDAY OF LENT

First Reading: Genesis 9: 8-15

8 God spoke to Noah and to his sons with him, saying, 9 "As for me, behold, I establish my covenant with you, and with your offspring after you, 10 and with every living creature that is with you: the birds, the livestock, and every animal of the earth with you, of all that go out of the ship, even every animal of the earth. 11 I will establish my covenant with you: All flesh will not be cut off any more by the waters of the flood. There will never again be a flood to destroy the earth." 12 God said, "This is the token of the covenant which I make between me and you and every living creature that is with you, for perpetual generations:

13 I set my rainbow in the cloud, and it will be a sign of a covenant between me and the earth. 14 When I bring a cloud over the earth, that the rainbow will be seen in the cloud, 15 I will remember my covenant, which is between me and you and every living creature of all flesh, and the waters will no more become a flood to destroy all flesh.

Responsorial Psalm: Psalms 25: 4-9

4 Show me your ways, Yahweh.
Teach me your paths.
5 Guide me in your truth, and teach me,
for you are the God of my salvation.
I wait for you all day long.
6 Yahweh, remember your tender mercies and your loving kindness,
for they are from old times.
7 Don't remember the sins of my youth, nor my transgressions.
Remember me according to your loving kindness,
for your goodness' sake, Yahweh.
8 Good and upright is Yahweh,
therefore he will instruct sinners in the way.
9 He will guide the humble in justice.
He will teach the humble his way.

Second Reading: First Peter 3: 18-22

18 Because Christ also suffered for sins once, the righteous for the unrighteous, that he might bring you to God, being put to death in the flesh, but made alive in the Spirit, 19 in whom he also went and preached to the spirits in prison, 20 who before were disobedient when God waited patiently in the days of Noah while the ship was being built. In it, few, that is, eight souls, were saved through water. 21 This is a symbol of baptism, which now saves you—not the putting away of the filth of the flesh, but the answer of a good conscience toward God—through the resurrection of Jesus Christ, 22 who is at the right hand of God, having gone into heaven, angels and authorities and powers being made subject to him.

Gospel: Mark 1: 12-15

12 Immediately the Spirit drove him out into the wilderness. 13 He was there in the wilderness forty days, tempted by Satan. He was with the wild animals; and the angels were serving him.

14 Now after John was taken into custody, Jesus came into Galilee, preaching the Good News of God's Kingdom, 15 and saying, "The time is fulfilled, and God's Kingdom is at hand! Repent, and believe in the Good News."

1. Invite the Holy Spirit into this reading, asking the Author of Scripture to speak to you through His Word
2. Read today's passage as many times as you need, take your time
3. Write down (below) what the Lord is saying to you today
4. Live with this Word in your heart through the day

_____

_____

Monday, February 19, 2024

First Reading: Leviticus 19: 1-2, 11-18

1 Yahweh spoke to Moses, saying, 2 "Speak to all the congregation of the children of Israel, and tell them, 'You shall be holy; for I, Yahweh your God, am holy.
11 " 'You shall not steal.
" 'You shall not lie.
" 'You shall not deceive one another.
12 " 'You shall not swear by my name falsely, and profane the name of your God. I am Yahweh.
13 " 'You shall not oppress your neighbor, nor rob him.
" 'The wages of a hired servant shall not remain with you all night until the morning.
14 " 'You shall not curse the deaf, nor put a stumbling block before the blind; but you shall fear your God. I am Yahweh.
15 " 'You shall do no injustice in judgment. You shall not be partial to the poor, nor show favoritism to the great; but you shall judge your neighbor in righteousness.
16 " 'You shall not go around as a slanderer among your people.
" 'You shall not endanger the life† of your neighbor. I am Yahweh.
17 " 'You shall not hate your brother in your heart. You shall surely rebuke your neighbor, and not bear sin because of him.
18 " 'You shall not take vengeance, nor bear any grudge against the children of your people; but you shall love your neighbor as yourself. I am Yahweh.

Responsorial Psalm: Psalms 19: 8, 9, 10

8 Yahweh's precepts are right, rejoicing the heart.
Yahweh's commandment is pure, enlightening the eyes.
9 The fear of Yahweh is clean, enduring forever.
Yahweh's ordinances are true, and righteous altogether.
10 They are more to be desired than gold, yes, than much fine gold,
sweeter also than honey and the extract of the honeycomb.

Gospel: Matthew 25: 31-46

31 "But when the Son of Man comes in his glory, and all the holy angels with him, then he will sit on the throne of his glory. 32 Before him all the nations will be gathered, and he will separate them one from another, as a shepherd separates the sheep from the goats. 33 He will set the sheep on his right hand, but the goats on the left. 34 Then the King will tell those on his right hand, 'Come, blessed of my Father, inherit the Kingdom prepared for you from the foundation of the world; 35 for I was hungry and you gave me food to eat. I was thirsty and you gave me drink. I was a stranger and you took me in. 36 I was naked and you clothed me. I was sick and you visited me. I was in prison and you came to me.'

37 "Then the righteous will answer him, saying, 'Lord, when did we see you hungry and feed you, or thirsty and give you a drink? 38 When did we see you as a stranger and take you in, or naked and clothe you? 39 When did we see you sick or in prison and come to you?'

40 "The King will answer them, 'Most certainly I tell you, because you did it to one of the least of these my brothers,§ you did it to me.' 41 Then he will say also to those on the left hand, 'Depart from me, you cursed, into the eternal fire which is prepared for the devil and his angels; 42 for I was hungry, and you didn't give me food to eat; I was thirsty, and you gave me no drink; 43 I was a stranger, and you didn't take me in; naked, and you didn't clothe me; sick, and in prison, and you didn't visit me.'

44 "Then they will also answer, saying, 'Lord, when did we see you hungry, or thirsty, or a stranger, or naked, or sick, or in prison, and didn't help you?'

45 "Then he will answer them, saying, 'Most certainly I tell you, because you didn't do it to one of the least of these, you didn't do it to me.' 46 These will go away into eternal punishment, but the righteous into eternal life."

1. Invite the Holy Spirit into this reading, asking the Author of Scripture to speak to you through His Word
2. Read today's passage as many times as you need, take your time
3. Write down (below) what the Lord is saying to you today
4. Live with this Word in your heart through the day

Tuesday, February 20, 2024

First Reading: Isaiah 55: 10-11

10 For as the rain comes down and the snow from the sky,
and doesn't return there, but waters the earth,
and makes it grow and bud,
and gives seed to the sower and bread to the eater;
11 so is my word that goes out of my mouth:
it will not return to me void,
but it will accomplish that which I please,
and it will prosper in the thing I sent it to do.

Responsorial Psalm: Psalms 34: 4-7, 16-19

4 I sought Yahweh, and he answered me,
and delivered me from all my fears.
5 They looked to him, and were radiant.
Their faces shall never be covered with shame.
6 This poor man cried, and Yahweh heard him,
and saved him out of all his troubles.
7 Yahweh's angel encamps around those who fear him,
and delivers them.
16 Yahweh's face is against those who do evil,
to cut off their memory from the earth.
17 The righteous cry, and Yahweh hears,
and delivers them out of all their troubles.
18 Yahweh is near to those who have a broken heart,
and saves those who have a crushed spirit.
19 Many are the afflictions of the righteous,
but Yahweh delivers him out of them all.

Gospel: Matthew 6: 7-15

7 In praying, don't use vain repetitions as the Gentiles do; for they think that they will be heard for their much speaking. 8 Therefore don't be like them, for your Father knows what things you need before you ask him. 9 Pray like this:

" 'Our Father in heaven, may your name be kept holy.

10 Let your Kingdom come.

Let your will be done on earth as it is in heaven.

11 Give us today our daily bread.

12 Forgive us our debts,

as we also forgive our debtors.

13 Bring us not into temptation,

but deliver us from the evil one.

For yours is the Kingdom, the power, and the glory forever. Amen.'‡

14 "For if you forgive men their trespasses, your heavenly Father will also forgive you. 15 But if you don't forgive men their trespasses, neither will your Father forgive your trespasses.

1. Invite the Holy Spirit into this reading, asking the Author of Scripture to speak to you through His Word
2. Read today's passage as many times as you need, take your time
3. Write down (below) what the Lord is saying to you today
4. Live with this Word in your heart through the day

_____

_____

Wednesday, February 21, 2024
Saint Peter Damian, Bishop and Doctor of the Church

First Reading: Jonah 3: 1-10

1 Yahweh's word came to Jonah the second time, saying, 2 "Arise, go to Nineveh, that great city, and preach to it the message that I give you."
3 So Jonah arose, and went to Nineveh, according to Yahweh's word. Now Nineveh was an exceedingly great city, three days' journey across. 4 Jonah began to enter into the city a day's journey, and he cried out, and said, "In forty days, Nineveh will be overthrown!"
5 The people of Nineveh believed God; and they proclaimed a fast and put on sackcloth, from their greatest even to their least. 6 The news reached the king of Nineveh, and he arose from his throne, took off his royal robe, covered himself with sackcloth, and sat in

ashes. 7 He made a proclamation and published through Nineveh by the decree of the king and his nobles, saying, "Let neither man nor animal, herd nor flock, taste anything; let them not feed, nor drink water; 8 but let them be covered with sackcloth, both man and animal, and let them cry mightily to God. Yes, let them turn everyone from his evil way and from the violence that is in his hands. 9 Who knows whether God will not turn and relent, and turn away from his fierce anger, so that we might not perish?"

10 God saw their works, that they turned from their evil way. God relented of the disaster which he said he would do to them, and he didn't do it.

Responsorial Psalm: Psalms 51: 3-4, 12-13, 18-19

3 For I know my transgressions.
My sin is constantly before me.
4 Against you, and you only, I have sinned,
and done that which is evil in your sight,
so you may be proved right when you speak,
and justified when you judge.
12 Restore to me the joy of your salvation.
Uphold me with a willing spirit.
13 Then I will teach transgressors your ways.
Sinners will be converted to you.
18 Do well in your good pleasure to Zion.
Build the walls of Jerusalem.
19 Then you will delight in the sacrifices of righteousness,
in burnt offerings and in whole burnt offerings.
Then they will offer bulls on your altar.

Gospel: Luke 11: 29-32

29 When the multitudes were gathering together to him, he began to say, "This is an evil generation. It seeks after a sign. No sign will be given to it but the sign of Jonah the prophet. 30 For even as Jonah became a sign to the Ninevites, so the Son of Man will also be to this generation. 31 The Queen of the South will rise up in the judgment with the men of this generation and will condemn them, for she came from the ends of the earth to hear the wisdom of Solomon; and behold, one greater than Solomon is here. 32 The men of Nineveh will stand up in the judgment with this generation, and will condemn it, for they repented at the preaching of Jonah; and behold, one greater than Jonah is here.

1. Invite the Holy Spirit into this reading, asking the Author of Scripture to speak to you through His Word
2. Read today's passage as many times as you need, take your time

3. Write down (below) what the Lord is saying to you today
4. Live with this Word in your heart through the day

Thursday, February 22, 2024
The Chair of Saint Peter the Apostle

First Reading: First Peter 5: 1-4

1 Therefore I exhort the elders among you, as a fellow elder and a witness of the sufferings of Christ, and who will also share in the glory that will be revealed: 2 shepherd the flock of God which is among you, exercising the oversight, not under compulsion, but voluntarily; not for dishonest gain, but willingly; 3 not as lording it over those entrusted to you, but making yourselves examples to the flock. 4 When the chief Shepherd is revealed, you will receive the crown of glory that doesn't fade away.

Responsorial Psalm: Psalms 23: 1-6

1 Yahweh is my shepherd;
I shall lack nothing.
2 He makes me lie down in green pastures.
He leads me beside still waters.
3 He restores my soul.
He guides me in the paths of righteousness for his name's sake.
4 Even though I walk through the valley of the shadow of death,
I will fear no evil, for you are with me.
Your rod and your staff,
they comfort me.
5 You prepare a table before me
in the presence of my enemies.
You anoint my head with oil.
My cup runs over.
6 Surely goodness and loving kindness shall follow me all the days of my life,
and I will dwell in Yahweh's house forever.

Gospel: Matthew 16: 13-19

13 Now when Jesus came into the parts of Caesarea Philippi, he asked his disciples, saying, "Who do men say that I, the Son of Man, am?"

14 They said, "Some say John the Baptizer, some, Elijah, and others, Jeremiah or one of the prophets."

15 He said to them, "But who do you say that I am?"

16 Simon Peter answered, "You are the Christ, the Son of the living God."

17 Jesus answered him, "Blessed are you, Simon Bar Jonah, for flesh and blood has not revealed this to you, but my Father who is in heaven. 18 I also tell you that you are Peter,† and on this rock ‡ I will build my assembly, and the gates of Hades§ will not prevail against it. 19 I will give to you the keys of the Kingdom of Heaven, and whatever you bind on earth will have been bound in heaven; and whatever you release on earth will have been released in heaven."

1. Invite the Holy Spirit into this reading, asking the Author of Scripture to speak to you through His Word
2. Read today's passage as many times as you need, take your time
3. Write down (below) what the Lord is saying to you today
4. Live with this Word in your heart through the day

_____

_____

Friday, February 23, 2024
Saint Polycarp, Bishop and Martyr

First Reading: Ezekiel 18: 21-28

21 "But if the wicked turns from all his sins that he has committed, and keeps all my statutes, and does that which is lawful and right, he shall surely live. He shall not die. 22 None of his transgressions that he has committed will be remembered against him. In his righteousness that he has done, he shall live. 23 Have I any pleasure in the death of the wicked?" says the Lord Yahweh, "and not rather that he should return from his way, and live?

24 "But when the righteous turns away from his righteousness, and commits iniquity, and does according to all the abominations that the wicked man does, should he live? None of

his righteous deeds that he has done will be remembered. In his trespass that he has trespassed, and in his sin that he has sinned, in them he shall die.

25 "Yet you say, 'The way of the Lord is not equal.' Hear now, house of Israel: Is my way not equal? Aren't your ways unequal? 26 When the righteous man turns away from his righteousness, and commits iniquity, and dies in it, then he dies in his iniquity that he has done. 27 Again, when the wicked man turns away from his wickedness that he has committed, and does that which is lawful and right, he will save his soul alive. 28 Because he considers, and turns away from all his transgressions that he has committed, he shall surely live. He shall not die.

Responsorial Psalm: Psalms 130: 1-8

1 Out of the depths I have cried to you, Yahweh.
2 Lord, hear my voice.
Let your ears be attentive to the voice of my petitions.
3 If you, Yah, kept a record of sins,
Lord, who could stand?
4 But there is forgiveness with you,
therefore you are feared.
5 I wait for Yahweh.
My soul waits.
I hope in his word.
6 My soul longs for the Lord more than watchmen long for the morning,
more than watchmen for the morning.
7 Israel, hope in Yahweh,
for there is loving kindness with Yahweh.
Abundant redemption is with him.
8 He will redeem Israel from all their sins.

Gospel: Matthew 5: 20-26

20 For I tell you that unless your righteousness exceeds that of the scribes and Pharisees, there is no way you will enter into the Kingdom of Heaven.
21 "You have heard that it was said to the ancient ones, 'You shall not murder;'* and 'Whoever murders will be in danger of the judgment.' 22 But I tell you that everyone who is angry with his brother without a cause † will be in danger of the judgment. Whoever says to his brother, 'Raca!' ‡ will be in danger of the council. Whoever says, 'You fool!' will be in danger of the fire of Gehenna.§
23 "If therefore you are offering your gift at the altar, and there remember that your brother has anything against you, 24 leave your gift there before the altar, and go your way. First be reconciled to your brother, and then come and offer your gift. 25 Agree with

your adversary quickly while you are with him on the way; lest perhaps the prosecutor deliver you to the judge, and the judge deliver you to the officer, and you be cast into prison. 26 Most certainly I tell you, you shall by no means get out of there until you have paid the last penny.

1. Invite the Holy Spirit into this reading, asking the Author of Scripture to speak to you through His Word
2. Read today's passage as many times as you need, take your time
3. Write down (below) what the Lord is saying to you today
4. Live with this Word in your heart through the day

_____

_____

Saturday, February 24, 2024

First Reading: Deuteronomy 26: 16-19

16 Today Yahweh your God commands you to do these statutes and ordinances. You shall therefore keep and do them with all your heart and with all your soul. 17 You have declared today that Yahweh is your God, and that you would walk in his ways, keep his statutes, his commandments, and his ordinances, and listen to his voice. 18 Yahweh has declared today that you are a people for his own possession, as he has promised you, and that you should keep all his commandments. 19 He will make you high above all nations that he has made, in praise, in name, and in honor, and that you may be a holy people to Yahweh your God, as he has spoken.

Responsorial Psalm: Psalms 119: 1-2, 4-5, 7-8

1 Blessed are those whose ways are blameless,
who walk according to Yahweh's law.
2 Blessed are those who keep his statutes,
who seek him with their whole heart.
4 You have commanded your precepts,
that we should fully obey them.
5 Oh that my ways were steadfast
to obey your statutes!
7 I will give thanks to you with uprightness of heart,

when I learn your righteous judgments.
8 I will observe your statutes.
Don't utterly forsake me.

Gospel: Matthew 5: 43-48

43 "You have heard that it was said, 'You shall love your neighbor * and hate your enemy.'‡ 44 But I tell you, love your enemies, bless those who curse you, do good to those who hate you, and pray for those who mistreat you and persecute you, 45 that you may be children of your Father who is in heaven. For he makes his sun to rise on the evil and the good, and sends rain on the just and the unjust. 46 For if you love those who love you, what reward do you have? Don't even the tax collectors do the same? 47 If you only greet your friends, what more do you do than others? Don't even the tax collectors§ do the same? 48 Therefore you shall be perfect, just as your Father in heaven is perfect.

1. Invite the Holy Spirit into this reading, asking the Author of Scripture to speak to you through His Word
2. Read today's passage as many times as you need, take your time
3. Write down (below) what the Lord is saying to you today
4. Live with this Word in your heart through the day

_____

_____

Sunday, February 25, 2024
Second Sunday Of Lent

First Reading: Genesis 22: 1-2, 9a, 10-13, 15-18

1 After these things, God tested Abraham, and said to him, "Abraham!"
He said, "Here I am."
2 He said, "Now take your son, your only son, Isaac, whom you love, and go into the land of Moriah. Offer him there as a burnt offering on one of the mountains which I will tell you of."
9 They came to the place which God had told him of.
10 Abraham stretched out his hand, and took the knife to kill his son.
11 Yahweh's angel called to him out of the sky, and said, "Abraham, Abraham!"
He said, "Here I am."

12 He said, "Don't lay your hand on the boy or do anything to him. For now I know that you fear God, since you have not withheld your son, your only son, from me."

13 Abraham lifted up his eyes, and looked, and saw that behind him was a ram caught in the thicket by his horns. Abraham went and took the ram, and offered him up for a burnt offering instead of his son.

15 Yahweh's angel called to Abraham a second time out of the sky, 16 and said, " 'I have sworn by myself,' says Yahweh, 'because you have done this thing, and have not withheld your son, your only son, 17 that I will bless you greatly, and I will multiply your offspring greatly like the stars of the heavens, and like the sand which is on the seashore. Your offspring will possess the gate of his enemies. 18 All the nations of the earth will be blessed by your offspring, because you have obeyed my voice.' "

Responsorial Psalm: Psalms 116: 10, 15-19

10 I believed, therefore I said,
"I was greatly afflicted."
15 Precious in Yahweh's sight is the death of his saints.
16 Yahweh, truly I am your servant.
I am your servant, the son of your servant girl.
You have freed me from my chains.
17 I will offer to you the sacrifice of thanksgiving,
and will call on Yahweh's name.
18 I will pay my vows to Yahweh,
yes, in the presence of all his people,
19 in the courts of Yahweh's house,
in the middle of you, Jerusalem.
Praise Yah!

Second Reading: Romans 8: 31b-34

If God is for us, who can be against us? 32 He who didn't spare his own Son, but delivered him up for us all, how would he not also with him freely give us all things? 33 Who could bring a charge against God's chosen ones? It is God who justifies. 34 Who is he who condemns? It is Christ who died, yes rather, who was raised from the dead, who is at the right hand of God, who also makes intercession for us.

Gospel: Mark 9: 2-10

2 After six days Jesus took with him Peter, James, and John, and brought them up onto a high mountain privately by themselves, and he was changed into another form in front of them. 3 His clothing became glistening, exceedingly white, like snow, such as no launderer

on earth can whiten them. 4 Elijah and Moses appeared to them, and they were talking with Jesus.

5 Peter answered Jesus, "Rabbi, it is good for us to be here. Let's make three tents: one for you, one for Moses, and one for Elijah." 6 For he didn't know what to say, for they were very afraid.

7 A cloud came, overshadowing them, and a voice came out of the cloud, "This is my beloved Son. Listen to him."

8 Suddenly looking around, they saw no one with them any more, except Jesus only.

9 As they were coming down from the mountain, he commanded them that they should tell no one what things they had seen, until after the Son of Man had risen from the dead.

10 They kept this saying to themselves, questioning what the "rising from the dead" meant.

1. Invite the Holy Spirit into this reading, asking the Author of Scripture to speak to you through His Word
2. Read today's passage as many times as you need, take your time
3. Write down (below) what the Lord is saying to you today
4. Live with this Word in your heart through the day

_____

_____

Monday, February 26, 2024

First Reading: Daniel 9: 4b-10

4 "Oh, Lord, the great and dreadful God, who keeps covenant and loving kindness with those who love him and keep his commandments, 5 we have sinned, and have dealt perversely, and have done wickedly, and have rebelled, even turning aside from your precepts and from your ordinances. 6 We haven't listened to your servants the prophets, who spoke in your name to our kings, our princes, and our fathers, and to all the people of the land.

7 "Lord, righteousness belongs to you, but to us confusion of face, as it is today; to the men of Judah, and to the inhabitants of Jerusalem, and to all Israel, who are near and who are far off, through all the countries where you have driven them, because of their trespass that they have trespassed against you. 8 Lord, to us belongs confusion of face, to our kings, to our princes, and to our fathers, because we have sinned against you. 9 To the Lord our God belong mercies and forgiveness, for we have rebelled against him. 10 We haven't obeyed Yahweh our God's voice, to walk in his laws, which he set before us by his servants the prophets.

Responsorial Psalm: Psalms 79: 8, 9, 11 and 13

8 Don't hold the iniquities of our forefathers against us.
Let your tender mercies speedily meet us,
for we are in desperate need.
9 Help us, God of our salvation, for the glory of your name.
Deliver us, and forgive our sins, for your name's sake.
11 Let the sighing of the prisoner come before you.
According to the greatness of your power, preserve those who are sentenced to death.
13 So we, your people and sheep of your pasture,
will give you thanks forever.
We will praise you forever, to all generations.

Gospel: Luke 6: 36-38

36 "Therefore be merciful,
even as your Father is also merciful.
37 Don't judge,
and you won't be judged.
Don't condemn,
and you won't be condemned.
Set free,
and you will be set free.
38 "Give, and it will be given to you: good measure, pressed down, shaken together, and running over, will be given to you.§ For with the same measure you measure it will be measured back to you."

1. Invite the Holy Spirit into this reading, asking the Author of Scripture to speak to you through His Word
2. Read today's passage as many times as you need, take your time
3. Write down (below) what the Lord is saying to you today
4. Live with this Word in your heart through the day

Tuesday, February 27, 2024
Saint Gregory of Narek, Abbot and Doctor of the Church

First Reading: Isaiah 1: 10, 16-20

10 Hear Yahweh's word, you rulers of Sodom!
Listen to the law of our God,§ you people of Gomorrah!
16 Wash yourselves. Make yourself clean.
Put away the evil of your doings from before my eyes.
Cease to do evil.
17 Learn to do well.
Seek justice.
Relieve the oppressed.
Defend the fatherless.
Plead for the widow."
 18 "Come now, and let's reason together," says Yahweh:
"Though your sins are as scarlet, they shall be as white as snow.
Though they are red like crimson, they shall be as wool.
19 If you are willing and obedient,
you will eat the good of the land;
20 but if you refuse and rebel, you will be devoured with the sword;
for Yahweh's mouth has spoken it."

Responsorial Psalm: Psalms 50: 8-9, 16bc-17, 21 and 23

8 I don't rebuke you for your sacrifices.
Your burnt offerings are continually before me.
9 I have no need for a bull from your stall,
nor male goats from your pens.
16b "What right do you have to declare my statutes,
that you have taken my covenant on your lips,
17 since you hate instruction,
and throw my words behind you?
21 You have done these things, and I kept silent.
You thought that I was just like you.
I will rebuke you, and accuse you in front of your eyes.
23 Whoever offers the sacrifice of thanksgiving glorifies me,
and prepares his way so that I will show God's salvation to him."

Gospel: Matthew 23: 1-12

1 Then Jesus spoke to the multitudes and to his disciples, 2 saying, "The scribes and the Pharisees sit on Moses' seat. 3 All things therefore whatever they tell you to observe, observe and do, but don't do their works; for they say, and don't do. 4 For they bind heavy

burdens that are grievous to be borne, and lay them on men's shoulders; but they themselves will not lift a finger to help them. 5 But they do all their works to be seen by men. They make their phylacteries† broad and enlarge the fringes‡ of their garments, 6 and love the place of honor at feasts, the best seats in the synagogues, 7 the salutations in the marketplaces, and to be called 'Rabbi, Rabbi'§ by men. 8 But you are not to be called 'Rabbi', for one is your teacher, the Christ, and all of you are brothers. 9 Call no man on the earth your father, for one is your Father, he who is in heaven. 10 Neither be called masters, for one is your master, the Christ. 11 But he who is greatest among you will be your servant. 12 Whoever exalts himself will be humbled, and whoever humbles himself will be exalted.

1. Invite the Holy Spirit into this reading, asking the Author of Scripture to speak to you through His Word
2. Read today's passage as many times as you need, take your time
3. Write down (below) what the Lord is saying to you today
4. Live with this Word in your heart through the day

_____

_____

Wednesday, February 28, 2024

First Reading: Jeremiah 18: 18-20

18 Then they said, "Come! Let's devise plans against Jeremiah; for the law won't perish from the priest, nor counsel from the wise, nor the word from the prophet. Come, and let's strike him with the tongue, and let's not give heed to any of his words."
19 Give heed to me, Yahweh,
and listen to the voice of those who contend with me.
20 Should evil be recompensed for good?
For they have dug a pit for my soul.
Remember how I stood before you to speak good for them,
to turn away your wrath from them.

Responsorial Psalm: Psalms 31: 5-6, 14-16

5 Into your hand I commend my spirit.
You redeem me, Yahweh, God of truth.

6 I hate those who regard lying vanities,

but I trust in Yahweh.

14 But I trust in you, Yahweh.

I said, "You are my God."

15 My times are in your hand.

Deliver me from the hand of my enemies, and from those who persecute me.

16 Make your face to shine on your servant.

Save me in your loving kindness.

Gospel: Matthew 20: 17-28

17 As Jesus was going up to Jerusalem, he took the twelve disciples aside, and on the way he said to them, 18 "Behold, we are going up to Jerusalem, and the Son of Man will be delivered to the chief priests and scribes, and they will condemn him to death, 19 and will hand him over to the Gentiles to mock, to scourge, and to crucify; and the third day he will be raised up."

20 Then the mother of the sons of Zebedee came to him with her sons, kneeling and asking a certain thing of him. 21 He said to her, "What do you want?"

She said to him, "Command that these, my two sons, may sit, one on your right hand and one on your left hand, in your Kingdom."

22 But Jesus answered, "You don't know what you are asking. Are you able to drink the cup that I am about to drink, and be baptized with the baptism that I am baptized with?"

They said to him, "We are able."

23 He said to them, "You will indeed drink my cup, and be baptized with the baptism that I am baptized with; but to sit on my right hand and on my left hand is not mine to give, but it is for whom it has been prepared by my Father."

24 When the ten heard it, they were indignant with the two brothers.

25 But Jesus summoned them, and said, "You know that the rulers of the nations lord it over them, and their great ones exercise authority over them. 26 It shall not be so among you; but whoever desires to become great among you shall be‡ your servant. 27 Whoever desires to be first among you shall be your bondservant, 28 even as the Son of Man came not to be served, but to serve, and to give his life as a ransom for many."

1. Invite the Holy Spirit into this reading, asking the Author of Scripture to speak to you through His Word

2. Read today's passage as many times as you need, take your time

3. Write down (below) what the Lord is saying to you today

4. Live with this Word in your heart through the day

_____

_____

Thursday, February 29, 2024

First Reading: Jeremiah 17: 5-10

5 Yahweh says:
"Cursed is the man who trusts in man,
relies on strength of flesh,
and whose heart departs from Yahweh.
6 For he will be like a bush in the desert,
and will not see when good comes,
but will inhabit the parched places in the wilderness,
an uninhabited salt land.
 7 "Blessed is the man who trusts in Yahweh,
and whose confidence is in Yahweh.
8 For he will be as a tree planted by the waters,
who spreads out its roots by the river,
and will not fear when heat comes,
but its leaf will be green,
and will not be concerned in the year of drought.
It won't cease from yielding fruit.
9 The heart is deceitful above all things
and it is exceedingly corrupt.
Who can know it?
 10 "I, Yahweh, search the mind.
I try the heart,
even to give every man according to his ways,
according to the fruit of his doings."

Responsorial Psalm: Psalms 1: 1-4 and 6

1 Blessed is the man who doesn't walk in the counsel of the wicked,
nor stand on the path of sinners,
nor sit in the seat of scoffers;
2 but his delight is in Yahweh's† law.
On his law he meditates day and night.
3 He will be like a tree planted by the streams of water,
that produces its fruit in its season,
whose leaf also does not wither.
Whatever he does shall prosper.
4 The wicked are not so,

but are like the chaff which the wind drives away.
6 For Yahweh knows the way of the righteous,
but the way of the wicked shall perish.

Gospel: Luke 16: 19-31

19 "Now there was a certain rich man, and he was clothed in purple and fine linen, living in luxury every day. 20 A certain beggar, named Lazarus, was taken to his gate, full of sores, 21 and desiring to be fed with the crumbs that fell from the rich man's table. Yes, even the dogs came and licked his sores. 22 The beggar died, and he was carried away by the angels to Abraham's bosom. The rich man also died and was buried. 23 In Hades,† he lifted up his eyes, being in torment, and saw Abraham far off, and Lazarus at his bosom. 24 He cried and said, 'Father Abraham, have mercy on me, and send Lazarus, that he may dip the tip of his finger in water and cool my tongue! For I am in anguish in this flame.'
25 "But Abraham said, 'Son, remember that you, in your lifetime, received your good things, and Lazarus, in the same way, bad things. But here he is now comforted and you are in anguish. 26 Besides all this, between us and you there is a great gulf fixed, that those who want to pass from here to you are not able, and that no one may cross over from there to us.'
27 "He said, 'I ask you therefore, father, that you would send him to my father's house—
28 for I have five brothers—that he may testify to them, so they won't also come into this place of torment.'
29 "But Abraham said to him, 'They have Moses and the prophets. Let them listen to them.'
30 "He said, 'No, father Abraham, but if one goes to them from the dead, they will repent.'
31 "He said to him, 'If they don't listen to Moses and the prophets, neither will they be persuaded if one rises from the dead.' "

1. Invite the Holy Spirit into this reading, asking the Author of Scripture to speak to you through His Word
2. Read today's passage as many times as you need, take your time
3. Write down (below) what the Lord is saying to you today
4. Live with this Word in your heart through the day

_____

_____

Friday, March 1, 2024

First Reading: Genesis 37: 3-4, 12-13a, 17b-28

3 Now Israel loved Joseph more than all his children, because he was the son of his old age, and he made him a tunic of many colors. 4 His brothers saw that their father loved him more than all his brothers, and they hated him, and couldn't speak peaceably to him.
12 His brothers went to feed their father's flock in Shechem. 13 Israel said to Joseph, "Aren't your brothers feeding the flock in Shechem? Come, and I will send you to them." He said to him, "Here I am."
17b Joseph went after his brothers, and found them in Dothan. 18 They saw him afar off, and before he came near to them, they conspired against him to kill him. 19 They said to one another, "Behold, this dreamer comes. 20 Come now therefore, and let's kill him, and cast him into one of the pits, and we will say, 'An evil animal has devoured him.' We will see what will become of his dreams."
21 Reuben heard it, and delivered him out of their hand, and said, "Let's not take his life."
22 Reuben said to them, "Shed no blood. Throw him into this pit that is in the wilderness, but lay no hand on him"—that he might deliver him out of their hand, to restore him to his father. 23 When Joseph came to his brothers, they stripped Joseph of his tunic, the tunic of many colors that was on him; 24 and they took him, and threw him into the pit. The pit was empty. There was no water in it.
25 They sat down to eat bread, and they lifted up their eyes and looked, and saw a caravan of Ishmaelites was coming from Gilead, with their camels bearing spices and balm and myrrh, going to carry it down to Egypt. 26 Judah said to his brothers, "What profit is it if we kill our brother and conceal his blood? 27 Come, and let's sell him to the Ishmaelites, and not let our hand be on him; for he is our brother, our flesh." His brothers listened to him. 28 Midianites who were merchants passed by, and they drew and lifted up Joseph out of the pit, and sold Joseph to the Ishmaelites for twenty pieces of silver. The merchants brought Joseph into Egypt.

Responsorial Psalm: Psalms 105: 16-21

16 He called for a famine on the land.
He destroyed the food supplies.
17 He sent a man before them.
Joseph was sold for a slave.
18 They bruised his feet with shackles.
His neck was locked in irons,
19 until the time that his word happened,
and Yahweh's word proved him true.
20 The king sent and freed him,
even the ruler of peoples, and let him go free.

21 He made him lord of his house,
and ruler of all of his possessions

Gospel: Matthew 21: 33-43, 45-46

33 "Hear another parable. There was a man who was a master of a household who planted a vineyard, set a hedge about it, dug a wine press in it, built a tower, leased it out to farmers, and went into another country. 34 When the season for the fruit came near, he sent his servants to the farmers to receive his fruit. 35 The farmers took his servants, beat one, killed another, and stoned another. 36 Again, he sent other servants more than the first; and they treated them the same way. 37 But afterward he sent to them his son, saying, 'They will respect my son.' 38 But the farmers, when they saw the son, said among themselves, 'This is the heir. Come, let's kill him and seize his inheritance.' 39 So they took him and threw him out of the vineyard, then killed him. 40 When therefore the lord of the vineyard comes, what will he do to those farmers?"
41 They told him, "He will miserably destroy those miserable men, and will lease out the vineyard to other farmers who will give him the fruit in its season."
42 Jesus said to them, "Did you never read in the Scriptures,
'The stone which the builders rejected
was made the head of the corner.
This was from the Lord.
It is marvelous in our eyes'?*
43 "Therefore I tell you, God's Kingdom will be taken away from you and will be given to a nation producing its fruit.
45 When the chief priests and the Pharisees heard his parables, they perceived that he spoke about them. 46 When they sought to seize him, they feared the multitudes, because they considered him to be a prophet.

1. Invite the Holy Spirit into this reading, asking the Author of Scripture to speak to you through His Word
2. Read today's passage as many times as you need, take your time
3. Write down (below) what the Lord is saying to you today
4. Live with this Word in your heart through the day

_____

_____

Saturday, March 2, 2024

First Reading: Micah 7: 14-15, 18-20

14 Shepherd your people with your staff,
the flock of your heritage,
who dwell by themselves in a forest.
Let them feed in the middle of fertile pasture land,
in Bashan and Gilead, as in the days of old.
15 "As in the days of your coming out of the land of Egypt,
I will show them marvelous things."
18 Who is a God like you, who pardons iniquity,
and passes over the disobedience of the remnant of his heritage?
He doesn't retain his anger forever,
because he delights in loving kindness.
19 He will again have compassion on us.
He will tread our iniquities under foot.
You will cast all their sins into the depths of the sea.
20 You will give truth to Jacob,
and mercy to Abraham,
as you have sworn to our fathers from the days of old.

Responsorial Psalm: Psalms 103: 1-4, 9-12

1 Praise Yahweh, my soul!
All that is within me, praise his holy name!
2 Praise Yahweh, my soul,
and don't forget all his benefits,
3 who forgives all your sins,
who heals all your diseases,
4 who redeems your life from destruction,
who crowns you with loving kindness and tender mercies,
9 He will not always accuse;
neither will he stay angry forever.
10 He has not dealt with us according to our sins,
nor repaid us for our iniquities.
11 For as the heavens are high above the earth,
so great is his loving kindness toward those who fear him.
12 As far as the east is from the west,
so far has he removed our transgressions from us.

Gospel: Luke 15: 1-3, 11-32

1 Now all the tax collectors and sinners were coming close to him to hear him. 2 The Pharisees and the scribes murmured, saying, "This man welcomes sinners, and eats with them."

3 He told them this parable:

11 He said, "A certain man had two sons. 12 The younger of them said to his father, 'Father, give me my share of your property.' So he divided his livelihood between them. 13 Not many days after, the younger son gathered all of this together and traveled into a far country. There he wasted his property with riotous living. 14 When he had spent all of it, there arose a severe famine in that country, and he began to be in need. 15 He went and joined himself to one of the citizens of that country, and he sent him into his fields to feed pigs. 16 He wanted to fill his belly with the pods that the pigs ate, but no one gave him any. 17 But when he came to himself, he said, 'How many hired servants of my father's have bread enough to spare, and I'm dying with hunger! 18 I will get up and go to my father, and will tell him, "Father, I have sinned against heaven and in your sight. 19 I am no more worthy to be called your son. Make me as one of your hired servants."'

20 "He arose and came to his father. But while he was still far off, his father saw him and was moved with compassion, and ran, fell on his neck, and kissed him. 21 The son said to him, 'Father, I have sinned against heaven and in your sight. I am no longer worthy to be called your son.'

22 "But the father said to his servants, 'Bring out the best robe and put it on him. Put a ring on his hand and sandals on his feet. 23 Bring the fattened calf, kill it, and let's eat and celebrate; 24 for this, my son, was dead and is alive again. He was lost and is found.' Then they began to celebrate.

25 "Now his elder son was in the field. As he came near to the house, he heard music and dancing. 26 He called one of the servants to him and asked what was going on. 27 He said to him, 'Your brother has come, and your father has killed the fattened calf, because he has received him back safe and healthy.' 28 But he was angry and would not go in. Therefore his father came out and begged him. 29 But he answered his father, 'Behold, these many years I have served you, and I never disobeyed a commandment of yours, but you never gave me a goat, that I might celebrate with my friends. 30 But when this your son came, who has devoured your living with prostitutes, you killed the fattened calf for him.'

31 "He said to him, 'Son, you are always with me, and all that is mine is yours. 32 But it was appropriate to celebrate and be glad, for this, your brother, was dead, and is alive again. He was lost, and is found.'"

1. Invite the Holy Spirit into this reading, asking the Author of Scripture to speak to you through His Word
2. Read today's passage as many times as you need, take your time
3. Write down (below) what the Lord is saying to you today
4. Live with this Word in your heart through the day

Sunday, March 3, 2024
Third Sunday of Lent

First Reading: Exodus 20: 1-17

1 God† spoke all these words, saying, 2 "I am Yahweh your God, who brought you out of the land of Egypt, out of the house of bondage.

3 "You shall have no other gods before me.

4 "You shall not make for yourselves an idol, nor any image of anything that is in the heavens above, or that is in the earth beneath, or that is in the water under the earth: 5 you shall not bow yourself down to them, nor serve them, for I, Yahweh your God, am a jealous God, visiting the iniquity of the fathers on the children, on the third and on the fourth generation of those who hate me, 6 and showing loving kindness to thousands of those who love me and keep my commandments.

7 "You shall not misuse the name of Yahweh your God,‡ for Yahweh will not hold him guiltless who misuses his name.

8 "Remember the Sabbath day, to keep it holy. 9 You shall labor six days, and do all your work, 10 but the seventh day is a Sabbath to Yahweh your God. You shall not do any work in it, you, nor your son, nor your daughter, your male servant, nor your female servant, nor your livestock, nor your stranger who is within your gates; 11 for in six days Yahweh made heaven and earth, the sea, and all that is in them, and rested the seventh day; therefore Yahweh blessed the Sabbath day, and made it holy.

12 "Honor your father and your mother, that your days may be long in the land which Yahweh your God gives you.

13 "You shall not murder.

14 "You shall not commit adultery.

15 "You shall not steal.

16 "You shall not give false testimony against your neighbor.

17 "You shall not covet your neighbor's house. You shall not covet your neighbor's wife, nor his male servant, nor his female servant, nor his ox, nor his donkey, nor anything that is your neighbor's."

Responsorial Psalm: Psalms 19: 8-11

8 Yahweh's precepts are right, rejoicing the heart.
Yahweh's commandment is pure, enlightening the eyes.
9 The fear of Yahweh is clean, enduring forever.
Yahweh's ordinances are true, and righteous altogether.
10 They are more to be desired than gold, yes, than much fine gold,
sweeter also than honey and the extract of the honeycomb.
11 Moreover your servant is warned by them.
In keeping them there is great reward.

Second Reading: First Corinthians 1: 22-25

22 For Jews ask for signs, Greeks seek after wisdom, 23 but we preach Christ crucified, a stumbling block to Jews and foolishness to Greeks, 24 but to those who are called, both Jews and Greeks, Christ is the power of God and the wisdom of God; 25 because the foolishness of God is wiser than men, and the weakness of God is stronger than men.

Gospel: John 2: 13-25

13 The Passover of the Jews was at hand, and Jesus went up to Jerusalem. 14 He found in the temple those who sold oxen, sheep, and doves, and the changers of money sitting. 15 He made a whip of cords and drove all out of the temple, both the sheep and the oxen; and he poured out the changers' money and overthrew their tables. 16 To those who sold the doves, he said, "Take these things out of here! Don't make my Father's house a marketplace!" 17 His disciples remembered that it was written, "Zeal for your house will eat me up."*
18 The Jews therefore answered him, "What sign do you show us, seeing that you do these things?"
19 Jesus answered them, "Destroy this temple, and in three days I will raise it up."
20 The Jews therefore said, "It took forty-six years to build this temple! Will you raise it up in three days?" 21 But he spoke of the temple of his body. 22 When therefore he was raised from the dead, his disciples remembered that he said this, and they believed the Scripture and the word which Jesus had said.
23 Now when he was in Jerusalem at the Passover, during the feast, many believed in his name, observing his signs which he did. 24 But Jesus didn't entrust himself to them, because he knew everyone, 25 and because he didn't need for anyone to testify concerning man; for he himself knew what was in man.

1. Invite the Holy Spirit into this reading, asking the Author of Scripture to speak to you through His Word
2. Read today's passage as many times as you need, take your time
3. Write down (below) what the Lord is saying to you today

Monday, March 4, 2024
Saint Casimir

First Reading: Second Kings 5: 1-15

1 Now Naaman, captain of the army of the king of Syria, was a great man with his master, and honorable, because by him Yahweh had given victory to Syria; he was also a mighty man of valor, but he was a leper. 2 The Syrians had gone out in bands, and had brought away captive out of the land of Israel a little girl, and she waited on Naaman's wife. 3 She said to her mistress, "I wish that my lord were with the prophet who is in Samaria! Then he would heal him of his leprosy."
4 Someone went in and told his lord, saying, "The girl who is from the land of Israel said this."
5 The king of Syria said, "Go now, and I will send a letter to the king of Israel."
He departed, and took with him ten talents† of silver, six thousand pieces of gold, and ten changes of clothing. 6 He brought the letter to the king of Israel, saying, "Now when this letter has come to you, behold, I have sent Naaman my servant to you, that you may heal him of his leprosy."
7 When the king of Israel had read the letter, he tore his clothes and said, "Am I God, to kill and to make alive, that this man sends to me to heal a man of his leprosy? But please consider and see how he seeks a quarrel against me."
8 It was so, when Elisha the man of God heard that the king of Israel had torn his clothes, that he sent to the king, saying, "Why have you torn your clothes? Let him come now to me, and he shall know that there is a prophet in Israel."
9 So Naaman came with his horses and with his chariots, and stood at the door of the house of Elisha. 10 Elisha sent a messenger to him, saying, "Go and wash in the Jordan seven times, and your flesh shall come again to you, and you shall be clean."
11 But Naaman was angry, and went away and said, "Behold, I thought, 'He will surely come out to me, and stand, and call on the name of Yahweh his God, and wave his hand over the place, and heal the leper.' 12 Aren't Abanah and Pharpar, the rivers of Damascus, better than all the waters of Israel? Couldn't I wash in them and be clean?" So he turned and went away in a rage.

13 His servants came near and spoke to him, and said, "My father, if the prophet had asked you do some great thing, wouldn't you have done it? How much rather then, when he says to you, 'Wash, and be clean'?"

14 Then went he down and dipped himself seven times in the Jordan, according to the saying of the man of God; and his flesh was restored like the flesh of a little child, and he was clean. 15 He returned to the man of God, he and all his company, and came, and stood before him; and he said, "See now, I know that there is no God in all the earth, but in Israel. Now therefore, please take a gift from your servant."

Responsorial Psalm: Psalms 42: 2, 3; 43: 3, 4

2 My soul thirsts for God, for the living God.
When shall I come and appear before God?
3 My tears have been my food day and night,
while they continually ask me, "Where is your God?"
3 Oh, send out your light and your truth.
Let them lead me.
Let them bring me to your holy hill,
to your tents.
4 Then I will go to the altar of God,
to God, my exceeding joy.
I will praise you on the harp, God, my God.

Gospel: Luke 4: 24-30

24 He said, "Most certainly I tell you, no prophet is acceptable in his hometown. 25 But truly I tell you, there were many widows in Israel in the days of Elijah, when the sky was shut up three years and six months, when a great famine came over all the land. 26 Elijah was sent to none of them, except to Zarephath, in the land of Sidon, to a woman who was a widow. 27 There were many lepers in Israel in the time of Elisha the prophet, yet not one of them was cleansed, except Naaman, the Syrian."

28 They were all filled with wrath in the synagogue as they heard these things. 29 They rose up, threw him out of the city, and led him to the brow of the hill that their city was built on, that they might throw him off the cliff. 30 But he, passing through the middle of them, went his way.

1. Invite the Holy Spirit into this reading, asking the Author of Scripture to speak to you through His Word
2. Read today's passage as many times as you need, take your time
3. Write down (below) what the Lord is saying to you today
4. Live with this Word in your heart through the day

Tuesday, March 5, 2024

First Reading: Daniel 3: 25, 34-43

25 He answered, "Look, I see four men loose, walking in the middle of the fire, and they are unharmed. The appearance of the fourth is like a son of the gods.‡"

Responsorial Psalm: Psalms 25: 4-9

4 Show me your ways, Yahweh.
Teach me your paths.
5 Guide me in your truth, and teach me,
for you are the God of my salvation.
I wait for you all day long.
6 Yahweh, remember your tender mercies and your loving kindness,
for they are from old times.
7 Don't remember the sins of my youth, nor my transgressions.
Remember me according to your loving kindness,
for your goodness' sake, Yahweh.
8 Good and upright is Yahweh,
therefore he will instruct sinners in the way.
9 He will guide the humble in justice.
He will teach the humble his way.

Gospel: Matthew 18: 21-35

21 Then Peter came and said to him, "Lord, how often shall my brother sin against me, and I forgive him? Until seven times?"
22 Jesus said to him, "I don't tell you until seven times, but, until seventy times seven. 23 Therefore the Kingdom of Heaven is like a certain king who wanted to settle accounts with his servants. 24 When he had begun to settle, one was brought to him who owed him ten thousand talents.§ 25 But because he couldn't pay, his lord commanded him to be sold, with his wife, his children, and all that he had, and payment to be made. 26 The servant therefore fell down and knelt before him, saying, 'Lord, have patience with me, and I will

repay you all!' 27 The lord of that servant, being moved with compassion, released him and forgave him the debt.

28 "But that servant went out and found one of his fellow servants who owed him one hundred denarii,† and he grabbed him and took him by the throat, saying, 'Pay me what you owe!'

29 "So his fellow servant fell down at his feet and begged him, saying, 'Have patience with me, and I will repay you!' 30 He would not, but went and cast him into prison until he should pay back that which was due. 31 So when his fellow servants saw what was done, they were exceedingly sorry, and came and told their lord all that was done. 32 Then his lord called him in and said to him, 'You wicked servant! I forgave you all that debt because you begged me. 33 Shouldn't you also have had mercy on your fellow servant, even as I had mercy on you?' 34 His lord was angry, and delivered him to the tormentors until he should pay all that was due to him. 35 So my heavenly Father will also do to you, if you don't each forgive your brother from your hearts for his misdeeds."

1. Invite the Holy Spirit into this reading, asking the Author of Scripture to speak to you through His Word
2. Read today's passage as many times as you need, take your time
3. Write down (below) what the Lord is saying to you today
4. Live with this Word in your heart through the day

_____

_____

Wednesday, March 6, 2024

First Reading: Deuteronomy 4: 1, 5-9

1 Now, Israel, listen to the statutes and to the ordinances which I teach you, to do them, that you may live and go in and possess the land which Yahweh, the God of your fathers, gives you.

5 Behold, I have taught you statutes and ordinances, even as Yahweh my God commanded me, that you should do so in the middle of the land where you go in to possess it. 6 Keep therefore and do them; for this is your wisdom and your understanding in the sight of the peoples who shall hear all these statutes and say, "Surely this great nation is a wise and understanding people." 7 For what great nation is there that has a god so near to them as Yahweh our God is whenever we call on him? 8 What great nation is there that has statutes and ordinances so righteous as all this law which I set before you today?

9 Only be careful, and keep your soul diligently, lest you forget the things which your eyes saw, and lest they depart from your heart all the days of your life; but make them known to your children and your children's children

Responsorial Psalm: Psalms 147: 12-13, 15-16, 19-20

12 Praise Yahweh, Jerusalem!
Praise your God, Zion!
13 For he has strengthened the bars of your gates.
He has blessed your children within you.
15 He sends out his commandment to the earth.
His word runs very swiftly.
16 He gives snow like wool,
and scatters frost like ashes.
19 He shows his word to Jacob,
his statutes and his ordinances to Israel.
20 He has not done this for just any nation.
They don't know his ordinances.
Praise Yah!

Gospel: Matthew 5: 17-19

17 "Don't think that I came to destroy the law or the prophets. I didn't come to destroy, but to fulfill. 18 For most certainly, I tell you, until heaven and earth pass away, not even one smallest letter‡ or one tiny pen stroke§ shall in any way pass away from the law, until all things are accomplished. 19 Therefore, whoever shall break one of these least commandments and teach others to do so, shall be called least in the Kingdom of Heaven; but whoever shall do and teach them shall be called great in the Kingdom of Heaven.

1. Invite the Holy Spirit into this reading, asking the Author of Scripture to speak to you through His Word
2. Read today's passage as many times as you need, take your time
3. Write down (below) what the Lord is saying to you today
4. Live with this Word in your heart through the day

Thursday, March 7, 2024
Saints Perpetua and Felicity, Martyrs

First Reading: Jeremiah 7: 23-28

23 but this thing I commanded them, saying, 'Listen to my voice, and I will be your God, and you shall be my people. Walk in all the way that I command you, that it may be well with you.' 24 But they didn't listen or turn their ear, but walked in their own counsels and in the stubbornness of their evil heart, and went backward, and not forward. 25 Since the day that your fathers came out of the land of Egypt to this day, I have sent to you all my servants the prophets, daily rising up early and sending them. 26 Yet they didn't listen to me or incline their ear, but made their neck stiff. They did worse than their fathers.
27 "You shall speak all these words to them, but they will not listen to you. You shall also call to them, but they will not answer you. 28 You shall tell them, 'This is the nation that has not listened to Yahweh their God's voice, nor received instruction. Truth has perished, and is cut off from their mouth.'

Responsorial Psalm: Psalms 95: 1-2, 6-9

1 Oh come, let's sing to Yahweh.
Let's shout aloud to the rock of our salvation!
2 Let's come before his presence with thanksgiving.
Let's extol him with songs!
6 Oh come, let's worship and bow down.
Let's kneel before Yahweh, our Maker,
7 for he is our God.
We are the people of his pasture,
and the sheep in his care.
Today, oh that you would hear his voice!
8 Don't harden your heart, as at Meribah,
as in the day of Massah in the wilderness,
9 when your fathers tempted me,
tested me, and saw my work.

Gospel: Luke 11: 14-23

14 He was casting out a demon, and it was mute. When the demon had gone out, the mute man spoke; and the multitudes marveled. 15 But some of them said, "He casts out demons by Beelzebul, the prince of the demons." 16 Others, testing him, sought from him a sign from heaven. 17 But he, knowing their thoughts, said to them, "Every kingdom divided against itself is brought to desolation. A house divided against itself falls. 18 If Satan also is divided against himself, how will his kingdom stand? For you say that I cast out demons by Beelzebul. 19 But if I cast out demons by Beelzebul, by whom do your children cast

them out? Therefore they will be your judges. 20 But if I by God's finger cast out demons, then God's Kingdom has come to you.

21 "When the strong man, fully armed, guards his own dwelling, his goods are safe. 22 But when someone stronger attacks him and overcomes him, he takes from him his whole armor in which he trusted, and divides his plunder.

23 "He who is not with me is against me. He who doesn't gather with me scatters.

1. Invite the Holy Spirit into this reading, asking the Author of Scripture to speak to you through His Word
2. Read today's passage as many times as you need, take your time
3. Write down (below) what the Lord is saying to you today
4. Live with this Word in your heart through the day

Friday, March 8, 2024
Saint John of God, Religious

First Reading: Hosea 14: 2-9

2 Take words with you, and return to Yahweh.
Tell him, "Forgive all our sins,
and accept that which is good;
so we offer bulls as we vowed of our lips.
3 Assyria can't save us.
We won't ride on horses;
neither will we say any more to the work of our hands, 'Our gods!'
for in you the fatherless finds mercy."
4 "I will heal their waywardness.
I will love them freely;
for my anger is turned away from them.
5 I will be like the dew to Israel.
He will blossom like the lily,
and send down his roots like Lebanon.
6 His branches will spread,
and his beauty will be like the olive tree,
and his fragrance like Lebanon.

7 Men will dwell in his shade.
They will revive like the grain,
and blossom like the vine.
Their fragrance will be like the wine of Lebanon.
8 Ephraim, what have I to do any more with idols?
I answer, and will take care of him.
I am like a green cypress tree;
from me your fruit is found."
 9 Who is wise, that he may understand these things?
Who is prudent, that he may know them?
For the ways of Yahweh are right,
and the righteous walk in them,
but the rebellious stumble in them.

Responsorial Psalm: Psalms 81: 6-11, 14

6 "I removed his shoulder from the burden.
His hands were freed from the basket.
7 You called in trouble, and I delivered you.
I answered you in the secret place of thunder.
I tested you at the waters of Meribah."
8 "Hear, my people, and I will testify to you,
Israel, if you would listen to me!
9 There shall be no strange god in you,
neither shall you worship any foreign god.
10 I am Yahweh, your God,
who brought you up out of the land of Egypt.
Open your mouth wide, and I will fill it.
11 But my people didn't listen to my voice.
Israel desired none of me.
14 I would soon subdue their enemies,
and turn my hand against their adversaries.

Gospel: Mark 12: 28-34

28 But if this is how God clothes the grass in the field, which today exists and tomorrow
is cast into the oven, how much more will he clothe you, O you of little faith?
29 "Don't seek what you will eat or what you will drink; neither be anxious. 30 For the
nations of the world seek after all of these things, but your Father knows that you need
these things. 31 But seek God's Kingdom, and all these things will be added to you.

32 "Don't be afraid, little flock, for it is your Father's good pleasure to give you the Kingdom. 33 Sell what you have and give gifts to the needy. Make for yourselves purses which don't grow old, a treasure in the heavens that doesn't fail, where no thief approaches and no moth destroys. 34 For where your treasure is, there will your heart be also.

1. Invite the Holy Spirit into this reading, asking the Author of Scripture to speak to you through His Word
2. Read today's passage as many times as you need, take your time
3. Write down (below) what the Lord is saying to you today
4. Live with this Word in your heart through the day

_____

_____

Saturday, March 9, 2024
Saint Frances of Rome, Religious

First Reading: Hosea 6: 1-6

1 "Come! Let's return to Yahweh;
for he has torn us to pieces,
and he will heal us;
he has injured us,
and he will bind up our wounds.
2 After two days he will revive us.
On the third day he will raise us up,
and we will live before him.
3 Let's acknowledge Yahweh.
Let's press on to know Yahweh.
As surely as the sun rises,
Yahweh will appear.
He will come to us like the rain,
like the spring rain that waters the earth."
4 "Ephraim, what shall I do to you?
Judah, what shall I do to you?
For your love is like a morning cloud,
and like the dew that disappears early.
5 Therefore I have cut them to pieces with the prophets;

I killed them with the words of my mouth.
Your judgments are like a flash of lightning.
6 For I desire mercy, and not sacrifice;
and the knowledge of God more than burnt offerings.

Responsorial Psalm: Psalms 51: 3-4, 18-19

3 For I know my transgressions.
My sin is constantly before me.
4 Against you, and you only, I have sinned,
and done that which is evil in your sight,
so you may be proved right when you speak,
and justified when you judge.
18 Do well in your good pleasure to Zion.
Build the walls of Jerusalem.
19 Then you will delight in the sacrifices of righteousness,
in burnt offerings and in whole burnt offerings.
Then they will offer bulls on your altar.

Gospel: Luke 18: 9-14

9 He also spoke this parable to certain people who were convinced of their own righteousness, and who despised all others: 10 "Two men went up into the temple to pray; one was a Pharisee, and the other was a tax collector. 11 The Pharisee stood and prayed by himself like this: 'God, I thank you that I am not like the rest of men: extortionists, unrighteous, adulterers, or even like this tax collector. 12 I fast twice a week. I give tithes of all that I get.' 13 But the tax collector, standing far away, wouldn't even lift up his eyes to heaven, but beat his breast, saying, 'God, be merciful to me, a sinner!' 14 I tell you, this man went down to his house justified rather than the other; for everyone who exalts himself will be humbled, but he who humbles himself will be exalted."

1. Invite the Holy Spirit into this reading, asking the Author of Scripture to speak to you through His Word
2. Read today's passage as many times as you need, take your time
3. Write down (below) what the Lord is saying to you today
4. Live with this Word in your heart through the day

_____

_____

Sunday, March 10, 2024
Fourth Sunday Of Lent

First Reading: Second Chronicles 36: 14-16, 19-23

14 Moreover all the chiefs of the priests and the people trespassed very greatly after all the abominations of the nations; and they polluted Yahweh's house which he had made holy in Jerusalem.
15 Yahweh, the God of their fathers, sent to them by his messengers, rising up early and sending, because he had compassion on his people and on his dwelling place; 16 but they mocked the messengers of God, despised his words, and scoffed at his prophets, until Yahweh's wrath arose against his people, until there was no remedy.
19 They burned God's house, broke down the wall of Jerusalem, burned all its palaces with fire, and destroyed all of its valuable vessels. 20 He carried those who had escaped from the sword away to Babylon, and they were servants to him and his sons until the reign of the kingdom of Persia, 21 to fulfill Yahweh's word by Jeremiah's mouth, until the land had enjoyed its Sabbaths. As long as it lay desolate, it kept Sabbath, to fulfill seventy years.
22 Now in the first year of Cyrus king of Persia, that Yahweh's word by the mouth of Jeremiah might be accomplished, Yahweh stirred up the spirit of Cyrus king of Persia, so that he made a proclamation throughout all his kingdom, and put it also in writing, saying,
23 "Cyrus king of Persia says, 'Yahweh, the God of heaven, has given all the kingdoms of the earth to me; and he has commanded me to build him a house in Jerusalem, which is in Judah. Whoever there is among you of all his people, Yahweh his God be with him, and let him go up.' "

Responsorial Psalm: Psalms 137: 1-6

1 By the rivers of Babylon, there we sat down.
Yes, we wept, when we remembered Zion.
2 On the willows in that land,
we hung up our harps.
3 For there, those who led us captive asked us for songs.
Those who tormented us demanded songs of joy:
"Sing us one of the songs of Zion!"
4 How can we sing Yahweh's song in a foreign land?
5 If I forget you, Jerusalem,
let my right hand forget its skill.
6 Let my tongue stick to the roof of my mouth if I don't remember you,
if I don't prefer Jerusalem above my chief joy.

Second Reading: Ephesians 2: 4-10

4 But God, being rich in mercy, for his great love with which he loved us, 5 even when we were dead through our trespasses, made us alive together with Christ—by grace you have been saved— 6 and raised us up with him, and made us to sit with him in the heavenly places in Christ Jesus, 7 that in the ages to come he might show the exceeding riches of his grace in kindness toward us in Christ Jesus; 8 for by grace you have been saved through faith, and that not of yourselves; it is the gift of God, 9 not of works, that no one would boast. 10 For we are his workmanship, created in Christ Jesus for good works, which God prepared before that we would walk in them.

Gospel: John 3: 14-21

14 As Moses lifted up the serpent in the wilderness, even so must the Son of Man be lifted up, 15 that whoever believes in him should not perish, but have eternal life. 16 For God so loved the world, that he gave his only born§ Son, that whoever believes in him should not perish, but have eternal life. 17 For God didn't send his Son into the world to judge the world, but that the world should be saved through him. 18 He who believes in him is not judged. He who doesn't believe has been judged already, because he has not believed in the name of the only born Son of God. 19 This is the judgment, that the light has come into the world, and men loved the darkness rather than the light, for their works were evil. 20 For everyone who does evil hates the light and doesn't come to the light, lest his works would be exposed. 21 But he who does the truth comes to the light, that his works may be revealed, that they have been done in God."

1. Invite the Holy Spirit into this reading, asking the Author of Scripture to speak to you through His Word
2. Read today's passage as many times as you need, take your time
3. Write down (below) what the Lord is saying to you today
4. Live with this Word in your heart through the day

_____

_____

Monday, March 11, 2024

First Reading: Isaiah 65: 17-21

17 "For, behold, I create new heavens and a new earth;
and the former things will not be remembered,
nor come into mind.
18 But be glad and rejoice forever in that which I create;
for, behold, I create Jerusalem to be a delight,
and her people a joy.
19 I will rejoice in Jerusalem,
and delight in my people;
and the voice of weeping and the voice of crying
will be heard in her no more.
20 "No more will there be an infant who only lives a few days,
nor an old man who has not filled his days;
for the child will die one hundred years old,
and the sinner being one hundred years old will be accursed.
21 They will build houses and inhabit them.
They will plant vineyards and eat their fruit.

Responsorial Psalm: Psalms 30: 2 and 4-6, 11-12a

2 Yahweh my God, I cried to you,
and you have healed me.
4 Sing praise to Yahweh, you saints of his.
Give thanks to his holy name.
5 For his anger is but for a moment.
His favor is for a lifetime.
Weeping may stay for the night,
but joy comes in the morning.
6 As for me, I said in my prosperity,
"I shall never be moved."
11 You have turned my mourning into dancing for me.
You have removed my sackcloth, and clothed me with gladness,
12 to the end that my heart may sing praise to you, and not be silent.

Gospel: John 4: 43-54

43 After the two days he went out from there and went into Galilee. 44 For Jesus himself testified that a prophet has no honor in his own country. 45 So when he came into Galilee, the Galileans received him, having seen all the things that he did in Jerusalem at the feast, for they also went to the feast. 46 Jesus came therefore again to Cana of Galilee, where he made the water into wine. There was a certain nobleman whose son was sick at Capernaum. 47 When he heard that Jesus had come out of Judea into Galilee, he went to

him and begged him that he would come down and heal his son, for he was at the point of death. 48 Jesus therefore said to him, "Unless you see signs and wonders, you will in no way believe."

49 The nobleman said to him, "Sir, come down before my child dies."

50 Jesus said to him, "Go your way. Your son lives." The man believed the word that Jesus spoke to him, and he went his way. 51 As he was going down, his servants met him and reported, saying "Your child lives!" 52 So he inquired of them the hour when he began to get better. They said therefore to him, "Yesterday at the seventh hour,§ the fever left him." 53 So the father knew that it was at that hour in which Jesus said to him, "Your son lives." He believed, as did his whole house. 54 This is again the second sign that Jesus did, having come out of Judea into Galilee.

1. Invite the Holy Spirit into this reading, asking the Author of Scripture to speak to you through His Word
2. Read today's passage as many times as you need, take your time
3. Write down (below) what the Lord is saying to you today
4. Live with this Word in your heart through the day

Tuesday, March 12, 2024

First Reading: Ezekiel 47: 1-9, 12

1 He brought me back to the door of the temple; and behold, waters flowed out from under the threshold of the temple eastward, for the front of the temple faced toward the east. The waters came down from underneath, from the right side of the temple, on the south of the altar. 2 Then he brought me out by the way of the gate northward, and led me around by the way outside to the outer gate, by the way of the gate that looks toward the east. Behold, waters ran out on the right side.

3 When the man went out eastward with the line in his hand, he measured one thousand cubits,† and he caused me to pass through the waters, waters that were to the ankles. 4 Again he measured one thousand, and caused me to pass through the waters, waters that were to the knees. Again he measured one thousand, and caused me to pass through waters that were to the waist. 5 Afterward he measured one thousand; and it was a river

that I could not pass through, for the waters had risen, waters to swim in, a river that could not be walked through.

6 He said to me, "Son of man, have you seen this?"

Then he brought me and caused me to return to the bank of the river. 7 Now when I had returned, behold, on the bank of the river were very many trees on the one side and on the other. 8 Then he said to me, "These waters flow out toward the eastern region and will go down into the Arabah. Then they will go toward the sea and flow into the sea which will be made to flow out; and the waters will be healed. 9 It will happen that every living creature which swarms, in every place where the rivers come, will live. Then there will be a very great multitude of fish; for these waters have come there, and the waters of the sea will be healed, and everything will live wherever the river comes. 12 By the river banks, on both sides, will grow every tree for food, whose leaf won't wither, neither will its fruit fail. It will produce new fruit every month, because its waters issue out of the sanctuary. Its fruit will be for food, and its leaf for healing."

Responsorial Psalm: Psalms 46: 2-3, 5-6, 8-9

2 Therefore we won't be afraid, though the earth changes,
though the mountains are shaken into the heart of the seas;
3 though its waters roar and are troubled,
though the mountains tremble with their swelling.
5 God is within her. She shall not be moved.
God will help her at dawn.
6 The nations raged. The kingdoms were moved.
He lifted his voice and the earth melted.
8 Come, see Yahweh's works,
what desolations he has made in the earth.
9 He makes wars cease to the end of the earth.
He breaks the bow, and shatters the spear.
He burns the chariots in the fire.

Gospel: John 5: 1-16

1 After these things, there was a feast of the Jews, and Jesus went up to Jerusalem. 2 Now in Jerusalem by the sheep gate, there is a pool, which is called in Hebrew, "Bethesda", having five porches. 3 In these lay a great multitude of those who were sick, blind, lame, or paralyzed, waiting for the moving of the water; 4 for an angel went down at certain times into the pool and stirred up the water. Whoever stepped in first after the stirring of the water was healed of whatever disease he had.† 5 A certain man was there who had been sick for thirty-eight years. 6 When Jesus saw him lying there, and knew that he had been sick for a long time, he asked him, "Do you want to be made well?"

7 The sick man answered him, "Sir, I have no one to put me into the pool when the water is stirred up, but while I'm coming, another steps down before me."

8 Jesus said to him, "Arise, take up your mat, and walk."

9 Immediately, the man was made well, and took up his mat and walked.

Now that day was a Sabbath. 10 So the Jews said to him who was cured, "It is the Sabbath. It is not lawful for you to carry the mat."

11 He answered them, "He who made me well said to me, 'Take up your mat and walk.' "

12 Then they asked him, "Who is the man who said to you, 'Take up your mat and walk'?"

13 But he who was healed didn't know who it was, for Jesus had withdrawn, a crowd being in the place.

14 Afterward Jesus found him in the temple and said to him, "Behold, you are made well. Sin no more, so that nothing worse happens to you."

15 The man went away, and told the Jews that it was Jesus who had made him well. 16 For this cause the Jews persecuted Jesus and sought to kill him, because he did these things on the Sabbath.

1. Invite the Holy Spirit into this reading, asking the Author of Scripture to speak to you through His Word
2. Read today's passage as many times as you need, take your time
3. Write down (below) what the Lord is saying to you today
4. Live with this Word in your heart through the day

_____

_____

Wednesday, March 13, 2024

First Reading: Isaiah 49: 8-15

8 Yahweh says, "I have answered you in an acceptable time.
I have helped you in a day of salvation.
I will preserve you and give you for a covenant of the people,
to raise up the land, to make them inherit the desolate heritage,
9 saying to those who are bound, 'Come out!';
to those who are in darkness, 'Show yourselves!'
"They shall feed along the paths,
and their pasture shall be on all treeless heights.
10 They shall not hunger nor thirst;

neither shall the heat nor sun strike them,

for he who has mercy on them will lead them.

He will guide them by springs of water.

11 I will make all my mountains a road,

and my highways shall be exalted.

12 Behold, these shall come from afar,

and behold, these from the north and from the west,

and these from the land of Sinim."

13 Sing, heavens, and be joyful, earth!

Break out into singing, mountains!

For Yahweh has comforted his people,

and will have compassion on his afflicted.

14 But Zion said, "Yahweh has forsaken me,

and the Lord has forgotten me."

15 "Can a woman forget her nursing child,

that she should not have compassion on the son of her womb?

Yes, these may forget,

yet I will not forget you!

Responsorial Psalm: Psalms 145: 8-9, 13cd-14, 17-18

8 Yahweh is gracious, merciful,

slow to anger, and of great loving kindness.

9 Yahweh is good to all.

13 His tender mercies are over all his works.

Yahweh is faithful in all his words,

and loving in all his deeds.‡

14 Yahweh upholds all who fall,

and raises up all those who are bowed down.

17 Yahweh is righteous in all his ways,

and gracious in all his works.

18 Yahweh is near to all those who call on him,

to all who call on him in truth.

Gospel: John 5: 17-30

17 But Jesus answered them, "My Father is still working, so I am working, too."
18 For this cause therefore the Jews sought all the more to kill him, because he not only broke the Sabbath, but also called God his own Father, making himself equal with God. 19 Jesus therefore answered them, "Most certainly, I tell you, the Son can do nothing of himself, but what he sees the Father doing. For whatever things he does, these the Son

also does likewise. 20 For the Father has affection for the Son, and shows him all things that he himself does. He will show him greater works than these, that you may marvel. 21 For as the Father raises the dead and gives them life, even so the Son also gives life to whom he desires. 22 For the Father judges no one, but he has given all judgment to the Son, 23 that all may honor the Son, even as they honor the Father. He who doesn't honor the Son doesn't honor the Father who sent him.

24 "Most certainly I tell you, he who hears my word and believes him who sent me has eternal life, and doesn't come into judgment, but has passed out of death into life. 25 Most certainly I tell you, the hour comes, and now is, when the dead will hear the Son of God's voice; and those who hear will live. 26 For as the Father has life in himself, even so he gave to the Son also to have life in himself. 27 He also gave him authority to execute judgment, because he is a son of man. 28 Don't marvel at this, for the hour comes in which all who are in the tombs will hear his voice 29 and will come out; those who have done good, to the resurrection of life; and those who have done evil, to the resurrection of judgment. 30 I can of myself do nothing. As I hear, I judge; and my judgment is righteous, because I don't seek my own will, but the will of my Father who sent me.

1. Invite the Holy Spirit into this reading, asking the Author of Scripture to speak to you through His Word
2. Read today's passage as many times as you need, take your time
3. Write down (below) what the Lord is saying to you today
4. Live with this Word in your heart through the day

Thursday, March 14, 2024

First Reading: Exodus 32: 7-14

7 Yahweh spoke to Moses, "Go, get down; for your people, whom you brought up out of the land of Egypt, have corrupted themselves! 8 They have turned away quickly out of the way which I commanded them. They have made themselves a molded calf, and have worshiped it, and have sacrificed to it, and said, 'These are your gods, Israel, which brought you up out of the land of Egypt.' "
9 Yahweh said to Moses, "I have seen these people, and behold, they are a stiff-necked people. 10 Now therefore leave me alone, that my wrath may burn hot against them, and that I may consume them; and I will make of you a great nation."

11 Moses begged Yahweh his God, and said, "Yahweh, why does your wrath burn hot against your people, that you have brought out of the land of Egypt with great power and with a mighty hand? 12 Why should the Egyptians talk, saying, 'He brought them out for evil, to kill them in the mountains, and to consume them from the surface of the earth'? Turn from your fierce wrath, and turn away from this evil against your people. 13 Remember Abraham, Isaac, and Israel, your servants, to whom you swore by your own self, and said to them, 'I will multiply your offspring† as the stars of the sky, and all this land that I have spoken of I will give to your offspring, and they shall inherit it forever.' " 14 So Yahweh turned away from the evil which he said he would do to his people.

Responsorial Psalm: Psalms 106: 19-23

19 They made a calf in Horeb,
and worshiped a molten image.
20 Thus they exchanged their glory
for an image of a bull that eats grass.
21 They forgot God, their Savior,
who had done great things in Egypt,
22 wondrous works in the land of Ham,
and awesome things by the Red Sea.
23 Therefore he said that he would destroy them,
had Moses, his chosen, not stood before him in the breach,
to turn away his wrath, so that he wouldn't destroy them.

Gospel: John 5: 31-47

31 "If I testify about myself, my witness is not valid. 32 It is another who testifies about me. I know that the testimony which he testifies about me is true. 33 You have sent to John, and he has testified to the truth. 34 But the testimony which I receive is not from man. However, I say these things that you may be saved. 35 He was the burning and shining lamp, and you were willing to rejoice for a while in his light. 36 But the testimony which I have is greater than that of John; for the works which the Father gave me to accomplish, the very works that I do, testify about me, that the Father has sent me. 37 The Father himself, who sent me, has testified about me. You have neither heard his voice at any time, nor seen his form. 38 You don't have his word living in you, because you don't believe him whom he sent.
39 "You search the Scriptures, because you think that in them you have eternal life; and these are they which testify about me. 40 Yet you will not come to me, that you may have life. 41 I don't receive glory from men. 42 But I know you, that you don't have God's love in yourselves. 43 I have come in my Father's name, and you don't receive me. If another

comes in his own name, you will receive him. 44 How can you believe, who receive glory from one another, and you don't seek the glory that comes from the only God?

45 "Don't think that I will accuse you to the Father. There is one who accuses you, even Moses, on whom you have set your hope. 46 For if you believed Moses, you would believe me; for he wrote about me. 47 But if you don't believe his writings, how will you believe my words?"

1. Invite the Holy Spirit into this reading, asking the Author of Scripture to speak to you through His Word
2. Read today's passage as many times as you need, take your time
3. Write down (below) what the Lord is saying to you today
4. Live with this Word in your heart through the day

_____

_____

Friday, March 15, 2024

First Reading: Wisdom 2: 1a, 12-22

1 For they said† within themselves, with unsound reasoning,
12 But let's lie in wait for the righteous man,
because he annoys us,
is contrary to our works,
reproaches us with sins against the law,
and charges us with sins against our training.
13 He professes to have knowledge of God,
and calls himself a child of the Lord.
14 He became to us a reproof of our thoughts.
15 He is grievous to us even to look at,
because his life is unlike other men's,
and his paths are strange.
16 We were regarded by him as something worthless,
and he abstains from our ways as from uncleanness.
He calls the latter end of the righteous happy.
He boasts that God is his father.
17 Let's see if his words are true.
Let's test what will happen at the end of his life.

18 For if the righteous man is God's son, he will uphold him,

and he will deliver him out of the hand of his adversaries.

19 Let's test him with insult and torture,

that we may find out how gentle he is,

and test his patience.

20 Let's condemn him to a shameful death,

for he will be protected, according to his words."

 21 Thus they reasoned, and they were led astray;

for their wickedness blinded them,

22 and they didn't know the mysteries of God,

neither did they hope for wages of holiness,

nor did they discern that there is a prize for blameless souls.

Responsorial Psalm: Psalms 34: 17-22

17 The righteous cry, and Yahweh hears,

and delivers them out of all their troubles.

18 Yahweh is near to those who have a broken heart,

and saves those who have a crushed spirit.

19 Many are the afflictions of the righteous,

but Yahweh delivers him out of them all.

20 He protects all of his bones.

Not one of them is broken.

21 Evil shall kill the wicked.

Those who hate the righteous shall be condemned.

22 Yahweh redeems the soul of his servants.

None of those who take refuge in him shall be condemned.

Gospel: John 7: 1-2, 10, 25-30

1 After these things, Jesus was walking in Galilee, for he wouldn't walk in Judea, because the Jews sought to kill him. 2 Now the feast of the Jews, the Feast of Booths, was at hand. 10 But when his brothers had gone up to the feast, then he also went up, not publicly, but as it were in secret.

25 Therefore some of them of Jerusalem said, "Isn't this he whom they seek to kill? 26 Behold, he speaks openly, and they say nothing to him. Can it be that the rulers indeed know that this is truly the Christ? 27 However, we know where this man comes from, but when the Christ comes, no one will know where he comes from."

28 Jesus therefore cried out in the temple, teaching and saying, "You both know me, and know where I am from. I have not come of myself, but he who sent me is true, whom you don't know. 29 I know him, because I am from him, and he sent me."

30 They sought therefore to take him; but no one laid a hand on him, because his hour had not yet come.

1. Invite the Holy Spirit into this reading, asking the Author of Scripture to speak to you through His Word
2. Read today's passage as many times as you need, take your time
3. Write down (below) what the Lord is saying to you today
4. Live with this Word in your heart through the day

Saturday, March 16, 2024

First Reading: Jeremiah 11: 18-20

18 Yahweh gave me knowledge of it, and I knew it. Then you showed me their doings. 19 But I was like a gentle lamb that is led to the slaughter. I didn't know that they had devised plans against me, saying,
"Let's destroy the tree with its fruit,
and let's cut him off from the land of the living,
that his name may be no more remembered."
20 But, Yahweh of Armies, who judges righteously,
who tests the heart and the mind,
I will see your vengeance on them;
for to you I have revealed my cause.

Responsorial Psalm: Psalms 7: 2-3, 9bc-12

2 lest they tear apart my soul like a lion,
ripping it in pieces, while there is no one to deliver.
3 Yahweh, my God, if I have done this,
if there is iniquity in my hands,
9b but establish the righteous;
their minds and hearts are searched by the righteous God.
10 My shield is with God,
who saves the upright in heart.
11 God is a righteous judge,

yes, a God who has indignation every day.

12 If a man doesn't repent, he will sharpen his sword;

he has bent and strung his bow.

Gospel: John 7: 40-53

40 Many of the multitude therefore, when they heard these words, said, "This is truly the prophet." 41 Others said, "This is the Christ." But some said, "What, does the Christ come out of Galilee? 42 Hasn't the Scripture said that the Christ comes of the offspring† of David, * and from Bethlehem,* the village where David was?" 43 So a division arose in the multitude because of him. 44 Some of them would have arrested him, but no one laid hands on him. 45 The officers therefore came to the chief priests and Pharisees; and they said to them, "Why didn't you bring him?"

46 The officers answered, "No man ever spoke like this man!"

47 The Pharisees therefore answered them, "You aren't also led astray, are you? 48 Have any of the rulers or any of the Pharisees believed in him? 49 But this multitude that doesn't know the law is cursed."

50 Nicodemus (he who came to him by night, being one of them) said to them, 51 "Does our law judge a man unless it first hears from him personally and knows what he does?"

52 They answered him, "Are you also from Galilee? Search and see that no prophet has arisen out of Galilee."*

53 Everyone went to his own house,

1. Invite the Holy Spirit into this reading, asking the Author of Scripture to speak to you through His Word
2. Read today's passage as many times as you need, take your time
3. Write down (below) what the Lord is saying to you today
4. Live with this Word in your heart through the day

_____

_____

Sunday, March 17, 2024
Fifth Sunday of Lent

First Reading: Jeremiah 31: 31-34

31 "Behold, the days come," says Yahweh, "that I will make a new covenant with the house of Israel, and with the house of Judah, 32 not according to the covenant that I made with their fathers in the day that I took them by the hand to bring them out of the land of Egypt, which covenant of mine they broke, although I was a husband to them," says Yahweh. 33 "But this is the covenant that I will make with the house of Israel after those days," says Yahweh:

"I will put my law in their inward parts,
and I will write it in their heart.
I will be their God,
and they shall be my people.
34 They will no longer each teach his neighbor,
and every man teach his brother, saying, 'Know Yahweh;'
for they will all know me,
from their least to their greatest," says Yahweh,
"for I will forgive their iniquity,
and I will remember their sin no more."

Responsorial Psalm: Psalms 51: 3-4, 12-15

3 For I know my transgressions.
My sin is constantly before me.
4 Against you, and you only, I have sinned,
and done that which is evil in your sight,
so you may be proved right when you speak,
and justified when you judge.
12 Restore to me the joy of your salvation.
Uphold me with a willing spirit.
13 Then I will teach transgressors your ways.
Sinners will be converted to you.
14 Deliver me from the guilt of bloodshed, O God, the God of my salvation.
My tongue will sing aloud of your righteousness.
15 Lord, open my lips.
My mouth will declare your praise.

Second Reading: Hebrews 5: 7-9

7 He, in the days of his flesh, having offered up prayers and petitions with strong crying and tears to him who was able to save him from death, and having been heard for his godly fear, 8 though he was a Son, yet learned obedience by the things which he suffered. 9 Having been made perfect, he became to all of those who obey him the author of eternal salvation

Gospel: John 12: 20-33

20 Now there were certain Greeks among those who went up to worship at the feast. 21 Therefore, these came to Philip, who was from Bethsaida of Galilee, and asked him, saying, "Sir, we want to see Jesus." 22 Philip came and told Andrew, and in turn, Andrew came with Philip, and they told Jesus.

23 Jesus answered them, "The time has come for the Son of Man to be glorified. 24 Most certainly I tell you, unless a grain of wheat falls into the earth and dies, it remains by itself alone. But if it dies, it bears much fruit. 25 He who loves his life will lose it. He who hates his life in this world will keep it to eternal life. 26 If anyone serves me, let him follow me. Where I am, there my servant will also be. If anyone serves me, the Father will honor him. 27 "Now my soul is troubled. What shall I say? 'Father, save me from this time'? But I came to this time for this cause. 28 Father, glorify your name!"

Then a voice came out of the sky, saying, "I have both glorified it and will glorify it again." 29 Therefore the multitude who stood by and heard it said that it had thundered. Others said, "An angel has spoken to him."

30 Jesus answered, "This voice hasn't come for my sake, but for your sakes. 31 Now is the judgment of this world. Now the prince of this world will be cast out. 32 And I, if I am lifted up from the earth, will draw all people to myself." 33 But he said this, signifying by what kind of death he should die.

1. Invite the Holy Spirit into this reading, asking the Author of Scripture to speak to you through His Word
2. Read today's passage as many times as you need, take your time
3. Write down (below) what the Lord is saying to you today
4. Live with this Word in your heart through the day

Monday, March 18, 2024
Saint Cyril of Jerusalem, Bishop and Doctor of the Church

First Reading: Daniel 13: 41c-62

41 Then the assembly believed them, as those who were elders of the people and judges; so they condemned her to death.

42 Then Susanna cried out with a loud voice, and said, "O everlasting God, you know the secrets, and know all things before they happen. 43 You know that they have testified falsely against me. Behold, I must die, even though I never did such things as these men have maliciously invented against me."

44 The Lord heard her voice. 45 Therefore when she was led away to be put to death, God raised up the holy spirit of a young youth, whose name was Daniel. 46 He cried with a loud voice, "I am clear from the blood of this woman!"

47 Then all the people turned them toward him, and said, "What do these words that you have spoken mean?"

48 So he, standing in the midst of them, said, "Are you all such fools, you sons of Israel, that without examination or knowledge of the truth you have condemned a daughter of Israel? 49 Return again to the place of judgment; for these have testified falsely against her."

50 Therefore all the people turned again in haste, and the elders said to him, "Come, sit down among us, and show it to us, seeing God has given you the honor of an elder."

51 Then Daniel said to them, "Put them far apart from each another, and I will examine them." 52 So when they were put apart one from another, he called one of them, and said to him, "O you who have become old in wickedness, now your sins have returned which you have committed before, 53 in pronouncing unjust judgment, condemning the innocent, and letting the guilty go free; although the Lord says, 'You shall not kill the innocent and righteous.' 54 Now then, if you saw her, tell me, under which tree did you see them companying together?"

He answered, "Under a mastick tree."

55 And Daniel said, "You have certainly lied against your own head; for even now the angel of God has received the sentence of God and will cut you in two." 56 So he put him aside, and commanded to bring the other, and said to him, "O you seed of Canaan, and not of Judah, beauty has deceived you, and lust has perverted your heart. 57 Thus you have dealt with the daughters of Israel, and they for fear were intimate with you; but the daughter of Judah would not tolerate your wickedness. 58 Now therefore tell me, under which tree did you take them being intimate together?"

He answered, "Under an evergreen oak tree."

59 Then Daniel said to him, "You have also certainly lied against your own head; for the angel of God waits with the sword to cut you in two, that he may destroy you."

60 With that, all the assembly cried out with a loud voice, and blessed God, who saves those who hope in him. 61 Then they arose against the two elders, for Daniel had convicted them of false testimony out of their own mouth. 62 According to the law of Moses they did to them what they maliciously intended to do to their neighbor. They put them to death, and the innocent blood was saved the same day.

Responsorial Psalm: Psalms 23: 1-6

1 Yahweh is my shepherd;

I shall lack nothing.

2 He makes me lie down in green pastures.

He leads me beside still waters.

3 He restores my soul.

He guides me in the paths of righteousness for his name's sake.

4 Even though I walk through the valley of the shadow of death,

I will fear no evil, for you are with me.

Your rod and your staff,

they comfort me.

5 You prepare a table before me

in the presence of my enemies.

You anoint my head with oil.

My cup runs over.

6 Surely goodness and loving kindness shall follow me all the days of my life,

and I will dwell in Yahweh's house forever.

Gospel: John 8: 1-11

1 but Jesus went to the Mount of Olives.

2 Now very early in the morning, he came again into the temple, and all the people came to him. He sat down and taught them. 3 The scribes and the Pharisees brought a woman taken in adultery. Having set her in the middle, 4 they told him, "Teacher, we found this woman in adultery, in the very act. 5 Now in our law, Moses commanded us to stone such women.* What then do you say about her?" 6 They said this testing him, that they might have something to accuse him of.

But Jesus stooped down and wrote on the ground with his finger. 7 But when they continued asking him, he looked up and said to them, "He who is without sin among you, let him throw the first stone at her." 8 Again he stooped down and wrote on the ground with his finger.

9 They, when they heard it, being convicted by their conscience, went out one by one, beginning from the oldest, even to the last. Jesus was left alone with the woman where she was, in the middle. 10 Jesus, standing up, saw her and said, "Woman, where are your accusers? Did no one condemn you?"

11 She said, "No one, Lord."

Jesus said, "Neither do I condemn you. Go your way. From now on, sin no more."

1. Invite the Holy Spirit into this reading, asking the Author of Scripture to speak to you through His Word

2. Read today's passage as many times as you need, take your time

3. Write down (below) what the Lord is saying to you today

<hr>

<hr>

Tuesday, March 19, 2024
Saint Joseph, Spouse of The Blessed Virgin Mary

First Reading: Second Samuel 7: 4-5a, 12-14a, 16

4 That same night, Yahweh's word came to Nathan, saying, 5 "Go and tell my servant David, 'Yahweh says, 12 When your days are fulfilled and you sleep with your fathers, I will set up your offspring after you, who will proceed out of your body, and I will establish his kingdom. 13 He will build a house for my name, and I will establish the throne of his kingdom forever. 14 I will be his father, and he will be my son.
16 Your house and your kingdom will be made sure forever before you. Your throne will be established forever."

Responsorial Psalm: Psalms 89: 2-5, 27 and 29

2 I indeed declare, "Love stands firm forever.
You established the heavens.
Your faithfulness is in them."
 3 "I have made a covenant with my chosen one,
I have sworn to David, my servant,
4 'I will establish your offspring forever,
and build up your throne to all generations.' "
5 The heavens will praise your wonders, Yahweh,
your faithfulness also in the assembly of the holy ones.
27 I will also appoint him my firstborn,
the highest of the kings of the earth.
29 I will also make his offspring endure forever,
and his throne as the days of heaven.

Second Reading: Romans 4: 13, 16-18, 22

13 For the promise to Abraham and to his offspring that he would be heir of the world wasn't through the law, but through the righteousness of faith.

16 For this cause it is of faith, that it may be according to grace, to the end that the promise may be sure to all the offspring, not to that only which is of the law, but to that also which is of the faith of Abraham, who is the father of us all. 17 As it is written, "I have made you a father of many nations."* This is in the presence of him whom he believed: God, who gives life to the dead, and calls the things that are not, as though they were. 18 Against hope, Abraham in hope believed, to the end that he might become a father of many nations, according to that which had been spoken, "So will your offspring be."
22 Therefore it also was "credited to him for righteousness."

Gospel: Matthew 1: 16, 18-21, 24

16 Jacob became the father of Joseph, the husband of Mary, from whom was born Jesus,§ who is called Christ.
18 Now the birth of Jesus Christ was like this: After his mother, Mary, was engaged to Joseph, before they came together, she was found pregnant by the Holy Spirit. 19 Joseph, her husband, being a righteous man, and not willing to make her a public example, intended to put her away secretly. 20 But when he thought about these things, behold,† an angel of the Lord appeared to him in a dream, saying, "Joseph, son of David, don't be afraid to take to yourself Mary as your wife, for that which is conceived in her is of the Holy Spirit. 21 She shall give birth to a son. You shall name him Jesus,‡ for it is he who shall save his people from their sins."
24 Joseph arose from his sleep, and did as the angel of the Lord commanded him, and took his wife to himself; 25 and didn't know her sexually until she had given birth to her firstborn son. He named him Jesus.

1. Invite the Holy Spirit into this reading, asking the Author of Scripture to speak to you through His Word
2. Read today's passage as many times as you need, take your time
3. Write down (below) what the Lord is saying to you today
4. Live with this Word in your heart through the day

_____

_____

Wednesday, March 20, 2024

First Reading: Daniel 3: 14-20, 91-92, 95

14 Nebuchadnezzar answered them, "Is it on purpose, Shadrach, Meshach, and Abednego, that you don't serve my god, nor worship the golden image which I have set up? 15 Now if you are ready whenever you hear the sound of the horn, flute, zither, lyre, harp, pipe, and all kinds of music to fall down and worship the image which I have made, good; but if you don't worship, you shall be cast the same hour into the middle of a burning fiery furnace. Who is that god who will deliver you out of my hands?"

16 Shadrach, Meshach, and Abednego answered the king, "Nebuchadnezzar, we have no need to answer you in this matter. 17 If it happens, our God whom we serve is able to deliver us from the burning fiery furnace; and he will deliver us out of your hand, O king. 18 But if not, let it be known to you, O king, that we will not serve your gods or worship the golden image which you have set up."

19 Then Nebuchadnezzar was full of fury, and the form of his appearance was changed against Shadrach, Meshach, and Abednego. He spoke, and commanded that they should heat the furnace seven times more than it was usually heated. 20 He commanded certain mighty men who were in his army to bind Shadrach, Meshach, and Abednego, and to cast them into the burning fiery furnace.

91 † Then Nebuchadnezzar the king was astonished and rose up in haste. He spoke and said to his counselors, "Didn't we cast three men bound into the middle of the fire?"

They answered the king, "True, O king."

92 He answered, "Look, I see four men loose, walking in the middle of the fire, and they are unharmed. The appearance of the fourth is like a son of the gods."

95 Nebuchadnezzar spoke and said, "Blessed be the God of Shadrach, Meshach, and Abednego, who has sent his angel and delivered his servants who trusted in him, and have changed the king's word, and have yielded their bodies, that they might not serve nor worship any god, except their own God.

Responsorial Psalm: Daniel 3: 52-56

52 "Blessed are you, O Lord, you God of our fathers, to be praised and exalted above all forever! 53 Blessed is your glorious and holy name, to be praised and exalted above all forever! 54 Blessed are you in the temple of your holy glory, to be praised and glorified above all forever! 55 Blessed are you who see the depths and sit upon the cherubim, to be praised and exalted above all forever. 56 Blessed are you on the throne of your kingdom, to be praised and extolled above all forever!

Gospel: John 8: 31-42

31 Jesus therefore said to those Jews who had believed him, "If you remain in my word, then you are truly my disciples. 32 You will know the truth, and the truth will make you free." *

33 They answered him, "We are Abraham's offspring, and have never been in bondage to anyone. How do you say, 'You will be made free'?"

34 Jesus answered them, "Most certainly I tell you, everyone who commits sin is the bondservant of sin. 35 A bondservant doesn't live in the house forever. A son remains forever.

36 If therefore the Son makes you free, you will be free indeed. 37 I know that you are Abraham's offspring, yet you seek to kill me, because my word finds no place in you. 38 I say the things which I have seen with my Father; and you also do the things which you have seen with your father."

39 They answered him, "Our father is Abraham."

Jesus said to them, "If you were Abraham's children, you would do the works of Abraham. 40 But now you seek to kill me, a man who has told you the truth which I heard from God. Abraham didn't do this. 41 You do the works of your father."

They said to him, "We were not born of sexual immorality. We have one Father, God."

42 Therefore Jesus said to them, "If God were your father, you would love me, for I came out and have come from God. For I haven't come of myself, but he sent me.

1. Invite the Holy Spirit into this reading, asking the Author of Scripture to speak to you through His Word
2. Read today's passage as many times as you need, take your time
3. Write down (below) what the Lord is saying to you today
4. Live with this Word in your heart through the day

Thursday, March 21, 2024

First Reading: Genesis 17: 3-9

3 Abram fell on his face. God talked with him, saying, 4 "As for me, behold, my covenant is with you. You will be the father of a multitude of nations. 5 Your name will no more be called Abram, but your name will be Abraham; for I have made you the father of a multitude of nations. 6 I will make you exceedingly fruitful, and I will make nations of you. Kings will come out of you. 7 I will establish my covenant between me and you and your offspring after you throughout their generations for an everlasting covenant, to be a God to you and to your offspring after you. 8 I will give to you, and to your offspring after you, the land where you are traveling, all the land of Canaan, for an everlasting possession. I will be their God."

9 God said to Abraham, "As for you, you shall keep my covenant, you and your offspring after you throughout their generations.

Responsorial Psalm: Psalms 105: 4-9

4 Seek Yahweh and his strength.
Seek his face forever more.

5 Remember his marvelous works that he has done:
his wonders, and the judgments of his mouth,
6 you offspring of Abraham, his servant,
you children of Jacob, his chosen ones.
7 He is Yahweh, our God.
His judgments are in all the earth.
8 He has remembered his covenant forever,
the word which he commanded to a thousand generations,
9 the covenant which he made with Abraham,
his oath to Isaac,

Gospel: John 8: 51-59

51 Most certainly, I tell you, if a person keeps my word, he will never see death."
52 Then the Jews said to him, "Now we know that you have a demon. Abraham died, as did the prophets; and you say, 'If a man keeps my word, he will never taste of death.' 53 Are you greater than our father Abraham, who died? The prophets died. Who do you make yourself out to be?"
54 Jesus answered, "If I glorify myself, my glory is nothing. It is my Father who glorifies me, of whom you say that he is our God. 55 You have not known him, but I know him. If I said, 'I don't know him,' I would be like you, a liar. But I know him and keep his word. 56 Your father Abraham rejoiced to see my day. He saw it and was glad."
57 The Jews therefore said to him, "You are not yet fifty years old! Have you seen Abraham?"
58 Jesus said to them, "Most certainly, I tell you, before Abraham came into existence, I AM.*"
59 Therefore they took up stones to throw at him, but Jesus hid himself and went out of the temple, having gone through the middle of them, and so passed by.

1. Invite the Holy Spirit into this reading, asking the Author of Scripture to speak to you through His Word
2. Read today's passage as many times as you need, take your time
3. Write down (below) what the Lord is saying to you today
4. Live with this Word in your heart through the day

_____   _____

_____

Friday, March 22, 2024

First Reading: Jeremiah 20: 10-13

10 For I have heard the defaming of many:

"Terror on every side!

Denounce, and we will denounce him!"

say all my familiar friends,

those who watch for my fall.

"Perhaps he will be persuaded,

and we will prevail against him,

and we will take our revenge on him."

11 But Yahweh is with me as an awesome mighty one.

Therefore my persecutors will stumble,

and they won't prevail.

They will be utterly disappointed

because they have not dealt wisely,

even with an everlasting dishonor which will never be forgotten.

12 But Yahweh of Armies, who tests the righteous,

who sees the heart and the mind,

let me see your vengeance on them,

for I have revealed my cause to you.

13 Sing to Yahweh!

Praise Yahweh,

for he has delivered the soul of the needy from the hand of evildoers.

Responsorial Psalm: Psalms 18: 2-7

2 Yahweh is my rock, my fortress, and my deliverer;

my God, my rock, in whom I take refuge;

my shield, and the horn of my salvation, my high tower.

3 I call on Yahweh, who is worthy to be praised;

and I am saved from my enemies.

4 The cords of death surrounded me.

The floods of ungodliness made me afraid.

5 The cords of Sheol† were around me.

The snares of death came on me.

6 In my distress I called on Yahweh,

and cried to my God.

He heard my voice out of his temple.

My cry before him came into his ears.

7 Then the earth shook and trembled.

The foundations also of the mountains quaked and were shaken,

because he was angry.

Gospel: John 10: 31-42

31 Therefore the Jews took up stones again to stone him. 32 Jesus answered them, "I have shown you many good works from my Father. For which of those works do you stone me?"

33 The Jews answered him, "We don't stone you for a good work, but for blasphemy, because you, being a man, make yourself God."

34 Jesus answered them, "Isn't it written in your law, 'I said, you are gods'?* 35 If he called them gods, to whom the word of God came (and the Scripture can't be broken), 36 do you say of him whom the Father sanctified and sent into the world, 'You blaspheme,' because I said, 'I am the Son of God'? 37 If I don't do the works of my Father, don't believe me. 38 But if I do them, though you don't believe me, believe the works, that you may know and believe that the Father is in me, and I in the Father."

39 They sought again to seize him, and he went out of their hand. 40 He went away again beyond the Jordan into the place where John was baptizing at first, and he stayed there. 41 Many came to him. They said, "John indeed did no sign, but everything that John said about this man is true." 42 Many believed in him there.

1. Invite the Holy Spirit into this reading, asking the Author of Scripture to speak to you through His Word
2. Read today's passage as many times as you need, take your time
3. Write down (below) what the Lord is saying to you today
4. Live with this Word in your heart through the day

_____

_____

Saturday, March 23, 2024
Saint Turibius of Mogrovejo, Bishop

First Reading: Ezekiel 37: 21-28

21 Say to them, 'The Lord Yahweh says: "Behold, I will take the children of Israel from among the nations where they have gone, and will gather them on every side, and bring them into their own land. 22 I will make them one nation in the land, on the mountains of Israel. One king will be king to them all. They will no longer be two nations. They won't be divided into two kingdoms any more at all. 23 They won't defile themselves any more with their idols, nor with their detestable things, nor with any of their transgressions; but I will save them out of all their dwelling places in which they have sinned, and will cleanse them. So they will be my people, and I will be their God.

24 " ' "My servant David will be king over them. They all will have one shepherd. They will also walk in my ordinances and observe my statutes, and do them. 25 They will dwell in the land that I have given to Jacob my servant, in which your fathers lived. They will dwell therein, they, and their children, and their children's children, forever. David my servant will be their

prince forever. 26 Moreover I will make a covenant of peace with them. It will be an everlasting covenant with them. I will place them, multiply them, and will set my sanctuary among them forever more. 27 My tent also will be with them. I will be their God, and they will be my people. 28 The nations will know that I am Yahweh who sanctifies Israel, when my sanctuary is among them forever more." ' "

Responsorial Psalm: Jeremiah 31: 10-13

10 "Hear Yahweh's word, you nations,
and declare it in the distant islands. Say,
'He who scattered Israel will gather him,
and keep him, as a shepherd does his flock.'
11 For Yahweh has ransomed Jacob,
and redeemed him from the hand of him who was stronger than he.
12 They will come and sing in the height of Zion,
and will flow to the goodness of Yahweh,
to the grain, to the new wine, to the oil,
and to the young of the flock and of the herd.
Their soul will be as a watered garden.
They will not sorrow any more at all.
13 Then the virgin will rejoice in the dance,
the young men and the old together;
for I will turn their mourning into joy,
and will comfort them, and make them rejoice from their sorrow.

Gospel: John 11: 45-56

45 Therefore many of the Jews who came to Mary and saw what Jesus did believed in him. 46 But some of them went away to the Pharisees and told them the things which Jesus had done. 47 The chief priests therefore and the Pharisees gathered a council, and said, "What are we doing? For this man does many signs. 48 If we leave him alone like this, everyone will believe in him, and the Romans will come and take away both our place and our nation."
49 But a certain one of them, Caiaphas, being high priest that year, said to them, "You know nothing at all, 50 nor do you consider that it is advantageous for us that one man should die for the people, and that the whole nation not perish." 51 Now he didn't say this of himself, but being high priest that year, he prophesied that Jesus would die for the nation, 52 and not for the nation only, but that he might also gather together into one the children of God who are scattered abroad. 53 So from that day forward they took counsel that they might put him to death. 54 Jesus therefore walked no more openly among the Jews, but departed from there into the country near the wilderness, to a city called Ephraim. He stayed there with his disciples.
55 Now the Passover of the Jews was at hand. Many went up from the country to Jerusalem before the Passover, to purify themselves. 56 Then they sought for Jesus and spoke with one

another as they stood in the temple, "What do you think—that he isn't coming to the feast at all?"

Sunday, March 24, 2024
PALM SUNDAY OF THE PASSION OF THE LORD

Procession: Mark 11: 1-10

1 When they came near to Jerusalem, to Bethsphage† and Bethany, at the Mount of Olives, he sent two of his disciples 2 and said to them, "Go your way into the village that is opposite you. Immediately as you enter into it, you will find a young donkey tied, on which no one has sat. Untie him and bring him. 3 If anyone asks you, 'Why are you doing this?' say, 'The Lord needs him;' and immediately he will send him back here."
4 They went away, and found a young donkey tied at the door outside in the open street, and they untied him. 5 Some of those who stood there asked them, "What are you doing, untying the young donkey?" 6 They said to them just as Jesus had said, and they let them go.
7 They brought the young donkey to Jesus and threw their garments on it, and Jesus sat on it. 8 Many spread their garments on the way, and others were cutting down branches from the trees and spreading them on the road. 9 Those who went in front and those who followed cried out, "Hosanna!‡ Blessed is he who comes in the name of the Lord!* 10 Blessed is the kingdom of our father David that is coming in the name of the Lord! Hosanna in the highest!"

First Reading: Isaiah 50: 4-7

4 The Lord Yahweh has given me the tongue of those who are taught,
that I may know how to sustain with words him who is weary.
He awakens morning by morning,
he awakens my ear to hear as those who are taught.
5 The Lord Yahweh has opened my ear.
I was not rebellious.
I have not turned back.
6 I gave my back to those who beat me,

and my cheeks to those who plucked off the hair.
I didn't hide my face from shame and spitting.
7 For the Lord Yahweh will help me.
Therefore I have not been confounded.
Therefore I have set my face like a flint,
and I know that I won't be disappointed.

Responsorial Psalm: Psalms 22: 8-9, 17-20, 23-24

8 "He trusts in Yahweh.
Let him deliver him.
Let him rescue him, since he delights in him."
9 But you brought me out of the womb.
You made me trust while at my mother's breasts.
17 I can count all of my bones.
They look and stare at me.
18 They divide my garments among them.
They cast lots for my clothing.
19 But don't be far off, Yahweh.
You are my help. Hurry to help me!
20 Deliver my soul from the sword,
my precious life from the power of the dog.
23 You who fear Yahweh, praise him!
All you descendants of Jacob, glorify him!
Stand in awe of him, all you descendants of Israel!
24 For he has not despised nor abhorred the affliction of the afflicted,
neither has he hidden his face from him;
but when he cried to him, he heard.

Second Reading: Philippians 2: 6-11

6 who, existing in the form of God, didn't consider equality with God a thing to be grasped, 7 but emptied himself, taking the form of a servant, being made in the likeness of men. 8 And being found in human form, he humbled himself, becoming obedient to the point of death, yes, the death of the cross. 9 Therefore God also highly exalted him, and gave to him the name which is above every name, 10 that at the name of Jesus every knee should bow, of those in heaven, those on earth, and those under the earth, 11 and that every tongue should confess that Jesus Christ is Lord, to the glory of God the Father.

Gospel: Mark 14: 1 – 15: 47

1 It was now two days before the Passover and the Feast of Unleavened Bread, and the chief priests and the scribes sought how they might seize him by deception and kill him. 2 For they said, "Not during the feast, because there might be a riot among the people."

3 While he was at Bethany, in the house of Simon the leper, as he sat at the table, a woman came having an alabaster jar of ointment of pure nard—very costly. She broke the jar and poured it over his head. 4 But there were some who were indignant among themselves, saying, "Why has this ointment been wasted? 5 For this might have been sold for more than three hundred denarii† and given to the poor." So they grumbled against her.

6 But Jesus said, "Leave her alone. Why do you trouble her? She has done a good work for me. 7 For you always have the poor with you, and whenever you want to, you can do them good; but you will not always have me. 8 She has done what she could. She has anointed my body beforehand for the burying. 9 Most certainly I tell you, wherever this Good News may be preached throughout the whole world, that which this woman has done will also be spoken of for a memorial of her."

10 Judas Iscariot, who was one of the twelve, went away to the chief priests, that he might deliver him to them. 11 They, when they heard it, were glad, and promised to give him money. He sought how he might conveniently deliver him.

12 On the first day of unleavened bread, when they sacrificed the Passover, his disciples asked him, "Where do you want us to go and prepare that you may eat the Passover?"

13 He sent two of his disciples and said to them, "Go into the city, and there a man carrying a pitcher of water will meet you. Follow him, 14 and wherever he enters in, tell the master of the house, 'The Teacher says, "Where is the guest room, where I may eat the Passover with my disciples?" ' 15 He will himself show you a large upper room furnished and ready. Get ready for us there."

16 His disciples went out, and came into the city, and found things as he had said to them, and they prepared the Passover.

17 When it was evening he came with the twelve. 18 As they sat and were eating, Jesus said, "Most certainly I tell you, one of you will betray me—he who eats with me."

19 They began to be sorrowful, and to ask him one by one, "Surely not I?" And another said, "Surely not I?"

20 He answered them, "It is one of the twelve, he who dips with me in the dish. 21 For the Son of Man goes as it is written about him, but woe to that man by whom the Son of Man is betrayed! It would be better for that man if he had not been born."

22 As they were eating, Jesus took bread, and when he had blessed it, he broke it and gave to them, and said, "Take, eat. This is my body."

23 He took the cup, and when he had given thanks, he gave to them. They all drank of it. 24 He said to them, "This is my blood of the new covenant, which is poured out for many. 25 Most certainly I tell you, I will no more drink of the fruit of the vine until that day when I drink it anew in God's Kingdom." 26 When they had sung a hymn, they went out to the Mount of Olives.

27 Jesus said to them, "All of you will be made to stumble because of me tonight, for it is written, 'I will strike the shepherd, and the sheep will be scattered.'* 28 However, after I am raised up, I will go before you into Galilee."

29 But Peter said to him, "Although all will be offended, yet I will not."

30 Jesus said to him, "Most certainly I tell you that you today, even this night, before the rooster crows twice, you will deny me three times."

31 But he spoke all the more, "If I must die with you, I will not deny you." They all said the same thing.

32 They came to a place which was named Gethsemane. He said to his disciples, "Sit here while I pray." 33 He took with him Peter, James, and John, and began to be greatly troubled and distressed. 34 He said to them, "My soul is exceedingly sorrowful, even to death. Stay here and watch."

35 He went forward a little, and fell on the ground, and prayed that if it were possible, the hour might pass away from him. 36 He said, "Abba,‡ Father, all things are possible to you. Please remove this cup from me. However, not what I desire, but what you desire."

37 He came and found them sleeping, and said to Peter, "Simon, are you sleeping? Couldn't you watch one hour? 38 Watch and pray, that you may not enter into temptation. The spirit indeed is willing, but the flesh is weak."

39 Again he went away and prayed, saying the same words. 40 Again he returned and found them sleeping, for their eyes were very heavy; and they didn't know what to answer him. 41 He came the third time and said to them, "Sleep on now, and take your rest. It is enough. The hour has come. Behold, the Son of Man is betrayed into the hands of sinners. 42 Arise! Let's get going. Behold, he who betrays me is at hand."

43 Immediately, while he was still speaking, Judas, one of the twelve, came—and with him a multitude with swords and clubs, from the chief priests, the scribes, and the elders. 44 Now he who betrayed him had given them a sign, saying, "Whomever I will kiss, that is he. Seize him, and lead him away safely." 45 When he had come, immediately he came to him and said, "Rabbi! Rabbi!" and kissed him. 46 They laid their hands on him and seized him. 47 But a certain one of those who stood by drew his sword and struck the servant of the high priest, and cut off his ear.

48 Jesus answered them, "Have you come out, as against a robber, with swords and clubs to seize me? 49 I was daily with you in the temple teaching, and you didn't arrest me. But this is so that the Scriptures might be fulfilled."

50 They all left him, and fled. 51 A certain young man followed him, having a linen cloth thrown around himself over his naked body. The young men grabbed him, 52 but he left the linen cloth and fled from them naked. 53 They led Jesus away to the high priest. All the chief priests, the elders, and the scribes came together with him.

54 Peter had followed him from a distance, until he came into the court of the high priest. He was sitting with the officers, and warming himself in the light of the fire. 55 Now the chief priests and the whole council sought witnesses against Jesus to put him to death, and found none. 56 For many gave false testimony against him, and their testimony didn't agree with each other. 57 Some stood up and gave false testimony against him, saying, 58 "We heard him say, 'I will destroy this temple that is made with hands, and in three days I will build another made without hands.' " 59 Even so, their testimony didn't agree.

60 The high priest stood up in the middle, and asked Jesus, "Have you no answer? What is it which these testify against you?" 61 But he stayed quiet, and answered nothing. Again the high priest asked him, "Are you the Christ, the Son of the Blessed?"

62 Jesus said, "I am. You will see the Son of Man sitting at the right hand of Power, and coming with the clouds of the sky."

63 The high priest tore his clothes and said, "What further need have we of witnesses? 64 You have heard the blasphemy! What do you think?" They all condemned him to be worthy of death. 65 Some began to spit on him, and to cover his face, and to beat him with fists, and to tell him, "Prophesy!" The officers struck him with the palms of their hands.

66 As Peter was in the courtyard below, one of the maids of the high priest came, 67 and seeing Peter warming himself, she looked at him and said, "You were also with the Nazarene, Jesus!"

68 But he denied it, saying, "I neither know nor understand what you are saying." He went out on the porch, and the rooster crowed.

69 The maid saw him and began again to tell those who stood by, "This is one of them." 70 But he again denied it. After a little while again those who stood by said to Peter, "You truly are one of them, for you are a Galilean, and your speech shows it." 71 But he began to curse and to swear, "I don't know this man of whom you speak!"

72 The rooster crowed the second time. Peter remembered the words that Jesus said to him, "Before the rooster crows twice, you will deny me three times." When he thought about that, he wept.

1 Immediately in the morning the chief priests, with the elders, scribes, and the whole council, held a consultation, bound Jesus, carried him away, and delivered him up to Pilate. 2 Pilate asked him, "Are you the King of the Jews?"

He answered, "So you say."

3 The chief priests accused him of many things. 4 Pilate again asked him, "Have you no answer? See how many things they testify against you!"

5 But Jesus made no further answer, so that Pilate marveled.

6 Now at the feast he used to release to them one prisoner, whomever they asked of him. 7 There was one called Barabbas, bound with his fellow insurgents, men who in the insurrection had committed murder. 8 The multitude, crying aloud, began to ask him to do as he always did for them. 9 Pilate answered them, saying, "Do you want me to release to you the King of the Jews?" 10 For he perceived that for envy the chief priests had delivered him up. 11 But the chief priests stirred up the multitude, that he should release Barabbas to them instead. 12 Pilate again asked them, "What then should I do to him whom you call the King of the Jews?"

13 They cried out again, "Crucify him!"

14 Pilate said to them, "Why, what evil has he done?"

But they cried out exceedingly, "Crucify him!"

15 Pilate, wishing to please the multitude, released Barabbas to them, and handed over Jesus, when he had flogged him, to be crucified.

16 The soldiers led him away within the court, which is the Praetorium; and they called together the whole cohort. 17 They clothed him with purple; and weaving a crown of thorns, they put it on him. 18 They began to salute him, "Hail, King of the Jews!" 19 They struck his head with a reed and spat on him, and bowing their knees, did homage to him. 20 When they

had mocked him, they took the purple cloak off him, and put his own garments on him. They led him out to crucify him.

21 They compelled one passing by, coming from the country, Simon of Cyrene, the father of Alexander and Rufus, to go with them that he might bear his cross. 22 They brought him to the place called Golgotha, which is, being interpreted, "The place of a skull." 23 They offered him wine mixed with myrrh to drink, but he didn't take it.

24 Crucifying him, they parted his garments among them, casting lots on them, what each should take. 25 It was the third hour† when they crucified him. 26 The superscription of his accusation was written over him: "THE KING OF THE JEWS." 27 With him they crucified two robbers, one on his right hand, and one on his left. 28 The Scripture was fulfilled which says, "He was counted with transgressors."‡

29 Those who passed by blasphemed him, wagging their heads and saying, "Ha! You who destroy the temple and build it in three days, 30 save yourself, and come down from the cross!" 31 Likewise, also the chief priests mocking among themselves with the scribes said, "He saved others. He can't save himself. 32 Let the Christ, the King of Israel, now come down from the cross, that we may see and believe him."§ Those who were crucified with him also insulted him.

33 When the sixth hour† had come, there was darkness over the whole land until the ninth hour.‡ 34 At the ninth hour Jesus cried with a loud voice, saying, "Eloi, Eloi, lama sabachthani?" which is, being interpreted, "My God, my God, why have you forsaken me?" *

35 Some of those who stood by, when they heard it, said, "Behold, he is calling Elijah."

36 One ran, and filling a sponge full of vinegar, put it on a reed and gave it to him to drink, saying, "Let him be. Let's see whether Elijah comes to take him down."

37 Jesus cried out with a loud voice, and gave up the spirit. 38 The veil of the temple was torn in two from the top to the bottom. 39 When the centurion, who stood by opposite him, saw that he cried out like this and breathed his last, he said, "Truly this man was the Son of God!"

40 There were also women watching from afar, among whom were both Mary Magdalene and Mary the mother of James the less and of Joses, and Salome; 41 who, when he was in Galilee, followed him and served him; and many other women who came up with him to Jerusalem.

42 When evening had now come, because it was the Preparation Day, that is, the day before the Sabbath, 43 Joseph of Arimathaea, a prominent council member who also himself was looking for God's Kingdom, came. He boldly went in to Pilate, and asked for Jesus' body. 44 Pilate was surprised to hear that he was already dead; and summoning the centurion, he asked him whether he had been dead long. 45 When he found out from the centurion, he granted the body to Joseph. 46 He bought a linen cloth, and taking him down, wound him in the linen cloth and laid him in a tomb which had been cut out of a rock. He rolled a stone against the door of the tomb. 47 Mary Magdalene and Mary the mother of Joses, saw where he was laid.

1. Invite the Holy Spirit into this reading, asking the Author of Scripture to speak to you through His Word
2. Read today's passage as many times as you need, take your time
3. Write down (below) what the Lord is saying to you today
4. Live with this Word in your heart through the day

Monday, March 25, 2024
Monday of Holy Week

First Reading: Isaiah 42: 1-7

1 "Behold, my servant, whom I uphold,
my chosen, in whom my soul delights:
I have put my Spirit on him.
He will bring justice to the nations.
2 He will not shout,
nor raise his voice,
nor cause it to be heard in the street.
3 He won't break a bruised reed.
He won't quench a dimly burning wick.
He will faithfully bring justice.
4 He will not fail nor be discouraged,
until he has set justice in the earth,
and the islands wait for his law."
5 God Yahweh,
he who created the heavens and stretched them out,
he who spread out the earth and that which comes out of it,
he who gives breath to its people and spirit to those who walk in it, says:
6 "I, Yahweh, have called you in righteousness.
I will hold your hand.
I will keep you,
and make you a covenant for the people,
as a light for the nations,
7 to open the blind eyes,
to bring the prisoners out of the dungeon,
and those who sit in darkness out of the prison.

Responsorial Psalm: Psalms 27: 1-3, 13-14

1 Yahweh is my light and my salvation.
Whom shall I fear?
Yahweh is the strength of my life.

Of whom shall I be afraid?
2 When evildoers came at me to eat up my flesh,
even my adversaries and my foes, they stumbled and fell.
3 Though an army should encamp against me,
my heart shall not fear.
Though war should rise against me,
even then I will be confident.
13 I am still confident of this:
I will see the goodness of Yahweh in the land of the living.
14 Wait for Yahweh.
Be strong, and let your heart take courage.
Yes, wait for Yahweh.

Gospel: John 12: 1-11

1 Then, six days before the Passover, Jesus came to Bethany, where Lazarus was, who had been dead, whom he raised from the dead. 2 So they made him a supper there. Martha served, but Lazarus was one of those who sat at the table with him. 3 Therefore Mary took a pound† of ointment of pure nard, very precious, and anointed Jesus' feet and wiped his feet with her hair. The house was filled with the fragrance of the ointment.
4 Then Judas Iscariot, Simon's son, one of his disciples, who would betray him, said, 5 "Why wasn't this ointment sold for three hundred denarii‡ and given to the poor?" 6 Now he said this, not because he cared for the poor, but because he was a thief, and having the money box, used to steal what was put into it.
7 But Jesus said, "Leave her alone. She has kept this for the day of my burial. 8 For you always have the poor with you, but you don't always have me."
9 A large crowd therefore of the Jews learned that he was there; and they came, not for Jesus' sake only, but that they might see Lazarus also, whom he had raised from the dead. 10 But the chief priests conspired to put Lazarus to death also, 11 because on account of him many of the Jews went away and believed in Jesus.

1. Invite the Holy Spirit into this reading, asking the Author of Scripture to speak to you through His Word
2. Read today's passage as many times as you need, take your time
3. Write down (below) what the Lord is saying to you today
4. Live with this Word in your heart through the day

_____

_____

Tuesday, March 26, 2024

Tuesday of Holy Week

First Reading: Isaiah 49: 1-6

1 Listen, islands, to me.
Listen, you peoples, from afar:
Yahweh has called me from the womb;
from the inside of my mother, he has mentioned my name.
2 He has made my mouth like a sharp sword.
He has hidden me in the shadow of his hand.
He has made me a polished shaft.
He has kept me close in his quiver.
3 He said to me, "You are my servant,
Israel, in whom I will be glorified."
4 But I said, "I have labored in vain.
I have spent my strength in vain for nothing;
yet surely the justice due to me is with Yahweh,
and my reward with my God."
5 Now Yahweh, he who formed me from the womb to be his servant,
says to bring Jacob again to him,
and to gather Israel to him,
for I am honorable in Yahweh's eyes,
and my God has become my strength.
6 Indeed, he says, "It is too light a thing that you should be my servant to raise up the tribes of Jacob,
and to restore the preserved of Israel.
I will also give you as a light to the nations,
that you may be my salvation to the end of the earth."

Responsorial Psalm: Psalms 71: 1-6, 15 and 17

1 In you, Yahweh, I take refuge.
Never let me be disappointed.
2 Deliver me in your righteousness, and rescue me.
Turn your ear to me, and save me.
3 Be to me a rock of refuge to which I may always go.
Give the command to save me,
for you are my rock and my fortress.
4 Rescue me, my God, from the hand of the wicked,
from the hand of the unrighteous and cruel man.
5 For you are my hope, Lord Yahweh,
my confidence from my youth.
6 I have relied on you from the womb.

You are he who took me out of my mother's womb.
I will always praise you.
15 My mouth will tell about your righteousness,
and of your salvation all day,
though I don't know its full measure.
17 God, you have taught me from my youth.
Until now, I have declared your wondrous works.

Gospel: John 13: 21-33, 36-38

21 When Jesus had said this, he was troubled in spirit, and testified, "Most certainly I tell you that one of you will betray me."
22 The disciples looked at one another, perplexed about whom he spoke. 23 One of his disciples, whom Jesus loved, was at the table, leaning against Jesus' breast. 24 Simon Peter therefore beckoned to him, and said to him, "Tell us who it is of whom he speaks."
25 He, leaning back, as he was, on Jesus' breast, asked him, "Lord, who is it?"
26 Jesus therefore answered, "It is he to whom I will give this piece of bread when I have dipped it." So when he had dipped the piece of bread, he gave it to Judas, the son of Simon Iscariot. 27 After the piece of bread, then Satan entered into him.
Then Jesus said to him, "What you do, do quickly."
28 Now nobody at the table knew why he said this to him. 29 For some thought, because Judas had the money box, that Jesus said to him, "Buy what things we need for the feast," or that he should give something to the poor. 30 Therefore having received that morsel, he went out immediately. It was night.
31 When he had gone out, Jesus said, "Now the Son of Man has been glorified, and God has been glorified in him. 32 If God has been glorified in him, God will also glorify him in himself, and he will glorify him immediately. 33 Little children, I will be with you a little while longer. You will seek me, and as I said to the Jews, 'Where I am going, you can't come,' so now I tell you.
36 Simon Peter said to him, "Lord, where are you going?"
Jesus answered, "Where I am going, you can't follow now, but you will follow afterwards."
37 Peter said to him, "Lord, why can't I follow you now? I will lay down my life for you."
38 Jesus answered him, "Will you lay down your life for me? Most certainly I tell you, the rooster won't crow until you have denied me three times.

1. Invite the Holy Spirit into this reading, asking the Author of Scripture to speak to you through His Word
2. Read today's passage as many times as you need, take your time
3. Write down (below) what the Lord is saying to you today
4. Live with this Word in your heart through the day

_____

_____

Wednesday, March 27, 2024
Wednesday of Holy Week

First Reading: Isaiah 50: 4-9a

4 The Lord Yahweh has given me the tongue of those who are taught,
that I may know how to sustain with words him who is weary.
He awakens morning by morning,
he awakens my ear to hear as those who are taught.
5 The Lord Yahweh has opened my ear.
I was not rebellious.
I have not turned back.
6 I gave my back to those who beat me,
and my cheeks to those who plucked off the hair.
I didn't hide my face from shame and spitting.
7 For the Lord Yahweh will help me.
Therefore I have not been confounded.
Therefore I have set my face like a flint,
and I know that I won't be disappointed.
8 He who justifies me is near.
Who will bring charges against me?
Let us stand up together.
Who is my adversary?
Let him come near to me.
9 Behold, the Lord Yahweh will help me!
Who is he who will condemn me?

Responsorial Psalm: Psalms 69: 8-10, 21-22, 31 and 33-34

8 I have become a stranger to my brothers,
an alien to my mother's children.
9 For the zeal of your house consumes me.
The reproaches of those who reproach you have fallen on me.
10 When I wept and I fasted,
that was to my reproach.
21 They also gave me poison for my food.
In my thirst, they gave me vinegar to drink.
22 Let their table before them become a snare.
May it become a retribution and a trap.
31 It will please Yahweh better than an ox,
or a bull that has horns and hoofs.
33 For Yahweh hears the needy,

and doesn't despise his captive people.
34 Let heaven and earth praise him;
the seas, and everything that moves therein!

Gospel: Matthew 26: 14-25

14 Then one of the twelve, who was called Judas Iscariot, went to the chief priests 15 and said, "What are you willing to give me if I deliver him to you?" So they weighed out for him thirty pieces of silver. 16 From that time he sought opportunity to betray him.

17 Now on the first day of unleavened bread, the disciples came to Jesus, saying to him, "Where do you want us to prepare for you to eat the Passover?"

18 He said, "Go into the city to a certain person, and tell him, 'The Teacher says, "My time is at hand. I will keep the Passover at your house with my disciples." ' "

19 The disciples did as Jesus commanded them, and they prepared the Passover.

20 Now when evening had come, he was reclining at the table with the twelve disciples. 21 As they were eating, he said, "Most certainly I tell you that one of you will betray me."

22 They were exceedingly sorrowful, and each began to ask him, "It isn't me, is it, Lord?"

23 He answered, "He who dipped his hand with me in the dish will betray me. 24 The Son of Man goes even as it is written of him, but woe to that man through whom the Son of Man is betrayed! It would be better for that man if he had not been born."

25 Judas, who betrayed him, answered, "It isn't me, is it, Rabbi?"
He said to him, "You said it."

1. Invite the Holy Spirit into this reading, asking the Author of Scripture to speak to you through His Word
2. Read today's passage as many times as you need, take your time
3. Write down (below) what the Lord is saying to you today
4. Live with this Word in your heart through the day

_____

_____

Thursday, March 28, 2024
Thursday of Holy Week (Holy Thursday)

First Reading: Exodus 12: 1-8, 11-14

1 Yahweh spoke to Moses and Aaron in the land of Egypt, saying, 2 "This month shall be to you the beginning of months. It shall be the first month of the year to you. 3 Speak to all the congregation of Israel, saying, 'On the tenth day of this month, they shall take to them every

man a lamb, according to their fathers' houses, a lamb for a household; 4 and if the household is too little for a lamb, then he and his neighbor next to his house shall take one according to the number of the souls. You shall make your count for the lamb according to what everyone can eat. 5 Your lamb shall be without defect, a male a year old. You shall take it from the sheep or from the goats. 6 You shall keep it until the fourteenth day of the same month; and the whole assembly of the congregation of Israel shall kill it at evening. 7 They shall take some of the blood, and put it on the two door posts and on the lintel, on the houses in which they shall eat it. 8 They shall eat the meat in that night, roasted with fire, with unleavened bread. They shall eat it with bitter herbs.

11 This is how you shall eat it: with your belt on your waist, your sandals on your feet, and your staff in your hand; and you shall eat it in haste: it is Yahweh's Passover. 12 For I will go through the land of Egypt in that night, and will strike all the firstborn in the land of Egypt, both man and animal. I will execute judgments against all the gods of Egypt. I am Yahweh. 13 The blood shall be to you for a token on the houses where you are. When I see the blood, I will pass over you, and no plague will be on you to destroy you when I strike the land of Egypt. 14 This day shall be a memorial for you. You shall keep it as a feast to Yahweh. You shall keep it as a feast throughout your generations by an ordinance forever.

Responsorial Psalm: Psalms 116: 12-13, 15-18

12 What will I give to Yahweh for all his benefits toward me?
13 I will take the cup of salvation, and call on Yahweh's name.
15 Precious in Yahweh's sight is the death of his saints.
16 Yahweh, truly I am your servant.
I am your servant, the son of your servant girl.
You have freed me from my chains.
17 I will offer to you the sacrifice of thanksgiving,
and will call on Yahweh's name.
18 I will pay my vows to Yahweh,
yes, in the presence of all his people,

Second Reading: First Corinthians 11: 23-26

23 For I received from the Lord that which also I delivered to you, that the Lord Jesus on the night in which he was betrayed took bread. 24 When he had given thanks, he broke it and said, "Take, eat. This is my body, which is broken for you. Do this in memory of me." 25 In the same way he also took the cup after supper, saying, "This cup is the new covenant in my blood. Do this, as often as you drink, in memory of me." 26 For as often as you eat this bread and drink this cup, you proclaim the Lord's death until he comes.

Gospel: John 13: 1-15

1 Now before the feast of the Passover, Jesus, knowing that his time had come that he would depart from this world to the Father, having loved his own who were in the world, he loved them to the end. 2 During supper, the devil having already put into the heart of Judas Iscariot, Simon's son, to betray him, 3 Jesus, knowing that the Father had given all things into his hands, and that he came from God and was going to God, 4 arose from supper, and laid aside his outer garments. He took a towel and wrapped a towel around his waist. 5 Then he poured water into the basin, and began to wash the disciples' feet and to wipe them with the towel that was wrapped around him. 6 Then he came to Simon Peter. He said to him, "Lord, do you wash my feet?"

7 Jesus answered him, "You don't know what I am doing now, but you will understand later."
8 Peter said to him, "You will never wash my feet!"
Jesus answered him, "If I don't wash you, you have no part with me."
9 Simon Peter said to him, "Lord, not my feet only, but also my hands and my head!"
10 Jesus said to him, "Someone who has bathed only needs to have his feet washed, but is completely clean. You are clean, but not all of you." 11 For he knew him who would betray him; therefore he said, "You are not all clean." 12 So when he had washed their feet, put his outer garment back on, and sat down again, he said to them, "Do you know what I have done to you? 13 You call me, 'Teacher' and 'Lord.' You say so correctly, for so I am. 14 If I then, the Lord and the Teacher, have washed your feet, you also ought to wash one another's feet. 15 For I have given you an example, that you should also do as I have done to you.

1. Invite the Holy Spirit into this reading, asking the Author of Scripture to speak to you through His Word
2. Read today's passage as many times as you need, take your time
3. Write down (below) what the Lord is saying to you today
4. Live with this Word in your heart through the day

_____

_____

Friday, March 29, 2024
Friday of the Passion of the Lord (Good Friday)

First Reading: Isaiah 52: 13 – 53: 12

13 Behold, my servant will deal wisely.
He will be exalted and lifted up,
and will be very high.
14 Just as many were astonished at you—
his appearance was marred more than any man, and his form more than the sons of men—

15 so he will cleanse† many nations.

Kings will shut their mouths at him;

for they will see that which had not been told them,

and they will understand that which they had not heard.

1 Who has believed our message?

To whom has Yahweh's arm been revealed?

2 For he grew up before him as a tender plant,

and as a root out of dry ground.

He has no good looks or majesty.

When we see him, there is no beauty that we should desire him.

3 He was despised

and rejected by men,

a man of suffering

and acquainted with disease.

He was despised as one from whom men hide their face;

and we didn't respect him.

4 Surely he has borne our sickness

and carried our suffering;

yet we considered him plagued,

struck by God, and afflicted.

5 But he was pierced for our transgressions.

He was crushed for our iniquities.

The punishment that brought our peace was on him;

and by his wounds we are healed.

6 All we like sheep have gone astray.

Everyone has turned to his own way;

and Yahweh has laid on him the iniquity of us all.

7 He was oppressed,

yet when he was afflicted he didn't open his mouth.

As a lamb that is led to the slaughter,

and as a sheep that before its shearers is silent,

so he didn't open his mouth.

8 He was taken away by oppression and judgment.

As for his generation,

who considered that he was cut off out of the land of the living

and stricken for the disobedience of my people?

9 They made his grave with the wicked,

and with a rich man in his death,

although he had done no violence,

nor was any deceit in his mouth.

10 Yet it pleased Yahweh to bruise him.

He has caused him to suffer.

When you make his soul an offering for sin,

he will see his offspring.
He will prolong his days
and Yahweh's pleasure will prosper in his hand.
11 After the suffering of his soul,
he will see the light† and be satisfied.
My righteous servant will justify many by the knowledge of himself;
and he will bear their iniquities.
12 Therefore I will give him a portion with the great.
He will divide the plunder with the strong,
because he poured out his soul to death
and was counted with the transgressors;
yet he bore the sins of many
and made intercession for the transgressors.

Responsorial Psalm: Psalms 31: 2, 6, 12-13, 15-16, 17, 24

2 Bow down your ear to me.
Deliver me speedily.
Be to me a strong rock,
a house of defense to save me.
6 I hate those who regard lying vanities,
but I trust in Yahweh.
12 I am forgotten from their hearts like a dead man.
I am like broken pottery.
13 For I have heard the slander of many, terror on every side,
while they conspire together against me,
they plot to take away my life.
15 My times are in your hand.
Deliver me from the hand of my enemies, and from those who persecute me.
16 Make your face to shine on your servant.
Save me in your loving kindness.
17 Let me not be disappointed, Yahweh, for I have called on you.
Let the wicked be disappointed.
Let them be silent in Sheol
24 Be strong, and let your heart take courage,
all you who hope in Yahweh.

Second Reading: Hebrews 4: 14-16; 5: 7-9

14 Having then a great high priest who has passed through the heavens, Jesus, the Son of God, let's hold tightly to our confession. 15 For we don't have a high priest who can't be touched with the feeling of our infirmities, but one who has been in all points tempted like we are, yet

without sin. 16 Let's therefore draw near with boldness to the throne of grace, that we may receive mercy and may find grace for help in time of need.

7 He, in the days of his flesh, having offered up prayers and petitions with strong crying and tears to him who was able to save him from death, and having been heard for his godly fear, 8 though he was a Son, yet learned obedience by the things which he suffered. 9 Having been made perfect, he became to all of those who obey him the author of eternal salvation

Gospel: John 18: 1 – 19: 42

1 When Jesus had spoken these words, he went out with his disciples over the brook Kidron, where there was a garden, into which he and his disciples entered. 2 Now Judas, who betrayed him, also knew the place, for Jesus often met there with his disciples. 3 Judas then, having taken a detachment of soldiers and officers from the chief priests and the Pharisees, came there with lanterns, torches, and weapons. 4 Jesus therefore, knowing all the things that were happening to him, went out and said to them, "Who are you looking for?"

5 They answered him, "Jesus of Nazareth."

Jesus said to them, "I am he."

Judas also, who betrayed him, was standing with them. 6 When therefore he said to them, "I am he," they went backward and fell to the ground.

7 Again therefore he asked them, "Who are you looking for?"

They said, "Jesus of Nazareth."

8 Jesus answered, "I told you that I am he. If therefore you seek me, let these go their way," 9 that the word might be fulfilled which he spoke, "Of those whom you have given me, I have lost none."*

10 Simon Peter therefore, having a sword, drew it, struck the high priest's servant, and cut off his right ear. The servant's name was Malchus. 11 Jesus therefore said to Peter, "Put the sword into its sheath. The cup which the Father has given me, shall I not surely drink it?"

12 So the detachment, the commanding officer, and the officers of the Jews seized Jesus and bound him, 13 and led him to Annas first, for he was father-in-law to Caiaphas, who was high priest that year. 14 Now it was Caiaphas who advised the Jews that it was expedient that one man should perish for the people.

15 Simon Peter followed Jesus, as did another disciple. Now that disciple was known to the high priest, and entered in with Jesus into the court of the high priest; 16 but Peter was standing at the door outside. So the other disciple, who was known to the high priest, went out and spoke to her who kept the door, and brought in Peter. 17 Then the maid who kept the door said to Peter, "Are you also one of this man's disciples?"

He said, "I am not."

18 Now the servants and the officers were standing there, having made a fire of coals, for it was cold. They were warming themselves. Peter was with them, standing and warming himself.

19 The high priest therefore asked Jesus about his disciples and about his teaching.

20 Jesus answered him, "I spoke openly to the world. I always taught in synagogues and in the temple, where the Jews always meet. I said nothing in secret. 21 Why do you ask me? Ask those who have heard me what I said to them. Behold, they know the things which I said."

22 When he had said this, one of the officers standing by slapped Jesus with his hand, saying, "Do you answer the high priest like that?"

23 Jesus answered him, "If I have spoken evil, testify of the evil; but if well, why do you beat me?"

24 Annas sent him bound to Caiaphas, the high priest.

25 Now Simon Peter was standing and warming himself. They said therefore to him, "You aren't also one of his disciples, are you?"

He denied it and said, "I am not."

26 One of the servants of the high priest, being a relative of him whose ear Peter had cut off, said, "Didn't I see you in the garden with him?"

27 Peter therefore denied it again, and immediately the rooster crowed.

28 They led Jesus therefore from Caiaphas into the Praetorium. It was early, and they themselves didn't enter into the Praetorium, that they might not be defiled, but might eat the Passover. 29 Pilate therefore went out to them and said, "What accusation do you bring against this man?"

30 They answered him, "If this man weren't an evildoer, we wouldn't have delivered him up to you."

31 Pilate therefore said to them, "Take him yourselves, and judge him according to your law." Therefore the Jews said to him, "It is illegal for us to put anyone to death," 32 that the word of Jesus might be fulfilled, which he spoke, signifying by what kind of death he should die.

33 Pilate therefore entered again into the Praetorium, called Jesus, and said to him, "Are you the King of the Jews?"

34 Jesus answered him, "Do you say this by yourself, or did others tell you about me?"

35 Pilate answered, "I'm not a Jew, am I? Your own nation and the chief priests delivered you to me. What have you done?"

36 Jesus answered, "My Kingdom is not of this world. If my Kingdom were of this world, then my servants would fight, that I wouldn't be delivered to the Jews. But now my Kingdom is not from here."

37 Pilate therefore said to him, "Are you a king then?"

Jesus answered, "You say that I am a king. For this reason I have been born, and for this reason I have come into the world, that I should testify to the truth. Everyone who is of the truth listens to my voice."

38 Pilate said to him, "What is truth?"

When he had said this, he went out again to the Jews, and said to them, "I find no basis for a charge against him. 39 But you have a custom that I should release someone to you at the Passover. Therefore, do you want me to release to you the King of the Jews?"

40 Then they all shouted again, saying, "Not this man, but Barabbas!" Now Barabbas was a robber.

1 So Pilate then took Jesus and flogged him. 2 The soldiers twisted thorns into a crown and put it on his head, and dressed him in a purple garment. 3 They kept saying, "Hail, King of the Jews!" and they kept slapping him.

4 Then Pilate went out again, and said to them, "Behold, I bring him out to you, that you may know that I find no basis for a charge against him."

5 Jesus therefore came out, wearing the crown of thorns and the purple garment. Pilate said to them, "Behold, the man!"

6 When therefore the chief priests and the officers saw him, they shouted, saying, "Crucify! Crucify!"

Pilate said to them, "Take him yourselves and crucify him, for I find no basis for a charge against him."

7 The Jews answered him, "We have a law, and by our law he ought to die, because he made himself the Son of God."

8 When therefore Pilate heard this saying, he was more afraid. 9 He entered into the Praetorium again, and said to Jesus, "Where are you from?" But Jesus gave him no answer. 10 Pilate therefore said to him, "Aren't you speaking to me? Don't you know that I have power to release you and have power to crucify you?"

11 Jesus answered, "You would have no power at all against me, unless it were given to you from above. Therefore he who delivered me to you has greater sin."

12 At this, Pilate was seeking to release him, but the Jews cried out, saying, "If you release this man, you aren't Caesar's friend! Everyone who makes himself a king speaks against Caesar!"

13 When Pilate therefore heard these words, he brought Jesus out and sat down on the judgment seat at a place called "The Pavement", but in Hebrew, "Gabbatha." 14 Now it was the Preparation Day of the Passover, at about the sixth hour.† He said to the Jews, "Behold, your King!"

15 They cried out, "Away with him! Away with him! Crucify him!"

Pilate said to them, "Shall I crucify your King?"

The chief priests answered, "We have no king but Caesar!"

16 So then he delivered him to them to be crucified. So they took Jesus and led him away. 17 He went out, bearing his cross, to the place called "The Place of a Skull", which is called in Hebrew, "Golgotha", 18 where they crucified him, and with him two others, on either side one, and Jesus in the middle. 19 Pilate wrote a title also, and put it on the cross. There was written, "JESUS OF NAZARETH, THE KING OF THE JEWS." 20 Therefore many of the Jews read this title, for the place where Jesus was crucified was near the city; and it was written in Hebrew, in Latin, and in Greek. 21 The chief priests of the Jews therefore said to Pilate, "Don't write, 'The King of the Jews,' but, 'he said, "I am King of the Jews." ' "22 Pilate answered, "What I have written, I have written."

23 Then the soldiers, when they had crucified Jesus, took his garments and made four parts, to every soldier a part; and also the tunic. Now the tunic was without seam, woven from the top throughout. 24 Then they said to one another, "Let's not tear it, but cast lots for it to decide whose it will be," that the Scripture might be fulfilled, which says,

"They parted my garments among them.
They cast lots for my clothing."*

Therefore the soldiers did these things.

25 But standing by Jesus' cross were his mother, his mother's sister, Mary the wife of Clopas, and Mary Magdalene. 26 Therefore when Jesus saw his mother, and the disciple whom he loved standing there, he said to his mother, "Woman, behold, your son!" 27 Then he said to the disciple, "Behold, your mother!" From that hour, the disciple took her to his own home. 28 After this, Jesus, seeing‡ that all things were now finished, that the Scripture might be fulfilled, said, "I am thirsty!" 29 Now a vessel full of vinegar was set there; so they put a sponge full of the vinegar on hyssop, and held it at his mouth. 30 When Jesus therefore had received the vinegar, he said, "It is finished!" Then he bowed his head and gave up his spirit.

31 Therefore the Jews, because it was the Preparation Day, so that the bodies wouldn't remain on the cross on the Sabbath (for that Sabbath was a special one), asked of Pilate that their legs might be broken and that they might be taken away. 32 Therefore the soldiers came and broke the legs of the first and of the other who was crucified with him; 33 but when they came to Jesus and saw that he was already dead, they didn't break his legs. 34 However, one of the soldiers pierced his side with a spear, and immediately blood and water came out. 35 He who has seen has testified, and his testimony is true. He knows that he tells the truth, that you may believe. 36 For these things happened that the Scripture might be fulfilled, "A bone of him will not be broken."* 37 Again another Scripture says, "They will look on him whom they pierced."* 38 After these things, Joseph of Arimathaea, being a disciple of Jesus, but secretly for fear of the Jews, asked of Pilate that he might take away Jesus' body. Pilate gave him permission. He came therefore and took away his body. 39 Nicodemus, who at first came to Jesus by night, also came bringing a mixture of myrrh and aloes, about a hundred Roman pounds.§ 40 So they took Jesus' body, and bound it in linen cloths with the spices, as the custom of the Jews is to bury. 41 Now in the place where he was crucified there was a garden. In the garden was a new tomb in which no man had ever yet been laid. 42 Then, because of the Jews' Preparation Day (for the tomb was near at hand), they laid Jesus there.

1. Invite the Holy Spirit into this reading, asking the Author of Scripture to speak to you through His Word
2. Read today's passage as many times as you need, take your time
3. Write down (below) what the Lord is saying to you today
4. Live with this Word in your heart through the day

_____

_____

Saturday, March 30, 2024
Holy Saturday

First Reading: Genesis 1: 1, 26-31a

1 In the beginning, God† created the heavens and the earth. 2 The earth was formless and empty. Darkness was on the surface of the deep and God's Spirit was hovering over the surface of the waters.

26 God said, "Let's make man in our image, after our likeness. Let them have dominion over the fish of the sea, and over the birds of the sky, and over the livestock, and over all the earth, and over every creeping thing that creeps on the earth." 27 God created man in his own image. In God's image he created him; male and female he created them. 28 God blessed them. God said to them, "Be fruitful, multiply, fill the earth, and subdue it. Have dominion over the fish of the sea, over the birds of the sky, and over every living thing that moves on the earth." 29 God said, "Behold,‡ I have given you every herb yielding seed, which is on the surface of all the earth, and every tree, which bears fruit yielding seed. It will be your food. 30 To every animal of the earth, and to every bird of the sky, and to everything that creeps on the earth, in which there is life, I have given every green herb for food;" and it was so.

31 God saw everything that he had made, and, behold, it was very good.

Responsorial Psalm: Psalms 104: 1-2, 5-6, 10, 12-14, 24, 35

1 Bless Yahweh, my soul.
Yahweh, my God, you are very great.
You are clothed with honor and majesty.
2 He covers himself with light as with a garment.
He stretches out the heavens like a curtain.
5 He laid the foundations of the earth,
that it should not be moved forever.
6 You covered it with the deep as with a cloak.
The waters stood above the mountains.
10 He sends springs into the valleys.
They run among the mountains.
12 The birds of the sky nest by them.
They sing among the branches.
13 He waters the mountains from his rooms.
The earth is filled with the fruit of your works.
14 He causes the grass to grow for the livestock,
and plants for man to cultivate,
that he may produce food out of the earth:
24 Yahweh, how many are your works!
In wisdom, you have made them all.
The earth is full of your riches.
35 Let sinners be consumed out of the earth.
Let the wicked be no more.
Bless Yahweh, my soul.
Praise Yah!

Second Reading: Genesis 22: 1-18

1 After these things, God tested Abraham, and said to him, "Abraham!"
He said, "Here I am."
2 He said, "Now take your son, your only son, Isaac, whom you love, and go into the land of Moriah. Offer him there as a burnt offering on one of the mountains which I will tell you of."
3 Abraham rose early in the morning, and saddled his donkey; and took two of his young men with him, and Isaac his son. He split the wood for the burnt offering, and rose up, and went to the place of which God had told him. 4 On the third day Abraham lifted up his eyes, and saw the place far off. 5 Abraham said to his young men, "Stay here with the donkey. The boy and I will go over there. We will worship, and come back to you." 6 Abraham took the wood of the burnt offering and laid it on Isaac his son. He took in his hand the fire and the knife. They both went together. 7 Isaac spoke to Abraham his father, and said, "My father?"
He said, "Here I am, my son."
He said, "Here is the fire and the wood, but where is the lamb for a burnt offering?"
8 Abraham said, "God will provide himself the lamb for a burnt offering, my son." So they both went together. 9 They came to the place which God had told him of. Abraham built the altar there, and laid the wood in order, bound Isaac his son, and laid him on the altar, on the wood. 10 Abraham stretched out his hand, and took the knife to kill his son.
11 Yahweh's angel called to him out of the sky, and said, "Abraham, Abraham!"
He said, "Here I am."
12 He said, "Don't lay your hand on the boy or do anything to him. For now I know that you fear God, since you have not withheld your son, your only son, from me."
13 Abraham lifted up his eyes, and looked, and saw that behind him was a ram caught in the thicket by his horns. Abraham went and took the ram, and offered him up for a burnt offering instead of his son. 14 Abraham called the name of that place "Yahweh Will Provide".† As it is said to this day, "On Yahweh's mountain, it will be provided."
15 Yahweh's angel called to Abraham a second time out of the sky, 16 and said, " 'I have sworn by myself,' says Yahweh, 'because you have done this thing, and have not withheld your son, your only son, 17 that I will bless you greatly, and I will multiply your offspring greatly like the stars of the heavens, and like the sand which is on the seashore. Your offspring will possess the gate of his enemies. 18 All the nations of the earth will be blessed by your offspring, because you have obeyed my voice.' "

Responsorial Psalm: Psalms 16: 5, 8-11

5 Yahweh assigned my portion and my cup.
You made my lot secure.
8 I have set Yahweh always before me.
Because he is at my right hand, I shall not be moved.
9 Therefore my heart is glad, and my tongue rejoices.
My body shall also dwell in safety.

10 For you will not leave my soul in Sheol,†
neither will you allow your holy one to see corruption.
11 You will show me the path of life.
In your presence is fullness of joy.
In your right hand there are pleasures forever more.

Third Reading: Exodus 14: 15 – 15: 1

15 Yahweh said to Moses, "Why do you cry to me? Speak to the children of Israel, that they go forward. 16 Lift up your rod, and stretch out your hand over the sea and divide it. Then the children of Israel shall go into the middle of the sea on dry ground. 17 Behold, I myself will harden the hearts of the Egyptians, and they will go in after them. I will get myself honor over Pharaoh, and over all his armies, over his chariots, and over his horsemen. 18 The Egyptians shall know that I am Yahweh when I have gotten myself honor over Pharaoh, over his chariots, and over his horsemen." 19 The angel of God, who went before the camp of Israel, moved and went behind them; and the pillar of cloud moved from before them, and stood behind them. 20 It came between the camp of Egypt and the camp of Israel. There was the cloud and the darkness, yet it gave light by night. One didn't come near the other all night.
21 Moses stretched out his hand over the sea, and Yahweh caused the sea to go back by a strong east wind all night, and made the sea dry land, and the waters were divided. 22 The children of Israel went into the middle of the sea on the dry ground; and the waters were a wall to them on their right hand and on their left. 23 The Egyptians pursued, and went in after them into the middle of the sea: all of Pharaoh's horses, his chariots, and his horsemen. 24 In the morning watch, Yahweh looked out on the Egyptian army through the pillar of fire and of cloud, and confused the Egyptian army. 25 He took off their chariot wheels, and they drove them heavily; so that the Egyptians said, "Let's flee from the face of Israel, for Yahweh fights for them against the Egyptians!"
26 Yahweh said to Moses, "Stretch out your hand over the sea, that the waters may come again on the Egyptians, on their chariots, and on their horsemen." 27 Moses stretched out his hand over the sea, and the sea returned to its strength when the morning appeared; and the Egyptians fled against it. Yahweh overthrew the Egyptians in the middle of the sea. 28 The waters returned, and covered the chariots and the horsemen, even all Pharaoh's army that went in after them into the sea. There remained not so much as one of them. 29 But the children of Israel walked on dry land in the middle of the sea, and the waters were a wall to them on their right hand and on their left. 30 Thus Yahweh saved Israel that day out of the hand of the Egyptians; and Israel saw the Egyptians dead on the seashore. 31 Israel saw the great work which Yahweh did to the Egyptians, and the people feared Yahweh; and they believed in Yahweh and in his servant Moses.
1 Then Moses and the children of Israel sang this song to Yahweh, and said,
"I will sing to Yahweh, for he has triumphed gloriously.
He has thrown the horse and his rider into the sea.
Responsorial Psalm: Exodus 15: 1-6, 17-18

1 Then Moses and the children of Israel sang this song to Yahweh, and said,
"I will sing to Yahweh, for he has triumphed gloriously.
He has thrown the horse and his rider into the sea.
2 Yah is my strength and song.
He has become my salvation.
This is my God, and I will praise him;
my father's God, and I will exalt him.
3 Yahweh is a man of war.
Yahweh is his name.
4 He has cast Pharaoh's chariots and his army into the sea.
His chosen captains are sunk in the Red Sea.
5 The deeps cover them.
They went down into the depths like a stone.
6 Your right hand, Yahweh, is glorious in power.
Your right hand, Yahweh, dashes the enemy in pieces.
17 You will bring them in, and plant them in the mountain of your inheritance,
the place, Yahweh, which you have made for yourself to dwell in:
the sanctuary, Lord, which your hands have established.
18 Yahweh will reign forever and ever."

Fourth Reading: Isaiah 54: 5-14

5 For your Maker is your husband; Yahweh of Armies is his name.
The Holy One of Israel is your Redeemer.
He will be called the God of the whole earth.
6 For Yahweh has called you as a wife forsaken and grieved in spirit,
even a wife of youth, when she is cast off," says your God.
 7 "For a small moment I have forsaken you,
but I will gather you with great mercies.
8 In overflowing wrath I hid my face from you for a moment,
but with everlasting loving kindness I will have mercy on you," says Yahweh your Redeemer.
 9 "For this is like the waters of Noah to me;
for as I have sworn that the waters of Noah will no more go over the earth,
so I have sworn that I will not be angry with you, nor rebuke you.
10 For the mountains may depart,
and the hills be removed,
but my loving kindness will not depart from you,
and my covenant of peace will not be removed,"
says Yahweh who has mercy on you.
 11 "You afflicted, tossed with storms, and not comforted,
behold, I will set your stones in beautiful colors,
and lay your foundations with sapphires.
12 I will make your pinnacles of rubies,

your gates of sparkling jewels,
and all your walls of precious stones.
13 All your children will be taught by Yahweh,
and your children's peace will be great.
14 You will be established in righteousness.
You will be far from oppression,
for you will not be afraid,
and far from terror,
for it shall not come near you.

Responsorial Psalm: Psalms 30: 2, 4-6, 11-12

2 Yahweh my God, I cried to you,
and you have healed me.
4 Sing praise to Yahweh, you saints of his.
Give thanks to his holy name.
5 For his anger is but for a moment.
His favor is for a lifetime.
Weeping may stay for the night,
but joy comes in the morning.
6 As for me, I said in my prosperity,
"I shall never be moved."
11 You have turned my mourning into dancing for me.
You have removed my sackcloth, and clothed me with gladness,
12 to the end that my heart may sing praise to you, and not be silent.
Yahweh my God, I will give thanks to you forever!

Fifth Reading: Isaiah 55: 1-11

1 "Hey! Come, everyone who thirsts, to the waters!
Come, he who has no money, buy, and eat!
Yes, come, buy wine and milk without money and without price.
2 Why do you spend money for that which is not bread,
and your labor for that which doesn't satisfy?
Listen diligently to me, and eat that which is good,
and let your soul delight itself in richness.
3 Turn your ear, and come to me.
Hear, and your soul will live.
I will make an everlasting covenant with you, even the sure mercies of David.
4 Behold, I have given him for a witness to the peoples,
a leader and commander to the peoples.
5 Behold, you shall call a nation that you don't know;
and a nation that didn't know you shall run to you,

because of Yahweh your God,
and for the Holy One of Israel;
for he has glorified you."
 6 Seek Yahweh while he may be found.
Call on him while he is near.
7 Let the wicked forsake his way,
and the unrighteous man his thoughts.
Let him return to Yahweh, and he will have mercy on him,
to our God, for he will freely pardon.
 8 "For my thoughts are not your thoughts,
and your ways are not my ways," says Yahweh.
9 "For as the heavens are higher than the earth,
so are my ways higher than your ways,
and my thoughts than your thoughts.
10 For as the rain comes down and the snow from the sky,
and doesn't return there, but waters the earth,
and makes it grow and bud,
and gives seed to the sower and bread to the eater;
11 so is my word that goes out of my mouth:
it will not return to me void,
but it will accomplish that which I please,
and it will prosper in the thing I sent it to do.

Responsorial Psalm: Isaiah 12: 2-6

2 Behold, God is my salvation. I will trust, and will not be afraid; for Yah, Yahweh, is my strength and song; and he has become my salvation." 3 Therefore with joy you will draw water out of the wells of salvation. 4 In that day you will say, "Give thanks to Yahweh! Call on his name! Declare his doings among the peoples! Proclaim that his name is exalted! 5 Sing to Yahweh, for he has done excellent things! Let this be known in all the earth! 6 Cry aloud and shout, you inhabitant of Zion, for the Holy One of Israel is great among you!"

Sixth Reading: Baruch 3: 9-15, 32 – 4: 4

9 Hear, O Israel, the commandments of life! Give ear to understand wisdom! 10 How is it, O Israel, that you are in your enemies' land, that you have become old in a strange country, that you are defiled with the dead, 11 that you are counted with those who are in Hades? 12 You have forsaken the fountain of wisdom. 13 If you had walked in the way of God, you would have dwelled in peace forever. 14 Learn where there is wisdom, where there is strength, and where there is understanding, that you may also know where there is length of days and life, where there is the light of the eyes and peace. 15 Who has found out her place? Who has come into her treasuries?

32 But he that knows all things knows her, he found her out with his understanding. He who prepared the earth for all time has filled it with four-footed beasts. 33 It is he who sends forth the light, and it goes. He called it, and it obeyed him with fear. 34 The stars shone in their watches, and were glad. When he called them, they said, "Here we are." They shone with gladness to him who made them. 35 This is our God. No other can be compared to him. 36 He has found out all the way of knowledge, and has given it to Jacob his servant and to Israel who is loved by him. 37 Afterward she appeared upon earth, and lived with men.

1 This is the book of God's commandments and the law that endures forever. All those who hold it fast will live, but those who leave it will die. 2 Turn, O Jacob, and take hold of it. Walk toward the shining of its light. 3 Don't give your glory to another, nor the things that are to your advantage to a foreign nation. 4 O Israel, we are happy; for the things that are pleasing to God are made known to us.

Responsorial Psalm: Psalms 19: 8-11

8 Yahweh's precepts are right, rejoicing the heart.
Yahweh's commandment is pure, enlightening the eyes.
9 The fear of Yahweh is clean, enduring forever.
Yahweh's ordinances are true, and righteous altogether.
10 They are more to be desired than gold, yes, than much fine gold,
sweeter also than honey and the extract of the honeycomb.
11 Moreover your servant is warned by them.
In keeping them there is great reward.

Seventh Reading: Ezekiel 36: 16-17a, 18-28

16 Moreover Yahweh's word came to me, saying, 17 "Son of man, when the house of Israel lived in their own land, they defiled it by their ways and by their deeds. 18 Therefore I poured out my wrath on them for the blood which they had poured out on the land, and because they had defiled it with their idols. 19 I scattered them among the nations, and they were dispersed through the countries. I judged them according to their way and according to their deeds. 20 When they came to the nations where they went, they profaned my holy name, in that men said of them, 'These are Yahweh's people, and have left his land.' 21 But I had respect for my holy name, which the house of Israel had profaned among the nations where they went.

22 "Therefore tell the house of Israel, 'The Lord Yahweh says: "I don't do this for your sake, house of Israel, but for my holy name, which you have profaned among the nations where you went. 23 I will sanctify my great name, which has been profaned among the nations, which you have profaned among them. Then the nations will know that I am Yahweh," says the Lord Yahweh, "when I am proven holy in you before their eyes.

24 " ' "For I will take you from among the nations and gather you out of all the countries, and will bring you into your own land. 25 I will sprinkle clean water on you, and you will be clean. I will cleanse you from all your filthiness and from all your idols. 26 I will also give you a new heart, and I will put a new spirit within you. I will take away the stony heart out of your flesh,

and I will give you a heart of flesh. 27 I will put my Spirit within you, and cause you to walk in my statutes. You will keep my ordinances and do them. 28 You will dwell in the land that I gave to your fathers. You will be my people, and I will be your God.

Responsorial Psalm: Psalms 42: 3, 5; 43: 3, 4

3 My tears have been my food day and night,
while they continually ask me, "Where is your God?"
5 Why are you in despair, my soul?
Why are you disturbed within me?
Hope in God!
For I shall still praise him for the saving help of his presence.
3 Oh, send out your light and your truth.
Let them lead me.
Let them bring me to your holy hill,
to your tents.
4 Then I will go to the altar of God,
to God, my exceeding joy.
I will praise you on the harp, God, my God.

Epistle Reading: Romans 6: 3-11

3 Or don't you know that all of us who were baptized into Christ Jesus were baptized into his death? 4 We were buried therefore with him through baptism into death, that just as Christ was raised from the dead through the glory of the Father, so we also might walk in newness of life.
5 For if we have become united with him in the likeness of his death, we will also be part of his resurrection; 6 knowing this, that our old man was crucified with him, that the body of sin might be done away with, so that we would no longer be in bondage to sin. 7 For he who has died has been freed from sin. 8 But if we died with Christ, we believe that we will also live with him, 9 knowing that Christ, being raised from the dead, dies no more. Death no longer has dominion over him! 10 For the death that he died, he died to sin one time; but the life that he lives, he lives to God. 11 Thus consider yourselves also to be dead to sin, but alive to God in Christ Jesus our Lord.

Responsorial Psalm: Psalms 118: 1-2, 16-17, 22-23

1 Give thanks to Yahweh, for he is good,
for his loving kindness endures forever.
2 Let Israel now say
that his loving kindness endures forever.
16 The right hand of Yahweh is exalted!
The right hand of Yahweh does valiantly!"

17 I will not die, but live,
and declare Yah's works.
22 The stone which the builders rejected
has become the cornerstone.†
23 This is Yahweh's doing.
It is marvelous in our eyes.

Gospel: Mark 16: 1-7

1 When the Sabbath was past, Mary Magdalene, and Mary the mother of James, and Salome bought spices, that they might come and anoint him. 2 Very early on the first day of the week, they came to the tomb when the sun had risen. 3 They were saying among themselves, "Who will roll away the stone from the door of the tomb for us?" 4 for it was very big. Looking up, they saw that the stone was rolled back.
5 Entering into the tomb, they saw a young man sitting on the right side, dressed in a white robe; and they were amazed. 6 He said to them, "Don't be amazed. You seek Jesus, the Nazarene, who has been crucified. He has risen! He is not here. See the place where they laid him! 7 But go, tell his disciples and Peter, 'He goes before you into Galilee. There you will see him, as he said to you.' "

1. Invite the Holy Spirit into this reading, asking the Author of Scripture to speak to you through His Word
2. Read today's passage as many times as you need, take your time
3. Write down (below) what the Lord is saying to you today
4. Live with this Word in your heart through the day

_____

_____

Sunday, March 31, 2024
EASTER SUNDAY OF THE RESURRECTION OF THE LORD

First Reading: Acts 10: 34a, 37-43

34 Peter opened his mouth and said, 37 you yourselves know what happened, which was proclaimed throughout all Judea, beginning from Galilee, after the baptism which John preached; 38 how God anointed Jesus of Nazareth with the Holy Spirit and with power, who went about doing good and healing all who were oppressed by the devil, for God was with him. 39 We are witnesses of everything he did both in the country of the Jews and in Jerusalem; whom they also‡ killed, hanging him on a tree. 40 God raised him up the third day and gave him to be revealed, 41 not to all the people, but to witnesses who were chosen before by God,

to us, who ate and drank with him after he rose from the dead. 42 He commanded us to preach to the people and to testify that this is he who is appointed by God as the Judge of the living and the dead. 43 All the prophets testify about him, that through his name everyone who believes in him will receive remission of sins."

Responsorial Psalm: Psalms 118: 1-2, 16-17, 22-23

1 Give thanks to Yahweh, for he is good,
for his loving kindness endures forever.
2 Let Israel now say
that his loving kindness endures forever.
16 The right hand of Yahweh is exalted!
The right hand of Yahweh does valiantly!"
17 I will not die, but live,
and declare Yah's works.
22 The stone which the builders rejected
has become the cornerstone.†
23 This is Yahweh's doing.
It is marvelous in our eyes.

Second Reading: Colossians 3: 1-4

1 If then you were raised together with Christ, seek the things that are above, where Christ is, seated on the right hand of God. 2 Set your mind on the things that are above, not on the things that are on the earth. 3 For you died, and your life is hidden with Christ in God. 4 When Christ, our life, is revealed, then you will also be revealed with him in glory.

Gospel: John 20: 1-9

1 Now on the first day of the week, Mary Magdalene went early, while it was still dark, to the tomb, and saw that the stone had been taken away from the tomb. 2 Therefore she ran and came to Simon Peter and to the other disciple whom Jesus loved, and said to them, "They have taken away the Lord out of the tomb, and we don't know where they have laid him!"
3 Therefore Peter and the other disciple went out, and they went toward the tomb. 4 They both ran together. The other disciple outran Peter and came to the tomb first. 5 Stooping and looking in, he saw the linen cloths lying there; yet he didn't enter in. 6 Then Simon Peter came, following him, and entered into the tomb. He saw the linen cloths lying, 7 and the cloth that had been on his head, not lying with the linen cloths, but rolled up in a place by itself. 8 So then the other disciple who came first to the tomb also entered in, and he saw and believed. 9 For as yet they didn't know the Scripture, that he must rise from the dead.

1. Invite the Holy Spirit into this reading, asking the Author of Scripture to speak to you through His Word
2. Read today's passage as many times as you need, take your time
3. Write down (below) what the Lord is saying to you today
4. Live with this Word in your heart through the day

Monday, April 1, 2024
Monday within the Octave of Easter

First Reading: Acts 2: 14, 22-33

14 But Peter, standing up with the eleven, lifted up his voice and spoke out to them, "You men of Judea and all you who dwell at Jerusalem, let this be known to you, and listen to my words. 22 "Men of Israel, hear these words! Jesus of Nazareth, a man approved by God to you by mighty works and wonders and signs which God did by him among you, even as you yourselves know, 23 him, being delivered up by the determined counsel and foreknowledge of God, you have taken by the hand of lawless men, crucified and killed; 24 whom God raised up, having freed him from the agony of death, because it was not possible that he should be held by it. 25 For David says concerning him,
'I saw the Lord always before my face,
for he is on my right hand, that I should not be moved.
26 Therefore my heart was glad, and my tongue rejoiced.
Moreover my flesh also will dwell in hope,
27 because you will not leave my soul in Hades,‡
neither will you allow your Holy One to see decay.
28 You made known to me the ways of life.
You will make me full of gladness with your presence.'*
29 "Brothers, I may tell you freely of the patriarch David, that he both died and was buried, and his tomb is with us to this day. 30 Therefore, being a prophet, and knowing that God had sworn with an oath to him that of the fruit of his body, according to the flesh, he would raise up the Christ§ to sit on his throne, 31 he foreseeing this, spoke about the resurrection of the Christ, that his soul wasn't left in Hades,† and his flesh didn't see decay. 32 This Jesus God raised up, to which we all are witnesses. 33 Being therefore exalted by the right hand of God, and having received from the Father the promise of the Holy Spirit, he has poured out this which you now see and hear.

Responsorial Psalm: Psalms 16: 1-2a and 5- 11

1 Preserve me, God, for I take refuge in you.
2 My soul, you have said to Yahweh, "You are my Lord.
5 Yahweh assigned my portion and my cup.
You made my lot secure.

6 The lines have fallen to me in pleasant places.
Yes, I have a good inheritance.
7 I will bless Yahweh, who has given me counsel.
Yes, my heart instructs me in the night seasons.
8 I have set Yahweh always before me.
Because he is at my right hand, I shall not be moved.
9 Therefore my heart is glad, and my tongue rejoices.
My body shall also dwell in safety.
10 For you will not leave my soul in Sheol,†
neither will you allow your holy one to see corruption.
11 You will show me the path of life.
In your presence is fullness of joy.
In your right hand there are pleasures forever more.

Gospel: Matthew 28: 8-15

8 They departed quickly from the tomb with fear and great joy, and ran to bring his disciples word. 9 As they went to tell his disciples, behold, Jesus met them, saying, "Rejoice!"
They came and took hold of his feet, and worshiped him.
10 Then Jesus said to them, "Don't be afraid. Go tell my brothers † that they should go into Galilee, and there they will see me."
11 Now while they were going, behold, some of the guards came into the city and told the chief priests all the things that had happened. 12 When they were assembled with the elders and had taken counsel, they gave a large amount of silver to the soldiers, 13 saying, "Say that his disciples came by night and stole him away while we slept. 14 If this comes to the governor's ears, we will persuade him and make you free of worry." 15 So they took the money and did as they were told. This saying was spread abroad among the Jews, and continues until today.

1. Invite the Holy Spirit into this reading, asking the Author of Scripture to speak to you through His Word
2. Read today's passage as many times as you need, take your time
3. Write down (below) what the Lord is saying to you today
4. Live with this Word in your heart through the day

First Reading: Acts 2: 36-41

36 "Let all the house of Israel therefore know certainly that God has made him both Lord and Christ, this Jesus whom you crucified."

37 Now when they heard this, they were cut to the heart, and said to Peter and the rest of the apostles, "Brothers, what shall we do?"

38 Peter said to them, "Repent and be baptized, every one of you, in the name of Jesus Christ for the forgiveness of sins, and you will receive the gift of the Holy Spirit. 39 For the promise is to you and to your children, and to all who are far off, even as many as the Lord our God will call to himself." 40 With many other words he testified and exhorted them, saying, "Save yourselves from this crooked generation!"

41 Then those who gladly received his word were baptized. There were added that day about three thousand souls.

Responsorial Psalm: Psalms 33: 4-5, 18-20 and 22

4 For Yahweh's word is right.
All his work is done in faithfulness.
5 He loves righteousness and justice.
The earth is full of the loving kindness of Yahweh.
18 Behold, Yahweh's eye is on those who fear him,
on those who hope in his loving kindness,
19 to deliver their soul from death,
to keep them alive in famine.
20 Our soul has waited for Yahweh.
He is our help and our shield.
22 Let your loving kindness be on us, Yahweh,
since we have hoped in you.

Gospel: John 20: 11-18

11 But Mary was standing outside at the tomb weeping. So as she wept, she stooped and looked into the tomb, 12 and she saw two angels in white sitting, one at the head and one at the feet, where the body of Jesus had lain. 13 They asked her, "Woman, why are you weeping?"
She said to them, "Because they have taken away my Lord, and I don't know where they have laid him." 14 When she had said this, she turned around and saw Jesus standing, and didn't know that it was Jesus.
15 Jesus said to her, "Woman, why are you weeping? Who are you looking for?"

She, supposing him to be the gardener, said to him, "Sir, if you have carried him away, tell me where you have laid him, and I will take him away."

16 Jesus said to her, "Mary."

She turned and said to him, "Rabboni!"† which is to say, "Teacher!"‡

17 Jesus said to her, "Don't hold me, for I haven't yet ascended to my Father; but go to my brothers and tell them, 'I am ascending to my Father and your Father, to my God and your God.'"

18 Mary Magdalene came and told the disciples that she had seen the Lord, and that he had said these things to her.

1. Invite the Holy Spirit into this reading, asking the Author of Scripture to speak to you through His Word
2. Read today's passage as many times as you need, take your time
3. Write down (below) what the Lord is saying to you today
4. Live with this Word in your heart through the day

Wednesday, April 3, 2024
Wednesday within the Octave of Easter

First Reading: Acts 3: 1-10

1 Peter and John were going up into the temple at the hour of prayer, the ninth hour.† 2 A certain man who was lame from his mother's womb was being carried, whom they laid daily at the door of the temple which is called Beautiful, to ask gifts for the needy of those who entered into the temple. 3 Seeing Peter and John about to go into the temple, he asked to receive gifts for the needy. 4 Peter, fastening his eyes on him, with John, said, "Look at us." 5 He listened to them, expecting to receive something from them. 6 But Peter said, "I have no silver or gold, but what I have, that I give you. In the name of Jesus Christ of Nazareth, get up and walk!" 7 He took him by the right hand and raised him up. Immediately his feet and his ankle bones received strength. 8 Leaping up, he stood and began to walk. He entered with them into the temple, walking, leaping, and praising God. 9 All the people saw him walking and praising God. 10 They recognized him, that it was he who used to sit begging for gifts for the needy at the Beautiful Gate of the temple. They were filled with wonder and amazement at what had happened to him.

Responsorial Psalm: Psalms 105: 1-4, 6-9

1 Give thanks to Yahweh! Call on his name!
Make his doings known among the peoples.
2 Sing to him, sing praises to him!
Tell of all his marvelous works.
3 Glory in his holy name.
Let the heart of those who seek Yahweh rejoice.
4 Seek Yahweh and his strength.
Seek his face forever more.
6 you offspring of Abraham, his servant,
you children of Jacob, his chosen ones.
7 He is Yahweh, our God.
His judgments are in all the earth.
8 He has remembered his covenant forever,
the word which he commanded to a thousand generations,
9 the covenant which he made with Abraham,
his oath to Isaac,

Gospel: Luke 24: 13-35

13 Behold, two of them were going that very day to a village named Emmaus, which was sixty stadia† from Jerusalem. 14 They talked with each other about all of these things which had happened. 15 While they talked and questioned together, Jesus himself came near, and went with them. 16 But their eyes were kept from recognizing him. 17 He said to them, "What are you talking about as you walk, and are sad?"
18 One of them, named Cleopas, answered him, "Are you the only stranger in Jerusalem who doesn't know the things which have happened there in these days?"
19 He said to them, "What things?"
They said to him, "The things concerning Jesus the Nazarene, who was a prophet mighty in deed and word before God and all the people; 20 and how the chief priests and our rulers delivered him up to be condemned to death, and crucified him. 21 But we were hoping that it was he who would redeem Israel. Yes, and besides all this, it is now the third day since these things happened. 22 Also, certain women of our company amazed us, having arrived early at the tomb; 23 and when they didn't find his body, they came saying that they had also seen a vision of angels, who said that he was alive. 24 Some of us went to the tomb and found it just like the women had said, but they didn't see him."
25 He said to them, "Foolish people, and slow of heart to believe in all that the prophets have spoken! 26 Didn't the Christ have to suffer these things and to enter into his glory?" 27 Beginning from Moses and from all the prophets, he explained to them in all the Scriptures the things concerning himself.
28 They came near to the village where they were going, and he acted like he would go further. 29 They urged him, saying, "Stay with us, for it is almost evening, and the day is almost over." He went in to stay with them. 30 When he had sat down at the table with them, he took the bread and gave thanks. Breaking it, he gave it to them. 31 Their eyes were opened and they

recognized him; then he vanished out of their sight. 32 They said to one another, "Weren't our hearts burning within us while he spoke to us along the way, and while he opened the Scriptures to us?" 33 They rose up that very hour, returned to Jerusalem, and found the eleven gathered together, and those who were with them, 34 saying, "The Lord is risen indeed, and has appeared to Simon!" 35 They related the things that happened along the way, and how he was recognized by them in the breaking of the bread.

1. Invite the Holy Spirit into this reading, asking the Author of Scripture to speak to you through His Word
2. Read today's passage as many times as you need, take your time
3. Write down (below) what the Lord is saying to you today
4. Live with this Word in your heart through the day

_____

_____

Thursday, April 4, 2024
Thursday within the Octave of Easter

First Reading: Acts 3: 11-26

11 As the lame man who was healed held on to Peter and John, all the people ran together to them in the porch that is called Solomon's, greatly wondering.
12 When Peter saw it, he responded to the people, "You men of Israel, why do you marvel at this man? Why do you fasten your eyes on us, as though by our own power or godliness we had made him walk? 13 The God of Abraham, Isaac, and Jacob, the God of our fathers, has glorified his Servant Jesus, whom you delivered up and denied in the presence of Pilate, when he had determined to release him. 14 But you denied the Holy and Righteous One and asked for a murderer to be granted to you, 15 and killed the Prince of life, whom God raised from the dead, to which we are witnesses. 16 By faith in his name, his name has made this man strong, whom you see and know. Yes, the faith which is through him has given him this perfect soundness in the presence of you all.
17 "Now, brothers,‡ I know that you did this in ignorance, as did also your rulers. 18 But the things which God announced by the mouth of all his prophets, that Christ should suffer, he thus fulfilled.
19 "Repent therefore, and turn again, that your sins may be blotted out, so that there may come times of refreshing from the presence of the Lord, 20 and that he may send Christ Jesus, who was ordained for you before, 21 whom heaven must receive until the times of restoration of all things, which God spoke long ago by the mouth of his holy prophets. 22 For Moses indeed said to the fathers, 'The Lord God will raise up a prophet for you from among your brothers,

like me. You shall listen to him in all things whatever he says to you. 23 It will be that every soul that will not listen to that prophet will be utterly destroyed from among the people.'* 24 Yes, and all the prophets from Samuel and those who followed after, as many as have spoken, also told of these days. 25 You are the children of the prophets, and of the covenant which God made with our fathers, saying to Abraham, 'All the families of the earth will be blessed through your offspring.'§* 26 God, having raised up his servant Jesus, sent him to you first to bless you, in turning away every one of you from your wickedness."

Responsorial Psalm: Psalms 8: 2 and 5-9

2 From the lips of babes and infants you have established strength,
because of your adversaries, that you might silence the enemy and the avenger.
5 For you have made him a little lower than the angels,†
and crowned him with glory and honor.
6 You make him ruler over the works of your hands.
You have put all things under his feet:
7 All sheep and cattle,
yes, and the animals of the field,
8 the birds of the sky, the fish of the sea,
and whatever passes through the paths of the seas.
9 Yahweh, our Lord,
how majestic is your name in all the earth!

Gospel: Luke 24: 35-48

35 They related the things that happened along the way, and how he was recognized by them in the breaking of the bread.
36 As they said these things, Jesus himself stood among them, and said to them, "Peace be to you."
37 But they were terrified and filled with fear, and supposed that they had seen a spirit.
38 He said to them, "Why are you troubled? Why do doubts arise in your hearts? 39 See my hands and my feet, that it is truly me. Touch me and see, for a spirit doesn't have flesh and bones, as you see that I have." 40 When he had said this, he showed them his hands and his feet. 41 While they still didn't believe for joy, and wondered, he said to them, "Do you have anything here to eat?"
42 They gave him a piece of a broiled fish and some honeycomb. 43 He took them, and ate in front of them. 44 He said to them, "This is what I told you while I was still with you, that all things which are written in the law of Moses, the prophets, and the psalms concerning me must be fulfilled."
45 Then he opened their minds, that they might understand the Scriptures. 46 He said to them, "Thus it is written, and thus it was necessary for the Christ to suffer and to rise from the dead the third day, 47 and that repentance and remission of sins should be preached in his name to all the nations, beginning at Jerusalem. 48 You are witnesses of these things.

1. Invite the Holy Spirit into this reading, asking the Author of Scripture to speak to you through His Word
2. Read today's passage as many times as you need, take your time
3. Write down (below) what the Lord is saying to you today
4. Live with this Word in your heart through the day

Friday, April 5, 2024
Friday within the Octave of Easter

First Reading: Acts 4: 1-12

1 As they spoke to the people, the priests and the captain of the temple and the Sadducees came to them, 2 being upset because they taught the people and proclaimed in Jesus the resurrection from the dead. 3 They laid hands on them, and put them in custody until the next day, for it was now evening. 4 But many of those who heard the word believed, and the number of the men came to be about five thousand.

5 In the morning, their rulers, elders, and scribes were gathered together in Jerusalem. 6 Annas the high priest was there, with Caiaphas, John, Alexander, and as many as were relatives of the high priest. 7 When they had stood Peter and John in the middle of them, they inquired, "By what power, or in what name, have you done this?"

8 Then Peter, filled with the Holy Spirit, said to them, "You rulers of the people and elders of Israel, 9 if we are examined today concerning a good deed done to a crippled man, by what means this man has been healed, 10 may it be known to you all, and to all the people of Israel, that in the name of Jesus Christ of Nazareth, whom you crucified, whom God raised from the dead, this man stands here before you whole in him. 11 He is 'the stone which was regarded as worthless by you, the builders, which has become the head of the corner.'* 12 There is salvation in no one else, for there is no other name under heaven that is given among men, by which we must be saved!"

Responsorial Psalm: Psalms 118: 1-2 and 4, 22-27a

1 Give thanks to Yahweh, for he is good,
for his loving kindness endures forever.
2 Let Israel now say
that his loving kindness endures forever.
4 Now let those who fear Yahweh say
that his loving kindness endures forever.

22 The stone which the builders rejected
has become the cornerstone.†
23 This is Yahweh's doing.
It is marvelous in our eyes.
24 This is the day that Yahweh has made.
We will rejoice and be glad in it!
25 Save us now, we beg you, Yahweh!
Yahweh, we beg you, send prosperity now.
26 Blessed is he who comes in Yahweh's name!
We have blessed you out of Yahweh's house.
27 Yahweh is God, and he has given us light.

Gospel: John 21: 1-14

1 After these things, Jesus revealed himself again to the disciples at the sea of Tiberias. He revealed himself this way. 2 Simon Peter, Thomas called Didymus,† Nathanael of Cana in Galilee, and the sons of Zebedee, and two others of his disciples were together. 3 Simon Peter said to them, "I'm going fishing."
They told him, "We are also coming with you." They immediately went out and entered into the boat. That night, they caught nothing. 4 But when day had already come, Jesus stood on the beach; yet the disciples didn't know that it was Jesus. 5 Jesus therefore said to them, "Children, have you anything to eat?"
They answered him, "No."
6 He said to them, "Cast the net on the right side of the boat, and you will find some."
They cast it therefore, and now they weren't able to draw it in for the multitude of fish. 7 That disciple therefore whom Jesus loved said to Peter, "It's the Lord!"
So when Simon Peter heard that it was the Lord, he wrapped his coat around himself (for he was naked), and threw himself into the sea. 8 But the other disciples came in the little boat (for they were not far from the land, but about two hundred cubits‡ away), dragging the net full of fish. 9 So when they got out on the land, they saw a fire of coals there, with fish and bread laid on it. 10 Jesus said to them, "Bring some of the fish which you have just caught."
11 Simon Peter went up, and drew the net to land, full of one hundred fifty-three great fish. Even though there were so many, the net wasn't torn.
12 Jesus said to them, "Come and eat breakfast!"
None of the disciples dared inquire of him, "Who are you?" knowing that it was the Lord.
13 Then Jesus came and took the bread, gave it to them, and the fish likewise. 14 This is now the third time that Jesus was revealed to his disciples after he had risen from the dead.

1. Invite the Holy Spirit into this reading, asking the Author of Scripture to speak to you through His Word
2. Read today's passage as many times as you need, take your time
3. Write down (below) what the Lord is saying to you today
4. Live with this Word in your heart through the day

Saturday, April 6, 2024
Saturday within the Octave of Easter

First Reading: Acts 4: 13-21

13 Now when they saw the boldness of Peter and John, and had perceived that they were unlearned and ignorant men, they marveled. They recognized that they had been with Jesus. 14 Seeing the man who was healed standing with them, they could say nothing against it. 15 But when they had commanded them to go aside out of the council, they conferred among themselves, 16 saying, "What shall we do to these men? Because indeed a notable miracle has been done through them, as can be plainly seen by all who dwell in Jerusalem, and we can't deny it. 17 But so that this spreads no further among the people, let's threaten them, that from now on they don't speak to anyone in this name." 18 They called them, and commanded them not to speak at all nor teach in the name of Jesus.

19 But Peter and John answered them, "Whether it is right in the sight of God to listen to you rather than to God, judge for yourselves, 20 for we can't help telling the things which we saw and heard."

21 When they had further threatened them, they let them go, finding no way to punish them, because of the people; for everyone glorified God for that which was done.

Responsorial Psalm: Psalms 118: 1 and 14-21

1 Give thanks to Yahweh, for he is good,
for his loving kindness endures forever.
14 Yah is my strength and song.
He has become my salvation.
15 The voice of rejoicing and salvation is in the tents of the righteous.
"The right hand of Yahweh does valiantly.
16 The right hand of Yahweh is exalted!
The right hand of Yahweh does valiantly!"
17 I will not die, but live,
and declare Yah's works.
18 Yah has punished me severely,
but he has not given me over to death.
19 Open to me the gates of righteousness.
I will enter into them.

I will give thanks to Yah.
20 This is the gate of Yahweh;
the righteous will enter into it.
21 I will give thanks to you, for you have answered me,
and have become my salvation.

Gospel: Mark 16: 9-15

9 §Now when he had risen early on the first day of the week, he appeared first to Mary Magdalene, from whom he had cast out seven demons. 10 She went and told those who had been with him, as they mourned and wept. 11 When they heard that he was alive and had been seen by her, they disbelieved.

12 After these things he was revealed in another form to two of them as they walked, on their way into the country. 13 They went away and told it to the rest. They didn't believe them, either.

14 Afterward he was revealed to the eleven themselves as they sat at the table; and he rebuked them for their unbelief and hardness of heart, because they didn't believe those who had seen him after he had risen. 15 He said to them, "Go into all the world and preach the Good News to the whole creation.

1. Invite the Holy Spirit into this reading, asking the Author of Scripture to speak to you through His Word
2. Read today's passage as many times as you need, take your time
3. Write down (below) what the Lord is saying to you today
4. Live with this Word in your heart through the day

_____

_____

Sunday, April 7, 2024
SECOND SUNDAY OF EASTER
SUNDAY OF DIVINE MERCY

First Reading: Acts 4: 32-35

32 The multitude of those who believed were of one heart and soul. Not one of them claimed that anything of the things which he possessed was his own, but they had all things in common. 33 With great power, the apostles gave their testimony of the resurrection of the Lord Jesus. Great grace was on them all. 34 For neither was there among them any who lacked, for as many as were owners of lands or houses sold them, and brought the proceeds of the things that were sold, 35 and laid them at the apostles' feet; and distribution was made to each, according as anyone had need.

Responsorial Psalm: Psalms 118: 2-4, 13-15, 22-24

2 Let Israel now say
that his loving kindness endures forever.
3 Let the house of Aaron now say
that his loving kindness endures forever.
4 Now let those who fear Yahweh say
that his loving kindness endures forever.
13 You pushed me back hard, to make me fall,
but Yahweh helped me.
14 Yah is my strength and song.
He has become my salvation.
15 The voice of rejoicing and salvation is in the tents of the righteous.
"The right hand of Yahweh does valiantly.
22 The stone which the builders rejected
has become the cornerstone.†
23 This is Yahweh's doing.
It is marvelous in our eyes.
24 This is the day that Yahweh has made.
We will rejoice and be glad in it!

Second Reading: First John 5: 1-6

1 Whoever believes that Jesus is the Christ has been born of God. Whoever loves the Father also loves the child who is born of him. 2 By this we know that we love the children of God, when we love God and keep his commandments. 3 For this is loving God, that we keep his commandments. His commandments are not grievous. 4 For whatever is born of God overcomes the world. This is the victory that has overcome the world: your faith. 5 Who is he who overcomes the world, but he who believes that Jesus is the Son of God?
6 This is he who came by water and blood, Jesus Christ; not with the water only, but with the water and the blood. It is the Spirit who testifies, because the Spirit is the truth.

Gospel: John 20: 19-31

19 When therefore it was evening on that day, the first day of the week, and when the doors were locked where the disciples were assembled, for fear of the Jews, Jesus came and stood in the middle and said to them, "Peace be to you."
20 When he had said this, he showed them his hands and his side. The disciples therefore were glad when they saw the Lord. 21 Jesus therefore said to them again, "Peace be to you. As the Father has sent me, even so I send you." 22 When he had said this, he breathed on them, and said to them, "Receive the Holy Spirit! 23 If you forgive anyone's sins, they have been forgiven them. If you retain anyone's sins, they have been retained."

24 But Thomas, one of the twelve, called Didymus,§ wasn't with them when Jesus came. 25 The other disciples therefore said to him, "We have seen the Lord!"

But he said to them, "Unless I see in his hands the print of the nails, put my finger into the print of the nails, and put my hand into his side, I will not believe."

26 After eight days, again his disciples were inside and Thomas was with them. Jesus came, the doors being locked, and stood in the middle, and said, "Peace be to you." 27 Then he said to Thomas, "Reach here your finger, and see my hands. Reach here your hand, and put it into my side. Don't be unbelieving, but believing."

28 Thomas answered him, "My Lord and my God!"

29 Jesus said to him, "Because you have seen me,† you have believed. Blessed are those who have not seen and have believed."

30 Therefore Jesus did many other signs in the presence of his disciples, which are not written in this book; 31 but these are written that you may believe that Jesus is the Christ, the Son of God, and that believing you may have life in his name.

1. Invite the Holy Spirit into this reading, asking the Author of Scripture to speak to you through His Word
2. Read today's passage as many times as you need, take your time
3. Write down (below) what the Lord is saying to you today
4. Live with this Word in your heart through the day

_____

_____

Monday, April 8, 2024
THE ANNUNCIATION OF THE LORD

First Reading: Isaiah 7: 10-14; 8: 10

10 Yahweh spoke again to Ahaz, saying, 11 "Ask a sign of Yahweh your God; ask it either in the depth, or in the height above."

12 But Ahaz said, "I won't ask. I won't tempt Yahweh."

13 He said, "Listen now, house of David. Is it not enough for you to try the patience of men, that you will try the patience of my God also? 14 Therefore the Lord himself will give you a sign. Behold, the virgin will conceive, and bear a son, and shall call his name Immanuel.

10 Take counsel together, and it will be brought to nothing; speak the word, and it will not stand, for God is with us."

Responsorial Psalm: Psalms 40: 7-11

7 Then I said, "Behold, I have come.
It is written about me in the book in the scroll.
8 I delight to do your will, my God.
Yes, your law is within my heart."
9 I have proclaimed glad news of righteousness in the great assembly.
Behold, I will not seal my lips, Yahweh, you know.
10 I have not hidden your righteousness within my heart.
I have declared your faithfulness and your salvation.
I have not concealed your loving kindness and your truth from the great assembly.
11 Don't withhold your tender mercies from me, Yahweh.
Let your loving kindness and your truth continually preserve me.

Second Reading: Hebrews 10: 4-10

4 For it is impossible that the blood of bulls and goats should take away sins. 5 Therefore when he comes into the world, he says,
"You didn't desire sacrifice and offering,
but you prepared a body for me.
6 You had no pleasure in whole burnt offerings and sacrifices for sin.
7 Then I said, 'Behold, I have come (in the scroll of the book it is written of me)
to do your will, O God.' "*
8 Previously saying, "Sacrifices and offerings and whole burnt offerings and sacrifices for sin you didn't desire, neither had pleasure in them" (those which are offered according to the law), 9 then he has said, "Behold, I have come to do your will." He takes away the first, that he may establish the second, 10 by which will we have been sanctified through the offering of the body of Jesus Christ once for all.

Gospel: Luke 1: 26-38

26 Now in the sixth month, the angel Gabriel was sent from God to a city of Galilee named Nazareth, 27 to a virgin pledged to be married to a man whose name was Joseph, of David's house. The virgin's name was Mary. 28 Having come in, the angel said to her, "Rejoice, you highly favored one! The Lord is with you. Blessed are you among women!"
29 But when she saw him, she was greatly troubled at the saying, and considered what kind of salutation this might be. 30 The angel said to her, "Don't be afraid, Mary, for you have found favor with God. 31 Behold, you will conceive in your womb and give birth to a son, and shall name him 'Jesus.' 32 He will be great and will be called the Son of the Most High. The Lord God will give him the throne of his father David, 33 and he will reign over the house of Jacob forever. There will be no end to his Kingdom."
34 Mary said to the angel, "How can this be, seeing I am a virgin?"
35 The angel answered her, "The Holy Spirit will come on you, and the power of the Most High will overshadow you. Therefore also the holy one who is born from you will be called the Son of God. 36 Behold, Elizabeth your relative also has conceived a son in her old age; and this is

the sixth month with her who was called barren. 37 For nothing spoken by God is impossible."‡

38 Mary said, "Behold, the servant of the Lord; let it be done to me according to your word." Then the angel departed from her.

1. Invite the Holy Spirit into this reading, asking the Author of Scripture to speak to you through His Word
2. Read today's passage as many times as you need, take your time
3. Write down (below) what the Lord is saying to you today
4. Live with this Word in your heart through the day

_____

_____

Tuesday, April 9, 2024

First Reading: Acts 4: 32-37

32 The multitude of those who believed were of one heart and soul. Not one of them claimed that anything of the things which he possessed was his own, but they had all things in common. 33 With great power, the apostles gave their testimony of the resurrection of the Lord Jesus. Great grace was on them all. 34 For neither was there among them any who lacked, for as many as were owners of lands or houses sold them, and brought the proceeds of the things that were sold, 35 and laid them at the apostles' feet; and distribution was made to each, according as anyone had need.
36 Joses, who by the apostles was also called Barnabas (which is, being interpreted, Son of Encouragement), a Levite, a man of Cyprus by race, 37 having a field, sold it and brought the money and laid it at the apostles' feet.

Responsorial Psalm: Psalms 93: 1-2, 5

1 Yahweh reigns!
He is clothed with majesty!
Yahweh is armed with strength.
The world also is established.
It can't be moved.
2 Your throne is established from long ago.
You are from everlasting.
5 Your statutes stand firm.
Holiness adorns your house,

Yahweh, forever more.

Gospel: John 3: 7b-15

7b 'You must be born anew.' 8 The wind‡ blows where it wants to, and you hear its sound, but don't know where it comes from and where it is going. So is everyone who is born of the Spirit."
9 Nicodemus answered him, "How can these things be?"
10 Jesus answered him, "Are you the teacher of Israel, and don't understand these things? 11 Most certainly I tell you, we speak that which we know and testify of that which we have seen, and you don't receive our witness. 12 If I told you earthly things and you don't believe, how will you believe if I tell you heavenly things? 13 No one has ascended into heaven but he who descended out of heaven, the Son of Man, who is in heaven. 14 As Moses lifted up the serpent in the wilderness, even so must the Son of Man be lifted up, 15 that whoever believes in him should not perish, but have eternal life.

1. Invite the Holy Spirit into this reading, asking the Author of Scripture to speak to you through His Word
2. Read today's passage as many times as you need, take your time
3. Write down (below) what the Lord is saying to you today
4. Live with this Word in your heart through the day

_____

_____

Wednesday, April 10, 2024

First Reading: Acts 5: 17-26

17 But the high priest rose up, and all those who were with him (which is the sect of the Sadducees), and they were filled with jealousy 18 and laid hands on the apostles, then put them in public custody. 19 But an angel of the Lord opened the prison doors by night, and brought them out and said, 20 "Go stand and speak in the temple to the people all the words of this life."
21 When they heard this, they entered into the temple about daybreak and taught. But the high priest and those who were with him came and called the council together, with all the senate of the children of Israel, and sent to the prison to have them brought. 22 But the officers who came didn't find them in the prison. They returned and reported, 23 "We found the prison shut and locked, and the guards standing before the doors, but when we opened them, we found no one inside!"
24 Now when the high priest, the captain of the temple, and the chief priests heard these words, they were very perplexed about them and what might become of this. 25 One came and

told them, "Behold, the men whom you put in prison are in the temple, standing and teaching the people." 26 Then the captain went with the officers, and brought them without violence, for they were afraid that the people might stone them.

Responsorial Psalm: Psalms 34: 2-9

2 My soul shall boast in Yahweh.
The humble shall hear of it and be glad.
3 Oh magnify Yahweh with me.
Let's exalt his name together.
4 I sought Yahweh, and he answered me,
and delivered me from all my fears.
5 They looked to him, and were radiant.
Their faces shall never be covered with shame.
6 This poor man cried, and Yahweh heard him,
and saved him out of all his troubles.
7 Yahweh's angel encamps around those who fear him,
and delivers them.
8 Oh taste and see that Yahweh is good.
Blessed is the man who takes refuge in him.
9 Oh fear Yahweh, you his saints,
for there is no lack with those who fear him.

Gospel: John 3: 16-21

16 For God so loved the world, that he gave his only born§ Son, that whoever believes in him should not perish, but have eternal life. 17 For God didn't send his Son into the world to judge the world, but that the world should be saved through him. 18 He who believes in him is not judged. He who doesn't believe has been judged already, because he has not believed in the name of the only born Son of God. 19 This is the judgment, that the light has come into the world, and men loved the darkness rather than the light, for their works were evil. 20 For everyone who does evil hates the light and doesn't come to the light, lest his works would be exposed. 21 But he who does the truth comes to the light, that his works may be revealed, that they have been done in God."

1. Invite the Holy Spirit into this reading, asking the Author of Scripture to speak to you through His Word
2. Read today's passage as many times as you need, take your time
3. Write down (below) what the Lord is saying to you today
4. Live with this Word in your heart through the day

_____

_____

Thursday, April 11, 2024
Saint Stanislaus, Bishop and Martyr

First Reading: Acts 5: 27-33

27 When they had brought them, they set them before the council. The high priest questioned them, 28 saying, "Didn't we strictly command you not to teach in this name? Behold, you have filled Jerusalem with your teaching, and intend to bring this man's blood on us."
29 But Peter and the apostles answered, "We must obey God rather than men. 30 The God of our fathers raised up Jesus, whom you killed, hanging him on a tree. 31 God exalted him with his right hand to be a Prince and a Savior, to give repentance to Israel, and remission of sins. 32 We are his witnesses of these things; and so also is the Holy Spirit, whom God has given to those who obey him."
33 But they, when they heard this, were cut to the heart, and were determined to kill them.

Responsorial Psalm: Psalms 34: 2 and 9, 17-20

2 My soul shall boast in Yahweh.
The humble shall hear of it and be glad.
9 Oh fear Yahweh, you his saints,
for there is no lack with those who fear him.
17 The righteous cry, and Yahweh hears,
and delivers them out of all their troubles.
18 Yahweh is near to those who have a broken heart,
and saves those who have a crushed spirit.
19 Many are the afflictions of the righteous,
but Yahweh delivers him out of them all.
20 He protects all of his bones.
Not one of them is broken.

Gospel: John 3: 31-36

31 "He who comes from above is above all. He who is from the earth belongs to the earth and speaks of the earth. He who comes from heaven is above all. 32 What he has seen and heard, of that he testifies; and no one receives his witness. 33 He who has received his witness has set his seal to this, that God is true. 34 For he whom God has sent speaks the words of God; for God gives the Spirit without measure. 35 The Father loves the Son, and has given all things into his hand. 36 One who believes in the Son has eternal life, but one who disobeys† the Son won't see life, but the wrath of God remains on him."

1. Invite the Holy Spirit into this reading, asking the Author of Scripture to speak to you through His Word

2. Read today's passage as many times as you need, take your time
3. Write down (below) what the Lord is saying to you today
4. Live with this Word in your heart through the day

Friday, April 12, 2024

First Reading: Acts 5: 34-42

34 But one stood up in the council, a Pharisee named Gamaliel, a teacher of the law, honored by all the people, and commanded to put the apostles out for a little while. 35 He said to them, "You men of Israel, be careful concerning these men, what you are about to do. 36 For before these days Theudas rose up, making himself out to be somebody; to whom a number of men, about four hundred, joined themselves. He was slain; and all, as many as obeyed him, were dispersed and came to nothing. 37 After this man, Judas of Galilee rose up in the days of the enrollment, and drew away some people after him. He also perished, and all, as many as obeyed him, were scattered abroad. 38 Now I tell you, withdraw from these men and leave them alone. For if this counsel or this work is of men, it will be overthrown. 39 But if it is of God, you will not be able to overthrow it, and you would be found even to be fighting against God!"
40 They agreed with him. Summoning the apostles, they beat them and commanded them not to speak in the name of Jesus, and let them go. 41 They therefore departed from the presence of the council, rejoicing that they were counted worthy to suffer dishonor for Jesus' name.
42 Every day, in the temple and at home, they never stopped teaching and preaching Jesus, the Christ.

Responsorial Psalm: Psalms 27: 1, 4, 13-14

1 Yahweh is my light and my salvation.
Whom shall I fear?
Yahweh is the strength of my life.
Of whom shall I be afraid?
4 One thing I have asked of Yahweh, that I will seek after:
that I may dwell in Yahweh's house all the days of my life,
to see Yahweh's beauty,
and to inquire in his temple.
13 I am still confident of this:
I will see the goodness of Yahweh in the land of the living.

14 Wait for Yahweh.
Be strong, and let your heart take courage.
Yes, wait for Yahweh.

Gospel: John 6: 1-15

1 After these things, Jesus went away to the other side of the sea of Galilee, which is also called the Sea of Tiberias. 2 A great multitude followed him, because they saw his signs which he did on those who were sick. 3 Jesus went up into the mountain, and he sat there with his disciples. 4 Now the Passover, the feast of the Jews, was at hand. 5 Jesus therefore, lifting up his eyes and seeing that a great multitude was coming to him, said to Philip, "Where are we to buy bread, that these may eat?" 6 He said this to test him, for he himself knew what he would do. 7 Philip answered him, "Two hundred denarii† worth of bread is not sufficient for them, that every one of them may receive a little."
8 One of his disciples, Andrew, Simon Peter's brother, said to him, 9 "There is a boy here who has five barley loaves and two fish, but what are these among so many?"
10 Jesus said, "Have the people sit down." Now there was much grass in that place. So the men sat down, in number about five thousand. 11 Jesus took the loaves, and having given thanks, he distributed to the disciples, and the disciples to those who were sitting down, likewise also of the fish as much as they desired. 12 When they were filled, he said to his disciples, "Gather up the broken pieces which are left over, that nothing be lost." 13 So they gathered them up, and filled twelve baskets with broken pieces from the five barley loaves, which were left over by those who had eaten. 14 When therefore the people saw the sign which Jesus did, they said, "This is truly the prophet who comes into the world." 15 Jesus therefore, perceiving that they were about to come and take him by force to make him king, withdrew again to the mountain by himself.

1. Invite the Holy Spirit into this reading, asking the Author of Scripture to speak to you through His Word
2. Read today's passage as many times as you need, take your time
3. Write down (below) what the Lord is saying to you today
4. Live with this Word in your heart through the day

Saturday, April 13, 2024
Saint Martin I, Pope and Martyr

First Reading: Acts 6: 1-7

1 Now in those days, when the number of the disciples was multiplying, a complaint arose from the Hellenists† against the Hebrews, because their widows were neglected in the daily service. 2 The twelve summoned the multitude of the disciples and said, "It is not appropriate for us to forsake the word of God and serve tables. 3 Therefore, select from among you, brothers, seven men of good report, full of the Holy Spirit and of wisdom, whom we may appoint over this business. 4 But we will continue steadfastly in prayer and in the ministry of the word."

5 These words pleased the whole multitude. They chose Stephen, a man full of faith and of the Holy Spirit, Philip, Prochorus, Nicanor, Timon, Parmenas, and Nicolaus, a proselyte of Antioch, 6 whom they set before the apostles. When they had prayed, they laid their hands on them.

7 The word of God increased and the number of the disciples greatly multiplied in Jerusalem. A great company of the priests were obedient to the faith.

Responsorial Psalm: Psalms 33: 1-2, 4-5, 18-19

1 Rejoice in Yahweh, you righteous!
Praise is fitting for the upright.
2 Give thanks to Yahweh with the lyre.
Sing praises to him with the harp of ten strings.
4 For Yahweh's word is right.
All his work is done in faithfulness.
5 He loves righteousness and justice.
The earth is full of the loving kindness of Yahweh.
18 Behold, Yahweh's eye is on those who fear him,
on those who hope in his loving kindness,
19 to deliver their soul from death,
to keep them alive in famine.

Gospel: John 6: 16-21

16 When evening came, his disciples went down to the sea. 17 They entered into the boat, and were going over the sea to Capernaum. It was now dark, and Jesus had not come to them. 18 The sea was tossed by a great wind blowing. 19 When therefore they had rowed about twenty-five or thirty stadia,‡ they saw Jesus walking on the sea* and drawing near to the boat; and they were afraid. 20 But he said to them, "It is I.§ Don't be afraid." 21 They were willing therefore to receive him into the boat. Immediately the boat was at the land where they were going.

1. Invite the Holy Spirit into this reading, asking the Author of Scripture to speak to you through His Word
2. Read today's passage as many times as you need, take your time
3. Write down (below) what the Lord is saying to you today

_____

_____

Sunday, April 14, 2024
THIRD SUNDAY OF EASTER

First Reading: Acts 3: 13-15, 17-19

13 The God of Abraham, Isaac, and Jacob, the God of our fathers, has glorified his Servant Jesus, whom you delivered up and denied in the presence of Pilate, when he had determined to release him. 14 But you denied the Holy and Righteous One and asked for a murderer to be granted to you, 15 and killed the Prince of life, whom God raised from the dead, to which we are witnesses.
17 "Now, brothers,‡ I know that you did this in ignorance, as did also your rulers. 18 But the things which God announced by the mouth of all his prophets, that Christ should suffer, he thus fulfilled.
19 "Repent therefore, and turn again, that your sins may be blotted out, so that there may come times of refreshing from the presence of the Lord

Responsorial Psalm: Psalms 4: 2, 4, 7-8

2 You sons of men, how long shall my glory be turned into dishonor?
Will you love vanity and seek after falsehood?
4 Stand in awe, and don't sin.
Search your own heart on your bed, and be still.
7 You have put gladness in my heart,
more than when their grain and their new wine are increased.
8 In peace I will both lay myself down and sleep,
for you alone, Yahweh, make me live in safety.

Second Reading: First John 2: 1-5a

1 My little children, I write these things to you so that you may not sin. If anyone sins, we have a Counselor† with the Father, Jesus Christ, the righteous. 2 And he is the atoning sacrifice‡ for our sins, and not for ours only, but also for the whole world. 3 This is how we know that we know him: if we keep his commandments. 4 One who says, "I know him," and doesn't keep his commandments, is a liar, and the truth isn't in him. 5a But God's love has most certainly been perfected in whoever keeps his word.

Gospel: Luke 24: 35-48

35 They related the things that happened along the way, and how he was recognized by them in the breaking of the bread.

36 As they said these things, Jesus himself stood among them, and said to them, "Peace be to you."

37 But they were terrified and filled with fear, and supposed that they had seen a spirit.

38 He said to them, "Why are you troubled? Why do doubts arise in your hearts? 39 See my hands and my feet, that it is truly me. Touch me and see, for a spirit doesn't have flesh and bones, as you see that I have." 40 When he had said this, he showed them his hands and his feet. 41 While they still didn't believe for joy, and wondered, he said to them, "Do you have anything here to eat?"

42 They gave him a piece of a broiled fish and some honeycomb. 43 He took them, and ate in front of them. 44 He said to them, "This is what I told you while I was still with you, that all things which are written in the law of Moses, the prophets, and the psalms concerning me must be fulfilled."

45 Then he opened their minds, that they might understand the Scriptures. 46 He said to them, "Thus it is written, and thus it was necessary for the Christ to suffer and to rise from the dead the third day, 47 and that repentance and remission of sins should be preached in his name to all the nations, beginning at Jerusalem. 48 You are witnesses of these things.

1. Invite the Holy Spirit into this reading, asking the Author of Scripture to speak to you through His Word
2. Read today's passage as many times as you need, take your time
3. Write down (below) what the Lord is saying to you today
4. Live with this Word in your heart through the day

_____

_____

Monday, April 15, 2024

First Reading: Acts 6: 8-15

8 Stephen, full of faith and power, performed great wonders and signs among the people. 9 But some of those who were of the synagogue called "The Libertines", and of the Cyrenians, of the Alexandrians, and of those of Cilicia and Asia arose, disputing with Stephen. 10 They weren't able to withstand the wisdom and the Spirit by which he spoke. 11 Then they secretly induced men to say, "We have heard him speak blasphemous words against Moses and God."

12 They stirred up the people, the elders, and the scribes, and came against him and seized him, then brought him in to the council, 13 and set up false witnesses who said, "This man never stops speaking blasphemous words against this holy place and the law. 14 For we have heard him say that this Jesus of Nazareth will destroy this place, and will change the customs which Moses delivered to us." 15 All who sat in the council, fastening their eyes on him, saw his face like it was the face of an angel.

Responsorial Psalm: Psalms 119: 23-24, 26-27, 29-30

23 Though princes sit and slander me,
your servant will meditate on your statutes.
24 Indeed your statutes are my delight,
and my counselors.
26 I declared my ways, and you answered me.
Teach me your statutes.
27 Let me understand the teaching of your precepts!
Then I will meditate on your wondrous works.
29 Keep me from the way of deceit.
Grant me your law graciously!
30 I have chosen the way of truth.
I have set your ordinances before me.

Gospel: John 6: 22-29

22 On the next day, the multitude that stood on the other side of the sea saw that there was no other boat there, except the one in which his disciples had embarked, and that Jesus hadn't entered with his disciples into the boat, but his disciples had gone away alone. 23 However, boats from Tiberias came near to the place where they ate the bread after the Lord had given thanks. 24 When the multitude therefore saw that Jesus wasn't there, nor his disciples, they themselves got into the boats and came to Capernaum, seeking Jesus. 25 When they found him on the other side of the sea, they asked him, "Rabbi, when did you come here?"
26 Jesus answered them, "Most certainly I tell you, you seek me, not because you saw signs, but because you ate of the loaves and were filled. 27 Don't work for the food which perishes, but for the food which remains to eternal life, which the Son of Man will give to you. For God the Father has sealed him."
28 They said therefore to him, "What must we do, that we may work the works of God?"
29 Jesus answered them, "This is the work of God, that you believe in him whom he has sent."

1. Invite the Holy Spirit into this reading, asking the Author of Scripture to speak to you through His Word
2. Read today's passage as many times as you need, take your time
3. Write down (below) what the Lord is saying to you today
4. Live with this Word in your heart through the day

Tuesday, April 16, 2024

First Reading: Acts 7: 51-60

51 "You stiff-necked and uncircumcised in heart and ears, you always resist the Holy Spirit! As your fathers did, so you do. 52 Which of the prophets didn't your fathers persecute? They killed those who foretold the coming of the Righteous One, of whom you have now become betrayers and murderers. 53 You received the law as it was ordained by angels, and didn't keep it!"
54 Now when they heard these things, they were cut to the heart, and they gnashed at him with their teeth. 55 But he, being full of the Holy Spirit, looked up steadfastly into heaven and saw the glory of God, and Jesus standing on the right hand of God, 56 and said, "Behold, I see the heavens opened and the Son of Man standing at the right hand of God!"
57 But they cried out with a loud voice and stopped their ears, then rushed at him with one accord. 58 They threw him out of the city and stoned him. The witnesses placed their garments at the feet of a young man named Saul. 59 They stoned Stephen as he called out, saying, "Lord Jesus, receive my spirit!" 60 He kneeled down and cried with a loud voice, "Lord, don't hold this sin against them!" When he had said this, he fell asleep.

Responsorial Psalm: Psalms 31: 3-4, 6-8a, 17 and 21

3 For you are my rock and my fortress,
therefore for your name's sake lead me and guide me.
4 Pluck me out of the net that they have laid secretly for me,
for you are my stronghold.
6 I hate those who regard lying vanities,
but I trust in Yahweh.
7 I will be glad and rejoice in your loving kindness,
for you have seen my affliction.
You have known my soul in adversities.
8 You have not shut me up into the hand of the enemy.
17 Let me not be disappointed, Yahweh, for I have called on you.
Let the wicked be disappointed.
Let them be silent in Sheol.
21 Praise be to Yahweh,
for he has shown me his marvelous loving kindness in a strong city.

Gospel: John 6: 30-35

30 They said therefore to him, "What then do you do for a sign, that we may see and believe you? What work do you do? 31 Our fathers ate the manna in the wilderness. As it is written, 'He gave them bread out of heaven† to eat.' "*

32 Jesus therefore said to them, "Most certainly, I tell you, it wasn't Moses who gave you the bread out of heaven, but my Father gives you the true bread out of heaven. 33 For the bread of God is that which comes down out of heaven and gives life to the world."

34 They said therefore to him, "Lord, always give us this bread."

35 Jesus said to them, "I am the bread of life. Whoever comes to me will not be hungry, and whoever believes in me will never be thirsty.

1. Invite the Holy Spirit into this reading, asking the Author of Scripture to speak to you through His Word
2. Read today's passage as many times as you need, take your time
3. Write down (below) what the Lord is saying to you today
4. Live with this Word in your heart through the day

Wednesday, April 17, 2024

First Reading: Acts 8: 1b-8

1b A great persecution arose against the assembly which was in Jerusalem in that day. They were all scattered abroad throughout the regions of Judea and Samaria, except for the apostles. 2 Devout men buried Stephen and lamented greatly over him. 3 But Saul ravaged the assembly, entering into every house and dragged both men and women off to prison. 4 Therefore those who were scattered abroad went around preaching the word. 5 Philip went down to the city of Samaria and proclaimed to them the Christ. 6 The multitudes listened with one accord to the things that were spoken by Philip when they heard and saw the signs which he did. 7 For unclean spirits came out of many of those who had them. They came out, crying with a loud voice. Many who had been paralyzed and lame were healed. 8 There was great joy in that city.

Responsorial Psalm: Psalms 66: 1-7a

1 Make a joyful shout to God, all the earth!

2 Sing to the glory of his name!
Offer glory and praise!
3 Tell God, "How awesome are your deeds!
Through the greatness of your power, your enemies submit themselves to you.
4 All the earth will worship you,
and will sing to you;
they will sing to your name."
5 Come, and see God's deeds—
awesome work on behalf of the children of men.
6 He turned the sea into dry land.
They went through the river on foot.
There, we rejoiced in him.
7 He rules by his might forever.
His eyes watch the nations.

Gospel: John 6: 35-40

35 Jesus said to them, "I am the bread of life. Whoever comes to me will not be hungry, and whoever believes in me will never be thirsty. 36 But I told you that you have seen me, and yet you don't believe. 37 All those whom the Father gives me will come to me. He who comes to me I will in no way throw out. 38 For I have come down from heaven, not to do my own will, but the will of him who sent me. 39 This is the will of my Father who sent me, that of all he has given to me I should lose nothing, but should raise him up at the last day. 40 This is the will of the one who sent me, that everyone who sees the Son and believes in him should have eternal life; and I will raise him up at the last day."

1. Invite the Holy Spirit into this reading, asking the Author of Scripture to speak to you through His Word
2. Read today's passage as many times as you need, take your time
3. Write down (below) what the Lord is saying to you today
4. Live with this Word in your heart through the day

_____

_____

Thursday, April 18, 2024

First Reading: Acts 8: 26-40

26 Then an angel of the Lord spoke to Philip, saying, "Arise, and go toward the south to the way that goes down from Jerusalem to Gaza. This is a desert."

27 He arose and went; and behold, there was a man of Ethiopia, a eunuch of great authority under Candace, queen of the Ethiopians, who was over all her treasure, who had come to Jerusalem to worship. 28 He was returning and sitting in his chariot, and was reading the prophet Isaiah.

29 The Spirit said to Philip, "Go near, and join yourself to this chariot."

30 Philip ran to him, and heard him reading Isaiah the prophet, and said, "Do you understand what you are reading?"

31 He said, "How can I, unless someone explains it to me?" He begged Philip to come up and sit with him. 32 Now the passage of the Scripture which he was reading was this,

"He was led as a sheep to the slaughter.

As a lamb before his shearer is silent,

so he doesn't open his mouth.

33 In his humiliation, his judgment was taken away.

Who will declare His generation?

For his life is taken from the earth."*

34 The eunuch answered Philip, "Who is the prophet talking about? About himself, or about someone else?"

35 Philip opened his mouth, and beginning from this Scripture, preached to him about Jesus.

36 As they went on the way, they came to some water; and the eunuch said, "Behold, here is water. What is keeping me from being baptized?"

37 † 38 He commanded the chariot to stand still, and they both went down into the water, both Philip and the eunuch, and he baptized him.

39 When they came up out of the water, the Spirit of the Lord caught Philip away, and the eunuch didn't see him any more, for he went on his way rejoicing. 40 But Philip was found at Azotus. Passing through, he preached the Good News to all the cities until he came to Caesarea.

Responsorial Psalm: Psalms 66: 8-9, 16-17, 20

8 Praise our God, you peoples!

Make the sound of his praise heard,

9 who preserves our life among the living,

and doesn't allow our feet to be moved.

16 Come and hear, all you who fear God.

I will declare what he has done for my soul.

17 I cried to him with my mouth.

He was extolled with my tongue.

20 Blessed be God, who has not turned away my prayer,

nor his loving kindness from me.

Gospel: John 6: 44-51

44 No one can come to me unless the Father who sent me draws him; and I will raise him up in the last day. 45 It is written in the prophets, 'They will all be taught by God.' * Therefore everyone who hears from the Father and has learned, comes to me. 46 Not that anyone has seen the Father, except he who is from God. He has seen the Father. 47 Most certainly, I tell you, he who believes in me has eternal life. 48 I am the bread of life. 49 Your fathers ate the manna in the wilderness and they died. 50 This is the bread which comes down out of heaven, that anyone may eat of it and not die. 51 I am the living bread which came down out of heaven. If anyone eats of this bread, he will live forever. Yes, the bread which I will give for the life of the world is my flesh."

1. Invite the Holy Spirit into this reading, asking the Author of Scripture to speak to you through His Word
2. Read today's passage as many times as you need, take your time
3. Write down (below) what the Lord is saying to you today
4. Live with this Word in your heart through the day

_____

_____

Friday, April 19, 2024

First Reading: Acts 9: 1-20

1 But Saul, still breathing threats and slaughter against the disciples of the Lord, went to the high priest 2 and asked for letters from him to the synagogues of Damascus, that if he found any who were of the Way, whether men or women, he might bring them bound to Jerusalem. 3 As he traveled, he got close to Damascus, and suddenly a light from the sky shone around him. 4 He fell on the earth, and heard a voice saying to him, "Saul, Saul, why do you persecute me?"
5 He said, "Who are you, Lord?"
The Lord said, "I am Jesus, whom you are persecuting.† 6 But‡ rise up and enter into the city, then you will be told what you must do."
7 The men who traveled with him stood speechless, hearing the sound, but seeing no one. 8 Saul arose from the ground, and when his eyes were opened, he saw no one. They led him by the hand and brought him into Damascus. 9 He was without sight for three days, and neither ate nor drank.
10 Now there was a certain disciple at Damascus named Ananias. The Lord said to him in a vision, "Ananias!"
He said, "Behold, it's me, Lord."

11 The Lord said to him, "Arise and go to the street which is called Straight, and inquire in the house of Judah§ for one named Saul, a man of Tarsus. For behold, he is praying, 12 and in a vision he has seen a man named Ananias coming in and laying his hands on him, that he might receive his sight."

13 But Ananias answered, "Lord, I have heard from many about this man, how much evil he did to your saints at Jerusalem. 14 Here he has authority from the chief priests to bind all who call on your name."

15 But the Lord said to him, "Go your way, for he is my chosen vessel to bear my name before the nations and kings, and the children of Israel. 16 For I will show him how many things he must suffer for my name's sake."

17 Ananias departed and entered into the house. Laying his hands on him, he said, "Brother Saul, the Lord, who appeared to you on the road by which you came, has sent me that you may receive your sight and be filled with the Holy Spirit." 18 Immediately something like scales fell from his eyes, and he received his sight. He arose and was baptized. 19 He took food and was strengthened.

Saul stayed several days with the disciples who were at Damascus. 20 Immediately in the synagogues he proclaimed the Christ, that he is the Son of God.

Responsorial Psalm: Psalms 117: 1, 2

1 Praise Yahweh, all you nations!
Extol him, all you peoples!
2 For his loving kindness is great toward us.
Yahweh's faithfulness endures forever.
Praise Yah!

Gospel: John 6: 52-59

52 The Jews therefore contended with one another, saying, "How can this man give us his flesh to eat?"

53 Jesus therefore said to them, "Most certainly I tell you, unless you eat the flesh of the Son of Man and drink his blood, you don't have life in yourselves. 54 He who eats my flesh and drinks my blood has eternal life, and I will raise him up at the last day. 55 For my flesh is food indeed, and my blood is drink indeed. 56 He who eats my flesh and drinks my blood lives in me, and I in him. 57 As the living Father sent me, and I live because of the Father, so he who feeds on me will also live because of me. 58 This is the bread which came down out of heaven—not as our fathers ate the manna and died. He who eats this bread will live forever." 59 He said these things in the synagogue, as he taught in Capernaum.

1. Invite the Holy Spirit into this reading, asking the Author of Scripture to speak to you through His Word
2. Read today's passage as many times as you need, take your time
3. Write down (below) what the Lord is saying to you today

Saturday, April 20, 2024

First Reading: Acts 9: 31-42

31 So the assemblies throughout all Judea, Galilee, and Samaria had peace and were built up. They were multiplied, walking in the fear of the Lord and in the comfort of the Holy Spirit.
32 As Peter went throughout all those parts, he came down also to the saints who lived at Lydda. 33 There he found a certain man named Aeneas, who had been bedridden for eight years because he was paralyzed. 34 Peter said to him, "Aeneas, Jesus Christ heals you. Get up and make your bed!" Immediately he arose. 35 All who lived at Lydda and in Sharon saw him, and they turned to the Lord.
36 Now there was at Joppa a certain disciple named Tabitha, which when translated means Dorcas.‡ This woman was full of good works and acts of mercy which she did. 37 In those days, she became sick and died. When they had washed her, they laid her in an upper room. 38 As Lydda was near Joppa, the disciples, hearing that Peter was there, sent two men§ to him, imploring him not to delay in coming to them. 39 Peter got up and went with them. When he had come, they brought him into the upper room. All the widows stood by him weeping, and showing the tunics and other garments which Dorcas had made while she was with them. 40 Peter sent them all out, and knelt down and prayed. Turning to the body, he said, "Tabitha, get up!" She opened her eyes, and when she saw Peter, she sat up. 41 He gave her his hand and raised her up. Calling the saints and widows, he presented her alive. 42 This became known throughout all Joppa, and many believed in the Lord.

Responsorial Psalm: Psalms 116: 12-17

12 What will I give to Yahweh for all his benefits toward me?
13 I will take the cup of salvation, and call on Yahweh's name.
14 I will pay my vows to Yahweh,
yes, in the presence of all his people.
15 Precious in Yahweh's sight is the death of his saints.
16 Yahweh, truly I am your servant.
I am your servant, the son of your servant girl.
You have freed me from my chains.
17 I will offer to you the sacrifice of thanksgiving,
and will call on Yahweh's name.

Gospel: John 6: 60-69

60 Therefore many of his disciples, when they heard this, said, "This is a hard saying! Who can listen to it?"

61 But Jesus knowing in himself that his disciples murmured at this, said to them, "Does this cause you to stumble? 62 Then what if you would see the Son of Man ascending to where he was before? 63 It is the spirit who gives life. The flesh profits nothing. The words that I speak to you are spirit, and are life. 64 But there are some of you who don't believe." For Jesus knew from the beginning who they were who didn't believe, and who it was who would betray him. 65 He said, "For this cause I have said to you that no one can come to me, unless it is given to him by my Father."

66 At this, many of his disciples went back and walked no more with him. 67 Jesus said therefore to the twelve, "You don't also want to go away, do you?"

68 Simon Peter answered him, "Lord, to whom would we go? You have the words of eternal life. 69 We have come to believe and know that you are the Christ, the Son of the living God."

1. Invite the Holy Spirit into this reading, asking the Author of Scripture to speak to you through His Word
2. Read today's passage as many times as you need, take your time
3. Write down (below) what the Lord is saying to you today
4. Live with this Word in your heart through the day

Sunday, April 21, 2024
FOURTH SUNDAY OF EASTER

First Reading: Acts 4: 8-12

8 Then Peter, filled with the Holy Spirit, said to them, "You rulers of the people and elders of Israel, 9 if we are examined today concerning a good deed done to a crippled man, by what means this man has been healed, 10 may it be known to you all, and to all the people of Israel, that in the name of Jesus Christ of Nazareth, whom you crucified, whom God raised from the dead, this man stands here before you whole in him. 11 He is 'the stone which was regarded as worthless by you, the builders, which has become the head of the corner.'* 12 There is salvation in no one else, for there is no other name under heaven that is given among men, by which we must be saved!"

Responsorial Psalm: Psalms 118: 1, 8-9, 21-23, 26, 28, 29

1 Give thanks to Yahweh, for he is good,
for his loving kindness endures forever.
8 It is better to take refuge in Yahweh,
than to put confidence in man.
9 It is better to take refuge in Yahweh,
than to put confidence in princes.
21 I will give thanks to you, for you have answered me,
and have become my salvation.
22 The stone which the builders rejected
has become the cornerstone.†
23 This is Yahweh's doing.
It is marvelous in our eyes.
26 Blessed is he who comes in Yahweh's name!
We have blessed you out of Yahweh's house.
28 You are my God, and I will give thanks to you.
You are my God, I will exalt you.
29 Oh give thanks to Yahweh, for he is good,
for his loving kindness endures forever.

Second Reading: First John 3: 1-2

1 See how great a love the Father has given to us, that we should be called children of God! For this cause the world doesn't know us, because it didn't know him. 2 Beloved, now we are children of God. It is not yet revealed what we will be; but we know that when he is revealed, we will be like him, for we will see him just as he is.

Gospel: John 10: 11-18

11 "I am the good shepherd.* The good shepherd lays down his life for the sheep. 12 He who is a hired hand, and not a shepherd, who doesn't own the sheep, sees the wolf coming, leaves the sheep, and flees. The wolf snatches the sheep and scatters them. 13 The hired hand flees because he is a hired hand and doesn't care for the sheep. 14 I am the good shepherd. I know my own, and I'm known by my own; 15 even as the Father knows me, and I know the Father. I lay down my life for the sheep. 16 I have other sheep which are not of this fold. I must bring them also, and they will hear my voice. They will become one flock with one shepherd. 17 Therefore the Father loves me, because I lay down my life, that I may take it again. 18 No one takes it away from me, but I lay it down by myself. I have power to lay it down, and I have power to take it again. I received this commandment from my Father."

1. Invite the Holy Spirit into this reading, asking the Author of Scripture to speak to you through His Word
2. Read today's passage as many times as you need, take your time

_____

_____

Monday, April 22, 2024

First Reading: Acts 11: 1-18

1 Now the apostles and the brothers† who were in Judea heard that the Gentiles had also received the word of God. 2 When Peter had come up to Jerusalem, those who were of the circumcision contended with him, 3 saying, "You went in to uncircumcised men and ate with them!"

4 But Peter began, and explained to them in order, saying, 5 "I was in the city of Joppa praying, and in a trance I saw a vision: a certain container descending, like it was a great sheet let down from heaven by four corners. It came as far as me. 6 When I had looked intently at it, I considered, and saw the four-footed animals of the earth, wild animals, creeping things, and birds of the sky. 7 I also heard a voice saying to me, 'Rise, Peter, kill and eat!' 8 But I said, 'Not so, Lord, for nothing unholy or unclean has ever entered into my mouth.' 9 But a voice answered me the second time out of heaven, 'What God has cleansed, don't you call unclean.' 10 This was done three times, and all were drawn up again into heaven. 11 Behold, immediately three men stood before the house where I was, having been sent from Caesarea to me. 12 The Spirit told me to go with them without discriminating. These six brothers also accompanied me, and we entered into the man's house. 13 He told us how he had seen the angel standing in his house and saying to him, 'Send to Joppa and get Simon, who is called Peter, 14 who will speak to you words by which you will be saved, you and all your house.' 15 As I began to speak, the Holy Spirit fell on them, even as on us at the beginning. 16 I remembered the word of the Lord, how he said, 'John indeed baptized in water, but you will be baptized in the Holy Spirit.' 17 If then God gave to them the same gift as us when we believed in the Lord Jesus Christ, who was I, that I could withstand God?"

18 When they heard these things, they held their peace and glorified God, saying, "Then God has also granted to the Gentiles repentance to life!"

Responsorial Psalm: Psalms 42: 2-3; 43: 3-4

2 My soul thirsts for God, for the living God.
When shall I come and appear before God?
3 My tears have been my food day and night,
while they continually ask me, "Where is your God?"

3 Oh, send out your light and your truth.
Let them lead me.
Let them bring me to your holy hill,
to your tents.
4 Then I will go to the altar of God,
to God, my exceeding joy.
I will praise you on the harp, God, my God.

Gospel: John 10: 1-10

1 "Most certainly, I tell you, one who doesn't enter by the door into the sheep fold, but climbs up some other way, is a thief and a robber. 2 But one who enters in by the door is the shepherd of the sheep. 3 The gatekeeper opens the gate for him, and the sheep listen to his voice. He calls his own sheep by name and leads them out. 4 Whenever he brings out his own sheep, he goes before them; and the sheep follow him, for they know his voice. 5 They will by no means follow a stranger, but will flee from him; for they don't know the voice of strangers." 6 Jesus spoke this parable to them, but they didn't understand what he was telling them.
7 Jesus therefore said to them again, "Most certainly, I tell you, I am the sheep's door. 8 All who came before me are thieves and robbers, but the sheep didn't listen to them. 9 I am the door. If anyone enters in by me, he will be saved, and will go in and go out and will find pasture. 10 The thief only comes to steal, kill, and destroy. I came that they may have life, and may have it abundantly.

1. Invite the Holy Spirit into this reading, asking the Author of Scripture to speak to you through His Word
2. Read today's passage as many times as you need, take your time
3. Write down (below) what the Lord is saying to you today
4. Live with this Word in your heart through the day

_____

_____

Tuesday, April 23, 2024
Saint George, Martyr; Saint Adalbert, Bishop and Martyr

First Reading: Acts 11: 19-26

19 They therefore who were scattered abroad by the oppression that arose about Stephen traveled as far as Phoenicia, Cyprus, and Antioch, speaking the word to no one except to Jews only. 20 But there were some of them, men of Cyprus and Cyrene, who, when they had come

to Antioch, spoke to the Hellenists,‡ preaching the Lord Jesus. 21 The hand of the Lord was with them, and a great number believed and turned to the Lord. 22 The report concerning them came to the ears of the assembly which was in Jerusalem. They sent out Barnabas to go as far as Antioch, 23 who, when he had come, and had seen the grace of God, was glad. He exhorted them all, that with purpose of heart they should remain near to the Lord. 24 For he was a good man, and full of the Holy Spirit and of faith, and many people were added to the Lord.

25 Barnabas went out to Tarsus to look for Saul. 26 When he had found him, he brought him to Antioch. For a whole year they were gathered together with the assembly, and taught many people. The disciples were first called Christians in Antioch.

Responsorial Psalm: Psalms 87: 1-7

1 His foundation is in the holy mountains.
2 Yahweh loves the gates of Zion more than all the dwellings of Jacob.
3 Glorious things are spoken about you, city of God.
4 I will record Rahab† and Babylon among those who acknowledge me.
Behold, Philistia, Tyre, and also Ethiopia:
"This one was born there."
5 Yes, of Zion it will be said, "This one and that one was born in her;"
the Most High himself will establish her.
6 Yahweh will count, when he writes up the peoples,
"This one was born there."
7 Those who sing as well as those who dance say,
"All my springs are in you."

Gospel: John 10: 22-30

22 It was the Feast of the Dedication† at Jerusalem. 23 It was winter, and Jesus was walking in the temple, in Solomon's porch. 24 The Jews therefore came around him and said to him, "How long will you hold us in suspense? If you are the Christ, tell us plainly."
25 Jesus answered them, "I told you, and you don't believe. The works that I do in my Father's name, these testify about me. 26 But you don't believe, because you are not of my sheep, as I told you. 27 My sheep hear my voice, and I know them, and they follow me. 28 I give eternal life to them. They will never perish, and no one will snatch them out of my hand. 29 My Father who has given them to me is greater than all. No one is able to snatch them out of my Father's hand. 30 I and the Father are one."

1. Invite the Holy Spirit into this reading, asking the Author of Scripture to speak to you through His Word
2. Read today's passage as many times as you need, take your time
3. Write down (below) what the Lord is saying to you today
4. Live with this Word in your heart through the day

Wednesday, April 24, 2024
Saint Fidelis of Sigmaringen, Priest and Martyr

First Reading: Acts 12: 24 – 13: 5

24 But the word of God grew and multiplied. 25 Barnabas and Saul returned to† Jerusalem when they had fulfilled their service, also taking with them John who was called Mark.
1 Now in the assembly that was at Antioch there were some prophets and teachers: Barnabas, Simeon who was called Niger, Lucius of Cyrene, Manaen the foster brother of Herod the tetrarch, and Saul. 2 As they served the Lord and fasted, the Holy Spirit said, "Separate Barnabas and Saul for me, for the work to which I have called them."
3 Then, when they had fasted and prayed and laid their hands on them, they sent them away.
4 So, being sent out by the Holy Spirit, they went down to Seleucia. From there they sailed to Cyprus. 5 When they were at Salamis, they proclaimed God's word in the Jewish synagogues. They also had John as their attendant.

Responsorial Psalm: Psalms 67: 2-3, 5- 7

2 That your way may be known on earth,
and your salvation among all nations,
3 let the peoples praise you, God.
Let all the peoples praise you.
5 Let the peoples praise you, God.
Let all the peoples praise you.
6 The earth has yielded its increase.
God, even our own God, will bless us.
7 God will bless us.
All the ends of the earth shall fear him.

Gospel: John 12: 44-50

44 Jesus cried out and said, "Whoever believes in me, believes not in me, but in him who sent me. 45 He who sees me sees him who sent me. 46 I have come as a light into the world, that whoever believes in me may not remain in the darkness. 47 If anyone listens to my sayings and doesn't believe, I don't judge him. For I came not to judge the world, but to save the world. 48 He who rejects me, and doesn't receive my sayings, has one who judges him. The word that I spoke will judge him in the last day. 49 For I spoke not from myself, but the Father who

sent me gave me a commandment, what I should say and what I should speak. 50 I know that his commandment is eternal life. The things therefore which I speak, even as the Father has said to me, so I speak."

Thursday, April 25, 2024
Saint Mark, Evangelist

First Reading: First Peter 5: 5b-14

5b Yes, all of you clothe yourselves with humility and subject yourselves to one another; for "God resists the proud, but gives grace to the humble."* 6 Humble yourselves therefore under the mighty hand of God, that he may exalt you in due time, 7 casting all your worries on him, because he cares for you.

8 Be sober and self-controlled. Be watchful. Your adversary, the devil, walks around like a roaring lion, seeking whom he may devour. 9 Withstand him steadfast in your faith, knowing that your brothers who are in the world are undergoing the same sufferings. 10 But may the God of all grace, who called you to his eternal glory by Christ Jesus, after you have suffered a little while, perfect, establish, strengthen, and settle you. 11 To him be the glory and the power forever and ever. Amen.

12 Through Silvanus, our faithful brother, as I consider him, I have written to you briefly, exhorting and testifying that this is the true grace of God in which you stand. 13 She who is in Babylon, chosen together with you, greets you. So does Mark, my son. 14 Greet one another with a kiss of love.

Peace be to all of you who are in Christ Jesus. Amen.

Responsorial Psalm: Psalms 89: 2-3, 6-7, 16-17

2 I indeed declare, "Love stands firm forever.
You established the heavens.
Your faithfulness is in them."
3 "I have made a covenant with my chosen one,
I have sworn to David, my servant,

6 For who in the skies can be compared to Yahweh?
Who among the sons of the heavenly beings is like Yahweh,
7 a very awesome God in the council of the holy ones,
to be feared above all those who are around him?
16 In your name they rejoice all day.
In your righteousness, they are exalted.
17 For you are the glory of their strength.
In your favor, our horn will be exalted.

Gospel: Mark 16: 15-20

15 He said to them, "Go into all the world and preach the Good News to the whole creation. 16 He who believes and is baptized will be saved; but he who disbelieves will be condemned. 17 These signs will accompany those who believe: in my name they will cast out demons; they will speak with new languages; 18 they will take up serpents; and if they drink any deadly thing, it will in no way hurt them; they will lay hands on the sick, and they will recover."
19 So then the Lord,† after he had spoken to them, was received up into heaven and sat down at the right hand of God. 20 They went out and preached everywhere, the Lord working with them and confirming the word by the signs that followed. Amen.

1. Invite the Holy Spirit into this reading, asking the Author of Scripture to speak to you through His Word
2. Read today's passage as many times as you need, take your time
3. Write down (below) what the Lord is saying to you today
4. Live with this Word in your heart through the day

_____

_____

Friday, April 26, 2024

First Reading: Acts 13: 26-33

26 "Brothers, children of the stock of Abraham, and those among you who fear God, the word of this salvation is sent out to you. 27 For those who dwell in Jerusalem, and their rulers, because they didn't know him, nor the voices of the prophets which are read every Sabbath, fulfilled them by condemning him. 28 Though they found no cause for death, they still asked Pilate to have him killed. 29 When they had fulfilled all things that were written about him, they took him down from the tree and laid him in a tomb. 30 But God raised him from the dead, 31 and he was seen for many days by those who came up with him from Galilee to

Jerusalem, who are his witnesses to the people. 32 We bring you good news of the promise made to the fathers, 33 that God has fulfilled this to us, their children, in that he raised up Jesus. As it is also written in the second psalm,
'You are my Son.
Today I have become your father.'

Responsorial Psalm: Psalms 2: 6-11ab

6 "Yet I have set my King on my holy hill of Zion."
7 I will tell of the decree:
Yahweh said to me, "You are my son.
Today I have become your father.
8 Ask of me, and I will give the nations for your inheritance,
the uttermost parts of the earth for your possession.
9 You shall break them with a rod of iron.
You shall dash them in pieces like a potter's vessel."
10 Now therefore be wise, you kings.
Be instructed, you judges of the earth.
11 Serve Yahweh with fear,
and rejoice with trembling.

Gospel: John 14: 1-6

1 "Don't let your heart be troubled. Believe in God. Believe also in me. 2 In my Father's house are many homes. If it weren't so, I would have told you. I am going to prepare a place for you. 3 If I go and prepare a place for you, I will come again and will receive you to myself; that where I am, you may be there also. 4 You know where I go, and you know the way."
5 Thomas said to him, "Lord, we don't know where you are going. How can we know the way?"
6 Jesus said to him, "I am the way, the truth, and the life. No one comes to the Father, except through me.

1. Invite the Holy Spirit into this reading, asking the Author of Scripture to speak to you through His Word
2. Read today's passage as many times as you need, take your time
3. Write down (below) what the Lord is saying to you today
4. Live with this Word in your heart through the day

Saturday, April 27, 2024

First Reading: Acts 13: 44-52

44 The next Sabbath, almost the whole city was gathered together to hear the word of God. 45 But when the Jews saw the multitudes, they were filled with jealousy, and contradicted the things which were spoken by Paul, and blasphemed.

46 Paul and Barnabas spoke out boldly, and said, "It was necessary that God's word should be spoken to you first. Since indeed you thrust it from yourselves, and judge yourselves unworthy of eternal life, behold, we turn to the Gentiles. 47 For so has the Lord commanded us, saying,
'I have set you as a light for the Gentiles,
that you should bring salvation to the uttermost parts of the earth.' "

48 As the Gentiles heard this, they were glad and glorified the word of God. As many as were appointed to eternal life believed. 49 The Lord's word was spread abroad throughout all the region. 50 But the Jews stirred up the devout and prominent women and the chief men of the city, and stirred up a persecution against Paul and Barnabas, and threw them out of their borders. 51 But they shook off the dust of their feet against them, and came to Iconium. 52 The disciples were filled with joy and with the Holy Spirit.

Responsorial Psalm: Psalms 98: 1-4

1 Sing to Yahweh a new song,
for he has done marvelous things!
His right hand and his holy arm have worked salvation for him.
2 Yahweh has made known his salvation.
He has openly shown his righteousness in the sight of the nations.
3 He has remembered his loving kindness and his faithfulness toward the house of Israel.
All the ends of the earth have seen the salvation of our God.
4 Make a joyful noise to Yahweh, all the earth!
Burst out and sing for joy, yes, sing praises!

Gospel: John 14: 7-14

7 If you had known me, you would have known my Father also. From now on, you know him and have seen him."
8 Philip said to him, "Lord, show us the Father, and that will be enough for us."
9 Jesus said to him, "Have I been with you such a long time, and do you not know me, Philip? He who has seen me has seen the Father. How do you say, 'Show us the Father'? 10 Don't you believe that I am in the Father, and the Father in me? The words that I tell you, I speak not from myself; but the Father who lives in me does his works. 11 Believe me that I am in the Father, and the Father in me; or else believe me for the very works' sake. 12 Most certainly I tell you, he who believes in me, the works that I do, he will do also; and he will do greater works than these, because I am going to my Father. 13 Whatever you will ask in my name, I

will do it, that the Father may be glorified in the Son. 14 If you will ask anything in my name, I will do it.

1. Invite the Holy Spirit into this reading, asking the Author of Scripture to speak to you through His Word
2. Read today's passage as many times as you need, take your time
3. Write down (below) what the Lord is saying to you today
4. Live with this Word in your heart through the day

_____

_____

Sunday, April 28, 2024
FIFTH SUNDAY OF EASTER

First Reading: Acts 9: 26-31

26 When Saul had come to Jerusalem, he tried to join himself to the disciples; but they were all afraid of him, not believing that he was a disciple. 27 But Barnabas took him and brought him to the apostles, and declared to them how he had seen the Lord on the way, and that he had spoken to him, and how at Damascus he had preached boldly in the name of Jesus. 28 He was with them entering into† Jerusalem, 29 preaching boldly in the name of the Lord Jesus.‡ He spoke and disputed against the Hellenists,§ but they were seeking to kill him. 30 When the brothers† knew it, they brought him down to Caesarea and sent him off to Tarsus.
31 So the assemblies throughout all Judea, Galilee, and Samaria had peace and were built up. They were multiplied, walking in the fear of the Lord and in the comfort of the Holy Spirit.

Responsorial Psalm: Psalms 22: 26-28, 30-31

26 The humble shall eat and be satisfied.
They shall praise Yahweh who seek after him.
Let your hearts live forever.
27 All the ends of the earth shall remember and turn to Yahweh.
All the relatives of the nations shall worship before you.
28 For the kingdom is Yahweh's.
He is the ruler over the nations.
30 Posterity shall serve him.
Future generations shall be told about the Lord.
31 They shall come and shall declare his righteousness to a people that shall be born,
for he has done it.

Second Reading: First John 3: 18-24

18 My little children, let's not love in word only, or with the tongue only, but in deed and truth. 19 And by this we know that we are of the truth and persuade our hearts before him, 20 because if our heart condemns us, God is greater than our heart, and knows all things. 21 Beloved, if our hearts don't condemn us, we have boldness toward God; 22 so whatever we ask, we receive from him, because we keep his commandments and do the things that are pleasing in his sight. 23 This is his commandment, that we should believe in the name of his Son, Jesus Christ, and love one another, even as he commanded. 24 He who keeps his commandments remains in him, and he in him. By this we know that he remains in us, by the Spirit which he gave us.

Gospel: John 15: 1-8

1 "I am the true vine, and my Father is the farmer. 2 Every branch in me that doesn't bear fruit, he takes away. Every branch that bears fruit, he prunes, that it may bear more fruit. 3 You are already pruned clean because of the word which I have spoken to you. 4 Remain in me, and I in you. As the branch can't bear fruit by itself unless it remains in the vine, so neither can you, unless you remain in me. 5 I am the vine. You are the branches. He who remains in me and I in him bears much fruit, for apart from me you can do nothing. 6 If a man doesn't remain in me, he is thrown out as a branch and is withered; and they gather them, throw them into the fire, and they are burned. 7 If you remain in me, and my words remain in you, you will ask whatever you desire, and it will be done for you.
8 "In this my Father is glorified, that you bear much fruit; and so you will be my disciples.

1. Invite the Holy Spirit into this reading, asking the Author of Scripture to speak to you through His Word
2. Read today's passage as many times as you need, take your time
3. Write down (below) what the Lord is saying to you today
4. Live with this Word in your heart through the day

_____

_____

Monday, April 29, 2024
Saint Catherine of Siena, Virgin and Doctor of the Church

First Reading: Acts 14: 5-18

5 When some of both the Gentiles and the Jews, with their rulers, made a violent attempt to mistreat and stone them, 6 they became aware of it and fled to the cities of Lycaonia, Lystra, Derbe, and the surrounding region. 7 There they preached the Good News.

8 At Lystra a certain man sat, impotent in his feet, a cripple from his mother's womb, who never had walked. 9 He was listening to Paul speaking, who, fastening eyes on him and seeing that he had faith to be made whole, 10 said with a loud voice, "Stand upright on your feet!" He leaped up and walked. 11 When the multitude saw what Paul had done, they lifted up their voice, saying in the language of Lycaonia, "The gods have come down to us in the likeness of men!" 12 They called Barnabas "Jupiter", and Paul "Mercury", because he was the chief speaker. 13 The priest of Jupiter, whose temple was in front of their city, brought oxen and garlands to the gates, and would have made a sacrifice along with the multitudes.

14 But when the apostles, Barnabas and Paul, heard of it, they tore their clothes and sprang into the multitude, crying out, 15 "Men, why are you doing these things? We also are men of the same nature as you, and bring you good news, that you should turn from these vain things to the living God, who made the sky, the earth, the sea, and all that is in them; 16 who in the generations gone by allowed all the nations to walk in their own ways. 17 Yet he didn't leave himself without witness, in that he did good and gave you‡ rains from the sky and fruitful seasons, filling our hearts with food and gladness."

18 Even saying these things, they hardly stopped the multitudes from making a sacrifice to them.

Responsorial Psalm: Psalms 115: 1-4, 15-16

1 Not to us, Yahweh, not to us,
but to your name give glory,
for your loving kindness, and for your truth's sake.
2 Why should the nations say,
"Where is their God, now?"
3 But our God is in the heavens.
He does whatever he pleases.
4 Their idols are silver and gold,
the work of men's hands.
15 Blessed are you by Yahweh,
who made heaven and earth.
16 The heavens are Yahweh's heavens,
but he has given the earth to the children of men.

Gospel: John 14: 21-26

21 One who has my commandments and keeps them, that person is one who loves me. One who loves me will be loved by my Father, and I will love him, and will reveal myself to him."
22 Judas (not Iscariot) said to him, "Lord, what has happened that you are about to reveal yourself to us, and not to the world?"

23 Jesus answered him, "If a man loves me, he will keep my word. My Father will love him, and we will come to him and make our home with him. 24 He who doesn't love me doesn't keep my words. The word which you hear isn't mine, but the Father's who sent me.
25 "I have said these things to you while still living with you. 26 But the Counselor, the Holy Spirit, whom the Father will send in my name, will teach you all things, and will remind you of all that I said to you.

1. Invite the Holy Spirit into this reading, asking the Author of Scripture to speak to you through His Word
2. Read today's passage as many times as you need, take your time
3. Write down (below) what the Lord is saying to you today
4. Live with this Word in your heart through the day

Tuesday, April 30, 2024
Saint Pius V, Pope

First Reading: Acts 14: 19-28

19 But some Jews from Antioch and Iconium came there, and having persuaded the multitudes, they stoned Paul and dragged him out of the city, supposing that he was dead.
20 But as the disciples stood around him, he rose up, and entered into the city. On the next day he went out with Barnabas to Derbe.
21 When they had preached the Good News to that city and had made many disciples, they returned to Lystra, Iconium, and Antioch, 22 strengthening the souls of the disciples, exhorting them to continue in the faith, and that through many afflictions we must enter into God's Kingdom. 23 When they had appointed elders for them in every assembly, and had prayed with fasting, they commended them to the Lord on whom they had believed.
24 They passed through Pisidia and came to Pamphylia. 25 When they had spoken the word in Perga, they went down to Attalia. 26 From there they sailed to Antioch, from where they had been committed to the grace of God for the work which they had fulfilled. 27 When they had arrived and had gathered the assembly together, they reported all the things that God had done with them, and that he had opened a door of faith to the nations. 28 They stayed there with the disciples for a long time.

Responsorial Psalm: Psalms 145: 10-13ab, 21

10 All your works will give thanks to you, Yahweh.

Your saints will extol you.
11 They will speak of the glory of your kingdom,
and talk about your power,
12 to make known to the sons of men his mighty acts,
the glory of the majesty of his kingdom.
13 Your kingdom is an everlasting kingdom.
Your dominion endures throughout all generations.
21 My mouth will speak the praise of Yahweh.
Let all flesh bless his holy name forever and ever.

Gospel: John 14: 27-31a

27 Peace I leave with you. My peace I give to you; not as the world gives, I give to you. Don't let your heart be troubled, neither let it be fearful. 28 You heard how I told you, 'I am going away, and I will come back to you.' If you loved me, you would have rejoiced because I said 'I am going to my Father;' for the Father is greater than I. 29 Now I have told you before it happens so that when it happens, you may believe. 30 I will no more speak much with you, for the prince of the world comes, and he has nothing in me. 31 But that the world may know that I love the Father, and as the Father commanded me, even so I do.

1. Invite the Holy Spirit into this reading, asking the Author of Scripture to speak to you through His Word
2. Read today's passage as many times as you need, take your time
3. Write down (below) what the Lord is saying to you today
4. Live with this Word in your heart through the day

Wednesday, May 1, 2024
Saint Joseph the Worker

First Reading: Acts 15: 1-6

1 Some men came down from Judea and taught the brothers,† "Unless you are circumcised after the custom of Moses, you can't be saved." 2 Therefore when Paul and Barnabas had no small discord and discussion with them, they appointed Paul, Barnabas, and some others of them to go up to Jerusalem to the apostles and elders about this question. 3 They, being sent on their way by the assembly, passed through both Phoenicia and Samaria, declaring the conversion of the Gentiles. They caused great joy to all the brothers. 4 When they had come

to Jerusalem, they were received by the assembly and the apostles and the elders, and they reported everything that God had done with them.

5 But some of the sect of the Pharisees who believed rose up, saying, "It is necessary to circumcise them, and to command them to keep the law of Moses."

6 The apostles and the elders were gathered together to see about this matter.

Responsorial Psalm: Psalms 122: 1-5

1 I was glad when they said to me,
"Let's go to Yahweh's house!"
2 Our feet are standing within your gates, Jerusalem!
3 Jerusalem is built as a city that is compact together,
4 where the tribes go up, even Yah's tribes,
according to an ordinance for Israel,
to give thanks to Yahweh's name.
5 For there are set thrones for judgment,
the thrones of David's house.

Gospel: Matthew 13: 54-58

54 Coming into his own country, he taught them in their synagogue, so that they were astonished and said, "Where did this man get this wisdom and these mighty works? 55 Isn't this the carpenter's son? Isn't his mother called Mary, and his brothers James, Joses, Simon, and Judas?† 56 Aren't all of his sisters with us? Where then did this man get all of these things?" 57 They were offended by him.

But Jesus said to them, "A prophet is not without honor, except in his own country and in his own house." 58 He didn't do many mighty works there because of their unbelief.

1. Invite the Holy Spirit into this reading, asking the Author of Scripture to speak to you through His Word
2. Read today's passage as many times as you need, take your time
3. Write down (below) what the Lord is saying to you today
4. Live with this Word in your heart through the day

_____

_____

Thursday, May 2, 2024
Saint Athanasius, Bishop and Doctor of the Church

First Reading: Acts 15: 7-21

7 When there had been much discussion, Peter rose up and said to them, "Brothers, you know that a good while ago God made a choice among you that by my mouth the nations should hear the word of the Good News and believe. 8 God, who knows the heart, testified about them, giving them the Holy Spirit, just like he did to us. 9 He made no distinction between us and them, cleansing their hearts by faith. 10 Now therefore why do you tempt God, that you should put a yoke on the neck of the disciples which neither our fathers nor we were able to bear? 11 But we believe that we are saved through the grace of the Lord Jesus,‡ just as they are."

12 All the multitude kept silence, and they listened to Barnabas and Paul reporting what signs and wonders God had done among the nations through them. 13 After they were silent, James answered, "Brothers, listen to me. 14 Simeon has reported how God first visited the nations to take out of them a people for his name. 15 This agrees with the words of the prophets. As it is written,

16 'After these things I will return.

I will again build the tabernacle of David, which has fallen.

I will again build its ruins.

I will set it up 17 that the rest of men may seek after the Lord:

all the Gentiles who are called by my name,

says the Lord, who does all these things.'*

18 "All of God's works are known to him from eternity. 19 Therefore my judgment is that we don't trouble those from among the Gentiles who turn to God, 20 but that we write to them that they abstain from the pollution of idols, from sexual immorality, from what is strangled, and from blood. 21 For Moses from generations of old has in every city those who preach him, being read in the synagogues every Sabbath."

Responsorial Psalm: Psalms 96: 1-3, 10

1 Sing to Yahweh a new song!

Sing to Yahweh, all the earth.

2 Sing to Yahweh!

Bless his name!

Proclaim his salvation from day to day!

3 Declare his glory among the nations,

his marvelous works among all the peoples.

10 Say among the nations, "Yahweh reigns."

The world is also established.

It can't be moved.

He will judge the peoples with equity.

Gospel: John 15: 9-11

9 Even as the Father has loved me, I also have loved you. Remain in my love. 10 If you keep my commandments, you will remain in my love, even as I have kept my Father's commandments and remain in his love. 11 I have spoken these things to you, that my joy may remain in you, and that your joy may be made full.

1. Invite the Holy Spirit into this reading, asking the Author of Scripture to speak to you through His Word
2. Read today's passage as many times as you need, take your time
3. Write down (below) what the Lord is saying to you today
4. Live with this Word in your heart through the day

_____

_____

Friday, May 3, 2024
Saints Philip and James, Apostles

First Reading: First Corinthians 15: 1-8

1 Now I declare to you, brothers, the Good News which I preached to you, which also you received, in which you also stand, 2 by which also you are saved, if you hold firmly the word which I preached to you—unless you believed in vain.
3 For I delivered to you first of all that which I also received: that Christ died for our sins according to the Scriptures, 4 that he was buried, that he was raised on the third day according to the Scriptures, 5 and that he appeared to Cephas, then to the twelve. 6 Then he appeared to over five hundred brothers at once, most of whom remain until now, but some have also fallen asleep. 7 Then he appeared to James, then to all the apostles, 8 and last of all, as to the child born at the wrong time, he appeared to me also.

Responsorial Psalm: Psalms 19: 2-5

2 Day after day they pour out speech,
and night after night they display knowledge.
3 There is no speech nor language
where their voice is not heard.
4 Their voice has gone out through all the earth,
their words to the end of the world.
In them he has set a tent for the sun,
5 which is as a bridegroom coming out of his room,
like a strong man rejoicing to run his course.

Gospel: John 14: 6-14

6 Jesus said to him, "I am the way, the truth, and the life. No one comes to the Father, except through me. 7 If you had known me, you would have known my Father also. From now on, you know him and have seen him."

8 Philip said to him, "Lord, show us the Father, and that will be enough for us."

9 Jesus said to him, "Have I been with you such a long time, and do you not know me, Philip? He who has seen me has seen the Father. How do you say, 'Show us the Father'? 10 Don't you believe that I am in the Father, and the Father in me? The words that I tell you, I speak not from myself; but the Father who lives in me does his works. 11 Believe me that I am in the Father, and the Father in me; or else believe me for the very works' sake. 12 Most certainly I tell you, he who believes in me, the works that I do, he will do also; and he will do greater works than these, because I am going to my Father. 13 Whatever you will ask in my name, I will do it, that the Father may be glorified in the Son. 14 If you will ask anything in my name, I will do it.

1. Invite the Holy Spirit into this reading, asking the Author of Scripture to speak to you through His Word
2. Read today's passage as many times as you need, take your time
3. Write down (below) what the Lord is saying to you today
4. Live with this Word in your heart through the day

_____

_____

Saturday, May 4, 2024

First Reading: Acts 16: 1-10

1 He came to Derbe and Lystra; and behold, a certain disciple was there, named Timothy, the son of a Jewess who believed, but his father was a Greek. 2 The brothers who were at Lystra and Iconium gave a good testimony about him. 3 Paul wanted to have him go out with him, and he took and circumcised him because of the Jews who were in those parts, for they all knew that his father was a Greek. 4 As they went on their way through the cities, they delivered the decrees to them to keep which had been ordained by the apostles and elders who were at Jerusalem. 5 So the assemblies were strengthened in the faith, and increased in number daily. 6 When they had gone through the region of Phrygia and Galatia, they were forbidden by the Holy Spirit to speak the word in Asia. 7 When they had come opposite Mysia, they tried to go into Bithynia, but the Spirit didn't allow them. 8 Passing by Mysia, they came down to Troas. 9 A vision appeared to Paul in the night. There was a man of Macedonia standing, begging him and saying, "Come over into Macedonia and help us." 10 When he had seen the vision,

immediately we sought to go out to Macedonia, concluding that the Lord had called us to preach the Good News to them.

Responsorial Psalm: Psalms 100: 2, 3, 5

2 Serve Yahweh with gladness.
Come before his presence with singing.
3 Know that Yahweh, he is God.
It is he who has made us, and we are his.
We are his people, and the sheep of his pasture.
5 For Yahweh is good.
His loving kindness endures forever,
his faithfulness to all generations.

Gospel: John 15: 18-21

18 If the world hates you, you know that it has hated me before it hated you. 19 If you were of the world, the world would love its own. But because you are not of the world, since I chose you out of the world, therefore the world hates you. 20 Remember the word that I said to you: 'A servant is not greater than his lord.'* If they persecuted me, they will also persecute you. If they kept my word, they will also keep yours. 21 But they will do all these things to you for my name's sake, because they don't know him who sent me.

1. Invite the Holy Spirit into this reading, asking the Author of Scripture to speak to you through His Word
2. Read today's passage as many times as you need, take your time
3. Write down (below) what the Lord is saying to you today
4. Live with this Word in your heart through the day

_____

_____

Sunday, May 5, 2024
SIXTH SUNDAY OF EASTER

First Reading: Acts 10: 25-26, 34-35, 44-48

25 When Peter entered, Cornelius met him, fell down at his feet, and worshiped him. 26 But Peter raised him up, saying, "Stand up! I myself am also a man."

34 Peter opened his mouth and said, "Truly I perceive that God doesn't show favoritism; 35 but in every nation he who fears him and works righteousness is acceptable to him.

44 While Peter was still speaking these words, the Holy Spirit fell on all those who heard the word. 45 They of the circumcision who believed were amazed, as many as came with Peter, because the gift of the Holy Spirit was also poured out on the Gentiles. 46 For they heard them speaking in other languages and magnifying God.

Then Peter answered, 47 "Can anyone forbid these people from being baptized with water? They have received the Holy Spirit just like us." 48 He commanded them to be baptized in the name of Jesus Christ. Then they asked him to stay some days.

Responsorial Psalm: Psalms 98: 1-4

1 Sing to Yahweh a new song,
for he has done marvelous things!
His right hand and his holy arm have worked salvation for him.
2 Yahweh has made known his salvation.
He has openly shown his righteousness in the sight of the nations.
3 He has remembered his loving kindness and his faithfulness toward the house of Israel.
All the ends of the earth have seen the salvation of our God.
4 Make a joyful noise to Yahweh, all the earth!
Burst out and sing for joy, yes, sing praises!

Second Reading: First John 4: 7-10

7 Beloved, let's love one another, for love is of God; and everyone who loves has been born of God and knows God. 8 He who doesn't love doesn't know God, for God is love. 9 By this God's love was revealed in us, that God has sent his only born† Son into the world that we might live through him. 10 In this is love, not that we loved God, but that he loved us, and sent his Son as the atoning sacrifice‡ for our sins.

Gospel: John 15: 9-17

9 Even as the Father has loved me, I also have loved you. Remain in my love. 10 If you keep my commandments, you will remain in my love, even as I have kept my Father's commandments and remain in his love. 11 I have spoken these things to you, that my joy may remain in you, and that your joy may be made full.

12 "This is my commandment, that you love one another, even as I have loved you. 13 Greater love has no one than this, that someone lay down his life for his friends. 14 You are my friends if you do whatever I command you. 15 No longer do I call you servants, for the servant doesn't know what his lord does. But I have called you friends, for everything that I heard from my Father, I have made known to you. 16 You didn't choose me, but I chose you and appointed you, that you should go and bear fruit, and that your fruit should remain; that whatever you will ask of the Father in my name, he may give it to you.

17 "I command these things to you, that you may love one another.

Monday, May 6, 2024

First Reading: Acts 16: 11-15

11 Setting sail therefore from Troas, we made a straight course to Samothrace, and the day following to Neapolis; 12 and from there to Philippi, which is a city of Macedonia, the foremost of the district, a Roman colony. We were staying some days in this city.
13 On the Sabbath day we went outside of the city by a riverside, where we supposed there was a place of prayer, and we sat down and spoke to the women who had come together. 14 A certain woman named Lydia, a seller of purple, of the city of Thyatira, one who worshiped God, heard us. The Lord opened her heart to listen to the things which were spoken by Paul. 15 When she and her household were baptized, she begged us, saying, "If you have judged me to be faithful to the Lord, come into my house and stay." So she persuaded us.

Responsorial Psalm: Psalms 149: 1b-6a and 9b

1b Sing to Yahweh a new song,
his praise in the assembly of the saints.
2 Let Israel rejoice in him who made them.
Let the children of Zion be joyful in their King.
3 Let them praise his name in the dance!
Let them sing praises to him with tambourine and harp!
4 For Yahweh takes pleasure in his people.
He crowns the humble with salvation.
5 Let the saints rejoice in honor.
Let them sing for joy on their beds.
6 May the high praises of God be in their mouths,
9b All his saints have this honor.
Praise Yah!

Gospel: John 15: 26 – 16: 4

26 "When the Counselor† has come, whom I will send to you from the Father, the Spirit of truth, who proceeds from the Father, he will testify about me. 27 You will also testify, because you have been with me from the beginning.

1 "I have said these things to you so that you wouldn't be caused to stumble. 2 They will put you out of the synagogues. Yes, the time is coming that whoever kills you will think that he offers service to God. 3 They will do these things† because they have not known the Father nor me. 4 But I have told you these things so that when the time comes, you may remember that I told you about them. I didn't tell you these things from the beginning, because I was with you.

1. Invite the Holy Spirit into this reading, asking the Author of Scripture to speak to you through His Word
2. Read today's passage as many times as you need, take your time
3. Write down (below) what the Lord is saying to you today
4. Live with this Word in your heart through the day

Tuesday, May 7, 2024

First Reading: Acts 16: 22-34

22 The multitude rose up together against them and the magistrates tore their clothes from them, then commanded them to be beaten with rods. 23 When they had laid many stripes on them, they threw them into prison, charging the jailer to keep them safely. 24 Having received such a command, he threw them into the inner prison and secured their feet in the stocks.

25 But about midnight Paul and Silas were praying and singing hymns to God, and the prisoners were listening to them. 26 Suddenly there was a great earthquake, so that the foundations of the prison were shaken; and immediately all the doors were opened, and everyone's bonds were loosened. 27 The jailer, being roused out of sleep and seeing the prison doors open, drew his sword and was about to kill himself, supposing that the prisoners had escaped. 28 But Paul cried with a loud voice, saying, "Don't harm yourself, for we are all here!" 29 He called for lights, sprang in, fell down trembling before Paul and Silas, 30 brought them out, and said, "Sirs, what must I do to be saved?"

31 They said, "Believe in the Lord Jesus Christ, and you will be saved, you and your household." 32 They spoke the word of the Lord to him, and to all who were in his house.

33 He took them the same hour of the night and washed their stripes, and was immediately baptized, he and all his household. 34 He brought them up into his house and set food before them, and rejoiced greatly with all his household, having believed in God.

Responsorial Psalm: Psalms 138: 1-3, 7c-8

1 I will give you thanks with my whole heart.
Before the gods,† I will sing praises to you.
2 I will bow down toward your holy temple,
and give thanks to your Name for your loving kindness and for your truth;
for you have exalted your Name and your Word above all.
3 In the day that I called, you answered me.
You encouraged me with strength in my soul.
7c Your right hand will save me.
8 Yahweh will fulfill that which concerns me.
Your loving kindness, Yahweh, endures forever.
Don't forsake the works of your own hands.

Gospel: John 16: 5-11

5 But now I am going to him who sent me, and none of you asks me, 'Where are you going?' 6 But because I have told you these things, sorrow has filled your heart. 7 Nevertheless I tell you the truth: It is to your advantage that I go away; for if I don't go away, the Counselor won't come to you. But if I go, I will send him to you. 8 When he has come, he will convict the world about sin, about righteousness, and about judgment; 9 about sin, because they don't believe in me; 10 about righteousness, because I am going to my Father, and you won't see me any more; 11 about judgment, because the prince of this world has been judged.

1. Invite the Holy Spirit into this reading, asking the Author of Scripture to speak to you through His Word
2. Read today's passage as many times as you need, take your time
3. Write down (below) what the Lord is saying to you today
4. Live with this Word in your heart through the day

_____

_____

Wednesday, May 8, 2024

First Reading: Acts 17: 15, 22 – 18: 1

15 But those who escorted Paul brought him as far as Athens. Receiving a commandment to Silas and Timothy that they should come to him very quickly, they departed.

22 Paul stood in the middle of the Areopagus and said, "You men of Athens, I perceive that you are very religious in all things. 23 For as I passed along and observed the objects of your worship, I also found an altar with this inscription: 'TO AN UNKNOWN GOD.' What therefore you worship in ignorance, I announce to you. 24 The God who made the world and all things in it, he, being Lord of heaven and earth, doesn't dwell in temples made with hands. 25 He isn't served by men's hands, as though he needed anything, seeing he himself gives to all life and breath and all things. 26 He made from one blood every nation of men to dwell on all the surface of the earth, having determined appointed seasons and the boundaries of their dwellings, 27 that they should seek the Lord, if perhaps they might reach out for him and find him, though he is not far from each one of us. 28 'For in him we live, move, and have our being.' As some of your own poets have said, 'For we are also his offspring.' 29 Being then the offspring of God, we ought not to think that the Divine Nature is like gold, or silver, or stone, engraved by art and design of man. 30 The times of ignorance therefore God overlooked. But now he commands that all people everywhere should repent, 31 because he has appointed a day in which he will judge the world in righteousness by the man whom he has ordained; of which he has given assurance to all men, in that he has raised him from the dead."

32 Now when they heard of the resurrection of the dead, some mocked; but others said, "We want to hear you again concerning this."

33 Thus Paul went out from among them. 34 But certain men joined with him and believed, including Dionysius the Areopagite, and a woman named Damaris, and others with them.

1 After these things Paul departed from Athens and came to Corinth.

Responsorial Psalm: Psalms 148: 1-2, 11-14

1 Praise Yah!
Praise Yahweh from the heavens!
Praise him in the heights!
2 Praise him, all his angels!
Praise him, all his army!
11 kings of the earth and all peoples,
princes and all judges of the earth,
12 both young men and maidens,
old men and children.
13 Let them praise Yahweh's name,
for his name alone is exalted.
His glory is above the earth and the heavens.
14 He has lifted up the horn of his people,
the praise of all his saints,
even of the children of Israel, a people near to him.
Praise Yah!

Gospel: John 16: 12-15

12 "I still have many things to tell you, but you can't bear them now. 13 However, when he, the Spirit of truth, has come, he will guide you into all truth, for he will not speak from himself; but whatever he hears, he will speak. He will declare to you things that are coming. 14 He will glorify me, for he will take from what is mine and will declare it to you. 15 All things that the Father has are mine; therefore I said that he takes‡ of mine and will declare it to you.

1. Invite the Holy Spirit into this reading, asking the Author of Scripture to speak to you through His Word
2. Read today's passage as many times as you need, take your time
3. Write down (below) what the Lord is saying to you today
4. Live with this Word in your heart through the day

Thursday, May 9, 2024

First Reading: Acts 18: 1-8

1 After these things Paul departed from Athens and came to Corinth. 2 He found a certain Jew named Aquila, a man of Pontus by race, who had recently come from Italy with his wife Priscilla, because Claudius had commanded all the Jews to depart from Rome. He came to them, 3 and because he practiced the same trade, he lived with them and worked, for by trade they were tent makers. 4 He reasoned in the synagogue every Sabbath and persuaded Jews and Greeks.
5 When Silas and Timothy came down from Macedonia, Paul was compelled by the Spirit, testifying to the Jews that Jesus was the Christ. 6 When they opposed him and blasphemed, he shook out his clothing and said to them, "Your blood be on your own heads! I am clean. From now on, I will go to the Gentiles!"
7 He departed there and went into the house of a certain man named Justus, one who worshiped God, whose house was next door to the synagogue. 8 Crispus, the ruler of the synagogue, believed in the Lord with all his house. Many of the Corinthians, when they heard, believed and were baptized.

Responsorial Psalm: Psalms 98: 1-4

1 Sing to Yahweh a new song,

for he has done marvelous things!
His right hand and his holy arm have worked salvation for him.
2 Yahweh has made known his salvation.
He has openly shown his righteousness in the sight of the nations.
3 He has remembered his loving kindness and his faithfulness toward the house of Israel.
All the ends of the earth have seen the salvation of our God.
4 Make a joyful noise to Yahweh, all the earth!
Burst out and sing for joy, yes, sing praises!

Gospel: John 16: 16-20

16 "A little while, and you will not see me. Again a little while, and you will see me."
17 Some of his disciples therefore said to one another, "What is this that he says to us, 'A little while, and you won't see me, and again a little while, and you will see me;' and, 'Because I go to the Father'?" 18 They said therefore, "What is this that he says, 'A little while'? We don't know what he is saying."
19 Therefore Jesus perceived that they wanted to ask him, and he said to them, "Do you inquire among yourselves concerning this, that I said, 'A little while, and you won't see me, and again a little while, and you will see me'? 20 Most certainly I tell you that you will weep and lament, but the world will rejoice. You will be sorrowful, but your sorrow will be turned into joy.

1. Invite the Holy Spirit into this reading, asking the Author of Scripture to speak to you through His Word
2. Read today's passage as many times as you need, take your time
3. Write down (below) what the Lord is saying to you today
4. Live with this Word in your heart through the day

_____

_____

Friday, May 10, 2024
Saint John of Avila, Priest and Doctor of the Church;
USA: Saint Damien de Veuster, Priest

First Reading: Acts 18: 9-18

9 The Lord said to Paul in the night by a vision, "Don't be afraid, but speak and don't be silent;
10 for I am with you, and no one will attack you to harm you, for I have many people in this city."

11 He lived there a year and six months, teaching the word of God among them. 12 But when Gallio was proconsul of Achaia, the Jews with one accord rose up against Paul and brought him before the judgment seat, 13 saying, "This man persuades men to worship God contrary to the law."

14 But when Paul was about to open his mouth, Gallio said to the Jews, "If indeed it were a matter of wrong or of wicked crime, you Jews, it would be reasonable that I should bear with you; 15 but if they are questions about words and names and your own law, look to it yourselves. For I don't want to be a judge of these matters." 16 So he drove them from the judgment seat.

17 Then all the Greeks seized Sosthenes, the ruler of the synagogue, and beat him before the judgment seat. Gallio didn't care about any of these things.

18 Paul, having stayed after this many more days, took his leave of the brothers,† and sailed from there for Syria, together with Priscilla and Aquila. He shaved his head in Cenchreae, for he had a vow.

Responsorial Psalm: Psalms 47: 2-7

2 For Yahweh Most High is awesome.
He is a great King over all the earth.
3 He subdues nations under us,
and peoples under our feet.
4 He chooses our inheritance for us,
the glory of Jacob whom he loved.
5 God has gone up with a shout,
Yahweh with the sound of a trumpet.
6 Sing praises to God! Sing praises!
Sing praises to our King! Sing praises!
7 For God is the King of all the earth.
Sing praises with understanding.

Gospel: John 16: 20-23

20 Most certainly I tell you that you will weep and lament, but the world will rejoice. You will be sorrowful, but your sorrow will be turned into joy. 21 A woman, when she gives birth, has sorrow because her time has come. But when she has delivered the child, she doesn't remember the anguish any more, for the joy that a human being is born into the world. 22 Therefore you now have sorrow, but I will see you again, and your heart will rejoice, and no one will take your joy away from you.

23 "In that day you will ask me no questions. Most certainly I tell you, whatever you may ask of the Father in my name, he will give it to you.

1. Invite the Holy Spirit into this reading, asking the Author of Scripture to speak to you through His Word

2. Read today's passage as many times as you need, take your time
3. Write down (below) what the Lord is saying to you today
4. Live with this Word in your heart through the day

Saturday, May 11, 2024

First Reading: Acts 18: 23-28

23 Having spent some time there, he departed and went through the region of Galatia and Phrygia, in order, establishing all the disciples. 24 Now a certain Jew named Apollos, an Alexandrian by race, an eloquent man, came to Ephesus. He was mighty in the Scriptures. 25 This man had been instructed in the way of the Lord; and being fervent in spirit, he spoke and taught accurately the things concerning Jesus, although he knew only the baptism of John. 26 He began to speak boldly in the synagogue. But when Priscilla and Aquila heard him, they took him aside, and explained to him the way of God more accurately.
27 When he had determined to pass over into Achaia, the brothers encouraged him; and wrote to the disciples to receive him. When he had come, he greatly helped those who had believed through grace; 28 for he powerfully refuted the Jews, publicly showing by the Scriptures that Jesus was the Christ.

Responsorial Psalm: Psalms 47: 2-3, 8-9

2 For Yahweh Most High is awesome.
He is a great King over all the earth.
3 He subdues nations under us,
and peoples under our feet.
8 God reigns over the nations.
God sits on his holy throne.
9 The princes of the peoples are gathered together,
the people of the God of Abraham.
For the shields of the earth belong to God.
He is greatly exalted!

Gospel: John 16: 23b-28

23b Most certainly I tell you, whatever you may ask of the Father in my name, he will give it to you. 24 Until now, you have asked nothing in my name. Ask, and you will receive, that your joy may be made full.

25 "I have spoken these things to you in figures of speech. But the time is coming when I will no more speak to you in figures of speech, but will tell you plainly about the Father. 26 In that day you will ask in my name; and I don't say to you that I will pray to the Father for you, 27 for the Father himself loves you, because you have loved me, and have believed that I came from God. 28 I came from the Father and have come into the world. Again, I leave the world and go to the Father."

1. Invite the Holy Spirit into this reading, asking the Author of Scripture to speak to you through His Word
2. Read today's passage as many times as you need, take your time
3. Write down (below) what the Lord is saying to you today
4. Live with this Word in your heart through the day

_____

_____

Sunday, May 12, 2024
Ascension of the Lord Solemnity (Seventh Sunday of Easter)

First Reading: Acts 1: 1-11

1 The first book I wrote, Theophilus, concerned all that Jesus began both to do and to teach, 2 until the day in which he was received up, after he had given commandment through the Holy Spirit to the apostles whom he had chosen. 3 To these he also showed himself alive after he suffered, by many proofs, appearing to them over a period of forty days and speaking about God's Kingdom. 4 Being assembled together with them, he commanded them, "Don't depart from Jerusalem, but wait for the promise of the Father, which you heard from me. 5 For John indeed baptized in water, but you will be baptized in the Holy Spirit not many days from now."
6 Therefore, when they had come together, they asked him, "Lord, are you now restoring the kingdom to Israel?"
7 He said to them, "It isn't for you to know times or seasons which the Father has set within his own authority. 8 But you will receive power when the Holy Spirit has come upon you. You will be witnesses to me in Jerusalem, in all Judea and Samaria, and to the uttermost parts of the earth."
9 When he had said these things, as they were looking, he was taken up, and a cloud received him out of their sight. 10 While they were looking steadfastly into the sky as he went, behold,† two men stood by them in white clothing, 11 who also said, "You men of Galilee, why do you stand looking into the sky? This Jesus, who was received up from you into the sky, will come back in the same way as you saw him going into the sky."

Responsorial Psalm: Psalms 47: 2-3, 6-9

2 For Yahweh Most High is awesome.
He is a great King over all the earth.
3 He subdues nations under us,
and peoples under our feet.
6 Sing praises to God! Sing praises!
Sing praises to our King! Sing praises!
7 For God is the King of all the earth.
Sing praises with understanding.
8 God reigns over the nations.
God sits on his holy throne.
9 The princes of the peoples are gathered together,
the people of the God of Abraham.
For the shields of the earth belong to God.
He is greatly exalted!

Second Reading: Ephesians 4: 1-13

1 I therefore, the prisoner in the Lord, beg you to walk worthily of the calling with which you were called, 2 with all lowliness and humility, with patience, bearing with one another in love, 3 being eager to keep the unity of the Spirit in the bond of peace. 4 There is one body and one Spirit, even as you also were called in one hope of your calling, 5 one Lord, one faith, one baptism, 6 one God and Father of all, who is over all and through all and in us all. 7 But to each one of us, the grace was given according to the measure of the gift of Christ. 8 Therefore he says,
"When he ascended on high,
he led captivity captive,
and gave gifts to people."*
9 Now this, "He ascended", what is it but that he also first descended into the lower parts of the earth? 10 He who descended is the one who also ascended far above all the heavens, that he might fill all things.
11 He gave some to be apostles; and some, prophets; and some, evangelists; and some, shepherds† and teachers; 12 for the perfecting of the saints, to the work of serving, to the building up of the body of Christ, 13 until we all attain to the unity of the faith and of the knowledge of the Son of God, to a full grown man, to the measure of the stature of the fullness of Christ

Gospel: Mark 16: 15-20

15 He said to them, "Go into all the world and preach the Good News to the whole creation. 16 He who believes and is baptized will be saved; but he who disbelieves will be condemned. 17 These signs will accompany those who believe: in my name they will cast out demons; they

will speak with new languages; 18 they will take up serpents; and if they drink any deadly thing, it will in no way hurt them; they will lay hands on the sick, and they will recover."

19 So then the Lord,† after he had spoken to them, was received up into heaven and sat down at the right hand of God. 20 They went out and preached everywhere, the Lord working with them and confirming the word by the signs that followed. Amen.

1. Invite the Holy Spirit into this reading, asking the Author of Scripture to speak to you through His Word
2. Read today's passage as many times as you need, take your time
3. Write down (below) what the Lord is saying to you today
4. Live with this Word in your heart through the day

_____

_____

Monday, May 13, 2024
Our Lady of Fatima

First Reading: Acts 19: 1-8

1 While Apollos was at Corinth, Paul, having passed through the upper country, came to Ephesus and found certain disciples. 2 He said to them, "Did you receive the Holy Spirit when you believed?"
They said to him, "No, we haven't even heard that there is a Holy Spirit."
3 He said, "Into what then were you baptized?"
They said, "Into John's baptism."
4 Paul said, "John indeed baptized with the baptism of repentance, saying to the people that they should believe in the one who would come after him, that is, in Christ Jesus."†
5 When they heard this, they were baptized in the name of the Lord Jesus. 6 When Paul had laid his hands on them, the Holy Spirit came on them and they spoke with other languages and prophesied. 7 They were about twelve men in all.
8 He entered into the synagogue and spoke boldly for a period of three months, reasoning and persuading about the things concerning God's Kingdom.

Responsorial Psalm: Psalms 68: 2-7

2 As smoke is driven away,
so drive them away.
As wax melts before the fire,
so let the wicked perish at the presence of God.

3 But let the righteous be glad.
Let them rejoice before God.
Yes, let them rejoice with gladness.
4 Sing to God! Sing praises to his name!
Extol him who rides on the clouds:
to Yah, his name!
Rejoice before him!
5 A father of the fatherless, and a defender of the widows,
is God in his holy habitation.
6 God sets the lonely in families.
He brings out the prisoners with singing,
but the rebellious dwell in a sun-scorched land.
7 God, when you went out before your people,
when you marched through the wilderness...

Gospel: John 16: 29-33

29 His disciples said to him, "Behold, now you are speaking plainly, and using no figures of speech. 30 Now we know that you know all things, and don't need for anyone to question you. By this we believe that you came from God."
31 Jesus answered them, "Do you now believe? 32 Behold, the time is coming, yes, and has now come, that you will be scattered, everyone to his own place, and you will leave me alone. Yet I am not alone, because the Father is with me. 33 I have told you these things, that in me you may have peace. In the world you have trouble; but cheer up! I have overcome the world."

1. Invite the Holy Spirit into this reading, asking the Author of Scripture to speak to you through His Word
2. Read today's passage as many times as you need, take your time
3. Write down (below) what the Lord is saying to you today
4. Live with this Word in your heart through the day

_____

_____

Tuesday, May 14, 2024
Saint Matthias, Apostle

First Reading: Acts 1: 15-17, 20-26

15 In these days, Peter stood up in the middle of the disciples (and the number of names was about one hundred twenty), and said, 16 "Brothers, it was necessary that this Scripture should be fulfilled, which the Holy Spirit spoke before by the mouth of David concerning Judas, who was guide to those who took Jesus. 17 For he was counted with us, and received his portion in this ministry.

20 For it is written in the book of Psalms,

'Let his habitation be made desolate.

Let no one dwell in it;'

and,

'Let another take his office.'

21 "Of the men therefore who have accompanied us all the time that the Lord Jesus went in and out among us, 22 beginning from the baptism of John to the day that he was received up from us, of these one must become a witness with us of his resurrection."

23 They put forward two: Joseph called Barsabbas, who was also called Justus, and Matthias. 24 They prayed and said, "You, Lord, who know the hearts of all men, show which one of these two you have chosen 25 to take part in this ministry and apostleship from which Judas fell away, that he might go to his own place." 26 They drew lots for them, and the lot fell on Matthias; and he was counted with the eleven apostles.

Responsorial Psalm: Psalms 113: 1-8

1 Praise Yah!

Praise, you servants of Yahweh,

praise Yahweh's name.

2 Blessed be Yahweh's name,

from this time forward and forever more.

3 From the rising of the sun to its going down,

Yahweh's name is to be praised.

4 Yahweh is high above all nations,

his glory above the heavens.

5 Who is like Yahweh, our God,

who has his seat on high,

6 who stoops down to see in heaven and in the earth?

7 He raises up the poor out of the dust,

and lifts up the needy from the ash heap,

8 that he may set him with princes,

even with the princes of his people.

Gospel: John 15: 9-17

9 Even as the Father has loved me, I also have loved you. Remain in my love. 10 If you keep my commandments, you will remain in my love, even as I have kept my Father's

commandments and remain in his love. 11 I have spoken these things to you, that my joy may remain in you, and that your joy may be made full.

12 "This is my commandment, that you love one another, even as I have loved you. 13 Greater love has no one than this, that someone lay down his life for his friends. 14 You are my friends if you do whatever I command you. 15 No longer do I call you servants, for the servant doesn't know what his lord does. But I have called you friends, for everything that I heard from my Father, I have made known to you. 16 You didn't choose me, but I chose you and appointed you, that you should go and bear fruit, and that your fruit should remain; that whatever you will ask of the Father in my name, he may give it to you.

17 "I command these things to you, that you may love one another.

1. Invite the Holy Spirit into this reading, asking the Author of Scripture to speak to you through His Word
2. Read today's passage as many times as you need, take your time
3. Write down (below) what the Lord is saying to you today
4. Live with this Word in your heart through the day

_____

_____

Wednesday, May 15, 2024
Saint Isidore

First Reading: Acts 20: 28-38

28 Take heed, therefore, to yourselves and to all the flock, in which the Holy Spirit has made you overseers, to shepherd the assembly of the Lord and§ God which he purchased with his own blood. 29 For I know that after my departure, vicious wolves will enter in among you, not sparing the flock. 30 Men will arise from among your own selves, speaking perverse things, to draw away the disciples after them. 31 Therefore watch, remembering that for a period of three years I didn't cease to admonish everyone night and day with tears. 32 Now, brothers,† I entrust you to God and to the word of his grace, which is able to build up and to give you the inheritance among all those who are sanctified. 33 I coveted no one's silver, gold, or clothing. 34 You yourselves know that these hands served my necessities, and those who were with me. 35 In all things I gave you an example, that so laboring you ought to help the weak, and to remember the words of the Lord Jesus, that he himself said, 'It is more blessed to give than to receive.' "

36 When he had spoken these things, he knelt down and prayed with them all. 37 They all wept freely, and fell on Paul's neck and kissed him, 38 sorrowing most of all because of the

word which he had spoken, that they should see his face no more. Then they accompanied him to the ship.

Responsorial Psalm: Psalms 68: 29-30, 33-35

29 Because of your temple at Jerusalem,
kings shall bring presents to you.
30 Rebuke the wild animal of the reeds,
the multitude of the bulls with the calves of the peoples.
Trample under foot the bars of silver.
Scatter the nations who delight in war.
33 to him who rides on the heaven of heavens, which are of old;
behold, he utters his voice, a mighty voice.
34 Ascribe strength to God!
His excellency is over Israel,
his strength is in the skies.
35 You are awesome, God, in your sanctuaries.
The God of Israel gives strength and power to his people.
Praise be to God!

Gospel: John 17: 11b-19

11b Holy Father, keep them through your name which you have given me, that they may be one, even as we are. 12 While I was with them in the world, I kept them in your name. I have kept those whom you have given me. None of them is lost except the son of destruction, that the Scripture might be fulfilled. 13 But now I come to you, and I say these things in the world, that they may have my joy made full in themselves. 14 I have given them your word. The world hated them because they are not of the world, even as I am not of the world. 15 I pray not that you would take them from the world, but that you would keep them from the evil one. 16 They are not of the world, even as I am not of the world. 17 Sanctify them in your truth. Your word is truth. 18 As you sent me into the world, even so I have sent them into the world. 19 For their sakes I sanctify myself, that they themselves also may be sanctified in truth.

1. Invite the Holy Spirit into this reading, asking the Author of Scripture to speak to you through His Word
2. Read today's passage as many times as you need, take your time
3. Write down (below) what the Lord is saying to you today
4. Live with this Word in your heart through the day

First Reading: Acts 22: 30; 23: 6-11

30 But on the next day, desiring to know the truth about why he was accused by the Jews, he freed him from the bonds and commanded the chief priests and all the council to come together, and brought Paul down and set him before them.

6 But when Paul perceived that the one part were Sadducees and the other Pharisees, he cried out in the council, "Men and brothers, I am a Pharisee, a son of Pharisees. Concerning the hope and resurrection of the dead I am being judged!"

7 When he had said this, an argument arose between the Pharisees and Sadducees, and the crowd was divided. 8 For the Sadducees say that there is no resurrection, nor angel, nor spirit; but the Pharisees confess all of these. 9 A great clamor arose, and some of the scribes of the Pharisees' part stood up, and contended, saying, "We find no evil in this man. But if a spirit or angel has spoken to him, let's not fight against God!"

10 When a great argument arose, the commanding officer, fearing that Paul would be torn in pieces by them, commanded the soldiers to go down and take him by force from among them and bring him into the barracks.

11 The following night, the Lord stood by him and said, "Cheer up, Paul, for as you have testified about me at Jerusalem, so you must testify also at Rome."

Responsorial Psalm: Psalms 16: 1-2a and 5, 7-11

1 Preserve me, God, for I take refuge in you.
2 My soul, you have said to Yahweh, "You are my Lord.
5 Yahweh assigned my portion and my cup.
You made my lot secure.
7 I will bless Yahweh, who has given me counsel.
Yes, my heart instructs me in the night seasons.
8 I have set Yahweh always before me.
Because he is at my right hand, I shall not be moved.
9 Therefore my heart is glad, and my tongue rejoices.
My body shall also dwell in safety.
10 For you will not leave my soul in Sheol,†
neither will you allow your holy one to see corruption.
11 You will show me the path of life.
In your presence is fullness of joy.
In your right hand there are pleasures forever more.

Gospel: John 17: 20-26

20 "Not for these only do I pray, but for those also who will believe in me through their word, 21 that they may all be one; even as you, Father, are in me, and I in you, that they also may be one in us; that the world may believe that you sent me. 22 The glory which you have given me, I have given to them, that they may be one, even as we are one, 23 I in them, and you in me, that they may be perfected into one, that the world may know that you sent me and loved them, even as you loved me. 24 Father, I desire that they also whom you have given me be with me where I am, that they may see my glory which you have given me, for you loved me before the foundation of the world. 25 Righteous Father, the world hasn't known you, but I knew you; and these knew that you sent me. 26 I made known to them your name, and will make it known; that the love with which you loved me may be in them, and I in them."

Friday, May 17, 2024

First Reading: Acts 25: 13-21

13 Now when some days had passed, King Agrippa and Bernice arrived at Caesarea and greeted Festus. 14 As he stayed there many days, Festus laid Paul's case before the king, saying, "There is a certain man left a prisoner by Felix; 15 about whom, when I was at Jerusalem, the chief priests and the elders of the Jews informed me, asking for a sentence against him. 16 I answered them that it is not the custom of the Romans to give up any man to destruction before the accused has met the accusers face to face and has had opportunity to make his defense concerning the matter laid against him. 17 When therefore they had come together here, I didn't delay, but on the next day sat on the judgment seat and commanded the man to be brought. 18 When the accusers stood up, they brought no charges against him of such things as I supposed; 19 but had certain questions against him about their own religion and about one Jesus, who was dead, whom Paul affirmed to be alive. 20 Being perplexed how to inquire concerning these things, I asked whether he was willing to go to Jerusalem and there be judged concerning these matters. 21 But when Paul had appealed to be kept for the decision of the emperor, I commanded him to be kept until I could send him to Caesar."

Responsorial Psalm: Psalms 103: 1-2, 11-12, 19-20ab

1 Praise Yahweh, my soul!

All that is within me, praise his holy name!

2 Praise Yahweh, my soul,

and don't forget all his benefits,

11 For as the heavens are high above the earth,

so great is his loving kindness toward those who fear him.

12 As far as the east is from the west,

so far has he removed our transgressions from us.

19 Yahweh has established his throne in the heavens.

His kingdom rules over all.

20 Praise Yahweh, you angels of his,

who are mighty in strength, who fulfill his word,

Gospel: John 21: 15-19

15 So when they had eaten their breakfast, Jesus said to Simon Peter, "Simon, son of Jonah, do you love me more than these?"

He said to him, "Yes, Lord; you know that I have affection for you."

He said to him, "Feed my lambs." 16 He said to him again a second time, "Simon, son of Jonah, do you love me?"

He said to him, "Yes, Lord; you know that I have affection for you."

He said to him, "Tend my sheep." 17 He said to him the third time, "Simon, son of Jonah, do you have affection for me?"

Peter was grieved because he asked him the third time, "Do you have affection for me?" He said to him, "Lord, you know everything. You know that I have affection for you."

Jesus said to him, "Feed my sheep. 18 Most certainly I tell you, when you were young, you dressed yourself and walked where you wanted to. But when you are old, you will stretch out your hands, and another will dress you and carry you where you don't want to go."

19 Now he said this, signifying by what kind of death he would glorify God. When he had said this, he said to him, "Follow me."

1. Invite the Holy Spirit into this reading, asking the Author of Scripture to speak to you through His Word

2. Read today's passage as many times as you need, take your time

3. Write down (below) what the Lord is saying to you today

4. Live with this Word in your heart through the day

Saturday, May 18, 2024
Saint John I, Pope and Martyr

First Reading: Acts 28: 16-20, 30-31

16 When we entered into Rome, the centurion delivered the prisoners to the captain of the guard, but Paul was allowed to stay by himself with the soldier who guarded him.
17 After three days Paul called together those who were the leaders of the Jews. When they had come together, he said to them, "I, brothers, though I had done nothing against the people or the customs of our fathers, still was delivered prisoner from Jerusalem into the hands of the Romans, 18 who, when they had examined me, desired to set me free, because there was no cause of death in me. 19 But when the Jews spoke against it, I was constrained to appeal to Caesar, not that I had anything about which to accuse my nation. 20 For this cause therefore I asked to see you and to speak with you. For because of the hope of Israel I am bound with this chain."
30 Paul stayed two whole years in his own rented house and received all who were coming to him, 31 preaching God's Kingdom and teaching the things concerning the Lord Jesus Christ with all boldness, without hindrance.

Responsorial Psalm: Psalms 11: 4, 5 and 7

4 Yahweh is in his holy temple.
Yahweh is on his throne in heaven.
His eyes observe.
His eyes examine the children of men.
5 Yahweh examines the righteous,
but his soul hates the wicked and him who loves violence.
7 For Yahweh is righteous.
He loves righteousness.
The upright shall see his face.

Gospel: John 21: 20-25

20 Then Peter, turning around, saw a disciple following. This was the disciple whom Jesus loved, the one who had also leaned on Jesus' breast at the supper and asked, "Lord, who is going to betray you?" 21 Peter, seeing him, said to Jesus, "Lord, what about this man?"
22 Jesus said to him, "If I desire that he stay until I come, what is that to you? You follow me."
23 This saying therefore went out among the brothers§ that this disciple wouldn't die. Yet Jesus didn't say to him that he wouldn't die, but, "If I desire that he stay until I come, what is that to you?"
24 This is the disciple who testifies about these things, and wrote these things. We know that his witness is true. 25 There are also many other things which Jesus did, which if they would

all be written, I suppose that even the world itself wouldn't have room for the books that would be written.

Sunday, May 19, 2024
PENTECOST SUNDAY

First Reading: Acts 2: 1-11

1 Now when the day of Pentecost had come, they were all with one accord in one place. 2 Suddenly there came from the sky a sound like the rushing of a mighty wind, and it filled all the house where they were sitting. 3 Tongues like fire appeared and were distributed to them, and one sat on each of them. 4 They were all filled with the Holy Spirit and began to speak with other languages, as the Spirit gave them the ability to speak.
5 Now there were dwelling in Jerusalem Jews, devout men, from every nation under the sky. 6 When this sound was heard, the multitude came together and were bewildered, because everyone heard them speaking in his own language. 7 They were all amazed and marveled, saying to one another, "Behold, aren't all these who speak Galileans? 8 How do we hear, everyone in our own native language? 9 Parthians, Medes, Elamites, and people from Mesopotamia, Judea, Cappadocia, Pontus, Asia, 10 Phrygia, Pamphylia, Egypt, the parts of Libya around Cyrene, visitors from Rome, both Jews and proselytes, 11 Cretans and Arabians—we hear them speaking in our languages the mighty works of God!"

Responsorial Psalm: Psalms 104: 1, 24, 29-31, 34

1 Bless Yahweh, my soul.
Yahweh, my God, you are very great.
You are clothed with honor and majesty.
24 Yahweh, how many are your works!
In wisdom, you have made them all.
The earth is full of your riches.
29 You hide your face; they are troubled.

You take away their breath; they die and return to the dust.
30 You send out your Spirit and they are created.
You renew the face of the ground.
31 Let Yahweh's glory endure forever.
Let Yahweh rejoice in his works.
34 Let my meditation be sweet to him.
I will rejoice in Yahweh.

Second Reading: First Corinthians 12: 3b-7, 12-13

3b No one can say, "Jesus is Lord," but by the Holy Spirit. 4 Now there are various kinds of gifts, but the same Spirit. 5 There are various kinds of service, and the same Lord. 6 There are various kinds of workings, but the same God who works all things in all. 7 But to each one is given the manifestation of the Spirit for the profit of all.
12 For as the body is one and has many members, and all the members of the body, being many, are one body; so also is Christ. 13 For in one Spirit we were all baptized into one body, whether Jews or Greeks, whether bond or free; and were all given to drink into one Spirit.

Gospel: John 20: 19-23

19 When therefore it was evening on that day, the first day of the week, and when the doors were locked where the disciples were assembled, for fear of the Jews, Jesus came and stood in the middle and said to them, "Peace be to you."
20 When he had said this, he showed them his hands and his side. The disciples therefore were glad when they saw the Lord. 21 Jesus therefore said to them again, "Peace be to you. As the Father has sent me, even so I send you." 22 When he had said this, he breathed on them, and said to them, "Receive the Holy Spirit! 23 If you forgive anyone's sins, they have been forgiven them. If you retain anyone's sins, they have been retained."

1. Invite the Holy Spirit into this reading, asking the Author of Scripture to speak to you through His Word
2. Read today's passage as many times as you need, take your time
3. Write down (below) what the Lord is saying to you today
4. Live with this Word in your heart through the day

_____

_____

Monday, May 20, 2024
The Blessed Virgin Mary, Mother of the Church

First Reading: Acts 1: 12-14

12 Then they returned to Jerusalem from the mountain called Olivet, which is near Jerusalem, a Sabbath day's journey away. 13 When they had come in, they went up into the upper room where they were staying, that is Peter, John, James, Andrew, Philip, Thomas, Bartholomew, Matthew, James the son of Alphaeus, Simon the Zealot, and Judas the son of James. 14 All these with one accord continued steadfastly in prayer and supplication, along with the women and Mary the mother of Jesus, and with his brothers.

Responsorial Psalm: Psalms 87: 1-3 and 5-7

1 His foundation is in the holy mountains.
2 Yahweh loves the gates of Zion more than all the dwellings of Jacob.
3 Glorious things are spoken about you, city of God.
5 Yes, of Zion it will be said, "This one and that one was born in her;"
the Most High himself will establish her.
6 Yahweh will count, when he writes up the peoples,
"This one was born there."
7 Those who sing as well as those who dance say,
"All my springs are in you."

Gospel: John 19: 25-34

25 But standing by Jesus' cross were his mother, his mother's sister, Mary the wife of Clopas, and Mary Magdalene. 26 Therefore when Jesus saw his mother, and the disciple whom he loved standing there, he said to his mother, "Woman, behold, your son!" 27 Then he said to the disciple, "Behold, your mother!" From that hour, the disciple took her to his own home. 28 After this, Jesus, seeing‡ that all things were now finished, that the Scripture might be fulfilled, said, "I am thirsty!" 29 Now a vessel full of vinegar was set there; so they put a sponge full of the vinegar on hyssop, and held it at his mouth. 30 When Jesus therefore had received the vinegar, he said, "It is finished!" Then he bowed his head and gave up his spirit. 31 Therefore the Jews, because it was the Preparation Day, so that the bodies wouldn't remain on the cross on the Sabbath (for that Sabbath was a special one), asked of Pilate that their legs might be broken and that they might be taken away. 32 Therefore the soldiers came and broke the legs of the first and of the other who was crucified with him; 33 but when they came to Jesus and saw that he was already dead, they didn't break his legs. 34 However, one of the soldiers pierced his side with a spear, and immediately blood and water came out.

1. Invite the Holy Spirit into this reading, asking the Author of Scripture to speak to you through His Word
2. Read today's passage as many times as you need, take your time
3. Write down (below) what the Lord is saying to you today

Tuesday, May 21, 2024
Saint Christopher Magallanes, Priest, and Companions, Martyrs

First Reading: James 4: 1-10

1 Where do wars and fightings among you come from? Don't they come from your pleasures that war in your members? 2 You lust, and don't have. You murder and covet, and can't obtain. You fight and make war. You don't have, because you don't ask. 3 You ask, and don't receive, because you ask with wrong motives, so that you may spend it on your pleasures. 4 You adulterers and adulteresses, don't you know that friendship with the world is hostility toward God? Whoever therefore wants to be a friend of the world makes himself an enemy of God. 5 Or do you think that the Scripture says in vain, "The Spirit who lives in us yearns jealously"? 6 But he gives more grace. Therefore it says, "God resists the proud, but gives grace to the humble."* 7 Be subject therefore to God. Resist the devil, and he will flee from you. 8 Draw near to God, and he will draw near to you. Cleanse your hands, you sinners. Purify your hearts, you double-minded. 9 Lament, mourn, and weep. Let your laughter be turned to mourning and your joy to gloom. 10 Humble yourselves in the sight of the Lord, and he will exalt you.

Responsorial Psalm: Psalms 55: 7-11a, 23

7 Behold, then I would wander far off.
I would lodge in the wilderness."
8 "I would hurry to a shelter from the stormy wind and storm."
9 Confuse them, Lord, and confound their language,
for I have seen violence and strife in the city.
10 Day and night they prowl around on its walls.
Malice and abuse are also within her.
11 Destructive forces are within her.
23 But you, God, will bring them down into the pit of destruction.
Bloodthirsty and deceitful men shall not live out half their days,
but I will trust in you.

Gospel: Mark 9: 30-37

30 They went out from there and passed through Galilee. He didn't want anyone to know it, 31 for he was teaching his disciples, and said to them, "The Son of Man is being handed over to the hands of men, and they will kill him; and when he is killed, on the third day he will rise again."

32 But they didn't understand the saying, and were afraid to ask him.

33 He came to Capernaum, and when he was in the house he asked them, "What were you arguing among yourselves on the way?"

34 But they were silent, for they had disputed with one another on the way about who was the greatest.

35 He sat down and called the twelve; and he said to them, "If any man wants to be first, he shall be last of all, and servant of all." 36 He took a little child and set him in the middle of them. Taking him in his arms, he said to them, 37 "Whoever receives one such little child in my name receives me; and whoever receives me, doesn't receive me, but him who sent me."

1. Invite the Holy Spirit into this reading, asking the Author of Scripture to speak to you through His Word
2. Read today's passage as many times as you need, take your time
3. Write down (below) what the Lord is saying to you today
4. Live with this Word in your heart through the day

Wednesday, May 22, 2024
Saint Rita of Cascia, Religious

First Reading: James 4: 13-17

13 Come now, you who say, "Today or tomorrow let's go into this city and spend a year there, trade, and make a profit." 14 Yet you don't know what your life will be like tomorrow. For what is your life? For you are a vapor that appears for a little time and then vanishes away. 15 For you ought to say, "If the Lord wills, we will both live, and do this or that." 16 But now you glory in your boasting. All such boasting is evil. 17 To him therefore who knows to do good and doesn't do it, to him it is sin.

Responsorial Psalm: Psalms 49: 2-3, 6-11

2 both low and high,
rich and poor together.
3 My mouth will speak words of wisdom.

My heart will utter understanding.
6 Those who trust in their wealth,
and boast in the multitude of their riches—
7 none of them can by any means redeem his brother,
nor give God a ransom for him.
8 For the redemption of their life is costly,
no payment is ever enough,
9 that he should live on forever,
that he should not see corruption.
10 For he sees that wise men die;
likewise the fool and the senseless perish,
and leave their wealth to others.
11 Their inward thought is that their houses will endure forever,
and their dwelling places to all generations.
They name their lands after themselves.

Gospel: Mark 9: 38-40

38 John said to him, "Teacher, we saw someone who doesn't follow us casting out demons in your name; and we forbade him, because he doesn't follow us."
39 But Jesus said, "Don't forbid him, for there is no one who will do a mighty work in my name and be able quickly to speak evil of me. 40 For whoever is not against us is on our side.

1. Invite the Holy Spirit into this reading, asking the Author of Scripture to speak to you through His Word
2. Read today's passage as many times as you need, take your time
3. Write down (below) what the Lord is saying to you today
4. Live with this Word in your heart through the day

_____

_____

Thursday, May 23, 2024

First Reading: James 5: 1-6

1 Come now, you rich, weep and howl for your miseries that are coming on you. 2 Your riches are corrupted and your garments are moth-eaten. 3 Your gold and your silver are corroded, and their corrosion will be for a testimony against you and will eat your flesh like fire. You have laid up your treasure in the last days. 4 Behold, the wages of the laborers who mowed your fields, which you have kept back by fraud, cry out; and the cries of those who reaped have

entered into the ears of the Lord of Armies.† 5 You have lived in luxury on the earth, and taken your pleasure. You have nourished your hearts as in a day of slaughter. 6 You have condemned and you have murdered the righteous one. He doesn't resist you.

Responsorial Psalm: Psalms 49: 14-20

14 They are appointed as a flock for Sheol.†
Death shall be their shepherd.
The upright shall have dominion over them in the morning.
Their beauty shall decay in Sheol,‡
far from their mansion.
15 But God will redeem my soul from the power of Sheol,§
for he will receive me.
16 Don't be afraid when a man is made rich,
when the glory of his house is increased;
17 for when he dies he will carry nothing away.
His glory won't descend after him.
18 Though while he lived he blessed his soul—
and men praise you when you do well for yourself—
19 he shall go to the generation of his fathers.
They shall never see the light.
20 A man who has riches without understanding,
is like the animals that perish.

Gospel: Mark 9: 41-50

41 For whoever will give you a cup of water to drink in my name because you are Christ's, most certainly I tell you, he will in no way lose his reward.
42 "Whoever will cause one of these little ones who believe in me to stumble, it would be better for him if he were thrown into the sea with a millstone hung around his neck. 43 If your hand causes you to stumble, cut it off. It is better for you to enter into life maimed, rather than having your two hands to go into Gehenna, † into the unquenchable fire, 44 'where their worm doesn't die, and the fire is not quenched.' *‡ 45 If your foot causes you to stumble, cut it off. It is better for you to enter into life lame, rather than having your two feet to be cast into Gehenna, § into the fire that will never be quenched— 46 'where their worm doesn't die, and the fire is not quenched.' † 47 If your eye causes you to stumble, throw it out. It is better for you to enter into God's Kingdom with one eye, rather than having two eyes to be cast into the Gehenna‡ of fire, 48 'where their worm doesn't die, and the fire is not quenched.' * 49 For everyone will be salted with fire, and every sacrifice will be seasoned with salt. 50 Salt is good, but if the salt has lost its saltiness, with what will you season it? Have salt in yourselves, and be at peace with one another."

1. Invite the Holy Spirit into this reading, asking the Author of Scripture to speak to you through His Word
2. Read today's passage as many times as you need, take your time
3. Write down (below) what the Lord is saying to you today
4. Live with this Word in your heart through the day

_____

_____

Friday, May 24, 2024

First Reading: James 5: 9-12

9 Don't grumble, brothers, against one another, so that you won't be judged. Behold, the judge stands at the door. 10 Take, brothers, for an example of suffering and of perseverance, the prophets who spoke in the name of the Lord. 11 Behold, we call them blessed who endured. You have heard of the perseverance of Job and have seen the Lord in the outcome, and how the Lord is full of compassion and mercy.
12 But above all things, my brothers, don't swear— not by heaven, or by the earth, or by any other oath; but let your "yes" be "yes", and your "no", "no", so that you don't fall into hypocrisy.

Responsorial Psalm: Psalms 103: 1-4, 8-9, 11-12

1 Praise Yahweh, my soul!
All that is within me, praise his holy name!
2 Praise Yahweh, my soul,
and don't forget all his benefits,
3 who forgives all your sins,
who heals all your diseases,
4 who redeems your life from destruction,
who crowns you with loving kindness and tender mercies,
8 Yahweh is merciful and gracious,
slow to anger, and abundant in loving kindness.
9 He will not always accuse;
neither will he stay angry forever.
11 For as the heavens are high above the earth,
so great is his loving kindness toward those who fear him.
12 As far as the east is from the west,
so far has he removed our transgressions from us.

Gospel: Mark 10: 1-12

1 He arose from there and came into the borders of Judea and beyond the Jordan. Multitudes came together to him again. As he usually did, he was again teaching them.

2 Pharisees came to him testing him, and asked him, "Is it lawful for a man to divorce his wife?"

3 He answered, "What did Moses command you?"

4 They said, "Moses allowed a certificate of divorce to be written, and to divorce her."

5 But Jesus said to them, "For your hardness of heart, he wrote you this commandment. 6 But from the beginning of the creation, God made them male and female.* 7 For this cause a man will leave his father and mother, and will join to his wife, 8 and the two will become one flesh,* so that they are no longer two, but one flesh. 9 What therefore God has joined together, let no man separate."

10 In the house, his disciples asked him again about the same matter. 11 He said to them, "Whoever divorces his wife and marries another commits adultery against her. 12 If a woman herself divorces her husband and marries another, she commits adultery."

1. Invite the Holy Spirit into this reading, asking the Author of Scripture to speak to you through His Word
2. Read today's passage as many times as you need, take your time
3. Write down (below) what the Lord is saying to you today
4. Live with this Word in your heart through the day

Saturday, May 25, 2024
Saint Bede the Venerable, Priest and Doctor of the Church;
Saint Gregory VII, Pope; Saint Mary Magdalene de' Pazzi, Virgin; BVM

First Reading: James 5: 13-20

13 Is any among you suffering? Let him pray. Is any cheerful? Let him sing praises. 14 Is any among you sick? Let him call for the elders of the assembly, and let them pray over him, anointing him with oil in the name of the Lord; 15 and the prayer of faith will heal him who is sick, and the Lord will raise him up. If he has committed sins, he will be forgiven. 16 Confess your sins to one another and pray for one another, that you may be healed. The insistent prayer of a righteous person is powerfully effective. 17 Elijah was a man with a nature like ours, and he prayed earnestly that it might not rain, and it didn't rain on the earth for three years and six months. 18 He prayed again, and the sky gave rain, and the earth produced its fruit.

19 Brothers, if any among you wanders from the truth and someone turns him back, 20 let him know that he who turns a sinner from the error of his way will save a soul from death and will cover a multitude of sins.

Responsorial Psalm: Psalms 141: 1-3 and 8

1 Yahweh, I have called on you.
Come to me quickly!
Listen to my voice when I call to you.
2 Let my prayer be set before you like incense;
the lifting up of my hands like the evening sacrifice.
3 Set a watch, Yahweh, before my mouth.
Keep the door of my lips.
8 For my eyes are on you, Yahweh, the Lord.
I take refuge in you.
Don't leave my soul destitute.

Gospel: Mark 10: 13-16

13 They were bringing to him little children, that he should touch them, but the disciples rebuked those who were bringing them. 14 But when Jesus saw it, he was moved with indignation and said to them, "Allow the little children to come to me! Don't forbid them, for God's Kingdom belongs to such as these. 15 Most certainly I tell you, whoever will not receive God's Kingdom like a little child, he will in no way enter into it." 16 He took them in his arms and blessed them, laying his hands on them.

1. Invite the Holy Spirit into this reading, asking the Author of Scripture to speak to you through His Word
2. Read today's passage as many times as you need, take your time
3. Write down (below) what the Lord is saying to you today
4. Live with this Word in your heart through the day

_____

_____

Sunday, May 26, 2024
THE MOST HOLY TRINITY

First Reading: Deuteronomy 4: 32-34, 39-40

32 For ask now of the days that are past, which were before you, since the day that God created man on the earth, and from the one end of the sky to the other, whether there has been anything as great as this thing is, or has been heard like it? 33 Did a people ever hear the voice of God speaking out of the middle of the fire, as you have heard, and live? 34 Or has God tried to go and take a nation for himself from among another nation, by trials, by signs, by wonders, by war, by a mighty hand, by an outstretched arm, and by great terrors, according to all that Yahweh your God did for you in Egypt before your eyes?

39 Know therefore today, and take it to heart, that Yahweh himself is God in heaven above and on the earth beneath. There is no one else. 40 You shall keep his statutes and his commandments which I command you today, that it may go well with you and with your children after you, and that you may prolong your days in the land which Yahweh your God gives you for all time.

Responsorial Psalm: Psalms 33: 4-6, 9, 18-20, 22

4 For Yahweh's word is right.
All his work is done in faithfulness.
5 He loves righteousness and justice.
The earth is full of the loving kindness of Yahweh.
6 By Yahweh's word, the heavens were made:
all their army by the breath of his mouth.
9 For he spoke, and it was done.
He commanded, and it stood firm.
18 Behold, Yahweh's eye is on those who fear him,
on those who hope in his loving kindness,
19 to deliver their soul from death,
to keep them alive in famine.
20 Our soul has waited for Yahweh.
He is our help and our shield.
22 Let your loving kindness be on us, Yahweh,
since we have hoped in you.

Second Reading: Romans 8: 14-17

14 For as many as are led by the Spirit of God, these are children of God. 15 For you didn't receive the spirit of bondage again to fear, but you received the Spirit of adoption, by whom we cry, "Abba!‡ Father!"

16 The Spirit himself testifies with our spirit that we are children of God; 17 and if children, then heirs—heirs of God and joint heirs with Christ, if indeed we suffer with him, that we may also be glorified with him.

Gospel: Matthew 28: 16-20

16 But the eleven disciples went into Galilee, to the mountain where Jesus had sent them. 17 When they saw him, they bowed down to him; but some doubted. 18 Jesus came to them and spoke to them, saying, "All authority has been given to me in heaven and on earth. 19 Go‡ and make disciples of all nations, baptizing them in the name of the Father and of the Son and of the Holy Spirit, 20 teaching them to observe all things that I commanded you. Behold, I am with you always, even to the end of the age." Amen.

1. Invite the Holy Spirit into this reading, asking the Author of Scripture to speak to you through His Word
2. Read today's passage as many times as you need, take your time
3. Write down (below) what the Lord is saying to you today
4. Live with this Word in your heart through the day

_____

_____

Monday, May 27, 2024
Saint Augustine of Canterbury, Bishop

First Reading: First Peter 1: 3-9

3 Blessed be the God and Father of our Lord Jesus Christ, who according to his great mercy caused us to be born again to a living hope through the resurrection of Jesus Christ from the dead, 4 to an incorruptible and undefiled inheritance that doesn't fade away, reserved in Heaven for you, 5 who by the power of God are guarded through faith for a salvation ready to be revealed in the last time. 6 In this you greatly rejoice, though now for a little while, if need be, you have been grieved in various trials, 7 that the proof of your faith, which is more precious than gold that perishes, even though it is tested by fire, may be found to result in praise, glory, and honor at the revelation of Jesus Christ— 8 whom, not having known, you love. In him, though now you don't see him, yet believing, you rejoice greatly with joy that is unspeakable and full of glory, 9 receiving the result of your faith, the salvation of your souls.

Responsorial Psalm: Psalms 111: 1-2, 5-6, 9 and 10c

1 Praise Yah!†
I will give thanks to Yahweh with my whole heart,
in the council of the upright, and in the congregation.
2 Yahweh's works are great,
pondered by all those who delight in them.
5 He has given food to those who fear him.

He always remembers his covenant.
6 He has shown his people the power of his works,
in giving them the heritage of the nations.
9 He has sent redemption to his people.
He has ordained his covenant forever.
His name is holy and awesome!
10c His praise endures forever!

Gospel: Mark 10: 17-27

17 As he was going out into the way, one ran to him, knelt before him, and asked him, "Good Teacher, what shall I do that I may inherit eternal life?"

18 Jesus said to him, "Why do you call me good? No one is good except one—God. 19 You know the commandments: 'Do not murder,' 'Do not commit adultery,' 'Do not steal,' 'Do not give false testimony,' 'Do not defraud,' 'Honor your father and mother.' "*

20 He said to him, "Teacher, I have observed all these things from my youth."

21 Jesus looking at him loved him, and said to him, "One thing you lack. Go, sell whatever you have and give to the poor, and you will have treasure in heaven; and come, follow me, taking up the cross."

22 But his face fell at that saying, and he went away sorrowful, for he was one who had great possessions.

23 Jesus looked around and said to his disciples, "How difficult it is for those who have riches to enter into God's Kingdom!"

24 The disciples were amazed at his words. But Jesus answered again, "Children, how hard it is for those who trust in riches to enter into God's Kingdom! 25 It is easier for a camel to go through a needle's eye than for a rich man to enter into God's Kingdom."

26 They were exceedingly astonished, saying to him, "Then who can be saved?"

27 Jesus, looking at them, said, "With men it is impossible, but not with God, for all things are possible with God."

1. Invite the Holy Spirit into this reading, asking the Author of Scripture to speak to you through His Word
2. Read today's passage as many times as you need, take your time
3. Write down (below) what the Lord is saying to you today
4. Live with this Word in your heart through the day

Tuesday, May 28, 2024

First Reading: First Peter 1: 10-16

10 Concerning this salvation, the prophets sought and searched diligently. They prophesied of the grace that would come to you, 11 searching for who or what kind of time the Spirit of Christ which was in them pointed to when he predicted the sufferings of Christ and the glories that would follow them. 12 To them it was revealed that they served not themselves, but you, in these things, which now have been announced to you through those who preached the Good News to you by the Holy Spirit sent out from heaven; which things angels desire to look into. 13 Therefore prepare your minds for action.‡ Be sober, and set your hope fully on the grace that will be brought to you at the revelation of Jesus Christ— 14 as children of obedience, not conforming yourselves according to your former lusts as in your ignorance, 15 but just as he who called you is holy, you yourselves also be holy in all of your behavior, 16 because it is written, "You shall be holy, for I am holy."

Responsorial Psalm: Psalms 98: 1-4

1 Sing to Yahweh a new song,
for he has done marvelous things!
His right hand and his holy arm have worked salvation for him.
2 Yahweh has made known his salvation.
He has openly shown his righteousness in the sight of the nations.
3 He has remembered his loving kindness and his faithfulness toward the house of Israel.
All the ends of the earth have seen the salvation of our God.
4 Make a joyful noise to Yahweh, all the earth!
Burst out and sing for joy, yes, sing praises!

Gospel: Mark 10: 28-31

28 Peter began to tell him, "Behold, we have left all and have followed you."
29 Jesus said, "Most certainly I tell you, there is no one who has left house, or brothers, or sisters, or father, or mother, or wife, or children, or land, for my sake, and for the sake of the Good News, 30 but he will receive one hundred times more now in this time: houses, brothers, sisters, mothers, children, and land, with persecutions; and in the age to come eternal life. 31 But many who are first will be last, and the last first."

1. Invite the Holy Spirit into this reading, asking the Author of Scripture to speak to you through His Word
2. Read today's passage as many times as you need, take your time
3. Write down (below) what the Lord is saying to you today
4. Live with this Word in your heart through the day

First Reading: First Peter 1: 18-25

18 knowing that you were redeemed, not with corruptible things like silver or gold, from the useless way of life handed down from your fathers, 19 but with precious blood, as of a lamb without blemish or spot, the blood of Christ, 20 who was foreknown indeed before the foundation of the world, but was revealed in this last age for your sake, 21 who through him are believers in God, who raised him from the dead and gave him glory, so that your faith and hope might be in God.

22 Seeing you have purified your souls in your obedience to the truth through the Spirit in sincere brotherly affection, love one another from the heart fervently, 23 having been born again, not of corruptible seed, but of incorruptible, through the word of God, which lives and remains forever. 24 For,

"All flesh is like grass,

and all of man's glory like the flower in the grass.

The grass withers, and its flower falls;

25 but the Lord's word endures forever."

This is the word of Good News which was preached to you.

Responsorial Psalm: Psalms 147: 12-15, 19-20

12 Praise Yahweh, Jerusalem!

Praise your God, Zion!

13 For he has strengthened the bars of your gates.

He has blessed your children within you.

14 He makes peace in your borders.

He fills you with the finest of the wheat.

15 He sends out his commandment to the earth.

His word runs very swiftly.

19 He shows his word to Jacob,

his statutes and his ordinances to Israel.

20 He has not done this for just any nation.

They don't know his ordinances.

Praise Yah!

Gospel: Mark 10: 32-45

32 They were on the way, going up to Jerusalem; and Jesus was going in front of them, and they were amazed; and those who followed were afraid. He again took the twelve, and began to tell them the things that were going to happen to him. 33 "Behold, we are going up to

Jerusalem. The Son of Man will be delivered to the chief priests and the scribes. They will condemn him to death, and will deliver him to the Gentiles. 34 They will mock him, spit on him, scourge him, and kill him. On the third day he will rise again."

35 James and John, the sons of Zebedee, came near to him, saying, "Teacher, we want you to do for us whatever we will ask."

36 He said to them, "What do you want me to do for you?"

37 They said to him, "Grant to us that we may sit, one at your right hand and one at your left hand, in your glory."

38 But Jesus said to them, "You don't know what you are asking. Are you able to drink the cup that I drink, and to be baptized with the baptism that I am baptized with?"

39 They said to him, "We are able."

Jesus said to them, "You shall indeed drink the cup that I drink, and you shall be baptized with the baptism that I am baptized with; 40 but to sit at my right hand and at my left hand is not mine to give, but for whom it has been prepared."

41 When the ten heard it, they began to be indignant toward James and John.

42 Jesus summoned them and said to them, "You know that they who are recognized as rulers over the nations lord it over them, and their great ones exercise authority over them. 43 But it shall not be so among you, but whoever wants to become great among you shall be your servant. 44 Whoever of you wants to become first among you shall be bondservant of all. 45 For the Son of Man also came not to be served but to serve, and to give his life as a ransom for many."

1. Invite the Holy Spirit into this reading, asking the Author of Scripture to speak to you through His Word
2. Read today's passage as many times as you need, take your time
3. Write down (below) what the Lord is saying to you today
4. Live with this Word in your heart through the day

_____

_____

Thursday, May 30, 2024

First Reading: First Peter 2: 2-5, 9-12

2 as newborn babies, long for the pure spiritual milk, that with it you may grow, 3 if indeed you have tasted that the Lord is gracious. 4 Come to him, a living stone, rejected indeed by men, but chosen by God, precious. 5 You also as living stones are built up as a spiritual house, to be a holy priesthood, to offer up spiritual sacrifices, acceptable to God through Jesus Christ.

9 But you are a chosen race, a royal priesthood, a holy nation, a people for God's own possession, that you may proclaim the excellence of him who called you out of darkness into his marvelous light. 10 In the past, you were not a people, but now are God's people, who had not obtained mercy, but now have obtained mercy.

11 Beloved, I beg you as foreigners and pilgrims to abstain from fleshly lusts which war against the soul, 12 having good behavior among the nations, so in that of which they speak against you as evildoers, they may see your good works and glorify God in the day of visitation.

Responsorial Psalm: Psalms 100: 2, 3, 4, 5

2 Serve Yahweh with gladness.
Come before his presence with singing.
3 Know that Yahweh, he is God.
It is he who has made us, and we are his.
We are his people, and the sheep of his pasture.
4 Enter into his gates with thanksgiving,
and into his courts with praise.
Give thanks to him, and bless his name.
5 For Yahweh is good.
His loving kindness endures forever,
his faithfulness to all generations.

Gospel: Mark 10: 46-52

46 They came to Jericho. As he went out from Jericho with his disciples and a great multitude, the son of Timaeus, Bartimaeus, a blind beggar, was sitting by the road. 47 When he heard that it was Jesus the Nazarene, he began to cry out and say, "Jesus, you son of David, have mercy on me!" 48 Many rebuked him, that he should be quiet, but he cried out much more, "You son of David, have mercy on me!"
49 Jesus stood still and said, "Call him."
They called the blind man, saying to him, "Cheer up! Get up. He is calling you!"
50 He, casting away his cloak, sprang up, and came to Jesus.
51 Jesus asked him, "What do you want me to do for you?"
The blind man said to him, "Rabboni,† that I may see again."
52 Jesus said to him, "Go your way. Your faith has made you well." Immediately he received his sight and followed Jesus on the way.

1. Invite the Holy Spirit into this reading, asking the Author of Scripture to speak to you through His Word
2. Read today's passage as many times as you need, take your time
3. Write down (below) what the Lord is saying to you today
4. Live with this Word in your heart through the day

Friday, May 31, 2024
The Visitation of the Blessed Virgin Mary

First Reading: Zephaniah 3: 14-18a

14 Sing, daughter of Zion! Shout, Israel! Be glad and rejoice with all your heart, daughter of Jerusalem. 15 Yahweh has taken away your judgments. He has thrown out your enemy. The King of Israel, Yahweh, is among you. You will not be afraid of evil any more. 16 In that day, it will be said to Jerusalem, "Don't be afraid, Zion. Don't let your hands be weak." 17 Yahweh, your God, is among you, a mighty one who will save. He will rejoice over you with joy. He will calm you in his love. He will rejoice over you with singing. 18 I will remove those who grieve about the appointed feasts from you.

Responsorial Psalm: Isaiah 12: 2-3, 4bcd, 5-6

2 Behold, God is my salvation. I will trust, and will not be afraid; for Yah, Yahweh, is my strength and song; and he has become my salvation." 3 Therefore with joy you will draw water out of the wells of salvation. 4b "Give thanks to Yahweh! Call on his name! Declare his doings among the peoples! Proclaim that his name is exalted! 5 Sing to Yahweh, for he has done excellent things! Let this be known in all the earth! 6 Cry aloud and shout, you inhabitant of Zion, for the Holy One of Israel is great among you!"

Gospel: Luke 1: 39-56

39 Mary arose in those days and went into the hill country with haste, into a city of Judah, 40 and entered into the house of Zacharias and greeted Elizabeth. 41 When Elizabeth heard Mary's greeting, the baby leaped in her womb; and Elizabeth was filled with the Holy Spirit. 42 She called out with a loud voice and said, "Blessed are you among women, and blessed is the fruit of your womb! 43 Why am I so favored, that the mother of my Lord should come to me? 44 For behold, when the voice of your greeting came into my ears, the baby leaped in my womb for joy! 45 Blessed is she who believed, for there will be a fulfillment of the things which have been spoken to her from the Lord!"
46 Mary said,
"My soul magnifies the Lord.
47 My spirit has rejoiced in God my Savior,
48 for he has looked at the humble state of his servant.

For behold, from now on, all generations will call me blessed.
49 For he who is mighty has done great things for me.
Holy is his name.
50 His mercy is for generations and generations on those who fear him.
51 He has shown strength with his arm.
He has scattered the proud in the imagination of their hearts.
52 He has put down princes from their thrones,
and has exalted the lowly.
53 He has filled the hungry with good things.
He has sent the rich away empty.
54 He has given help to Israel, his servant, that he might remember mercy,
55 as he spoke to our fathers,
to Abraham and his offspring§ forever."
56 Mary stayed with her about three months, and then returned to her house.

1. Invite the Holy Spirit into this reading, asking the Author of Scripture to speak to you through His Word
2. Read today's passage as many times as you need, take your time
3. Write down (below) what the Lord is saying to you today
4. Live with this Word in your heart through the day

_____

_____

Saturday, June 1, 2024
Saint Justin, Martyr

First Reading: Jude 1: 17, 20b-25

17 But you, beloved, remember the words which have been spoken before by the apostles of our Lord Jesus Christ.
20 But you, beloved, keep building up yourselves on your most holy faith, praying in the Holy Spirit. 21 Keep yourselves in God's love, looking for the mercy of our Lord Jesus Christ to eternal life. 22 On some have compassion, making a distinction, 23 and some save, snatching them out of the fire with fear, hating even the clothing stained by the flesh.
24 Now to him who is able to keep them† from stumbling, and to present you faultless before the presence of his glory in great joy, 25 to God our Savior, who alone is wise, be glory and majesty, dominion and power, both now and forever. Amen.

Responsorial Psalm: Psalms 63: 2-6

2 So I have seen you in the sanctuary,
watching your power and your glory.
3 Because your loving kindness is better than life,
my lips shall praise you.
4 So I will bless you while I live.
I will lift up my hands in your name.
5 My soul shall be satisfied as with the richest food.
My mouth shall praise you with joyful lips,
6 when I remember you on my bed,
and think about you in the night watches.

Gospel: Mark 11: 27-33

27 They came again to Jerusalem, and as he was walking in the temple, the chief priests, the scribes, and the elders came to him, 28 and they began saying to him, "By what authority do you do these things? Or who gave you this authority to do these things?"
29 Jesus said to them, "I will ask you one question. Answer me, and I will tell you by what authority I do these things. 30 The baptism of John—was it from heaven, or from men? Answer me."
31 They reasoned with themselves, saying, "If we should say, 'From heaven;' he will say, 'Why then did you not believe him?' 32 If we should say, 'From men' "—they feared the people, for all held John to really be a prophet. 33 They answered Jesus, "We don't know."
Jesus said to them, "Neither will I tell you by what authority I do these things."

1. Invite the Holy Spirit into this reading, asking the Author of Scripture to speak to you through His Word
2. Read today's passage as many times as you need, take your time
3. Write down (below) what the Lord is saying to you today
4. Live with this Word in your heart through the day

_____

_____

Sunday, June 2, 2024
THE MOST HOLY BODY AND BLOOD OF CHRIST
(Corpus Christi)

First Reading: Exodus 24: 3-8

3 Moses came and told the people all Yahweh's words, and all the ordinances; and all the people answered with one voice, and said, "All the words which Yahweh has spoken will we do."

4 Moses wrote all Yahweh's words, then rose up early in the morning and built an altar at the base of the mountain, with twelve pillars for the twelve tribes of Israel. 5 He sent young men of the children of Israel, who offered burnt offerings and sacrificed peace offerings of cattle to Yahweh. 6 Moses took half of the blood and put it in basins, and half of the blood he sprinkled on the altar. 7 He took the book of the covenant and read it in the hearing of the people, and they said, "We will do all that Yahweh has said, and be obedient."

8 Moses took the blood, and sprinkled it on the people, and said, "Look, this is the blood of the covenant, which Yahweh has made with you concerning all these words."

Responsorial Psalm: Psalms 116: 12-13, 15-18

12 What will I give to Yahweh for all his benefits toward me?
13 I will take the cup of salvation, and call on Yahweh's name.
15 Precious in Yahweh's sight is the death of his saints.
16 Yahweh, truly I am your servant.
I am your servant, the son of your servant girl.
You have freed me from my chains.
17 I will offer to you the sacrifice of thanksgiving,
and will call on Yahweh's name.
18 I will pay my vows to Yahweh,
yes, in the presence of all his people,

Second Reading: Hebrews 9: 11-15

11 But Christ having come as a high priest of the coming good things, through the greater and more perfect tabernacle, not made with hands, that is to say, not of this creation, 12 nor yet through the blood of goats and calves, but through his own blood, entered in once for all into the Holy Place, having obtained eternal redemption. 13 For if the blood of goats and bulls, and the ashes of a heifer sprinkling those who have been defiled, sanctify to the cleanness of the flesh, 14 how much more will the blood of Christ, who through the eternal Spirit offered himself without defect to God, cleanse your conscience from dead works to serve the living God? 15 For this reason he is the mediator of a new covenant, since a death has occurred for the redemption of the transgressions that were under the first covenant, that those who have been called may receive the promise of the eternal inheritance.

Gospel: Mark 14: 12-16, 22-26

12 On the first day of unleavened bread, when they sacrificed the Passover, his disciples asked him, "Where do you want us to go and prepare that you may eat the Passover?"

13 He sent two of his disciples and said to them, "Go into the city, and there a man carrying a pitcher of water will meet you. Follow him, 14 and wherever he enters in, tell the master of the house, 'The Teacher says, "Where is the guest room, where I may eat the Passover with my disciples?" ' 15 He will himself show you a large upper room furnished and ready. Get ready for us there."

16 His disciples went out, and came into the city, and found things as he had said to them, and they prepared the Passover.

22 As they were eating, Jesus took bread, and when he had blessed it, he broke it and gave to them, and said, "Take, eat. This is my body."

23 He took the cup, and when he had given thanks, he gave to them. They all drank of it. 24 He said to them, "This is my blood of the new covenant, which is poured out for many. 25 Most certainly I tell you, I will no more drink of the fruit of the vine until that day when I drink it anew in God's Kingdom." 26 When they had sung a hymn, they went out to the Mount of Olives.

1. Invite the Holy Spirit into this reading, asking the Author of Scripture to speak to you through His Word
2. Read today's passage as many times as you need, take your time
3. Write down (below) what the Lord is saying to you today
4. Live with this Word in your heart through the day

Monday, June 3, 2024
Saint Charles Lwanga and Companions, Martyrs

First Reading: Second Peter 1: 2-7

2 Grace to you and peace be multiplied in the knowledge of God and of Jesus our Lord, 3 seeing that his divine power has granted to us all things that pertain to life and godliness, through the knowledge of him who called us by his own glory and virtue, 4 by which he has granted to us his precious and exceedingly great promises; that through these you may become partakers of the divine nature, having escaped from the corruption that is in the world by lust. 5 Yes, and for this very cause adding on your part all diligence, in your faith supply moral excellence; and in moral excellence, knowledge; 6 and in knowledge, self-control; and in self-control, perseverance; and in perseverance, godliness; 7 and in godliness, brotherly affection; and in brotherly affection, love.

Responsorial Psalm: Psalms 91: 1-2, 14-16

1 He who dwells in the secret place of the Most High
will rest in the shadow of the Almighty.
2 I will say of Yahweh, "He is my refuge and my fortress;
my God, in whom I trust."
14 "Because he has set his love on me, therefore I will deliver him.
I will set him on high, because he has known my name.
15 He will call on me, and I will answer him.
I will be with him in trouble.
I will deliver him, and honor him.
16 I will satisfy him with long life,
and show him my salvation."

Gospel: Mark 12: 1-12

1 He began to speak to them in parables. "A man planted a vineyard, put a hedge around it, dug a pit for the wine press, built a tower, rented it out to a farmer, and went into another country. 2 When it was time, he sent a servant to the farmer to get from the farmer his share of the fruit of the vineyard. 3 They took him, beat him, and sent him away empty. 4 Again, he sent another servant to them; and they threw stones at him, wounded him in the head, and sent him away shamefully treated. 5 Again he sent another, and they killed him, and many others, beating some, and killing some. 6 Therefore still having one, his beloved son, he sent him last to them, saying, 'They will respect my son.' 7 But those farmers said among themselves, 'This is the heir. Come, let's kill him, and the inheritance will be ours.' 8 They took him, killed him, and cast him out of the vineyard. 9 What therefore will the lord of the vineyard do? He will come and destroy the farmers, and will give the vineyard to others. 10 Haven't you even read this Scripture:
'The stone which the builders rejected
was made the head of the corner.
11 This was from the Lord.
It is marvelous in our eyes'?"*
12 They tried to seize him, but they feared the multitude; for they perceived that he spoke the parable against them. They left him and went away.

1. Invite the Holy Spirit into this reading, asking the Author of Scripture to speak to you through His Word
2. Read today's passage as many times as you need, take your time
3. Write down (below) what the Lord is saying to you today
4. Live with this Word in your heart through the day

Tuesday, June 4, 2024

First Reading: Second Peter 3: 12-15a, 17-18

12 looking for and earnestly desiring the coming of the day of God, which will cause the burning heavens to be dissolved, and the elements will melt with fervent heat? 13 But, according to his promise, we look for new heavens and a new earth, in which righteousness dwells.
14 Therefore, beloved, seeing that you look for these things, be diligent to be found in peace, without defect and blameless in his sight. 15 Regard the patience of our Lord as salvation;
17 You therefore, beloved, knowing these things beforehand, beware, lest being carried away with the error of the wicked, you fall from your own steadfastness. 18 But grow in the grace and knowledge of our Lord and Savior Jesus Christ. To him be the glory both now and forever. Amen.

Responsorial Psalm: Psalms 90: 2-4, 10, 14 and 16

2 Before the mountains were born,
before you had formed the earth and the world,
even from everlasting to everlasting, you are God.
3 You turn man to destruction, saying,
"Return, you children of men."
4 For a thousand years in your sight are just like yesterday when it is past,
like a watch in the night.
10 The days of our years are seventy,
or even by reason of strength eighty years;
yet their pride is but labor and sorrow,
for it passes quickly, and we fly away.
14 Satisfy us in the morning with your loving kindness,
that we may rejoice and be glad all our days.
16 Let your work appear to your servants,
your glory to their children.

Gospel: Mark 12: 13-17

13 They sent some of the Pharisees and the Herodians to him, that they might trap him with words. 14 When they had come, they asked him, "Teacher, we know that you are honest, and don't defer to anyone; for you aren't partial to anyone, but truly teach the way of God. Is it lawful to pay taxes to Caesar, or not? 15 Shall we give, or shall we not give?"
But he, knowing their hypocrisy, said to them, "Why do you test me? Bring me a denarius, that I may see it."
16 They brought it.

He said to them, "Whose is this image and inscription?"

They said to him, "Caesar's."

17 Jesus answered them, "Render to Caesar the things that are Caesar's, and to God the things that are God's."

They marveled greatly at him.

1. Invite the Holy Spirit into this reading, asking the Author of Scripture to speak to you through His Word
2. Read today's passage as many times as you need, take your time
3. Write down (below) what the Lord is saying to you today
4. Live with this Word in your heart through the day

Wednesday, June 5, 2024
Saint Boniface, Bishop and Martyr

First Reading: Second Timothy 1: 1-3, 6-12

1 Paul, an apostle of Jesus Christ† through the will of God, according to the promise of the life which is in Christ Jesus, 2 to Timothy, my beloved child: Grace, mercy, and peace, from God the Father and Christ Jesus our Lord.

3 I thank God, whom I serve as my forefathers did, with a pure conscience. How unceasing is my memory of you in my petitions, night and day

6 For this cause, I remind you that you should stir up the gift of God which is in you through the laying on of my hands. 7 For God didn't give us a spirit of fear, but of power, love, and self-control. 8 Therefore don't be ashamed of the testimony of our Lord, nor of me his prisoner; but endure hardship for the Good News according to the power of God, 9 who saved us and called us with a holy calling, not according to our works, but according to his own purpose and grace, which was given to us in Christ Jesus before times eternal, 10 but has now been revealed by the appearing of our Savior, Christ Jesus, who abolished death, and brought life and immortality to light through the Good News. 11 For this I was appointed as a preacher, an apostle, and a teacher of the Gentiles. 12 For this cause I also suffer these things.

Yet I am not ashamed, for I know him whom I have believed, and I am persuaded that he is able to guard that which I have committed to him against that day.

Responsorial Psalm: Psalms 123: 1b-2

1 I lift up my eyes to you,

you who sit in the heavens.

2 Behold, as the eyes of servants look to the hand of their master,

as the eyes of a maid to the hand of her mistress,

so our eyes look to Yahweh, our God,

until he has mercy on us.

Gospel: Mark 12: 18-27

18 Some Sadducees, who say that there is no resurrection, came to him. They asked him, saying, 19 "Teacher, Moses wrote to us, 'If a man's brother dies and leaves a wife behind him, and leaves no children, that his brother should take his wife and raise up offspring for his brother.' 20 There were seven brothers. The first took a wife, and dying left no offspring. 21 The second took her, and died, leaving no children behind him. The third likewise; 22 and the seven took her and left no children. Last of all the woman also died. 23 In the resurrection, when they rise, whose wife will she be of them? For the seven had her as a wife."

24 Jesus answered them, "Isn't this because you are mistaken, not knowing the Scriptures nor the power of God? 25 For when they will rise from the dead, they neither marry nor are given in marriage, but are like angels in heaven. 26 But about the dead, that they are raised, haven't you read in the book of Moses about the Bush, how God spoke to him, saying, 'I am the God of Abraham, the God of Isaac, and the God of Jacob'?* 27 He is not the God of the dead, but of the living. You are therefore badly mistaken."

1. Invite the Holy Spirit into this reading, asking the Author of Scripture to speak to you through His Word
2. Read today's passage as many times as you need, take your time
3. Write down (below) what the Lord is saying to you today
4. Live with this Word in your heart through the day

Thursday, June 6, 2024
Saint Norbert, Bishop

First Reading: Second Timothy 2: 8-15

8 Remember Jesus Christ, risen from the dead, of the offspring† of David, according to my Good News, 9 in which I suffer hardship to the point of chains as a criminal. But God's word isn't chained. 10 Therefore I endure all things for the chosen ones' sake, that they also may obtain the salvation which is in Christ Jesus with eternal glory. 11 This saying is trustworthy:

"For if we died with him,
we will also live with him.
12 If we endure,
we will also reign with him.
If we deny him,
he also will deny us.
13 If we are faithless,
he remains faithful;
for he can't deny himself."

14 Remind them of these things, charging them in the sight of the Lord that they don't argue about words to no profit, to the subverting of those who hear.

15 Give diligence to present yourself approved by God, a workman who doesn't need to be ashamed, properly handling the Word of Truth.

Responsorial Psalm: Psalms 25: 4-5ab, 8-10 and 14

4 Show me your ways, Yahweh.
Teach me your paths.
5 Guide me in your truth, and teach me,
for you are the God of my salvation.
8 Good and upright is Yahweh,
therefore he will instruct sinners in the way.
9 He will guide the humble in justice.
He will teach the humble his way.
10 All the paths of Yahweh are loving kindness and truth
to such as keep his covenant and his testimonies.
14 The friendship of Yahweh is with those who fear him.
He will show them his covenant.

Gospel: Mark 12: 28-34

28 One of the scribes came and heard them questioning together, and knowing that he had answered them well, asked him, "Which commandment is the greatest of all?"

29 Jesus answered, "The greatest is: 'Hear, Israel, the Lord our God, the Lord is one. 30 You shall love the Lord your God with all your heart, with all your soul, with all your mind, and with all your strength.'* This is the first commandment. 31 The second is like this: 'You shall love your neighbor as yourself.'* There is no other commandment greater than these."

32 The scribe said to him, "Truly, teacher, you have said well that he is one, and there is none other but he; 33 and to love him with all the heart, with all the understanding, all the soul, and with all the strength, and to love his neighbor as himself, is more important than all whole burnt offerings and sacrifices."

34 When Jesus saw that he answered wisely, he said to him, "You are not far from God's Kingdom."

No one dared ask him any question after that.

_____

_____

Friday, June 7, 2024
THE MOST SACRED HEART OF JESUS

First Reading: Hosea 11: 1, 3-4, 8c-9

1 "When Israel was a child, then I loved him,
and called my son out of Egypt.
3 Yet I taught Ephraim to walk.
I took them by their arms,
but they didn't know that I healed them.
4 I drew them with cords of a man, with ties of love;
and I was to them like those who lift up the yoke on their necks;
and I bent down to him and I fed him.
8c How can I make you like Admah?
How can I make you like Zeboiim?
My heart is turned within me,
my compassion is aroused.
9 I will not execute the fierceness of my anger.
I will not return to destroy Ephraim,
for I am God, and not man—the Holy One among you.
I will not come in wrath.

Responsorial Psalm: Isaiah 12: 2-6

2 Behold, God is my salvation. I will trust, and will not be afraid; for Yah, Yahweh, is my strength and song; and he has become my salvation." 3 Therefore with joy you will draw water out of the wells of salvation. 4 In that day you will say, "Give thanks to Yahweh! Call on his name! Declare his doings among the peoples! Proclaim that his name is exalted! 5 Sing to

Yahweh, for he has done excellent things! Let this be known in all the earth! 6 Cry aloud and shout, you inhabitant of Zion, for the Holy One of Israel is great among you!"

Second Reading: Ephesians 3: 8-12, 14-19

8 To me, the very least of all saints, was this grace given, to preach to the Gentiles the unsearchable riches of Christ, 9 and to make all men see what is the administration† of the mystery which for ages has been hidden in God, who created all things through Jesus Christ, 10 to the intent that now through the assembly the manifold wisdom of God might be made known to the principalities and the powers in the heavenly places, 11 according to the eternal purpose which he accomplished in Christ Jesus our Lord. 12 In him we have boldness and access in confidence through our faith in him.
14 For this cause, I bow my knees to the Father of our Lord Jesus Christ, 15 from whom every family in heaven and on earth is named, 16 that he would grant you, according to the riches of his glory, that you may be strengthened with power through his Spirit in the inner person, 17 that Christ may dwell in your hearts through faith, to the end that you, being rooted and grounded in love, 18 may be strengthened to comprehend with all the saints what is the width and length and height and depth, 19 and to know Christ's love which surpasses knowledge, that you may be filled with all the fullness of God.

Gospel: John 19: 31-37

31 Therefore the Jews, because it was the Preparation Day, so that the bodies wouldn't remain on the cross on the Sabbath (for that Sabbath was a special one), asked of Pilate that their legs might be broken and that they might be taken away. 32 Therefore the soldiers came and broke the legs of the first and of the other who was crucified with him; 33 but when they came to Jesus and saw that he was already dead, they didn't break his legs. 34 However, one of the soldiers pierced his side with a spear, and immediately blood and water came out. 35 He who has seen has testified, and his testimony is true. He knows that he tells the truth, that you may believe. 36 For these things happened that the Scripture might be fulfilled, "A bone of him will not be broken."* 37 Again another Scripture says, "They will look on him whom they pierced."

1. Invite the Holy Spirit into this reading, asking the Author of Scripture to speak to you through His Word
2. Read today's passage as many times as you need, take your time
3. Write down (below) what the Lord is saying to you today
4. Live with this Word in your heart through the day

_____

_____

Saturday, June 8, 2024
The Immaculate Heart of the Blessed Virgin Mary

First Reading: Second Timothy 4: 1-8

1 I command you therefore before God and the Lord Jesus Christ, who will judge the living and the dead at his appearing and his Kingdom: 2 preach the word; be urgent in season and out of season; reprove, rebuke, and exhort with all patience and teaching. 3 For the time will come when they will not listen to the sound doctrine, but having itching ears, will heap up for themselves teachers after their own lusts, 4 and will turn away their ears from the truth, and turn away to fables. 5 But you be sober in all things, suffer hardship, do the work of an evangelist, and fulfill your ministry.

6 For I am already being offered, and the time of my departure has come. 7 I have fought the good fight. I have finished the course. I have kept the faith. 8 From now on, the crown of righteousness is stored up for me, which the Lord, the righteous judge, will give to me on that day; and not to me only, but also to all those who have loved his appearing.

Responsorial Psalm: Psalms 71: 8-9, 14-17, 22

8 My mouth shall be filled with your praise,
with your honor all day long.
9 Don't reject me in my old age.
Don't forsake me when my strength fails.
14 But I will always hope,
and will add to all of your praise.
15 My mouth will tell about your righteousness,
and of your salvation all day,
though I don't know its full measure.
16 I will come with the mighty acts of the Lord Yahweh.
I will make mention of your righteousness, even of yours alone.
17 God, you have taught me from my youth.
Until now, I have declared your wondrous works.
22 I will also praise you with the harp for your faithfulness, my God.
I sing praises to you with the lyre, Holy One of Israel.

Gospel: Luke 2: 41-51

41 His parents went every year to Jerusalem at the feast of the Passover. 42 When he was twelve years old, they went up to Jerusalem according to the custom of the feast; 43 and when they had fulfilled the days, as they were returning, the boy Jesus stayed behind in Jerusalem. Joseph and his mother didn't know it, 44 but supposing him to be in the company, they went a day's journey; and they looked for him among their relatives and acquaintances. 45 When

they didn't find him, they returned to Jerusalem, looking for him. 46 After three days they found him in the temple, sitting in the middle of the teachers, both listening to them and asking them questions. 47 All who heard him were amazed at his understanding and his answers. 48 When they saw him, they were astonished; and his mother said to him, "Son, why have you treated us this way? Behold, your father and I were anxiously looking for you."

49 He said to them, "Why were you looking for me? Didn't you know that I must be in my Father's house?" 50 They didn't understand the saying which he spoke to them. 51 And he went down with them and came to Nazareth. He was subject to them, and his mother kept all these sayings in her heart.

1. Invite the Holy Spirit into this reading, asking the Author of Scripture to speak to you through His Word
2. Read today's passage as many times as you need, take your time
3. Write down (below) what the Lord is saying to you today
4. Live with this Word in your heart through the day

_____

_____

Sunday, June 9, 2024
TENTH SUNDAY IN ORDINARY TIME

First Reading: Genesis 3: 9-15

9 Yahweh God called to the man, and said to him, "Where are you?"
10 The man said, "I heard your voice in the garden, and I was afraid, because I was naked; so I hid myself."
11 God said, "Who told you that you were naked? Have you eaten from the tree that I commanded you not to eat from?"
12 The man said, "The woman whom you gave to be with me, she gave me fruit from the tree, and I ate it."
13 Yahweh God said to the woman, "What have you done?"
The woman said, "The serpent deceived me, and I ate."
14 Yahweh God said to the serpent,
"Because you have done this,
you are cursed above all livestock,
and above every animal of the field.
You shall go on your belly
and you shall eat dust all the days of your life.
15 I will put hostility between you and the woman,

and between your offspring and her offspring.
He will bruise your head,
and you will bruise his heel."

Responsorial Psalm: Psalms 130: 1-8

1 Out of the depths I have cried to you, Yahweh.
2 Lord, hear my voice.
Let your ears be attentive to the voice of my petitions.
3 If you, Yah, kept a record of sins,
Lord, who could stand?
4 But there is forgiveness with you,
therefore you are feared.
5 I wait for Yahweh.
My soul waits.
I hope in his word.
6 My soul longs for the Lord more than watchmen long for the morning,
more than watchmen for the morning.
7 Israel, hope in Yahweh,
for there is loving kindness with Yahweh.
Abundant redemption is with him.
8 He will redeem Israel from all their sins.

Second Reading: Second Corinthians 4: 13 – 5:1

13 But having the same spirit of faith, according to that which is written, "I believed, and therefore I spoke."* We also believe, and therefore we also speak, 14 knowing that he who raised the Lord Jesus will raise us also with Jesus, and will present us with you. 15 For all things are for your sakes, that the grace, being multiplied through the many, may cause the thanksgiving to abound to the glory of God.
16 Therefore we don't faint, but though our outward person is decaying, yet our inward person is renewed day by day. 17 For our light affliction, which is for the moment, works for us more and more exceedingly an eternal weight of glory, 18 while we don't look at the things which are seen, but at the things which are not seen. For the things which are seen are temporal, but the things which are not seen are eternal.
1 For we know that if the earthly house of our tent is dissolved, we have a building from God, a house not made with hands, eternal, in the heavens.

Gospel: Mark 3: 20-35

20 The multitude came together again, so that they could not so much as eat bread. 21 When his friends heard it, they went out to seize him; for they said, "He is insane." 22 The scribes who came down from Jerusalem said, "He has Beelzebul," and, "By the prince of the demons he casts out the demons."

23 He summoned them and said to them in parables, "How can Satan cast out Satan? 24 If a kingdom is divided against itself, that kingdom cannot stand. 25 If a house is divided against itself, that house cannot stand. 26 If Satan has risen up against himself, and is divided, he can't stand, but has an end. 27 But no one can enter into the house of the strong man to plunder unless he first binds the strong man; then he will plunder his house.

28 "Most certainly I tell you, all sins of the descendants of man will be forgiven, including their blasphemies with which they may blaspheme; 29 but whoever may blaspheme against the Holy Spirit never has forgiveness, but is subject to eternal condemnation."† 30 —because they said, "He has an unclean spirit."

31 His mother and his brothers came, and standing outside, they sent to him, calling him. 32 A multitude was sitting around him, and they told him, "Behold, your mother, your brothers, and your sisters‡ are outside looking for you."

33 He answered them, "Who are my mother and my brothers?" 34 Looking around at those who sat around him, he said, "Behold, my mother and my brothers! 35 For whoever does the will of God is my brother, my sister, and mother."

1. Invite the Holy Spirit into this reading, asking the Author of Scripture to speak to you through His Word
2. Read today's passage as many times as you need, take your time
3. Write down (below) what the Lord is saying to you today
4. Live with this Word in your heart through the day

_____

_____

Monday, June 10, 2024

First Reading: First Kings 17: 1-6

1 Elijah the Tishbite, who was one of the settlers of Gilead, said to Ahab, "As Yahweh, the God of Israel, lives, before whom I stand, there shall not be dew nor rain these years, but according to my word."

2 Then Yahweh's word came to him, saying, 3 "Go away from here, turn eastward, and hide yourself by the brook Cherith, that is before the Jordan. 4 You shall drink from the brook. I have commanded the ravens to feed you there." 5 So he went and did according to Yahweh's word, for he went and lived by the brook Cherith that is before the Jordan. 6 The ravens brought him bread and meat in the morning, and bread and meat in the evening; and he drank from the brook.

Responsorial Psalm: Psalms 121: 1-8

1 I will lift up my eyes to the hills.
Where does my help come from?
2 My help comes from Yahweh,
who made heaven and earth.
3 He will not allow your foot to be moved.
He who keeps you will not slumber.
4 Behold, he who keeps Israel
will neither slumber nor sleep.
5 Yahweh is your keeper.
Yahweh is your shade on your right hand.
6 The sun will not harm you by day,
nor the moon by night.
7 Yahweh will keep you from all evil.
He will keep your soul.
8 Yahweh will keep your going out and your coming in,
from this time forward, and forever more.

Gospel: Matthew 5: 1-12

1 Seeing the multitudes, he went up onto the mountain. When he had sat down, his disciples
came to him. 2 He opened his mouth and taught them, saying,
3 "Blessed are the poor in spirit,
for theirs is the Kingdom of Heaven.*
4 Blessed are those who mourn,
for they shall be comforted.*
5 Blessed are the gentle,
for they shall inherit the earth.†*
6 Blessed are those who hunger and thirst for righteousness,
for they shall be filled.
7 Blessed are the merciful,
for they shall obtain mercy.
8 Blessed are the pure in heart,
for they shall see God.
9 Blessed are the peacemakers,
for they shall be called children of God.
10 Blessed are those who have been persecuted for righteousness' sake,
for theirs is the Kingdom of Heaven.
11 "Blessed are you when people reproach you, persecute you, and say all kinds of evil against
you falsely, for my sake. 12 Rejoice, and be exceedingly glad, for great is your reward in
heaven. For that is how they persecuted the prophets who were before you.

1. Invite the Holy Spirit into this reading, asking the Author of Scripture to speak to you through His Word
2. Read today's passage as many times as you need, take your time
3. Write down (below) what the Lord is saying to you today
4. Live with this Word in your heart through the day

Tuesday, June 11, 2024
Saint Barnabas, Apostle

First Reading: Acts 11: 21b-26; 13: 1-3

21 The hand of the Lord was with them, and a great number believed and turned to the Lord. 22 The report concerning them came to the ears of the assembly which was in Jerusalem. They sent out Barnabas to go as far as Antioch, 23 who, when he had come, and had seen the grace of God, was glad. He exhorted them all, that with purpose of heart they should remain near to the Lord. 24 For he was a good man, and full of the Holy Spirit and of faith, and many people were added to the Lord.

25 Barnabas went out to Tarsus to look for Saul. 26 When he had found him, he brought him to Antioch. For a whole year they were gathered together with the assembly, and taught many people. The disciples were first called Christians in Antioch.

1 Now in the assembly that was at Antioch there were some prophets and teachers: Barnabas, Simeon who was called Niger, Lucius of Cyrene, Manaen the foster brother of Herod the tetrarch, and Saul. 2 As they served the Lord and fasted, the Holy Spirit said, "Separate Barnabas and Saul for me, for the work to which I have called them."

3 Then, when they had fasted and prayed and laid their hands on them, they sent them away.

Responsorial Psalm: Psalms 98: 1-6

1 Sing to Yahweh a new song,
for he has done marvelous things!
His right hand and his holy arm have worked salvation for him.
2 Yahweh has made known his salvation.
He has openly shown his righteousness in the sight of the nations.
3 He has remembered his loving kindness and his faithfulness toward the house of Israel.
All the ends of the earth have seen the salvation of our God.
4 Make a joyful noise to Yahweh, all the earth!
Burst out and sing for joy, yes, sing praises!

5 Sing praises to Yahweh with the harp,
with the harp and the voice of melody.
6 With trumpets and sound of the ram's horn,
make a joyful noise before the King, Yahweh.

Gospel: Matthew 5: 13-16

13 "You are the salt of the earth, but if the salt has lost its flavor, with what will it be salted? It is then good for nothing, but to be cast out and trodden under the feet of men.
14 You are the light of the world. A city located on a hill can't be hidden. 15 Neither do you light a lamp and put it under a measuring basket, but on a stand; and it shines to all who are in the house. 16 Even so, let your light shine before men, that they may see your good works and glorify your Father who is in heaven.

1. Invite the Holy Spirit into this reading, asking the Author of Scripture to speak to you through His Word
2. Read today's passage as many times as you need, take your time
3. Write down (below) what the Lord is saying to you today
4. Live with this Word in your heart through the day

_____

_____

Wednesday, June 12, 2024

First Reading: First Kings 18: 20-39

20 So Ahab sent to all the children of Israel, and gathered the prophets together to Mount Carmel. 21 Elijah came near to all the people, and said, "How long will you waver between the two sides? If Yahweh is God, follow him; but if Baal, then follow him."
The people didn't say a word.
22 Then Elijah said to the people, "I, even I only, am left as a prophet of Yahweh; but Baal's prophets are four hundred fifty men. 23 Let them therefore give us two bulls; and let them choose one bull for themselves, and cut it in pieces, and lay it on the wood, and put no fire under; and I will dress the other bull, and lay it on the wood, and put no fire under it. 24 You call on the name of your god, and I will call on Yahweh's name. The God who answers by fire, let him be God."
All the people answered, "What you say is good."
25 Elijah said to the prophets of Baal, "Choose one bull for yourselves, and dress it first, for you are many; and call on the name of your god, but put no fire under it."

26 They took the bull which was given them, and they dressed it, and called on the name of Baal from morning even until noon, saying, "Baal, hear us!" But there was no voice, and nobody answered. They leaped about the altar which was made.

27 At noon, Elijah mocked them, and said, "Cry aloud, for he is a god. Either he is deep in thought, or he has gone somewhere, or he is on a journey, or perhaps he sleeps and must be awakened."

28 They cried aloud, and cut themselves in their way with knives and lances until the blood gushed out on them. 29 When midday was past, they prophesied until the time of the evening offering; but there was no voice, no answer, and nobody paid attention.

30 Elijah said to all the people, "Come near to me!"; and all the people came near to him. He repaired Yahweh's altar that had been thrown down. 31 Elijah took twelve stones, according to the number of the tribes of the sons of Jacob, to whom Yahweh's word came, saying, "Israel shall be your name." 32 With the stones he built an altar in Yahweh's name. He made a trench around the altar large enough to contain two seahs† of seed. 33 He put the wood in order, and cut the bull in pieces and laid it on the wood. He said, "Fill four jars with water, and pour it on the burnt offering and on the wood." 34 He said, "Do it a second time;" and they did it the second time. He said, "Do it a third time;" and they did it the third time. 35 The water ran around the altar; and he also filled the trench with water.

36 At the time of the evening offering, Elijah the prophet came near and said, "Yahweh, the God of Abraham, of Isaac, and of Israel, let it be known today that you are God in Israel and that I am your servant, and that I have done all these things at your word. 37 Hear me, Yahweh, hear me, that this people may know that you, Yahweh, are God, and that you have turned their heart back again."

38 Then Yahweh's fire fell and consumed the burnt offering, the wood, the stones, and the dust; and it licked up the water that was in the trench. 39 When all the people saw it, they fell on their faces. They said, "Yahweh, he is God! Yahweh, he is God!"

Responsorial Psalm: Psalms 16: 1b-2ab, 4, 5ab and 8, 11

1 Preserve me, God, for I take refuge in you.
2 My soul, you have said to Yahweh, "You are my Lord.
Apart from you I have no good thing."
4 Their sorrows shall be multiplied who give gifts to another god.
Their drink offerings of blood I will not offer,
nor take their names on my lips.
5 Yahweh assigned my portion and my cup.
You made my lot secure.
8 I have set Yahweh always before me.
Because he is at my right hand, I shall not be moved.
11 You will show me the path of life.
In your presence is fullness of joy.
In your right hand there are pleasures forever more.

Gospel: Matthew 5: 17-19

17 "Don't think that I came to destroy the law or the prophets. I didn't come to destroy, but to fulfill. 18 For most certainly, I tell you, until heaven and earth pass away, not even one smallest letter‡ or one tiny pen stroke§ shall in any way pass away from the law, until all things are accomplished. 19 Therefore, whoever shall break one of these least commandments and teach others to do so, shall be called least in the Kingdom of Heaven; but whoever shall do and teach them shall be called great in the Kingdom of Heaven.

1. Invite the Holy Spirit into this reading, asking the Author of Scripture to speak to you through His Word
2. Read today's passage as many times as you need, take your time
3. Write down (below) what the Lord is saying to you today
4. Live with this Word in your heart through the day

Thursday, June 13, 2024
Saint Anthony of Padua, Priest and Doctor of the Church

First Reading: First Kings 18: 41-46

41 Elijah said to Ahab, "Get up, eat and drink; for there is the sound of abundance of rain."
42 So Ahab went up to eat and to drink. Elijah went up to the top of Carmel; and he bowed himself down on the earth, and put his face between his knees. 43 He said to his servant, "Go up now and look toward the sea."
He went up and looked, then said, "There is nothing."
He said, "Go again" seven times.
44 On the seventh time, he said, "Behold, a small cloud, like a man's hand, is rising out of the sea."
He said, "Go up, tell Ahab, 'Get ready and go down, so that the rain doesn't stop you.' "
45 In a little while, the sky grew black with clouds and wind, and there was a great rain. Ahab rode, and went to Jezreel. 46 Yahweh's hand was on Elijah; and he tucked his cloak into his belt and ran before Ahab to the entrance of Jezreel.

Responsorial Psalm: Psalms 65: 10-13

10 You drench its furrows.
You level its ridges.

You soften it with showers.
You bless it with a crop.
11 You crown the year with your bounty.
Your carts overflow with abundance.
12 The wilderness grasslands overflow.
The hills are clothed with gladness.
13 The pastures are covered with flocks.
The valleys also are clothed with grain.
They shout for joy!
They also sing.

Gospel: Matthew 5: 20-26

20 For I tell you that unless your righteousness exceeds that of the scribes and Pharisees, there is no way you will enter into the Kingdom of Heaven.
21 "You have heard that it was said to the ancient ones, 'You shall not murder;'* and 'Whoever murders will be in danger of the judgment.' 22 But I tell you that everyone who is angry with his brother without a cause † will be in danger of the judgment. Whoever says to his brother, 'Raca!' ‡ will be in danger of the council. Whoever says, 'You fool!' will be in danger of the fire of Gehenna.§
23 "If therefore you are offering your gift at the altar, and there remember that your brother has anything against you, 24 leave your gift there before the altar, and go your way. First be reconciled to your brother, and then come and offer your gift. 25 Agree with your adversary quickly while you are with him on the way; lest perhaps the prosecutor deliver you to the judge, and the judge deliver you to the officer, and you be cast into prison. 26 Most certainly I tell you, you shall by no means get out of there until you have paid the last penny.

1. Invite the Holy Spirit into this reading, asking the Author of Scripture to speak to you through His Word
2. Read today's passage as many times as you need, take your time
3. Write down (below) what the Lord is saying to you today
4. Live with this Word in your heart through the day

Friday, June 14, 2024

First Reading: First Kings 19: 9a, 11-16

9 He came to a cave there, and camped there; and behold, Yahweh's word came to him, and he said to him, "What are you doing here, Elijah?"

10 He said, "I have been very jealous for Yahweh, the God of Armies; for the children of Israel have forsaken your covenant, thrown down your altars, and killed your prophets with the sword. I, even I only, am left; and they seek my life, to take it away."

11 He said, "Go out and stand on the mountain before Yahweh."

Behold, Yahweh passed by, and a great and strong wind tore the mountains and broke in pieces the rocks before Yahweh; but Yahweh was not in the wind. After the wind there was an earthquake; but Yahweh was not in the earthquake. 12 After the earthquake a fire passed; but Yahweh was not in the fire. After the fire, there was a still small voice. 13 When Elijah heard it, he wrapped his face in his mantle, went out, and stood in the entrance of the cave. Behold, a voice came to him, and said, "What are you doing here, Elijah?"

14 He said, "I have been very jealous for Yahweh, the God of Armies; for the children of Israel have forsaken your covenant, thrown down your altars, and killed your prophets with the sword. I, even I only, am left; and they seek my life, to take it away."

15 Yahweh said to him, "Go, return on your way to the wilderness of Damascus. When you arrive, anoint Hazael to be king over Syria. 16 Anoint Jehu the son of Nimshi to be king over Israel; and anoint Elisha the son of Shaphat of Abel Meholah to be prophet in your place.

Responsorial Psalm: Psalms 27: 7-9, 13-14

7 Hear, Yahweh, when I cry with my voice.
Have mercy also on me, and answer me.
8 When you said, "Seek my face,"
my heart said to you, "I will seek your face, Yahweh."
9 Don't hide your face from me.
Don't put your servant away in anger.
You have been my help.
Don't abandon me,
neither forsake me, God of my salvation.
13 I am still confident of this:
I will see the goodness of Yahweh in the land of the living.
14 Wait for Yahweh.
Be strong, and let your heart take courage.
Yes, wait for Yahweh.

Gospel: Matthew 5: 27-32

27 "You have heard that it was said, ‡ 'You shall not commit adultery;'* 28 but I tell you that everyone who gazes at a woman to lust after her has committed adultery with her already in his heart. 29 If your right eye causes you to stumble, pluck it out and throw it away from you. For it is more profitable for you that one of your members should perish than for your whole body to be cast into Gehenna.§ 30 If your right hand causes you to stumble, cut it off, and

throw it away from you. For it is more profitable for you that one of your members should perish, than for your whole body to be cast into Gehenna.†

31 "It was also said, 'Whoever shall put away his wife, let him give her a writing of divorce,'* 32 but I tell you that whoever puts away his wife, except for the cause of sexual immorality, makes her an adulteress; and whoever marries her when she is put away commits adultery.

1. Invite the Holy Spirit into this reading, asking the Author of Scripture to speak to you through His Word
2. Read today's passage as many times as you need, take your time
3. Write down (below) what the Lord is saying to you today
4. Live with this Word in your heart through the day

_____

_____

Saturday, June 15, 2024

First Reading: First Kings 19: 19-21

19 So he departed from there and found Elisha the son of Shaphat, who was plowing with twelve yoke of oxen before him, and he with the twelfth. Elijah went over to him and put his mantle on him. 20 Elisha left the oxen and ran after Elijah, and said, "Let me please kiss my father and my mother, and then I will follow you."
He said to him, "Go back again; for what have I done to you?"
21 He returned from following him, and took the yoke of oxen, killed them, and boiled their meat with the oxen's equipment, and gave to the people; and they ate. Then he arose, and went after Elijah, and served him.

Responsorial Psalm: Psalms 16: 1b-2a and 5, 7-10

1 Preserve me, God, for I take refuge in you.
2 My soul, you have said to Yahweh, "You are my Lord.
5 Yahweh assigned my portion and my cup.
You made my lot secure.
7 I will bless Yahweh, who has given me counsel.
Yes, my heart instructs me in the night seasons.
8 I have set Yahweh always before me.
Because he is at my right hand, I shall not be moved.
9 Therefore my heart is glad, and my tongue rejoices.
My body shall also dwell in safety.

10 For you will not leave my soul in Sheol,†
neither will you allow your holy one to see corruption.

Gospel: Matthew 5: 33-37

33 "Again you have heard that it was said to the ancient ones, 'You shall not make false vows, but shall perform to the Lord your vows,'* 34 but I tell you, don't swear at all: neither by heaven, for it is the throne of God; 35 nor by the earth, for it is the footstool of his feet; nor by Jerusalem, for it is the city of the great King. 36 Neither shall you swear by your head, for you can't make one hair white or black. 37 But let your 'Yes' be 'Yes' and your 'No' be 'No.' Whatever is more than these is of the evil one.

1. Invite the Holy Spirit into this reading, asking the Author of Scripture to speak to you through His Word
2. Read today's passage as many times as you need, take your time
3. Write down (below) what the Lord is saying to you today
4. Live with this Word in your heart through the day

_____

_____

Sunday, June 16, 2024
ELEVENTH SUNDAY IN ORDINARY TIME

First Reading: Ezekiel 17: 22-24

22 "The Lord Yahweh says: 'I will also take some of the lofty top of the cedar, and will plant it. I will crop off from the topmost of its young twigs a tender one, and I will plant it on a high and lofty mountain. 23 I will plant it in the mountain of the height of Israel; and it will produce boughs, and bear fruit, and be a good cedar. Birds of every kind will dwell in the shade of its branches. 24 All the trees of the field will know that I, Yahweh, have brought down the high tree, have exalted the low tree, have dried up the green tree, and have made the dry tree flourish.
" 'I, Yahweh, have spoken and have done it.' "

Responsorial Psalm: Psalms 92: 2-3, 13-15

2 to proclaim your loving kindness in the morning,
and your faithfulness every night,
3 with the ten-stringed lute, with the harp,

and with the melody of the lyre.

13 They are planted in Yahweh's house.
They will flourish in our God's courts.

14 They will still produce fruit in old age.
They will be full of sap and green,

15 to show that Yahweh is upright.
He is my rock,
and there is no unrighteousness in him.

Second Reading: Second Corinthians 5: 6-10

6 Therefore we are always confident and know that while we are at home in the body, we are absent from the Lord; 7 for we walk by faith, not by sight. 8 We are courageous, I say, and are willing rather to be absent from the body and to be at home with the Lord. 9 Therefore also we make it our aim, whether at home or absent, to be well pleasing to him. 10 For we must all be revealed before the judgment seat of Christ that each one may receive the things in the body according to what he has done, whether good or bad.

Gospel: Mark 4: 26-34

26 He said, "God's Kingdom is as if a man should cast seed on the earth, 27 and should sleep and rise night and day, and the seed should spring up and grow, though he doesn't know how. 28 For the earth bears fruit by itself: first the blade, then the ear, then the full grain in the ear. 29 But when the fruit is ripe, immediately he puts in the sickle, because the harvest has come." 30 He said, "How will we liken God's Kingdom? Or with what parable will we illustrate it? 31 It's like a grain of mustard seed, which, when it is sown in the earth, though it is less than all the seeds that are on the earth, 32 yet when it is sown, grows up and becomes greater than all the herbs, and puts out great branches, so that the birds of the sky can lodge under its shadow." 33 With many such parables he spoke the word to them, as they were able to hear it. 34 Without a parable he didn't speak to them; but privately to his own disciples he explained everything.

1. Invite the Holy Spirit into this reading, asking the Author of Scripture to speak to you through His Word
2. Read today's passage as many times as you need, take your time
3. Write down (below) what the Lord is saying to you today
4. Live with this Word in your heart through the day

_____

_____

First Reading: First Kings 21: 1-16

1 After these things, Naboth the Jezreelite had a vineyard which was in Jezreel, next to the palace of Ahab king of Samaria. 2 Ahab spoke to Naboth, saying, "Give me your vineyard, that I may have it for a garden of herbs, because it is near my house; and I will give you for it a better vineyard than it. Or, if it seems good to you, I will give you its worth in money."
3 Naboth said to Ahab, "May Yahweh forbid me, that I should give the inheritance of my fathers to you!"
4 Ahab came into his house sullen and angry because of the word which Naboth the Jezreelite had spoken to him, for he had said, "I will not give you the inheritance of my fathers." He laid himself down on his bed, and turned away his face, and would eat no bread. 5 But Jezebel his wife came to him, and said to him, "Why is your spirit so sad that you eat no bread?"
6 He said to her, "Because I spoke to Naboth the Jezreelite, and said to him, 'Give me your vineyard for money; or else, if it pleases you, I will give you another vineyard for it.' He answered, 'I will not give you my vineyard.' "
7 Jezebel his wife said to him, "Do you now govern the kingdom of Israel? Arise, and eat bread, and let your heart be merry. I will give you the vineyard of Naboth the Jezreelite." 8 So she wrote letters in Ahab's name and sealed them with his seal, and sent the letters to the elders and to the nobles who were in his city, who lived with Naboth. 9 She wrote in the letters, saying, "Proclaim a fast, and set Naboth on high among the people. 10 Set two men, wicked fellows, before him, and let them testify against him, saying, 'You cursed God and the king!' Then carry him out, and stone him to death."
11 The men of his city, even the elders and the nobles who lived in his city, did as Jezebel had instructed them in the letters which she had written and sent to them. 12 They proclaimed a fast, and set Naboth on high among the people. 13 The two men, the wicked fellows, came in and sat before him. The wicked fellows testified against him, even against Naboth, in the presence of the people, saying, "Naboth cursed God and the king!" Then they carried him out of the city and stoned him to death with stones. 14 Then they sent to Jezebel, saying, "Naboth has been stoned and is dead."
15 When Jezebel heard that Naboth had been stoned and was dead, Jezebel said to Ahab, "Arise, take possession of the vineyard of Naboth the Jezreelite, which he refused to give you for money; for Naboth is not alive, but dead."
16 When Ahab heard that Naboth was dead, Ahab rose up to go down to the vineyard of Naboth the Jezreelite, to take possession of it.

Responsorial Psalm: Psalms 5: 2-3ab, 4b-7

2 Listen to the voice of my cry, my King and my God,
for I pray to you.
3 Yahweh, in the morning you will hear my voice.

In the morning I will lay my requests before you, and will watch expectantly.

4 bEvil can't live with you.

5 The arrogant will not stand in your sight.

You hate all workers of iniquity.

6 You will destroy those who speak lies.

Yahweh abhors the bloodthirsty and deceitful man.

7 But as for me, in the abundance of your loving kindness I will come into your house.

I will bow toward your holy temple in reverence of you.

Gospel: Matthew 5: 38-42

38 "You have heard that it was said, 'An eye for an eye, and a tooth for a tooth.'* 39 But I tell you, don't resist him who is evil; but whoever strikes you on your right cheek, turn to him the other also. 40 If anyone sues you to take away your coat, let him have your cloak also. 41 Whoever compels you to go one mile, go with him two. 42 Give to him who asks you, and don't turn away him who desires to borrow from you.

1. Invite the Holy Spirit into this reading, asking the Author of Scripture to speak to you through His Word
2. Read today's passage as many times as you need, take your time
3. Write down (below) what the Lord is saying to you today
4. Live with this Word in your heart through the day

Tuesday, June 18, 2024

First Reading: First Kings 21: 17-29

17 Yahweh's word came to Elijah the Tishbite, saying, 18 "Arise, go down to meet Ahab king of Israel, who dwells in Samaria. Behold, he is in the vineyard of Naboth, where he has gone down to take possession of it. 19 You shall speak to him, saying, 'Yahweh says, "Have you killed and also taken possession?" ' You shall speak to him, saying, 'Yahweh says, "In the place where dogs licked the blood of Naboth, dogs will lick your blood, even yours." ' "

20 Ahab said to Elijah, "Have you found me, my enemy?"

He answered, "I have found you, because you have sold yourself to do that which is evil in Yahweh's sight. 21 Behold, I will bring evil on you, and will utterly sweep you away and will cut off from Ahab everyone who urinates against a wall,† and him who is shut up and him who is left at large in Israel. 22 I will make your house like the house of Jeroboam the son of Nebat, and like the house of Baasha the son of Ahijah, for the provocation with which you have provoked me to anger, and have made Israel to sin." 23 Yahweh also spoke of Jezebel, saying, "The dogs will eat Jezebel by the rampart of Jezreel. 24 The dogs will eat he who dies of Ahab in the city; and the birds of the sky will eat he who dies in the field."

25 But there was no one like Ahab, who sold himself to do that which was evil in Yahweh's sight, whom Jezebel his wife stirred up. 26 He did very abominably in following idols, according to all that the Amorites did, whom Yahweh cast out before the children of Israel.

27 When Ahab heard those words, he tore his clothes, put sackcloth on his body, fasted, lay in sackcloth, and went about despondently.

28 Yahweh's word came to Elijah the Tishbite, saying, 29 "See how Ahab humbles himself before me? Because he humbles himself before me, I will not bring the evil in his days; but I will bring the evil on his house in his son's day."

Responsorial Psalm: Psalms 51: 3-4, 5-6ab, 11 and 16

3 For I know my transgressions.
My sin is constantly before me.
4 Against you, and you only, I have sinned,
and done that which is evil in your sight,
so you may be proved right when you speak,
and justified when you judge.
5 Behold, I was born in iniquity.
My mother conceived me in sin.
6 Behold, you desire truth in the inward parts.
You teach me wisdom in the inmost place.
11 Don't throw me from your presence,
and don't take your Holy Spirit from me.
16 For you don't delight in sacrifice, or else I would give it.
You have no pleasure in burnt offering.

Gospel: Matthew 5: 43-48

43 "You have heard that it was said, 'You shall love your neighbor * and hate your enemy.'‡ 44 But I tell you, love your enemies, bless those who curse you, do good to those who hate you, and pray for those who mistreat you and persecute you, 45 that you may be children of your Father who is in heaven. For he makes his sun to rise on the evil and the good, and sends rain on the just and the unjust. 46 For if you love those who love you, what reward do you have? Don't even the tax collectors do the same? 47 If you only greet your friends, what more do you do than others? Don't even the tax collectors§ do the same? 48 Therefore you shall be perfect, just as your Father in heaven is perfect.

1. Invite the Holy Spirit into this reading, asking the Author of Scripture to speak to you through His Word

2. Read today's passage as many times as you need, take your time
3. Write down (below) what the Lord is saying to you today
4. Live with this Word in your heart through the day

Wednesday, June 19, 2024
Saint Romuald, Abbot

First Reading: Second Kings 2: 1, 6-14

1 When Yahweh was about to take Elijah up by a whirlwind into heaven, Elijah went with Elisha from Gilgal.
6 Elijah said to him, "Please wait here, for Yahweh has sent me to the Jordan."
He said, "As Yahweh lives, and as your soul lives, I will not leave you." Then they both went on. 7 Fifty men of the sons of the prophets went and stood opposite them at a distance; and they both stood by the Jordan. 8 Elijah took his mantle, and rolled it up, and struck the waters; and they were divided here and there, so that they both went over on dry ground. 9 When they had gone over, Elijah said to Elisha, "Ask what I shall do for you, before I am taken from you." Elisha said, "Please let a double portion of your spirit be on me."
10 He said, "You have asked a hard thing. If you see me when I am taken from you, it will be so for you; but if not, it will not be so."
11 As they continued on and talked, behold, a chariot of fire and horses of fire separated them; and Elijah went up by a whirlwind into heaven. 12 Elisha saw it, and he cried, "My father, my father, the chariots of Israel and its horsemen!"
He saw him no more. Then he took hold of his own clothes and tore them in two pieces. 13 He also took up Elijah's mantle that fell from him, and went back and stood by the bank of the Jordan. 14 He took Elijah's mantle that fell from him, and struck the waters, and said, "Where is Yahweh, the God of Elijah?" When he also had struck the waters, they were divided apart, and Elisha went over.

Responsorial Psalm: Psalms 31: 20, 21, 24

20 In the shelter of your presence you will hide them from the plotting of man.
You will keep them secretly in a dwelling away from the strife of tongues.
21 Praise be to Yahweh,
for he has shown me his marvelous loving kindness in a strong city.
24 Be strong, and let your heart take courage,
all you who hope in Yahweh.

Gospel: Matthew 6: 1-6, 16-18

1 "Be careful that you don't do your charitable giving† before men, to be seen by them, or else you have no reward from your Father who is in heaven. 2 Therefore, when you do merciful deeds, don't sound a trumpet before yourself, as the hypocrites do in the synagogues and in the streets, that they may get glory from men. Most certainly I tell you, they have received their reward. 3 But when you do merciful deeds, don't let your left hand know what your right hand does, 4 so that your merciful deeds may be in secret, then your Father who sees in secret will reward you openly.

5 "When you pray, you shall not be as the hypocrites, for they love to stand and pray in the synagogues and in the corners of the streets, that they may be seen by men. Most certainly, I tell you, they have received their reward. 6 But you, when you pray, enter into your inner room, and having shut your door, pray to your Father who is in secret; and your Father who sees in secret will reward you openly.

16 "Moreover when you fast, don't be like the hypocrites, with sad faces. For they disfigure their faces that they may be seen by men to be fasting. Most certainly I tell you, they have received their reward. 17 But you, when you fast, anoint your head and wash your face, 18 so that you are not seen by men to be fasting, but by your Father who is in secret; and your Father, who sees in secret, will reward you.

1. Invite the Holy Spirit into this reading, asking the Author of Scripture to speak to you through His Word
2. Read today's passage as many times as you need, take your time
3. Write down (below) what the Lord is saying to you today
4. Live with this Word in your heart through the day

_____

_____

Thursday, June 20, 2024

First Reading: Sirach 48: 1-14

1 Then Elijah arose, the prophet like fire.
His word burned like a torch.
2 He brought a famine upon them,
and by his zeal made them few in number.
3 By the word of the Lord he shut up the heavens.
He brought down fire three times.

4 How you were glorified, O Elijah, in your wondrous deeds!
Whose glory is like yours?
5 You raised up a dead man from death,
from Hades, by the word of the Most High.
6 You brought down kings to destruction,
and honorable men from their sickbeds.
7 You heard rebuke in Sinai,
and judgments of vengeance in Horeb.
8 You anointed kings for retribution,
and prophets to succeed after you.
9 You were taken up in a tempest of fire,
in a chariot of fiery horses.
10 You were recorded for reproofs in their seasons,
to pacify anger, before it broke out into wrath,
to turn the heart of the father to the son,
and to restore the tribes of Jacob.
11 Blessed are those who saw you,
and those who have been beautified with love;
for we also shall surely live.
12 Elijah was wrapped in a whirlwind.
Elisha was filled with his spirit.
In his days he was not moved by the fear of any ruler,
and no one brought him into subjection.
13 Nothing was too hard for him.
When he was buried, his body prophesied.
14 As in his life he did wonders,
so his works were also marvelous in death.

Responsorial Psalm: Psalms 97: 1-7

1 Yahweh reigns!
Let the earth rejoice!
Let the multitude of islands be glad!
2 Clouds and darkness are around him.
Righteousness and justice are the foundation of his throne.
3 A fire goes before him,
and burns up his adversaries on every side.
4 His lightning lights up the world.
The earth sees, and trembles.
5 The mountains melt like wax at the presence of Yahweh,
at the presence of the Lord of the whole earth.
6 The heavens declare his righteousness.
All the peoples have seen his glory.

7 Let all them be shamed who serve engraved images,
who boast in their idols.
Worship him, all you gods!

Gospel: Matthew 6: 7-15

7 In praying, don't use vain repetitions as the Gentiles do; for they think that they will be heard for their much speaking. 8 Therefore don't be like them, for your Father knows what things you need before you ask him. 9 Pray like this:
" 'Our Father in heaven, may your name be kept holy.
10 Let your Kingdom come.
Let your will be done on earth as it is in heaven.
11 Give us today our daily bread.
12 Forgive us our debts,
as we also forgive our debtors.
13 Bring us not into temptation,
but deliver us from the evil one.
For yours is the Kingdom, the power, and the glory forever. Amen.'‡
14 "For if you forgive men their trespasses, your heavenly Father will also forgive you. 15 But if you don't forgive men their trespasses, neither will your Father forgive your trespasses.

1. Invite the Holy Spirit into this reading, asking the Author of Scripture to speak to you through His Word
2. Read today's passage as many times as you need, take your time
3. Write down (below) what the Lord is saying to you today
4. Live with this Word in your heart through the day

_____

_____

Friday, June 21, 2024
Saint Aloysius Gonzaga, Religious

First Reading: Second Kings 11: 1-4, 9-18, 20

1 Now when Athaliah the mother of Ahaziah saw that her son was dead, she arose and destroyed all the royal offspring. 2 But Jehosheba, the daughter of King Joram, sister of Ahaziah, took Joash the son of Ahaziah, and stole him away from among the king's sons who were slain, even him and his nurse, and put them in the bedroom; and they hid him from

Athaliah, so that he was not slain. 3 He was with her hidden in Yahweh's house six years while Athaliah reigned over the land.

4 In the seventh year Jehoiada sent and fetched the captains over hundreds of the Carites and of the guard, and brought them to him into Yahweh's house; and he made a covenant with them, and made a covenant with them in Yahweh's house, and showed them the king's son.

9 The captains over hundreds did according to all that Jehoiada the priest commanded; and they each took his men, those who were to come in on the Sabbath with those who were to go out on the Sabbath, and came to Jehoiada the priest. 10 The priest delivered to the captains over hundreds the spears and shields that had been King David's, which were in Yahweh's house. 11 The guard stood, every man with his weapons in his hand, from the right side of the house to the left side of the house, along by the altar and the house, around the king. 12 Then he brought out the king's son, and put the crown on him, and gave him the covenant; and they made him king and anointed him; and they clapped their hands, and said, "Long live the king!"

13 When Athaliah heard the noise of the guard and of the people, she came to the people into Yahweh's house; 14 and she looked, and behold, the king stood by the pillar, as the tradition was, with the captains and the trumpets by the king; and all the people of the land rejoiced, and blew trumpets. Then Athaliah tore her clothes and cried, "Treason! Treason!"

15 Jehoiada the priest commanded the captains of hundreds who were set over the army, and said to them, "Bring her out between the ranks. Kill anyone who follows her with the sword." For the priest said, "Don't let her be slain in Yahweh's house." 16 So they seized her; and she went by the way of the horses' entry to the king's house, and she was slain there.

17 Jehoiada made a covenant between Yahweh and the king and the people, that they should be Yahweh's people; also between the king and the people. 18 All the people of the land went to the house of Baal, and broke it down. They broke his altars and his images in pieces thoroughly, and killed Mattan the priest of Baal before the altars. The priest appointed officers over Yahweh's house.

20 So all the people of the land rejoiced, and the city was quiet. They had slain Athaliah with the sword at the king's house.

Responsorial Psalm: Psalms 132: 11-14, 17-18

11 Yahweh has sworn to David in truth.
He will not turn from it:
"I will set the fruit of your body on your throne.
12 If your children will keep my covenant,
my testimony that I will teach them,
their children also will sit on your throne forever more."
13 For Yahweh has chosen Zion.
He has desired it for his habitation.
14 "This is my resting place forever.
I will live here, for I have desired it.
17 I will make the horn of David to bud there.
I have ordained a lamp for my anointed.
18 I will clothe his enemies with shame,

but on himself, his crown will shine."

Gospel: Matthew 6: 19-23

19 "Don't lay up treasures for yourselves on the earth, where moth and rust consume, and where thieves break through and steal; 20 but lay up for yourselves treasures in heaven, where neither moth nor rust consume, and where thieves don't break through and steal; 21 for where your treasure is, there your heart will be also.
22 "The lamp of the body is the eye. If therefore your eye is sound, your whole body will be full of light. 23 But if your eye is evil, your whole body will be full of darkness. If therefore the light that is in you is darkness, how great is the darkness!

1. Invite the Holy Spirit into this reading, asking the Author of Scripture to speak to you through His Word
2. Read today's passage as many times as you need, take your time
3. Write down (below) what the Lord is saying to you today
4. Live with this Word in your heart through the day

Saturday, June 22, 2024
Saint Paulinus of Nola, Bishop; Saints John Fisher, Bishop,
and Thomas More, Martyrs; BVM

First Reading: Second Chronicles 24: 17-25

17 Now after the death of Jehoiada, the princes of Judah came and bowed down to the king. Then the king listened to them. 18 They abandoned the house of Yahweh, the God of their fathers, and served the Asherah poles and the idols, so wrath came on Judah and Jerusalem for this their guiltiness. 19 Yet he sent prophets to them to bring them again to Yahweh, and they testified against them; but they would not listen.
20 The Spirit of God came on Zechariah the son of Jehoiada the priest; and he stood above the people, and said to them, "God says, 'Why do you disobey Yahweh's commandments, so that you can't prosper? Because you have forsaken Yahweh, he has also forsaken you.'"
21 They conspired against him, and stoned him with stones at the commandment of the king in the court of Yahweh's house. 22 Thus Joash the king didn't remember the kindness which Jehoiada his father had done to him, but killed his son. When he died, he said, "May Yahweh look at it, and repay it."
23 At the end of the year, the army of the Syrians came up against him. They came to Judah and Jerusalem, and destroyed all the princes of the people from among the people, and sent all their plunder to the king of Damascus. 24 For the army of the Syrians came with a small

company of men; and Yahweh delivered a very great army into their hand, because they had forsaken Yahweh, the God of their fathers. So they executed judgment on Joash.

25 When they had departed from him (for they left him seriously wounded), his own servants conspired against him for the blood of the sons of Jehoiada the priest, and killed him on his bed, and he died. They buried him in David's city, but they didn't bury him in the tombs of the kings.

Responsorial Psalm: Psalms 89: 4-5, 29-34

4 'I will establish your offspring forever,
and build up your throne to all generations.' "
5 The heavens will praise your wonders, Yahweh,
your faithfulness also in the assembly of the holy ones.
29 I will also make his offspring endure forever,
and his throne as the days of heaven.
30 If his children forsake my law,
and don't walk in my ordinances;
31 if they break my statutes,
and don't keep my commandments;
32 then I will punish their sin with the rod,
and their iniquity with stripes.
33 But I will not completely take my loving kindness from him,
nor allow my faithfulness to fail.
34 I will not break my covenant,
nor alter what my lips have uttered.

Gospel: Matthew 6: 24-34

24 "No one can serve two masters, for either he will hate the one and love the other, or else he will be devoted to one and despise the other. You can't serve both God and Mammon. 25 Therefore I tell you, don't be anxious for your life: what you will eat, or what you will drink; nor yet for your body, what you will wear. Isn't life more than food, and the body more than clothing? 26 See the birds of the sky, that they don't sow, neither do they reap, nor gather into barns. Your heavenly Father feeds them. Aren't you of much more value than they?

27 "Which of you by being anxious, can add one moment§ to his lifespan? 28 Why are you anxious about clothing? Consider the lilies of the field, how they grow. They don't toil, neither do they spin, 29 yet I tell you that even Solomon in all his glory was not dressed like one of these. 30 But if God so clothes the grass of the field, which today exists and tomorrow is thrown into the oven, won't he much more clothe you, you of little faith?

31 "Therefore don't be anxious, saying, 'What will we eat?', 'What will we drink?' or, 'With what will we be clothed?' 32 For the Gentiles seek after all these things; for your heavenly Father knows that you need all these things. 33 But seek first God's Kingdom and his

righteousness; and all these things will be given to you as well. 34 Therefore don't be anxious for tomorrow, for tomorrow will be anxious for itself. Each day's own evil is sufficient.

1. Invite the Holy Spirit into this reading, asking the Author of Scripture to speak to you through His Word
2. Read today's passage as many times as you need, take your time
3. Write down (below) what the Lord is saying to you today
4. Live with this Word in your heart through the day

Sunday, June 23, 2024
TWELFTH SUNDAY IN ORDINARY TIME

First Reading: Job 38: 1, 8-11

1 Then Yahweh answered Job out of the whirlwind,
8 "Or who shut up the sea with doors,
when it broke out of the womb,
9 when I made clouds its garment,
and wrapped it in thick darkness,
10 marked out for it my bound,
set bars and doors,
11 and said, 'You may come here, but no further.
Your proud waves shall be stopped here'?

Responsorial Psalm: Psalms 107: 23-26, 28-31

23 Those who go down to the sea in ships,
who do business in great waters,
24 these see Yahweh's deeds,
and his wonders in the deep.
25 For he commands, and raises the stormy wind,
which lifts up its waves.
26 They mount up to the sky; they go down again to the depths.
Their soul melts away because of trouble.
28 Then they cry to Yahweh in their trouble,
and he brings them out of their distress.
29 He makes the storm a calm,

so that its waves are still.
30 Then they are glad because it is calm,
so he brings them to their desired haven.
31 Let them praise Yahweh for his loving kindness,
for his wonderful deeds for the children of men!

Second Reading: Second Corinthians 5: 14-17

14 For the love of Christ compels us; because we judge thus: that one died for all, therefore all died. 15 He died for all, that those who live should no longer live to themselves, but to him who for their sakes died and rose again.
16 Therefore we know no one according to the flesh from now on. Even though we have known Christ according to the flesh, yet now we know him so no more. 17 Therefore if anyone is in Christ, he is a new creation. The old things have passed away. Behold,† all things have become new.

Gospel: Mark 4: 35-41

35 On that day, when evening had come, he said to them, "Let's go over to the other side." 36 Leaving the multitude, they took him with them, even as he was, in the boat. Other small boats were also with him. 37 A big wind storm arose, and the waves beat into the boat, so much that the boat was already filled. 38 He himself was in the stern, asleep on the cushion; and they woke him up and asked him, "Teacher, don't you care that we are dying?"
39 He awoke and rebuked the wind, and said to the sea, "Peace! Be still!" The wind ceased and there was a great calm. 40 He said to them, "Why are you so afraid? How is it that you have no faith?"
41 They were greatly afraid and said to one another, "Who then is this, that even the wind and the sea obey him?"

1. Invite the Holy Spirit into this reading, asking the Author of Scripture to speak to you through His Word
2. Read today's passage as many times as you need, take your time
3. Write down (below) what the Lord is saying to you today
4. Live with this Word in your heart through the day

Monday, June 24, 2024
THE NATIVITY OF SAINT JOHN THE BAPTIST

First Reading: Isaiah 49: 1-6

1 Listen, islands, to me.
Listen, you peoples, from afar:
Yahweh has called me from the womb;
from the inside of my mother, he has mentioned my name.
2 He has made my mouth like a sharp sword.
He has hidden me in the shadow of his hand.
He has made me a polished shaft.
He has kept me close in his quiver.
3 He said to me, "You are my servant,
Israel, in whom I will be glorified."
4 But I said, "I have labored in vain.
I have spent my strength in vain for nothing;
yet surely the justice due to me is with Yahweh,
and my reward with my God."
5 Now Yahweh, he who formed me from the womb to be his servant,
says to bring Jacob again to him,
and to gather Israel to him,
for I am honorable in Yahweh's eyes,
and my God has become my strength.
6 Indeed, he says, "It is too light a thing that you should be my servant to raise up the tribes
of Jacob,
and to restore the preserved of Israel.
I will also give you as a light to the nations,
that you may be my salvation to the end of the earth."

Responsorial Psalm: Psalms 139: 1b-3, 13-15

1 Yahweh, you have searched me,
and you know me.
2 You know my sitting down and my rising up.
You perceive my thoughts from afar.
3 You search out my path and my lying down,
and are acquainted with all my ways.
13 For you formed my inmost being.
You knit me together in my mother's womb.
14 I will give thanks to you,
for I am fearfully and wonderfully made.
Your works are wonderful.
My soul knows that very well.
15 My frame wasn't hidden from you,

when I was made in secret,
woven together in the depths of the earth.

Second Reading: Acts 13: 22-26

22 When he had removed him, he raised up David to be their king, to whom he also testified, 'I have found David the son of Jesse, a man after my heart, who will do all my will.' 23 From this man's offspring, God has brought salvation‡ to Israel according to his promise, 24 before his coming, when John had first preached the baptism of repentance to Israel.§ 25 As John was fulfilling his course, he said, 'What do you suppose that I am? I am not he. But behold, one comes after me, the sandals of whose feet I am not worthy to untie.'
26 "Brothers, children of the stock of Abraham, and those among you who fear God, the word of this salvation is sent out to you.

Gospel: Luke 1: 57-66, 80

57 Now the time that Elizabeth should give birth was fulfilled, and she gave birth to a son. 58 Her neighbors and her relatives heard that the Lord had magnified his mercy toward her, and they rejoiced with her. 59 On the eighth day, they came to circumcise the child; and they would have called him Zacharias, after the name of his father. 60 His mother answered, "Not so; but he will be called John."
61 They said to her, "There is no one among your relatives who is called by this name." 62 They made signs to his father, what he would have him called.
63 He asked for a writing tablet, and wrote, "His name is John."
They all marveled. 64 His mouth was opened immediately and his tongue freed, and he spoke, blessing God. 65 Fear came on all who lived around them, and all these sayings were talked about throughout all the hill country of Judea. 66 All who heard them laid them up in their heart, saying, "What then will this child be?" The hand of the Lord was with him.
80 The child was growing and becoming strong in spirit, and was in the desert until the day of his public appearance to Israel.

1. Invite the Holy Spirit into this reading, asking the Author of Scripture to speak to you through His Word
2. Read today's passage as many times as you need, take your time
3. Write down (below) what the Lord is saying to you today
4. Live with this Word in your heart through the day

Tuesday, June 25, 2024

First Reading: Second Kings 19: 9b-11, 14-21, 31-35a, 36

9 When he heard it said of Tirhakah king of Ethiopia, "Behold, he has come out to fight against you," he sent messengers again to Hezekiah, saying, 10 "Tell Hezekiah king of Judah this: 'Don't let your God in whom you trust deceive you, saying, Jerusalem will not be given into the hand of the king of Assyria. 11 Behold, you have heard what the kings of Assyria have done to all lands, by destroying them utterly. Will you be delivered?

14 Hezekiah received the letter from the hand of the messengers and read it. Then Hezekiah went up to Yahweh's house, and spread it before Yahweh. 15 Hezekiah prayed before Yahweh, and said, "Yahweh, the God of Israel, who are enthroned above the cherubim, you are the God, even you alone, of all the kingdoms of the earth. You have made heaven and earth. 16 Incline your ear, Yahweh, and hear. Open your eyes, Yahweh, and see. Hear the words of Sennacherib, which he has sent to defy the living God. 17 Truly, Yahweh, the kings of Assyria have laid waste the nations and their lands, 18 and have cast their gods into the fire; for they were no gods, but the work of men's hands, wood and stone. Therefore they have destroyed them. 19 Now therefore, Yahweh our God, save us, I beg you, out of his hand, that all the kingdoms of the earth may know that you, Yahweh, are God alone."

20 Then Isaiah the son of Amoz sent to Hezekiah, saying, "Yahweh, the God of Israel, says 'You have prayed to me against Sennacherib king of Assyria, and I have heard you. 21 This is the word that Yahweh has spoken concerning him: 'The virgin daughter of Zion has despised you and ridiculed you. The daughter of Jerusalem has shaken her head at you.

31 For out of Jerusalem a remnant will go out, and out of Mount Zion those who shall escape. Yahweh's zeal will perform this.

32 "Therefore Yahweh says concerning the king of Assyria, 'He will not come to this city, nor shoot an arrow there. He will not come before it with shield, nor cast up a mound against it. 33 He will return the same way that he came, and he will not come to this city,' says Yahweh. 34 'For I will defend this city to save it, for my own sake and for my servant David's sake.' "

35a That night, Yahweh's angel went out and struck one hundred eighty-five thousand in the camp of the Assyrians.

36 So Sennacherib king of Assyria departed, went home, and lived at Nineveh.

Responsorial Psalm: Psalms 48: 2-4, 10-11

2 Beautiful in elevation, the joy of the whole earth,
is Mount Zion, on the north sides,
the city of the great King.
3 God has shown himself in her citadels as a refuge.
4 For, behold, the kings assembled themselves,
they passed by together.
10 As is your name, God,
so is your praise to the ends of the earth.

Your right hand is full of righteousness.
11 Let Mount Zion be glad!
Let the daughters of Judah rejoice because of your judgments.
Gospel: Matthew 7: 6, 12-14

6 "Don't give that which is holy to the dogs, neither throw your pearls before the pigs, lest perhaps they trample them under their feet, and turn and tear you to pieces.
12 Therefore, whatever you desire for men to do to you, you shall also do to them; for this is the law and the prophets.
13 "Enter in by the narrow gate; for the gate is wide and the way is broad that leads to destruction, and there are many who enter in by it. 14 How† narrow is the gate and the way is restricted that leads to life! There are few who find it.

1. Invite the Holy Spirit into this reading, asking the Author of Scripture to speak to you through His Word
2. Read today's passage as many times as you need, take your time
3. Write down (below) what the Lord is saying to you today
4. Live with this Word in your heart through the day

_____

_____

Wednesday, June 26, 2024

First Reading: Second Kings 22: 8-13; 23: 1-3

8 Hilkiah the high priest said to Shaphan the scribe, "I have found the book of the law in Yahweh's house." Hilkiah delivered the book to Shaphan, and he read it. 9 Shaphan the scribe came to the king, and brought the king word again, and said, "Your servants have emptied out the money that was found in the house, and have delivered it into the hands of the workmen who have the oversight of Yahweh's house." 10 Shaphan the scribe told the king, saying, "Hilkiah the priest has delivered a book to me." Then Shaphan read it before the king.
11 When the king had heard the words of the book of the law, he tore his clothes. 12 The king commanded Hilkiah the priest, Ahikam the son of Shaphan, Achbor the son of Micaiah, Shaphan the scribe, and Asaiah the king's servant, saying, 13 "Go inquire of Yahweh for me, and for the people, and for all Judah, concerning the words of this book that is found; for great is Yahweh's wrath that is kindled against us, because our fathers have not listened to the words of this book, to do according to all that which is written concerning us."
1 The king sent, and they gathered to him all the elders of Judah and of Jerusalem. 2 The king went up to Yahweh's house, and all the men of Judah and all the inhabitants of Jerusalem with him—with the priests, the prophets, and all the people, both small and great; and he read in

their hearing all the words of the book of the covenant which was found in Yahweh's house. 3 The king stood by the pillar and made a covenant before Yahweh to walk after Yahweh and to keep his commandments, his testimonies, and his statutes with all his heart and all his soul, to confirm the words of this covenant that were written in this book; and all the people agreed to the covenant.

Responsorial Psalm: Psalms 119: 33, 34, 36, 37, 40

33 Teach me, Yahweh, the way of your statutes.
I will keep them to the end.
34 Give me understanding, and I will keep your law.
Yes, I will obey it with my whole heart.
36 Turn my heart toward your statutes,
not toward selfish gain.
37 Turn my eyes away from looking at worthless things.
Revive me in your ways.
40 Behold, I long for your precepts!
Revive me in your righteousness.

Gospel: Matthew 7: 15-20

15 "Beware of false prophets, who come to you in sheep's clothing, but inwardly are ravening wolves. 16 By their fruits you will know them. Do you gather grapes from thorns or figs from thistles? 17 Even so, every good tree produces good fruit, but the corrupt tree produces evil fruit. 18 A good tree can't produce evil fruit, neither can a corrupt tree produce good fruit. 19 Every tree that doesn't grow good fruit is cut down and thrown into the fire. 20 Therefore by their fruits you will know them.

1. Invite the Holy Spirit into this reading, asking the Author of Scripture to speak to you through His Word
2. Read today's passage as many times as you need, take your time
3. Write down (below) what the Lord is saying to you today
4. Live with this Word in your heart through the day

_____

_____

Thursday, June 27, 2024
Saint Cyril of Alexandria, Bishop and Doctor of the Church

First Reading: Second Kings 24: 8-17

8 Jehoiachin was eighteen years old when he began to reign, and he reigned in Jerusalem three months. His mother's name was Nehushta the daughter of Elnathan of Jerusalem. 9 He did that which was evil in Yahweh's sight, according to all that his father had done. 10 At that time the servants of Nebuchadnezzar king of Babylon came up to Jerusalem, and the city was besieged. 11 Nebuchadnezzar king of Babylon came to the city while his servants were besieging it, 12 and Jehoiachin the king of Judah went out to the king of Babylon—he, his mother, his servants, his princes, and his officers; and the king of Babylon captured him in the eighth year of his reign. 13 He carried out from there all the treasures of Yahweh's house and the treasures of the king's house, and cut in pieces all the vessels of gold which Solomon king of Israel had made in Yahweh's temple, as Yahweh had said. 14 He carried away all Jerusalem, and all the princes, and all the mighty men of valor, even ten thousand captives, and all the craftsmen and the smiths. No one remained except the poorest people of the land. 15 He carried away Jehoiachin to Babylon, with the king's mother, the king's wives, his officers, and the chief men of the land. He carried them into captivity from Jerusalem to Babylon. 16 All the men of might, even seven thousand, and the craftsmen and the smiths one thousand, all of them strong and fit for war, even them the king of Babylon brought captive to Babylon. 17 The king of Babylon made Mattaniah, Jehoiachin's father's brother, king in his place, and changed his name to Zedekiah.

Responsorial Psalm: Psalms 79: 1b-5, 8, 9

1 God, the nations have come into your inheritance.
They have defiled your holy temple.
They have laid Jerusalem in heaps.
2 They have given the dead bodies of your servants to be food for the birds of the sky,
the flesh of your saints to the animals of the earth.
3 They have shed their blood like water around Jerusalem.
There was no one to bury them.
4 We have become a reproach to our neighbors,
a scoffing and derision to those who are around us.
5 How long, Yahweh?
Will you be angry forever?
Will your jealousy burn like fire?
8 Don't hold the iniquities of our forefathers against us.
Let your tender mercies speedily meet us,
for we are in desperate need.
9 Help us, God of our salvation, for the glory of your name.
Deliver us, and forgive our sins, for your name's sake.

Gospel: Matthew 7: 21-29

21 "Not everyone who says to me, 'Lord, Lord,' will enter into the Kingdom of Heaven, but he who does the will of my Father who is in heaven. 22 Many will tell me in that day, 'Lord, Lord, didn't we prophesy in your name, in your name cast out demons, and in your name do many mighty works?' 23 Then I will tell them, 'I never knew you. Depart from me, you who work iniquity.'

24 "Everyone therefore who hears these words of mine and does them, I will liken him to a wise man who built his house on a rock. 25 The rain came down, the floods came, and the winds blew and beat on that house; and it didn't fall, for it was founded on the rock. 26 Everyone who hears these words of mine and doesn't do them will be like a foolish man who built his house on the sand. 27 The rain came down, the floods came, and the winds blew and beat on that house; and it fell—and its fall was great."

28 When Jesus had finished saying these things, the multitudes were astonished at his teaching, 29 for he taught them with authority, and not like the scribes.

1. Invite the Holy Spirit into this reading, asking the Author of Scripture to speak to you through His Word
2. Read today's passage as many times as you need, take your time
3. Write down (below) what the Lord is saying to you today
4. Live with this Word in your heart through the day

_____

_____

Friday, June 28, 2024
Saint Irenaeus, Bishop and Martyr

First Reading: Second Kings 25: 1-12

1 In the ninth year of his reign, in the tenth month, in the tenth day of the month, Nebuchadnezzar king of Babylon came, he and all his army, against Jerusalem, and encamped against it; and they built forts against it around it. 2 So the city was besieged until the eleventh year of King Zedekiah. 3 On the ninth day of the fourth month, the famine was severe in the city, so that there was no bread for the people of the land. 4 Then a breach was made in the city, and all the men of war fled by night by the way of the gate between the two walls, which was by the king's garden (now the Chaldeans were against the city around it); and the king went by the way of the Arabah. 5 But the Chaldean army pursued the king, and overtook him in the plains of Jericho; and all his army was scattered from him. 6 Then they captured the king and carried him up to the king of Babylon to Riblah; and they passed judgment on him. 7 They killed Zedekiah's sons before his eyes, then put out Zedekiah's eyes, bound him in fetters, and carried him to Babylon.

8 Now in the fifth month, on the seventh day of the month, which was the nineteenth year of King Nebuchadnezzar king of Babylon, Nebuzaradan the captain of the guard, a servant of the king of Babylon, came to Jerusalem. 9 He burned Yahweh's house, the king's house, and all the houses of Jerusalem. He burned every great house with fire. 10 All the army of the Chaldeans, who were with the captain of the guard, broke down the walls around Jerusalem. 11 Nebuzaradan the captain of the guard carried away captive the rest of the people who were left in the city and those who had deserted to the king of Babylon—all the rest of the multitude. 12 But the captain of the guard left some of the poorest of the land to work the vineyards and fields.

Responsorial Psalm: Psalms 137: 1-6

1 By the rivers of Babylon, there we sat down.
Yes, we wept, when we remembered Zion.
2 On the willows in that land,
we hung up our harps.
3 For there, those who led us captive asked us for songs.
Those who tormented us demanded songs of joy:
"Sing us one of the songs of Zion!"
4 How can we sing Yahweh's song in a foreign land?
5 If I forget you, Jerusalem,
let my right hand forget its skill.
6 Let my tongue stick to the roof of my mouth if I don't remember you,
if I don't prefer Jerusalem above my chief joy.

Gospel: Matthew 8: 1-4

1 When he came down from the mountain, great multitudes followed him. 2 Behold, a leper came to him and worshiped him, saying, "Lord, if you want to, you can make me clean."
3 Jesus stretched out his hand and touched him, saying, "I want to. Be made clean." Immediately his leprosy was cleansed. 4 Jesus said to him, "See that you tell nobody; but go, show yourself to the priest, and offer the gift that Moses commanded, as a testimony to them."

1. Invite the Holy Spirit into this reading, asking the Author of Scripture to speak to you through His Word
2. Read today's passage as many times as you need, take your time
3. Write down (below) what the Lord is saying to you today
4. Live with this Word in your heart through the day

First Reading: Acts 12: 1-11

1 Now about that time, King Herod stretched out his hands to oppress some of the assembly. 2 He killed James, the brother of John, with the sword. 3 When he saw that it pleased the Jews, he proceeded to seize Peter also. This was during the days of unleavened bread. 4 When he had arrested him, he put him in prison and delivered him to four squads of four soldiers each to guard him, intending to bring him out to the people after the Passover. 5 Peter therefore was kept in the prison, but constant prayer was made by the assembly to God for him. 6 The same night when Herod was about to bring him out, Peter was sleeping between two soldiers, bound with two chains. Guards in front of the door kept the prison.

7 And behold, an angel of the Lord stood by him, and a light shone in the cell. He struck Peter on the side and woke him up, saying, "Stand up quickly!" His chains fell off his hands. 8 The angel said to him, "Get dressed and put on your sandals." He did so. He said to him, "Put on your cloak and follow me." 9 And he went out and followed him. He didn't know that what was being done by the angel was real, but thought he saw a vision. 10 When they were past the first and the second guard, they came to the iron gate that leads into the city, which opened to them by itself. They went out and went down one street, and immediately the angel departed from him.

11 When Peter had come to himself, he said, "Now I truly know that the Lord has sent out his angel and delivered me out of the hand of Herod, and from everything the Jewish people were expecting."

Responsorial Psalm: Psalms 34: 2-9

2 My soul shall boast in Yahweh.
The humble shall hear of it and be glad.
3 Oh magnify Yahweh with me.
Let's exalt his name together.
4 I sought Yahweh, and he answered me,
and delivered me from all my fears.
5 They looked to him, and were radiant.
Their faces shall never be covered with shame.
6 This poor man cried, and Yahweh heard him,
and saved him out of all his troubles.
7 Yahweh's angel encamps around those who fear him,
and delivers them.
8 Oh taste and see that Yahweh is good.
Blessed is the man who takes refuge in him.
9 Oh fear Yahweh, you his saints,

for there is no lack with those who fear him.

Second Reading: Second Timothy 4: 6-8, 17-18

6 For I am already being offered, and the time of my departure has come. 7 I have fought the good fight. I have finished the course. I have kept the faith. 8 From now on, the crown of righteousness is stored up for me, which the Lord, the righteous judge, will give to me on that day; and not to me only, but also to all those who have loved his appearing.
17 But the Lord stood by me and strengthened me, that through me the message might be fully proclaimed, and that all the Gentiles might hear. So I was delivered out of the mouth of the lion. 18 And the Lord will deliver me from every evil work and will preserve me for his heavenly Kingdom. To him be the glory forever and ever. Amen.

Gospel: Matthew 16: 13-19

13 Now when Jesus came into the parts of Caesarea Philippi, he asked his disciples, saying, "Who do men say that I, the Son of Man, am?"
14 They said, "Some say John the Baptizer, some, Elijah, and others, Jeremiah or one of the prophets."
15 He said to them, "But who do you say that I am?"
16 Simon Peter answered, "You are the Christ, the Son of the living God."
17 Jesus answered him, "Blessed are you, Simon Bar Jonah, for flesh and blood has not revealed this to you, but my Father who is in heaven. 18 I also tell you that you are Peter,† and on this rock ‡ I will build my assembly, and the gates of Hades§ will not prevail against it. 19 I will give to you the keys of the Kingdom of Heaven, and whatever you bind on earth will have been bound in heaven; and whatever you release on earth will have been released in heaven."

1. Invite the Holy Spirit into this reading, asking the Author of Scripture to speak to you through His Word
2. Read today's passage as many times as you need, take your time
3. Write down (below) what the Lord is saying to you today
4. Live with this Word in your heart through the day

Sunday, June 30, 2024
THIRTEENTH SUNDAY IN ORDINARY TIME

First Reading: Wisdom 1: 13-15; 2: 23-24

13 because God didn't make death,
neither does he delight when the living perish.
14 For he created all things that they might have being.
The generative powers of the world are wholesome,
and there is no poison of destruction in them,
nor has Hades‡ royal dominion upon earth;
15 for righteousness is immortal,
23 Because God created man for incorruption,
and made him an image of his own everlastingness;
24 but death entered into the world by the envy of the devil,
and those who belong to him experience it.

Responsorial Psalm: Psalms 30: 2, 4-6, 11- 12

2 Yahweh my God, I cried to you,
and you have healed me.
4 Sing praise to Yahweh, you saints of his.
Give thanks to his holy name.
5 For his anger is but for a moment.
His favor is for a lifetime.
Weeping may stay for the night,
but joy comes in the morning.
6 As for me, I said in my prosperity,
"I shall never be moved."
11 You have turned my mourning into dancing for me.
You have removed my sackcloth, and clothed me with gladness,
12 to the end that my heart may sing praise to you, and not be silent.
Yahweh my God, I will give thanks to you forever!

Second Reading: Second Corinthians 8: 7, 9, 13-15

7 But as you abound in everything—in faith, utterance, knowledge, all earnestness, and in your love to us—see that you also abound in this grace.
9 For you know the grace of our Lord Jesus Christ, that though he was rich, yet for your sakes he became poor, that you through his poverty might become rich.
13 For this is not that others may be eased and you distressed, 14 but for equality. Your abundance at this present time supplies their lack, that their abundance also may become a supply for your lack, that there may be equality. 15 As it is written, "He who gathered much had nothing left over, and he who gathered little had no lack."

Gospel: Mark 5: 21-43

21 When Jesus had crossed back over in the boat to the other side, a great multitude was gathered to him; and he was by the sea. 22 Behold, one of the rulers of the synagogue, Jairus by name, came; and seeing him, he fell at his feet 23 and begged him much, saying, "My little daughter is at the point of death. Please come and lay your hands on her, that she may be made healthy, and live."

24 He went with him, and a great multitude followed him, and they pressed upon him on all sides. 25 A certain woman who had a discharge of blood for twelve years, 26 and had suffered many things by many physicians, and had spent all that she had, and was no better, but rather grew worse, 27 having heard the things concerning Jesus, came up behind him in the crowd and touched his clothes. 28 For she said, "If I just touch his clothes, I will be made well." 29 Immediately the flow of her blood was dried up, and she felt in her body that she was healed of her affliction.

30 Immediately Jesus, perceiving in himself that the power had gone out from him, turned around in the crowd and asked, "Who touched my clothes?"

31 His disciples said to him, "You see the multitude pressing against you, and you say, 'Who touched me?'"

32 He looked around to see her who had done this thing. 33 But the woman, fearing and trembling, knowing what had been done to her, came and fell down before him, and told him all the truth.

34 He said to her, "Daughter, your faith has made you well. Go in peace, and be cured of your disease."

35 While he was still speaking, people came from the synagogue ruler's house, saying, "Your daughter is dead. Why bother the Teacher any more?"

36 But Jesus, when he heard the message spoken, immediately said to the ruler of the synagogue, "Don't be afraid, only believe." 37 He allowed no one to follow him except Peter, James, and John the brother of James. 38 He came to the synagogue ruler's house, and he saw an uproar, weeping, and great wailing. 39 When he had entered in, he said to them, "Why do you make an uproar and weep? The child is not dead, but is asleep."

40 They ridiculed him. But he, having put them all out, took the father of the child, her mother, and those who were with him, and went in where the child was lying. 41 Taking the child by the hand, he said to her, "Talitha cumi!" which means, being interpreted, "Girl, I tell you, get up!" 42 Immediately the girl rose up and walked, for she was twelve years old. They were amazed with great amazement. 43 He strictly ordered them that no one should know this, and commanded that something should be given to her to eat.

1. Invite the Holy Spirit into this reading, asking the Author of Scripture to speak to you through His Word
2. Read today's passage as many times as you need, take your time
3. Write down (below) what the Lord is saying to you today
4. Live with this Word in your heart through the day

Monday, July 1, 2024

Saint Junípero Serra, Priest

First Reading: Amos 2: 6-10, 13-16

6 Yahweh says:
"For three transgressions of Israel, yes, for four,
I will not turn away its punishment,
because they have sold the righteous for silver,
and the needy for a pair of sandals;
7 They trample the heads of the poor into the dust of the earth
and deny justice to the oppressed.
A man and his father use the same maiden, to profane my holy name.
8 They lay themselves down beside every altar on clothes taken in pledge.
In the house of their God† they drink the wine of those who have been fined.
9 Yet I destroyed the Amorite before them,
whose height was like the height of the cedars,
and he was strong as the oaks;
yet I destroyed his fruit from above,
and his roots from beneath.
10 Also I brought you up out of the land of Egypt
and led you forty years in the wilderness,
to possess the land of the Amorite.
13 Behold,‡ I will crush you in your place,
as a cart crushes that is full of grain.
14 Flight will perish from the swift.
The strong won't strengthen his force.
The mighty won't deliver himself.
15 He who handles the bow won't stand.
He who is swift of foot won't escape.
He who rides the horse won't deliver himself.
16 He who is courageous among the mighty
will flee away naked on that day,"
says Yahweh.

Responsorial Psalm: Psalms 50: 16bc-23

16b "What right do you have to declare my statutes,
that you have taken my covenant on your lips,
17 since you hate instruction,
and throw my words behind you?
18 When you saw a thief, you consented with him,

and have participated with adulterers.
19 "You give your mouth to evil.
Your tongue frames deceit.
20 You sit and speak against your brother.
You slander your own mother's son.
21 You have done these things, and I kept silent.
You thought that I was just like you.
I will rebuke you, and accuse you in front of your eyes.
22 "Now consider this, you who forget God,
lest I tear you into pieces, and there be no one to deliver.
23 Whoever offers the sacrifice of thanksgiving glorifies me,
and prepares his way so that I will show God's salvation to him."

Gospel: Matthew 8: 18-22

18 Now when Jesus saw great multitudes around him, he gave the order to depart to the other side.
19 A scribe came and said to him, "Teacher, I will follow you wherever you go."
20 Jesus said to him, "The foxes have holes and the birds of the sky have nests, but the Son of Man has nowhere to lay his head."
21 Another of his disciples said to him, "Lord, allow me first to go and bury my father."
22 But Jesus said to him, "Follow me, and leave the dead to bury their own dead."

1. Invite the Holy Spirit into this reading, asking the Author of Scripture to speak to you through His Word
2. Read today's passage as many times as you need, take your time
3. Write down (below) what the Lord is saying to you today
4. Live with this Word in your heart through the day

_____

_____

Tuesday, July 2, 2024

First Reading: Amos 3: 1-8; 4: 11-12

1 Hear this word that Yahweh has spoken against you, children of Israel, against the whole family which I brought up out of the land of Egypt, saying:
2 "I have only chosen you of all the families of the earth.
Therefore I will punish you for all of your sins."

3 Do two walk together,
unless they have agreed?
4 Will a lion roar in the thicket,
when he has no prey?
Does a young lion cry out of his den,
if he has caught nothing?
5 Can a bird fall in a trap on the earth,
where no snare is set for him?
Does a snare spring up from the ground,
when there is nothing to catch?
6 Does the trumpet alarm sound in a city,
without the people being afraid?
Does evil happen to a city,
and Yahweh hasn't done it?
7 Surely the Lord Yahweh will do nothing,
unless he reveals his secret to his servants the prophets.
8 The lion has roared.
Who will not fear?
The Lord Yahweh has spoken.
Who can but prophesy?
11 "I have overthrown some of you,
as when God overthrew Sodom and Gomorrah,
and you were like a burning stick plucked out of the fire;
yet you haven't returned to me," says Yahweh.
12 "Therefore I will do this to you, Israel;
because I will do this to you,
prepare to meet your God, Israel.

Responsorial Psalm: Psalms 5: 4b-8

4 For you are not a God who has pleasure in wickedness.
Evil can't live with you.
5 The arrogant will not stand in your sight.
You hate all workers of iniquity.
6 You will destroy those who speak lies.
Yahweh abhors the bloodthirsty and deceitful man.
7 But as for me, in the abundance of your loving kindness I will come into your house.
I will bow toward your holy temple in reverence of you.
8 Lead me, Yahweh, in your righteousness because of my enemies.
Make your way straight before my face.

Gospel: Matthew 8: 23-27

23 When he got into a boat, his disciples followed him. 24 Behold, a violent storm came up on the sea, so much that the boat was covered with the waves; but he was asleep. 25 The disciples came to him and woke him up, saying, "Save us, Lord! We are dying!"

26 He said to them, "Why are you fearful, O you of little faith?" Then he got up, rebuked the wind and the sea, and there was a great calm.

27 The men marveled, saying, "What kind of man is this, that even the wind and the sea obey him?"

1. Invite the Holy Spirit into this reading, asking the Author of Scripture to speak to you through His Word
2. Read today's passage as many times as you need, take your time
3. Write down (below) what the Lord is saying to you today
4. Live with this Word in your heart through the day

Wednesday, July 3, 2024
Saint Thomas, Apostle

First Reading: Ephesians 2: 19-22

19 So then you are no longer strangers and foreigners, but you are fellow citizens with the saints and of the household of God, 20 being built on the foundation of the apostles and prophets, Christ Jesus himself being the chief cornerstone; 21 in whom the whole building, fitted together, grows into a holy temple in the Lord; 22 in whom you also are built together for a habitation of God in the Spirit.

Responsorial Psalm: Psalms 117: 1bc, 2

1 Praise Yahweh, all you nations!
Extol him, all you peoples!
2 For his loving kindness is great toward us.
Yahweh's faithfulness endures forever.
Praise Yah!

Gospel: John 20: 24-29

24 But Thomas, one of the twelve, called Didymus,§ wasn't with them when Jesus came. 25 The other disciples therefore said to him, "We have seen the Lord!"

But he said to them, "Unless I see in his hands the print of the nails, put my finger into the print of the nails, and put my hand into his side, I will not believe."

26 After eight days, again his disciples were inside and Thomas was with them. Jesus came, the doors being locked, and stood in the middle, and said, "Peace be to you." 27 Then he said to Thomas, "Reach here your finger, and see my hands. Reach here your hand, and put it into my side. Don't be unbelieving, but believing."

28 Thomas answered him, "My Lord and my God!"

29 Jesus said to him, "Because you have seen me,† you have believed. Blessed are those who have not seen and have believed."

1. Invite the Holy Spirit into this reading, asking the Author of Scripture to speak to you through His Word
2. Read today's passage as many times as you need, take your time
3. Write down (below) what the Lord is saying to you today
4. Live with this Word in your heart through the day

_____

_____

Thursday, July 4, 2024
USA: Independence Day

First Reading: Amos 7: 10-17

10 Then Amaziah the priest of Bethel sent to Jeroboam king of Israel, saying, "Amos has conspired against you in the middle of the house of Israel. The land is not able to bear all his words. 11 For Amos says, 'Jeroboam will die by the sword, and Israel shall surely be led away captive out of his land.' "

12 Amaziah also said to Amos, "You seer, go, flee away into the land of Judah, and there eat bread, and prophesy there, 13 but don't prophesy again any more at Bethel; for it is the king's sanctuary, and it is a royal house!"

14 Then Amos answered Amaziah, "I was no prophet, neither was I a prophet's son, but I was a herdsman, and a farmer of sycamore figs; 15 and Yahweh took me from following the flock, and Yahweh said to me, 'Go, prophesy to my people Israel.' 16 Now therefore listen to Yahweh's word: 'You say, Don't prophesy against Israel, and don't preach against the house of Isaac.' 17 Therefore Yahweh says: 'Your wife shall be a prostitute in the city, and your sons and your daughters shall fall by the sword, and your land shall be divided by line; and you yourself shall die in a land that is unclean, and Israel shall surely be led away captive out of his land.' "

Responsorial Psalm: Psalms 19: 8- 11

8 Yahweh's precepts are right, rejoicing the heart.
Yahweh's commandment is pure, enlightening the eyes.
9 The fear of Yahweh is clean, enduring forever.
Yahweh's ordinances are true, and righteous altogether.
10 They are more to be desired than gold, yes, than much fine gold,
sweeter also than honey and the extract of the honeycomb.
11 Moreover your servant is warned by them.
In keeping them there is great reward.

Gospel: Matthew 9: 1-8

1 He entered into a boat and crossed over, and came into his own city. 2 Behold, they brought to him a man who was paralyzed, lying on a bed. Jesus, seeing their faith, said to the paralytic, "Son, cheer up! Your sins are forgiven you."
3 Behold, some of the scribes said to themselves, "This man blasphemes."
4 Jesus, knowing their thoughts, said, "Why do you think evil in your hearts? 5 For which is easier, to say, 'Your sins are forgiven;' or to say, 'Get up, and walk'? 6 But that you may know that the Son of Man has authority on earth to forgive sins—" (then he said to the paralytic), "Get up, and take up your mat, and go to your house."
7 He arose and departed to his house. 8 But when the multitudes saw it, they marveled and glorified God, who had given such authority to men.

1. Invite the Holy Spirit into this reading, asking the Author of Scripture to speak to you through His Word
2. Read today's passage as many times as you need, take your time
3. Write down (below) what the Lord is saying to you today
4. Live with this Word in your heart through the day

_____

_____

Friday, July 5, 2024
Saint Anthony Zaccaria, Priest; USA: Saint Elizabeth of Portugal

First Reading: Amos 8: 4-6, 9-12

4 Hear this, you who desire to swallow up the needy,

and cause the poor of the land to fail,
5 saying, 'When will the new moon be gone, that we may sell grain?
And the Sabbath, that we may market wheat,
making the ephah† small, and the shekel‡ large,
and dealing falsely with balances of deceit;
6 that we may buy the poor for silver,
and the needy for a pair of sandals,
and sell the sweepings with the wheat?' "
9 It will happen in that day," says the Lord Yahweh,
"that I will cause the sun to go down at noon,
and I will darken the earth in the clear day.
10 I will turn your feasts into mourning,
and all your songs into lamentation;
and I will make you wear sackcloth on all your bodies,
and baldness on every head.
I will make it like the mourning for an only son,
and its end like a bitter day.
11 Behold, the days come," says the Lord Yahweh,
"that I will send a famine in the land,
not a famine of bread,
nor a thirst for water,
but of hearing Yahweh's words.
12 They will wander from sea to sea,
and from the north even to the east;
they will run back and forth to seek Yahweh's word,
and will not find it.

Responsorial Psalm: Psalms 119: 2, 10, 20, 30, 40, 131

2 Blessed are those who keep his statutes,
who seek him with their whole heart.
10 With my whole heart I have sought you.
Don't let me wander from your commandments.
20 My soul is consumed with longing for your ordinances at all times.
30 I have chosen the way of truth.
I have set your ordinances before me.
40 Behold, I long for your precepts!
Revive me in your righteousness.
131 I opened my mouth wide and panted,
for I longed for your commandments.

Gospel: Matthew 9: 9-13

9 As Jesus passed by from there, he saw a man called Matthew sitting at the tax collection office. He said to him, "Follow me." He got up and followed him. 10 As he sat in the house, behold, many tax collectors and sinners came and sat down with Jesus and his disciples. 11 When the Pharisees saw it, they said to his disciples, "Why does your teacher eat with tax collectors and sinners?"

12 When Jesus heard it, he said to them, "Those who are healthy have no need for a physician, but those who are sick do. 13 But you go and learn what this means: 'I desire mercy, and not sacrifice,'* for I came not to call the righteous, but sinners to repentance."

1. Invite the Holy Spirit into this reading, asking the Author of Scripture to speak to you through His Word
2. Read today's passage as many times as you need, take your time
3. Write down (below) what the Lord is saying to you today
4. Live with this Word in your heart through the day

Saturday, July 6, 2024
Saint Maria Goretti, Virgin and Martyr; BVM

First Reading: Amos 9: 11-15

11 In that day I will raise up the tent of David who is fallen and close up its breaches, and I will raise up its ruins, and I will build it as in the days of old, 12 that they may possess the remnant of Edom and all the nations who are called by my name," says Yahweh who does this.
13 "Behold, the days come," says Yahweh,
"that the plowman shall overtake the reaper,
and the one treading grapes him who sows seed;
and sweet wine will drip from the mountains,
and flow from the hills.
14 I will bring my people Israel back from captivity,
and they will rebuild the ruined cities, and inhabit them;
and they will plant vineyards, and drink wine from them.
They shall also make gardens,
and eat their fruit.
15 I will plant them on their land,
and they will no more be plucked up out of their land which I have given them,"
says Yahweh your God.

Responsorial Psalm: Psalms 85: 9ab-13

9 Surely his salvation is near those who fear him,
that glory may dwell in our land.
10 Mercy and truth meet together.
Righteousness and peace have kissed each other.
11 Truth springs out of the earth.
Righteousness has looked down from heaven.
12 Yes, Yahweh will give that which is good.
Our land will yield its increase.
13 Righteousness goes before him,
and prepares the way for his steps.

Gospel: Matthew 9: 14-17

14 Then John's disciples came to him, saying, "Why do we and the Pharisees fast often, but your disciples don't fast?"
15 Jesus said to them, "Can the friends of the bridegroom mourn as long as the bridegroom is with them? But the days will come when the bridegroom will be taken away from them, and then they will fast. 16 No one puts a piece of unshrunk cloth on an old garment; for the patch would tear away from the garment, and a worse hole is made. 17 Neither do people put new wine into old wine skins, or else the skins would burst, and the wine be spilled, and the skins ruined. No, they put new wine into fresh wine skins, and both are preserved."

1. Invite the Holy Spirit into this reading, asking the Author of Scripture to speak to you through His Word
2. Read today's passage as many times as you need, take your time
3. Write down (below) what the Lord is saying to you today
4. Live with this Word in your heart through the day

_____

_____

Sunday, July 7, 2024
FOURTEENTH SUNDAY IN ORDINARY TIME

First Reading: Ezekiel 2: 2-5

2 The Spirit entered into me when he spoke to me, and set me on my feet; and I heard him who spoke to me.

3 He said to me, "Son of man, I send you to the children of Israel, to a nation of rebels who have rebelled against me. They and their fathers have transgressed against me even to this very day. 4 The children are impudent and stiff-hearted. I am sending you to them, and you shall tell them, 'This is what the Lord† Yahweh says.' 5 They, whether they will hear, or whether they will refuse—for they are a rebellious house—yet they will know that there has been a prophet among them.

Responsorial Psalm: Psalms 123: 1-4

1 I lift up my eyes to you,
you who sit in the heavens.
2 Behold, as the eyes of servants look to the hand of their master,
as the eyes of a maid to the hand of her mistress,
so our eyes look to Yahweh, our God,
until he has mercy on us.
3 Have mercy on us, Yahweh, have mercy on us,
for we have endured much contempt.
4 Our soul is exceedingly filled with the scoffing of those who are at ease,
with the contempt of the proud.

Second Reading: Second Corinthians 12: 7-10

7 By reason of the exceeding greatness of the revelations, that I should not be exalted excessively, a thorn in the flesh was given to me: a messenger of Satan to torment me, that I should not be exalted excessively. 8 Concerning this thing, I begged the Lord three times that it might depart from me. 9 He has said to me, "My grace is sufficient for you, for my power is made perfect in weakness." Most gladly therefore I will rather glory in my weaknesses, that the power of Christ may rest on me.
10 Therefore I take pleasure in weaknesses, in injuries, in necessities, in persecutions, and in distresses, for Christ's sake. For when I am weak, then am I strong.

Gospel: Mark 6: 1-6

1 He went out from there. He came into his own country, and his disciples followed him. 2 When the Sabbath had come, he began to teach in the synagogue, and many hearing him were astonished, saying, "Where did this man get these things?" and, "What is the wisdom that is given to this man, that such mighty works come about by his hands? 3 Isn't this the carpenter, the son of Mary and brother of James, Joses, Judah, and Simon? Aren't his sisters here with us?" So they were offended at him.
4 Jesus said to them, "A prophet is not without honor, except in his own country, and among his own relatives, and in his own house." 5 He could do no mighty work there, except that he laid his hands on a few sick people and healed them. 6 He marveled because of their unbelief.

1. Invite the Holy Spirit into this reading, asking the Author of Scripture to speak to you through His Word
2. Read today's passage as many times as you need, take your time
3. Write down (below) what the Lord is saying to you today
4. Live with this Word in your heart through the day

_____

_____

Monday, July 8, 2024

First Reading: Hosea 2: 16-18, 21-22

16 It will be in that day," says Yahweh,
"that you will call me 'my husband,'
and no longer call me 'my master.'
17 For I will take away the names of the Baals out of her mouth,
and they will no longer be mentioned by name.
18 In that day I will make a covenant for them with the animals of the field,
and with the birds of the sky,
and with the creeping things of the ground.
I will break the bow, the sword, and the battle out of the land,
and will make them lie down safely.
21 It will happen in that day, that I will respond," says Yahweh.
"I will respond to the heavens,
and they will respond to the earth;
22 and the earth will respond to the grain, and the new wine, and the oil;
and they will respond to Jezreel.

Responsorial Psalm: Psalms 145: 2-9

2 Every day I will praise you.
I will extol your name forever and ever.
3 Great is Yahweh, and greatly to be praised!
His greatness is unsearchable.
4 One generation will commend your works to another,
and will declare your mighty acts.
5 I will meditate on the glorious majesty of your honor,
on your wondrous works.
6 Men will speak of the might of your awesome acts.

I will declare your greatness.
7 They will utter the memory of your great goodness,
and will sing of your righteousness.
8 Yahweh is gracious, merciful,
slow to anger, and of great loving kindness.
9 Yahweh is good to all.
His tender mercies are over all his works.

Gospel: Matthew 9: 18-26

18 While he told these things to them, behold, a ruler came and worshiped him, saying, "My daughter has just died, but come and lay your hand on her, and she will live."
19 Jesus got up and followed him, as did his disciples. 20 Behold, a woman who had a discharge of blood for twelve years came behind him, and touched the fringe‡ of his garment; 21 for she said within herself, "If I just touch his garment, I will be made well."
22 But Jesus, turning around and seeing her, said, "Daughter, cheer up! Your faith has made you well." And the woman was made well from that hour.
23 When Jesus came into the ruler's house and saw the flute players and the crowd in noisy disorder, 24 he said to them, "Make room, because the girl isn't dead, but sleeping."
They were ridiculing him. 25 But when the crowd was sent out, he entered in, took her by the hand, and the girl arose. 26 The report of this went out into all that land.

1. Invite the Holy Spirit into this reading, asking the Author of Scripture to speak to you through His Word
2. Read today's passage as many times as you need, take your time
3. Write down (below) what the Lord is saying to you today
4. Live with this Word in your heart through the day

_____

_____

Tuesday, July 9, 2024
Saint Augustine Zhao Rong, Priest, and Companions, Martyrs

First Reading: Hosea 8: 4-7, 11-13

4 They have set up kings, but not by me.
They have made princes, and I didn't approve.
Of their silver and their gold they have made themselves idols,
that they may be cut off.

5 Let Samaria throw out his calf idol!
My anger burns against them!
How long will it be until they are capable of purity?
6 For this is even from Israel!
The workman made it, and it is no God;
indeed, the calf of Samaria shall be broken in pieces.
7 For they sow the wind,
and they will reap the whirlwind.
He has no standing grain.
The stalk will yield no head.
If it does yield, strangers will swallow it up.
11 Because Ephraim has multiplied altars for sinning,
they became for him altars for sinning.
12 I wrote for him the many things of my law,
but they were regarded as a strange thing.
13 As for the sacrifices of my offerings,
they sacrifice meat and eat it,
but Yahweh doesn't accept them.
Now he will remember their iniquity,
and punish their sins.
They will return to Egypt.

Responsorial Psalm: Psalms 115: 3-10

3 But our God is in the heavens.
He does whatever he pleases.
4 Their idols are silver and gold,
the work of men's hands.
5 They have mouths, but they don't speak.
They have eyes, but they don't see.
6 They have ears, but they don't hear.
They have noses, but they don't smell.
7 They have hands, but they don't feel.
They have feet, but they don't walk,
neither do they speak through their throat.
8 Those who make them will be like them;
yes, everyone who trusts in them.
9 Israel, trust in Yahweh!
He is their help and their shield.
10 House of Aaron, trust in Yahweh!
He is their help and their shield.

Gospel: Matthew 9: 32-38

32 As they went out, behold, a mute man who was demon possessed was brought to him. 33 When the demon was cast out, the mute man spoke. The multitudes marveled, saying, "Nothing like this has ever been seen in Israel!"

34 But the Pharisees said, "By the prince of the demons, he casts out demons."

35 Jesus went about all the cities and the villages, teaching in their synagogues and preaching the Good News of the Kingdom, and healing every disease and every sickness among the people. 36 But when he saw the multitudes, he was moved with compassion for them because they were harassed§ and scattered, like sheep without a shepherd. 37 Then he said to his disciples, "The harvest indeed is plentiful, but the laborers are few. 38 Pray therefore that the Lord of the harvest will send out laborers into his harvest."

1. Invite the Holy Spirit into this reading, asking the Author of Scripture to speak to you through His Word
2. Read today's passage as many times as you need, take your time
3. Write down (below) what the Lord is saying to you today
4. Live with this Word in your heart through the day

Wednesday, July 10, 2024

First Reading: Hosea 10: 1-3, 7-8, 12

1 Israel is a luxuriant vine that produces his fruit.
According to the abundance of his fruit he has multiplied his altars.
As their land has prospered, they have adorned their sacred stones.
2 Their heart is divided.
Now they will be found guilty.
He will demolish their altars.
He will destroy their sacred stones.
3 Surely now they will say, "We have no king; for we don't fear Yahweh;
and the king, what can he do for us?"
7 Samaria and her king float away
like a twig on the water.
8 The high places also of Aven, the sin of Israel, will be destroyed.
The thorn and the thistle will come up on their altars.
They will tell the mountains, "Cover us!" and the hills, "Fall on us!"
12 Sow to yourselves in righteousness,

reap according to kindness.
Break up your fallow ground,
for it is time to seek Yahweh,
until he comes and rains righteousness on you.

Responsorial Psalm: Psalms 105: 2-7

2 Sing to him, sing praises to him!
Tell of all his marvelous works.
3 Glory in his holy name.
Let the heart of those who seek Yahweh rejoice.
4 Seek Yahweh and his strength.
Seek his face forever more.
5 Remember his marvelous works that he has done:
his wonders, and the judgments of his mouth,
6 you offspring of Abraham, his servant,
you children of Jacob, his chosen ones.
7 He is Yahweh, our God.
His judgments are in all the earth.

Gospel: Matthew 10: 1-7

1 He called to himself his twelve disciples, and gave them authority over unclean spirits, to cast them out, and to heal every disease and every sickness. 2 Now the names of the twelve apostles are these. The first, Simon, who is called Peter; Andrew, his brother; James the son of Zebedee; John, his brother; 3 Philip; Bartholomew; Thomas; Matthew the tax collector; James the son of Alphaeus; Lebbaeus, who was also called† Thaddaeus; 4 Simon the Zealot; and Judas Iscariot, who also betrayed him.
5 Jesus sent these twelve out and commanded them, saying, "Don't go among the Gentiles, and don't enter into any city of the Samaritans. 6 Rather, go to the lost sheep of the house of Israel. 7 As you go, preach, saying, 'The Kingdom of Heaven is at hand!'

1. Invite the Holy Spirit into this reading, asking the Author of Scripture to speak to you through His Word
2. Read today's passage as many times as you need, take your time
3. Write down (below) what the Lord is saying to you today
4. Live with this Word in your heart through the day

_____

_____

Thursday, July 11, 2024
Saint Benedict, Abbot

First Reading: Hosea 11: 1-4, 8c-9

1 "When Israel was a child, then I loved him,
and called my son out of Egypt.
2 They called to them, so they went from them.
They sacrificed to the Baals,
and burned incense to engraved images.
3 Yet I taught Ephraim to walk.
I took them by their arms,
but they didn't know that I healed them.
4 I drew them with cords of a man, with ties of love;
and I was to them like those who lift up the yoke on their necks;
and I bent down to him and I fed him.
8c How can I make you like Admah?
How can I make you like Zeboiim?
My heart is turned within me,
my compassion is aroused.
9 I will not execute the fierceness of my anger.
I will not return to destroy Ephraim,
for I am God, and not man—the Holy One among you.
I will not come in wrath.

Responsorial Psalm: Psalms 80: 2ac and 3b, 15-16

2 Before Ephraim, Benjamin, and Manasseh, stir up your might!
Come to save us!
3 Turn us again, God.
Cause your face to shine,
and we will be saved.
15 the stock which your right hand planted,
the branch that you made strong for yourself.
16 It's burned with fire.
It's cut down.
They perish at your rebuke.

Gospel: Matthew 10: 7-15

7 As you go, preach, saying, 'The Kingdom of Heaven is at hand!' 8 Heal the sick, cleanse the lepers,‡ and cast out demons. Freely you received, so freely give. 9 Don't take any gold, silver,

or brass in your money belts. 10 Take no bag for your journey, neither two coats, nor sandals, nor staff: for the laborer is worthy of his food. 11 Into whatever city or village you enter, find out who in it is worthy, and stay there until you go on. 12 As you enter into the household, greet it. 13 If the household is worthy, let your peace come on it, but if it isn't worthy, let your peace return to you. 14 Whoever doesn't receive you or hear your words, as you go out of that house or that city, shake the dust off your feet. 15 Most certainly I tell you, it will be more tolerable for the land of Sodom and Gomorrah in the day of judgment than for that city.

1. Invite the Holy Spirit into this reading, asking the Author of Scripture to speak to you through His Word
2. Read today's passage as many times as you need, take your time
3. Write down (below) what the Lord is saying to you today
4. Live with this Word in your heart through the day

Friday, July 12, 2024

First Reading: Hosea 14: 2-9

2 Take words with you, and return to Yahweh.
Tell him, "Forgive all our sins,
and accept that which is good;
so we offer bulls as we vowed of our lips.
3 Assyria can't save us.
We won't ride on horses;
neither will we say any more to the work of our hands, 'Our gods!'
for in you the fatherless finds mercy."
4 "I will heal their waywardness.
I will love them freely;
for my anger is turned away from them.
5 I will be like the dew to Israel.
He will blossom like the lily,
and send down his roots like Lebanon.
6 His branches will spread,
and his beauty will be like the olive tree,
and his fragrance like Lebanon.
7 Men will dwell in his shade.
They will revive like the grain,
and blossom like the vine.

Their fragrance will be like the wine of Lebanon.
8 Ephraim, what have I to do any more with idols?
I answer, and will take care of him.
I am like a green cypress tree;
from me your fruit is found."
9 Who is wise, that he may understand these things?
Who is prudent, that he may know them?
For the ways of Yahweh are right,
and the righteous walk in them,
but the rebellious stumble in them.

Responsorial Psalm: Psalms 51: 3-4, 8-9, 12-14 and 17

3 For I know my transgressions.
My sin is constantly before me.
4 Against you, and you only, I have sinned,
and done that which is evil in your sight,
so you may be proved right when you speak,
and justified when you judge.
8 Let me hear joy and gladness,
that the bones which you have broken may rejoice.
9 Hide your face from my sins,
and blot out all of my iniquities.
12 Restore to me the joy of your salvation.
Uphold me with a willing spirit.
13 Then I will teach transgressors your ways.
Sinners will be converted to you.
14 Deliver me from the guilt of bloodshed, O God, the God of my salvation.
My tongue will sing aloud of your righteousness.
17 The sacrifices of God are a broken spirit.
O God, you will not despise a broken and contrite heart.

Gospel: Matthew 10: 16-23

16 "Behold, I send you out as sheep among wolves. Therefore be wise as serpents and harmless as doves. 17 But beware of men, for they will deliver you up to councils, and in their synagogues they will scourge you. 18 Yes, and you will be brought before governors and kings for my sake, for a testimony to them and to the nations. 19 But when they deliver you up, don't be anxious how or what you will say, for it will be given you in that hour what you will say. 20 For it is not you who speak, but the Spirit of your Father who speaks in you.
21 "Brother will deliver up brother to death, and the father his child. Children will rise up against parents and cause them to be put to death. 22 You will be hated by all men for my name's sake, but he who endures to the end will be saved. 23 But when they persecute you in

this city, flee into the next, for most certainly I tell you, you will not have gone through the cities of Israel until the Son of Man has come.

Saturday, July 13, 2024
Saint Henry; BVM

First Reading: Isaiah 6: 1-8

1 In the year that King Uzziah died, I saw the Lord sitting on a throne, high and lifted up; and his train filled the temple. 2 Above him stood the seraphim. Each one had six wings. With two he covered his face. With two he covered his feet. With two he flew. 3 One called to another, and said,
"Holy, holy, holy, is Yahweh of Armies!
The whole earth is full of his glory!"
4 The foundations of the thresholds shook at the voice of him who called, and the house was filled with smoke. 5 Then I said, "Woe is me! For I am undone, because I am a man of unclean lips and I live among a people of unclean lips, for my eyes have seen the King, Yahweh of Armies!"
6 Then one of the seraphim flew to me, having a live coal in his hand, which he had taken with the tongs from off the altar. 7 He touched my mouth with it, and said, "Behold, this has touched your lips; and your iniquity is taken away, and your sin forgiven."
8 I heard the Lord's voice, saying, "Whom shall I send, and who will go for us?"
Then I said, "Here I am. Send me!"

Responsorial Psalm: Psalms 93: 1- 5

1 Yahweh reigns!
He is clothed with majesty!
Yahweh is armed with strength.
The world also is established.
It can't be moved.

2 Your throne is established from long ago.
You are from everlasting.
3 The floods have lifted up, Yahweh,
the floods have lifted up their voice.
The floods lift up their waves.
4 Above the voices of many waters,
the mighty breakers of the sea,
Yahweh on high is mighty.
5 Your statutes stand firm.
Holiness adorns your house,
Yahweh, forever more.

Gospel: Matthew 10: 24-33

24 "A disciple is not above his teacher, nor a servant above his lord. 25 It is enough for the disciple that he be like his teacher, and the servant like his lord. If they have called the master of the house Beelzebul,§ how much more those of his household! 26 Therefore don't be afraid of them, for there is nothing covered that will not be revealed, or hidden that will not be known. 27 What I tell you in the darkness, speak in the light; and what you hear whispered in the ear, proclaim on the housetops. 28 Don't be afraid of those who kill the body, but are not able to kill the soul. Rather, fear him who is able to destroy both soul and body in Gehenna.†
29 "Aren't two sparrows sold for an assarion coin?‡ Not one of them falls to the ground apart from your Father's will. 30 But the very hairs of your head are all numbered. 31 Therefore don't be afraid. You are of more value than many sparrows. 32 Everyone therefore who confesses me before men, I will also confess him before my Father who is in heaven. 33 But whoever denies me before men, I will also deny him before my Father who is in heaven.

1. Invite the Holy Spirit into this reading, asking the Author of Scripture to speak to you through His Word
2. Read today's passage as many times as you need, take your time
3. Write down (below) what the Lord is saying to you today
4. Live with this Word in your heart through the day

Sunday, July 14, 2024
FIFTEENTH SUNDAY IN ORDINARY TIME

First Reading: Amos 7: 12-15

12 Amaziah also said to Amos, "You seer, go, flee away into the land of Judah, and there eat bread, and prophesy there, 13 but don't prophesy again any more at Bethel; for it is the king's sanctuary, and it is a royal house!"

14 Then Amos answered Amaziah, "I was no prophet, neither was I a prophet's son, but I was a herdsman, and a farmer of sycamore figs; 15 and Yahweh took me from following the flock, and Yahweh said to me, 'Go, prophesy to my people Israel.'

Responsorial Psalm: Psalms 85: 9-13

9 Surely his salvation is near those who fear him,
that glory may dwell in our land.
10 Mercy and truth meet together.
Righteousness and peace have kissed each other.
11 Truth springs out of the earth.
Righteousness has looked down from heaven.
12 Yes, Yahweh will give that which is good.
Our land will yield its increase.
13 Righteousness goes before him,
and prepares the way for his steps.

Second Reading: Ephesians 1: 3-14

3 Blessed be the God and Father of our Lord Jesus Christ, who has blessed us with every spiritual blessing in the heavenly places in Christ, 4 even as he chose us in him before the foundation of the world, that we would be holy and without defect before him in love, 5 having predestined us for adoption as children through Jesus Christ to himself, according to the good pleasure of his desire, 6 to the praise of the glory of his grace, by which he freely gave us favor in the Beloved. 7 In him we have our redemption through his blood, the forgiveness of our trespasses, according to the riches of his grace 8 which he made to abound toward us in all wisdom and prudence, 9 making known to us the mystery of his will, according to his good pleasure which he purposed in him 10 to an administration of the fullness of the times, to sum up all things in Christ, the things in the heavens and the things on the earth, in him. 11 We were also assigned an inheritance in him, having been foreordained according to the purpose of him who does all things after the counsel of his will, 12 to the end that we should be to the praise of his glory, we who had before hoped in Christ. 13 In him you also, having heard the word of the truth, the Good News of your salvation—in whom, having also believed, you were sealed with the promised Holy Spirit, 14 who is a pledge of our inheritance, to the redemption of God's own possession, to the praise of his glory.

Gospel: Mark 6: 7-13

7 He called to himself the twelve, and began to send them out two by two; and he gave them authority over the unclean spirits. 8 He commanded them that they should take nothing for their journey, except a staff only: no bread, no wallet, no money in their purse, 9 but to wear sandals, and not put on two tunics. 10 He said to them, "Wherever you enter into a house, stay there until you depart from there. 11 Whoever will not receive you nor hear you, as you depart from there, shake off the dust that is under your feet for a testimony against them. Assuredly, I tell you, it will be more tolerable for Sodom and Gomorrah in the day of judgment than for that city!"

12 They went out and preached that people should repent. 13 They cast out many demons, and anointed many with oil who were sick and healed them.

1. Invite the Holy Spirit into this reading, asking the Author of Scripture to speak to you through His Word
2. Read today's passage as many times as you need, take your time
3. Write down (below) what the Lord is saying to you today
4. Live with this Word in your heart through the day

_____

_____

Monday, July 15, 2024
Saint Bonaventure, Bishop and Doctor of the Church

First Reading: Isaiah 1: 10-17

10 Hear Yahweh's word, you rulers of Sodom!
Listen to the law of our God,§ you people of Gomorrah!
11 "What are the multitude of your sacrifices to me?", says Yahweh.
"I have had enough of the burnt offerings of rams
and the fat of fed animals.
I don't delight in the blood of bulls,
or of lambs,
or of male goats.
12 When you come to appear before me,
who has required this at your hand, to trample my courts?
13 Bring no more vain offerings.
Incense is an abomination to me.
New moons, Sabbaths, and convocations—
I can't stand evil assemblies.
14 My soul hates your New Moons and your appointed feasts.

They are a burden to me.

I am weary of bearing them.

15 When you spread out your hands, I will hide my eyes from you.

Yes, when you make many prayers, I will not hear.

Your hands are full of blood.

16 Wash yourselves. Make yourself clean.

Put away the evil of your doings from before my eyes.

Cease to do evil.

17 Learn to do well.

Seek justice.

Relieve the oppressed.

Defend the fatherless.

Plead for the widow."

Responsorial Psalm: Psalms 50: 8-9, 16bc-17, 21 and 23

8 I don't rebuke you for your sacrifices.

Your burnt offerings are continually before me.

9 I have no need for a bull from your stall,

nor male goats from your pens.

16 But to the wicked God says,

"What right do you have to declare my statutes,

that you have taken my covenant on your lips,

17 since you hate instruction,

and throw my words behind you?

21 You have done these things, and I kept silent.

You thought that I was just like you.

I will rebuke you, and accuse you in front of your eyes.

23 Whoever offers the sacrifice of thanksgiving glorifies me,

and prepares his way so that I will show God's salvation to him."

Gospel: Matthew 10: 34 – 11: 1

34 "Don't think that I came to send peace on the earth. I didn't come to send peace, but a sword. 35 For I came to set a man at odds against his father, and a daughter against her mother, and a daughter-in-law against her mother-in-law. 36 A man's foes will be those of his own household.* 37 He who loves father or mother more than me is not worthy of me; and he who loves son or daughter more than me isn't worthy of me. 38 He who doesn't take his cross and follow after me isn't worthy of me. 39 He who seeks his life will lose it; and he who loses his life for my sake will find it.

40 "He who receives you receives me, and he who receives me receives him who sent me. 41 He who receives a prophet in the name of a prophet will receive a prophet's reward. He who receives a righteous man in the name of a righteous man will receive a righteous man's reward.

42 Whoever gives one of these little ones just a cup of cold water to drink in the name of a disciple, most certainly I tell you, he will in no way lose his reward."

1 When Jesus had finished directing his twelve disciples, he departed from there to teach and preach in their cities.

1. Invite the Holy Spirit into this reading, asking the Author of Scripture to speak to you through His Word
2. Read today's passage as many times as you need, take your time
3. Write down (below) what the Lord is saying to you today
4. Live with this Word in your heart through the day

_____

_____

Tuesday, July 16, 2024
Our Lady of Mount Carmel

First Reading: Isaiah 7: 1-9

1 In the days of Ahaz the son of Jotham, the son of Uzziah, king of Judah, Rezin the king of Syria and Pekah the son of Remaliah, king of Israel, went up to Jerusalem to war against it, but could not prevail against it. 2 David's house was told, "Syria is allied with Ephraim." His heart trembled, and the heart of his people, as the trees of the forest tremble with the wind.
3 Then Yahweh said to Isaiah, "Go out now to meet Ahaz, you, and Shearjashub your son, at the end of the conduit of the upper pool, on the highway of the fuller's field. 4 Tell him, 'Be careful, and keep calm. Don't be afraid, neither let your heart be faint because of these two tails of smoking torches, for the fierce anger of Rezin and Syria, and of the son of Remaliah. 5 Because Syria, Ephraim, and the son of Remaliah, have plotted evil against you, saying, 6 "Let's go up against Judah, and tear it apart, and let's divide it among ourselves, and set up a king within it, even the son of Tabeel." 7 This is what the Lord Yahweh says: "It shall not stand, neither shall it happen." 8 For the head of Syria is Damascus, and the head of Damascus is Rezin. Within sixty-five years Ephraim shall be broken in pieces, so that it shall not be a people. 9 The head of Ephraim is Samaria, and the head of Samaria is Remaliah's son. If you will not believe, surely you shall not be established.' "

Responsorial Psalm: Psalms 48: 2-8

2 Beautiful in elevation, the joy of the whole earth,
is Mount Zion, on the north sides,
the city of the great King.

3 God has shown himself in her citadels as a refuge.
4 For, behold, the kings assembled themselves,
they passed by together.
5 They saw it, then they were amazed.
They were dismayed.
They hurried away.
6 Trembling took hold of them there,
pain, as of a woman in travail.
7 With the east wind, you break the ships of Tarshish.
8 As we have heard, so we have seen,
in the city of Yahweh of Armies, in the city of our God.
God will establish it forever.

Gospel: Matthew 11: 20-24

20 Then he began to denounce the cities in which most of his mighty works had been done, because they didn't repent. 21 "Woe to you, Chorazin! Woe to you, Bethsaida! For if the mighty works had been done in Tyre and Sidon which were done in you, they would have repented long ago in sackcloth and ashes. 22 But I tell you, it will be more tolerable for Tyre and Sidon on the day of judgment than for you. 23 You, Capernaum, who are exalted to heaven, you will go down to Hades. § For if the mighty works had been done in Sodom which were done in you, it would have remained until today. 24 But I tell you that it will be more tolerable for the land of Sodom on the day of judgment, than for you."

1. Invite the Holy Spirit into this reading, asking the Author of Scripture to speak to you through His Word
2. Read today's passage as many times as you need, take your time
3. Write down (below) what the Lord is saying to you today
4. Live with this Word in your heart through the day

———————————————————————————————————————

———————————————————————————————————————

Wednesday, July 17, 2024

First Reading: Isaiah 10: 5-7, 13b-16

5 Alas Assyrian, the rod of my anger, the staff in whose hand is my indignation! 6 I will send him against a profane nation, and against the people who anger me I will give him a command to take the plunder and to take the prey, and to tread them down like the mire of the streets.

7 However, he doesn't mean so, neither does his heart think so; but it is in his heart to destroy, and to cut off not a few nations.

13 For he has said, "By the strength of my hand I have done it, and by my wisdom, for I have understanding. I have removed the boundaries of the peoples, and have robbed their treasures. Like a valiant man I have brought down their rulers. 14 My hand has found the riches of the peoples like a nest, and like one gathers eggs that are abandoned, I have gathered all the earth. There was no one who moved their wing, or that opened their mouth, or chirped."

15 Should an ax brag against him who chops with it? Should a saw exalt itself above him who saws with it? As if a rod should lift those who lift it up, or as if a staff should lift up someone who is not wood. 16 Therefore the Lord, Yahweh of Armies, will send among his fat ones leanness; and under his glory a burning will be kindled like the burning of fire.

Responsorial Psalm: Psalms 94: 5-10, 14-15

5 They break your people in pieces, Yahweh,
and afflict your heritage.
6 They kill the widow and the alien,
and murder the fatherless.
7 They say, "Yah will not see,
neither will Jacob's God consider."
8 Consider, you senseless among the people;
you fools, when will you be wise?
9 He who implanted the ear, won't he hear?
He who formed the eye, won't he see?
10 He who disciplines the nations, won't he punish?
He who teaches man knows.
14 For Yahweh won't reject his people,
neither will he forsake his inheritance.
15 For judgment will return to righteousness.
All the upright in heart shall follow it.

Gospel: Matthew 11: 25-27

25 At that time, Jesus answered, "I thank you, Father, Lord of heaven and earth, that you hid these things from the wise and understanding, and revealed them to infants. 26 Yes, Father, for so it was well-pleasing in your sight. 27 All things have been delivered to me by my Father. No one knows the Son, except the Father; neither does anyone know the Father, except the Son and he to whom the Son desires to reveal him.

1. Invite the Holy Spirit into this reading, asking the Author of Scripture to speak to you through His Word
2. Read today's passage as many times as you need, take your time
3. Write down (below) what the Lord is saying to you today

Thursday, July 18, 2024
USA: Saint Camillus de Lellis, Priest

First Reading: Isaiah 26: 7-9, 11, 16-19

7 The way of the just is uprightness.
You who are upright make the path of the righteous level.
8 Yes, in the way of your judgments, Yahweh, we have waited for you.
Your name and your renown are the desire of our soul.
9 With my soul I have desired you in the night.
Yes, with my spirit within me I will seek you earnestly;
for when your judgments are in the earth, the inhabitants of the world learn righteousness.
11 Yahweh, your hand is lifted up, yet they don't see;
but they will see your zeal for the people and be disappointed.
Yes, fire will consume your adversaries.
16 Yahweh, in trouble they have visited you.
They poured out a prayer when your chastening was on them.
17 Just as a woman with child, who draws near the time of her delivery,
is in pain and cries out in her pangs,
so we have been before you, Yahweh.
18 We have been with child.
We have been in pain.
We gave birth, it seems, only to wind.
We have not worked any deliverance in the earth;
neither have the inhabitants of the world fallen.
19 Your dead shall live.
Their dead bodies shall arise.
Awake and sing, you who dwell in the dust;
for your dew is like the dew of herbs,
and the earth will cast out the departed spirits.

Responsorial Psalm: Psalms 102: 13-21

13 You will arise and have mercy on Zion,
for it is time to have pity on her.

Yes, the set time has come.
14 For your servants take pleasure in her stones,
and have pity on her dust.
15 So the nations will fear Yahweh's name,
all the kings of the earth your glory.
16 For Yahweh has built up Zion.
He has appeared in his glory.
17 He has responded to the prayer of the destitute,
and has not despised their prayer.
18 This will be written for the generation to come.
A people which will be created will praise Yah,
19 for he has looked down from the height of his sanctuary.
From heaven, Yahweh saw the earth,
20 to hear the groans of the prisoner,
to free those who are condemned to death,
21 that men may declare Yahweh's name in Zion,
and his praise in Jerusalem,

Gospel: Matthew 11: 28-30

28 "Come to me, all you who labor and are heavily burdened, and I will give you rest. 29 Take my yoke upon you and learn from me, for I am gentle and humble in heart; and you will find rest for your souls. 30 For my yoke is easy, and my burden is light."

1. Invite the Holy Spirit into this reading, asking the Author of Scripture to speak to you through His Word
2. Read today's passage as many times as you need, take your time
3. Write down (below) what the Lord is saying to you today
4. Live with this Word in your heart through the day

_____

_____

Friday, July 19, 2024

First Reading: Isaiah 38: 1-6, 21-22, 7-8

1 In those days Hezekiah was sick and near death. Isaiah the prophet, the son of Amoz, came to him, and said to him, "Yahweh says, 'Set your house in order, for you will die, and not live.' "

2 Then Hezekiah turned his face to the wall and prayed to Yahweh, 3 and said, "Remember now, Yahweh, I beg you, how I have walked before you in truth and with a perfect heart, and have done that which is good in your sight." Then Hezekiah wept bitterly.

4 Then Yahweh's word came to Isaiah, saying, 5 "Go, and tell Hezekiah, 'Yahweh, the God of David your father, says, "I have heard your prayer. I have seen your tears. Behold, I will add fifteen years to your life. 6 I will deliver you and this city out of the hand of the king of Assyria, and I will defend this city.

21 Now Isaiah had said, "Let them take a cake of figs, and lay it for a poultice on the boil, and he shall recover." 22 Hezekiah also had said, "What is the sign that I will go up to Yahweh's house?"

7 This shall be the sign to you from Yahweh, that Yahweh will do this thing that he has spoken. 8 Behold, I will cause the shadow on the sundial, which has gone down on the sundial of Ahaz with the sun, to return backward ten steps." ' " So the sun returned ten steps on the sundial on which it had gone down.

Responsorial Psalm: Isaiah 38: 10, 11, 12abcd, 16

10 I said, "In the middle of my life I go into the gates of Sheol.†
I am deprived of the residue of my years."
11 I said, "I won't see Yah,
Yah in the land of the living.
I will see man no more with the inhabitants of the world.
12 My dwelling is removed,
and is carried away from me like a shepherd's tent.
I have rolled up my life like a weaver.
He will cut me off from the loom.
From day even to night you will make an end of me.
16 Lord, men live by these things;
and my spirit finds life in all of them.
You restore me, and cause me to live.

Gospel: Matthew 12: 1-8

1 At that time, Jesus went on the Sabbath day through the grain fields. His disciples were hungry and began to pluck heads of grain and to eat. 2 But the Pharisees, when they saw it, said to him, "Behold, your disciples do what is not lawful to do on the Sabbath."

3 But he said to them, "Haven't you read what David did when he was hungry, and those who were with him: 4 how he entered into God's house and ate the show bread, which was not lawful for him to eat, nor for those who were with him, but only for the priests?* 5 Or have you not read in the law that on the Sabbath day the priests in the temple profane the Sabbath and are guiltless? 6 But I tell you that one greater than the temple is here. 7 But if you had known what this means, 'I desire mercy, and not sacrifice,'* you wouldn't have condemned the guiltless. 8 For the Son of Man is Lord of the Sabbath."

1. Invite the Holy Spirit into this reading, asking the Author of Scripture to speak to you through His Word
2. Read today's passage as many times as you need, take your time
3. Write down (below) what the Lord is saying to you today
4. Live with this Word in your heart through the day

_____

_____

Saturday, July 20, 2024
Saint Apollinaris, Bishop and Martyr; BVM

First Reading: Micah 2: 1-5

1 Woe to those who devise iniquity
and work evil on their beds!
When the morning is light, they practice it,
because it is in the power of their hand.
2 They covet fields and seize them,
and houses, then take them away.
They oppress a man and his house,
even a man and his heritage.
3 Therefore Yahweh says:
"Behold, I am planning against these people a disaster,
from which you will not remove your necks,
neither will you walk haughtily,
for it is an evil time.
4 In that day they will take up a parable against you,
and lament with a doleful lamentation, saying,
'We are utterly ruined!
My people's possession is divided up.
Indeed he takes it from me and assigns our fields to traitors!'"
5 Therefore you will have no one who divides the land by lot in Yahweh's assembly.

Responsorial Psalm: Psalms 10: 1-4, 7-8, 14

1 Why do you stand far off, Yahweh?
Why do you hide yourself in times of trouble?
2 In arrogance, the wicked hunt down the weak.

They are caught in the schemes that they devise.
3 For the wicked boasts of his heart's cravings.
He blesses the greedy and condemns Yahweh.
4 The wicked, in the pride of his face,
has no room in his thoughts for God.
7 His mouth is full of cursing, deceit, and oppression.
Under his tongue is mischief and iniquity.
8 He lies in wait near the villages.
From ambushes, he murders the innocent.
His eyes are secretly set against the helpless.
14 But you do see trouble and grief.
You consider it to take it into your hand.
You help the victim and the fatherless.

Gospel: Matthew 12: 14-21

14 But the Pharisees went out and conspired against him, how they might destroy him.
15 Jesus, perceiving that, withdrew from there. Great multitudes followed him; and he healed them all, 16 and commanded them that they should not make him known, 17 that it might be fulfilled which was spoken through Isaiah the prophet, saying,
18 "Behold, my servant whom I have chosen,
my beloved in whom my soul is well pleased.
I will put my Spirit on him.
He will proclaim justice to the nations.
19 He will not strive, nor shout,
neither will anyone hear his voice in the streets.
20 He won't break a bruised reed.
He won't quench a smoking flax,
until he leads justice to victory.
21 In his name, the nations will hope."

1. Invite the Holy Spirit into this reading, asking the Author of Scripture to speak to you through His Word
2. Read today's passage as many times as you need, take your time
3. Write down (below) what the Lord is saying to you today
4. Live with this Word in your heart through the day

_____

_____

Sunday, July 21, 2024
SIXTEENTH SUNDAY IN ORDINARY TIME

First Reading: Jeremiah 23: 1-6

1 "Woe to the shepherds who destroy and scatter the sheep of my pasture!" says Yahweh. 2 Therefore Yahweh, the God of Israel, says against the shepherds who feed my people: "You have scattered my flock, driven them away, and have not visited them. Behold, I will visit on you the evil of your doings," says Yahweh. 3 "I will gather the remnant of my flock out of all the countries where I have driven them, and will bring them again to their folds; and they will be fruitful and multiply. 4 I will set up shepherds over them who will feed them. They will no longer be afraid or dismayed, neither will any be lacking," says Yahweh.
5 "Behold, the days come," says Yahweh,
"that I will raise to David a righteous Branch;
and he will reign as king and deal wisely,
and will execute justice and righteousness in the land.
6 In his days Judah will be saved,
and Israel will dwell safely.
This is his name by which he will be called:
Yahweh our righteousness.

Responsorial Psalm: Psalms 23: 1-6

1 Yahweh is my shepherd;
I shall lack nothing.
2 He makes me lie down in green pastures.
He leads me beside still waters.
3 He restores my soul.
He guides me in the paths of righteousness for his name's sake.
4 Even though I walk through the valley of the shadow of death,
I will fear no evil, for you are with me.
Your rod and your staff,
they comfort me.
5 You prepare a table before me
in the presence of my enemies.
You anoint my head with oil.
My cup runs over.
6 Surely goodness and loving kindness shall follow me all the days of my life,
and I will dwell in Yahweh's house forever.

Second Reading: Ephesians 2: 13-18

13 But now in Christ Jesus you who once were far off are made near in the blood of Christ. 14 For he is our peace, who made both one, and broke down the middle wall of separation, 15 having abolished in his flesh the hostility, the law of commandments contained in ordinances, that he might create in himself one new man of the two, making peace, 16 and might reconcile them both in one body to God through the cross, having killed the hostility through it. 17 He came and preached peace to you who were far off and to those who were near. 18 For through him we both have our access in one Spirit to the Father.

Gospel: Mark 6: 30-34

30 The apostles gathered themselves together to Jesus, and they told him all things, whatever they had done, and whatever they had taught. 31 He said to them, "Come away into a deserted place, and rest awhile." For there were many coming and going, and they had no leisure so much as to eat. 32 They went away in the boat to a deserted place by themselves. 33 They† saw them going, and many recognized him and ran there on foot from all the cities. They arrived before them and came together to him. 34 Jesus came out, saw a great multitude, and he had compassion on them because they were like sheep without a shepherd; and he began to teach them many things.

1. Invite the Holy Spirit into this reading, asking the Author of Scripture to speak to you through His Word
2. Read today's passage as many times as you need, take your time
3. Write down (below) what the Lord is saying to you today
4. Live with this Word in your heart through the day

_____

_____

Monday, July 22, 2024
Saint Mary Magdalene

First Reading: Second Corinthians 5: 14-17

14 For the love of Christ compels us; because we judge thus: that one died for all, therefore all died. 15 He died for all, that those who live should no longer live to themselves, but to him who for their sakes died and rose again.
16 Therefore we know no one according to the flesh from now on. Even though we have known Christ according to the flesh, yet now we know him so no more. 17 Therefore if anyone is in Christ, he is a new creation. The old things have passed away. Behold,† all things have become new.

Responsorial Psalm: Psalms 63: 2-6, 8-9

2 So I have seen you in the sanctuary,
watching your power and your glory.
3 Because your loving kindness is better than life,
my lips shall praise you.
4 So I will bless you while I live.
I will lift up my hands in your name.
5 My soul shall be satisfied as with the richest food.
My mouth shall praise you with joyful lips,
6 when I remember you on my bed,
and think about you in the night watches.
8 My soul stays close to you.
Your right hand holds me up.
9 But those who seek my soul to destroy it
shall go into the lower parts of the earth.

Gospel: John 20: 1-2, 11-18

1 Now on the first day of the week, Mary Magdalene went early, while it was still dark, to the tomb, and saw that the stone had been taken away from the tomb. 2 Therefore she ran and came to Simon Peter and to the other disciple whom Jesus loved, and said to them, "They have taken away the Lord out of the tomb, and we don't know where they have laid him!"

11 But Mary was standing outside at the tomb weeping. So as she wept, she stooped and looked into the tomb, 12 and she saw two angels in white sitting, one at the head and one at the feet, where the body of Jesus had lain. 13 They asked her, "Woman, why are you weeping?"

She said to them, "Because they have taken away my Lord, and I don't know where they have laid him." 14 When she had said this, she turned around and saw Jesus standing, and didn't know that it was Jesus.

15 Jesus said to her, "Woman, why are you weeping? Who are you looking for?"

She, supposing him to be the gardener, said to him, "Sir, if you have carried him away, tell me where you have laid him, and I will take him away."

16 Jesus said to her, "Mary."

She turned and said to him, "Rabboni!"† which is to say, "Teacher!"‡

17 Jesus said to her, "Don't hold me, for I haven't yet ascended to my Father; but go to my brothers and tell them, 'I am ascending to my Father and your Father, to my God and your God.'"

18 Mary Magdalene came and told the disciples that she had seen the Lord, and that he had said these things to her.

1. Invite the Holy Spirit into this reading, asking the Author of Scripture to speak to you through His Word
2. Read today's passage as many times as you need, take your time

3. Write down (below) what the Lord is saying to you today
4. Live with this Word in your heart through the day

Tuesday, July 23, 2024
Saint Bridget, Religious

First Reading: Micah 7: 14-15, 18-20

14 Shepherd your people with your staff,
the flock of your heritage,
who dwell by themselves in a forest.
Let them feed in the middle of fertile pasture land,
in Bashan and Gilead, as in the days of old.
15 "As in the days of your coming out of the land of Egypt,
I will show them marvelous things."
18 Who is a God like you, who pardons iniquity,
and passes over the disobedience of the remnant of his heritage?
He doesn't retain his anger forever,
because he delights in loving kindness.
19 He will again have compassion on us.
He will tread our iniquities under foot.
You will cast all their sins into the depths of the sea.
20 You will give truth to Jacob,
and mercy to Abraham,
as you have sworn to our fathers from the days of old.

Responsorial Psalm: Psalms 85: 2-8

2 You have forgiven the iniquity of your people.
You have covered all their sin.
3 You have taken away all your wrath.
You have turned from the fierceness of your anger.
4 Turn us, God of our salvation,
and cause your indignation toward us to cease.
5 Will you be angry with us forever?
Will you draw out your anger to all generations?
6 Won't you revive us again,

that your people may rejoice in you?

7 Show us your loving kindness, Yahweh.

Grant us your salvation.

8 I will hear what God, Yahweh, will speak,

for he will speak peace to his people, his saints;

but let them not turn again to folly.

Gospel: Matthew 12: 46-50

46 While he was yet speaking to the multitudes, behold, his mother and his brothers stood outside, seeking to speak to him. 47 One said to him, "Behold, your mother and your brothers stand outside, seeking to speak to you."

48 But he answered him who spoke to him, "Who is my mother? Who are my brothers?" 49 He stretched out his hand toward his disciples, and said, "Behold, my mother and my brothers! 50 For whoever does the will of my Father who is in heaven, he is my brother, and sister, and mother."

1. Invite the Holy Spirit into this reading, asking the Author of Scripture to speak to you through His Word

2. Read today's passage as many times as you need, take your time

3. Write down (below) what the Lord is saying to you today

4. Live with this Word in your heart through the day

_____

_____

Wedneday, July 24, 2024
Saint Sharbel Makhlūf, Priest

First Reading: Jeremiah 1: 1, 4-10

1 The words of Jeremiah the son of Hilkiah, one of the priests who were in Anathoth in the land of Benjamin.

4 Now Yahweh's word came to me, saying,

5 "Before I formed you in the womb, I knew you.

Before you were born, I sanctified you.

I have appointed you a prophet to the nations."

6 Then I said, "Ah, Lord‡ Yahweh! Behold,§ I don't know how to speak; for I am a child."

7 But Yahweh said to me, "Don't say, 'I am a child;' for you must go to whomever I send you, and you must say whatever I command you. 8 Don't be afraid because of them, for I am with you to rescue you," says Yahweh.

9 Then Yahweh stretched out his hand and touched my mouth. Then Yahweh said to me, "Behold, I have put my words in your mouth. 10 Behold, I have today set you over the nations and over the kingdoms, to uproot and to tear down, to destroy and to overthrow, to build and to plant."

Responsorial Psalm: Psalms 71: 1-2, 3-4a, 5-6ab, 15 and 17

1 In you, Yahweh, I take refuge.
Never let me be disappointed.
2 Deliver me in your righteousness, and rescue me.
Turn your ear to me, and save me.
3 Be to me a rock of refuge to which I may always go.
Give the command to save me,
for you are my rock and my fortress.
4 Rescue me, my God, from the hand of the wicked,
from the hand of the unrighteous and cruel man.
5 For you are my hope, Lord Yahweh,
my confidence from my youth.
6 I have relied on you from the womb.
You are he who took me out of my mother's womb.
15 My mouth will tell about your righteousness,
and of your salvation all day,
though I don't know its full measure.
17 God, you have taught me from my youth.
Until now, I have declared your wondrous works.

Gospel: Matthew 13: 1-9

1 On that day Jesus went out of the house and sat by the seaside. 2 Great multitudes gathered to him, so that he entered into a boat and sat; and all the multitude stood on the beach. 3 He spoke to them many things in parables, saying, "Behold, a farmer went out to sow. 4 As he sowed, some seeds fell by the roadside, and the birds came and devoured them. 5 Others fell on rocky ground, where they didn't have much soil, and immediately they sprang up, because they had no depth of earth. 6 When the sun had risen, they were scorched. Because they had no root, they withered away. 7 Others fell among thorns. The thorns grew up and choked them. 8 Others fell on good soil and yielded fruit: some one hundred times as much, some sixty, and some thirty. 9 He who has ears to hear, let him hear."

1. Invite the Holy Spirit into this reading, asking the Author of Scripture to speak to you through His Word

2. Read today's passage as many times as you need, take your time
3. Write down (below) what the Lord is saying to you today
4. Live with this Word in your heart through the day

_____

_____

Thursday, July 25, 2024
Saint James, Apostle

First Reading: Second Corinthians 4: 7-15

7 But we have this treasure in clay vessels, that the exceeding greatness of the power may be of God and not from ourselves. 8 We are pressed on every side, yet not crushed; perplexed, yet not to despair; 9 pursued, yet not forsaken; struck down, yet not destroyed; 10 always carrying in the body the putting to death of the Lord Jesus, that the life of Jesus may also be revealed in our body. 11 For we who live are always delivered to death for Jesus' sake, that the life also of Jesus may be revealed in our mortal flesh. 12 So then death works in us, but life in you.

13 But having the same spirit of faith, according to that which is written, "I believed, and therefore I spoke."* We also believe, and therefore we also speak, 14 knowing that he who raised the Lord Jesus will raise us also with Jesus, and will present us with you. 15 For all things are for your sakes, that the grace, being multiplied through the many, may cause the thanksgiving to abound to the glory of God.

Responsorial Psalm: Psalms 126: 1bc-6

1 When Yahweh brought back those who returned to Zion,
we were like those who dream.
2 Then our mouth was filled with laughter,
and our tongue with singing.
Then they said among the nations,
"Yahweh has done great things for them."
3 Yahweh has done great things for us,
and we are glad.
4 Restore our fortunes again, Yahweh,
like the streams in the Negev.
5 Those who sow in tears will reap in joy.
6 He who goes out weeping, carrying seed for sowing,
will certainly come again with joy, carrying his sheaves.

Gospel: Matthew 20: 20-28

20 Then the mother of the sons of Zebedee came to him with her sons, kneeling and asking a certain thing of him. 21 He said to her, "What do you want?"

She said to him, "Command that these, my two sons, may sit, one on your right hand and one on your left hand, in your Kingdom."

22 But Jesus answered, "You don't know what you are asking. Are you able to drink the cup that I am about to drink, and be baptized with the baptism that I am baptized with?"

They said to him, "We are able."

23 He said to them, "You will indeed drink my cup, and be baptized with the baptism that I am baptized with; but to sit on my right hand and on my left hand is not mine to give, but it is for whom it has been prepared by my Father."

24 When the ten heard it, they were indignant with the two brothers.

25 But Jesus summoned them, and said, "You know that the rulers of the nations lord it over them, and their great ones exercise authority over them. 26 It shall not be so among you; but whoever desires to become great among you shall be‡ your servant. 27 Whoever desires to be first among you shall be your bondservant, 28 even as the Son of Man came not to be served, but to serve, and to give his life as a ransom for many."

1. Invite the Holy Spirit into this reading, asking the Author of Scripture to speak to you through His Word
2. Read today's passage as many times as you need, take your time
3. Write down (below) what the Lord is saying to you today
4. Live with this Word in your heart through the day

Friday, July 26, 2024
Saints Joachim and Anne, Parents of the Blessed Virgin Mary

First Reading: Jeremiah 3: 14-17

14 "Return, backsliding children," says Yahweh, "for I am a husband to you. I will take one of you from a city, and two from a family, and I will bring you to Zion. 15 I will give you shepherds according to my heart, who will feed you with knowledge and understanding. 16 It will come to pass, when you are multiplied and increased in the land in those days," says Yahweh, "they will no longer say, 'the ark of Yahweh's covenant!' It will not come to mind. They won't remember it. They won't miss it, nor will another be made. 17 At that time they will call

Jerusalem 'Yahweh's Throne;' and all the nations will be gathered to it, to Yahweh's name, to Jerusalem. They will no longer walk after the stubbornness of their evil heart.

Responsorial Psalm: Jeremiah 31: 10, 11-12abcd, 13

10 "Hear Yahweh's word, you nations,
and declare it in the distant islands. Say,
'He who scattered Israel will gather him,
and keep him, as a shepherd does his flock.'
11 For Yahweh has ransomed Jacob,
and redeemed him from the hand of him who was stronger than he.
12 They will come and sing in the height of Zion,
and will flow to the goodness of Yahweh,
to the grain, to the new wine, to the oil,
and to the young of the flock and of the herd.
Their soul will be as a watered garden.
They will not sorrow any more at all.
13 Then the virgin will rejoice in the dance,
the young men and the old together;
for I will turn their mourning into joy,
and will comfort them, and make them rejoice from their sorrow.

Gospel: Matthew 13: 18-23

18 "Hear, then, the parable of the farmer. 19 When anyone hears the word of the Kingdom and doesn't understand it, the evil one comes and snatches away that which has been sown in his heart. This is what was sown by the roadside. 20 What was sown on the rocky places, this is he who hears the word and immediately with joy receives it; 21 yet he has no root in himself, but endures for a while. When oppression or persecution arises because of the word, immediately he stumbles. 22 What was sown among the thorns, this is he who hears the word, but the cares of this age and the deceitfulness of riches choke the word, and he becomes unfruitful. 23 What was sown on the good ground, this is he who hears the word and understands it, who most certainly bears fruit and produces, some one hundred times as much, some sixty, and some thirty."

1. Invite the Holy Spirit into this reading, asking the Author of Scripture to speak to you through His Word
2. Read today's passage as many times as you need, take your time
3. Write down (below) what the Lord is saying to you today
4. Live with this Word in your heart through the day

_____

_____

Saturday, July 27, 2024

First Reading: Jeremiah 7: 1-11

1 The word that came to Jeremiah from Yahweh, saying, 2 "Stand in the gate of Yahweh's house, and proclaim this word there, and say, 'Hear Yahweh's word, all you of Judah, who enter in at these gates to worship Yahweh.' "

3 Yahweh of Armies, the God of Israel says, "Amend your ways and your doings, and I will cause you to dwell in this place. 4 Don't trust in lying words, saying, 'Yahweh's temple, Yahweh's temple, Yahweh's temple, are these.' 5 For if you thoroughly amend your ways and your doings, if you thoroughly execute justice between a man and his neighbor; 6 if you don't oppress the foreigner, the fatherless, and the widow, and don't shed innocent blood in this place, and don't walk after other gods to your own hurt, 7 then I will cause you to dwell in this place, in the land that I gave to your fathers, from of old even forever more. 8 Behold, you trust in lying words that can't profit. 9 Will you steal, murder, commit adultery, swear falsely, burn incense to Baal, and walk after other gods that you have not known, 10 then come and stand before me in this house, which is called by my name, and say, 'We are delivered,' that you may do all these abominations? 11 Has this house, which is called by my name, become a den of robbers in your eyes? Behold, I myself have seen it," says Yahweh.

Responsorial Psalm: Psalms 84: 3, 4, 5-6a and 8a, 11

3 Yes, the sparrow has found a home,
and the swallow a nest for herself, where she may have her young,
near your altars, Yahweh of Armies, my King, and my God.
4 Blessed are those who dwell in your house.
They are always praising you.
Selah.
5 Blessed are those whose strength is in you,
who have set their hearts on a pilgrimage.
6 Passing through the valley of Weeping, they make it a place of springs.
8 Yahweh, God of Armies, hear my prayer.
11 For Yahweh God is a sun and a shield.
Yahweh will give grace and glory.
He withholds no good thing from those who walk blamelessly.

Gospel: Matthew 13: 24-30

24 He set another parable before them, saying, "The Kingdom of Heaven is like a man who sowed good seed in his field, 25 but while people slept, his enemy came and sowed darnel weeds† also among the wheat, and went away. 26 But when the blade sprang up and produced

grain, then the darnel weeds appeared also. 27 The servants of the householder came and said to him, 'Sir, didn't you sow good seed in your field? Where did these darnel weeds come from?'
28 "He said to them, 'An enemy has done this.'
"The servants asked him, 'Do you want us to go and gather them up?'
29 "But he said, 'No, lest perhaps while you gather up the darnel weeds, you root up the wheat with them. 30 Let both grow together until the harvest, and in the harvest time I will tell the reapers, "First, gather up the darnel weeds, and bind them in bundles to burn them; but gather the wheat into my barn." ' "

1. Invite the Holy Spirit into this reading, asking the Author of Scripture to speak to you through His Word
2. Read today's passage as many times as you need, take your time
3. Write down (below) what the Lord is saying to you today
4. Live with this Word in your heart through the day

Sunday, July 28, 2024
SEVENTEENTH SUNDAY IN ORDINARY TIME

First Reading: Second Kings 4: 42-44

42 A man from Baal Shalishah came, and brought the man of God some bread of the first fruits: twenty loaves of barley and fresh ears of grain in his sack. Elisha said, "Give to the people, that they may eat."
43 His servant said, "What, should I set this before a hundred men?"
But he said, "Give it to the people, that they may eat; for Yahweh says, 'They will eat, and will have some left over.' "
44 So he set it before them and they ate and had some left over, according to Yahweh's word.

Responsorial Psalm: Psalms 145: 10-11, 15-18

10 All your works will give thanks to you, Yahweh.
Your saints will extol you.
11 They will speak of the glory of your kingdom,
and talk about your power,
15 The eyes of all wait for you.
You give them their food in due season.
16 You open your hand,

and satisfy the desire of every living thing.

17 Yahweh is righteous in all his ways,

and gracious in all his works.

18 Yahweh is near to all those who call on him,

to all who call on him in truth.

Second Reading: Ephesians 4: 1-6

1 I therefore, the prisoner in the Lord, beg you to walk worthily of the calling with which you were called, 2 with all lowliness and humility, with patience, bearing with one another in love, 3 being eager to keep the unity of the Spirit in the bond of peace. 4 There is one body and one Spirit, even as you also were called in one hope of your calling, 5 one Lord, one faith, one baptism, 6 one God and Father of all, who is over all and through all and in us all.

Gospel: John 6: 1-15

1 After these things, Jesus went away to the other side of the sea of Galilee, which is also called the Sea of Tiberias. 2 A great multitude followed him, because they saw his signs which he did on those who were sick. 3 Jesus went up into the mountain, and he sat there with his disciples. 4 Now the Passover, the feast of the Jews, was at hand. 5 Jesus therefore, lifting up his eyes and seeing that a great multitude was coming to him, said to Philip, "Where are we to buy bread, that these may eat?" 6 He said this to test him, for he himself knew what he would do. 7 Philip answered him, "Two hundred denarii† worth of bread is not sufficient for them, that every one of them may receive a little."

8 One of his disciples, Andrew, Simon Peter's brother, said to him, 9 "There is a boy here who has five barley loaves and two fish, but what are these among so many?"

10 Jesus said, "Have the people sit down." Now there was much grass in that place. So the men sat down, in number about five thousand. 11 Jesus took the loaves, and having given thanks, he distributed to the disciples, and the disciples to those who were sitting down, likewise also of the fish as much as they desired. 12 When they were filled, he said to his disciples, "Gather up the broken pieces which are left over, that nothing be lost." 13 So they gathered them up, and filled twelve baskets with broken pieces from the five barley loaves, which were left over by those who had eaten. 14 When therefore the people saw the sign which Jesus did, they said, "This is truly the prophet who comes into the world." 15 Jesus therefore, perceiving that they were about to come and take him by force to make him king, withdrew again to the mountain by himself.

1. Invite the Holy Spirit into this reading, asking the Author of Scripture to speak to you through His Word
2. Read today's passage as many times as you need, take your time
3. Write down (below) what the Lord is saying to you today
4. Live with this Word in your heart through the day

Monday, July 29, 2024
Saints Martha, Mary and Lazarus

First Reading: Jeremiah 13: 1-11

1 Yahweh said to me, "Go, and buy yourself a linen belt, and put it on your waist, and don't put it in water."
2 So I bought a belt according to Yahweh's word, and put it on my waist.
3 Yahweh's word came to me the second time, saying, 4 "Take the belt that you have bought, which is on your waist, and arise, go to the Euphrates, and hide it there in a cleft of the rock."
5 So I went and hid it by the Euphrates, as Yahweh commanded me.
6 After many days, Yahweh said to me, "Arise, go to the Euphrates, and take the belt from there, which I commanded you to hide there."
7 Then I went to the Euphrates, and dug, and took the belt from the place where I had hidden it; and behold, the belt was ruined. It was profitable for nothing.
8 Then Yahweh's word came to me, saying, 9 "Yahweh says, 'In this way I will ruin the pride of Judah, and the great pride of Jerusalem. 10 This evil people, who refuse to hear my words, who walk in the stubbornness of their heart, and have gone after other gods to serve them and to worship them, will even be as this belt, which is profitable for nothing. 11 For as the belt clings to the waist of a man, so I have caused the whole house of Israel and the whole house of Judah to cling to me,' says Yahweh; 'that they may be to me for a people, for a name, for praise, and for glory; but they would not hear.'

Responsorial Psalm: Deuteronomy 32: 18-21

18 Of the Rock who became your father, you are unmindful,
and have forgotten God who gave you birth.
19 Yahweh saw and abhorred,
because of the provocation of his sons and his daughters.
20 He said, "I will hide my face from them.
I will see what their end will be;
for they are a very perverse generation,
children in whom is no faithfulness.
21 They have moved me to jealousy with that which is not God.
They have provoked me to anger with their vanities.
I will move them to jealousy with those who are not a people.

I will provoke them to anger with a foolish nation.

Gospel: John 11: 19-27

19 Many of the Jews had joined the women around Martha and Mary, to console them concerning their brother. 20 Then when Martha heard that Jesus was coming, she went and met him, but Mary stayed in the house. 21 Therefore Martha said to Jesus, "Lord, if you would have been here, my brother wouldn't have died. 22 Even now I know that whatever you ask of God, God will give you."
23 Jesus said to her, "Your brother will rise again."
24 Martha said to him, "I know that he will rise again in the resurrection at the last day."
25 Jesus said to her, "I am the resurrection and the life. He who believes in me will still live, even if he dies. 26 Whoever lives and believes in me will never die. Do you believe this?"
27 She said to him, "Yes, Lord. I have come to believe that you are the Christ, God's Son, he who comes into the world."

1. Invite the Holy Spirit into this reading, asking the Author of Scripture to speak to you through His Word
2. Read today's passage as many times as you need, take your time
3. Write down (below) what the Lord is saying to you today
4. Live with this Word in your heart through the day

_____

_____

Tuesday, July 30, 2024
Saint Peter Chrysologus, Bishop and Doctor of the Church

First Reading: Jeremiah 14: 17-22

17 "You shall say this word to them:
" 'Let my eyes run down with tears night and day,
and let them not cease;
for the virgin daughter of my people is broken with a great breach,
with a very grievous wound.
18 If I go out into the field,
then behold, the slain with the sword!
If I enter into the city,
then behold, those who are sick with famine!
For both the prophet and the priest go about in the land,
and have no knowledge.' "

19 Have you utterly rejected Judah?
Has your soul loathed Zion?
Why have you struck us, and there is no healing for us?
We looked for peace, but no good came;
and for a time of healing, and behold, dismay!
20 We acknowledge, Yahweh, our wickedness,
and the iniquity of our fathers;
for we have sinned against you.
21 Do not abhor us, for your name's sake.
Do not disgrace the throne of your glory.
Remember, and don't break your covenant with us.
22 Are there any among the vanities of the nations that can cause rain?
Or can the sky give showers?
Aren't you he, Yahweh our God?
Therefore we will wait for you;
for you have made all these things.

Responsorial Psalm: Psalms 79: 8, 9, 11 and 13

8 Don't hold the iniquities of our forefathers against us.
Let your tender mercies speedily meet us,
for we are in desperate need.
9 Help us, God of our salvation, for the glory of your name.
Deliver us, and forgive our sins, for your name's sake.
11 Let the sighing of the prisoner come before you.
According to the greatness of your power, preserve those who are sentenced to death.
13 So we, your people and sheep of your pasture,
will give you thanks forever.
We will praise you forever, to all generations.

Gospel: Matthew 13: 36-43

36 Then Jesus sent the multitudes away, and went into the house. His disciples came to him, saying, "Explain to us the parable of the darnel weeds of the field."
37 He answered them, "He who sows the good seed is the Son of Man, 38 the field is the world, the good seeds are the children of the Kingdom, and the darnel weeds are the children of the evil one. 39 The enemy who sowed them is the devil. The harvest is the end of the age, and the reapers are angels. 40 As therefore the darnel weeds are gathered up and burned with fire; so will it be at the end of this age. 41 The Son of Man will send out his angels, and they will gather out of his Kingdom all things that cause stumbling and those who do iniquity, 42 and will cast them into the furnace of fire. There will be weeping and gnashing of teeth. 43 Then the righteous will shine like the sun in the Kingdom of their Father. He who has ears to hear, let him hear.

Wednesday, July 31, 2024
Saint Ignatius of Loyola, Priest

First Reading: Jeremiah 15: 10, 16-21

10 Woe is me, my mother, that you have borne me, a man of strife,
and a man of contention to the whole earth!
I have not lent, neither have men lent to me;
yet every one of them curses me.
16 Your words were found,
and I ate them.
Your words were to me a joy and the rejoicing of my heart,
for I am called by your name, Yahweh, God of Armies.
17 I didn't sit in the assembly of those who make merry and rejoice.
I sat alone because of your hand,
for you have filled me with indignation.
18 Why is my pain perpetual,
and my wound incurable,
which refuses to be healed?
Will you indeed be to me as a deceitful brook,
like waters that fail?
19 Therefore Yahweh says,
"If you return, then I will bring you again,
that you may stand before me;
and if you take out the precious from the vile,
you will be as my mouth.
They will return to you,
but you will not return to them.
20 I will make you to this people a fortified bronze wall.
They will fight against you,

but they will not prevail against you;
for I am with you to save you
and to deliver you," says Yahweh.
21 "I will deliver you out of the hand of the wicked,
and I will redeem you out of the hand of the terrible."

Responsorial Psalm: Psalms 59: 2-4, 10-11, 17

2 Deliver me from the workers of iniquity.
Save me from the bloodthirsty men.
3 For, behold, they lie in wait for my soul.
The mighty gather themselves together against me,
not for my disobedience, nor for my sin, Yahweh.
4 I have done no wrong, yet they are ready to attack me.
Rise up, behold, and help me!
10 My God will go before me with his loving kindness.
God will let me look at my enemies in triumph.
11 Don't kill them, or my people may forget.
Scatter them by your power, and bring them down, Lord our shield.
17 To you, my strength, I will sing praises.
For God is my high tower, the God of my mercy.

Gospel: Matthew 13: 44-46

44 "Again, the Kingdom of Heaven is like treasure hidden in the field, which a man found and hid. In his joy, he goes and sells all that he has and buys that field.
45 "Again, the Kingdom of Heaven is like a man who is a merchant seeking fine pearls, 46 who having found one pearl of great price, he went and sold all that he had and bought it.

1. Invite the Holy Spirit into this reading, asking the Author of Scripture to speak to you through His Word
2. Read today's passage as many times as you need, take your time
3. Write down (below) what the Lord is saying to you today
4. Live with this Word in your heart through the day

Thursday, August 1, 2024
Saint Alphonsus Liguori, Bishop and Doctor of the Church

First Reading: Jeremiah 18: 1-6

1 The word which came to Jeremiah from Yahweh, saying, 2 "Arise, and go down to the potter's house, and there I will cause you to hear my words."
3 Then I went down to the potter's house, and behold, he was making something on the wheels. 4 When the vessel that he made of the clay was marred in the hand of the potter, he made it again another vessel, as seemed good to the potter to make it.
5 Then Yahweh's word came to me, saying, 6 "House of Israel, can't I do with you as this potter?" says Yahweh. "Behold, as the clay in the potter's hand, so are you in my hand, house of Israel.

Responsorial Psalm: Psalms 146: 1b-6ab

1b Praise Yahweh, my soul.
2 While I live, I will praise Yahweh.
I will sing praises to my God as long as I exist.
3 Don't put your trust in princes,
in a son of man in whom there is no help.
4 His spirit departs, and he returns to the earth.
In that very day, his thoughts perish.
5 Happy is he who has the God of Jacob for his help,
whose hope is in Yahweh, his God,
6 who made heaven and earth,
the sea, and all that is in them;
who keeps truth forever;

Gospel: Matthew 13: 47-53

47 "Again, the Kingdom of Heaven is like a dragnet that was cast into the sea and gathered some fish of every kind, 48 which, when it was filled, fishermen drew up on the beach. They sat down and gathered the good into containers, but the bad they threw away. 49 So it will be in the end of the world.§ The angels will come and separate the wicked from among the righteous, 50 and will cast them into the furnace of fire. There will be weeping and gnashing of teeth." 51 Jesus said to them, "Have you understood all these things?"
They answered him, "Yes, Lord."
52 He said to them, "Therefore every scribe who has been made a disciple in the Kingdom of Heaven is like a man who is a householder, who brings out of his treasure new and old things."
53 When Jesus had finished these parables, he departed from there.

1. Invite the Holy Spirit into this reading, asking the Author of Scripture to speak to you through His Word
2. Read today's passage as many times as you need, take your time

3. Write down (below) what the Lord is saying to you today
4. Live with this Word in your heart through the day

_____

_____

Friday, August 2, 2024
Saint Eusebius of Vercelli, Bishop; Saint Peter Julian Eymard, Priest

First Reading: Jeremiah 26: 1-9

1 In the beginning of the reign of Jehoiakim the son of Josiah, king of Judah, this word came from Yahweh: 2 "Yahweh says: 'Stand in the court of Yahweh's house, and speak to all the cities of Judah which come to worship in Yahweh's house, all the words that I command you to speak to them. Don't omit a word. 3 It may be they will listen, and every man turn from his evil way, that I may relent from the evil which I intend to do to them because of the evil of their doings.' " 4 You shall tell them, "Yahweh says: 'If you will not listen to me, to walk in my law which I have set before you, 5 to listen to the words of my servants the prophets whom I send to you, even rising up early and sending them—but you have not listened— 6 then I will make this house like Shiloh, and will make this city a curse to all the nations of the earth.' "
7 The priests and the prophets and all the people heard Jeremiah speaking these words in Yahweh's house. 8 When Jeremiah had finished speaking all that Yahweh had commanded him to speak to all the people, the priests and the prophets and all the people seized him, saying, "You shall surely die! 9 Why have you prophesied in Yahweh's name, saying, 'This house will be like Shiloh, and this city will be desolate, without inhabitant'?" All the people were crowded around Jeremiah in Yahweh's house.

Responsorial Psalm: Psalms 69: 5, 8-10, 14

5 God, you know my foolishness.
My sins aren't hidden from you.
8 I have become a stranger to my brothers,
an alien to my mother's children.
9 For the zeal of your house consumes me.
The reproaches of those who reproach you have fallen on me.
10 When I wept and I fasted,
that was to my reproach.
14 Deliver me out of the mire, and don't let me sink.
Let me be delivered from those who hate me, and out of the deep waters.

Gospel: Matthew 13: 54-58

54 Coming into his own country, he taught them in their synagogue, so that they were astonished and said, "Where did this man get this wisdom and these mighty works? 55 Isn't this the carpenter's son? Isn't his mother called Mary, and his brothers James, Joses, Simon, and Judas?† 56 Aren't all of his sisters with us? Where then did this man get all of these things?" 57 They were offended by him.
But Jesus said to them, "A prophet is not without honor, except in his own country and in his own house." 58 He didn't do many mighty works there because of their unbelief.

1. Invite the Holy Spirit into this reading, asking the Author of Scripture to speak to you through His Word
2. Read today's passage as many times as you need, take your time
3. Write down (below) what the Lord is saying to you today
4. Live with this Word in your heart through the day

_____

_____

Saturday, August 3, 2024

First Reading: Jeremiah 26: 11-16, 24

11 Then the priests and the prophets spoke to the princes and to all the people, saying, "This man is worthy of death, for he has prophesied against this city, as you have heard with your ears."
12 Then Jeremiah spoke to all the princes and to all the people, saying, "Yahweh sent me to prophesy against this house and against this city all the words that you have heard. 13 Now therefore amend your ways and your doings, and obey Yahweh your God's voice; then Yahweh will relent from the evil that he has pronounced against you. 14 But as for me, behold, I am in your hand. Do with me what is good and right in your eyes. 15 Only know for certain that if you put me to death, you will bring innocent blood on yourselves, on this city, and on its inhabitants; for in truth Yahweh has sent me to you to speak all these words in your ears."
16 Then the princes and all the people said to the priests and to the prophets: "This man is not worthy of death; for he has spoken to us in the name of Yahweh our God."
24 But the hand of Ahikam the son of Shaphan was with Jeremiah, so that they didn't give him into the hand of the people to put him to death.

Responsorial Psalm: Psalms 69: 15-16, 30-31, 33-34

15 Don't let the flood waters overwhelm me,

neither let the deep swallow me up.

Don't let the pit shut its mouth on me.

16 Answer me, Yahweh, for your loving kindness is good.

According to the multitude of your tender mercies, turn to me.

30 I will praise the name of God with a song,

and will magnify him with thanksgiving.

31 It will please Yahweh better than an ox,

or a bull that has horns and hoofs.

33 For Yahweh hears the needy,

and doesn't despise his captive people.

34 Let heaven and earth praise him;

the seas, and everything that moves therein!

Gospel: Matthew 14: 1-12

1 At that time, Herod the tetrarch heard the report concerning Jesus, 2 and said to his servants, "This is John the Baptizer. He is risen from the dead. That is why these powers work in him." 3 For Herod had arrested John, bound him, and put him in prison for the sake of Herodias, his brother Philip's wife. 4 For John said to him, "It is not lawful for you to have her." 5 When he would have put him to death, he feared the multitude, because they counted him as a prophet. 6 But when Herod's birthday came, the daughter of Herodias danced among them and pleased Herod. 7 Therefore he promised with an oath to give her whatever she should ask. 8 She, being prompted by her mother, said, "Give me here on a platter the head of John the Baptizer."

9 The king was grieved, but for the sake of his oaths and of those who sat at the table with him, he commanded it to be given, 10 and he sent and beheaded John in the prison. 11 His head was brought on a platter and given to the young lady; and she brought it to her mother. 12 His disciples came, took the body, and buried it. Then they went and told Jesus.

1. Invite the Holy Spirit into this reading, asking the Author of Scripture to speak to you through His Word
2. Read today's passage as many times as you need, take your time
3. Write down (below) what the Lord is saying to you today
4. Live with this Word in your heart through the day

Sunday, August 4, 2024
EIGHTEENTH SUNDAY IN ORDINARY TIME

First Reading: Exodus 16: 2-4, 12-15

2 The whole congregation of the children of Israel murmured against Moses and against Aaron in the wilderness; 3 and the children of Israel said to them, "We wish that we had died by Yahweh's hand in the land of Egypt, when we sat by the meat pots, when we ate our fill of bread, for you have brought us out into this wilderness to kill this whole assembly with hunger."

4 Then Yahweh said to Moses, "Behold, I will rain bread from the sky for you, and the people shall go out and gather a day's portion every day, that I may test them, whether they will walk in my law or not.

12 "I have heard the murmurings of the children of Israel. Speak to them, saying, 'At evening you shall eat meat, and in the morning you shall be filled with bread. Then you will know that I am Yahweh your God.'"

13 In the evening, quail came up and covered the camp; and in the morning the dew lay around the camp. 14 When the dew that lay had gone, behold, on the surface of the wilderness was a small round thing, small as the frost on the ground. 15 When the children of Israel saw it, they said to one another, "What is it?" For they didn't know what it was. Moses said to them, "It is the bread which Yahweh has given you to eat.

Responsorial Psalm: Psalms 78: 3-4, 23-25, 54

3 which we have heard and known,
and our fathers have told us.
4 We will not hide them from their children,
telling to the generation to come the praises of Yahweh,
his strength, and his wondrous deeds that he has done.
23 Yet he commanded the skies above,
and opened the doors of heaven.
24 He rained down manna on them to eat,
and gave them food from the sky.
25 Man ate the bread of angels.
He sent them food to the full.
54 He brought them to the border of his sanctuary,
to this mountain, which his right hand had taken.

Second Reading: Ephesians 4: 17, 20-24

17 This I say therefore, and testify in the Lord, that you no longer walk as the rest of the Gentiles also walk, in the futility of their mind,
20 But you didn't learn Christ that way, 21 if indeed you heard him and were taught in him, even as truth is in Jesus: 22 that you put away, as concerning your former way of life, the old man that grows corrupt after the lusts of deceit, 23 and that you be renewed in the spirit of

your mind, 24 and put on the new man, who in the likeness of God has been created in righteousness and holiness of truth.

Gospel: John 6: 24-35

24 When the multitude therefore saw that Jesus wasn't there, nor his disciples, they themselves got into the boats and came to Capernaum, seeking Jesus. 25 When they found him on the other side of the sea, they asked him, "Rabbi, when did you come here?"
26 Jesus answered them, "Most certainly I tell you, you seek me, not because you saw signs, but because you ate of the loaves and were filled. 27 Don't work for the food which perishes, but for the food which remains to eternal life, which the Son of Man will give to you. For God the Father has sealed him."
28 They said therefore to him, "What must we do, that we may work the works of God?"
29 Jesus answered them, "This is the work of God, that you believe in him whom he has sent."
30 They said therefore to him, "What then do you do for a sign, that we may see and believe you? What work do you do? 31 Our fathers ate the manna in the wilderness. As it is written, 'He gave them bread out of heaven† to eat.' "*
32 Jesus therefore said to them, "Most certainly, I tell you, it wasn't Moses who gave you the bread out of heaven, but my Father gives you the true bread out of heaven. 33 For the bread of God is that which comes down out of heaven and gives life to the world."
34 They said therefore to him, "Lord, always give us this bread."
35 Jesus said to them, "I am the bread of life. Whoever comes to me will not be hungry, and whoever believes in me will never be thirsty.

1. Invite the Holy Spirit into this reading, asking the Author of Scripture to speak to you through His Word
2. Read today's passage as many times as you need, take your time
3. Write down (below) what the Lord is saying to you today
4. Live with this Word in your heart through the day

Monday, August 5, 2024
The Dedication of the Basilica of Saint Mary Major

First Reading: Jeremiah 28: 1-17

1 That same year, in the beginning of the reign of Zedekiah king of Judah, in the fourth year, in the fifth month, Hananiah the son of Azzur, the prophet, who was of Gibeon, spoke to me in Yahweh's house, in the presence of the priests and of all the people, saying, 2 "Yahweh of

Armies, the God of Israel, says, 'I have broken the yoke of the king of Babylon. 3 Within two full years I will bring again into this place all the vessels of Yahweh's house that Nebuchadnezzar king of Babylon took away from this place and carried to Babylon. 4 I will bring again to this place Jeconiah the son of Jehoiakim, king of Judah, with all the captives of Judah, who went to Babylon,' says Yahweh; 'for I will break the yoke of the king of Babylon.' "

5 Then the prophet Jeremiah said to the prophet Hananiah in the presence of the priests, and in the presence of all the people who stood in Yahweh's house, 6 even the prophet Jeremiah said, "Amen! May Yahweh do so. May Yahweh perform your words which you have prophesied, to bring again the vessels of Yahweh's house, and all those who are captives, from Babylon to this place. 7 Nevertheless listen now to this word that I speak in your ears, and in the ears of all the people: 8 The prophets who have been before me and before you of old prophesied against many countries, and against great kingdoms, of war, of evil, and of pestilence. 9 As for the prophet who prophesies of peace, when the word of the prophet happens, then the prophet will be known, that Yahweh has truly sent him."

10 Then Hananiah the prophet took the bar from off the prophet Jeremiah's neck, and broke it. 11 Hananiah spoke in the presence of all the people, saying, "Yahweh says: 'Even so I will break the yoke of Nebuchadnezzar king of Babylon from off the neck of all the nations within two full years.' " Then the prophet Jeremiah went his way.

12 Then Yahweh's word came to Jeremiah, after Hananiah the prophet had broken the bar from off the neck of the prophet Jeremiah, saying, 13 "Go, and tell Hananiah, saying, 'Yahweh says, "You have broken the bars of wood, but you have made in their place bars of iron." 14 For Yahweh of Armies, the God of Israel says, "I have put a yoke of iron on the neck of all these nations, that they may serve Nebuchadnezzar king of Babylon; and they will serve him. I have also given him the animals of the field." ' "

15 Then the prophet Jeremiah said to Hananiah the prophet, "Listen, Hananiah! Yahweh has not sent you, but you make this people trust in a lie. 16 Therefore Yahweh says, 'Behold, I will send you away from off the surface of the earth. This year you will die, because you have spoken rebellion against Yahweh.' "

17 So Hananiah the prophet died the same year in the seventh month.

Responsorial Psalm: Psalms 119: 29, 43, 79, 80, 95, 102

29 Keep me from the way of deceit.
Grant me your law graciously!
43 Don't snatch the word of truth out of my mouth,
for I put my hope in your ordinances.
79 Let those who fear you turn to me.
They will know your statutes.
80 Let my heart be blameless toward your decrees,
that I may not be disappointed.
95 The wicked have waited for me, to destroy me.
I will consider your statutes.
102 I have not turned away from your ordinances,

for you have taught me.

Gospel: Matthew 14: 13-21

13 Now when Jesus heard this, he withdrew from there in a boat to a deserted place apart. When the multitudes heard it, they followed him on foot from the cities.

14 Jesus went out, and he saw a great multitude. He had compassion on them and healed their sick. 15 When evening had come, his disciples came to him, saying, "This place is deserted, and the hour is already late. Send the multitudes away, that they may go into the villages, and buy themselves food."

16 But Jesus said to them, "They don't need to go away. You give them something to eat."

17 They told him, "We only have here five loaves and two fish."

18 He said, "Bring them here to me." 19 He commanded the multitudes to sit down on the grass; and he took the five loaves and the two fish, and looking up to heaven, he blessed, broke and gave the loaves to the disciples; and the disciples gave to the multitudes. 20 They all ate and were filled. They took up twelve baskets full of that which remained left over from the broken pieces. 21 Those who ate were about five thousand men, in addition to women and children.

1. Invite the Holy Spirit into this reading, asking the Author of Scripture to speak to you through His Word
2. Read today's passage as many times as you need, take your time
3. Write down (below) what the Lord is saying to you today
4. Live with this Word in your heart through the day

_____

_____

Tuesday, August 6, 2024
The Transfiguration of the Lord

First Reading: Daniel 7: 9-10, 13-14

9 "I watched until thrones were placed,
and one who was ancient of days sat.
His clothing was white as snow,
and the hair of his head like pure wool.
His throne was fiery flames,
and its wheels burning fire.
10 A fiery stream issued and came out from before him.

Thousands of thousands ministered to him.

Ten thousand times ten thousand stood before him.

The judgment was set.

The books were opened.

13 "I saw in the night visions, and behold, there came with the clouds of the sky one like a son of man, and he came even to the Ancient of Days, and they brought him near before him. 14 Dominion was given him, and glory, and a kingdom, that all the peoples, nations, and languages should serve him. His dominion is an everlasting dominion, which will not pass away, and his kingdom one that will not be destroyed.

Responsorial Psalm: Psalms 97: 1-2, 5-6, 9

1 Yahweh reigns!

Let the earth rejoice!

Let the multitude of islands be glad!

2 Clouds and darkness are around him.

Righteousness and justice are the foundation of his throne.

5 The mountains melt like wax at the presence of Yahweh,

at the presence of the Lord of the whole earth.

6 The heavens declare his righteousness.

All the peoples have seen his glory.

9 For you, Yahweh, are most high above all the earth.

You are exalted far above all gods.

Second Reading: Second Peter 1: 16-19

16 For we didn't follow cunningly devised fables when we made known to you the power and coming of our Lord Jesus Christ, but we were eyewitnesses of his majesty. 17 For he received from God the Father honor and glory when the voice came to him from the Majestic Glory, "This is my beloved Son, in whom I am well pleased."* 18 We heard this voice come out of heaven when we were with him on the holy mountain.

19 We have the more sure word of prophecy; and you do well that you heed it as to a lamp shining in a dark place, until the day dawns and the morning star arises in your hearts,

Gospel: Mark 9: 2-10

2 After six days Jesus took with him Peter, James, and John, and brought them up onto a high mountain privately by themselves, and he was changed into another form in front of them. 3 His clothing became glistening, exceedingly white, like snow, such as no launderer on earth can whiten them. 4 Elijah and Moses appeared to them, and they were talking with Jesus.

5 Peter answered Jesus, "Rabbi, it is good for us to be here. Let's make three tents: one for you, one for Moses, and one for Elijah." 6 For he didn't know what to say, for they were very afraid.

7 A cloud came, overshadowing them, and a voice came out of the cloud, "This is my beloved Son. Listen to him."

8 Suddenly looking around, they saw no one with them any more, except Jesus only.

9 As they were coming down from the mountain, he commanded them that they should tell no one what things they had seen, until after the Son of Man had risen from the dead. 10 They kept this saying to themselves, questioning what the "rising from the dead" meant.

1. Invite the Holy Spirit into this reading, asking the Author of Scripture to speak to you through His Word
2. Read today's passage as many times as you need, take your time
3. Write down (below) what the Lord is saying to you today
4. Live with this Word in your heart through the day

Wednesday, August 7, 2024
Saint Sixtus II, Pope, and Companions, Martyrs; Saint Cajetan, Priest

First Reading: Jeremiah 31: 1-7

1 "At that time," says Yahweh, "I will be the God of all the families of Israel, and they will be my people."

2 Yahweh says, "The people who survive the sword found favor in the wilderness; even Israel, when I went to cause him to rest."

3 Yahweh appeared of old to me, saying,

"Yes, I have loved you with an everlasting love.

Therefore I have drawn you with loving kindness.

4 I will build you again,

and you will be built, O virgin of Israel.

You will again be adorned with your tambourines,

and will go out in the dances of those who make merry.

5 Again you will plant vineyards on the mountains of Samaria.

The planters will plant,

and will enjoy its fruit.

6 For there will be a day that the watchmen on the hills of Ephraim cry,

'Arise! Let's go up to Zion to Yahweh our God.' "

7 For Yahweh says,

"Sing with gladness for Jacob,

and shout for the chief of the nations.

Publish, praise, and say,

'Yahweh, save your people,
the remnant of Israel!'

Responsorial Psalm: Jeremiah 31: 10- 13

10 "Hear Yahweh's word, you nations,
and declare it in the distant islands. Say,
'He who scattered Israel will gather him,
and keep him, as a shepherd does his flock.'
11 For Yahweh has ransomed Jacob,
and redeemed him from the hand of him who was stronger than he.
12 They will come and sing in the height of Zion,
and will flow to the goodness of Yahweh,
to the grain, to the new wine, to the oil,
and to the young of the flock and of the herd.
Their soul will be as a watered garden.
They will not sorrow any more at all.
13 Then the virgin will rejoice in the dance,
the young men and the old together;
for I will turn their mourning into joy,
and will comfort them, and make them rejoice from their sorrow.

Gospel: Matthew 15: 21-28

21 Jesus went out from there and withdrew into the region of Tyre and Sidon. 22 Behold, a Canaanite woman came out from those borders and cried, saying, "Have mercy on me, Lord, you son of David! My daughter is severely possessed by a demon!"
23 But he answered her not a word.
His disciples came and begged him, saying, "Send her away; for she cries after us."
24 But he answered, "I wasn't sent to anyone but the lost sheep of the house of Israel."
25 But she came and worshiped him, saying, "Lord, help me."
26 But he answered, "It is not appropriate to take the children's bread and throw it to the dogs."
27 But she said, "Yes, Lord, but even the dogs eat the crumbs which fall from their masters' table."
28 Then Jesus answered her, "Woman, great is your faith! Be it done to you even as you desire." And her daughter was healed from that hour.

1. Invite the Holy Spirit into this reading, asking the Author of Scripture to speak to you through His Word
2. Read today's passage as many times as you need, take your time
3. Write down (below) what the Lord is saying to you today
4. Live with this Word in your heart through the day

Thursday, August 8, 2024
Saint Dominic, Priest

First Reading: Jeremiah 31: 31-34

31 "Behold, the days come," says Yahweh, "that I will make a new covenant with the house of Israel, and with the house of Judah, 32 not according to the covenant that I made with their fathers in the day that I took them by the hand to bring them out of the land of Egypt, which covenant of mine they broke, although I was a husband to them," says Yahweh. 33 "But this is the covenant that I will make with the house of Israel after those days," says Yahweh:

"I will put my law in their inward parts,
and I will write it in their heart.
I will be their God,
and they shall be my people.
34 They will no longer each teach his neighbor,
and every man teach his brother, saying, 'Know Yahweh;'
for they will all know me,
from their least to their greatest," says Yahweh,
"for I will forgive their iniquity,
and I will remember their sin no more."

Responsorial Psalm: Psalms 51: 12-15, 18-19

12 Restore to me the joy of your salvation.
Uphold me with a willing spirit.
13 Then I will teach transgressors your ways.
Sinners will be converted to you.
14 Deliver me from the guilt of bloodshed, O God, the God of my salvation.
My tongue will sing aloud of your righteousness.
15 Lord, open my lips.
My mouth will declare your praise.
18 Do well in your good pleasure to Zion.
Build the walls of Jerusalem.
19 Then you will delight in the sacrifices of righteousness,
in burnt offerings and in whole burnt offerings.
Then they will offer bulls on your altar.

Gospel: Matthew 16: 13-23

13 Now when Jesus came into the parts of Caesarea Philippi, he asked his disciples, saying, "Who do men say that I, the Son of Man, am?"
14 They said, "Some say John the Baptizer, some, Elijah, and others, Jeremiah or one of the prophets."
15 He said to them, "But who do you say that I am?"
16 Simon Peter answered, "You are the Christ, the Son of the living God."
17 Jesus answered him, "Blessed are you, Simon Bar Jonah, for flesh and blood has not revealed this to you, but my Father who is in heaven. 18 I also tell you that you are Peter,† and on this rock ‡ I will build my assembly, and the gates of Hades§ will not prevail against it. 19 I will give to you the keys of the Kingdom of Heaven, and whatever you bind on earth will have been bound in heaven; and whatever you release on earth will have been released in heaven." 20 Then he commanded the disciples that they should tell no one that he was Jesus the Christ.
21 From that time, Jesus began to show his disciples that he must go to Jerusalem and suffer many things from the elders, chief priests, and scribes, and be killed, and the third day be raised up.
22 Peter took him aside and began to rebuke him, saying, "Far be it from you, Lord! This will never be done to you."
23 But he turned and said to Peter, "Get behind me, Satan! You are a stumbling block to me, for you are not setting your mind on the things of God, but on the things of men."

1. Invite the Holy Spirit into this reading, asking the Author of Scripture to speak to you through His Word
2. Read today's passage as many times as you need, take your time
3. Write down (below) what the Lord is saying to you today
4. Live with this Word in your heart through the day

_____

_____

Friday, August 9, 2024
Saint Teresa Benedicta of the Cross, Virgin and Martyr

First Reading: Nahum 2: 1, 3; 3: 1-3, 6-7

1 He who dashes in pieces has come up against you. Keep the fortress! Watch the way! Strengthen your waist! Fortify your power mightily!

3 The shield of his mighty men is made red. The valiant men are in scarlet. The chariots flash with steel in the day of his preparation, and the pine spears are brandished.

1 Woe to the bloody city! It is all full of lies and robbery—no end to the prey. 2 The noise of the whip, the noise of the rattling of wheels, prancing horses, and bounding chariots, 3 the horseman charging, and the flashing sword, the glittering spear, and a multitude of slain, and a great heap of corpses, and there is no end of the bodies. They stumble on their bodies

6 I will throw abominable filth on you and make you vile, and will make you a spectacle. 7 It will happen that all those who look at you will flee from you, and say, 'Nineveh is laid waste! Who will mourn for her?' Where will I seek comforters for you?"

Responsorial Psalm: Deuteronomy 32: 35cd-36ab, 39abcd, 41

35 Vengeance is mine, and recompense,
at the time when their foot slides,
for the day of their calamity is at hand.
Their doom rushes at them."
36 For Yahweh will judge his people,
and have compassion on his servants,
when he sees that their power is gone,
that there is no one remaining, shut up or left at large.
39 "See now that I myself am he.
There is no god with me.
I kill and I make alive.
I wound and I heal.
There is no one who can deliver out of my hand.
41 if I sharpen my glittering sword,
my hand grasps it in judgment;
I will take vengeance on my adversaries,
and will repay those who hate me.

Gospel: Matthew 16: 24-28

24 Then Jesus said to his disciples, "If anyone desires to come after me, let him deny himself, take up his cross, and follow me. 25 For whoever desires to save his life will lose it, and whoever will lose his life for my sake will find it. 26 For what will it profit a man if he gains the whole world and forfeits his life? Or what will a man give in exchange for his life? 27 For the Son of Man will come in the glory of his Father with his angels, and then he will render to everyone according to his deeds. 28 Most certainly I tell you, there are some standing here who will in no way taste of death until they see the Son of Man coming in his Kingdom."

1. Invite the Holy Spirit into this reading, asking the Author of Scripture to speak to you through His Word
2. Read today's passage as many times as you need, take your time

_____

_____

Saturday, August 10, 2024
Saint Lawrence, Deacon and Martyr

First Reading: Second Corinthians 9: 6-10

6 Remember this: he who sows sparingly will also reap sparingly. He who sows bountifully will also reap bountifully. 7 Let each man give according as he has determined in his heart, not grudgingly or under compulsion, for God loves a cheerful giver. 8 And God is able to make all grace abound to you, that you, always having all sufficiency in everything, may abound to every good work. 9 As it is written,
"He has scattered abroad. He has given to the poor.
His righteousness remains forever."*
10 Now may he who supplies seed to the sower and bread for food, supply and multiply your seed for sowing, and increase the fruits of your righteousness,

Responsorial Psalm: Psalms 112: 1-2, 5-9

1 Praise Yah!†
Blessed is the man who fears Yahweh,
who delights greatly in his commandments.
2 His offspring will be mighty in the land.
The generation of the upright will be blessed.
5 It is well with the man who deals graciously and lends.
He will maintain his cause in judgment.
6 For he will never be shaken.
The righteous will be remembered forever.
7 He will not be afraid of evil news.
His heart is steadfast, trusting in Yahweh.
8 His heart is established.
He will not be afraid in the end when he sees his adversaries.
9 He has dispersed, he has given to the poor.
His righteousness endures forever.
His horn will be exalted with honor.

Gospel: John 12: 24-26

24 Most certainly I tell you, unless a grain of wheat falls into the earth and dies, it remains by itself alone. But if it dies, it bears much fruit. 25 He who loves his life will lose it. He who hates his life in this world will keep it to eternal life. 26 If anyone serves me, let him follow me. Where I am, there my servant will also be. If anyone serves me, the Father will honor him.

1. Invite the Holy Spirit into this reading, asking the Author of Scripture to speak to you through His Word
2. Read today's passage as many times as you need, take your time
3. Write down (below) what the Lord is saying to you today
4. Live with this Word in your heart through the day

_____

_____

Sunday, August 11, 2024
NINETEENTH SUNDAY IN ORDINARY TIME

First Reading: First Kings 19: 4-8

4 But he himself went a day's journey into the wilderness, and came and sat down under a juniper tree. Then he requested for himself that he might die, and said, "It is enough. Now, O Yahweh, take away my life; for I am not better than my fathers."
5 He lay down and slept under a juniper tree; and behold, an angel touched him, and said to him, "Arise and eat!"
6 He looked, and behold, there was at his head a cake baked on the coals, and a jar of water. He ate and drank, and lay down again. 7 Yahweh's angel came again the second time, and touched him, and said, "Arise and eat, because the journey is too great for you."
8 He arose, and ate and drank, and went in the strength of that food forty days and forty nights to Horeb, God's Mountain.

Responsorial Psalm: Psalms 34: 2-9

2 My soul shall boast in Yahweh.
The humble shall hear of it and be glad.
3 Oh magnify Yahweh with me.
Let's exalt his name together.
4 I sought Yahweh, and he answered me,
and delivered me from all my fears.

5 They looked to him, and were radiant.
Their faces shall never be covered with shame.
6 This poor man cried, and Yahweh heard him,
and saved him out of all his troubles.
7 Yahweh's angel encamps around those who fear him,
and delivers them.
8 Oh taste and see that Yahweh is good.
Blessed is the man who takes refuge in him.
9 Oh fear Yahweh, you his saints,
for there is no lack with those who fear him.

Second Reading: Ephesians 4: 30 – 5: 2

30 Don't grieve the Holy Spirit of God, in whom you were sealed for the day of redemption. 31 Let all bitterness, wrath, anger, outcry, and slander be put away from you, with all malice. 32 And be kind to one another, tender hearted, forgiving each other, just as God also in Christ forgave you.
1 Be therefore imitators of God, as beloved children. 2 Walk in love, even as Christ also loved us and gave himself up for us, an offering and a sacrifice to God for a sweet-smelling fragrance.

Gospel: John 6: 41-51

41 The Jews therefore murmured concerning him, because he said, "I am the bread which came down out of heaven." 42 They said, "Isn't this Jesus, the son of Joseph, whose father and mother we know? How then does he say, 'I have come down out of heaven'?"
43 Therefore Jesus answered them, "Don't murmur among yourselves. 44 No one can come to me unless the Father who sent me draws him; and I will raise him up in the last day. 45 It is written in the prophets, 'They will all be taught by God.' * Therefore everyone who hears from the Father and has learned, comes to me. 46 Not that anyone has seen the Father, except he who is from God. He has seen the Father. 47 Most certainly, I tell you, he who believes in me has eternal life. 48 I am the bread of life. 49 Your fathers ate the manna in the wilderness and they died. 50 This is the bread which comes down out of heaven, that anyone may eat of it and not die. 51 I am the living bread which came down out of heaven. If anyone eats of this bread, he will live forever. Yes, the bread which I will give for the life of the world is my flesh."

1. Invite the Holy Spirit into this reading, asking the Author of Scripture to speak to you through His Word
2. Read today's passage as many times as you need, take your time
3. Write down (below) what the Lord is saying to you today
4. Live with this Word in your heart through the day

Monday, August 12, 2024
Saint Jane Frances de Chantal, Religious

First Reading: Ezekiel 1: 2-5, 24-28c

2 In the fifth of the month, which was the fifth year of King Jehoiachin's captivity, 3 Yahweh's‡ word came to Ezekiel the priest, the son of Buzi, in the land of the Chaldeans by the river Chebar; and Yahweh's hand was there on him.

4 I looked, and behold,§ a stormy wind came out of the north: a great cloud, with flashing lightning, and a brightness around it, and out of the middle of it as it were glowing metal, out of the middle of the fire. 5 Out of its center came the likeness of four living creatures. This was their appearance: They had the likeness of a man.

24 When they went, I heard the noise of their wings like the noise of great waters, like the voice of the Almighty, a noise of tumult like the noise of an army. When they stood, they let down their wings.

25 There was a voice above the expanse that was over their heads. When they stood, they let down their wings. 26 Above the expanse that was over their heads was the likeness of a throne, as the appearance of a sapphire† stone. On the likeness of the throne was a likeness as the appearance of a man on it above. 27 I saw as it were glowing metal, as the appearance of fire within it all around, from the appearance of his waist and upward; and from the appearance of his waist and downward I saw as it were the appearance of fire, and there was brightness around him. 28 As the appearance of the rainbow that is in the cloud in the day of rain, so was the appearance of the brightness all around.

This was the appearance of the likeness of Yahweh's glory. When I saw it, I fell on my face, and I heard a voice of one that spoke.

Responsorial Psalm: Psalms 148: 1-2, 11-14

1 Praise Yah!
Praise Yahweh from the heavens!
Praise him in the heights!
2 Praise him, all his angels!
Praise him, all his army!
11 kings of the earth and all peoples,
princes and all judges of the earth,
12 both young men and maidens,
old men and children.
13 Let them praise Yahweh's name,
for his name alone is exalted.
His glory is above the earth and the heavens.
14 He has lifted up the horn of his people,
the praise of all his saints,

even of the children of Israel, a people near to him.
Praise Yah!

Gospel: Matthew 17: 22-27

22 While they were staying in Galilee, Jesus said to them, "The Son of Man is about to be delivered up into the hands of men, 23 and they will kill him, and the third day he will be raised up."
They were exceedingly sorry.
24 When they had come to Capernaum, those who collected the didrachma coins§ came to Peter, and said, "Doesn't your teacher pay the didrachma?" 25 He said, "Yes."
When he came into the house, Jesus anticipated him, saying, "What do you think, Simon? From whom do the kings of the earth receive toll or tribute? From their children, or from strangers?"
26 Peter said to him, "From strangers."
Jesus said to him, "Therefore the children are exempt. 27 But, lest we cause them to stumble, go to the sea, cast a hook, and take up the first fish that comes up. When you have opened its mouth, you will find a stater coin.† Take that, and give it to them for me and you."

1. Invite the Holy Spirit into this reading, asking the Author of Scripture to speak to you through His Word
2. Read today's passage as many times as you need, take your time
3. Write down (below) what the Lord is saying to you today
4. Live with this Word in your heart through the day

_____

_____

Tuesday, August 13, 2024
Saints Pontian, Pope, and Hippolytus, Priest, Martyrs

First Reading: Ezekiel 2: 8 – 3: 4

8 But you, son of man, hear what I tell you. Don't be rebellious like that rebellious house. Open your mouth, and eat that which I give you."
9 When I looked, behold, a hand was stretched out to me; and behold, a scroll of a book was in it. 10 He spread it before me. It was written within and without; and lamentations, mourning, and woe were written in it.
1 He said to me, "Son of man, eat what you find. Eat this scroll, and go, speak to the house of Israel."

2 So I opened my mouth, and he caused me to eat the scroll.

3 He said to me, "Son of man, eat this scroll that I give you and fill your belly and your bowels with it."

Then I ate it. It was as sweet as honey in my mouth.

4 He said to me, "Son of man, go to the house of Israel, and speak my words to them.

Responsorial Psalm: Psalms 119: 14, 24, 72, 103, 111, 131

14 I have rejoiced in the way of your testimonies,

as much as in all riches.

24 Indeed your statutes are my delight,

and my counselors.

72 The law of your mouth is better to me than thousands of pieces of gold and silver.

103 How sweet are your promises to my taste,

more than honey to my mouth!

111 I have taken your testimonies as a heritage forever,

for they are the joy of my heart.

131 I opened my mouth wide and panted,

for I longed for your commandments.

Gospel: Matthew 18: 1-5, 10, 12-14

1 In that hour the disciples came to Jesus, saying, "Who then is greatest in the Kingdom of Heaven?"

2 Jesus called a little child to himself, and set him in the middle of them 3 and said, "Most certainly I tell you, unless you turn and become as little children, you will in no way enter into the Kingdom of Heaven. 4 Whoever therefore humbles himself as this little child is the greatest in the Kingdom of Heaven. 5 Whoever receives one such little child in my name receives me,

10 See that you don't despise one of these little ones, for I tell you that in heaven their angels always see the face of my Father who is in heaven.

12 "What do you think? If a man has one hundred sheep, and one of them goes astray, doesn't he leave the ninety-nine, go to the mountains, and seek that which has gone astray? 13 If he finds it, most certainly I tell you, he rejoices over it more than over the ninety-nine which have not gone astray. 14 Even so it is not the will of your Father who is in heaven that one of these little ones should perish.

1. Invite the Holy Spirit into this reading, asking the Author of Scripture to speak to you through His Word

2. Read today's passage as many times as you need, take your time

3. Write down (below) what the Lord is saying to you today

4. Live with this Word in your heart through the day

Wednesday, August 14, 2024
Saint Maximilian Kolbe, Priest and Martyr

First Reading: Ezekiel 9: 1-7; 10: 18-22

1 Then he cried in my ears with a loud voice, saying, "Cause those who are in charge of the city to draw near, each man with his destroying weapon in his hand." 2 Behold, six men came from the way of the upper gate, which lies toward the north, every man with his slaughter weapon in his hand. One man in the middle of them was clothed in linen, with a writer's inkhorn by his side. They went in, and stood beside the bronze altar.

3 The glory of the God of Israel went up from the cherub, whereupon it was, to the threshold of the house; and he called to the man clothed in linen, who had the writer's inkhorn by his side. 4 Yahweh said to him, "Go through the middle of the city, through the middle of Jerusalem, and set a mark on the foreheads of the men that sigh and that cry over all the abominations that are done within it."

5 To the others he said in my hearing, "Go through the city after him, and strike. Don't let your eye spare, neither have pity. 6 Kill utterly the old man, the young man, the virgin, little children and women; but don't come near any man on whom is the mark. Begin at my sanctuary."

Then they began at the old men who were before the house.

7 He said to them, "Defile the house, and fill the courts with the slain. Go out!"

They went out, and struck in the city.

18 Yahweh's glory went out from over the threshold of the house and stood over the cherubim. 19 The cherubim lifted up their wings and mounted up from the earth in my sight when they went out, with the wheels beside them. Then they stood at the door of the east gate of Yahweh's house; and the glory of the God of Israel was over them above.

20 This is the living creature that I saw under the God of Israel by the river Chebar; and I knew that they were cherubim. 21 Every one had four faces, and every one four wings. The likeness of the hands of a man was under their wings. 22 As for the likeness of their faces, they were the faces which I saw by the river Chebar, their appearances and themselves. They each went straight forward.

Responsorial Psalm: Psalms 113: 1-6

1 Praise Yah!
Praise, you servants of Yahweh,
praise Yahweh's name.
2 Blessed be Yahweh's name,

from this time forward and forever more.
3 From the rising of the sun to its going down,
Yahweh's name is to be praised.
4 Yahweh is high above all nations,
his glory above the heavens.
5 Who is like Yahweh, our God,
who has his seat on high,
6 who stoops down to see in heaven and in the earth?

Gospel: Matthew 18: 15-20

15 "If your brother sins against you, go, show him his fault between you and him alone. If he listens to you, you have gained back your brother. 16 But if he doesn't listen, take one or two more with you, that at the mouth of two or three witnesses every word may be established.* 17 If he refuses to listen to them, tell it to the assembly. If he refuses to hear the assembly also, let him be to you as a Gentile or a tax collector. 18 Most certainly I tell you, whatever things you bind on earth will have been bound in heaven, and whatever things you release on earth will have been released in heaven. 19 Again, assuredly I tell you, that if two of you will agree on earth concerning anything that they will ask, it will be done for them by my Father who is in heaven. 20 For where two or three are gathered together in my name, there I am in the middle of them."

1. Invite the Holy Spirit into this reading, asking the Author of Scripture to speak to you through His Word
2. Read today's passage as many times as you need, take your time
3. Write down (below) what the Lord is saying to you today
4. Live with this Word in your heart through the day

_____

_____

Thursday, August 15, 2024
THE ASSUMPTION OF THE BLESSED VIRGIN MARY

First Reading: Revelation 11: 19a; 12: 1-6a, 10ab

19 God's temple that is in heaven was opened, and the ark of the Lord's covenant was seen in his temple.

1 A great sign was seen in heaven: a woman clothed with the sun, and the moon under her feet, and on her head a crown of twelve stars. 2 She was with child. She cried out in pain, laboring to give birth.

3 Another sign was seen in heaven. Behold, a great red dragon, having seven heads and ten horns, and on his heads seven crowns. 4 His tail drew one third of the stars of the sky, and threw them to the earth. The dragon stood before the woman who was about to give birth, so that when she gave birth he might devour her child. 5 She gave birth to a son, a male child, who is to rule all the nations with a rod of iron. Her child was caught up to God and to his throne. 6 The woman fled into the wilderness, where she has a place prepared by God, that there they may nourish her one thousand two hundred sixty days.

10 I heard a loud voice in heaven, saying, "Now the salvation, the power, and the Kingdom of our God, and the authority of his Christ has come; for the accuser of our brothers has been thrown down, who accuses them before our God day and night.

Responsorial Psalm: Psalms 45: 10, 11, 12, 16

10 Listen, daughter, consider, and turn your ear.
Forget your own people, and also your father's house.
11 So the king will desire your beauty,
honor him, for he is your lord.
12 The daughter of Tyre comes with a gift.
The rich among the people entreat your favor.
16 Your sons will take the place of your fathers.
You shall make them princes in all the earth.

Second Reading: First Corinthians 15: 20-27

20 But now Christ has been raised from the dead. He became the first fruit of those who are asleep. 21 For since death came by man, the resurrection of the dead also came by man. 22 For as in Adam all die, so also in Christ all will be made alive. 23 But each in his own order: Christ the first fruits, then those who are Christ's at his coming. 24 Then the end comes, when he will deliver up the Kingdom to God the Father, when he will have abolished all rule and all authority and power. 25 For he must reign until he has put all his enemies under his feet. 26 The last enemy that will be abolished is death. 27 For, "He put all things in subjection under his feet."* But when he says, "All things are put in subjection", it is evident that he is excepted who subjected all things to him.

Gospel: Luke 1: 39-56

39 Mary arose in those days and went into the hill country with haste, into a city of Judah, 40 and entered into the house of Zacharias and greeted Elizabeth. 41 When Elizabeth heard Mary's greeting, the baby leaped in her womb; and Elizabeth was filled with the Holy Spirit. 42 She called out with a loud voice and said, "Blessed are you among women, and blessed is

the fruit of your womb! 43 Why am I so favored, that the mother of my Lord should come to me? 44 For behold, when the voice of your greeting came into my ears, the baby leaped in my womb for joy! 45 Blessed is she who believed, for there will be a fulfillment of the things which have been spoken to her from the Lord!"

46 Mary said,

"My soul magnifies the Lord.

47 My spirit has rejoiced in God my Savior,

48 for he has looked at the humble state of his servant.

For behold, from now on, all generations will call me blessed.

49 For he who is mighty has done great things for me.

Holy is his name.

50 His mercy is for generations and generations on those who fear him.

51 He has shown strength with his arm.

He has scattered the proud in the imagination of their hearts.

52 He has put down princes from their thrones,

and has exalted the lowly.

53 He has filled the hungry with good things.

He has sent the rich away empty.

54 He has given help to Israel, his servant, that he might remember mercy,

55 as he spoke to our fathers,

to Abraham and his offspring§ forever."

56 Mary stayed with her about three months, and then returned to her house.

1. Invite the Holy Spirit into this reading, asking the Author of Scripture to speak to you through His Word
2. Read today's passage as many times as you need, take your time
3. Write down (below) what the Lord is saying to you today
4. Live with this Word in your heart through the day

_____

_____

Friday, August 16, 2024
Saint Stephen of Hungary

First Reading: Ezekiel 16: 59-63

59 " 'For the Lord Yahweh says: "I will also deal with you as you have done, who have despised the oath in breaking the covenant. 60 Nevertheless I will remember my covenant with you in the days of your youth, and I will establish an everlasting covenant with you. 61 Then you will remember your ways and be ashamed when you receive your sisters, your elder sisters and

your younger; and I will give them to you for daughters, but not by your covenant. 62 I will establish my covenant with you. Then you will know that I am Yahweh; 63 that you may remember, and be confounded, and never open your mouth any more because of your shame, when I have forgiven you all that you have done," says the Lord Yahweh.' "

Responsorial Psalm: Isaiah 12: 2-6

2 Behold, God is my salvation. I will trust, and will not be afraid; for Yah, Yahweh, is my strength and song; and he has become my salvation." 3 Therefore with joy you will draw water out of the wells of salvation. 4 In that day you will say, "Give thanks to Yahweh! Call on his name! Declare his doings among the peoples! Proclaim that his name is exalted! 5 Sing to Yahweh, for he has done excellent things! Let this be known in all the earth! 6 Cry aloud and shout, you inhabitant of Zion, for the Holy One of Israel is great among you!"

Gospel: Matthew 19: 3-12

3 Pharisees came to him, testing him and saying, "Is it lawful for a man to divorce his wife for any reason?"
4 He answered, "Haven't you read that he who made them from the beginning made them male and female,* 5 and said, 'For this cause a man shall leave his father and mother, and shall be joined to his wife; and the two shall become one flesh'?* 6 So that they are no more two, but one flesh. What therefore God has joined together, don't let man tear apart."
7 They asked him, "Why then did Moses command us to give her a certificate of divorce and divorce her?"
8 He said to them, "Moses, because of the hardness of your hearts, allowed you to divorce your wives, but from the beginning it has not been so. 9 I tell you that whoever divorces his wife, except for sexual immorality, and marries another, commits adultery; and he who marries her when she is divorced commits adultery."
10 His disciples said to him, "If this is the case of the man with his wife, it is not expedient to marry."
11 But he said to them, "Not all men can receive this saying, but those to whom it is given. 12 For there are eunuchs who were born that way from their mother's womb, and there are eunuchs who were made eunuchs by men; and there are eunuchs who made themselves eunuchs for the Kingdom of Heaven's sake. He who is able to receive it, let him receive it."

1. Invite the Holy Spirit into this reading, asking the Author of Scripture to speak to you through His Word
2. Read today's passage as many times as you need, take your time
3. Write down (below) what the Lord is saying to you today
4. Live with this Word in your heart through the day

_____

_____

Saturday, August 17, 2024
Saint Stephen of Hungary

First Reading: Ezekiel 18: 1-10, 13b, 30-32

1 Yahweh's word came to me again, saying, 2 "What do you mean, that you use this proverb concerning the land of Israel, saying,
'The fathers have eaten sour grapes,
and the children's teeth are set on edge'?
3 "As I live," says the Lord Yahweh, "you shall not use this proverb any more in Israel. 4 Behold, all souls are mine; as the soul of the father, so also the soul of the son is mine. The soul who sins, he shall die.
5 "But if a man is just,
and does that which is lawful and right,
6 and has not eaten on the mountains,
hasn't lifted up his eyes to the idols of the house of Israel,
hasn't defiled his neighbor's wife,
hasn't come near a woman in her impurity,
7 and has not wronged any,
but has restored to the debtor his pledge,
has taken nothing by robbery,
has given his bread to the hungry,
and has covered the naked with a garment;
8 he who hasn't lent to them with interest,
hasn't taken any increase from them,
who has withdrawn his hand from iniquity,
has executed true justice between man and man,
9 has walked in my statutes,
and has kept my ordinances,
to deal truly;
he is just,
he shall surely live," says the Lord Yahweh.
10 "If he fathers a son who is a robber who sheds blood, and who does any one of these things,
13 has lent with interest,
and has taken increase from the poor,
shall he then live? He shall not live. He has done all these abominations. He shall surely die. His blood will be on him.
30 "Therefore I will judge you, house of Israel, everyone according to his ways," says the Lord Yahweh. "Return, and turn yourselves from all your transgressions, so iniquity will not be your ruin. 31 Cast away from you all your transgressions in which you have transgressed; and make yourself a new heart and a new spirit. For why will you die, house of Israel? 32 For I have no

pleasure in the death of him who dies," says the Lord Yahweh. "Therefore turn yourselves, and live!

Responsorial Psalm: Psalms 51: 12-15, 18-19

12 Restore to me the joy of your salvation.
Uphold me with a willing spirit.
13 Then I will teach transgressors your ways.
Sinners will be converted to you.
14 Deliver me from the guilt of bloodshed, O God, the God of my salvation.
My tongue will sing aloud of your righteousness.
15 Lord, open my lips.
My mouth will declare your praise.
18 Do well in your good pleasure to Zion.
Build the walls of Jerusalem.
19 Then you will delight in the sacrifices of righteousness,
in burnt offerings and in whole burnt offerings.
Then they will offer bulls on your altar.

Gospel: Matthew 19: 13-15

13 Then little children were brought to him that he should lay his hands on them and pray; and the disciples rebuked them. 14 But Jesus said, "Allow the little children, and don't forbid them to come to me; for the Kingdom of Heaven belongs to ones like these." 15 He laid his hands on them, and departed from there.

1. Invite the Holy Spirit into this reading, asking the Author of Scripture to speak to you through His Word
2. Read today's passage as many times as you need, take your time
3. Write down (below) what the Lord is saying to you today
4. Live with this Word in your heart through the day

_____

_____

Sunday, August 18, 2024
TWENTIETH SUNDAY IN ORDINARY TIME

First Reading: Proverbs 9: 1-6

1 Wisdom has built her house.
She has carved out her seven pillars.
2 She has prepared her meat.
She has mixed her wine.
She has also set her table.
3 She has sent out her maidens.
She cries from the highest places of the city:
4 "Whoever is simple, let him turn in here!"
As for him who is void of understanding, she says to him,
5 "Come, eat some of my bread,
Drink some of the wine which I have mixed!
6 Leave your simple ways, and live.
Walk in the way of understanding."

Responsorial Psalm: Psalms 34: 2-3, 10-15

2 My soul shall boast in Yahweh.
The humble shall hear of it and be glad.
3 Oh magnify Yahweh with me.
Let's exalt his name together.
10 The young lions do lack, and suffer hunger,
but those who seek Yahweh shall not lack any good thing.
11 Come, you children, listen to me.
I will teach you the fear of Yahweh.
12 Who is someone who desires life,
and loves many days, that he may see good?
13 Keep your tongue from evil,
and your lips from speaking lies.
14 Depart from evil, and do good.
Seek peace, and pursue it.
15 Yahweh's eyes are toward the righteous.
His ears listen to their cry.

Second Reading: Ephesians 5: 15-20

15 Therefore watch carefully how you walk, not as unwise, but as wise, 16 redeeming the time, because the days are evil. 17 Therefore, don't be foolish, but understand what the will of the Lord is. 18 Don't be drunken with wine, in which is dissipation, but be filled with the Spirit, 19 speaking to one another in psalms, hymns, and spiritual songs; singing and making melody in your heart to the Lord; 20 giving thanks always concerning all things in the name of our Lord Jesus Christ to God, even the Father;

Gospel: John 6: 51-58

51 I am the living bread which came down out of heaven. If anyone eats of this bread, he will live forever. Yes, the bread which I will give for the life of the world is my flesh."

52 The Jews therefore contended with one another, saying, "How can this man give us his flesh to eat?"

53 Jesus therefore said to them, "Most certainly I tell you, unless you eat the flesh of the Son of Man and drink his blood, you don't have life in yourselves. 54 He who eats my flesh and drinks my blood has eternal life, and I will raise him up at the last day. 55 For my flesh is food indeed, and my blood is drink indeed. 56 He who eats my flesh and drinks my blood lives in me, and I in him. 57 As the living Father sent me, and I live because of the Father, so he who feeds on me will also live because of me. 58 This is the bread which came down out of heaven—not as our fathers ate the manna and died. He who eats this bread will live forever."

1. Invite the Holy Spirit into this reading, asking the Author of Scripture to speak to you through His Word
2. Read today's passage as many times as you need, take your time
3. Write down (below) what the Lord is saying to you today
4. Live with this Word in your heart through the day

———————————————————————————————————

———————————————————————————————————

Monday, August 19, 2024
Saint John Eudes, Priest

First Reading: Ezekiel 24: 15-23

15 Also Yahweh's word came to me, saying, 16 "Son of man, behold, I will take away from you the desire of your eyes with one stroke; yet you shall neither mourn nor weep, neither shall your tears run down. 17 Sigh, but not aloud. Make no mourning for the dead. Bind your headdress on you, and put your sandals on your feet. Don't cover your lips, and don't eat mourner's bread."

18 So I spoke to the people in the morning, and at evening my wife died. So I did in the morning as I was commanded.

19 The people asked me, "Won't you tell us what these things mean to us, that you act like this?"

20 Then I said to them, "Yahweh's word came to me, saying, 21 'Speak to the house of Israel, "The Lord Yahweh says: 'Behold, I will profane my sanctuary, the pride of your power, the desire of your eyes, and that which your soul pities; and your sons and your daughters whom you have left behind will fall by the sword. 22 You will do as I have done. You won't cover your lips or eat mourner's bread. 23 Your turbans will be on your heads, and your sandals on your

feet. You won't mourn or weep; but you will pine away in your iniquities, and moan one toward another.

Responsorial Psalm: Deuteronomy 32: 18-19, 20, 21

18 Of the Rock who became your father, you are unmindful,
and have forgotten God who gave you birth.
19 Yahweh saw and abhorred,
because of the provocation of his sons and his daughters.
20 He said, "I will hide my face from them.
I will see what their end will be;
for they are a very perverse generation,
children in whom is no faithfulness.
21 They have moved me to jealousy with that which is not God.
They have provoked me to anger with their vanities.
I will move them to jealousy with those who are not a people.
I will provoke them to anger with a foolish nation.

Gospel: Matthew 19: 16-22

16 Behold, one came to him and said, "Good teacher, what good thing shall I do, that I may have eternal life?"
17 He said to him, "Why do you call me good?† No one is good but one, that is, God. But if you want to enter into life, keep the commandments."
18 He said to him, "Which ones?"
Jesus said, " 'You shall not murder.' 'You shall not commit adultery.' 'You shall not steal.' 'You shall not offer false testimony.' 19 'Honor your father and your mother.'* And, 'You shall love your neighbor as yourself.' "*
20 The young man said to him, "All these things I have observed from my youth. What do I still lack?"
21 Jesus said to him, "If you want to be perfect, go, sell what you have, and give to the poor, and you will have treasure in heaven; and come, follow me." 22 But when the young man heard this, he went away sad, for he was one who had great possessions.

1. Invite the Holy Spirit into this reading, asking the Author of Scripture to speak to you through His Word
2. Read today's passage as many times as you need, take your time
3. Write down (below) what the Lord is saying to you today
4. Live with this Word in your heart through the day

First Reading: Ezekiel 28: 1-10

1 Yahweh's word came again to me, saying, 2 "Son of man, tell the prince of Tyre, 'The Lord Yahweh says:
"Because your heart is lifted up,
and you have said, 'I am a god,
I sit in the seat of God,
in the middle of the seas;'
yet you are man,
and no god,
though you set your heart as the heart of a god—
3 behold, you are wiser than Daniel.
There is no secret that is hidden from you.
4 By your wisdom and by your understanding you have gotten yourself riches,
and have gotten gold and silver into your treasuries.
5 By your great wisdom
and by your trading you have increased your riches,
and your heart is lifted up because of your riches—"
6 " 'therefore the Lord Yahweh says:
"Because you have set your heart as the heart of God,
7 therefore, behold, I will bring strangers on you,
the terrible of the nations.
They will draw their swords against the beauty of your wisdom.
They will defile your brightness.
8 They will bring you down to the pit.
You will die the death of those who are slain
in the heart of the seas.
9 Will you yet say before him who kills you, 'I am God'?
But you are man, and not God,
in the hand of him who wounds you.
10 You will die the death of the uncircumcised
by the hand of strangers;
for I have spoken it," says the Lord Yahweh.' "

Responsorial Psalm: Deuteronomy 32: 26-28, 30, 35cd-36ab

26 I said that I would scatter them afar.
I would make their memory to cease from among men;
27 were it not that I feared the provocation of the enemy,

lest their adversaries should judge wrongly,
lest they should say, 'Our hand is exalted;
Yahweh has not done all this.' "
28 For they are a nation void of counsel.
There is no understanding in them.
30 How could one chase a thousand,
and two put ten thousand to flight,
unless their Rock had sold them,
and Yahweh had delivered them up?
35 Vengeance is mine, and recompense,
at the time when their foot slides,
for the day of their calamity is at hand.
Their doom rushes at them."
36 For Yahweh will judge his people,
and have compassion on his servants,
when he sees that their power is gone,
that there is no one remaining, shut up or left at large.

Gospel: Matthew 19: 23-30

23 Jesus said to his disciples, "Most certainly I say to you, a rich man will enter into the Kingdom of Heaven with difficulty. 24 Again I tell you, it is easier for a camel to go through a needle's eye than for a rich man to enter into God's Kingdom."
25 When the disciples heard it, they were exceedingly astonished, saying, "Who then can be saved?"
26 Looking at them, Jesus said, "With men this is impossible, but with God all things are possible."
27 Then Peter answered, "Behold, we have left everything and followed you. What then will we have?"
28 Jesus said to them, "Most certainly I tell you that you who have followed me, in the regeneration when the Son of Man will sit on the throne of his glory, you also will sit on twelve thrones, judging the twelve tribes of Israel. 29 Everyone who has left houses, or brothers, or sisters, or father, or mother, or wife, or children, or lands, for my name's sake, will receive one hundred times, and will inherit eternal life. 30 But many will be last who are first, and first who are last.

1. Invite the Holy Spirit into this reading, asking the Author of Scripture to speak to you through His Word
2. Read today's passage as many times as you need, take your time
3. Write down (below) what the Lord is saying to you today
4. Live with this Word in your heart through the day

First Reading: Ezekiel 34: 1-11

1 Yahweh's word came to me, saying, 2 "Son of man, prophesy against the shepherds of Israel. Prophesy, and tell them, even the shepherds, 'The Lord Yahweh says: "Woe to the shepherds of Israel who feed themselves! Shouldn't the shepherds feed the sheep? 3 You eat the fat. You clothe yourself with the wool. You kill the fatlings, but you don't feed the sheep. 4 You haven't strengthened the diseased. You haven't healed that which was sick. You haven't bound up that which was broken. You haven't brought back that which was driven away. You haven't sought that which was lost, but you have ruled over them with force and with rigor. 5 They were scattered, because there was no shepherd. They became food to all the animals of the field, and were scattered. 6 My sheep wandered through all the mountains and on every high hill. Yes, my sheep were scattered on all the surface of the earth. There was no one who searched or sought."

7 " 'Therefore, you shepherds, hear Yahweh's word: 8 "As I live," says the Lord Yahweh, "surely because my sheep became a prey, and my sheep became food to all the animals of the field, because there was no shepherd, and my shepherds didn't search for my sheep, but the shepherds fed themselves, and didn't feed my sheep, 9 therefore, you shepherds, hear Yahweh's word!" 10 The Lord Yahweh says: "Behold, I am against the shepherds. I will require my sheep at their hand, and cause them to cease from feeding the sheep. The shepherds won't feed themselves any more. I will deliver my sheep from their mouth, that they may not be food for them."

11 " 'For the Lord Yahweh says: "Behold, I myself, even I, will search for my sheep, and will seek them out

Responsorial Psalm: Psalms 23: 1-6

1 Yahweh is my shepherd;
I shall lack nothing.
2 He makes me lie down in green pastures.
He leads me beside still waters.
3 He restores my soul.
He guides me in the paths of righteousness for his name's sake.
4 Even though I walk through the valley of the shadow of death,
I will fear no evil, for you are with me.
Your rod and your staff,
they comfort me.
5 You prepare a table before me
in the presence of my enemies.
You anoint my head with oil.

My cup runs over.
6 Surely goodness and loving kindness shall follow me all the days of my life,
and I will dwell in Yahweh's house forever.

Gospel: Matthew 20: 1-16

1 "For the Kingdom of Heaven is like a man who was the master of a household, who went out early in the morning to hire laborers for his vineyard. 2 When he had agreed with the laborers for a denarius† a day, he sent them into his vineyard. 3 He went out about the third hour,‡ and saw others standing idle in the marketplace. 4 He said to them, 'You also go into the vineyard, and whatever is right I will give you.' So they went their way. 5 Again he went out about the sixth and the ninth hour,§ and did likewise. 6 About the eleventh hour† he went out and found others standing idle. He said to them, 'Why do you stand here all day idle?'
7 "They said to him, 'Because no one has hired us.'
"He said to them, 'You also go into the vineyard, and you will receive whatever is right.'
8 "When evening had come, the lord of the vineyard said to his manager, 'Call the laborers and pay them their wages, beginning from the last to the first.' 9 "When those who were hired at about the eleventh hour came, they each received a denarius. 10 When the first came, they supposed that they would receive more; and they likewise each received a denarius. 11 When they received it, they murmured against the master of the household, 12 saying, 'These last have spent one hour, and you have made them equal to us who have borne the burden of the day and the scorching heat!'
13 "But he answered one of them, 'Friend, I am doing you no wrong. Didn't you agree with me for a denarius? 14 Take that which is yours, and go your way. It is my desire to give to this last just as much as to you. 15 Isn't it lawful for me to do what I want to with what I own? Or is your eye evil, because I am good?' 16 So the last will be first, and the first last. For many are called, but few are chosen."

1. Invite the Holy Spirit into this reading, asking the Author of Scripture to speak to you through His Word
2. Read today's passage as many times as you need, take your time
3. Write down (below) what the Lord is saying to you today
4. Live with this Word in your heart through the day

_____

_____

Thursday, August 22, 2024
The Queenship of the Blessed Virgin Mary

First Reading: Ezekiel 36: 23-28

23 I will sanctify my great name, which has been profaned among the nations, which you have profaned among them. Then the nations will know that I am Yahweh," says the Lord Yahweh, "when I am proven holy in you before their eyes.

24 " ' "For I will take you from among the nations and gather you out of all the countries, and will bring you into your own land. 25 I will sprinkle clean water on you, and you will be clean. I will cleanse you from all your filthiness and from all your idols. 26 I will also give you a new heart, and I will put a new spirit within you. I will take away the stony heart out of your flesh, and I will give you a heart of flesh. 27 I will put my Spirit within you, and cause you to walk in my statutes. You will keep my ordinances and do them. 28 You will dwell in the land that I gave to your fathers. You will be my people, and I will be your God.

Responsorial Psalm: Psalms 51: 12-15, 18-19

12 Restore to me the joy of your salvation.
Uphold me with a willing spirit.
13 Then I will teach transgressors your ways.
Sinners will be converted to you.
14 Deliver me from the guilt of bloodshed, O God, the God of my salvation.
My tongue will sing aloud of your righteousness.
15 Lord, open my lips.
My mouth will declare your praise.
18 Do well in your good pleasure to Zion.
Build the walls of Jerusalem.
19 Then you will delight in the sacrifices of righteousness,
in burnt offerings and in whole burnt offerings.
Then they will offer bulls on your altar.

Gospel: Matthew 22: 1-14

1 Jesus answered and spoke to them again in parables, saying, 2 "The Kingdom of Heaven is like a certain king, who made a wedding feast for his son, 3 and sent out his servants to call those who were invited to the wedding feast, but they would not come. 4 Again he sent out other servants, saying, 'Tell those who are invited, "Behold, I have prepared my dinner. My cattle and my fatlings are killed, and all things are ready. Come to the wedding feast!" ' 5 But they made light of it, and went their ways, one to his own farm, another to his merchandise; 6 and the rest grabbed his servants, treated them shamefully, and killed them. 7 When the king heard that, he was angry, and sent his armies, destroyed those murderers, and burned their city.

8 "Then he said to his servants, 'The wedding is ready, but those who were invited weren't worthy. 9 Go therefore to the intersections of the highways, and as many as you may find,

invite to the wedding feast.' 10 Those servants went out into the highways and gathered together as many as they found, both bad and good. The wedding was filled with guests.

11 "But when the king came in to see the guests, he saw there a man who didn't have on wedding clothing, 12 and he said to him, 'Friend, how did you come in here not wearing wedding clothing?' He was speechless. 13 Then the king said to the servants, 'Bind him hand and foot, take him away, and throw him into the outer darkness. That is where the weeping and grinding of teeth will be.' 14 For many are called, but few chosen."

1. Invite the Holy Spirit into this reading, asking the Author of Scripture to speak to you through His Word
2. Read today's passage as many times as you need, take your time
3. Write down (below) what the Lord is saying to you today
4. Live with this Word in your heart through the day

Friday, August 23, 2024
Saint Rose of Lima, Virgin

First Reading: Ezekiel 37: 1-14

1 Yahweh's hand was on me, and he brought me out in Yahweh's Spirit, and set me down in the middle of the valley; and it was full of bones. 2 He caused me to pass by them all around; and behold, there were very many in the open valley, and behold, they were very dry. 3 He said to me, "Son of man, can these bones live?"

I answered, "Lord Yahweh, you know."

4 Again he said to me, "Prophesy over these bones, and tell them, 'You dry bones, hear Yahweh's word. 5 The Lord Yahweh says to these bones: "Behold, I will cause breath to enter into you, and you will live. 6 I will lay sinews on you, and will bring up flesh on you, and cover you with skin, and put breath in you, and you will live. Then you will know that I am Yahweh." ' "

7 So I prophesied as I was commanded. As I prophesied, there was a noise, and behold, there was an earthquake. Then the bones came together, bone to its bone. 8 I saw, and, behold, there were sinews on them, and flesh came up, and skin covered them above; but there was no breath in them.

9 Then he said to me, "Prophesy to the wind, prophesy, son of man, and tell the wind, 'The Lord Yahweh says: "Come from the four winds, breath, and breathe on these slain, that they may live." ' "

10 So I prophesied as he commanded me, and the breath came into them, and they lived, and stood up on their feet, an exceedingly great army.

11 Then he said to me, "Son of man, these bones are the whole house of Israel. Behold, they say, 'Our bones are dried up, and our hope is lost. We are completely cut off.' 12 Therefore prophesy, and tell them, 'The Lord Yahweh says: "Behold, I will open your graves, and cause you to come up out of your graves, my people; and I will bring you into the land of Israel. 13 You will know that I am Yahweh, when I have opened your graves and caused you to come up out of your graves, my people. 14 I will put my Spirit in you, and you will live. Then I will place you in your own land; and you will know that I, Yahweh, have spoken it and performed it," says Yahweh.' "

Responsorial Psalm: Psalms 107: 2-9

2 Let the redeemed by Yahweh say so,
whom he has redeemed from the hand of the adversary,
3 and gathered out of the lands,
from the east and from the west,
from the north and from the south.
4 They wandered in the wilderness in a desert way.
They found no city to live in.
5 Hungry and thirsty,
their soul fainted in them.
6 Then they cried to Yahweh in their trouble,
and he delivered them out of their distresses.
7 He led them also by a straight way,
that they might go to a city to live in.
8 Let them praise Yahweh for his loving kindness,
for his wonderful deeds to the children of men!
9 For he satisfies the longing soul.
He fills the hungry soul with good.

Gospel: Matthew 22: 34-40

34 But the Pharisees, when they heard that he had silenced the Sadducees, gathered themselves together. 35 One of them, a lawyer, asked him a question, testing him. 36 "Teacher, which is the greatest commandment in the law?"

37 Jesus said to him, " 'You shall love the Lord your God with all your heart, with all your soul, and with all your mind.'* 38 This is the first and great commandment. 39 A second likewise is this, 'You shall love your neighbor as yourself.'* 40 The whole law and the prophets depend on these two commandments."

1. Invite the Holy Spirit into this reading, asking the Author of Scripture to speak to you through His Word
2. Read today's passage as many times as you need, take your time
3. Write down (below) what the Lord is saying to you today
4. Live with this Word in your heart through the day

Saturday, August 24, 2024
Saint Bartholomew, Apostle

First Reading: Revelation 21: 9b-14

9 One of the seven angels who had the seven bowls which were loaded with the seven last plagues came, and he spoke with me, saying, "Come here. I will show you the bride, the Lamb's wife." 10 He carried me away in the Spirit to a great and high mountain, and showed me the holy city, Jerusalem, coming down out of heaven from God, 11 having the glory of God. Her light was like a most precious stone, like a jasper stone, clear as crystal; 12 having a great and high wall with twelve gates, and at the gates twelve angels, and names written on them, which are the names of the twelve tribes of the children of Israel. 13 On the east were three gates, and on the north three gates, and on the south three gates, and on the west three gates. 14 The wall of the city had twelve foundations, and on them twelve names of the twelve Apostles of the Lamb.

Responsorial Psalm: Psalms 145: 10-13, 17-18

10 All your works will give thanks to you, Yahweh.
Your saints will extol you.
11 They will speak of the glory of your kingdom,
and talk about your power,
12 to make known to the sons of men his mighty acts,
the glory of the majesty of his kingdom.
13 Your kingdom is an everlasting kingdom.
Your dominion endures throughout all generations.
Yahweh is faithful in all his words,
and loving in all his deeds.‡
17 Yahweh is righteous in all his ways,
and gracious in all his works.
18 Yahweh is near to all those who call on him,

to all who call on him in truth.
Gospel: John 1: 45-51

45 Philip found Nathanael, and said to him, "We have found him of whom Moses in the law and also the prophets, wrote: Jesus of Nazareth, the son of Joseph."
46 Nathanael said to him, "Can any good thing come out of Nazareth?"
Philip said to him, "Come and see."
47 Jesus saw Nathanael coming to him, and said about him, "Behold, an Israelite indeed, in whom is no deceit!"
48 Nathanael said to him, "How do you know me?"
Jesus answered him, "Before Philip called you, when you were under the fig tree, I saw you."
49 Nathanael answered him, "Rabbi, you are the Son of God! You are King of Israel!"
50 Jesus answered him, "Because I told you, 'I saw you underneath the fig tree,' do you believe? You will see greater things than these!" 51 He said to him, "Most certainly, I tell you all, hereafter you will see heaven opened, and the angels of God ascending and descending on the Son of Man."

1. Invite the Holy Spirit into this reading, asking the Author of Scripture to speak to you through His Word
2. Read today's passage as many times as you need, take your time
3. Write down (below) what the Lord is saying to you today
4. Live with this Word in your heart through the day

_____

_____

Sunday, August 25, 2024
TWENTY-FIRST SUNDAY IN ORDINARY TIME

First Reading: Joshua 24: 1-2a, 15-17, 18b

1 Joshua gathered all the tribes of Israel to Shechem, and called for the elders of Israel, for their heads, for their judges, and for their officers; and they presented themselves before God.
2 Joshua said to all the people, "Yahweh, the God of Israel, says, 'Your fathers lived of old time beyond the River, even Terah, the father of Abraham, and the father of Nahor. They served other gods.
15 If it seems evil to you to serve Yahweh, choose today whom you will serve; whether the gods which your fathers served that were beyond the River, or the gods of the Amorites, in whose land you dwell; but as for me and my house, we will serve Yahweh."

16 The people answered, "Far be it from us that we should forsake Yahweh, to serve other gods; 17 for it is Yahweh our God who brought us and our fathers up out of the land of Egypt, from the house of bondage, and who did those great signs in our sight, and preserved us in all the way in which we went, and among all the peoples through the middle of whom we passed. 18 Yahweh drove out from before us all the peoples, even the Amorites who lived in the land. Therefore we also will serve Yahweh; for he is our God."

Responsorial Psalm: Psalms 34: 2-3, 16-22

2 My soul shall boast in Yahweh.
The humble shall hear of it and be glad.
3 Oh magnify Yahweh with me.
Let's exalt his name together.
16 Yahweh's face is against those who do evil,
to cut off their memory from the earth.
17 The righteous cry, and Yahweh hears,
and delivers them out of all their troubles.
18 Yahweh is near to those who have a broken heart,
and saves those who have a crushed spirit.
19 Many are the afflictions of the righteous,
but Yahweh delivers him out of them all.
20 He protects all of his bones.
Not one of them is broken.
21 Evil shall kill the wicked.
Those who hate the righteous shall be condemned.
22 Yahweh redeems the soul of his servants.
None of those who take refuge in him shall be condemned.

Second Reading: Ephesians 5: 21-32

21 subjecting yourselves to one another in the fear of Christ.
22 Wives, be subject to your own husbands, as to the Lord. 23 For the husband is the head of the wife, as Christ also is the head of the assembly, being himself the savior of the body. 24 But as the assembly is subject to Christ, so let the wives also be to their own husbands in everything.
25 Husbands, love your wives, even as Christ also loved the assembly and gave himself up for her, 26 that he might sanctify her, having cleansed her by the washing of water with the word, 27 that he might present the assembly to himself gloriously, not having spot or wrinkle or any such thing, but that she should be holy and without defect. 28 Even so husbands also ought to love their own wives as their own bodies. He who loves his own wife loves himself. 29 For no man ever hated his own flesh, but nourishes and cherishes it, even as the Lord also does the assembly, 30 because we are members of his body, of his flesh and bones. 31 "For this cause a

man will leave his father and mother and will be joined to his wife. Then the two will become one flesh."* 32 This mystery is great, but I speak concerning Christ and the assembly.

Gospel: John 6: 60-69

60 Therefore many of his disciples, when they heard this, said, "This is a hard saying! Who can listen to it?"

61 But Jesus knowing in himself that his disciples murmured at this, said to them, "Does this cause you to stumble? 62 Then what if you would see the Son of Man ascending to where he was before? 63 It is the spirit who gives life. The flesh profits nothing. The words that I speak to you are spirit, and are life. 64 But there are some of you who don't believe." For Jesus knew from the beginning who they were who didn't believe, and who it was who would betray him. 65 He said, "For this cause I have said to you that no one can come to me, unless it is given to him by my Father."

66 At this, many of his disciples went back and walked no more with him. 67 Jesus said therefore to the twelve, "You don't also want to go away, do you?"

68 Simon Peter answered him, "Lord, to whom would we go? You have the words of eternal life. 69 We have come to believe and know that you are the Christ, the Son of the living God."

1. Invite the Holy Spirit into this reading, asking the Author of Scripture to speak to you through His Word
2. Read today's passage as many times as you need, take your time
3. Write down (below) what the Lord is saying to you today
4. Live with this Word in your heart through the day

_____

_____

Monday, August 26, 2024

First Reading: Second Thessalonians 1: 1-5, 11-12

1 Paul, Silvanus, and Timothy, to the assembly of the Thessalonians in God our Father and the Lord Jesus Christ: 2 Grace to you and peace from God our Father and the Lord Jesus Christ. 3 We are bound to always give thanks to God for you, brothers,† even as it is appropriate, because your faith grows exceedingly, and the love of each and every one of you toward one another abounds, 4 so that we ourselves boast about you in the assemblies of God for your perseverance and faith in all your persecutions and in the afflictions which you endure. 5 This is an obvious sign of the righteous judgment of God, to the end that you may be counted worthy of God's Kingdom, for which you also suffer.

11 To this end we also pray always for you that our God may count you worthy of your calling, and fulfill every desire of goodness and work of faith with power, 12 that the name of our Lord Jesus‡ may be glorified in you, and you in him, according to the grace of our God and the Lord Jesus Christ.

Responsorial Psalm: Psalms 96: 1-5

1 Sing to Yahweh a new song!
Sing to Yahweh, all the earth.
2 Sing to Yahweh!
Bless his name!
Proclaim his salvation from day to day!
3 Declare his glory among the nations,
his marvelous works among all the peoples.
4 For Yahweh is great, and greatly to be praised!
He is to be feared above all gods.
5 For all the gods of the peoples are idols,
but Yahweh made the heavens.

Gospel: Matthew 23: 13-22

13 "Woe to you, scribes and Pharisees, hypocrites! For you devour widows' houses, and as a pretense you make long prayers. Therefore you will receive greater condemnation.
14 "But woe to you, scribes and Pharisees, hypocrites! Because you shut up the Kingdom of Heaven against men; for you don't enter in yourselves, neither do you allow those who are entering in to enter.† 15 Woe to you, scribes and Pharisees, hypocrites! For you travel around by sea and land to make one proselyte; and when he becomes one, you make him twice as much a son of Gehenna‡ as yourselves.
16 "Woe to you, you blind guides, who say, 'Whoever swears by the temple, it is nothing; but whoever swears by the gold of the temple, he is obligated.' 17 You blind fools! For which is greater, the gold or the temple that sanctifies the gold? 18 And, 'Whoever swears by the altar, it is nothing; but whoever swears by the gift that is on it, he is obligated.' 19 You blind fools! For which is greater, the gift, or the altar that sanctifies the gift? 20 He therefore who swears by the altar, swears by it and by everything on it. 21 He who swears by the temple, swears by it and by him who has been living§ in it. 22 He who swears by heaven, swears by the throne of God and by him who sits on it.

1. Invite the Holy Spirit into this reading, asking the Author of Scripture to speak to you through His Word
2. Read today's passage as many times as you need, take your time
3. Write down (below) what the Lord is saying to you today
4. Live with this Word in your heart through the day

Tuesday, August 27, 2024
Saint Monica

First Reading: Second Thessalonians 2: 1-3a, 14-17

1 Now, brothers, concerning the coming of our Lord Jesus Christ and our gathering together to him, we ask you 2 not to be quickly shaken in your mind or troubled, either by spirit or by word or by letter as if from us, saying that the day of Christ has already come. 3 Let no one deceive you in any way. For it will not be unless the rebellion† comes first, and the man of sin is revealed, the son of destruction.

14 to which he called you through our Good News, for the obtaining of the glory of our Lord Jesus Christ. 15 So then, brothers, stand firm and hold the traditions which you were taught by us, whether by word or by letter.

16 Now our Lord Jesus Christ himself, and God our Father, who loved us and gave us eternal comfort and good hope through grace, 17 comfort your hearts and establish you in every good work and word.

Responsorial Psalm: Psalms 96: 10-13

10 Say among the nations, "Yahweh reigns."
The world is also established.
It can't be moved.
He will judge the peoples with equity.
11 Let the heavens be glad, and let the earth rejoice.
Let the sea roar, and its fullness!
12 Let the field and all that is in it exult!
Then all the trees of the woods shall sing for joy
13 before Yahweh; for he comes,
for he comes to judge the earth.
He will judge the world with righteousness,
the peoples with his truth.

Gospel: Matthew 23: 23-26

23 "Woe to you, scribes and Pharisees, hypocrites! For you tithe mint, dill, and cumin,† and have left undone the weightier matters of the law: justice, mercy, and faith. But you ought to have done these, and not to have left the other undone. 24 You blind guides, who strain out a gnat, and swallow a camel!

25 "Woe to you, scribes and Pharisees, hypocrites! For you clean the outside of the cup and of the platter, but within they are full of extortion and unrighteousness.‡ 26 You blind Pharisee, first clean the inside of the cup and of the platter, that its outside may become clean also.

1. Invite the Holy Spirit into this reading, asking the Author of Scripture to speak to you through His Word
2. Read today's passage as many times as you need, take your time
3. Write down (below) what the Lord is saying to you today
4. Live with this Word in your heart through the day

_____

_____

Wednesday, August 28, 2024
Saint Augustine, Bishop and Doctor of the Church

First Reading: Second Thessalonians 3: 6-10, 16-18

6 Now we command you, brothers, in the name of our Lord Jesus Christ, that you withdraw yourselves from every brother who walks in rebellion and not after the tradition which they received from us. 7 For you know how you ought to imitate us. For we didn't behave ourselves rebelliously among you, 8 neither did we eat bread from anyone's hand without paying for it, but in labor and travail worked night and day, that we might not burden any of you. 9 This was not because we don't have the right, but to make ourselves an example to you, that you should imitate us. 10 For even when we were with you, we commanded you this: "If anyone is not willing to work, don't let him eat."
16 Now may the Lord of peace himself give you peace at all times in all ways. The Lord be with you all.
17 I, Paul, write this greeting with my own hand, which is the sign in every letter. This is how I write. 18 The grace of our Lord Jesus Christ be with you all. Amen.

Responsorial Psalm: Psalms 128: 1-2, 4-5

1 Blessed is everyone who fears Yahweh,
who walks in his ways.
2 For you will eat the labor of your hands.
You will be happy, and it will be well with you.
4 Behold, this is how the man who fears Yahweh is blessed.
5 May Yahweh bless you out of Zion,
and may you see the good of Jerusalem all the days of your life.

Gospel: Matthew 23: 27-32

27 "Woe to you, scribes and Pharisees, hypocrites! For you are like whitened tombs, which outwardly appear beautiful, but inwardly are full of dead men's bones and of all uncleanness. 28 Even so you also outwardly appear righteous to men, but inwardly you are full of hypocrisy and iniquity.

29 "Woe to you, scribes and Pharisees, hypocrites! For you build the tombs of the prophets and decorate the tombs of the righteous, 30 and say, 'If we had lived in the days of our fathers, we wouldn't have been partakers with them in the blood of the prophets.' 31 Therefore you testify to yourselves that you are children of those who killed the prophets. 32 Fill up, then, the measure of your fathers.

1. Invite the Holy Spirit into this reading, asking the Author of Scripture to speak to you through His Word
2. Read today's passage as many times as you need, take your time
3. Write down (below) what the Lord is saying to you today
4. Live with this Word in your heart through the day

Thursday, August 29, 2024
The Passion of Saint John the Baptist

First Reading: First Corinthians 1: 1-9

1 Paul, called to be an apostle of Jesus Christ† through the will of God, and our brother Sosthenes, 2 to the assembly of God which is at Corinth—those who are sanctified in Christ Jesus, called saints, with all who call on the name of our Lord Jesus Christ in every place, both theirs and ours: 3 Grace to you and peace from God our Father and the Lord Jesus Christ.

4 I always thank my God concerning you for the grace of God which was given you in Christ Jesus, 5 that in everything you were enriched in him, in all speech and all knowledge— 6 even as the testimony of Christ was confirmed in you— 7 so that you come behind in no gift, waiting for the revelation of our Lord Jesus Christ, 8 who will also confirm you until the end, blameless in the day of our Lord Jesus Christ. 9 God is faithful, through whom you were called into the fellowship of his Son, Jesus Christ our Lord.

Responsorial Psalm: Psalms 145: 2-7

2 Every day I will praise you.
I will extol your name forever and ever.
3 Great is Yahweh, and greatly to be praised!

His greatness is unsearchable.
4 One generation will commend your works to another,
and will declare your mighty acts.
5 I will meditate on the glorious majesty of your honor,
on your wondrous works.
6 Men will speak of the might of your awesome acts.
I will declare your greatness.
7 They will utter the memory of your great goodness,
and will sing of your righteousness.

Gospel: Mark 6: 17-29

17 For Herod himself had sent out and arrested John and bound him in prison for the sake of Herodias, his brother Philip's wife, for he had married her. 18 For John had said to Herod, "It is not lawful for you to have your brother's wife." 19 Herodias set herself against him and desired to kill him, but she couldn't, 20 for Herod feared John, knowing that he was a righteous and holy man, and kept him safe. When he heard him, he did many things, and he heard him gladly.

21 Then a convenient day came when Herod on his birthday made a supper for his nobles, the high officers, and the chief men of Galilee. 22 When the daughter of Herodias herself came in and danced, she pleased Herod and those sitting with him. The king said to the young lady, "Ask me whatever you want, and I will give it to you." 23 He swore to her, "Whatever you ask of me, I will give you, up to half of my kingdom."

24 She went out and said to her mother, "What shall I ask?"
She said, "The head of John the Baptizer."

25 She came in immediately with haste to the king and requested, "I want you to give me right now the head of John the Baptizer on a platter."

26 The king was exceedingly sorry, but for the sake of his oaths and of his dinner guests, he didn't wish to refuse her. 27 Immediately the king sent out a soldier of his guard and commanded to bring John's head; and he went and beheaded him in the prison, 28 and brought his head on a platter, and gave it to the young lady; and the young lady gave it to her mother.

29 When his disciples heard this, they came and took up his corpse and laid it in a tomb.

1. Invite the Holy Spirit into this reading, asking the Author of Scripture to speak to you through His Word
2. Read today's passage as many times as you need, take your time
3. Write down (below) what the Lord is saying to you today
4. Live with this Word in your heart through the day

_____

_____

Friday, August 30, 2024

First Reading: First Corinthians 1: 17-25

17 For Christ sent me not to baptize, but to preach the Good News—not in wisdom of words, so that the cross of Christ wouldn't be made void. 18 For the word of the cross is foolishness to those who are dying, but to us who are being saved it is the power of God. 19 For it is written,
"I will destroy the wisdom of the wise.
I will bring the discernment of the discerning to nothing."*
20 Where is the wise? Where is the scribe? Where is the debater of this age? Hasn't God made foolish the wisdom of this world? 21 For seeing that in the wisdom of God, the world through its wisdom didn't know God, it was God's good pleasure through the foolishness of the preaching to save those who believe. 22 For Jews ask for signs, Greeks seek after wisdom, 23 but we preach Christ crucified, a stumbling block to Jews and foolishness to Greeks, 24 but to those who are called, both Jews and Greeks, Christ is the power of God and the wisdom of God; 25 because the foolishness of God is wiser than men, and the weakness of God is stronger than men.

Responsorial Psalm: Psalms 33: 1-2, 4-5, 10-11

1 Rejoice in Yahweh, you righteous!
Praise is fitting for the upright.
2 Give thanks to Yahweh with the lyre.
Sing praises to him with the harp of ten strings.
4 For Yahweh's word is right.
All his work is done in faithfulness.
5 He loves righteousness and justice.
The earth is full of the loving kindness of Yahweh.
10 Yahweh brings the counsel of the nations to nothing.
He makes the thoughts of the peoples to be of no effect.
11 The counsel of Yahweh stands fast forever,
the thoughts of his heart to all generations.

Gospel: Matthew 25: 1-13

1 "Then the Kingdom of Heaven will be like ten virgins who took their lamps and went out to meet the bridegroom. 2 Five of them were foolish, and five were wise. 3 Those who were foolish, when they took their lamps, took no oil with them, 4 but the wise took oil in their vessels with their lamps. 5 Now while the bridegroom delayed, they all slumbered and slept. 6 But at midnight there was a cry, 'Behold! The bridegroom is coming! Come out to meet him!' 7 Then all those virgins arose, and trimmed their lamps.† 8 The foolish said to the wise,

'Give us some of your oil, for our lamps are going out.' 9 But the wise answered, saying, 'What if there isn't enough for us and you? You go rather to those who sell, and buy for yourselves.' 10 While they went away to buy, the bridegroom came, and those who were ready went in with him to the wedding feast, and the door was shut. 11 Afterward the other virgins also came, saying, 'Lord, Lord, open to us.' 12 But he answered, 'Most certainly I tell you, I don't know you.' 13 Watch therefore, for you don't know the day nor the hour in which the Son of Man is coming.

1. Invite the Holy Spirit into this reading, asking the Author of Scripture to speak to you through His Word
2. Read today's passage as many times as you need, take your time
3. Write down (below) what the Lord is saying to you today
4. Live with this Word in your heart through the day

_____

_____

Saturday, August 31, 2024

First Reading: First Corinthians 1: 26-31

26 For you see your calling, brothers, that not many are wise according to the flesh, not many mighty, and not many noble; 27 but God chose the foolish things of the world that he might put to shame those who are wise. God chose the weak things of the world that he might put to shame the things that are strong. 28 God chose the lowly things of the world, and the things that are despised, and the things that don't exist, that he might bring to nothing the things that exist, 29 that no flesh should boast before God. 30 Because of him, you are in Christ Jesus, who was made to us wisdom from God, and righteousness and sanctification, and redemption, 31 that, as it is written, "He who boasts, let him boast in the Lord."

Responsorial Psalm: Psalms 33: 12-13, 18-21

12 Blessed is the nation whose God is Yahweh,
the people whom he has chosen for his own inheritance.
13 Yahweh looks from heaven.
He sees all the sons of men.
18 Behold, Yahweh's eye is on those who fear him,
on those who hope in his loving kindness,
19 to deliver their soul from death,
to keep them alive in famine.

20 Our soul has waited for Yahweh.
He is our help and our shield.
21 For our heart rejoices in him,
because we have trusted in his holy name.

Gospel: Matthew 25: 14-30

14 "For it is like a man going into another country, who called his own servants and entrusted his goods to them. 15 To one he gave five talents,‡ to another two, to another one, to each according to his own ability. Then he went on his journey. 16 Immediately he who received the five talents went and traded with them, and made another five talents. 17 In the same way, he also who got the two gained another two. 18 But he who received the one talent went away and dug in the earth and hid his lord's money.

19 "Now after a long time the lord of those servants came, and settled accounts with them. 20 He who received the five talents came and brought another five talents, saying, 'Lord, you delivered to me five talents. Behold, I have gained another five talents in addition to them.'

21 "His lord said to him, 'Well done, good and faithful servant. You have been faithful over a few things, I will set you over many things. Enter into the joy of your lord.'

22 "He also who got the two talents came and said, 'Lord, you delivered to me two talents. Behold, I have gained another two talents in addition to them.'

23 "His lord said to him, 'Well done, good and faithful servant. You have been faithful over a few things. I will set you over many things. Enter into the joy of your lord.'

24 "He also who had received the one talent came and said, 'Lord, I knew you that you are a hard man, reaping where you didn't sow, and gathering where you didn't scatter. 25 I was afraid, and went away and hid your talent in the earth. Behold, you have what is yours.'

26 "But his lord answered him, 'You wicked and slothful servant. You knew that I reap where I didn't sow, and gather where I didn't scatter. 27 You ought therefore to have deposited my money with the bankers, and at my coming I should have received back my own with interest. 28 Take away therefore the talent from him and give it to him who has the ten talents. 29 For to everyone who has will be given, and he will have abundance, but from him who doesn't have, even that which he has will be taken away. 30 Throw out the unprofitable servant into the outer darkness, where there will be weeping and gnashing of teeth.'

1. Invite the Holy Spirit into this reading, asking the Author of Scripture to speak to you through His Word
2. Read today's passage as many times as you need, take your time
3. Write down (below) what the Lord is saying to you today
4. Live with this Word in your heart through the day

_____

_____

Sunday, September 1, 2024
TWENTY-SECOND SUNDAY IN ORDINARY TIME

First Reading: Deuteronomy 4: 1-2, 6-8

1 Now, Israel, listen to the statutes and to the ordinances which I teach you, to do them, that you may live and go in and possess the land which Yahweh, the God of your fathers, gives you. 2 You shall not add to the word which I command you, neither shall you take away from it, that you may keep the commandments of Yahweh your God which I command you. 6 Keep therefore and do them; for this is your wisdom and your understanding in the sight of the peoples who shall hear all these statutes and say, "Surely this great nation is a wise and understanding people." 7 For what great nation is there that has a god so near to them as Yahweh our God is whenever we call on him? 8 What great nation is there that has statutes and ordinances so righteous as all this law which I set before you today?

Responsorial Psalm: Psalms 15: 2-5

2 He who walks blamelessly and does what is right,
and speaks truth in his heart;
3 he who doesn't slander with his tongue,
nor does evil to his friend,
nor casts slurs against his fellow man;
4 in whose eyes a vile man is despised,
but who honors those who fear Yahweh;
he who keeps an oath even when it hurts, and doesn't change;
5 he who doesn't lend out his money for usury,
nor take a bribe against the innocent.

Second Reading: James 1: 17-18, 21b-22, 27

17 Every good gift and every perfect gift is from above, coming down from the Father of lights, with whom can be no variation nor turning shadow. 18 Of his own will he gave birth to us by the word of truth, that we should be a kind of first fruits of his creatures.
21 Therefore, putting away all filthiness and overflowing of wickedness, receive with humility the implanted word, which is able to save your souls.§
22 But be doers of the word, and not only hearers, deluding your own selves.
27 Pure religion and undefiled before our God and Father is this: to visit the fatherless and widows in their affliction, and to keep oneself unstained by the world.

Gospel: Mark 7: 1-8, 14-15, 21-23

1 Then the Pharisees and some of the scribes gathered together to him, having come from Jerusalem. 2 Now when they saw some of his disciples eating bread with defiled, that is

unwashed, hands, they found fault. 3 (For the Pharisees and all the Jews don't eat unless they wash their hands and forearms, holding to the tradition of the elders. 4 They don't eat when they come from the marketplace unless they bathe themselves, and there are many other things which they have received to hold to: washings of cups, pitchers, bronze vessels, and couches.) 5 The Pharisees and the scribes asked him, "Why don't your disciples walk according to the tradition of the elders, but eat their bread with unwashed hands?"

6 He answered them, "Well did Isaiah prophesy of you hypocrites, as it is written,

'This people honors me with their lips,

but their heart is far from me.

7 They worship me in vain,

teaching as doctrines the commandments of men.'*

8 "For you set aside the commandment of God, and hold tightly to the tradition of men—the washing of pitchers and cups, and you do many other such things."

14 He called all the multitude to himself and said to them, "Hear me, all of you, and understand. 15 There is nothing from outside of the man that going into him can defile him; but the things which proceed out of the man are those that defile the man.

21 For from within, out of the hearts of men, proceed evil thoughts, adulteries, sexual sins, murders, thefts, 22 covetings, wickedness, deceit, lustful desires, an evil eye, blasphemy, pride, and foolishness. 23 All these evil things come from within and defile the man."

1. Invite the Holy Spirit into this reading, asking the Author of Scripture to speak to you through His Word
2. Read today's passage as many times as you need, take your time
3. Write down (below) what the Lord is saying to you today
4. Live with this Word in your heart through the day

_____

_____

Monday, September 2, 2024

First Reading: First Corinthians 2: 1-5

1 When I came to you, brothers, I didn't come with excellence of speech or of wisdom, proclaiming to you the testimony of God. 2 For I determined not to know anything among you except Jesus Christ and him crucified. 3 I was with you in weakness, in fear, and in much trembling. 4 My speech and my preaching were not in persuasive words of human wisdom, but in demonstration of the Spirit and of power, 5 that your faith wouldn't stand in the wisdom of men, but in the power of God.

Responsorial Psalm: Psalms 119: 97-102

97 How I love your law!
It is my meditation all day.
98 Your commandments make me wiser than my enemies,
for your commandments are always with me.
99 I have more understanding than all my teachers,
for your testimonies are my meditation.
100 I understand more than the aged,
because I have kept your precepts.
101 I have kept my feet from every evil way,
that I might observe your word.
102 I have not turned away from your ordinances,
for you have taught me.

Gospel: Luke 4: 16-30

16 He came to Nazareth, where he had been brought up. He entered, as was his custom, into the synagogue on the Sabbath day, and stood up to read. 17 The book of the prophet Isaiah was handed to him. He opened the book, and found the place where it was written,
18 "The Spirit of the Lord is on me,
because he has anointed me to preach good news to the poor.
He has sent me to heal the broken hearted,†
to proclaim release to the captives,
recovering of sight to the blind,
to deliver those who are crushed,
19 and to proclaim the acceptable year of the Lord."*
20 He closed the book, gave it back to the attendant, and sat down. The eyes of all in the synagogue were fastened on him. 21 He began to tell them, "Today, this Scripture has been fulfilled in your hearing."
22 All testified about him and wondered at the gracious words which proceeded out of his mouth; and they said, "Isn't this Joseph's son?"
23 He said to them, "Doubtless you will tell me this proverb, 'Physician, heal yourself! Whatever we have heard done at Capernaum, do also here in your hometown.' " 24 He said, "Most certainly I tell you, no prophet is acceptable in his hometown. 25 But truly I tell you, there were many widows in Israel in the days of Elijah, when the sky was shut up three years and six months, when a great famine came over all the land. 26 Elijah was sent to none of them, except to Zarephath, in the land of Sidon, to a woman who was a widow. 27 There were many lepers in Israel in the time of Elisha the prophet, yet not one of them was cleansed, except Naaman, the Syrian."
28 They were all filled with wrath in the synagogue as they heard these things. 29 They rose up, threw him out of the city, and led him to the brow of the hill that their city was built on,

that they might throw him off the cliff. 30 But he, passing through the middle of them, went his way.

Tuesday, September 3, 2024
Saint Gregory the Great, Pope and Doctor of the Church

First Reading: First Corinthians 2: 10b-16

10 But to us, God revealed them through the Spirit. For the Spirit searches all things, yes, the deep things of God. 11 For who among men knows the things of a man except the spirit of the man which is in him? Even so, no one knows the things of God except God's Spirit. 12 But we received not the spirit of the world, but the Spirit which is from God, that we might know the things that were freely given to us by God. 13 We also speak these things, not in words which man's wisdom teaches but which the Holy Spirit teaches, comparing spiritual things with spiritual things. 14 Now the natural man doesn't receive the things of God's Spirit, for they are foolishness to him; and he can't know them, because they are spiritually discerned. 15 But he who is spiritual discerns all things, and he himself is to be judged by no one. 16 "For who has known the mind of the Lord that he should instruct him?" * But we have Christ's mind.

Responsorial Psalm: Psalms 145: 8-14

8 Yahweh is gracious, merciful,
slow to anger, and of great loving kindness.
9 Yahweh is good to all.
His tender mercies are over all his works.
10 All your works will give thanks to you, Yahweh.
Your saints will extol you.
11 They will speak of the glory of your kingdom,
and talk about your power,
12 to make known to the sons of men his mighty acts,
the glory of the majesty of his kingdom.
13 Your kingdom is an everlasting kingdom.

Your dominion endures throughout all generations.
Yahweh is faithful in all his words,
and loving in all his deeds.‡
14 Yahweh upholds all who fall,
and raises up all those who are bowed down.

Gospel: Luke 4: 31-37

31 He came down to Capernaum, a city of Galilee. He was teaching them on the Sabbath day, 32 and they were astonished at his teaching, for his word was with authority. 33 In the synagogue there was a man who had a spirit of an unclean demon; and he cried out with a loud voice, 34 saying, "Ah! what have we to do with you, Jesus of Nazareth? Have you come to destroy us? I know who you are: the Holy One of God!"
35 Jesus rebuked him, saying, "Be silent and come out of him!" When the demon had thrown him down in the middle of them, he came out of him, having done him no harm.
36 Amazement came on all and they spoke together, one with another, saying, "What is this word? For with authority and power he commands the unclean spirits, and they come out!"
37 News about him went out into every place of the surrounding region.

1. Invite the Holy Spirit into this reading, asking the Author of Scripture to speak to you through His Word
2. Read today's passage as many times as you need, take your time
3. Write down (below) what the Lord is saying to you today
4. Live with this Word in your heart through the day

_____

_____

Wednesday, September 4, 2024

First Reading: First Corinthians 3: 1-9

1 Brothers, I couldn't speak to you as to spiritual, but as to fleshly, as to babies in Christ. 2 I fed you with milk, not with solid food, for you weren't yet ready. Indeed, you aren't ready even now, 3 for you are still fleshly. For insofar as there is jealousy, strife, and factions among you, aren't you fleshly, and don't you walk in the ways of men? 4 For when one says, "I follow Paul," and another, "I follow Apollos," aren't you fleshly?
5 Who then is Apollos, and who is Paul, but servants through whom you believed, and each as the Lord gave to him? 6 I planted. Apollos watered. But God gave the increase. 7 So then neither he who plants is anything, nor he who waters, but God who gives the increase. 8 Now

he who plants and he who waters are the same, but each will receive his own reward according to his own labor. 9 For we are God's fellow workers. You are God's farming, God's building.

Responsorial Psalm: Psalms 33: 12-15, 20-21

12 Blessed is the nation whose God is Yahweh,
the people whom he has chosen for his own inheritance.
13 Yahweh looks from heaven.
He sees all the sons of men.
14 From the place of his habitation he looks out on all the inhabitants of the earth,
15 he who fashions all of their hearts;
and he considers all of their works.
20 Our soul has waited for Yahweh.
He is our help and our shield.
21 For our heart rejoices in him,
because we have trusted in his holy name.

Gospel: Luke 4: 38-44

38 He rose up from the synagogue and entered into Simon's house. Simon's mother-in-law was afflicted with a great fever, and they begged him to help her. 39 He stood over her and rebuked the fever, and it left her. Immediately she rose up and served them. 40 When the sun was setting, all those who had any sick with various diseases brought them to him; and he laid his hands on every one of them, and healed them. 41 Demons also came out of many, crying out and saying, "You are the Christ, the Son of God!" Rebuking them, he didn't allow them to speak, because they knew that he was the Christ.
42 When it was day, he departed and went into an uninhabited place and the multitudes looked for him, and came to him, and held on to him, so that he wouldn't go away from them. 43 But he said to them, "I must preach the good news of God's Kingdom to the other cities also. For this reason I have been sent." 44 He was preaching in the synagogues of Galilee.

1. Invite the Holy Spirit into this reading, asking the Author of Scripture to speak to you through His Word
2. Read today's passage as many times as you need, take your time
3. Write down (below) what the Lord is saying to you today
4. Live with this Word in your heart through the day

_____

_____

Thursday, September 5, 2024

First Reading: First Corinthians 3: 18-23

18 Let no one deceive himself. If anyone thinks that he is wise among you in this world, let him become a fool that he may become wise. 19 For the wisdom of this world is foolishness with God. For it is written, "He has taken the wise in their craftiness."* 20 And again, "The Lord knows the reasoning of the wise, that it is worthless."* 21 Therefore let no one boast in men. For all things are yours, 22 whether Paul, or Apollos, or Cephas, or the world, or life, or death, or things present, or things to come. All are yours, 23 and you are Christ's, and Christ is God's.

Responsorial Psalm: Psalms 24: 1bc-6

1 The earth is Yahweh's, with its fullness;
the world, and those who dwell in it.
2 For he has founded it on the seas,
and established it on the floods.
3 Who may ascend to Yahweh's hill?
Who may stand in his holy place?
4 He who has clean hands and a pure heart;
who has not lifted up his soul to falsehood,
and has not sworn deceitfully.
5 He shall receive a blessing from Yahweh,
righteousness from the God of his salvation.
6 This is the generation of those who seek Him,
who seek your face—even Jacob.

Gospel: Luke 5: 1-11

1 Now while the multitude pressed on him and heard the word of God, he was standing by the lake of Gennesaret. 2 He saw two boats standing by the lake, but the fishermen had gone out of them and were washing their nets. 3 He entered into one of the boats, which was Simon's, and asked him to put out a little from the land. He sat down and taught the multitudes from the boat.
4 When he had finished speaking, he said to Simon, "Put out into the deep and let down your nets for a catch."
5 Simon answered him, "Master, we worked all night and caught nothing; but at your word I will let down the net." 6 When they had done this, they caught a great multitude of fish, and their net was breaking. 7 They beckoned to their partners in the other boat, that they should come and help them. They came and filled both boats, so that they began to sink. 8 But Simon Peter, when he saw it, fell down at Jesus' knees, saying, "Depart from me, for I am a sinful

man, Lord." 9 For he was amazed, and all who were with him, at the catch of fish which they had caught; 10 and so also were James and John, sons of Zebedee, who were partners with Simon.

Jesus said to Simon, "Don't be afraid. From now on you will be catching people alive."

11 When they had brought their boats to land, they left everything, and followed him.

1. Invite the Holy Spirit into this reading, asking the Author of Scripture to speak to you through His Word
2. Read today's passage as many times as you need, take your time
3. Write down (below) what the Lord is saying to you today
4. Live with this Word in your heart through the day

Friday, September 6, 2024

First Reading: First Corinthians 4: 1-5

1 So let a man think of us as Christ's servants and stewards of God's mysteries. 2 Here, moreover, it is required of stewards that they be found faithful. 3 But with me it is a very small thing that I should be judged by you, or by a human court. Yes, I don't even judge my own self. 4 For I know nothing against myself. Yet I am not justified by this, but he who judges me is the Lord. 5 Therefore judge nothing before the time, until the Lord comes, who will both bring to light the hidden things of darkness and reveal the counsels of the hearts. Then each man will get his praise from God.

Responsorial Psalm: Psalms 37: 3-6, 27-28, 39-40

3 Trust in Yahweh, and do good.
Dwell in the land, and enjoy safe pasture.
4 Also delight yourself in Yahweh,
and he will give you the desires of your heart.
5 Commit your way to Yahweh.
Trust also in him, and he will do this:
6 he will make your righteousness shine out like light,
and your justice as the noon day sun.
27 Depart from evil, and do good.
Live securely forever.
28 For Yahweh loves justice,

and doesn't forsake his saints.
They are preserved forever,
but the children of the wicked shall be cut off.
39 But the salvation of the righteous is from Yahweh.
He is their stronghold in the time of trouble.
40 Yahweh helps them and rescues them.
He rescues them from the wicked and saves them,
because they have taken refuge in him.

Gospel: Luke 5: 33-39

33 They said to him, "Why do John's disciples often fast and pray, likewise also the disciples of the Pharisees, but yours eat and drink?"
34 He said to them, "Can you make the friends of the bridegroom fast while the bridegroom is with them? 35 But the days will come when the bridegroom will be taken away from them. Then they will fast in those days."
36 He also told a parable to them. "No one puts a piece from a new garment on an old garment, or else he will tear the new, and also the piece from the new will not match the old. 37 No one puts new wine into old wine skins, or else the new wine will burst the skins, and it will be spilled and the skins will be destroyed. 38 But new wine must be put into fresh wine skins, and both are preserved. 39 No man having drunk old wine immediately desires new, for he says, 'The old is better.' "

1. Invite the Holy Spirit into this reading, asking the Author of Scripture to speak to you through His Word
2. Read today's passage as many times as you need, take your time
3. Write down (below) what the Lord is saying to you today
4. Live with this Word in your heart through the day

_____

_____

Saturday, September 7, 2024

First Reading: First Corinthians 4: 6b-15

6 Now these things, brothers, I have in a figure transferred to myself and Apollos for your sakes, that in us you might learn not to think beyond the things which are written, that none of you be puffed up against one another. 7 For who makes you different? And what do you have that you didn't receive? But if you did receive it, why do you boast as if you had not received it?

8 You are already filled. You have already become rich. You have come to reign without us. Yes, and I wish that you did reign, that we also might reign with you! 9 For I think that God has displayed us, the apostles, last of all, like men sentenced to death. For we are made a spectacle to the world, both to angels and men. 10 We are fools for Christ's sake, but you are wise in Christ. We are weak, but you are strong. You have honor, but we have dishonor. 11 Even to this present hour we hunger, thirst, are naked, are beaten, and have no certain dwelling place. 12 We toil, working with our own hands. When people curse us, we bless. Being persecuted, we endure. 13 Being defamed, we entreat. We are made as the filth of the world, the dirt wiped off by all, even until now.

14 I don't write these things to shame you, but to admonish you as my beloved children. 15 For though you have ten thousand tutors in Christ, you don't have many fathers. For in Christ Jesus, I became your father through the Good News.

Responsorial Psalm: Psalms 145: 17-21

17 Yahweh is righteous in all his ways,
and gracious in all his works.
18 Yahweh is near to all those who call on him,
to all who call on him in truth.
19 He will fulfill the desire of those who fear him.
He also will hear their cry, and will save them.
20 Yahweh preserves all those who love him,
but he will destroy all the wicked.
21 My mouth will speak the praise of Yahweh.
Let all flesh bless his holy name forever and ever.

Gospel: Luke 6: 1-5

1 Now on the second Sabbath after the first, he was going through the grain fields. His disciples plucked the heads of grain and ate, rubbing them in their hands. 2 But some of the Pharisees said to them, "Why do you do that which is not lawful to do on the Sabbath day?"
3 Jesus, answering them, said, "Haven't you read what David did when he was hungry, he and those who were with him, 4 how he entered into God's house, and took and ate the show bread, and gave also to those who were with him, which is not lawful to eat except for the priests alone?" 5 He said to them, "The Son of Man is lord of the Sabbath."

1. Invite the Holy Spirit into this reading, asking the Author of Scripture to speak to you through His Word
2. Read today's passage as many times as you need, take your time
3. Write down (below) what the Lord is saying to you today
4. Live with this Word in your heart through the day

Sunday, September 8, 2024
TWENTY-THIRD SUNDAY IN ORDINARY TIME

First Reading: Isaiah 35: 4-7a

4 Tell those who have a fearful heart, "Be strong!
Don't be afraid!
Behold, your God will come with vengeance, God's retribution.
He will come and save you.
5 Then the eyes of the blind will be opened,
and the ears of the deaf will be unstopped.
6 Then the lame man will leap like a deer,
and the tongue of the mute will sing;
for waters will break out in the wilderness,
and streams in the desert.
7 The burning sand will become a pool,
and the thirsty ground springs of water.

Responsorial Psalm: Psalms 146: 7-10

7 who executes justice for the oppressed;
who gives food to the hungry.
Yahweh frees the prisoners.
8 Yahweh opens the eyes of the blind.
Yahweh raises up those who are bowed down.
Yahweh loves the righteous.
9 Yahweh preserves the foreigners.
He upholds the fatherless and widow,
but he turns the way of the wicked upside down.
10 Yahweh will reign forever;
your God, O Zion, to all generations.
Praise Yah!

Second Reading: James 2: 1-5

1 My brothers, don't hold the faith of our glorious Lord Jesus Christ with partiality. 2 For if a man with a gold ring, in fine clothing, comes into your synagogue,† and a poor man in filthy clothing also comes in, 3 and you pay special attention to him who wears the fine clothing and say, "Sit here in a good place;" and you tell the poor man, "Stand there," or "Sit by my footstool" 4 haven't you shown partiality among yourselves, and become judges with evil thoughts? 5 Listen, my beloved brothers. Didn't God choose those who are poor in this world to be rich in faith and heirs of the Kingdom which he promised to those who love him?

Gospel: Mark 7: 31-37

31 Again he departed from the borders of Tyre and Sidon, and came to the sea of Galilee through the middle of the region of Decapolis. 32 They brought to him one who was deaf and had an impediment in his speech. They begged him to lay his hand on him. 33 He took him aside from the multitude privately and put his fingers into his ears; and he spat and touched his tongue. 34 Looking up to heaven, he sighed, and said to him, "Ephphatha!" that is, "Be opened!" 35 Immediately his ears were opened, and the impediment of his tongue was released, and he spoke clearly. 36 He commanded them that they should tell no one, but the more he commanded them, so much the more widely they proclaimed it. 37 They were astonished beyond measure, saying, "He has done all things well. He makes even the deaf hear and the mute speak!"

1. Invite the Holy Spirit into this reading, asking the Author of Scripture to speak to you through His Word
2. Read today's passage as many times as you need, take your time
3. Write down (below) what the Lord is saying to you today
4. Live with this Word in your heart through the day

_____

_____

Monday, September 9, 2024
Saint Peter Claver, Priest

First Reading: First Corinthians 5: 1-8

1 It is actually reported that there is sexual immorality among you, and such sexual immorality as is not even named among the Gentiles, that one has his father's wife. 2 You are arrogant, and didn't mourn instead, that he who had done this deed might be removed from among you. 3 For I most certainly, as being absent in body but present in spirit, have already, as though I were present, judged him who has done this thing. 4 In the name of our Lord Jesus Christ, when you are gathered together with my spirit with the power of our Lord Jesus Christ, 5 you are to deliver such a one to Satan for the destruction of the flesh, that the spirit may be saved in the day of the Lord Jesus.
6 Your boasting is not good. Don't you know that a little yeast leavens the whole lump? 7 Purge out the old yeast, that you may be a new lump, even as you are unleavened. For indeed Christ, our Passover, has been sacrificed in our place. 8 Therefore let's keep the feast, not with old

yeast, neither with the yeast of malice and wickedness, but with the unleavened bread of sincerity and truth.

Responsorial Psalm: Psalms 5: 5-7, 12

5 The arrogant will not stand in your sight.
You hate all workers of iniquity.
6 You will destroy those who speak lies.
Yahweh abhors the bloodthirsty and deceitful man.
7 But as for me, in the abundance of your loving kindness I will come into your house.
I will bow toward your holy temple in reverence of you.
12 For you will bless the righteous.
Yahweh, you will surround him with favor as with a shield.

Gospel: Luke 6: 6-11

6 It also happened on another Sabbath that he entered into the synagogue and taught. There was a man there, and his right hand was withered. 7 The scribes and the Pharisees watched him, to see whether he would heal on the Sabbath, that they might find an accusation against him. 8 But he knew their thoughts; and he said to the man who had the withered hand, "Rise up and stand in the middle." He arose and stood. 9 Then Jesus said to them, "I will ask you something: Is it lawful on the Sabbath to do good, or to do harm? To save a life, or to kill?" 10 He looked around at them all, and said to the man, "Stretch out your hand." He did, and his hand was restored as sound as the other. 11 But they were filled with rage, and talked with one another about what they might do to Jesus.

1. Invite the Holy Spirit into this reading, asking the Author of Scripture to speak to you through His Word
2. Read today's passage as many times as you need, take your time
3. Write down (below) what the Lord is saying to you today
4. Live with this Word in your heart through the day

_____

_____

Tuesday, September 10, 2024

First Reading: First Corinthians 6: 1-11

1 Dare any of you, having a matter against his neighbor, go to law before the unrighteous, and not before the saints? 2 Don't you know that the saints will judge the world? And if the world

is judged by you, are you unworthy to judge the smallest matters? 3 Don't you know that we will judge angels? How much more, things that pertain to this life? 4 If then you have to judge things pertaining to this life, do you set them to judge who are of no account in the assembly? 5 I say this to move you to shame. Isn't there even one wise man among you who would be able to decide between his brothers? 6 But brother goes to law with brother, and that before unbelievers! 7 Therefore it is already altogether a defect in you that you have lawsuits one with another. Why not rather be wronged? Why not rather be defrauded? 8 No, but you yourselves do wrong and defraud, and that against your brothers.

9 Or don't you know that the unrighteous will not inherit God's Kingdom? Don't be deceived. Neither the sexually immoral, nor idolaters, nor adulterers, nor male prostitutes, nor homosexuals, 10 nor thieves, nor covetous, nor drunkards, nor slanderers, nor extortionists, will inherit God's Kingdom. 11 Some of you were such, but you were washed. You were sanctified. You were justified in the name of the Lord Jesus, and in the Spirit of our God.

Responsorial Psalm: Psalms 149: 1b-6a and 9b

1 Praise Yahweh!
Sing to Yahweh a new song,
his praise in the assembly of the saints.
2 Let Israel rejoice in him who made them.
Let the children of Zion be joyful in their King.
3 Let them praise his name in the dance!
Let them sing praises to him with tambourine and harp!
4 For Yahweh takes pleasure in his people.
He crowns the humble with salvation.
5 Let the saints rejoice in honor.
Let them sing for joy on their beds.
6 May the high praises of God be in their mouths,
and a two-edged sword in their hand,
9b All his saints have this honor.
Praise Yah!

Gospel: Luke 6: 12-19

12 In these days, he went out to the mountain to pray, and he continued all night in prayer to God. 13 When it was day, he called his disciples, and from them he chose twelve, whom he also named apostles: 14 Simon, whom he also named Peter; Andrew, his brother; James; John; Philip; Bartholomew; 15 Matthew; Thomas; James the son of Alphaeus; Simon who was called the Zealot; 16 Judas the son of James; and Judas Iscariot, who also became a traitor.
17 He came down with them and stood on a level place, with a crowd of his disciples and a great number of the people from all Judea and Jerusalem and the sea coast of Tyre and Sidon, who came to hear him and to be healed of their diseases, 18 as well as those who were troubled

by unclean spirits; and they were being healed. 19 All the multitude sought to touch him, for power came out of him and healed them all.

Wednesday, September 11, 2024

First Reading: First Corinthians 7: 25-31

25 Now concerning virgins, I have no commandment from the Lord, but I give my judgment as one who has obtained mercy from the Lord to be trustworthy. 26 Therefore I think that because of the distress that is on us, it's good for a man to remain as he is. 27 Are you bound to a wife? Don't seek to be freed. Are you free from a wife? Don't seek a wife. 28 But if you marry, you have not sinned. If a virgin marries, she has not sinned. Yet such will have oppression in the flesh, and I want to spare you. 29 But I say this, brothers: the time is short. From now on, both those who have wives may be as though they had none; 30 and those who weep, as though they didn't weep; and those who rejoice, as though they didn't rejoice; and those who buy, as though they didn't possess; 31 and those who use the world, as not using it to the fullest. For the mode of this world passes away.

Responsorial Psalm: Psalms 45: 11-12, 14-17

11 So the king will desire your beauty,
honor him, for he is your lord.
12 The daughter of Tyre comes with a gift.
The rich among the people entreat your favor.
14 She shall be led to the king in embroidered work.
The virgins, her companions who follow her, shall be brought to you.
15 With gladness and rejoicing they shall be led.
They shall enter into the king's palace.
16 Your sons will take the place of your fathers.
You shall make them princes in all the earth.
17 I will make your name to be remembered in all generations.

Therefore the peoples shall give you thanks forever and ever.

Gospel: Luke 6: 20-26

20 He lifted up his eyes to his disciples, and said:
"Blessed are you who are poor,
for God's Kingdom is yours.
21 Blessed are you who hunger now,
for you will be filled.
Blessed are you who weep now,
for you will laugh.
22 Blessed are you when men hate you, and when they exclude and mock you, and throw out your name as evil, for the Son of Man's sake.
23 Rejoice in that day and leap for joy, for behold, your reward is great in heaven, for their fathers did the same thing to the prophets.
24 "But woe to you who are rich!
For you have received your consolation.
25 Woe to you, you who are full now,
for you will be hungry.
Woe to you who laugh now,
for you will mourn and weep.
26 Woe,† when‡ men speak well of you,
for their fathers did the same thing to the false prophets.

1. Invite the Holy Spirit into this reading, asking the Author of Scripture to speak to you through His Word
2. Read today's passage as many times as you need, take your time
3. Write down (below) what the Lord is saying to you today
4. Live with this Word in your heart through the day

_____

_____

Thursday, September 12, 2024
The Most Holy Name of Mary

First Reading: First Corinthians 8: 1b-7, 11-13

1 Now concerning things sacrificed to idols: We know that we all have knowledge. Knowledge puffs up, but love builds up. 2 But if anyone thinks that he knows anything, he doesn't yet know as he ought to know. 3 But anyone who loves God is known by him.

4 Therefore concerning the eating of things sacrificed to idols, we know that no idol is anything in the world, and that there is no other God but one. 5 For though there are things that are called "gods", whether in the heavens or on earth—as there are many "gods" and many "lords"— 6 yet to us there is one God, the Father, of whom are all things, and we for him; and one Lord, Jesus Christ, through whom are all things, and we live through him.

7 However, that knowledge isn't in all men. But some, with consciousness of an idol until now, eat as of a thing sacrificed to an idol, and their conscience, being weak, is defiled.

11 And through your knowledge, he who is weak perishes, the brother for whose sake Christ died. 12 Thus, sinning against the brothers, and wounding their conscience when it is weak, you sin against Christ. 13 Therefore, if food causes my brother to stumble, I will eat no meat forever more, that I don't cause my brother to stumble.

Responsorial Psalm: Psalms 139: 1b-3, 13-14ab, 23-24

1 Yahweh, you have searched me,
and you know me.
2 You know my sitting down and my rising up.
You perceive my thoughts from afar.
3 You search out my path and my lying down,
and are acquainted with all my ways.
13 For you formed my inmost being.
You knit me together in my mother's womb.
14 I will give thanks to you,
for I am fearfully and wonderfully made.
Your works are wonderful.
My soul knows that very well.
23 Search me, God, and know my heart.
Try me, and know my thoughts.
24 See if there is any wicked way in me,
and lead me in the everlasting way.

Gospel: Luke 6: 27-38

27 "But I tell you who hear: love your enemies, do good to those who hate you, 28 bless those who curse you, and pray for those who mistreat you. 29 To him who strikes you on the cheek, offer also the other; and from him who takes away your cloak, don't withhold your coat also. 30 Give to everyone who asks you, and don't ask him who takes away your goods to give them back again.
31 "As you would like people to do to you, do exactly so to them.

32 "If you love those who love you, what credit is that to you? For even sinners love those who love them. 33 If you do good to those who do good to you, what credit is that to you? For even sinners do the same. 34 If you lend to those from whom you hope to receive, what credit is that to you? Even sinners lend to sinners, to receive back as much. 35 But love your enemies, and do good, and lend, expecting nothing back; and your reward will be great, and you will be children of the Most High; for he is kind toward the unthankful and evil.

36 "Therefore be merciful,

even as your Father is also merciful.

37 Don't judge,

and you won't be judged.

Don't condemn,

and you won't be condemned.

Set free,

and you will be set free.

38 "Give, and it will be given to you: good measure, pressed down, shaken together, and running over, will be given to you.§ For with the same measure you measure it will be measured back to you."

1. Invite the Holy Spirit into this reading, asking the Author of Scripture to speak to you through His Word
2. Read today's passage as many times as you need, take your time
3. Write down (below) what the Lord is saying to you today
4. Live with this Word in your heart through the day

_____

_____

Friday, September 13, 2024
Saint John Chrysostom, Bishop and Doctor of the Church

First Reading: First Corinthians 9: 16-19, 22b-27

16 For if I preach the Good News, I have nothing to boast about, for necessity is laid on me; but woe is to me if I don't preach the Good News. 17 For if I do this of my own will, I have a reward. But if not of my own will, I have a stewardship entrusted to me. 18 What then is my reward? That when I preach the Good News, I may present the Good News of Christ without charge, so as not to abuse my authority in the Good News.

19 For though I was free from all, I brought myself under bondage to all, that I might gain the more.

22 To the weak I became as weak, that I might gain the weak. I have become all things to all men, that I may by all means save some. 23 Now I do this for the sake of the Good News, that I may be a joint partaker of it. 24 Don't you know that those who run in a race all run, but one receives the prize? Run like that, so that you may win. 25 Every man who strives in the games exercises self-control in all things. Now they do it to receive a corruptible crown, but we an incorruptible. 26 I therefore run like that, not aimlessly. I fight like that, not beating the air, 27 but I beat my body and bring it into submission, lest by any means, after I have preached to others, I myself should be disqualified.

Responsorial Psalm: Psalms 84: 3-6, 12

3 Yes, the sparrow has found a home,
and the swallow a nest for herself, where she may have her young,
near your altars, Yahweh of Armies, my King, and my God.
4 Blessed are those who dwell in your house.
They are always praising you.
5 Blessed are those whose strength is in you,
who have set their hearts on a pilgrimage.
6 Passing through the valley of Weeping, they make it a place of springs.
Yes, the autumn rain covers it with blessings.
12 Yahweh of Armies,
blessed is the man who trusts in you.

Gospel: Luke 6: 39-42

39 He spoke a parable to them. "Can the blind guide the blind? Won't they both fall into a pit? 40 A disciple is not above his teacher, but everyone when he is fully trained will be like his teacher. 41 Why do you see the speck of chaff that is in your brother's eye, but don't consider the beam that is in your own eye? 42 Or how can you tell your brother, 'Brother, let me remove the speck of chaff that is in your eye,' when you yourself don't see the beam that is in your own eye? You hypocrite! First remove the beam from your own eye, and then you can see clearly to remove the speck of chaff that is in your brother's eye.

1. Invite the Holy Spirit into this reading, asking the Author of Scripture to speak to you through His Word
2. Read today's passage as many times as you need, take your time
3. Write down (below) what the Lord is saying to you today
4. Live with this Word in your heart through the day

First Reading: Numbers 21: 4b-9

4 They traveled from Mount Hor by the way to the Red Sea, to go around the land of Edom. The soul of the people was very discouraged because of the journey. 5 The people spoke against God and against Moses: "Why have you brought us up out of Egypt to die in the wilderness? For there is no bread, there is no water, and our soul loathes this disgusting food!"
6 Yahweh sent venomous snakes among the people, and they bit the people. Many people of Israel died. 7 The people came to Moses, and said, "We have sinned, because we have spoken against Yahweh and against you. Pray to Yahweh, that he take away the serpents from us." Moses prayed for the people.
8 Yahweh said to Moses, "Make a venomous snake, and set it on a pole. It shall happen that everyone who is bitten, when he sees it, shall live." 9 Moses made a serpent of bronze, and set it on the pole. If a serpent had bitten any man, when he looked at the serpent of bronze, he lived.

Responsorial Psalm: Psalms 78: 1bc-2, 34-38

1 Hear my teaching, my people.
Turn your ears to the words of my mouth.
2 I will open my mouth in a parable.
I will utter dark sayings of old,
34 When he killed them, then they inquired after him.
They returned and sought God earnestly.
35 They remembered that God was their rock,
the Most High God, their redeemer.
36 But they flattered him with their mouth,
and lied to him with their tongue.
37 For their heart was not right with him,
neither were they faithful in his covenant.
38 But he, being merciful, forgave iniquity, and didn't destroy them.
Yes, many times he turned his anger away,
and didn't stir up all his wrath.

Second Reading: Philippians 2: 6-11

6 who, existing in the form of God, didn't consider equality with God a thing to be grasped, 7 but emptied himself, taking the form of a servant, being made in the likeness of men. 8 And being found in human form, he humbled himself, becoming obedient to the point of death, yes, the death of the cross. 9 Therefore God also highly exalted him, and gave to him the name

which is above every name, 10 that at the name of Jesus every knee should bow, of those in heaven, those on earth, and those under the earth, 11 and that every tongue should confess that Jesus Christ is Lord, to the glory of God the Father.

Gospel: John 3: 13-17

13 No one has ascended into heaven but he who descended out of heaven, the Son of Man, who is in heaven. 14 As Moses lifted up the serpent in the wilderness, even so must the Son of Man be lifted up, 15 that whoever believes in him should not perish, but have eternal life. 16 For God so loved the world, that he gave his only born§ Son, that whoever believes in him should not perish, but have eternal life. 17 For God didn't send his Son into the world to judge the world, but that the world should be saved through him.

1. Invite the Holy Spirit into this reading, asking the Author of Scripture to speak to you through His Word
2. Read today's passage as many times as you need, take your time
3. Write down (below) what the Lord is saying to you today
4. Live with this Word in your heart through the day

_____

_____

Sunday, September 15, 2024
TWENTY-FOURTH SUNDAY IN ORDINARY TIME

First Reading: Isaiah 50: 5-9a

5 The Lord Yahweh has opened my ear.
I was not rebellious.
I have not turned back.
6 I gave my back to those who beat me,
and my cheeks to those who plucked off the hair.
I didn't hide my face from shame and spitting.
7 For the Lord Yahweh will help me.
Therefore I have not been confounded.
Therefore I have set my face like a flint,
and I know that I won't be disappointed.
8 He who justifies me is near.
Who will bring charges against me?
Let us stand up together.

Who is my adversary?
Let him come near to me.
9 Behold, the Lord Yahweh will help me!
Who is he who will condemn me?
Behold, they will all grow old like a garment.
The moths will eat them up.

Responsorial Psalm: Psalms 116: 1-6, 8-9

1 I love Yahweh, because he listens to my voice,
and my cries for mercy.
2 Because he has turned his ear to me,
therefore I will call on him as long as I live.
3 The cords of death surrounded me,
the pains of Sheol† got a hold of me.
I found trouble and sorrow.
4 Then I called on Yahweh's name:
"Yahweh, I beg you, deliver my soul."
5 Yahweh is gracious and righteous.
Yes, our God is merciful.
6 Yahweh preserves the simple.
I was brought low, and he saved me.
8 For you have delivered my soul from death,
my eyes from tears,
and my feet from falling.
9 I will walk before Yahweh in the land of the living.

Second Reading: James 2: 14-18

14 What good is it, my brothers, if a man says he has faith, but has no works? Can faith save him? 15 And if a brother or sister is naked and in lack of daily food, 16 and one of you tells them, "Go in peace. Be warmed and filled;" yet you didn't give them the things the body needs, what good is it? 17 Even so faith, if it has no works, is dead in itself. 18 Yes, a man will say, "You have faith, and I have works." Show me your faith without works, and I will show you my faith by my works.

Gospel: Mark 8: 27-35

27 Jesus went out, with his disciples, into the villages of Caesarea Philippi. On the way he asked his disciples, "Who do men say that I am?"
28 They told him, "John the Baptizer, and others say Elijah, but others, one of the prophets."
29 He said to them, "But who do you say that I am?"
Peter answered, "You are the Christ."

30 He commanded them that they should tell no one about him. 31 He began to teach them that the Son of Man must suffer many things, and be rejected by the elders, the chief priests, and the scribes, and be killed, and after three days rise again. 32 He spoke to them openly. Peter took him and began to rebuke him. 33 But he, turning around and seeing his disciples, rebuked Peter, and said, "Get behind me, Satan! For you have in mind not the things of God, but the things of men."

34 He called the multitude to himself with his disciples and said to them, "Whoever wants to come after me, let him deny himself, and take up his cross, and follow me. 35 For whoever wants to save his life will lose it; and whoever will lose his life for my sake and the sake of the Good News will save it.

1. Invite the Holy Spirit into this reading, asking the Author of Scripture to speak to you through His Word
2. Read today's passage as many times as you need, take your time
3. Write down (below) what the Lord is saying to you today
4. Live with this Word in your heart through the day

_____

_____

Monday, September 16, 2024
Saints Cornelius, Pope, and Cyprian, Bishop, Martyrs

First Reading: First Corinthians 11: 17-26, 33

17 But in giving you this command I don't praise you, because you come together not for the better but for the worse. 18 For first of all, when you come together in the assembly, I hear that divisions exist among you, and I partly believe it. 19 For there also must be factions among you, that those who are approved may be revealed among you. 20 When therefore you assemble yourselves together, it is not the Lord's supper that you eat. 21 For in your eating each one takes his own supper first. One is hungry, and another is drunken. 22 What, don't you have houses to eat and to drink in? Or do you despise God's assembly and put them to shame who don't have enough? What shall I tell you? Shall I praise you? In this I don't praise you.

23 For I received from the Lord that which also I delivered to you, that the Lord Jesus on the night in which he was betrayed took bread. 24 When he had given thanks, he broke it and said, "Take, eat. This is my body, which is broken for you. Do this in memory of me." 25 In the same way he also took the cup after supper, saying, "This cup is the new covenant in my blood. Do this, as often as you drink, in memory of me." 26 For as often as you eat this bread and drink this cup, you proclaim the Lord's death until he comes.

33 Therefore, my brothers, when you come together to eat, wait for one another.

Responsorial Psalm: Psalms 40: 7-10, 17

7 Then I said, "Behold, I have come.
It is written about me in the book in the scroll.
8 I delight to do your will, my God.
Yes, your law is within my heart."
9 I have proclaimed glad news of righteousness in the great assembly.
Behold, I will not seal my lips, Yahweh, you know.
10 I have not hidden your righteousness within my heart.
I have declared your faithfulness and your salvation.
I have not concealed your loving kindness and your truth from the great assembly.
17 But I am poor and needy.
May the Lord think about me.
You are my help and my deliverer.
Don't delay, my God.

Gospel: Luke 7: 1-10

1 After he had finished speaking in the hearing of the people, he entered into Capernaum. 2 A certain centurion's servant, who was dear to him, was sick and at the point of death. 3 When he heard about Jesus, he sent to him elders of the Jews, asking him to come and save his servant. 4 When they came to Jesus, they begged him earnestly, saying, "He is worthy for you to do this for him, 5 for he loves our nation, and he built our synagogue for us." 6 Jesus went with them. When he was now not far from the house, the centurion sent friends to him, saying to him, "Lord, don't trouble yourself, for I am not worthy for you to come under my roof. 7 Therefore I didn't even think myself worthy to come to you; but say the word, and my servant will be healed. 8 For I also am a man placed under authority, having under myself soldiers. I tell this one, 'Go!' and he goes; and to another, 'Come!' and he comes; and to my servant, 'Do this,' and he does it."
9 When Jesus heard these things, he marveled at him, and turned and said to the multitude who followed him, "I tell you, I have not found such great faith, no, not in Israel." 10 Those who were sent, returning to the house, found that the servant who had been sick was well.

1. Invite the Holy Spirit into this reading, asking the Author of Scripture to speak to you through His Word
2. Read today's passage as many times as you need, take your time
3. Write down (below) what the Lord is saying to you today
4. Live with this Word in your heart through the day

Tuesday, September 17, 2024
Saint Robert Bellarmine, Bishop and Doctor of the Church;
Saint Hildegard of Bingen, Virgin and Doctor of the Church

First Reading: First Corinthians 12: 12-14, 27-31a

12 For as the body is one and has many members, and all the members of the body, being many, are one body; so also is Christ. 13 For in one Spirit we were all baptized into one body, whether Jews or Greeks, whether bond or free; and were all given to drink into one Spirit. 14 For the body is not one member, but many.

27 Now you are the body of Christ, and members individually. 28 God has set some in the assembly: first apostles, second prophets, third teachers, then miracle workers, then gifts of healings, helps, governments, and various kinds of languages. 29 Are all apostles? Are all prophets? Are all teachers? Are all miracle workers? 30 Do all have gifts of healings? Do all speak with various languages? Do all interpret? 31 But earnestly desire the best gifts. Moreover, I show a most excellent way to you.

Responsorial Psalm: Psalms 100: 1b-5

1 Shout for joy to Yahweh, all you lands!
2 Serve Yahweh with gladness.
Come before his presence with singing.
3 Know that Yahweh, he is God.
It is he who has made us, and we are his.
We are his people, and the sheep of his pasture.
4 Enter into his gates with thanksgiving,
and into his courts with praise.
Give thanks to him, and bless his name.
5 For Yahweh is good.
His loving kindness endures forever,
his faithfulness to all generations.

Gospel: Luke 7: 11-17

11 Soon afterwards, he went to a city called Nain. Many of his disciples, along with a great multitude, went with him. 12 Now when he came near to the gate of the city, behold, one who was dead was carried out, the only born† son of his mother, and she was a widow. Many people of the city were with her. 13 When the Lord saw her, he had compassion on her and said to her, "Don't cry." 14 He came near and touched the coffin, and the bearers stood still. He said, "Young man, I tell you, arise!" 15 He who was dead sat up and began to speak. Then he gave him to his mother.

16 Fear took hold of all, and they glorified God, saying, "A great prophet has arisen among us!" and, "God has visited his people!" 17 This report went out concerning him in the whole of Judea and in all the surrounding region.

1. Invite the Holy Spirit into this reading, asking the Author of Scripture to speak to you through His Word
2. Read today's passage as many times as you need, take your time
3. Write down (below) what the Lord is saying to you today
4. Live with this Word in your heart through the day

_____

_____

Wednesday, September 18, 2024

First Reading: First Corinthians 12: 31 – 13: 13

31 But earnestly desire the best gifts. Moreover, I show a most excellent way to you.
1 If I speak with the languages of men and of angels, but don't have love, I have become sounding brass or a clanging cymbal. 2 If I have the gift of prophecy, and know all mysteries and all knowledge, and if I have all faith, so as to remove mountains, but don't have love, I am nothing. 3 If I give away all my goods to feed the poor, and if I give my body to be burned, but don't have love, it profits me nothing.
4 Love is patient and is kind. Love doesn't envy. Love doesn't brag, is not proud, 5 doesn't behave itself inappropriately, doesn't seek its own way, is not provoked, takes no account of evil; 6 doesn't rejoice in unrighteousness, but rejoices with the truth; 7 bears all things, believes all things, hopes all things, and endures all things.
8 Love never fails. But where there are prophecies, they will be done away with. Where there are various languages, they will cease. Where there is knowledge, it will be done away with. 9 For we know in part and we prophesy in part; 10 but when that which is complete has come, then that which is partial will be done away with. 11 When I was a child, I spoke as a child, I felt as a child, I thought as a child. Now that I have become a man, I have put away childish things. 12 For now we see in a mirror, dimly, but then face to face. Now I know in part, but then I will know fully, even as I was also fully known. 13 But now faith, hope, and love remain—these three. The greatest of these is love.

Responsorial Psalm: Psalms 33: 2-5, 12 and 22

2 Give thanks to Yahweh with the lyre.
Sing praises to him with the harp of ten strings.

3 Sing to him a new song.
Play skillfully with a shout of joy!
4 For Yahweh's word is right.
All his work is done in faithfulness.
5 He loves righteousness and justice.
The earth is full of the loving kindness of Yahweh.
12 Blessed is the nation whose God is Yahweh,
the people whom he has chosen for his own inheritance.
22 Let your loving kindness be on us, Yahweh,
since we have hoped in you.

Gospel: Luke 7: 31-35

31 ‡ "To what then should I compare the people of this generation? What are they like? 32 They are like children who sit in the marketplace and call to one another, saying, 'We piped to you, and you didn't dance. We mourned, and you didn't weep.' 33 For John the Baptizer came neither eating bread nor drinking wine, and you say, 'He has a demon.' 34 The Son of Man has come eating and drinking, and you say, 'Behold, a glutton and a drunkard, a friend of tax collectors and sinners!' 35 Wisdom is justified by all her children."

1. Invite the Holy Spirit into this reading, asking the Author of Scripture to speak to you through His Word
2. Read today's passage as many times as you need, take your time
3. Write down (below) what the Lord is saying to you today
4. Live with this Word in your heart through the day

_____

_____

Thursday, September 19, 2024
Saint Januarius, Bishop and Martyr

First Reading: First Corinthians 15: 1-11

1 Now I declare to you, brothers, the Good News which I preached to you, which also you received, in which you also stand, 2 by which also you are saved, if you hold firmly the word which I preached to you—unless you believed in vain.
3 For I delivered to you first of all that which I also received: that Christ died for our sins according to the Scriptures, 4 that he was buried, that he was raised on the third day according to the Scriptures, 5 and that he appeared to Cephas, then to the twelve. 6 Then he appeared to

over five hundred brothers at once, most of whom remain until now, but some have also fallen asleep. 7 Then he appeared to James, then to all the apostles, 8 and last of all, as to the child born at the wrong time, he appeared to me also. 9 For I am the least of the apostles, who is not worthy to be called an apostle, because I persecuted the assembly of God. 10 But by the grace of God I am what I am. His grace which was given to me was not futile, but I worked more than all of them; yet not I, but the grace of God which was with me. 11 Whether then it is I or they, so we preach, and so you believed.

Responsorial Psalm: Psalms 118: 1b-2, 16ab-17, 28

1 Give thanks to Yahweh, for he is good,
for his loving kindness endures forever.
2 Let Israel now say
that his loving kindness endures forever.
16 The right hand of Yahweh is exalted!
The right hand of Yahweh does valiantly!"
17 I will not die, but live,
and declare Yah's works.
28 You are my God, and I will give thanks to you.
You are my God, I will exalt you.

Gospel: Luke 7: 36-50

36 One of the Pharisees invited him to eat with him. He entered into the Pharisee's house and sat at the table. 37 Behold, a woman in the city who was a sinner, when she knew that he was reclining in the Pharisee's house, brought an alabaster jar of ointment. 38 Standing behind at his feet weeping, she began to wet his feet with her tears, and she wiped them with the hair of her head, kissed his feet, and anointed them with the ointment. 39 Now when the Pharisee who had invited him saw it, he said to himself, "This man, if he were a prophet, would have perceived who and what kind of woman this is who touches him, that she is a sinner."
40 Jesus answered him, "Simon, I have something to tell you."
He said, "Teacher, say on."
41 "A certain lender had two debtors. The one owed five hundred denarii, and the other fifty. 42 When they couldn't pay, he forgave them both. Which of them therefore will love him most?"
43 Simon answered, "He, I suppose, to whom he forgave the most."
He said to him, "You have judged correctly." 44 Turning to the woman, he said to Simon, "Do you see this woman? I entered into your house, and you gave me no water for my feet, but she has wet my feet with her tears, and wiped them with the hair of her head. 45 You gave me no kiss, but she, since the time I came in, has not ceased to kiss my feet. 46 You didn't anoint my head with oil, but she has anointed my feet with ointment. 47 Therefore I tell you, her sins, which are many, are forgiven, for she loved much. But one to whom little is forgiven, loves little." 48 He said to her, "Your sins are forgiven."

49 Those who sat at the table with him began to say to themselves, "Who is this who even forgives sins?"

50 He said to the woman, "Your faith has saved you. Go in peace."

1. Invite the Holy Spirit into this reading, asking the Author of Scripture to speak to you through His Word
2. Read today's passage as many times as you need, take your time
3. Write down (below) what the Lord is saying to you today
4. Live with this Word in your heart through the day

Friday, September 20, 2024
Saints Andrew Kim Tae-gŏn, Priest, and Paul Chŏng Ha-sang, red and Companions, Martyrs

First Reading: First Corinthians 15: 12-20

12 Now if Christ is preached, that he has been raised from the dead, how do some among you say that there is no resurrection of the dead? 13 But if there is no resurrection of the dead, neither has Christ been raised. 14 If Christ has not been raised, then our preaching is in vain and your faith also is in vain. 15 Yes, we are also found false witnesses of God, because we testified about God that he raised up Christ, whom he didn't raise up if it is true that the dead are not raised. 16 For if the dead aren't raised, neither has Christ been raised. 17 If Christ has not been raised, your faith is vain; you are still in your sins. 18 Then they also who are fallen asleep in Christ have perished. 19 If we have only hoped in Christ in this life, we are of all men most pitiable.

20 But now Christ has been raised from the dead. He became the first fruit of those who are asleep.

Responsorial Psalm: Psalms 17: 1bcd, 6-7, 8b and 15

1 Hear, Yahweh, my righteous plea.
Give ear to my prayer that doesn't go out of deceitful lips.
6 I have called on you, for you will answer me, God.
Turn your ear to me.
Hear my speech.
7 Show your marvelous loving kindness,
you who save those who take refuge by your right hand from their enemies.
8 Keep me as the apple of your eye.

Hide me under the shadow of your wings,
15 As for me, I shall see your face in righteousness.
I shall be satisfied, when I awake, with seeing your form.

Gospel: Luke 8: 1-3

1 Soon afterwards, he went about through cities and villages, preaching and bringing the good news of God's Kingdom. With him were the twelve, 2 and certain women who had been healed of evil spirits and infirmities: Mary who was called Magdalene, from whom seven demons had gone out; 3 and Joanna, the wife of Chuzas, Herod's steward; Susanna; and many others who served them† from their possessions.

1. Invite the Holy Spirit into this reading, asking the Author of Scripture to speak to you through His Word
2. Read today's passage as many times as you need, take your time
3. Write down (below) what the Lord is saying to you today
4. Live with this Word in your heart through the day

_____

_____

Saturday, September 21, 2024
Saint Matthew, Apostle and Evangelist

First Reading: Ephesians 4: 1-7, 11-13

1 I therefore, the prisoner in the Lord, beg you to walk worthily of the calling with which you were called, 2 with all lowliness and humility, with patience, bearing with one another in love, 3 being eager to keep the unity of the Spirit in the bond of peace. 4 There is one body and one Spirit, even as you also were called in one hope of your calling, 5 one Lord, one faith, one baptism, 6 one God and Father of all, who is over all and through all and in us all. 7 But to each one of us, the grace was given according to the measure of the gift of Christ.
11 He gave some to be apostles; and some, prophets; and some, evangelists; and some, shepherds† and teachers; 12 for the perfecting of the saints, to the work of serving, to the building up of the body of Christ, 13 until we all attain to the unity of the faith and of the knowledge of the Son of God, to a full grown man, to the measure of the stature of the fullness of Christ,

Responsorial Psalm: Psalms 19: 2-5

2 Day after day they pour out speech,
and night after night they display knowledge.
3 There is no speech nor language
where their voice is not heard.
4 Their voice has gone out through all the earth,
their words to the end of the world.
In them he has set a tent for the sun,
5 which is as a bridegroom coming out of his room,
like a strong man rejoicing to run his course.

Gospel: Matthew 9: 9-13

9 As Jesus passed by from there, he saw a man called Matthew sitting at the tax collection office. He said to him, "Follow me." He got up and followed him. 10 As he sat in the house, behold, many tax collectors and sinners came and sat down with Jesus and his disciples. 11 When the Pharisees saw it, they said to his disciples, "Why does your teacher eat with tax collectors and sinners?"
12 When Jesus heard it, he said to them, "Those who are healthy have no need for a physician, but those who are sick do. 13 But you go and learn what this means: 'I desire mercy, and not sacrifice,'* for I came not to call the righteous, but sinners to repentance."

1. Invite the Holy Spirit into this reading, asking the Author of Scripture to speak to you through His Word
2. Read today's passage as many times as you need, take your time
3. Write down (below) what the Lord is saying to you today
4. Live with this Word in your heart through the day

_____

_____

Sunday, September 22, 2024
TWENTY-FIFTH SUNDAY IN ORDINARY TIME

First Reading: Wisdom 2: 12, 17-20

12 But let's lie in wait for the righteous man,
because he annoys us,
is contrary to our works,
reproaches us with sins against the law,

and charges us with sins against our training.

17 Let's see if his words are true.

Let's test what will happen at the end of his life.

18 For if the righteous man is God's son, he will uphold him,

and he will deliver him out of the hand of his adversaries.

19 Let's test him with insult and torture,

that we may find out how gentle he is,

and test his patience.

20 Let's condemn him to a shameful death,

for he will be protected, according to his words."

Responsorial Psalm: Psalms 54: 3-7

3 For strangers have risen up against me.

Violent men have sought after my soul.

They haven't set God before them.

4 Behold, God is my helper.

The Lord is the one who sustains my soul.

5 He will repay the evil to my enemies.

Destroy them in your truth.

6 With a free will offering, I will sacrifice to you.

I will give thanks to your name, Yahweh, for it is good.

7 For he has delivered me out of all trouble.

My eye has seen triumph over my enemies.

Second Reading: James 3: 16 – 4: 3

16 For where jealousy and selfish ambition are, there is confusion and every evil deed. 17 But the wisdom that is from above is first pure, then peaceful, gentle, reasonable, full of mercy and good fruits, without partiality, and without hypocrisy. 18 Now the fruit of righteousness is sown in peace by those who make peace.

1 Where do wars and fightings among you come from? Don't they come from your pleasures that war in your members? 2 You lust, and don't have. You murder and covet, and can't obtain. You fight and make war. You don't have, because you don't ask. 3 You ask, and don't receive, because you ask with wrong motives, so that you may spend it on your pleasures.

Gospel: Mark 9: 30-37

30 Then their eyes were opened. Jesus strictly commanded them, saying, "See that no one knows about this." 31 But they went out and spread abroad his fame in all that land.

32 As they went out, behold, a mute man who was demon possessed was brought to him. 33 When the demon was cast out, the mute man spoke. The multitudes marveled, saying, "Nothing like this has ever been seen in Israel!"

34 But the Pharisees said, "By the prince of the demons, he casts out demons."

35 Jesus went about all the cities and the villages, teaching in their synagogues and preaching the Good News of the Kingdom, and healing every disease and every sickness among the people. 36 But when he saw the multitudes, he was moved with compassion for them because they were harassed§ and scattered, like sheep without a shepherd. 37 Then he said to his disciples, "The harvest indeed is plentiful, but the laborers are few.

1. Invite the Holy Spirit into this reading, asking the Author of Scripture to speak to you through His Word
2. Read today's passage as many times as you need, take your time
3. Write down (below) what the Lord is saying to you today
4. Live with this Word in your heart through the day

Monday, September 23, 2024
Saint Pio of Pietrelcina, Priest

First Reading: Proverbs 3: 27-34

27 Don't withhold good from those to whom it is due,
when it is in the power of your hand to do it.
28 Don't say to your neighbor, "Go, and come again;
tomorrow I will give it to you,"
when you have it by you.
29 Don't devise evil against your neighbor,
since he dwells securely by you.
30 Don't strive with a man without cause,
if he has done you no harm.
31 Don't envy the man of violence.
Choose none of his ways.
32 For the perverse is an abomination to Yahweh,
but his friendship is with the upright.
33 Yahweh's curse is in the house of the wicked,
but he blesses the habitation of the righteous.
34 Surely he mocks the mockers,
but he gives grace to the humble.

Responsorial Psalm: Psalms 15: 2-5

2 He who walks blamelessly and does what is right,
and speaks truth in his heart;
3 he who doesn't slander with his tongue,
nor does evil to his friend,
nor casts slurs against his fellow man;
4 in whose eyes a vile man is despised,
but who honors those who fear Yahweh;
he who keeps an oath even when it hurts, and doesn't change;
5 he who doesn't lend out his money for usury,
nor take a bribe against the innocent.

Gospel: Luke 8: 16-18

16 "No one, when he has lit a lamp, covers it with a container or puts it under a bed; but puts it on a stand, that those who enter in may see the light. 17 For nothing is hidden that will not be revealed, nor anything secret that will not be known and come to light. 18 Be careful therefore how you hear. For whoever has, to him will be given; and whoever doesn't have, from him will be taken away even that which he thinks he has."

1. Invite the Holy Spirit into this reading, asking the Author of Scripture to speak to you through His Word
2. Read today's passage as many times as you need, take your time
3. Write down (below) what the Lord is saying to you today
4. Live with this Word in your heart through the day

_____

_____

Tuesday, September 24, 2024

First Reading: Proverbs 21: 1-6, 10-13

1 The king's heart is in Yahweh's hand like the watercourses.
He turns it wherever he desires.
2 Every way of a man is right in his own eyes,
but Yahweh weighs the hearts.
3 To do righteousness and justice
is more acceptable to Yahweh than sacrifice.

4 A high look and a proud heart,
the lamp of the wicked, is sin.
5 The plans of the diligent surely lead to profit;
and everyone who is hasty surely rushes to poverty.
6 Getting treasures by a lying tongue
is a fleeting vapor for those who seek death.
10 The soul of the wicked desires evil;
his neighbor finds no mercy in his eyes.
11 When the mocker is punished, the simple gains wisdom.
When the wise is instructed, he receives knowledge.
12 The Righteous One considers the house of the wicked,
and brings the wicked to ruin.
13 Whoever stops his ears at the cry of the poor,
he will also cry out, but shall not be heard.

Responsorial Psalm: Psalms 119: 1, 27, 30, 34, 35, 44

1 Blessed are those whose ways are blameless,
who walk according to Yahweh's law.
27 Let me understand the teaching of your precepts!
Then I will meditate on your wondrous works.
30 I have chosen the way of truth.
I have set your ordinances before me.
34 Give me understanding, and I will keep your law.
Yes, I will obey it with my whole heart.
35 Direct me in the path of your commandments,
for I delight in them.
44 So I will obey your law continually,
forever and ever.

Gospel: Luke 8: 19-21

19 His mother and brothers came to him, and they could not come near him for the crowd. 20 Some people told him, "Your mother and your brothers stand outside, desiring to see you." 21 But he answered them, "My mother and my brothers are these who hear the word of God and do it."

1. Invite the Holy Spirit into this reading, asking the Author of Scripture to speak to you through His Word
2. Read today's passage as many times as you need, take your time
3. Write down (below) what the Lord is saying to you today
4. Live with this Word in your heart through the day

Wednesday, September 25, 2024

First Reading: Proverbs 30: 5-9

5 "Every word of God is flawless.
He is a shield to those who take refuge in him.
6 Don't you add to his words,
lest he reprove you, and you be found a liar.
7 "Two things I have asked of you.
Don't deny me before I die.
8 Remove far from me falsehood and lies.
Give me neither poverty nor riches.
Feed me with the food that is needful for me,
9 lest I be full, deny you, and say, 'Who is Yahweh?'
or lest I be poor, and steal,
and so dishonor the name of my God.

Responsorial Psalm: Psalms 119: 29, 72, 89, 101, 104, 163

29 Keep me from the way of deceit.
Grant me your law graciously!
72 The law of your mouth is better to me than thousands of pieces of gold and silver.
89 Yahweh, your word is settled in heaven forever.
101 I have kept my feet from every evil way,
that I might observe your word.
104 Through your precepts, I get understanding;
therefore I hate every false way.
163 I hate and abhor falsehood.
I love your law.

Gospel: Luke 9: 1-6

1 He called the twelve† together and gave them power and authority over all demons, and to cure diseases. 2 He sent them out to preach God's Kingdom and to heal the sick. 3 He said to them, "Take nothing for your journey—no staffs, nor wallet, nor bread, nor money. Don't have two tunics each. 4 Into whatever house you enter, stay there, and depart from there. 5 As

many as don't receive you, when you depart from that city, shake off even the dust from your feet for a testimony against them."

6 They departed and went throughout the villages, preaching the Good News and healing everywhere.

Thursday, September 26, 2024
Saints Cosmas and Damian, Martyrs

First Reading: Ecclesiastes 1: 2-11

2 "Vanity of vanities," says the Preacher; "Vanity of vanities, all is vanity." 3 What does man gain from all his labor in which he labors under the sun? 4 One generation goes, and another generation comes; but the earth remains forever. 5 The sun also rises, and the sun goes down, and hurries to its place where it rises. 6 The wind goes toward the south, and turns around to the north. It turns around continually as it goes, and the wind returns again to its courses. 7 All the rivers run into the sea, yet the sea is not full. To the place where the rivers flow, there they flow again. 8 All things are full of weariness beyond uttering. The eye is not satisfied with seeing, nor the ear filled with hearing. 9 That which has been is that which shall be, and that which has been done is that which shall be done; and there is no new thing under the sun. 10 Is there a thing of which it may be said, "Behold,† this is new"? It has been long ago, in the ages which were before us. 11 There is no memory of the former; neither shall there be any memory of the latter that are to come, among those that shall come after.

Responsorial Psalm: Psalms 90: 3-6, 12-14 and 17bc

3 You turn man to destruction, saying,
"Return, you children of men."
4 For a thousand years in your sight are just like yesterday when it is past,
like a watch in the night.
5 You sweep them away as they sleep.
In the morning they sprout like new grass.

6 In the morning it sprouts and springs up.
By evening, it is withered and dry.
12 So teach us to count our days,
that we may gain a heart of wisdom.
13 Relent, Yahweh!§
How long?
Have compassion on your servants!
14 Satisfy us in the morning with your loving kindness,
that we may rejoice and be glad all our days.
17b Establish the work of our hands for us.
Yes, establish the work of our hands.

Gospel: Luke 9: 7-9

7 Now Herod the tetrarch heard of all that was done by him; and he was very perplexed, because it was said by some that John had risen from the dead, 8 and by some that Elijah had appeared, and by others that one of the old prophets had risen again. 9 Herod said, "I beheaded John, but who is this about whom I hear such things?" He sought to see him.

1. Invite the Holy Spirit into this reading, asking the Author of Scripture to speak to you through His Word
2. Read today's passage as many times as you need, take your time
3. Write down (below) what the Lord is saying to you today
4. Live with this Word in your heart through the day

_____

_____

Friday, September 27, 2024
Saint Vincent de Paul, Priest

First Reading: Ecclesiastes 3: 1-11

1 For everything there is a season, and a time for every purpose under heaven:
2 a time to be born, and a time to die; a time to plant, and a time to pluck up that which is planted;
3 a time to kill, and a time to heal; a time to break down, and a time to build up;
4 a time to weep, and a time to laugh; a time to mourn, and a time to dance;
5 a time to cast away stones, and a time to gather stones together; a time to embrace,
and a time to refrain from embracing;

6 a time to seek, and a time to lose; a time to keep, and a time to cast away;

7 a time to tear, and a time to sew; a time to keep silence, and a time to speak;

8 a time to love, and a time to hate; a time for war, and a time for peace.

9 What profit has he who works in that in which he labors? 10 I have seen the burden which God has given to the sons of men to be afflicted with. 11 He has made everything beautiful in its time. He has also set eternity in their hearts, yet so that man can't find out the work that God has done from the beginning even to the end.

Responsorial Psalm: Psalms 144: 1b-4

1 Blessed be Yahweh, my rock,
who trains my hands to war,
and my fingers to battle—
2 my loving kindness, my fortress,
my high tower, my deliverer,
my shield, and he in whom I take refuge,
who subdues my people under me.
3 Yahweh, what is man, that you care for him?
Or the son of man, that you think of him?
4 Man is like a breath.
His days are like a shadow that passes away.

Gospel: Luke 9: 18-22

18 As he was praying alone, the disciples were near him, and he asked them, "Who do the multitudes say that I am?"

19 They answered, " 'John the Baptizer,' but others say, 'Elijah,' and others, that one of the old prophets has risen again."

20 He said to them, "But who do you say that I am?"

Peter answered, "The Christ of God."

21 But he warned them and commanded them to tell this to no one, 22 saying, "The Son of Man must suffer many things, and be rejected by the elders, chief priests, and scribes, and be killed, and the third day be raised up."

1. Invite the Holy Spirit into this reading, asking the Author of Scripture to speak to you through His Word
2. Read today's passage as many times as you need, take your time
3. Write down (below) what the Lord is saying to you today
4. Live with this Word in your heart through the day

Saturday, September 28, 2024
Saint Wenceslaus, Martyr; Saint Lawrence Ruiz
and Companions, Martyrs; BVM

First Reading: Ecclesiastes 11: 9 – 12: 8

9 Rejoice, young man, in your youth,
and let your heart cheer you in the days of your youth,
and walk in the ways of your heart,
and in the sight of your eyes;
but know that for all these things God will bring you into judgment.
10 Therefore remove sorrow from your heart,
and put away evil from your flesh;
for youth and the dawn of life are vanity.
1 Remember also your Creator in the days of your youth,
before the evil days come, and the years draw near,
when you will say, "I have no pleasure in them;"
2 Before the sun, the light, the moon, and the stars are darkened,
and the clouds return after the rain;
3 in the day when the keepers of the house shall tremble,
and the strong men shall bow themselves,
and the grinders cease because they are few,
and those who look out of the windows are darkened,
4 and the doors shall be shut in the street;
when the sound of the grinding is low,
and one shall rise up at the voice of a bird,
and all the daughters of music shall be brought low;
5 yes, they shall be afraid of heights,
and terrors will be on the way;
and the almond tree shall blossom,
and the grasshopper shall be a burden,
and desire shall fail;
because man goes to his everlasting home,
and the mourners go about the streets;
6 before the silver cord is severed,
or the golden bowl is broken,
or the pitcher is broken at the spring,
or the wheel broken at the cistern,
7 and the dust returns to the earth as it was,
and the spirit returns to God who gave it.
8 "Vanity of vanities," says the Preacher.
"All is vanity!"

Responsorial Psalm: Psalms 90: 3-6, 12-14 and 17

3 You turn man to destruction, saying,
"Return, you children of men."
4 For a thousand years in your sight are just like yesterday when it is past,
like a watch in the night.
5 You sweep them away as they sleep.
In the morning they sprout like new grass.
6 In the morning it sprouts and springs up.
By evening, it is withered and dry.
12 So teach us to count our days,
that we may gain a heart of wisdom.
13 Relent, Yahweh!§
How long?
Have compassion on your servants!
14 Satisfy us in the morning with your loving kindness,
that we may rejoice and be glad all our days.
17 Let the favor of the Lord our God be on us.
Establish the work of our hands for us.
Yes, establish the work of our hands.

Gospel: Luke 9: 43b-45

43 They were all astonished at the majesty of God.
But while all were marveling at all the things which Jesus did, he said to his disciples, 44 "Let these words sink into your ears, for the Son of Man will be delivered up into the hands of men."
45 But they didn't understand this saying. It was concealed from them, that they should not perceive it, and they were afraid to ask him about this saying.

1. Invite the Holy Spirit into this reading, asking the Author of Scripture to speak to you through His Word
2. Read today's passage as many times as you need, take your time
3. Write down (below) what the Lord is saying to you today
4. Live with this Word in your heart through the day

_____

_____

Sunday, September 29, 2024
TWENTY-SIXTH SUNDAY IN ORDINARY TIME

First Reading: Numbers 11: 25-29

25 Yahweh came down in the cloud, and spoke to him, and took of the Spirit that was on him, and put it on the seventy elders. When the Spirit rested on them, they prophesied, but they did so no more. 26 But two men remained in the camp. The name of one was Eldad, and the name of the other Medad; and the Spirit rested on them. They were of those who were written, but had not gone out to the Tent; and they prophesied in the camp. 27 A young man ran, and told Moses, and said, "Eldad and Medad are prophesying in the camp!"
28 Joshua the son of Nun, the servant of Moses, one of his chosen men, answered, "My lord Moses, forbid them!"
29 Moses said to him, "Are you jealous for my sake? I wish that all Yahweh's people were prophets, that Yahweh would put his Spirit on them!"

Responsorial Psalm: Psalms 19: 8, 10, 12-13, 14

8 Yahweh's precepts are right, rejoicing the heart.
Yahweh's commandment is pure, enlightening the eyes.
10 They are more to be desired than gold, yes, than much fine gold,
sweeter also than honey and the extract of the honeycomb.
12 Who can discern his errors?
Forgive me from hidden errors.
13 Keep back your servant also from presumptuous sins.
Let them not have dominion over me.
Then I will be upright.
I will be blameless and innocent of great transgression.
14 Let the words of my mouth and the meditation of my heart
be acceptable in your sight,
Yahweh, my rock, and my redeemer.

Second Reading: James 5: 1-6

1 Come now, you rich, weep and howl for your miseries that are coming on you. 2 Your riches are corrupted and your garments are moth-eaten. 3 Your gold and your silver are corroded, and their corrosion will be for a testimony against you and will eat your flesh like fire. You have laid up your treasure in the last days. 4 Behold, the wages of the laborers who mowed your fields, which you have kept back by fraud, cry out; and the cries of those who reaped have entered into the ears of the Lord of Armies.† 5 You have lived in luxury on the earth, and taken your pleasure. You have nourished your hearts as in a day of slaughter. 6 You have condemned and you have murdered the righteous one. He doesn't resist you.

Gospel: Mark 9: 38-43, 45, 47-48

38 John said to him, "Teacher, we saw someone who doesn't follow us casting out demons in your name; and we forbade him, because he doesn't follow us."

39 But Jesus said, "Don't forbid him, for there is no one who will do a mighty work in my name and be able quickly to speak evil of me. 40 For whoever is not against us is on our side. 41 For whoever will give you a cup of water to drink in my name because you are Christ's, most certainly I tell you, he will in no way lose his reward.

42 "Whoever will cause one of these little ones who believe in me to stumble, it would be better for him if he were thrown into the sea with a millstone hung around his neck. 43 If your hand causes you to stumble, cut it off. It is better for you to enter into life maimed, rather than having your two hands to go into Gehenna, † into the unquenchable fire, 45 If your foot causes you to stumble, cut it off. It is better for you to enter into life lame, rather than having your two feet to be cast into Gehenna, § into the fire that will never be quenched—47 If your eye causes you to stumble, throw it out. It is better for you to enter into God's Kingdom with one eye, rather than having two eyes to be cast into the Gehenna‡ of fire, 48 'where their worm doesn't die, and the fire is not quenched.'

1. Invite the Holy Spirit into this reading, asking the Author of Scripture to speak to you through His Word
2. Read today's passage as many times as you need, take your time
3. Write down (below) what the Lord is saying to you today
4. Live with this Word in your heart through the day

_____

_____

Monday, September 30, 2024
Saint Jerome, Priest and Doctor of the Church

First Reading: Job 1: 6-22

6 Now on the day when God's sons came to present themselves before Yahweh,‡ Satan also came among them. 7 Yahweh said to Satan, "Where have you come from?"
Then Satan answered Yahweh, and said, "From going back and forth in the earth, and from walking up and down in it."
8 Yahweh said to Satan, "Have you considered my servant, Job? For there is no one like him in the earth, a blameless and an upright man, one who fears God, and turns away from evil."
9 Then Satan answered Yahweh, and said, "Does Job fear God for nothing? 10 Haven't you made a hedge around him, and around his house, and around all that he has, on every side? You have blessed the work of his hands, and his substance is increased in the land. 11 But stretch out your hand now, and touch all that he has, and he will renounce you to your face."

12 Yahweh said to Satan, "Behold,§ all that he has is in your power. Only on himself don't stretch out your hand."

So Satan went out from the presence of Yahweh. 13 It fell on a day when his sons and his daughters were eating and drinking wine in their oldest brother's house, 14 that a messenger came to Job, and said, "The oxen were plowing, and the donkeys feeding beside them, 15 and the Sabeans attacked, and took them away. Yes, they have killed the servants with the edge of the sword, and I alone have escaped to tell you."

16 While he was still speaking, another also came and said, "The fire of God has fallen from the sky, and has burned up the sheep and the servants, and consumed them, and I alone have escaped to tell you."

17 While he was still speaking, another also came and said, "The Chaldeans made three bands, and swept down on the camels, and have taken them away, yes, and killed the servants with the edge of the sword; and I alone have escaped to tell you."

18 While he was still speaking, there came also another, and said, "Your sons and your daughters were eating and drinking wine in their oldest brother's house, 19 and behold, there came a great wind from the wilderness, and struck the four corners of the house, and it fell on the young men, and they are dead. I alone have escaped to tell you."

20 Then Job arose, and tore his robe, and shaved his head, and fell down on the ground, and worshiped. 21 He said, "Naked I came out of my mother's womb, and naked will I return there. Yahweh gave, and Yahweh has taken away. Blessed be Yahweh's name." 22 In all this, Job didn't sin, nor charge God with wrongdoing.

Responsorial Psalm: Psalms 17: 1bcd, 2-3, 6-7

1b Give ear to my prayer that doesn't go out of deceitful lips.
2 Let my sentence come out of your presence.
Let your eyes look on equity.
3 You have proved my heart.
You have visited me in the night.
You have tried me, and found nothing.
I have resolved that my mouth shall not disobey.
6 I have called on you, for you will answer me, God.
Turn your ear to me.
Hear my speech.
7 Show your marvelous loving kindness,
you who save those who take refuge by your right hand from their enemies.

Gospel: Luke 9: 46-50

46 An argument arose among them about which of them was the greatest. 47 Jesus, perceiving the reasoning of their hearts, took a little child, and set him by his side, 48 and said to them, "Whoever receives this little child in my name receives me. Whoever receives me receives him who sent me. For whoever is least among you all, this one will be great."

49 John answered, "Master, we saw someone casting out demons in your name, and we forbade him, because he doesn't follow with us."

50 Jesus said to him, "Don't forbid him, for he who is not against us is for us."

1. Invite the Holy Spirit into this reading, asking the Author of Scripture to speak to you through His Word
2. Read today's passage as many times as you need, take your time
3. Write down (below) what the Lord is saying to you today
4. Live with this Word in your heart through the day

Tuesday, October 1, 2024
Saint Thérèse of the Child Jesus, Virgin and Doctor of the Church

First Reading: Job 3: 1-3, 11-17, 20-23

1 After this Job opened his mouth, and cursed the day of his birth. 2 Job answered:
3 "Let the day perish in which I was born,
the night which said, 'There is a boy conceived.'
11 "Why didn't I die from the womb?
Why didn't I give up the spirit when my mother bore me?
12 Why did the knees receive me?
Or why the breast, that I should nurse?
13 For now I should have lain down and been quiet.
I should have slept, then I would have been at rest,
14 with kings and counselors of the earth,
who built up waste places for themselves;
15 or with princes who had gold,
who filled their houses with silver;
16 or as a hidden untimely birth I had not been,
as infants who never saw light.
17 There the wicked cease from troubling.
There the weary are at rest.
20 "Why is light given to him who is in misery,
life to the bitter in soul,
21 who long for death, but it doesn't come;
and dig for it more than for hidden treasures,
22 who rejoice exceedingly,

and are glad, when they can find the grave?
23 Why is light given to a man whose way is hidden,
whom God has hedged in?

Responsorial Psalm: Psalms 88: 2-8

2 Let my prayer enter into your presence.
Turn your ear to my cry.
3 For my soul is full of troubles.
My life draws near to Sheol.†
4 I am counted among those who go down into the pit.
I am like a man who has no help,
5 set apart among the dead,
like the slain who lie in the grave,
whom you remember no more.
They are cut off from your hand.
6 You have laid me in the lowest pit,
in the darkest depths.
7 Your wrath lies heavily on me.
You have afflicted me with all your waves.
8 You have taken my friends from me.
You have made me an abomination to them.
I am confined, and I can't escape.

Gospel: Luke 9: 51-56

51 It came to pass, when the days were near that he should be taken up, he intently set his face to go to Jerusalem 52 and sent messengers before his face. They went and entered into a village of the Samaritans, so as to prepare for him. 53 They didn't receive him, because he was traveling with his face set toward Jerusalem. 54 When his disciples, James and John, saw this, they said, "Lord, do you want us to command fire to come down from the sky and destroy them, just as Elijah did?"
55 But he turned and rebuked them, "You don't know of what kind of spirit you are. 56 For the Son of Man didn't come to destroy men's lives, but to save them."
They went to another village.

1. Invite the Holy Spirit into this reading, asking the Author of Scripture to speak to you through His Word
2. Read today's passage as many times as you need, take your time
3. Write down (below) what the Lord is saying to you today
4. Live with this Word in your heart through the day

Wednesday, October 2, 2024
The Holy Guardian Angels

First Reading: Job 9: 1-12, 14-16

1 Then Job answered,
2 "Truly I know that it is so,
but how can man be just with God?
3 If he is pleased to contend with him,
he can't answer him one time in a thousand.
4 God is wise in heart, and mighty in strength.
Who has hardened himself against him and prospered?
5 He removes the mountains, and they don't know it,
when he overturns them in his anger.
6 He shakes the earth out of its place.
Its pillars tremble.
7 He commands the sun and it doesn't rise,
and seals up the stars.
8 He alone stretches out the heavens,
and treads on the waves of the sea.
9 He makes the Bear, Orion, and the Pleiades,
and the rooms of the south.
10 He does great things past finding out;
yes, marvelous things without number.
11 Behold, he goes by me, and I don't see him.
He passes on also, but I don't perceive him.
12 Behold, he snatches away.
Who can hinder him?
Who will ask him, 'What are you doing?'
14 How much less will I answer him,
and choose my words to argue with him?
15 Though I were righteous, yet I wouldn't answer him.
I would make supplication to my judge.
16 If I had called, and he had answered me,
yet I wouldn't believe that he listened to my voice.

Responsorial Psalm: Psalms 88: 10bc-15

10 Do you show wonders to the dead?
Do the departed spirits rise up and praise you?
11 Is your loving kindness declared in the grave?
Or your faithfulness in Destruction?
12 Are your wonders made known in the dark?
Or your righteousness in the land of forgetfulness?
13 But to you, Yahweh, I have cried.
In the morning, my prayer comes before you.
14 Yahweh, why do you reject my soul?
Why do you hide your face from me?
15 I am afflicted and ready to die from my youth up.
While I suffer your terrors, I am distracted.

Gospel: Matthew 18: 1-5, 10

1 In that hour the disciples came to Jesus, saying, "Who then is greatest in the Kingdom of Heaven?"
2 Jesus called a little child to himself, and set him in the middle of them 3 and said, "Most certainly I tell you, unless you turn and become as little children, you will in no way enter into the Kingdom of Heaven. 4 Whoever therefore humbles himself as this little child is the greatest in the Kingdom of Heaven. 5 Whoever receives one such little child in my name receives me,
10 See that you don't despise one of these little ones, for I tell you that in heaven their angels always see the face of my Father who is in heaven. 11 For the Son of Man came to save that which was lost.

1. Invite the Holy Spirit into this reading, asking the Author of Scripture to speak to you through His Word
2. Read today's passage as many times as you need, take your time
3. Write down (below) what the Lord is saying to you today
4. Live with this Word in your heart through the day

_____

_____

Thursday, October 3, 2024

First Reading: Job 19: 21-27

21 "Have pity on me. Have pity on me, you my friends,
for the hand of God has touched me.
22 Why do you persecute me as God,
and are not satisfied with my flesh?
23 "Oh that my words were now written!
Oh that they were inscribed in a book!
24 That with an iron pen and lead
they were engraved in the rock forever!
25 But as for me, I know that my Redeemer lives.
In the end, he will stand upon the earth.
26 After my skin is destroyed,
then I will see God in my flesh,
27 whom I, even I, will see on my side.
My eyes will see, and not as a stranger.
"My heart is consumed within me.

Responsorial Psalm: Psalms 27: 7-9, 13-14

7 Hear, Yahweh, when I cry with my voice.
Have mercy also on me, and answer me.
8 When you said, "Seek my face,"
my heart said to you, "I will seek your face, Yahweh."
9 Don't hide your face from me.
Don't put your servant away in anger.
You have been my help.
Don't abandon me,
neither forsake me, God of my salvation.
13 I am still confident of this:
I will see the goodness of Yahweh in the land of the living.
14 Wait for Yahweh.
Be strong, and let your heart take courage.
Yes, wait for Yahweh.

Gospel: Luke 10: 1-12

1 Now after these things, the Lord also appointed seventy others, and sent them two by two ahead of him† into every city and place where he was about to come. 2 Then he said to them, "The harvest is indeed plentiful, but the laborers are few. Pray therefore to the Lord of the harvest, that he may send out laborers into his harvest. 3 Go your ways. Behold, I send you out as lambs among wolves. 4 Carry no purse, nor wallet, nor sandals. Greet no one on the way. 5 Into whatever house you enter, first say, 'Peace be to this house.' 6 If a son of peace is there, your peace will rest on him; but if not, it will return to you. 7 Remain in that same

house, eating and drinking the things they give, for the laborer is worthy of his wages. Don't go from house to house. 8 Into whatever city you enter and they receive you, eat the things that are set before you. 9 Heal the sick who are there and tell them, 'God's Kingdom has come near to you.' 10 But into whatever city you enter and they don't receive you, go out into its streets and say, 11 'Even the dust from your city that clings to us, we wipe off against you. Nevertheless know this, that God's Kingdom has come near to you.' 12 I tell you, it will be more tolerable in that day for Sodom than for that city.

1. Invite the Holy Spirit into this reading, asking the Author of Scripture to speak to you through His Word
2. Read today's passage as many times as you need, take your time
3. Write down (below) what the Lord is saying to you today
4. Live with this Word in your heart through the day

_____

_____

Friday, October 4, 2024
Saint Francis of Assisi

First Reading: Job 38: 1, 12-21; 40: 3-5

1 Then Yahweh answered Job out of the whirlwind,
12 "Have you commanded the morning in your days,
and caused the dawn to know its place,
13 that it might take hold of the ends of the earth,
and shake the wicked out of it?
14 It is changed as clay under the seal,
and presented as a garment.
15 From the wicked, their light is withheld.
The high arm is broken.
 16 "Have you entered into the springs of the sea?
Or have you walked in the recesses of the deep?
17 Have the gates of death been revealed to you?
Or have you seen the gates of the shadow of death?
18 Have you comprehended the earth in its width?
Declare, if you know it all.
 19 "What is the way to the dwelling of light?
As for darkness, where is its place,
20 that you should take it to its bound,

that you should discern the paths to its house?
21 Surely you know, for you were born then,
and the number of your days is great!
3 Then Job answered Yahweh,
4 "Behold, I am of small account. What will I answer you?
I lay my hand on my mouth.
5 I have spoken once, and I will not answer;
Yes, twice, but I will proceed no further."

Responsorial Psalm: Psalms 139: 1-3, 7-10, 13-14ab

1 Yahweh, you have searched me,
and you know me.
2 You know my sitting down and my rising up.
You perceive my thoughts from afar.
3 You search out my path and my lying down,
and are acquainted with all my ways.
7 Where could I go from your Spirit?
Or where could I flee from your presence?
8 If I ascend up into heaven, you are there.
If I make my bed in Sheol,† behold, you are there!
9 If I take the wings of the dawn,
and settle in the uttermost parts of the sea,
10 even there your hand will lead me,
and your right hand will hold me.
13 For you formed my inmost being.
You knit me together in my mother's womb.
14 I will give thanks to you,
for I am fearfully and wonderfully made.
Your works are wonderful.
My soul knows that very well.

Gospel: Luke 10: 13-16

13 "Woe to you, Chorazin! Woe to you, Bethsaida! For if the mighty works had been done in Tyre and Sidon which were done in you, they would have repented long ago, sitting in sackcloth and ashes. 14 But it will be more tolerable for Tyre and Sidon in the judgment than for you. 15 You, Capernaum, who are exalted to heaven, will be brought down to Hades. ‡ 16 Whoever listens to you listens to me, and whoever rejects you rejects me. Whoever rejects me rejects him who sent me."

1. Invite the Holy Spirit into this reading, asking the Author of Scripture to speak to you through His Word

2. Read today's passage as many times as you need, take your time
3. Write down (below) what the Lord is saying to you today
4. Live with this Word in your heart through the day

Saturday, October 5, 2024
Saint Faustina Kowalska, Virgin;
USA: Blessed Francis Xavier Seelos, Priest

First Reading: Job 42: 1-3, 5-6, 12-17

1 Then Job answered Yahweh:
2 "I know that you can do all things,
and that no purpose of yours can be restrained.
3 You asked, 'Who is this who hides counsel without knowledge?'
therefore I have uttered that which I didn't understand,
things too wonderful for me, which I didn't know.
5 I had heard of you by the hearing of the ear,
but now my eye sees you.
6 Therefore I abhor myself,
and repent in dust and ashes."
12 So Yahweh blessed the latter end of Job more than his beginning. He had fourteen thousand sheep, six thousand camels, one thousand yoke of oxen, and a thousand female donkeys. 13 He had also seven sons and three daughters. 14 He called the name of the first, Jemimah; and the name of the second, Keziah; and the name of the third, Keren Happuch. 15 In all the land were no women found so beautiful as the daughters of Job. Their father gave them an inheritance among their brothers. 16 After this Job lived one hundred forty years, and saw his sons, and his sons' sons, to four generations. 17 So Job died, being old and full of days.

Responsorial Psalm: Psalms 119: 66, 71, 75, 91, 125, 130

65 You have treated your servant well,
according to your word, Yahweh.
71 It is good for me that I have been afflicted,
that I may learn your statutes.
75 Yahweh, I know that your judgments are righteous,
that in faithfulness you have afflicted me.
91 Your laws remain to this day,
for all things serve you.

125 I am your servant. Give me understanding,
that I may know your testimonies.
130 The entrance of your words gives light.
It gives understanding to the simple.

Gospel: Luke 10: 17-24

17 The seventy returned with joy, saying, "Lord, even the demons are subject to us in your name!"

18 He said to them, "I saw Satan having fallen like lightning from heaven. 19 Behold, I give you authority to tread on serpents and scorpions, and over all the power of the enemy. Nothing will in any way hurt you. 20 Nevertheless, don't rejoice in this, that the spirits are subject to you, but rejoice that your names are written in heaven."

21 In that same hour, Jesus rejoiced in the Holy Spirit, and said, "I thank you, O Father, Lord of heaven and earth, that you have hidden these things from the wise and understanding, and revealed them to little children. Yes, Father, for so it was well-pleasing in your sight."

22 Turning to the disciples, he said, "All things have been delivered to me by my Father. No one knows who the Son is, except the Father, and who the Father is, except the Son, and he to whomever the Son desires to reveal him."

23 Turning to the disciples, he said privately, "Blessed are the eyes which see the things that you see, 24 for I tell you that many prophets and kings desired to see the things which you see, and didn't see them, and to hear the things which you hear, and didn't hear them."

1. Invite the Holy Spirit into this reading, asking the Author of Scripture to speak to you through His Word
2. Read today's passage as many times as you need, take your time
3. Write down (below) what the Lord is saying to you today
4. Live with this Word in your heart through the day

Sunday, October 6, 2024
TWENTY-SEVENTH SUNDAY IN ORDINARY TIME

First Reading: Genesis 2: 18-24

18 Yahweh God said, "It is not good for the man to be alone. I will make him a helper comparable to§ him." 19 Out of the ground Yahweh God formed every animal of the field, and every bird of the sky, and brought them to the man to see what he would call them. Whatever the man called every living creature became its name. 20 The man gave names to all livestock,

and to the birds of the sky, and to every animal of the field; but for man there was not found a helper comparable to him. 21 Yahweh God caused the man to fall into a deep sleep. As the man slept, he took one of his ribs, and closed up the flesh in its place. 22 Yahweh God made a woman from the rib which he had taken from the man, and brought her to the man. 23 The man said, "This is now bone of my bones, and flesh of my flesh. She will be called 'woman,' because she was taken out of Man." 24 Therefore a man will leave his father and his mother, and will join with his wife, and they will be one flesh.

Responsorial Psalm: Psalms 128: 1-6

1 Blessed is everyone who fears Yahweh,
who walks in his ways.
2 For you will eat the labor of your hands.
You will be happy, and it will be well with you.
3 Your wife will be as a fruitful vine in the innermost parts of your house,
your children like olive shoots around your table.
4 Behold, this is how the man who fears Yahweh is blessed.
5 May Yahweh bless you out of Zion,
and may you see the good of Jerusalem all the days of your life.
6 Yes, may you see your children's children.
Peace be upon Israel.

Second Reading: Hebrews 2: 9-11

9 But we see him who has been made a little lower than the angels, Jesus, because of the suffering of death crowned with glory and honor, that by the grace of God he should taste of death for everyone.
10 For it became him, for whom are all things and through whom are all things, in bringing many children to glory, to make the author of their salvation perfect through sufferings. 11 For both he who sanctifies and those who are sanctified are all from one, for which cause he is not ashamed to call them brothers,

Gospel: Mark 10: 2-16

2 Pharisees came to him testing him, and asked him, "Is it lawful for a man to divorce his wife?"
3 He answered, "What did Moses command you?"
4 They said, "Moses allowed a certificate of divorce to be written, and to divorce her."
5 But Jesus said to them, "For your hardness of heart, he wrote you this commandment. 6 But from the beginning of the creation, God made them male and female.* 7 For this cause a man will leave his father and mother, and will join to his wife, 8 and the two will become one flesh,* so that they are no longer two, but one flesh. 9 What therefore God has joined together, let no man separate."

10 In the house, his disciples asked him again about the same matter. 11 He said to them, "Whoever divorces his wife and marries another commits adultery against her. 12 If a woman herself divorces her husband and marries another, she commits adultery."

13 They were bringing to him little children, that he should touch them, but the disciples rebuked those who were bringing them. 14 But when Jesus saw it, he was moved with indignation and said to them, "Allow the little children to come to me! Don't forbid them, for God's Kingdom belongs to such as these. 15 Most certainly I tell you, whoever will not receive God's Kingdom like a little child, he will in no way enter into it." 16 He took them in his arms and blessed them, laying his hands on them.

1. Invite the Holy Spirit into this reading, asking the Author of Scripture to speak to you through His Word
2. Read today's passage as many times as you need, take your time
3. Write down (below) what the Lord is saying to you today
4. Live with this Word in your heart through the day

_____

_____

Monday, October 7, 2024
Our Lady of the Rosary

First Reading: Galatians 1: 6-12

6 I marvel that you are so quickly deserting him who called you in the grace of Christ to a different "good news", 7 but there isn't another "good news." Only there are some who trouble you and want to pervert the Good News of Christ. 8 But even though we, or an angel from heaven, should preach to you any "good news" other than that which we preached to you, let him be cursed. 9 As we have said before, so I now say again: if any man preaches to you any "good news" other than that which you received, let him be cursed.

10 For am I now seeking the favor of men, or of God? Or am I striving to please men? For if I were still pleasing men, I wouldn't be a servant of Christ.

11 But I make known to you, brothers, concerning the Good News which was preached by me, that it is not according to man. 12 For I didn't receive it from man, nor was I taught it, but it came to me through revelation of Jesus Christ.

Responsorial Psalm: Psalms 111: 1b-2, 7-9 and 10c

1b I will give thanks to Yahweh with my whole heart,
in the council of the upright, and in the congregation.

2 Yahweh's works are great,
pondered by all those who delight in them.
7 The works of his hands are truth and justice.
All his precepts are sure.
8 They are established forever and ever.
They are done in truth and uprightness.
9 He has sent redemption to his people.
He has ordained his covenant forever.
His name is holy and awesome!
10c His praise endures forever!

Gospel: Luke 10: 25-37

25 Behold, a certain lawyer stood up and tested him, saying, "Teacher, what shall I do to inherit eternal life?"
26 He said to him, "What is written in the law? How do you read it?"
27 He answered, "You shall love the Lord your God with all your heart, with all your soul, with all your strength, and with all your mind;* and your neighbor as yourself."*
28 He said to him, "You have answered correctly. Do this, and you will live."
29 But he, desiring to justify himself, asked Jesus, "Who is my neighbor?"
30 Jesus answered, "A certain man was going down from Jerusalem to Jericho, and he fell among robbers, who both stripped him and beat him, and departed, leaving him half dead. 31 By chance a certain priest was going down that way. When he saw him, he passed by on the other side. 32 In the same way a Levite also, when he came to the place and saw him, passed by on the other side. 33 But a certain Samaritan, as he traveled, came where he was. When he saw him, he was moved with compassion, 34 came to him, and bound up his wounds, pouring on oil and wine. He set him on his own animal, brought him to an inn, and took care of him. 35 On the next day, when he departed, he took out two denarii, gave them to the host, and said to him, 'Take care of him. Whatever you spend beyond that, I will repay you when I return.' 36 Now which of these three do you think seemed to be a neighbor to him who fell among the robbers?"
37 He said, "He who showed mercy on him."
Then Jesus said to him, "Go and do likewise."

1. Invite the Holy Spirit into this reading, asking the Author of Scripture to speak to you through His Word
2. Read today's passage as many times as you need, take your time
3. Write down (below) what the Lord is saying to you today
4. Live with this Word in your heart through the day

_____

_____

Tuesday, October 8, 2024

First Reading: Galatians 1: 13-24

13 For you have heard of my way of living in time past in the Jews' religion, how that beyond measure I persecuted the assembly of God and ravaged it. 14 I advanced in the Jews' religion beyond many of my own age among my countrymen, being more exceedingly zealous for the traditions of my fathers. 15 But when it was the good pleasure of God, who separated me from my mother's womb and called me through his grace, 16 to reveal his Son in me, that I might preach him among the Gentiles, I didn't immediately confer with flesh and blood, 17 nor did I go up to Jerusalem to those who were apostles before me, but I went away into Arabia. Then I returned to Damascus.

18 Then after three years I went up to Jerusalem to visit Peter, and stayed with him fifteen days. 19 But of the other apostles I saw no one except James, the Lord's brother. 20 Now about the things which I write to you, behold,§ before God, I'm not lying. 21 Then I came to the regions of Syria and Cilicia. 22 I was still unknown by face to the assemblies of Judea which were in Christ, 23 but they only heard, "He who once persecuted us now preaches the faith that he once tried to destroy." 24 So they glorified God in me.

Responsorial Psalm: Psalms 139: 1b-3, 13-15

1 Yahweh, you have searched me,
and you know me.
2 You know my sitting down and my rising up.
You perceive my thoughts from afar.
3 You search out my path and my lying down,
and are acquainted with all my ways.
13 For you formed my inmost being.
You knit me together in my mother's womb.
14 I will give thanks to you,
for I am fearfully and wonderfully made.
Your works are wonderful.
My soul knows that very well.
15 My frame wasn't hidden from you,
when I was made in secret,
woven together in the depths of the earth.

Gospel: Luke 10: 38-42

38 As they went on their way, he entered into a certain village, and a certain woman named Martha received him into her house. 39 She had a sister called Mary, who also sat at Jesus' feet and heard his word. 40 But Martha was distracted with much serving, and she came up

to him, and said, "Lord, don't you care that my sister left me to serve alone? Ask her therefore to help me."

41 Jesus answered her, "Martha, Martha, you are anxious and troubled about many things, 42 but one thing is needed. Mary has chosen the good part, which will not be taken away from her."

Wednesday, October 9, 2024
Saint Denis, Bishop, and Companions, Martyrs; Saint John Leonardi, Priest

First Reading: Galatians 2: 1-2, 7-14

1 Then after a period of fourteen years I went up again to Jerusalem with Barnabas, taking Titus also with me. 2 I went up by revelation, and I laid before them the Good News which I preach among the Gentiles, but privately before those who were respected, for fear that I might be running, or had run, in vain.

7 but to the contrary, when they saw that I had been entrusted with the Good News for the uncircumcised, even as Peter with the Good News for the circumcised— 8 for he who worked through Peter in the apostleship with the circumcised also worked through me with the Gentiles— 9 and when they perceived the grace that was given to me, James and Cephas and John, those who were reputed to be pillars, gave to Barnabas and me the right hand of fellowship, that we should go to the Gentiles, and they to the circumcision. 10 They only asked us to remember the poor—which very thing I was also zealous to do.

11 But when Peter came to Antioch, I resisted him to his face, because he stood condemned. 12 For before some people came from James, he ate with the Gentiles. But when they came, he drew back and separated himself, fearing those who were of the circumcision. 13 And the rest of the Jews joined him in his hypocrisy, so that even Barnabas was carried away with their hypocrisy. 14 But when I saw that they didn't walk uprightly according to the truth of the Good News, I said to Peter before them all, "If you, being a Jew, live as the Gentiles do, and not as the Jews do, why do you compel the Gentiles to live as the Jews do?

Responsorial Psalm: Psalms 117: 1bc, 2

1 Praise Yahweh, all you nations!
Extol him, all you peoples!
2 For his loving kindness is great toward us.
Yahweh's faithfulness endures forever.
Praise Yah!

Gospel: Luke 11: 1-4

1 When he finished praying in a certain place, one of his disciples said to him, "Lord, teach us to pray, just as John also taught his disciples."
2 He said to them, "When you pray, say,
'Our Father in heaven,
may your name be kept holy.
May your Kingdom come.
May your will be done on earth, as it is in heaven.
3 Give us day by day our daily bread.
4 Forgive us our sins,
for we ourselves also forgive everyone who is indebted to us.
Bring us not into temptation,
but deliver us from the evil one.' "

1. Invite the Holy Spirit into this reading, asking the Author of Scripture to speak to you through His Word
2. Read today's passage as many times as you need, take your time
3. Write down (below) what the Lord is saying to you today
4. Live with this Word in your heart through the day

_____

_____

Thursday, October 10, 2024

First Reading: Galatians 3: 1-5

1 Foolish Galatians, who has bewitched you not to obey the truth, before whose eyes Jesus Christ was openly portrayed among you as crucified? 2 I just want to learn this from you: Did you receive the Spirit by the works of the law, or by hearing of faith? 3 Are you so foolish? Having begun in the Spirit, are you now completed in the flesh? 4 Did you suffer so many

things in vain, if it is indeed in vain? 5 He therefore who supplies the Spirit to you and does miracles among you, does he do it by the works of the law, or by hearing of faith?

Responsorial Psalm: Luke 1: 69-75

69 and has raised up a horn of salvation for us in the house of his servant David
70 (as he spoke by the mouth of his holy prophets who have been from of old),
71 salvation from our enemies and from the hand of all who hate us;
72 to show mercy toward our fathers,
to remember his holy covenant,
73 the oath which he swore to Abraham our father,
74 to grant to us that we, being delivered out of the hand of our enemies,
should serve him without fear,
75 in holiness and righteousness before him all the days of our life.

Gospel: Luke 11: 5-13

5 He said to them, "Which of you, if you go to a friend at midnight and tell him, 'Friend, lend me three loaves of bread, 6 for a friend of mine has come to me from a journey, and I have nothing to set before him,' 7 and he from within will answer and say, 'Don't bother me. The door is now shut, and my children are with me in bed. I can't get up and give it to you'? 8 I tell you, although he will not rise and give it to him because he is his friend, yet because of his persistence, he will get up and give him as many as he needs.
9 "I tell you, keep asking, and it will be given you. Keep seeking, and you will find. Keep knocking, and it will be opened to you. 10 For everyone who asks receives. He who seeks finds. To him who knocks it will be opened.
11 "Which of you fathers, if your son asks for bread, will give him a stone? Or if he asks for a fish, he won't give him a snake instead of a fish, will he? 12 Or if he asks for an egg, he won't give him a scorpion, will he? 13 If you then, being evil, know how to give good gifts to your children, how much more will your heavenly Father give the Holy Spirit to those who ask him?"

1. Invite the Holy Spirit into this reading, asking the Author of Scripture to speak to you through His Word
2. Read today's passage as many times as you need, take your time
3. Write down (below) what the Lord is saying to you today
4. Live with this Word in your heart through the day

_____

_____

Friday, October 11, 2024
Saint John XXIII, Pope

First Reading: Galatians 3: 7-14

7 Know therefore that those who are of faith are children of Abraham. 8 The Scripture, foreseeing that God would justify the Gentiles by faith, preached the Good News beforehand to Abraham, saying, "In you all the nations will be blessed."* 9 So then, those who are of faith are blessed with the faithful Abraham.
10 For as many as are of the works of the law are under a curse. For it is written, "Cursed is everyone who doesn't continue in all things that are written in the book of the law, to do them."* 11 Now that no man is justified by the law before God is evident, for, "The righteous will live by faith."* 12 The law is not of faith, but, "The man who does them will live by them."* 13 Christ redeemed us from the curse of the law, having become a curse for us. For it is written, "Cursed is everyone who hangs on a tree,"* 14 that the blessing of Abraham might come on the Gentiles through Christ Jesus, that we might receive the promise of the Spirit through faith.

Responsorial Psalm: Psalms 111: 1b-6

1b I will give thanks to Yahweh with my whole heart,
in the council of the upright, and in the congregation.
2 Yahweh's works are great,
pondered by all those who delight in them.
3 His work is honor and majesty.
His righteousness endures forever.
4 He has caused his wonderful works to be remembered.
Yahweh is gracious and merciful.
5 He has given food to those who fear him.
He always remembers his covenant.
6 He has shown his people the power of his works,
in giving them the heritage of the nations.

Gospel: Luke 11: 15-26

15 But some of them said, "He casts out demons by Beelzebul, the prince of the demons." 16 Others, testing him, sought from him a sign from heaven. 17 But he, knowing their thoughts, said to them, "Every kingdom divided against itself is brought to desolation. A house divided against itself falls. 18 If Satan also is divided against himself, how will his kingdom stand? For you say that I cast out demons by Beelzebul. 19 But if I cast out demons by Beelzebul, by

whom do your children cast them out? Therefore they will be your judges. 20 But if I by God's finger cast out demons, then God's Kingdom has come to you.

21 "When the strong man, fully armed, guards his own dwelling, his goods are safe. 22 But when someone stronger attacks him and overcomes him, he takes from him his whole armor in which he trusted, and divides his plunder.

23 "He who is not with me is against me. He who doesn't gather with me scatters.

24 The unclean spirit, when he has gone out of the man, passes through dry places, seeking rest; and finding none, he says, 'I will turn back to my house from which I came out.' 25 When he returns, he finds it swept and put in order. 26 Then he goes and takes seven other spirits more evil than himself, and they enter in and dwell there. The last state of that man becomes worse than the first."

1. Invite the Holy Spirit into this reading, asking the Author of Scripture to speak to you through His Word
2. Read today's passage as many times as you need, take your time
3. Write down (below) what the Lord is saying to you today
4. Live with this Word in your heart through the day

_____

_____

Saturday, October 12, 2024

First Reading: Galatians 3: 22-29

2 But the Scripture imprisoned all things under sin, that the promise by faith in Jesus Christ might be given to those who believe.

23 But before faith came, we were kept in custody under the law, confined for the faith which should afterwards be revealed. 24 So that the law has become our tutor to bring us to Christ, that we might be justified by faith. 25 But now that faith has come, we are no longer under a tutor. 26 For you are all children of God, through faith in Christ Jesus. 27 For as many of you as were baptized into Christ have put on Christ. 28 There is neither Jew nor Greek, there is neither slave nor free man, there is neither male nor female; for you are all one in Christ Jesus. 29 If you are Christ's, then you are Abraham's offspring and heirs according to promise.

Responsorial Psalm: Psalms 105: 2-7

2 Sing to him, sing praises to him!
Tell of all his marvelous works.
3 Glory in his holy name.

Let the heart of those who seek Yahweh rejoice.
4 Seek Yahweh and his strength.
Seek his face forever more.
5 Remember his marvelous works that he has done:
his wonders, and the judgments of his mouth,
6 you offspring of Abraham, his servant,
you children of Jacob, his chosen ones.
7 He is Yahweh, our God.
His judgments are in all the earth.

Gospel: Luke 11: 27-28

27 It came to pass, as he said these things, a certain woman out of the multitude lifted up her voice and said to him, "Blessed is the womb that bore you, and the breasts which nursed you!"
28 But he said, "On the contrary, blessed are those who hear the word of God, and keep it."

1. Invite the Holy Spirit into this reading, asking the Author of Scripture to speak to you through His Word
2. Read today's passage as many times as you need, take your time
3. Write down (below) what the Lord is saying to you today
4. Live with this Word in your heart through the day

_____

_____

Sunday, October 13, 2024
TWENTY-EIGHTH SUNDAY IN ORDINARY TIME

First Reading: Wisdom 7: 7-11

7 For this cause I prayed, and understanding was given to me.
I asked, and a spirit of wisdom came to me.
8 I preferred her before sceptres and thrones.
I considered riches nothing in comparison to her.
9 Neither did I liken to her any priceless gem,
because all gold in her presence is a little sand,
and silver will be considered as clay before her.
10 I loved her more than health and beauty,
and I chose to have her rather than light,
because her bright shining is never laid to sleep.

11 All good things came to me with her,
and innumerable riches are in her hands.

Responsorial Psalm: Psalms 90: 12-17

12 So teach us to count our days,
that we may gain a heart of wisdom.
13 Relent, Yahweh!§
How long?
Have compassion on your servants!
14 Satisfy us in the morning with your loving kindness,
that we may rejoice and be glad all our days.
15 Make us glad for as many days as you have afflicted us,
for as many years as we have seen evil.
16 Let your work appear to your servants,
your glory to their children.
17 Let the favor of the Lord our God be on us.
Establish the work of our hands for us.
Yes, establish the work of our hands.

Second Reading: Hebrews 4: 12-13

12 For the word of God is living and active, and sharper than any two-edged sword, piercing even to the dividing of soul and spirit, of both joints and marrow, and is able to discern the thoughts and intentions of the heart. 13 There is no creature that is hidden from his sight, but all things are naked and laid open before the eyes of him to whom we must give an account.

Gospel: Mark 10: 17-30

17 As he was going out into the way, one ran to him, knelt before him, and asked him, "Good Teacher, what shall I do that I may inherit eternal life?"
18 Jesus said to him, "Why do you call me good? No one is good except one—God. 19 You know the commandments: 'Do not murder,' 'Do not commit adultery,' 'Do not steal,' 'Do not give false testimony,' 'Do not defraud,' 'Honor your father and mother.' "*
20 He said to him, "Teacher, I have observed all these things from my youth."
21 Jesus looking at him loved him, and said to him, "One thing you lack. Go, sell whatever you have and give to the poor, and you will have treasure in heaven; and come, follow me, taking up the cross."
22 But his face fell at that saying, and he went away sorrowful, for he was one who had great possessions.
23 Jesus looked around and said to his disciples, "How difficult it is for those who have riches to enter into God's Kingdom!"

24 The disciples were amazed at his words. But Jesus answered again, "Children, how hard it is for those who trust in riches to enter into God's Kingdom! 25 It is easier for a camel to go through a needle's eye than for a rich man to enter into God's Kingdom."

26 They were exceedingly astonished, saying to him, "Then who can be saved?"

27 Jesus, looking at them, said, "With men it is impossible, but not with God, for all things are possible with God."

28 Peter began to tell him, "Behold, we have left all and have followed you."

29 Jesus said, "Most certainly I tell you, there is no one who has left house, or brothers, or sisters, or father, or mother, or wife, or children, or land, for my sake, and for the sake of the Good News, 30 but he will receive one hundred times more now in this time: houses, brothers, sisters, mothers, children, and land, with persecutions; and in the age to come eternal life.

1. Invite the Holy Spirit into this reading, asking the Author of Scripture to speak to you through His Word
2. Read today's passage as many times as you need, take your time
3. Write down (below) what the Lord is saying to you today
4. Live with this Word in your heart through the day

_____

_____

Monday, October 14, 2024
Saint Callistus I, Pope and Martyr

First Reading: Galatians 4: 22-24, 26-27, 31 – 5: 1

22 For it is written that Abraham had two sons, one by the servant, and one by the free woman. 23 However, the son by the servant was born according to the flesh, but the son by the free woman was born through promise. 24 These things contain an allegory, for these are two covenants. One is from Mount Sinai, bearing children to bondage, which is Hagar.

26 But the Jerusalem that is above is free, which is the mother of us all. 27 For it is written,
"Rejoice, you barren who don't bear.
Break out and shout, you who don't travail.
For the desolate women have more children than her who has a husband."

31 So then, brothers, we are not children of a servant, but of the free woman.

1 Stand firm therefore in the liberty by which Christ has made us free, and don't be entangled again with a yoke of bondage.

Responsorial Psalm: Psalms 113: 1b-7

1b Praise, you servants of Yahweh,
praise Yahweh's name.
2 Blessed be Yahweh's name,
from this time forward and forever more.
3 From the rising of the sun to its going down,
Yahweh's name is to be praised.
4 Yahweh is high above all nations,
his glory above the heavens.
5 Who is like Yahweh, our God,
who has his seat on high,
6 who stoops down to see in heaven and in the earth?
7 He raises up the poor out of the dust,
and lifts up the needy from the ash heap,

Gospel: Luke 11: 29-32

29 When the multitudes were gathering together to him, he began to say, "This is an evil generation. It seeks after a sign. No sign will be given to it but the sign of Jonah the prophet. 30 For even as Jonah became a sign to the Ninevites, so the Son of Man will also be to this generation. 31 The Queen of the South will rise up in the judgment with the men of this generation and will condemn them, for she came from the ends of the earth to hear the wisdom of Solomon; and behold, one greater than Solomon is here. 32 The men of Nineveh will stand up in the judgment with this generation, and will condemn it, for they repented at the preaching of Jonah; and behold, one greater than Jonah is here.

1. Invite the Holy Spirit into this reading, asking the Author of Scripture to speak to you through His Word
2. Read today's passage as many times as you need, take your time
3. Write down (below) what the Lord is saying to you today
4. Live with this Word in your heart through the day

_____

_____

Tuesday, October 15, 2024
Saint Teresa of Jesus, Virgin and Doctor of the Church

First Reading: Galatians 5: 1-6

1 Stand firm therefore in the liberty by which Christ has made us free, and don't be entangled again with a yoke of bondage.

2 Behold, I, Paul, tell you that if you receive circumcision, Christ will profit you nothing. 3 Yes, I testify again to every man who receives circumcision that he is a debtor to do the whole law. 4 You are alienated from Christ, you who desire to be justified by the law. You have fallen away from grace. 5 For we through the Spirit, by faith wait for the hope of righteousness. 6 For in Christ Jesus neither circumcision nor uncircumcision amounts to anything, but faith working through love.

Responsorial Psalm: Psalms 119: 41, 43, 44, 45, 47, 48

41 Let your loving kindness also come to me, Yahweh,
your salvation, according to your word.
43 Don't snatch the word of truth out of my mouth,
for I put my hope in your ordinances.
44 So I will obey your law continually,
forever and ever.
45 I will walk in liberty,
for I have sought your precepts.
47 I will delight myself in your commandments,
because I love them.
48 I reach out my hands for your commandments, which I love.
I will meditate on your statutes.

Gospel: Luke 11: 37-41

37 Now as he spoke, a certain Pharisee asked him to dine with him. He went in and sat at the table. 38 When the Pharisee saw it, he marveled that he had not first washed himself before dinner. 39 The Lord said to him, "Now you Pharisees cleanse the outside of the cup and of the platter, but your inward part is full of extortion and wickedness. 40 You foolish ones, didn't he who made the outside make the inside also? 41 But give for gifts to the needy those things which are within, and behold, all things will be clean to you.

1. Invite the Holy Spirit into this reading, asking the Author of Scripture to speak to you through His Word
2. Read today's passage as many times as you need, take your time
3. Write down (below) what the Lord is saying to you today
4. Live with this Word in your heart through the day

_____

_____

First Reading: Galatians 5: 18-25

18 But if you are led by the Spirit, you are not under the law. 19 Now the deeds of the flesh are obvious, which are: adultery, sexual immorality, uncleanness, lustfulness, 20 idolatry, sorcery, hatred, strife, jealousies, outbursts of anger, rivalries, divisions, heresies, 21 envy, murders, drunkenness, orgies, and things like these; of which I forewarn you, even as I also forewarned you, that those who practice such things will not inherit God's Kingdom.
22 But the fruit of the Spirit is love, joy, peace, patience, kindness, goodness, faith,† 23 gentleness, and self-control. Against such things there is no law. 24 Those who belong to Christ have crucified the flesh with its passions and lusts.
25 If we live by the Spirit, let's also walk by the Spirit.

Responsorial Psalm: Psalms 1: 1-2, 3, 4 and 6

1 Blessed is the man who doesn't walk in the counsel of the wicked,
nor stand on the path of sinners,
nor sit in the seat of scoffers;
2 but his delight is in Yahweh's† law.
On his law he meditates day and night.
3 He will be like a tree planted by the streams of water,
that produces its fruit in its season,
whose leaf also does not wither.
Whatever he does shall prosper.
4 The wicked are not so,
but are like the chaff which the wind drives away.
6 For Yahweh knows the way of the righteous,
but the way of the wicked shall perish.

Gospel: Luke 11: 42-46

42 But woe to you Pharisees! For you tithe mint and rue and every herb, but you bypass justice and God's love. You ought to have done these, and not to have left the other undone. 43 Woe to you Pharisees! For you love the best seats in the synagogues and the greetings in the marketplaces. 44 Woe to you, scribes and Pharisees, hypocrites! For you are like hidden graves, and the men who walk over them don't know it."
45 One of the lawyers answered him, "Teacher, in saying this you insult us also."
46 He said, "Woe to you lawyers also! For you load men with burdens that are difficult to carry, and you yourselves won't even lift one finger to help carry those burdens.

1. Invite the Holy Spirit into this reading, asking the Author of Scripture to speak to you through His Word
2. Read today's passage as many times as you need, take your time
3. Write down (below) what the Lord is saying to you today
4. Live with this Word in your heart through the day

_____

_____

Thursday, October 17, 2024
Saint Ignatius of Antioch, Bishop and Martyr

First Reading: Ephesians 1: 1-10

1 Paul, an apostle of Christ† Jesus through the will of God, to the saints who are at Ephesus, and the faithful in Christ Jesus: 2 Grace to you and peace from God our Father and the Lord Jesus Christ.

3 Blessed be the God and Father of our Lord Jesus Christ, who has blessed us with every spiritual blessing in the heavenly places in Christ, 4 even as he chose us in him before the foundation of the world, that we would be holy and without defect before him in love, 5 having predestined us for adoption as children through Jesus Christ to himself, according to the good pleasure of his desire, 6 to the praise of the glory of his grace, by which he freely gave us favor in the Beloved. 7 In him we have our redemption through his blood, the forgiveness of our trespasses, according to the riches of his grace 8 which he made to abound toward us in all wisdom and prudence, 9 making known to us the mystery of his will, according to his good pleasure which he purposed in him 10 to an administration of the fullness of the times, to sum up all things in Christ, the things in the heavens and the things on the earth, in him.

Responsorial Psalm: Psalms 98: 1-6

1 Sing to Yahweh a new song,
for he has done marvelous things!
His right hand and his holy arm have worked salvation for him.
2 Yahweh has made known his salvation.
He has openly shown his righteousness in the sight of the nations.
3 He has remembered his loving kindness and his faithfulness toward the house of Israel.
All the ends of the earth have seen the salvation of our God.
4 Make a joyful noise to Yahweh, all the earth!
Burst out and sing for joy, yes, sing praises!

5 Sing praises to Yahweh with the harp,
with the harp and the voice of melody.
6 With trumpets and sound of the ram's horn,
make a joyful noise before the King, Yahweh.

Gospel: Luke 11: 47-54

47 Woe to you! For you build the tombs of the prophets, and your fathers killed them. 48 So you testify and consent to the works of your fathers. For they killed them, and you build their tombs. 49 Therefore also the wisdom of God said, 'I will send to them prophets and apostles; and some of them they will kill and persecute, 50 that the blood of all the prophets, which was shed from the foundation of the world, may be required of this generation, 51 from the blood of Abel to the blood of Zachariah, who perished between the altar and the sanctuary.' Yes, I tell you, it will be required of this generation. 52 Woe to you lawyers! For you took away the key of knowledge. You didn't enter in yourselves, and those who were entering in, you hindered."
53 As he said these things to them, the scribes and the Pharisees began to be terribly angry, and to draw many things out of him, 54 lying in wait for him, and seeking to catch him in something he might say, that they might accuse him.

1. Invite the Holy Spirit into this reading, asking the Author of Scripture to speak to you through His Word
2. Read today's passage as many times as you need, take your time
3. Write down (below) what the Lord is saying to you today
4. Live with this Word in your heart through the day

_____

_____

Friday, October 18, 2024
Saint Luke, Evangelist

First Reading: Second Timothy 4: 10-17b

10 for Demas left me, having loved this present world, and went to Thessalonica; Crescens to Galatia; and Titus to Dalmatia. 11 Only Luke is with me. Take Mark and bring him with you, for he is useful to me for service. 12 But I sent Tychicus to Ephesus. 13 Bring the cloak that I left at Troas with Carpus when you come—and the books, especially the parchments. 14 Alexander the coppersmith did much evil to me. The Lord will repay him according to his deeds. 15 Beware of him, for he greatly opposed our words.

16 At my first defense, no one came to help me, but all left me. May it not be held against them. 17 But the Lord stood by me and strengthened me, that through me the message might be fully proclaimed, and that all the Gentiles might hear.

Responsorial Psalm: Psalms 145: 10-13, 17-18

10 All your works will give thanks to you, Yahweh.
Your saints will extol you.
11 They will speak of the glory of your kingdom,
and talk about your power,
12 to make known to the sons of men his mighty acts,
the glory of the majesty of his kingdom.
13 Your kingdom is an everlasting kingdom.
Your dominion endures throughout all generations.
Yahweh is faithful in all his words,
and loving in all his deeds.‡
17 Yahweh is righteous in all his ways,
and gracious in all his works.
18 Yahweh is near to all those who call on him,
to all who call on him in truth.

Gospel: Luke 10: 1-9

1 Now after these things, the Lord also appointed seventy others, and sent them two by two ahead of him† into every city and place where he was about to come. 2 Then he said to them, "The harvest is indeed plentiful, but the laborers are few. Pray therefore to the Lord of the harvest, that he may send out laborers into his harvest. 3 Go your ways. Behold, I send you out as lambs among wolves. 4 Carry no purse, nor wallet, nor sandals. Greet no one on the way. 5 Into whatever house you enter, first say, 'Peace be to this house.' 6 If a son of peace is there, your peace will rest on him; but if not, it will return to you. 7 Remain in that same house, eating and drinking the things they give, for the laborer is worthy of his wages. Don't go from house to house. 8 Into whatever city you enter and they receive you, eat the things that are set before you. 9 Heal the sick who are there and tell them, 'God's Kingdom has come near to you.'

1. Invite the Holy Spirit into this reading, asking the Author of Scripture to speak to you through His Word
2. Read today's passage as many times as you need, take your time
3. Write down (below) what the Lord is saying to you today
4. Live with this Word in your heart through the day

_____

_____

Saturday, October 19, 2024
Saints John de Brébeuf and Isaac Jogues, Priests, red
and Companions, Martyrs

First Reading: Ephesians 1: 15-23

15 For this cause I also, having heard of the faith in the Lord Jesus which is among you and the love which you have toward all the saints, 16 don't cease to give thanks for you, making mention of you in my prayers, 17 that the God of our Lord Jesus Christ, the Father of glory, may give to you a spirit of wisdom and revelation in the knowledge of him, 18 having the eyes of your hearts‡ enlightened, that you may know what is the hope of his calling, and what are the riches of the glory of his inheritance in the saints, 19 and what is the exceeding greatness of his power toward us who believe, according to that working of the strength of his might 20 which he worked in Christ when he raised him from the dead and made him to sit at his right hand in the heavenly places, 21 far above all rule, authority, power, dominion, and every name that is named, not only in this age, but also in that which is to come. 22 He put all things in subjection under his feet, and gave him to be head over all things for the assembly, 23 which is his body, the fullness of him who fills all in all.

Responsorial Psalm: Psalms 8: 2-7

2 From the lips of babes and infants you have established strength,
because of your adversaries, that you might silence the enemy and the avenger.
3 When I consider your heavens, the work of your fingers,
the moon and the stars, which you have ordained,
4 what is man, that you think of him?
What is the son of man, that you care for him?
5 For you have made him a little lower than the angels,†
and crowned him with glory and honor.
6 You make him ruler over the works of your hands.
You have put all things under his feet:
7 All sheep and cattle,
yes, and the animals of the field,

Gospel: Luke 12: 8-12

8 "I tell you, everyone who confesses me before men, the Son of Man will also confess before the angels of God; 9 but he who denies me in the presence of men will be denied in the presence of God's angels. 10 Everyone who speaks a word against the Son of Man will be

forgiven, but those who blaspheme against the Holy Spirit will not be forgiven. 11 When they bring you before the synagogues, the rulers, and the authorities, don't be anxious how or what you will answer or what you will say; 12 for the Holy Spirit will teach you in that same hour what you must say."

1. Invite the Holy Spirit into this reading, asking the Author of Scripture to speak to you through His Word
2. Read today's passage as many times as you need, take your time
3. Write down (below) what the Lord is saying to you today
4. Live with this Word in your heart through the day

_____

_____

Sunday, October 20, 2024
TWENTY-NINTH SUNDAY IN ORDINARY TIME

First Reading: Isaiah 53: 10-11

10 Yet it pleased Yahweh to bruise him.
He has caused him to suffer.
When you make his soul an offering for sin,
he will see his offspring.
He will prolong his days
and Yahweh's pleasure will prosper in his hand.
11 After the suffering of his soul,
he will see the light† and be satisfied.
My righteous servant will justify many by the knowledge of himself;
and he will bear their iniquities.

Responsorial Psalm: Psalms 33: 4-5, 18-20, 22

4 For Yahweh's word is right.
All his work is done in faithfulness.
5 He loves righteousness and justice.
The earth is full of the loving kindness of Yahweh.
18 Behold, Yahweh's eye is on those who fear him,
on those who hope in his loving kindness,
19 to deliver their soul from death,
to keep them alive in famine.

20 Our soul has waited for Yahweh.
He is our help and our shield.
22 Let your loving kindness be on us, Yahweh,
since we have hoped in you.

Second Reading: Hebrews 4: 14-16

14 Having then a great high priest who has passed through the heavens, Jesus, the Son of God, let's hold tightly to our confession. 15 For we don't have a high priest who can't be touched with the feeling of our infirmities, but one who has been in all points tempted like we are, yet without sin. 16 Let's therefore draw near with boldness to the throne of grace, that we may receive mercy and may find grace for help in time of need.

Gospel: Mark 10: 42-45

42 Jesus summoned them and said to them, "You know that they who are recognized as rulers over the nations lord it over them, and their great ones exercise authority over them. 43 But it shall not be so among you, but whoever wants to become great among you shall be your servant. 44 Whoever of you wants to become first among you shall be bondservant of all. 45 For the Son of Man also came not to be served but to serve, and to give his life as a ransom for many."

1. Invite the Holy Spirit into this reading, asking the Author of Scripture to speak to you through His Word
2. Read today's passage as many times as you need, take your time
3. Write down (below) what the Lord is saying to you today
4. Live with this Word in your heart through the day

_____

_____

Monday, October 21, 2024

First Reading: Ephesians 2: 1-10

1 You were made alive when you were dead in transgressions and sins, 2 in which you once walked according to the course of this world, according to the prince of the power of the air, the spirit who now works in the children of disobedience. 3 We also all once lived among them in the lusts of our flesh, doing the desires of the flesh and of the mind, and were by nature children of wrath, even as the rest. 4 But God, being rich in mercy, for his great love with which

he loved us, 5 even when we were dead through our trespasses, made us alive together with Christ—by grace you have been saved— 6 and raised us up with him, and made us to sit with him in the heavenly places in Christ Jesus, 7 that in the ages to come he might show the exceeding riches of his grace in kindness toward us in Christ Jesus; 8 for by grace you have been saved through faith, and that not of yourselves; it is the gift of God, 9 not of works, that no one would boast. 10 For we are his workmanship, created in Christ Jesus for good works, which God prepared before that we would walk in them.

Responsorial Psalm: Psalms 100: 2-5

2 Serve Yahweh with gladness.
Come before his presence with singing.
3 Know that Yahweh, he is God.
It is he who has made us, and we are his.
We are his people, and the sheep of his pasture.
4 Enter into his gates with thanksgiving,
and into his courts with praise.
Give thanks to him, and bless his name.
5 For Yahweh is good.
His loving kindness endures forever,
his faithfulness to all generations.

Gospel: Luke 12: 13-21

13 One of the multitude said to him, "Teacher, tell my brother to divide the inheritance with me."
14 But he said to him, "Man, who made me a judge or an arbitrator over you?" 15 He said to them, "Beware! Keep yourselves from covetousness, for a man's life doesn't consist of the abundance of the things which he possesses."
16 He spoke a parable to them, saying, "The ground of a certain rich man produced abundantly. 17 He reasoned within himself, saying, 'What will I do, because I don't have room to store my crops?' 18 He said, 'This is what I will do. I will pull down my barns, build bigger ones, and there I will store all my grain and my goods. 19 I will tell my soul, "Soul, you have many goods laid up for many years. Take your ease, eat, drink, and be merry."'
20 "But God said to him, 'You foolish one, tonight your soul is required of you. The things which you have prepared—whose will they be?' 21 So is he who lays up treasure for himself, and is not rich toward God."

1. Invite the Holy Spirit into this reading, asking the Author of Scripture to speak to you through His Word
2. Read today's passage as many times as you need, take your time
3. Write down (below) what the Lord is saying to you today
4. Live with this Word in your heart through the day

Tuesday, October 22, 2024
Saint John Paul II, Pope

First Reading: Ephesians 2: 12-22

12 that you were at that time separate from Christ, alienated from the commonwealth of Israel, and strangers from the covenants of the promise, having no hope and without God in the world. 13 But now in Christ Jesus you who once were far off are made near in the blood of Christ. 14 For he is our peace, who made both one, and broke down the middle wall of separation, 15 having abolished in his flesh the hostility, the law of commandments contained in ordinances, that he might create in himself one new man of the two, making peace, 16 and might reconcile them both in one body to God through the cross, having killed the hostility through it. 17 He came and preached peace to you who were far off and to those who were near. 18 For through him we both have our access in one Spirit to the Father. 19 So then you are no longer strangers and foreigners, but you are fellow citizens with the saints and of the household of God, 20 being built on the foundation of the apostles and prophets, Christ Jesus himself being the chief cornerstone; 21 in whom the whole building, fitted together, grows into a holy temple in the Lord; 22 in whom you also are built together for a habitation of God in the Spirit.

Responsorial Psalm: Psalms 85: 9ab-13

9 Surely his salvation is near those who fear him,
that glory may dwell in our land.
10 Mercy and truth meet together.
Righteousness and peace have kissed each other.
11 Truth springs out of the earth.
Righteousness has looked down from heaven.
12 Yes, Yahweh will give that which is good.
Our land will yield its increase.
13 Righteousness goes before him,
and prepares the way for his steps.

Gospel: Luke 12: 35-38

35 "Let your waist be dressed and your lamps burning. 36 Be like men watching for their lord when he returns from the wedding feast, that when he comes and knocks, they may immediately open to him. 37 Blessed are those servants whom the lord will find watching when he comes. Most certainly I tell you that he will dress himself, make them recline, and will come and serve them. 38 They will be blessed if he comes in the second or third watch and finds them so.

Wednesday, October 23, 2024
Saint John of Capistrano, Priest

First Reading: Ephesians 3: 2-12

2 if it is so that you have heard of the administration of that grace of God which was given me toward you, 3 how that by revelation the mystery was made known to me, as I wrote before in few words, 4 by which, when you read, you can perceive my understanding in the mystery of Christ, 5 which in other generations was not made known to the children of men, as it has now been revealed to his holy apostles and prophets in the Spirit, 6 that the Gentiles are fellow heirs and fellow members of the body, and fellow partakers of his promise in Christ Jesus through the Good News, 7 of which I was made a servant according to the gift of that grace of God which was given me according to the working of his power. 8 To me, the very least of all saints, was this grace given, to preach to the Gentiles the unsearchable riches of Christ, 9 and to make all men see what is the administration† of the mystery which for ages has been hidden in God, who created all things through Jesus Christ, 10 to the intent that now through the assembly the manifold wisdom of God might be made known to the principalities and the powers in the heavenly places, 11 according to the eternal purpose which he accomplished in Christ Jesus our Lord. 12 In him we have boldness and access in confidence through our faith in him.

Responsorial Psalm: Isaiah 12: 2-3, 4bcd, 5-6

2 Behold, God is my salvation. I will trust, and will not be afraid; for Yah, Yahweh, is my strength and song; and he has become my salvation." 3 Therefore with joy you will draw water out of the wells of salvation. 4b "Give thanks to Yahweh! Call on his name! Declare his doings among the peoples! Proclaim that his name is exalted! 5 Sing to Yahweh, for he has done excellent things! Let this be known in all the earth! 6 Cry aloud and shout, you inhabitant of Zion, for the Holy One of Israel is great among you!"

Gospel: Luke 12: 39-48

39 But know this, that if the master of the house had known in what hour the thief was coming, he would have watched and not allowed his house to be broken into. 40 Therefore be ready also, for the Son of Man is coming in an hour that you don't expect him."
41 Peter said to him, "Lord, are you telling this parable to us, or to everybody?"
42 The Lord said, "Who then is the faithful and wise steward, whom his lord will set over his household, to give them their portion of food at the right times? 43 Blessed is that servant whom his lord will find doing so when he comes. 44 Truly I tell you that he will set him over all that he has. 45 But if that servant says in his heart, 'My lord delays his coming,' and begins to beat the menservants and the maidservants, and to eat and drink and to be drunken, 46 then the lord of that servant will come in a day when he isn't expecting him and in an hour that he doesn't know, and will cut him in two, and place his portion with the unfaithful. 47 That servant who knew his lord's will, and didn't prepare nor do what he wanted, will be beaten with many stripes, 48 but he who didn't know, and did things worthy of stripes, will be beaten with few stripes. To whomever much is given, of him will much be required; and to whom much was entrusted, of him more will be asked.

1. Invite the Holy Spirit into this reading, asking the Author of Scripture to speak to you through His Word
2. Read today's passage as many times as you need, take your time
3. Write down (below) what the Lord is saying to you today
4. Live with this Word in your heart through the day

_____

_____

Thursday, October 24, 2024
Saint Anthony Mary Claret, Bishop

First Reading: Ephesians 3: 14-21

14 For this cause, I bow my knees to the Father of our Lord Jesus Christ, 15 from whom every family in heaven and on earth is named, 16 that he would grant you, according to the riches of his glory, that you may be strengthened with power through his Spirit in the inner person, 17 that Christ may dwell in your hearts through faith, to the end that you, being rooted and grounded in love, 18 may be strengthened to comprehend with all the saints what is the width and length and height and depth, 19 and to know Christ's love which surpasses knowledge, that you may be filled with all the fullness of God.

20 Now to him who is able to do exceedingly abundantly above all that we ask or think, according to the power that works in us, 21 to him be the glory in the assembly and in Christ Jesus to all generations, forever and ever. Amen.

Responsorial Psalm: Psalms 33: 1-2, 4-5, 11-12, 18-19

1 Rejoice in Yahweh, you righteous!
Praise is fitting for the upright.
2 Give thanks to Yahweh with the lyre.
Sing praises to him with the harp of ten strings.
4 For Yahweh's word is right.
All his work is done in faithfulness.
5 He loves righteousness and justice.
The earth is full of the loving kindness of Yahweh.
11 The counsel of Yahweh stands fast forever,
the thoughts of his heart to all generations.
12 Blessed is the nation whose God is Yahweh,
the people whom he has chosen for his own inheritance.
18 Behold, Yahweh's eye is on those who fear him,
on those who hope in his loving kindness,
19 to deliver their soul from death,
to keep them alive in famine.

Gospel: Luke 12: 49-53

49 "I came to throw fire on the earth. I wish it were already kindled. 50 But I have a baptism to be baptized with, and how distressed I am until it is accomplished! 51 Do you think that I have come to give peace in the earth? I tell you, no, but rather division. 52 For from now on, there will be five in one house divided, three against two, and two against three. 53 They will be divided, father against son, and son against father; mother against daughter, and daughter against her mother; mother-in-law against her daughter-in-law, and daughter-in-law against her mother-in-law."

1. Invite the Holy Spirit into this reading, asking the Author of Scripture to speak to you through His Word
2. Read today's passage as many times as you need, take your time

3. Write down (below) what the Lord is saying to you today
4. Live with this Word in your heart through the day

Friday, October 25, 2024

First Reading: Ephesians 4: 1-6

1 I therefore, the prisoner in the Lord, beg you to walk worthily of the calling with which you were called, 2 with all lowliness and humility, with patience, bearing with one another in love, 3 being eager to keep the unity of the Spirit in the bond of peace. 4 There is one body and one Spirit, even as you also were called in one hope of your calling, 5 one Lord, one faith, one baptism, 6 one God and Father of all, who is over all and through all and in us all.

Responsorial Psalm: Psalms 24: 1-6

1 The earth is Yahweh's, with its fullness;
the world, and those who dwell in it.
2 For he has founded it on the seas,
and established it on the floods.
3 Who may ascend to Yahweh's hill?
Who may stand in his holy place?
4 He who has clean hands and a pure heart;
who has not lifted up his soul to falsehood,
and has not sworn deceitfully.
5 He shall receive a blessing from Yahweh,
righteousness from the God of his salvation.
6 This is the generation of those who seek Him,
who seek your face—even Jacob.

Gospel: Luke 12: 54-59

54 He said to the multitudes also, "When you see a cloud rising from the west, immediately you say, 'A shower is coming,' and so it happens. 55 When a south wind blows, you say, 'There will be a scorching heat,' and it happens. 56 You hypocrites! You know how to interpret the appearance of the earth and the sky, but how is it that you don't interpret this time?
57 "Why don't you judge for yourselves what is right? 58 For when you are going with your adversary before the magistrate, try diligently on the way to be released from him, lest perhaps he drag you to the judge, and the judge deliver you to the officer, and the officer throw you

into prison. 59 I tell you, you will by no means get out of there until you have paid the very last penny.†"

Saturday, October 26, 2024

First Reading: Ephesians 4: 7-16

7 But to each one of us, the grace was given according to the measure of the gift of Christ. 8 Therefore he says,
"When he ascended on high,
he led captivity captive,
and gave gifts to people."*
9 Now this, "He ascended", what is it but that he also first descended into the lower parts of the earth? 10 He who descended is the one who also ascended far above all the heavens, that he might fill all things.
11 He gave some to be apostles; and some, prophets; and some, evangelists; and some, shepherds† and teachers; 12 for the perfecting of the saints, to the work of serving, to the building up of the body of Christ, 13 until we all attain to the unity of the faith and of the knowledge of the Son of God, to a full grown man, to the measure of the stature of the fullness of Christ, 14 that we may no longer be children, tossed back and forth and carried about with every wind of doctrine, by the trickery of men, in craftiness, after the wiles of error; 15 but speaking truth in love, we may grow up in all things into him who is the head, Christ, 16 from whom all the body, being fitted and knit together through that which every joint supplies, according to the working in measure of each individual part, makes the body increase to the building up of itself in love.

Responsorial Psalm: Psalms 122: 1-5

1 I was glad when they said to me,
"Let's go to Yahweh's house!"
2 Our feet are standing within your gates, Jerusalem!

3 Jerusalem is built as a city that is compact together,
4 where the tribes go up, even Yah's tribes,
according to an ordinance for Israel,
to give thanks to Yahweh's name.
5 For there are set thrones for judgment,
the thrones of David's house.

Gospel: Luke 13: 1-9

1 Now there were some present at the same time who told him about the Galileans whose blood Pilate had mixed with their sacrifices. 2 Jesus answered them, "Do you think that these Galileans were worse sinners than all the other Galileans, because they suffered such things? 3 I tell you, no, but unless you repent, you will all perish in the same way. 4 Or those eighteen on whom the tower in Siloam fell and killed them—do you think that they were worse offenders than all the men who dwell in Jerusalem? 5 I tell you, no, but, unless you repent, you will all perish in the same way."
6 He spoke this parable. "A certain man had a fig tree planted in his vineyard, and he came seeking fruit on it and found none. 7 He said to the vine dresser, 'Behold, these three years I have come looking for fruit on this fig tree, and found none. Cut it down! Why does it waste the soil?' 8 He answered, 'Lord, leave it alone this year also, until I dig around it and fertilize it. 9 If it bears fruit, fine; but if not, after that, you can cut it down.'"

1. Invite the Holy Spirit into this reading, asking the Author of Scripture to speak to you through His Word
2. Read today's passage as many times as you need, take your time
3. Write down (below) what the Lord is saying to you today
4. Live with this Word in your heart through the day

_____

_____

Sunday, October 27, 2024
THIRTIETH SUNDAY IN ORDINARY TIME

First Reading: Jeremiah 31: 7-9

7 For Yahweh says,
"Sing with gladness for Jacob,
and shout for the chief of the nations.
Publish, praise, and say,

'Yahweh, save your people,
the remnant of Israel!'
8 Behold, I will bring them from the north country,
and gather them from the uttermost parts of the earth,
along with the blind and the lame,
the woman with child and her who travails with child together.
They will return as a great company.
9 They will come with weeping.
I will lead them with petitions.
I will cause them to walk by rivers of waters,
in a straight way in which they won't stumble;
for I am a father to Israel.
Ephraim is my firstborn.

Responsorial Psalm: Psalms 126: 1-6

1 When Yahweh brought back those who returned to Zion,
we were like those who dream.
2 Then our mouth was filled with laughter,
and our tongue with singing.
Then they said among the nations,
"Yahweh has done great things for them."
3 Yahweh has done great things for us,
and we are glad.
4 Restore our fortunes again, Yahweh,
like the streams in the Negev.
5 Those who sow in tears will reap in joy.
6 He who goes out weeping, carrying seed for sowing,
will certainly come again with joy, carrying his sheaves.

Second Reading: Hebrews 5: 1-6

1 For every high priest, being taken from among men, is appointed for men in things pertaining to God, that he may offer both gifts and sacrifices for sins. 2 The high priest can deal gently with those who are ignorant and going astray, because he himself is also surrounded with weakness. 3 Because of this, he must offer sacrifices for sins for the people, as well as for himself. 4 Nobody takes this honor on himself, but he is called by God, just like Aaron was. 5 So also Christ didn't glorify himself to be made a high priest, but it was he who said to him,
"You are my Son.
Today I have become your father."*
6 As he says also in another place,
"You are a priest forever,

after the order of Melchizedek."

Gospel: Mark 10: 46-52

46 They came to Jericho. As he went out from Jericho with his disciples and a great multitude, the son of Timaeus, Bartimaeus, a blind beggar, was sitting by the road. 47 When he heard that it was Jesus the Nazarene, he began to cry out and say, "Jesus, you son of David, have mercy on me!" 48 Many rebuked him, that he should be quiet, but he cried out much more, "You son of David, have mercy on me!"
49 Jesus stood still and said, "Call him."
They called the blind man, saying to him, "Cheer up! Get up. He is calling you!"
50 He, casting away his cloak, sprang up, and came to Jesus.
51 Jesus asked him, "What do you want me to do for you?"
The blind man said to him, "Rabboni,† that I may see again."
52 Jesus said to him, "Go your way. Your faith has made you well." Immediately he received his sight and followed Jesus on the way.

1. Invite the Holy Spirit into this reading, asking the Author of Scripture to speak to you through His Word
2. Read today's passage as many times as you need, take your time
3. Write down (below) what the Lord is saying to you today
4. Live with this Word in your heart through the day

_____

_____

Monday, October 28, 2024
Saints Simon and Jude, Apostles

First Reading: Ephesians 2: 19-22

19 So then you are no longer strangers and foreigners, but you are fellow citizens with the saints and of the household of God, 20 being built on the foundation of the apostles and prophets, Christ Jesus himself being the chief cornerstone; 21 in whom the whole building, fitted together, grows into a holy temple in the Lord; 22 in whom you also are built together for a habitation of God in the Spirit.

Responsorial Psalm: Psalms 19: 2-5

2 Day after day they pour out speech,

and night after night they display knowledge.
3 There is no speech nor language
where their voice is not heard.
4 Their voice has gone out through all the earth,
their words to the end of the world.
In them he has set a tent for the sun,
5 which is as a bridegroom coming out of his room,
like a strong man rejoicing to run his course.

Gospel: Luke 6: 12-16

12 In these days, he went out to the mountain to pray, and he continued all night in prayer to God. 13 When it was day, he called his disciples, and from them he chose twelve, whom he also named apostles: 14 Simon, whom he also named Peter; Andrew, his brother; James; John; Philip; Bartholomew; 15 Matthew; Thomas; James the son of Alphaeus; Simon who was called the Zealot; 16 Judas the son of James; and Judas Iscariot, who also became a traitor.

1. Invite the Holy Spirit into this reading, asking the Author of Scripture to speak to you through His Word
2. Read today's passage as many times as you need, take your time
3. Write down (below) what the Lord is saying to you today
4. Live with this Word in your heart through the day

_____

_____

Tuesday, October 29, 2024
Saints Simon and Jude, Apostles

First Reading: Ephesians 5: 21-33

21 subjecting yourselves to one another in the fear of Christ.
22 Wives, be subject to your own husbands, as to the Lord. 23 For the husband is the head of the wife, as Christ also is the head of the assembly, being himself the savior of the body. 24 But as the assembly is subject to Christ, so let the wives also be to their own husbands in everything.
25 Husbands, love your wives, even as Christ also loved the assembly and gave himself up for her, 26 that he might sanctify her, having cleansed her by the washing of water with the word, 27 that he might present the assembly to himself gloriously, not having spot or wrinkle or any such thing, but that she should be holy and without defect. 28 Even so husbands also ought to

love their own wives as their own bodies. He who loves his own wife loves himself. 29 For no man ever hated his own flesh, but nourishes and cherishes it, even as the Lord also does the assembly, 30 because we are members of his body, of his flesh and bones. 31 "For this cause a man will leave his father and mother and will be joined to his wife. Then the two will become one flesh."* 32 This mystery is great, but I speak concerning Christ and the assembly. 33 Nevertheless each of you must also love his own wife even as himself; and let the wife see that she respects her husband.

Responsorial Psalm: Psalms 128: 1-5

1 Blessed is everyone who fears Yahweh,
who walks in his ways.
2 For you will eat the labor of your hands.
You will be happy, and it will be well with you.
3 Your wife will be as a fruitful vine in the innermost parts of your house,
your children like olive shoots around your table.
4 Behold, this is how the man who fears Yahweh is blessed.
5 May Yahweh bless you out of Zion,
and may you see the good of Jerusalem all the days of your life.

Gospel: Luke 13: 18-21

18 He said, "What is God's Kingdom like? To what shall I compare it? 19 It is like a grain of mustard seed which a man took and put in his own garden. It grew and became a large tree, and the birds of the sky live in its branches."
20 Again he said, "To what shall I compare God's Kingdom? 21 It is like yeast, which a woman took and hid in three measures † of flour, until it was all leavened."

1. Invite the Holy Spirit into this reading, asking the Author of Scripture to speak to you through His Word
2. Read today's passage as many times as you need, take your time
3. Write down (below) what the Lord is saying to you today
4. Live with this Word in your heart through the day

_____

_____

Wednesday, October 30, 2024

First Reading: Ephesians 6: 1-9

1 Children, obey your parents in the Lord, for this is right. 2 "Honor your father and mother," which is the first commandment with a promise: 3 "that it may be well with you, and you may live long on the earth." *

4 You fathers, don't provoke your children to wrath, but nurture them in the discipline and instruction of the Lord.

5 Servants, be obedient to those who according to the flesh are your masters, with fear and trembling, in singleness of your heart, as to Christ, 6 not in the way of service only when eyes are on you, as men pleasers, but as servants of Christ, doing the will of God from the heart, 7 with good will doing service as to the Lord and not to men, 8 knowing that whatever good thing each one does, he will receive the same good again from the Lord, whether he is bound or free.

9 You masters, do the same things to them, and give up threatening, knowing that he who is both their Master and yours is in heaven, and there is no partiality with him.

Responsorial Psalm: Psalms 145: 10-14

10 All your works will give thanks to you, Yahweh.
Your saints will extol you.
11 They will speak of the glory of your kingdom,
and talk about your power,
12 to make known to the sons of men his mighty acts,
the glory of the majesty of his kingdom.
13 Your kingdom is an everlasting kingdom.
Your dominion endures throughout all generations.
Yahweh is faithful in all his words,
and loving in all his deeds.‡
14 Yahweh upholds all who fall,
and raises up all those who are bowed down.

Gospel: Luke 13: 22-30

22 He went on his way through cities and villages, teaching, and traveling on to Jerusalem. 23 One said to him, "Lord, are they few who are saved?"
He said to them, 24 "Strive to enter in by the narrow door, for many, I tell you, will seek to enter in and will not be able. 25 When once the master of the house has risen up and has shut the door, and you begin to stand outside and to knock at the door, saying, 'Lord, Lord, open to us!' then he will answer and tell you, 'I don't know you or where you come from.' 26 Then you will begin to say, 'We ate and drank in your presence, and you taught in our streets.' 27 He will say, 'I tell you, I don't know where you come from. Depart from me, all you workers of iniquity.' 28 There will be weeping and gnashing of teeth when you see Abraham, Isaac, Jacob, and all the prophets in God's Kingdom, and yourselves being thrown outside. 29 They will come from the east, west, north, and south, and will sit down in God's Kingdom. 30 Behold,

there are some who are last who will be first, and there are some who are first who will be last."

_____

_____

Thursday, October 31, 2024

First Reading: Ephesians 6: 10-20

10 Finally, be strong in the Lord and in the strength of his might. 11 Put on the whole armor of God, that you may be able to stand against the wiles of the devil. 12 For our wrestling is not against flesh and blood, but against the principalities, against the powers, against the world's rulers of the darkness of this age, and against the spiritual forces of wickedness in the heavenly places. 13 Therefore put on the whole armor of God, that you may be able to withstand in the evil day, and having done all, to stand. 14 Stand therefore, having the utility belt of truth buckled around your waist, and having put on the breastplate of righteousness, 15 and having fitted your feet with the preparation of the Good News of peace, 16 above all, taking up the shield of faith, with which you will be able to quench all the fiery darts of the evil one. 17 And take the helmet of salvation, and the sword of the Spirit, which is the word† of God; 18 with all prayer and requests, praying at all times in the Spirit, and being watchful to this end in all perseverance and requests for all the saints. 19 Pray for me, that utterance may be given to me in opening my mouth, to make known with boldness the mystery of the Good News, 20 for which I am an ambassador in chains; that in it I may speak boldly, as I ought to speak.

Responsorial Psalm: Psalms 144: 1-2, 9-10

1 Blessed be Yahweh, my rock,
who trains my hands to war,
and my fingers to battle—
2 my loving kindness, my fortress,
my high tower, my deliverer,
my shield, and he in whom I take refuge,
who subdues my people under me.

9 I will sing a new song to you, God.
On a ten-stringed lyre, I will sing praises to you.
10 You are he who gives salvation to kings,
who rescues David, his servant, from the deadly sword.

Gospel: Luke 13: 31-35

31 On that same day, some Pharisees came, saying to him, "Get out of here and go away, for Herod wants to kill you."
32 He said to them, "Go and tell that fox, 'Behold, I cast out demons and perform cures today and tomorrow, and the third day I complete my mission. 33 Nevertheless I must go on my way today and tomorrow and the next day, for it can't be that a prophet would perish outside of Jerusalem.'
34 "Jerusalem, Jerusalem, you who kills the prophets and stones those who are sent to her! How often I wanted to gather your children together, like a hen gathers her own brood under her wings, and you refused! 35 Behold, your house is left to you desolate. I tell you, you will not see me until you say, 'Blessed is he who comes in the name of the Lord!' "

1. Invite the Holy Spirit into this reading, asking the Author of Scripture to speak to you through His Word
2. Read today's passage as many times as you need, take your time
3. Write down (below) what the Lord is saying to you today
4. Live with this Word in your heart through the day

Friday, November 1, 2024
ALL SAINTS

First Reading: Revelation 7: 2-4, 9-14

2 I saw another angel ascend from the sunrise, having the seal of the living God. He cried with a loud voice to the four angels to whom it was given to harm the earth and the sea, 3 saying, "Don't harm the earth, the sea, or the trees, until we have sealed the bondservants of our God on their foreheads!" 4 I heard the number of those who were sealed, one hundred forty-four thousand, sealed out of every tribe of the children of Israel
9 After these things I looked, and behold, a great multitude which no man could count, out of every nation and of all tribes, peoples, and languages, standing before the throne and before the Lamb, dressed in white robes, with palm branches in their hands. 10 They cried with a loud voice, saying, "Salvation be to our God, who sits on the throne, and to the Lamb!"

11 All the angels were standing around the throne, the elders, and the four living creatures; and they fell on their faces before his throne, and worshiped God, 12 saying, "Amen! Blessing, glory, wisdom, thanksgiving, honor, power, and might, be to our God forever and ever! Amen."

13 One of the elders answered, saying to me, "These who are arrayed in the white robes, who are they, and where did they come from?"

14 I told him, "My lord, you know."

He said to me, "These are those who came out of the great suffering.† They washed their robes and made them white in the Lamb's blood.

Responsorial Psalm: Psalms 24: 1b-6

1 The earth is Yahweh's, with its fullness;
the world, and those who dwell in it.
2 For he has founded it on the seas,
and established it on the floods.
 3 Who may ascend to Yahweh's hill?
Who may stand in his holy place?
4 He who has clean hands and a pure heart;
who has not lifted up his soul to falsehood,
and has not sworn deceitfully.
5 He shall receive a blessing from Yahweh,
righteousness from the God of his salvation.
6 This is the generation of those who seek Him,
who seek your face—even Jacob.

Second Reading: First John 3: 1-3

1 See how great a love the Father has given to us, that we should be called children of God! For this cause the world doesn't know us, because it didn't know him. 2 Beloved, now we are children of God. It is not yet revealed what we will be; but we know that when he is revealed, we will be like him, for we will see him just as he is. 3 Everyone who has this hope set on him purifies himself, even as he is pure.

Gospel: Matthew 5: 1-12a

1 Seeing the multitudes, he went up onto the mountain. When he had sat down, his disciples came to him. 2 He opened his mouth and taught them, saying,
3 "Blessed are the poor in spirit,
for theirs is the Kingdom of Heaven.*
4 Blessed are those who mourn,
for they shall be comforted.*
5 Blessed are the gentle,
for they shall inherit the earth.†*
6 Blessed are those who hunger and thirst for righteousness,

for they shall be filled.
7 Blessed are the merciful,
for they shall obtain mercy.
8 Blessed are the pure in heart,
for they shall see God.
9 Blessed are the peacemakers,
for they shall be called children of God.
10 Blessed are those who have been persecuted for righteousness' sake,
for theirs is the Kingdom of Heaven.
11 "Blessed are you when people reproach you, persecute you, and say all kinds of evil against you falsely, for my sake. 12 Rejoice, and be exceedingly glad, for great is your reward in heaven. For that is how they persecuted the prophets who were before you.

1. Invite the Holy Spirit into this reading, asking the Author of Scripture to speak to you through His Word
2. Read today's passage as many times as you need, take your time
3. Write down (below) what the Lord is saying to you today
4. Live with this Word in your heart through the day

_____

_____

Saturday, November 2, 2024
The Commemoration of All the Faithful Departed
(All Souls' Day)

First Reading: Wisdom 3: 1-9

1 But the souls of the righteous are in the hand of God,
and no torment will touch them.
2 In the eyes of the foolish they seemed to have died.
Their departure was considered a disaster,
3 and their travel away from us ruin,
but they are in peace.
4 For even if in the sight of men they are punished,
their hope is full of immortality.
5 Having borne a little chastening, they will receive great good;
because God tested them, and found them worthy of himself.
6 He tested them like gold in the furnace,
and he accepted them as a whole burnt offering.

7 In the time of their visitation they will shine.
They will run back and forth like sparks among stubble.
8 They will judge nations and have dominion over peoples.
The Lord will reign over them forever.
9 Those who trust him will understand truth.
The faithful will live with him in love,
because grace and mercy are with his chosen ones.

Responsorial Psalm: Psalms 23: 1-6

1 Yahweh is my shepherd;
I shall lack nothing.
2 He makes me lie down in green pastures.
He leads me beside still waters.
3 He restores my soul.
He guides me in the paths of righteousness for his name's sake.
4 Even though I walk through the valley of the shadow of death,
I will fear no evil, for you are with me.
Your rod and your staff,
they comfort me.
5 You prepare a table before me
in the presence of my enemies.
You anoint my head with oil.
My cup runs over.
6 Surely goodness and loving kindness shall follow me all the days of my life,
and I will dwell in Yahweh's house forever.

Second Reading: Romans 5: 5-11

5 and hope doesn't disappoint us, because God's love has been poured into our hearts through the Holy Spirit who was given to us.
6 For while we were yet weak, at the right time Christ died for the ungodly. 7 For one will hardly die for a righteous man. Yet perhaps for a good person someone would even dare to die. 8 But God commends his own love toward us, in that while we were yet sinners, Christ died for us.
9 Much more then, being now justified by his blood, we will be saved from God's wrath through him. 10 For if while we were enemies, we were reconciled to God through the death of his Son, much more, being reconciled, we will be saved by his life.
11 Not only so, but we also rejoice in God through our Lord Jesus Christ, through whom we have now received the reconciliation.

Gospel: John 6: 37-40

37 All those whom the Father gives me will come to me. He who comes to me I will in no way throw out. 38 For I have come down from heaven, not to do my own will, but the will of him who sent me. 39 This is the will of my Father who sent me, that of all he has given to me I should lose nothing, but should raise him up at the last day. 40 This is the will of the one who sent me, that everyone who sees the Son and believes in him should have eternal life; and I will raise him up at the last day."

1. Invite the Holy Spirit into this reading, asking the Author of Scripture to speak to you through His Word
2. Read today's passage as many times as you need, take your time
3. Write down (below) what the Lord is saying to you today
4. Live with this Word in your heart through the day

_____

_____

Sunday, November 3, 2024
THIRTY-FIRST SUNDAY IN ORDINARY TIME

First Reading: Deuteronomy 6: 2-6

2 that you might fear Yahweh your God, to keep all his statutes and his commandments, which I command you—you, your son, and your son's son, all the days of your life; and that your days may be prolonged. 3 Hear therefore, Israel, and observe to do it, that it may be well with you, and that you may increase mightily, as Yahweh, the God of your fathers, has promised to you, in a land flowing with milk and honey.
4 Hear, Israel: Yahweh is our God. Yahweh is one. 5 You shall love Yahweh your God with all your heart, with all your soul, and with all your might. 6 These words, which I command you today, shall be on your heart;

Responsorial Psalm: Psalms 18: 2-4, 47, 50

2 Yahweh is my rock, my fortress, and my deliverer;
my God, my rock, in whom I take refuge;
my shield, and the horn of my salvation, my high tower.
3 I call on Yahweh, who is worthy to be praised;
and I am saved from my enemies.
4 The cords of death surrounded me.
The floods of ungodliness made me afraid.
47 even the God who executes vengeance for me,

and subdues peoples under me.
50 He gives great deliverance to his king,
and shows loving kindness to his anointed,
to David and to his offspring,‡ forever more.

Second Reading: Hebrews 7: 23-28

23 Many, indeed, have been made priests, because they are hindered from continuing by death. 24 But he, because he lives forever, has his priesthood unchangeable. 25 Therefore he is also able to save to the uttermost those who draw near to God through him, seeing that he lives forever to make intercession for them.
26 For such a high priest was fitting for us: holy, guiltless, undefiled, separated from sinners, and made higher than the heavens; 27 who doesn't need, like those high priests, to offer up sacrifices daily, first for his own sins, and then for the sins of the people. For he did this once for all, when he offered up himself. 28 For the law appoints men as high priests who have weakness, but the word of the oath, which came after the law, appoints a Son forever who has been perfected.

Gospel: Mark 12: 28b-34

28 One of the scribes came and heard them questioning together, and knowing that he had answered them well, asked him, "Which commandment is the greatest of all?"
29 Jesus answered, "The greatest is: 'Hear, Israel, the Lord our God, the Lord is one. 30 You shall love the Lord your God with all your heart, with all your soul, with all your mind, and with all your strength.'* This is the first commandment. 31 The second is like this: 'You shall love your neighbor as yourself.'* There is no other commandment greater than these."
32 The scribe said to him, "Truly, teacher, you have said well that he is one, and there is none other but he; 33 and to love him with all the heart, with all the understanding, all the soul, and with all the strength, and to love his neighbor as himself, is more important than all whole burnt offerings and sacrifices."
34 When Jesus saw that he answered wisely, he said to him, "You are not far from God's Kingdom."
No one dared ask him any question after that.

1. Invite the Holy Spirit into this reading, asking the Author of Scripture to speak to you through His Word
2. Read today's passage as many times as you need, take your time
3. Write down (below) what the Lord is saying to you today
4. Live with this Word in your heart through the day

_____

_____

Monday, November 4, 2024
Saint Charles Borromeo, Bishop

First Reading: Philippians 2: 1-4

1 If therefore there is any exhortation in Christ, if any consolation of love, if any fellowship of the Spirit, if any tender mercies and compassion, 2 make my joy full by being like-minded, having the same love, being of one accord, of one mind; 3 doing nothing through rivalry or through conceit, but in humility, each counting others better than himself; 4 each of you not just looking to his own things, but each of you also to the things of others.

Responsorial Psalm: Psalms 131: 1-3

1 Yahweh, my heart isn't arrogant, nor my eyes lofty;
nor do I concern myself with great matters,
or things too wonderful for me.
2 Surely I have stilled and quieted my soul,
like a weaned child with his mother,
like a weaned child is my soul within me.
3 Israel, hope in Yahweh,
from this time forward and forever more.

Gospel: Luke 14: 12-14

12 He also said to the one who had invited him, "When you make a dinner or a supper, don't call your friends, nor your brothers, nor your kinsmen, nor rich neighbors, or perhaps they might also return the favor, and pay you back. 13 But when you make a feast, ask the poor, the maimed, the lame, or the blind; 14 and you will be blessed, because they don't have the resources to repay you. For you will be repaid in the resurrection of the righteous."

1. Invite the Holy Spirit into this reading, asking the Author of Scripture to speak to you through His Word
2. Read today's passage as many times as you need, take your time
3. Write down (below) what the Lord is saying to you today
4. Live with this Word in your heart through the day

_____

_____

Tuesday, November 5, 2024

First Reading: Philippians 2: 5-11

5 Have this in your mind, which was also in Christ Jesus, 6 who, existing in the form of God, didn't consider equality with God a thing to be grasped, 7 but emptied himself, taking the form of a servant, being made in the likeness of men. 8 And being found in human form, he humbled himself, becoming obedient to the point of death, yes, the death of the cross. 9 Therefore God also highly exalted him, and gave to him the name which is above every name, 10 that at the name of Jesus every knee should bow, of those in heaven, those on earth, and those under the earth, 11 and that every tongue should confess that Jesus Christ is Lord, to the glory of God the Father.

Responsorial Psalm: Psalms 22: 26b-31

26 The humble shall eat and be satisfied.
They shall praise Yahweh who seek after him.
Let your hearts live forever.
27 All the ends of the earth shall remember and turn to Yahweh.
All the relatives of the nations shall worship before you.
28 For the kingdom is Yahweh's.
He is the ruler over the nations.
29 All the rich ones of the earth shall eat and worship.
All those who go down to the dust shall bow before him,
even he who can't keep his soul alive.
30 Posterity shall serve him.
Future generations shall be told about the Lord.
31 They shall come and shall declare his righteousness to a people that shall be born,
for he has done it.

Gospel: Luke 14: 15-24

15 When one of those who sat at the table with him heard these things, he said to him, "Blessed is he who will feast in God's Kingdom!"
16 But he said to him, "A certain man made a great supper, and he invited many people. 17 He sent out his servant at supper time to tell those who were invited, 'Come, for everything is ready now.' 18 They all as one began to make excuses.
"The first said to him, 'I have bought a field, and I must go and see it. Please have me excused.'
19 "Another said, 'I have bought five yoke of oxen, and I must go try them out. Please have me excused.'
20 "Another said, 'I have married a wife, and therefore I can't come.'

21 "That servant came, and told his lord these things. Then the master of the house, being angry, said to his servant, 'Go out quickly into the streets and lanes of the city, and bring in the poor, maimed, blind, and lame.'

Wednesday, November 6, 2024

First Reading: Philippians 2: 12-18

12 So then, my beloved, even as you have always obeyed, not only in my presence, but now much more in my absence, work out your own salvation with fear and trembling. 13 For it is God who works in you both to will and to work for his good pleasure.
14 Do all things without complaining and arguing, 15 that you may become blameless and harmless, children of God without defect in the middle of a crooked and perverse generation, among whom you are seen as lights in the world, 16 holding up the word of life, that I may have something to boast in the day of Christ that I didn't run in vain nor labor in vain. 17 Yes, and if I am poured out on the sacrifice and service of your faith, I am glad and rejoice with you all. 18 In the same way, you also should be glad and rejoice with me.

Responsorial Psalm: Psalms 27: 1, 4, 13-14

1 Yahweh is my light and my salvation.
Whom shall I fear?
Yahweh is the strength of my life.
Of whom shall I be afraid?
4 One thing I have asked of Yahweh, that I will seek after:
that I may dwell in Yahweh's house all the days of my life,
to see Yahweh's beauty,
and to inquire in his temple.
13 I am still confident of this:
I will see the goodness of Yahweh in the land of the living.
14 Wait for Yahweh.

Be strong, and let your heart take courage.
Yes, wait for Yahweh.

Gospel: Luke 14: 25-33

25 Now great multitudes were going with him. He turned and said to them, 26 "If anyone comes to me, and doesn't disregard‡ his own father, mother, wife, children, brothers, and sisters, yes, and his own life also, he can't be my disciple. 27 Whoever doesn't bear his own cross and come after me, can't be my disciple. 28 For which of you, desiring to build a tower, doesn't first sit down and count the cost, to see if he has enough to complete it? 29 Or perhaps, when he has laid a foundation and isn't able to finish, everyone who sees begins to mock him, 30 saying, 'This man began to build and wasn't able to finish.' 31 Or what king, as he goes to encounter another king in war, will not sit down first and consider whether he is able with ten thousand to meet him who comes against him with twenty thousand? 32 Or else, while the other is yet a great way off, he sends an envoy and asks for conditions of peace. 33 So therefore, whoever of you who doesn't renounce all that he has, he can't be my disciple.

1. Invite the Holy Spirit into this reading, asking the Author of Scripture to speak to you through His Word
2. Read today's passage as many times as you need, take your time
3. Write down (below) what the Lord is saying to you today
4. Live with this Word in your heart through the day

_____

_____

Thursday, November 7, 2024

First Reading: Philippians 3: 3-8a

3 For we are the circumcision, who worship God in the Spirit, and rejoice in Christ Jesus, and have no confidence in the flesh; 4 though I myself might have confidence even in the flesh. If any other man thinks that he has confidence in the flesh, I yet more: 5 circumcised the eighth day, of the stock of Israel, of the tribe of Benjamin, a Hebrew of Hebrews; concerning the law, a Pharisee; 6 concerning zeal, persecuting the assembly; concerning the righteousness which is in the law, found blameless.
7 However, I consider those things that were gain to me as a loss for Christ. 8 Yes most certainly, and I count all things to be a loss for the excellency of the knowledge of Christ Jesus, my Lord, for whom I suffered the loss of all things, and count them nothing but refuse, that I may gain Christ

Responsorial Psalm: Psalms 105: 2-7

2 Sing to him, sing praises to him!
Tell of all his marvelous works.
3 Glory in his holy name.
Let the heart of those who seek Yahweh rejoice.
4 Seek Yahweh and his strength.
Seek his face forever more.
5 Remember his marvelous works that he has done:
his wonders, and the judgments of his mouth,
6 you offspring of Abraham, his servant,
you children of Jacob, his chosen ones.
7 He is Yahweh, our God.
His judgments are in all the earth.

Gospel: Luke 15: 1-10

1 Now all the tax collectors and sinners were coming close to him to hear him. 2 The Pharisees and the scribes murmured, saying, "This man welcomes sinners, and eats with them."
3 He told them this parable: 4 "Which of you men, if you had one hundred sheep and lost one of them, wouldn't leave the ninety-nine in the wilderness and go after the one that was lost, until he found it? 5 When he has found it, he carries it on his shoulders, rejoicing. 6 When he comes home, he calls together his friends and his neighbors, saying to them, 'Rejoice with me, for I have found my sheep which was lost!' 7 I tell you that even so there will be more joy in heaven over one sinner who repents, than over ninety-nine righteous people who need no repentance.
8 "Or what woman, if she had ten drachma† coins, if she lost one drachma coin, wouldn't light a lamp, sweep the house, and seek diligently until she found it? 9 When she has found it, she calls together her friends and neighbors, saying, 'Rejoice with me, for I have found the drachma which I had lost!' 10 Even so, I tell you, there is joy in the presence of the angels of God over one sinner repenting."

1. Invite the Holy Spirit into this reading, asking the Author of Scripture to speak to you through His Word
2. Read today's passage as many times as you need, take your time
3. Write down (below) what the Lord is saying to you today
4. Live with this Word in your heart through the day

Friday, November 8, 2024

First Reading: Philippians 3: 17 – 4: 1

17 Brothers, be imitators together of me, and note those who walk this way, even as you have us for an example. 18 For many walk, of whom I told you often, and now tell you even weeping, as the enemies of the cross of Christ, 19 whose end is destruction, whose god is the belly, and whose glory is in their shame, who think about earthly things. 20 For our citizenship is in heaven, from where we also wait for a Savior, the Lord Jesus Christ, 21 who will change the body of our humiliation to be conformed to the body of his glory, according to the working by which he is able even to subject all things to himself.
1 Therefore, my brothers, beloved and longed for, my joy and crown, stand firm in the Lord in this way, my beloved.

Responsorial Psalm: Psalms 122: 1-5

1 I was glad when they said to me,
"Let's go to Yahweh's house!"
2 Our feet are standing within your gates, Jerusalem!
3 Jerusalem is built as a city that is compact together,
4 where the tribes go up, even Yah's tribes,
according to an ordinance for Israel,
to give thanks to Yahweh's name.
5 For there are set thrones for judgment,
the thrones of David's house.

Gospel: Luke 16: 1-8

1 He also said to his disciples, "There was a certain rich man who had a manager. An accusation was made to him that this man was wasting his possessions. 2 He called him, and said to him, 'What is this that I hear about you? Give an accounting of your management, for you can no longer be manager.'
3 "The manager said within himself, 'What will I do, seeing that my lord is taking away the management position from me? I don't have strength to dig. I am ashamed to beg. 4 I know what I will do, so that when I am removed from management, they may receive me into their houses.' 5 Calling each one of his lord's debtors to him, he said to the first, 'How much do you owe to my lord?' 6 He said, 'A hundred batos† of oil.' He said to him, 'Take your bill, and sit down quickly and write fifty.' 7 Then he said to another, 'How much do you owe?' He said, 'A hundred cors‡ of wheat.' He said to him, 'Take your bill, and write eighty.'
8 "His lord commended the dishonest manager because he had done wisely, for the children of this world are, in their own generation, wiser than the children of the light.

_____

_____

Saturday, November 9, 2024
The Dedication of the Lateran Basilica

First Reading: Ezekiel 47: 1-2, 8-9, 12

1 He brought me back to the door of the temple; and behold, waters flowed out from under the threshold of the temple eastward, for the front of the temple faced toward the east. The waters came down from underneath, from the right side of the temple, on the south of the altar. 2 Then he brought me out by the way of the gate northward, and led me around by the way outside to the outer gate, by the way of the gate that looks toward the east. Behold, waters ran out on the right side.

8 Then he said to me, "These waters flow out toward the eastern region and will go down into the Arabah. Then they will go toward the sea and flow into the sea which will be made to flow out; and the waters will be healed. 9 It will happen that every living creature which swarms, in every place where the rivers come, will live. Then there will be a very great multitude of fish; for these waters have come there, and the waters of the sea will be healed, and everything will live wherever the river comes.

12 By the river banks, on both sides, will grow every tree for food, whose leaf won't wither, neither will its fruit fail. It will produce new fruit every month, because its waters issue out of the sanctuary. Its fruit will be for food, and its leaf for healing."

Responsorial Psalm: Psalms 46: 2-3, 5-6, 8-9

2 Therefore we won't be afraid, though the earth changes,
though the mountains are shaken into the heart of the seas;
3 though its waters roar and are troubled,
though the mountains tremble with their swelling.
5 God is within her. She shall not be moved.
God will help her at dawn.
6 The nations raged. The kingdoms were moved.
He lifted his voice and the earth melted.

8 Come, see Yahweh's works,
what desolations he has made in the earth.
9 He makes wars cease to the end of the earth.
He breaks the bow, and shatters the spear.
He burns the chariots in the fire.

Second Reading: First Corinthians 3: 9c-11, 16-17

9c You are God's farming, God's building. 10 According to the grace of God which was given to me, as a wise master builder I laid a foundation, and another builds on it. But let each man be careful how he builds on it. 11 For no one can lay any other foundation than that which has been laid, which is Jesus Christ.
16 Don't you know that you are God's temple and that God's Spirit lives in you? 17 If anyone destroys God's temple, God will destroy him; for God's temple is holy, which you are.

Gospel: John 2: 13-22

13 The Passover of the Jews was at hand, and Jesus went up to Jerusalem. 14 He found in the temple those who sold oxen, sheep, and doves, and the changers of money sitting. 15 He made a whip of cords and drove all out of the temple, both the sheep and the oxen; and he poured out the changers' money and overthrew their tables. 16 To those who sold the doves, he said, "Take these things out of here! Don't make my Father's house a marketplace!" 17 His disciples remembered that it was written, "Zeal for your house will eat me up."*
18 The Jews therefore answered him, "What sign do you show us, seeing that you do these things?"
19 Jesus answered them, "Destroy this temple, and in three days I will raise it up."
20 The Jews therefore said, "It took forty-six years to build this temple! Will you raise it up in three days?" 21 But he spoke of the temple of his body. 22 When therefore he was raised from the dead, his disciples remembered that he said this, and they believed the Scripture and the word which Jesus had said.

1. Invite the Holy Spirit into this reading, asking the Author of Scripture to speak to you through His Word
2. Read today's passage as many times as you need, take your time
3. Write down (below) what the Lord is saying to you today
4. Live with this Word in your heart through the day

_____

_____

Sunday, November 10, 2024
THIRTY-SECOND SUNDAY IN ORDINARY TIME

First Reading: First Kings 17: 10-16

10 So he arose and went to Zarephath; and when he came to the gate of the city, behold, a widow was there gathering sticks. He called to her and said, "Please get me a little water in a jar, that I may drink."

11 As she was going to get it, he called to her and said, "Please bring me a morsel of bread in your hand."

12 She said, "As Yahweh your God lives, I don't have anything baked, but only a handful of meal in a jar and a little oil in a jar. Behold, I am gathering two sticks, that I may go in and bake it for me and my son, that we may eat it, and die."

13 Elijah said to her, "Don't be afraid. Go and do as you have said; but make me a little cake from it first, and bring it out to me, and afterward make some for you and for your son. 14 For Yahweh, the God of Israel, says, 'The jar of meal will not run out, and the jar of oil will not fail, until the day that Yahweh sends rain on the earth.' "

15 She went and did according to the saying of Elijah; and she, he, and her household ate many days. 16 The jar of meal didn't run out and the jar of oil didn't fail, according to Yahweh's word, which he spoke by Elijah.

Responsorial Psalm: Psalms 146: 7-10

7 who executes justice for the oppressed;
who gives food to the hungry.
Yahweh frees the prisoners.
8 Yahweh opens the eyes of the blind.
Yahweh raises up those who are bowed down.
Yahweh loves the righteous.
9 Yahweh preserves the foreigners.
He upholds the fatherless and widow,
but he turns the way of the wicked upside down.
10 Yahweh will reign forever;
your God, O Zion, to all generations.
Praise Yah!

Second Reading: Hebrews 9: 24-28

24 For Christ hasn't entered into holy places made with hands, which are representations of the true, but into heaven itself, now to appear in the presence of God for us; 25 nor yet that he should offer himself often, as the high priest enters into the holy place year by year with blood not his own, 26 or else he must have suffered often since the foundation of the world. But now

513

once at the end of the ages, he has been revealed to put away sin by the sacrifice of himself. 27 Inasmuch as it is appointed for men to die once, and after this, judgment, 28 so Christ also, having been offered once to bear the sins of many, will appear a second time, not to deal with sin, but to save those who are eagerly waiting for him.

Gospel: Mark 12: 41-44

41 Jesus sat down opposite the treasury and saw how the multitude cast money into the treasury. Many who were rich cast in much. 42 A poor widow came and she cast in two small brass coins,† which equal a quadrans coin.‡ 43 He called his disciples to himself and said to them, "Most certainly I tell you, this poor widow gave more than all those who are giving into the treasury, 44 for they all gave out of their abundance, but she, out of her poverty, gave all that she had to live on."

1. Invite the Holy Spirit into this reading, asking the Author of Scripture to speak to you through His Word
2. Read today's passage as many times as you need, take your time
3. Write down (below) what the Lord is saying to you today
4. Live with this Word in your heart through the day

_____

_____

Monday, November 11, 2024
Saint Martin of Tours, Bishop

First Reading: Titus 1: 1-9

1 Paul, a servant of God and an apostle of Jesus Christ,† according to the faith of God's chosen ones and the knowledge of the truth which is according to godliness, 2 in hope of eternal life, which God, who can't lie, promised before time began; 3 but in his own time revealed his word in the message with which I was entrusted according to the commandment of God our Savior, 4 to Titus, my true child according to a common faith: Grace, mercy, and peace from God the Father and the Lord Jesus Christ our Savior.
5 I left you in Crete for this reason, that you would set in order the things that were lacking and appoint elders in every city, as I directed you— 6 if anyone is blameless, the husband of one wife, having children who believe, who are not accused of loose or unruly behavior. 7 For the overseer must be blameless, as God's steward, not self-pleasing, not easily angered, not given to wine, not violent, not greedy for dishonest gain; 8 but given to hospitality, a lover of good, sober minded, fair, holy, self-controlled, 9 holding to the faithful word which is

according to the teaching, that he may be able to exhort in the sound doctrine, and to convict those who contradict him.

Responsorial Psalm: Psalms 24: 1b-6

1 The earth is Yahweh's, with its fullness;
the world, and those who dwell in it.
2 For he has founded it on the seas,
and established it on the floods.
3 Who may ascend to Yahweh's hill?
Who may stand in his holy place?
4 He who has clean hands and a pure heart;
who has not lifted up his soul to falsehood,
and has not sworn deceitfully.
5 He shall receive a blessing from Yahweh,
righteousness from the God of his salvation.
6 This is the generation of those who seek Him,
who seek your face—even Jacob.

Gospel: Luke 17: 1-6

1 He said to the disciples, "It is impossible that no occasions of stumbling should come, but woe to him through whom they come! 2 It would be better for him if a millstone were hung around his neck, and he were thrown into the sea, rather than that he should cause one of these little ones to stumble. 3 Be careful. If your brother sins against you, rebuke him. If he repents, forgive him. 4 If he sins against you seven times in the day, and seven times returns, saying, 'I repent,' you shall forgive him."
5 The apostles said to the Lord, "Increase our faith."
6 The Lord said, "If you had faith like a grain of mustard seed, you would tell this sycamore tree, 'Be uprooted and be planted in the sea,' and it would obey you.

1. Invite the Holy Spirit into this reading, asking the Author of Scripture to speak to you through His Word
2. Read today's passage as many times as you need, take your time
3. Write down (below) what the Lord is saying to you today
4. Live with this Word in your heart through the day

Tuesday, November 12, 2024
Saint Josaphat, Bishop and Martyr

First Reading: Titus 2: 1-8, 11-14

1 But say the things which fit sound doctrine, 2 that older men should be temperate, sensible, sober minded, sound in faith, in love, and in perseverance, 3 and that older women likewise be reverent in behavior, not slanderers nor enslaved to much wine, teachers of that which is good, 4 that they may train the young wives to love their husbands, to love their children, 5 to be sober minded, chaste, workers at home, kind, being in subjection to their own husbands, that God's word may not be blasphemed.

6 Likewise, exhort the younger men to be sober minded. 7 In all things show yourself an example of good works. In your teaching, show integrity, seriousness, incorruptibility, 8 and soundness of speech that can't be condemned, that he who opposes you may be ashamed, having no evil thing to say about us.

11 For the grace of God has appeared, bringing salvation to all men, 12 instructing us to the intent that, denying ungodliness and worldly lusts, we would live soberly, righteously, and godly in this present age; 13 looking for the blessed hope and appearing of the glory of our great God and Savior, Jesus Christ, 14 who gave himself for us, that he might redeem us from all iniquity and purify for himself a people for his own possession, zealous for good works.

Responsorial Psalm: Psalms 37: 3-4, 18 and 23, 27 and 29

3 Trust in Yahweh, and do good.
Dwell in the land, and enjoy safe pasture.
4 Also delight yourself in Yahweh,
and he will give you the desires of your heart.
18 Yahweh knows the days of the perfect.
Their inheritance shall be forever.
23 A man's steps are established by Yahweh.
He delights in his way.
27 Depart from evil, and do good.
Live securely forever.
29 The righteous shall inherit the land,
and live in it forever.

Gospel: Luke 17: 7-10

7 But who is there among you, having a servant plowing or keeping sheep, that will say when he comes in from the field, 'Come immediately and sit down at the table'? 8 Wouldn't he rather tell him, 'Prepare my supper, clothe yourself properly, and serve me while I eat and drink. Afterward you shall eat and drink'? 9 Does he thank that servant because he did the

things that were commanded? I think not. 10 Even so you also, when you have done all the things that are commanded you, say, 'We are unworthy servants. We have done our duty.' "

1. Invite the Holy Spirit into this reading, asking the Author of Scripture to speak to you through His Word
2. Read today's passage as many times as you need, take your time
3. Write down (below) what the Lord is saying to you today
4. Live with this Word in your heart through the day

Wednesday, November 13, 2024
Saint Frances Xavier Cabrini, Virgin

First Reading: Titus 3: 1-7

1 Remind them to be in subjection to rulers and to authorities, to be obedient, to be ready for every good work, 2 to speak evil of no one, not to be contentious, to be gentle, showing all humility toward all men. 3 For we were also once foolish, disobedient, deceived, serving various lusts and pleasures, living in malice and envy, hateful, and hating one another. 4 But when the kindness of God our Savior and his love toward mankind appeared, 5 not by works of righteousness which we did ourselves, but according to his mercy, he saved us through the washing of regeneration and renewing by the Holy Spirit, 6 whom he poured out on us richly through Jesus Christ our Savior; 7 that being justified by his grace, we might be made heirs according to the hope of eternal life.

Responsorial Psalm: Psalms 23: 1b-6

1 Yahweh is my shepherd;
I shall lack nothing.
2 He makes me lie down in green pastures.
He leads me beside still waters.
3 He restores my soul.
He guides me in the paths of righteousness for his name's sake.
4 Even though I walk through the valley of the shadow of death,
I will fear no evil, for you are with me.
Your rod and your staff,
they comfort me.
5 You prepare a table before me

in the presence of my enemies.
You anoint my head with oil.
My cup runs over.
6 Surely goodness and loving kindness shall follow me all the days of my life,
and I will dwell in Yahweh's house forever.

Gospel: Luke 17: 11-19

11 As he was on his way to Jerusalem, he was passing along the borders of Samaria and Galilee.
12 As he entered into a certain village, ten men who were lepers met him, who stood at a distance. 13 They lifted up their voices, saying, "Jesus, Master, have mercy on us!"
14 When he saw them, he said to them, "Go and show yourselves to the priests." As they went, they were cleansed. 15 One of them, when he saw that he was healed, turned back, glorifying God with a loud voice. 16 He fell on his face at Jesus' feet, giving him thanks; and he was a Samaritan.
17 Jesus answered, "Weren't the ten cleansed? But where are the nine? 18 Were there none found who returned to give glory to God, except this foreigner?" 19 Then he said to him, "Get up, and go your way. Your faith has healed you."

1. Invite the Holy Spirit into this reading, asking the Author of Scripture to speak to you through His Word
2. Read today's passage as many times as you need, take your time
3. Write down (below) what the Lord is saying to you today
4. Live with this Word in your heart through the day

_____

_____

Thursday, November 14, 2024

First Reading: Philemon 1: 7-20

7 For we have much joy and comfort in your love, because the hearts of the saints have been refreshed through you, brother.
8 Therefore though I have all boldness in Christ to command you that which is appropriate, 9 yet for love's sake I rather appeal to you, being such a one as Paul, the aged, but also a prisoner of Jesus Christ. 10 I appeal to you for my child Onesimus, whom I have become the father of in my chains,‡ 11 who once was useless to you, but now is useful to you and to me. 12 I am sending him back. Therefore receive him, that is, my own heart, 13 whom I desired to keep with me, that on your behalf he might serve me in my chains for the Good News. 14 But I was

willing to do nothing without your consent, that your goodness would not be as of necessity, but of free will. 15 For perhaps he was therefore separated from you for a while that you would have him forever, 16 no longer as a slave, but more than a slave, a beloved brother—especially to me, but how much rather to you, both in the flesh and in the Lord.

17 If then you count me a partner, receive him as you would receive me. 18 But if he has wronged you at all or owes you anything, put that to my account. 19 I, Paul, write this with my own hand: I will repay it (not to mention to you that you owe to me even your own self besides). 20 Yes, brother, let me have joy from you in the Lord. Refresh my heart in the Lord.

Responsorial Psalm: Psalms 146: 7-10

7 who executes justice for the oppressed;
who gives food to the hungry.
Yahweh frees the prisoners.
8 Yahweh opens the eyes of the blind.
Yahweh raises up those who are bowed down.
Yahweh loves the righteous.
9 Yahweh preserves the foreigners.
He upholds the fatherless and widow,
but he turns the way of the wicked upside down.
10 Yahweh will reign forever;
your God, O Zion, to all generations.
Praise Yah!

Gospel: Luke 17: 20-25

20 Being asked by the Pharisees when God's Kingdom would come, he answered them, "God's Kingdom doesn't come with observation; 21 neither will they say, 'Look, here!' or, 'Look, there!' for behold, God's Kingdom is within you."
22 He said to the disciples, "The days will come when you will desire to see one of the days of the Son of Man, and you will not see it. 23 They will tell you, 'Look, here!' or 'Look, there!' Don't go away or follow after them, 24 for as the lightning, when it flashes out of one part under the sky, shines to another part under the sky, so will the Son of Man be in his day. 25 But first, he must suffer many things and be rejected by this generation.

1. Invite the Holy Spirit into this reading, asking the Author of Scripture to speak to you through His Word
2. Read today's passage as many times as you need, take your time
3. Write down (below) what the Lord is saying to you today
4. Live with this Word in your heart through the day

Friday, November 15, 2024
Saint Albert the Great, Bishop and Doctor of the Church

First Reading: Second John 1: 4-9

4 I rejoice greatly that I have found some of your children walking in truth, even as we have been commanded by the Father. 5 Now I beg you, dear lady, not as though I wrote to you a new commandment, but that which we had from the beginning, that we love one another. 6 This is love, that we should walk according to his commandments. This is the commandment, even as you heard from the beginning, that you should walk in it.
7 For many deceivers have gone out into the world, those who don't confess that Jesus Christ came in the flesh. This is the deceiver and the Antichrist. 8 Watch yourselves, that we don't lose the things which we have accomplished, but that we receive a full reward. 9 Whoever transgresses and doesn't remain in the teaching of Christ doesn't have God. He who remains in the teaching has both the Father and the Son.

Responsorial Psalm: Psalms 119: 1, 2, 10, 11, 17, 18

1 Blessed are those whose ways are blameless,
who walk according to Yahweh's law.
2 Blessed are those who keep his statutes,
who seek him with their whole heart.
10 With my whole heart I have sought you.
Don't let me wander from your commandments.
11 I have hidden your word in my heart,
that I might not sin against you.
17 Do good to your servant.
I will live and I will obey your word.
18 Open my eyes,
that I may see wondrous things out of your law.

Gospel: Luke 17: 26-37

26 As it was in the days of Noah, even so it will also be in the days of the Son of Man. 27 They ate, they drank, they married, and they were given in marriage until the day that Noah entered into the ship, and the flood came and destroyed them all. 28 Likewise, even as it was in the days of Lot: they ate, they drank, they bought, they sold, they planted, they built; 29 but in the day that Lot went out from Sodom, it rained fire and sulfur from the sky and destroyed them all. 30 It will be the same way in the day that the Son of Man is revealed. 31 In that day, he who will be on the housetop and his goods in the house, let him not go down to take them away. Let him who is in the field likewise not turn back. 32 Remember Lot's wife! 33 Whoever seeks to save his life loses it, but whoever loses his life preserves it. 34 I tell you, in that night

there will be two people in one bed. One will be taken and the other will be left. 35 There will be two grinding grain together. One will be taken and the other will be left." 36
37 They, answering, asked him, "Where, Lord?"
He said to them, "Where the body is, there the vultures will also be gathered together."

1. Invite the Holy Spirit into this reading, asking the Author of Scripture to speak to you through His Word
2. Read today's passage as many times as you need, take your time
3. Write down (below) what the Lord is saying to you today
4. Live with this Word in your heart through the day

_____

_____

Saturday, November 16, 2024
Saint Margaret of Scotland; Saint Gertrude, Virgin; BVM

First Reading: Third John 1: 5-8

5 Beloved, you do a faithful work in whatever you accomplish for those who are brothers and strangers. 6 They have testified about your love before the assembly. You will do well to send them forward on their journey in a way worthy of God, 7 because for the sake of the Name they went out, taking nothing from the Gentiles. 8 We therefore ought to receive such, that we may be fellow workers for the truth.

Responsorial Psalm: Psalms 112: 1-6

1 Praise Yah!†
Blessed is the man who fears Yahweh,
who delights greatly in his commandments.
2 His offspring will be mighty in the land.
The generation of the upright will be blessed.
3 Wealth and riches are in his house.
His righteousness endures forever.
4 Light dawns in the darkness for the upright,
gracious, merciful, and righteous.
5 It is well with the man who deals graciously and lends.
He will maintain his cause in judgment.
6 For he will never be shaken.

The righteous will be remembered forever.

Gospel: Luke 18: 1-8

1 He also spoke a parable to them that they must always pray and not give up, 2 saying, "There was a judge in a certain city who didn't fear God and didn't respect man. 3 A widow was in that city, and she often came to him, saying, 'Defend me from my adversary!' 4 He wouldn't for a while; but afterward he said to himself, 'Though I neither fear God nor respect man, 5 yet because this widow bothers me, I will defend her, or else she will wear me out by her continual coming.' "
6 The Lord said, "Listen to what the unrighteous judge says. 7 Won't God avenge his chosen ones who are crying out to him day and night, and yet he exercises patience with them? 8 I tell you that he will avenge them quickly. Nevertheless, when the Son of Man comes, will he find faith on the earth?"

1. Invite the Holy Spirit into this reading, asking the Author of Scripture to speak to you through His Word
2. Read today's passage as many times as you need, take your time
3. Write down (below) what the Lord is saying to you today
4. Live with this Word in your heart through the day

_____

_____

Sunday, November 17, 2024
THIRTY-THIRD SUNDAY IN ORDINARY TIME'

First Reading: Daniel 12: 1-3

1 "At that time Michael will stand up, the great prince who stands for the children of your people; and there will be a time of trouble, such as never was since there was a nation even to that same time. At that time your people will be delivered, everyone who is found written in the book. 2 Many of those who sleep in the dust of the earth will awake, some to everlasting life, and some to shame and everlasting contempt. 3 Those who are wise will shine as the brightness of the expanse. Those who turn many to righteousness will shine as the stars forever and ever.

Responsorial Psalm: Psalms 16: 5, 8- 11

5 Yahweh assigned my portion and my cup.

You made my lot secure.

8 I have set Yahweh always before me.

Because he is at my right hand, I shall not be moved.

9 Therefore my heart is glad, and my tongue rejoices.

My body shall also dwell in safety.

10 For you will not leave my soul in Sheol,†

neither will you allow your holy one to see corruption.

11 You will show me the path of life.

In your presence is fullness of joy.

In your right hand there are pleasures forever more.

Second Reading: Hebrews 10: 11-14, 18

11 Every priest indeed stands day by day serving and offering often the same sacrifices, which can never take away sins, 12 but he, when he had offered one sacrifice for sins forever, sat down on the right hand of God, 13 from that time waiting until his enemies are made the footstool of his feet. 14 For by one offering he has perfected forever those who are being sanctified.

18 Now where remission of these is, there is no more offering for sin.

Gospel: Mark 13: 24-32

24 But in those days, after that oppression, the sun will be darkened, the moon will not give its light, 25 the stars will be falling from the sky, and the powers that are in the heavens will be shaken.* 26 Then they will see the Son of Man coming in clouds with great power and glory. 27 Then he will send out his angels, and will gather together his chosen ones from the four winds, from the ends of the earth to the ends of the sky.

28 "Now from the fig tree, learn this parable. When the branch has now become tender and produces its leaves, you know that the summer is near; 29 even so you also, when you see these things coming to pass, know that it is near, at the doors. 30 Most certainly I say to you, this generation‡ will not pass away until all these things happen. 31 Heaven and earth will pass away, but my words will not pass away.

32 "But of that day or that hour no one knows—not even the angels in heaven, nor the Son, but only the Father.

1. Invite the Holy Spirit into this reading, asking the Author of Scripture to speak to you through His Word

2. Read today's passage as many times as you need, take your time

3. Write down (below) what the Lord is saying to you today

4. Live with this Word in your heart through the day

Monday, November 18, 2024
The Dedication of the Basilicas of Saints Peter and Paul, Apostles;
USA: Saint Rose Philippine Duchesne, Virgin

First Reading: Revelation 1: 1-4; 2: 1-5

1 This is the Revelation of Jesus Christ,† which God gave him to show to his servants the things which must happen soon, which he sent and made known by his angel‡ to his servant, John,
2 who testified to God's word and of the testimony of Jesus Christ, about everything that he saw.
3 Blessed is he who reads and those who hear the words of the prophecy, and keep the things that are written in it, for the time is near.
4 John, to the seven assemblies that are in Asia: Grace to you and peace from God, who is and who was and who is to come; and from the seven Spirits who are before his throne;
1 "To the angel of the assembly in Ephesus write:
"He who holds the seven stars in his right hand, he who walks among the seven golden lamp stands says these things:
2 "I know your works, and your toil and perseverance, and that you can't tolerate evil men, and have tested those who call themselves apostles, and they are not, and found them false. 3 You have perseverance and have endured for my name's sake, and have † not grown weary. 4 But I have this against you, that you left your first love. 5 Remember therefore from where you have fallen, and repent and do the first works; or else I am coming to you swiftly, and will move your lamp stand out of its place, unless you repent.

Responsorial Psalm: Psalms 1: 1-4 and 6

1 Blessed is the man who doesn't walk in the counsel of the wicked,
nor stand on the path of sinners,
nor sit in the seat of scoffers;
2 but his delight is in Yahweh's† law.
On his law he meditates day and night.
3 He will be like a tree planted by the streams of water,
that produces its fruit in its season,
whose leaf also does not wither.
Whatever he does shall prosper.
4 The wicked are not so,
but are like the chaff which the wind drives away.
6 For Yahweh knows the way of the righteous,
but the way of the wicked shall perish.

Gospel: Luke 18: 35-43

35 As he came near Jericho, a certain blind man sat by the road, begging. 36 Hearing a multitude going by, he asked what this meant. 37 They told him that Jesus of Nazareth was passing by. 38 He cried out, "Jesus, you son of David, have mercy on me!" 39 Those who led the way rebuked him, that he should be quiet; but he cried out all the more, "You son of David, have mercy on me!"

40 Standing still, Jesus commanded him to be brought to him. When he had come near, he asked him, 41 "What do you want me to do?"

He said, "Lord, that I may see again."

42 Jesus said to him, "Receive your sight. Your faith has healed you."

43 Immediately he received his sight and followed him, glorifying God. All the people, when they saw it, praised God.

1. Invite the Holy Spirit into this reading, asking the Author of Scripture to speak to you through His Word
2. Read today's passage as many times as you need, take your time
3. Write down (below) what the Lord is saying to you today
4. Live with this Word in your heart through the day

Tuesday, November 19, 2024

First Reading: Revelation 3: 1-6, 14-22

1 "And to the angel of the assembly in Sardis write:
"He who has the seven Spirits of God and the seven stars says these things:
"I know your works, that you have a reputation of being alive, but you are dead. 2 Wake up and strengthen the things that remain, which you were about to throw away,† for I have found no works of yours perfected before my God. 3 Remember therefore how you have received and heard. Keep it and repent. If therefore you won't watch, I will come as a thief, and you won't know what hour I will come upon you. 4 Nevertheless you have a few names in Sardis that didn't defile their garments. They will walk with me in white, for they are worthy. 5 He who overcomes will be arrayed in white garments, and I will in no way blot his name out of the book of life, and I will confess his name before my Father, and before his angels. 6 He who has an ear, let him hear what the Spirit says to the assemblies.

14 "To the angel of the assembly in Laodicea write:
"The Amen, the Faithful and True Witness, the Beginning‡ of God's creation, says these things:

15 "I know your works, that you are neither cold nor hot. I wish you were cold or hot. 16 So, because you are lukewarm, and neither hot nor cold, I will vomit you out of my mouth. 17 Because you say, 'I am rich, and have gotten riches, and have need of nothing,' and don't know that you are the wretched one, miserable, poor, blind, and naked; 18 I counsel you to buy from me gold refined by fire, that you may become rich; and white garments, that you may clothe yourself, and that the shame of your nakedness may not be revealed; and eye salve to anoint your eyes, that you may see. 19 As many as I love, I reprove and chasten. Be zealous therefore, and repent. 20 Behold, I stand at the door and knock. If anyone hears my voice and opens the door, then I will come in to him and will dine with him, and he with me. 21 He who overcomes, I will give to him to sit down with me on my throne, as I also overcame and sat down with my Father on his throne. 22 He who has an ear, let him hear what the Spirit says to the assemblies."

Responsorial Psalm: Psalms 15: 2-5

2 He who walks blamelessly and does what is right,
and speaks truth in his heart;
3 he who doesn't slander with his tongue,
nor does evil to his friend,
nor casts slurs against his fellow man;
4 in whose eyes a vile man is despised,
but who honors those who fear Yahweh;
he who keeps an oath even when it hurts, and doesn't change;
5 he who doesn't lend out his money for usury,
nor take a bribe against the innocent.

Gospel: Luke 19: 1-10

1 He entered and was passing through Jericho. 2 There was a man named Zacchaeus. He was a chief tax collector, and he was rich. 3 He was trying to see who Jesus was, and couldn't because of the crowd, because he was short. 4 He ran on ahead and climbed up into a sycamore tree to see him, for he was going to pass that way. 5 When Jesus came to the place, he looked up and saw him, and said to him, "Zacchaeus, hurry and come down, for today I must stay at your house." 6 He hurried, came down, and received him joyfully. 7 When they saw it, they all murmured, saying, "He has gone in to lodge with a man who is a sinner."
8 Zacchaeus stood and said to the Lord, "Behold, Lord, half of my goods I give to the poor. If I have wrongfully exacted anything of anyone, I restore four times as much."
9 Jesus said to him, "Today, salvation has come to this house, because he also is a son of Abraham. 10 For the Son of Man came to seek and to save that which was lost."

1. Invite the Holy Spirit into this reading, asking the Author of Scripture to speak to you through His Word
2. Read today's passage as many times as you need, take your time

3. Write down (below) what the Lord is saying to you today
4. Live with this Word in your heart through the day

_____

_____

Wednesday, November 20, 2024

First Reading: Revelation 4: 1-11

1 After these things I looked and saw a door opened in heaven; and the first voice that I heard, like a trumpet speaking with me, was one saying, "Come up here, and I will show you the things which must happen after this."
2 Immediately I was in the Spirit. Behold, there was a throne set in heaven, and one sitting on the throne 3 that looked like a jasper stone and a sardius. There was a rainbow around the throne, like an emerald to look at. 4 Around the throne were twenty-four thrones. On the thrones were twenty-four elders sitting, dressed in white garments, with crowns of gold on their heads. 5 Out of the throne proceed lightnings, sounds, and thunders. There were seven lamps of fire burning before his throne, which are the seven Spirits of God. 6 Before the throne was something like a sea of glass, similar to crystal. In the middle of the throne, and around the throne were four living creatures full of eyes before and behind. 7 The first creature was like a lion, the second creature like a calf, the third creature had a face like a man, and the fourth was like a flying eagle. 8 The four living creatures, each one of them having six wings, are full of eyes around and within. They have no rest day and night, saying, "Holy, holy, holy† is the Lord God, the Almighty, who was and who is and who is to come!"
9 When the living creatures give glory, honor, and thanks to him who sits on the throne, to him who lives forever and ever, 10 the twenty-four elders fall down before him who sits on the throne and worship him who lives forever and ever, and throw their crowns before the throne, saying, 11 "Worthy are you, our Lord and God, the Holy One,‡ to receive the glory, the honor, and the power, for you created all things, and because of your desire they existed and were created!"

Responsorial Psalm: Psalms 150: 1b-6

1 Praise God in his sanctuary!
Praise him in his heavens for his acts of power!
2 Praise him for his mighty acts!
Praise him according to his excellent greatness!
3 Praise him with the sounding of the trumpet!
Praise him with harp and lyre!

4 Praise him with tambourine and dancing!
Praise him with stringed instruments and flute!
5 Praise him with loud cymbals!
Praise him with resounding cymbals!
6 Let everything that has breath praise Yah!
Praise Yah!

Gospel: Luke 19: 11-28

11 As they heard these things, he went on and told a parable, because he was near Jerusalem, and they supposed that God's Kingdom would be revealed immediately. 12 He said therefore, "A certain nobleman went into a far country to receive for himself a kingdom and to return. 13 He called ten servants of his and gave them ten mina coins, † and told them, 'Conduct business until I come.' 14 But his citizens hated him, and sent an envoy after him, saying, 'We don't want this man to reign over us.'

15 "When he had come back again, having received the kingdom, he commanded these servants, to whom he had given the money, to be called to him, that he might know what they had gained by conducting business. 16 The first came before him, saying, 'Lord, your mina has made ten more minas.'

17 "He said to him, 'Well done, you good servant! Because you were found faithful with very little, you shall have authority over ten cities.'

18 "The second came, saying, 'Your mina, Lord, has made five minas.'

19 "So he said to him, 'And you are to be over five cities.'

20 Another came, saying, 'Lord, behold, your mina, which I kept laid away in a handkerchief, 21 for I feared you, because you are an exacting man. You take up that which you didn't lay down, and reap that which you didn't sow.'

22 "He said to him, 'Out of your own mouth I will judge you, you wicked servant! You knew that I am an exacting man, taking up that which I didn't lay down and reaping that which I didn't sow. 23 Then why didn't you deposit my money in the bank, and at my coming, I might have earned interest on it?' 24 He said to those who stood by, 'Take the mina away from him and give it to him who has the ten minas.'

25 "They said to him, 'Lord, he has ten minas!' 26 'For I tell you that to everyone who has, will more be given; but from him who doesn't have, even that which he has will be taken away from him. 27 But bring those enemies of mine who didn't want me to reign over them here, and kill them before me.' " 28 Having said these things, he went on ahead, going up to Jerusalem.

1. Invite the Holy Spirit into this reading, asking the Author of Scripture to speak to you through His Word
2. Read today's passage as many times as you need, take your time
3. Write down (below) what the Lord is saying to you today
4. Live with this Word in your heart through the day

Thursday, November 21, 2024

The Presentation of the Blessed Virgin Mary

First Reading: Revelation 5: 1-10

1 I saw, in the right hand of him who sat on the throne, a book written inside and outside, sealed shut with seven seals. 2 I saw a mighty angel proclaiming with a loud voice, "Who is worthy to open the book, and to break its seals?" 3 No one in heaven above, or on the earth, or under the earth, was able to open the book or to look in it. 4 Then I wept much, because no one was found worthy to open the book or to look in it. 5 One of the elders said to me, "Don't weep. Behold, the Lion who is of the tribe of Judah, the Root of David, has overcome: he who opens the book and its seven seals."

6 I saw in the middle of the throne and of the four living creatures, and in the middle of the elders, a Lamb standing, as though it had been slain, having seven horns and seven eyes, which are the seven Spirits of God, sent out into all the earth. 7 Then he came, and he took it out of the right hand of him who sat on the throne. 8 Now when he had taken the book, the four living creatures and the twenty-four elders fell down before the Lamb, each one having a harp, and golden bowls full of incense, which are the prayers of the saints. 9 They sang a new song, saying,

"You are worthy to take the book
and to open its seals,
for you were killed,
and bought us for God with your blood
out of every tribe, language, people, and nation,
10 and made us kings and priests to our God;
and we will reign on the earth."

Responsorial Psalm: Psalms 149: 1b-6a and 9b

1 Sing to Yahweh a new song,
his praise in the assembly of the saints.
2 Let Israel rejoice in him who made them.
Let the children of Zion be joyful in their King.
3 Let them praise his name in the dance!
Let them sing praises to him with tambourine and harp!
4 For Yahweh takes pleasure in his people.
He crowns the humble with salvation.
5 Let the saints rejoice in honor.

Let them sing for joy on their beds.
6 May the high praises of God be in their mouths,
9b All his saints have this honor.
Praise Yah!

Gospel: Luke 19: 41-44

41 When he came near, he saw the city and wept over it, 42 saying, "If you, even you, had known today the things which belong to your peace! But now, they are hidden from your eyes. 43 For the days will come on you when your enemies will throw up a barricade against you, surround you, hem you in on every side, 44 and will dash you and your children within you to the ground. They will not leave in you one stone on another, because you didn't know the time of your visitation."

1. Invite the Holy Spirit into this reading, asking the Author of Scripture to speak to you through His Word
2. Read today's passage as many times as you need, take your time
3. Write down (below) what the Lord is saying to you today
4. Live with this Word in your heart through the day

_____

_____

Friday, November 22, 2024
Saint Cecilia, Virgin and Martyr

First Reading: Revelation 10: 8-11

8 The voice which I heard from heaven, again speaking with me, said, "Go, take the book which is open in the hand of the angel who stands on the sea and on the land."
9 I went to the angel, telling him to give me the little book.
He said to me, "Take it and eat it. It will make your stomach bitter, but in your mouth it will be as sweet as honey."
10 I took the little book out of the angel's hand, and ate it. It was as sweet as honey in my mouth. When I had eaten it, my stomach was made bitter. 11 They† told me, "You must prophesy again over many peoples, nations, languages, and kings."

Responsorial Psalm: Psalms 119: 14, 24, 72, 103, 111, 131

14 I have rejoiced in the way of your testimonies,
as much as in all riches.
24 Indeed your statutes are my delight,
and my counselors.
72 The law of your mouth is better to me than thousands of pieces of gold and silver.
103 How sweet are your promises to my taste,
more than honey to my mouth!
111 I have taken your testimonies as a heritage forever,
for they are the joy of my heart.
131 I opened my mouth wide and panted,
for I longed for your commandments.

Gospel: Luke 19: 45-48

45 He entered into the temple and began to drive out those who bought and sold in it, 46 saying to them, "It is written, 'My house is a house of prayer,' * but you have made it a 'den of robbers'!" *
47 He was teaching daily in the temple, but the chief priests, the scribes, and the leading men among the people sought to destroy him. 48 They couldn't find what they might do, for all the people hung on to every word that he said.

1. Invite the Holy Spirit into this reading, asking the Author of Scripture to speak to you through His Word
2. Read today's passage as many times as you need, take your time
3. Write down (below) what the Lord is saying to you today
4. Live with this Word in your heart through the day

_____

_____

Saturday, November 23, 2024
Saint Clement I, Pope and Martyr; Saint Columban, Abbot;
USA: Blessed Miguel Agustín Pro, Priest and Martyr; BVM

First Reading: Revelation 11: 4-12

4 These are the two olive trees and the two lamp stands, standing before the Lord of the earth.
5 If anyone desires to harm them, fire proceeds out of their mouth and devours their enemies. If anyone desires to harm them, he must be killed in this way. 6 These have the power to shut up the sky, that it may not rain during the days of their prophecy. They have power over the

waters, to turn them into blood, and to strike the earth with every plague, as often as they desire.

7 When they have finished their testimony, the beast that comes up out of the abyss will make war with them, and overcome them, and kill them. 8 Their dead bodies will be in the street of the great city, which spiritually is called Sodom and Egypt, where also their Lord was crucified. 9 From among the peoples, tribes, languages, and nations, people will look at their dead bodies for three and a half days, and will not allow their dead bodies to be laid in a tomb. 10 Those who dwell on the earth will rejoice over them, and they will be glad. They will give gifts to one another, because these two prophets tormented those who dwell on the earth.

11 After the three and a half days, the breath of life from God entered into them, and they stood on their feet. Great fear fell on those who saw them. 12 I heard a loud voice from heaven saying to them, "Come up here!" They went up into heaven in a cloud, and their enemies saw them.

Responsorial Psalm: Psalms 144: 1, 2, 9-10

1 Blessed be Yahweh, my rock,
who trains my hands to war,
and my fingers to battle—
2 my loving kindness, my fortress,
my high tower, my deliverer,
my shield, and he in whom I take refuge,
who subdues my people under me.
9 I will sing a new song to you, God.
On a ten-stringed lyre, I will sing praises to you.
10 You are he who gives salvation to kings,
who rescues David, his servant, from the deadly sword.

Gospel: Luke 20: 27-40

27 Some of the Sadducees came to him, those who deny that there is a resurrection. 28 They asked him, "Teacher, Moses wrote to us that if a man's brother dies having a wife, and he is childless, his brother should take the wife and raise up children for his brother. 29 There were therefore seven brothers. The first took a wife, and died childless. 30 The second took her as wife, and he died childless. 31 The third took her, and likewise the seven all left no children, and died. 32 Afterward the woman also died. 33 Therefore in the resurrection whose wife of them will she be? For the seven had her as a wife."

34 Jesus said to them, "The children of this age marry and are given in marriage. 35 But those who are considered worthy to attain to that age and the resurrection from the dead neither marry nor are given in marriage. 36 For they can't die any more, for they are like the angels and are children of God, being children of the resurrection. 37 But that the dead are raised, even Moses showed at the bush, when he called the Lord 'The God of Abraham, the God of Isaac, and the God of Jacob.' * 38 Now he is not the God of the dead, but of the living, for all are alive to him."

39 Some of the scribes answered, "Teacher, you speak well." 40 They didn't dare to ask him any more questions.

1. Invite the Holy Spirit into this reading, asking the Author of Scripture to speak to you through His Word
2. Read today's passage as many times as you need, take your time
3. Write down (below) what the Lord is saying to you today
4. Live with this Word in your heart through the day

Sunday, November 24, 2024
OUR LORD JESUS CHRIST, KING OF THE UNIVERSE

First Reading: Daniel 7: 13-14

13 "I saw in the night visions, and behold, there came with the clouds of the sky one like a son of man, and he came even to the Ancient of Days, and they brought him near before him. 14 Dominion was given him, and glory, and a kingdom, that all the peoples, nations, and languages should serve him. His dominion is an everlasting dominion, which will not pass away, and his kingdom one that will not be destroyed.

Responsorial Psalm: Psalms 93: 1-2, 5

1 Yahweh reigns!
He is clothed with majesty!
Yahweh is armed with strength.
The world also is established.
It can't be moved.
2 Your throne is established from long ago.
You are from everlasting.
5 Your statutes stand firm.
Holiness adorns your house,
Yahweh, forever more.

Second Reading: Revelation 1: 5-8

5 and from Jesus Christ, the faithful witness, the firstborn of the dead, and the ruler of the kings of the earth. To him who loves us, and washed us from our sins by his blood— 6 and he

made us to be a Kingdom, priests* to his God and Father—to him be the glory and the dominion forever and ever. Amen.

7 Behold,§ he is coming with the clouds, and every eye will see him, including those who pierced him. All the tribes of the earth will mourn over him. Even so, Amen.

8 "I am the Alpha and the Omega,†" says the Lord God,‡ "who is and who was and who is to come, the Almighty."

Gospel: John 18: 33b-37

33 Pilate therefore entered again into the Praetorium, called Jesus, and said to him, "Are you the King of the Jews?"

34 Jesus answered him, "Do you say this by yourself, or did others tell you about me?"

35 Pilate answered, "I'm not a Jew, am I? Your own nation and the chief priests delivered you to me. What have you done?"

36 Jesus answered, "My Kingdom is not of this world. If my Kingdom were of this world, then my servants would fight, that I wouldn't be delivered to the Jews. But now my Kingdom is not from here."

37 Pilate therefore said to him, "Are you a king then?"

Jesus answered, "You say that I am a king. For this reason I have been born, and for this reason I have come into the world, that I should testify to the truth. Everyone who is of the truth listens to my voice."

1. Invite the Holy Spirit into this reading, asking the Author of Scripture to speak to you through His Word
2. Read today's passage as many times as you need, take your time
3. Write down (below) what the Lord is saying to you today
4. Live with this Word in your heart through the day

_____

_____

Monday, November 25, 2024
Saint Catherine of Alexandria, Virgin and Martyr

First Reading: Revelation 14: 1-3, 4b-5

1 I saw, and behold, the Lamb standing on Mount Zion, and with him a number, one hundred forty-four thousand, having his name and the name of his Father written on their foreheads. 2 I heard a sound from heaven like the sound of many waters and like the sound of a great thunder. The sound which I heard was like that of harpists playing on their harps. 3 They sing

a new song before the throne and before the four living creatures and the elders. No one could learn the song except the one hundred forty-four thousand, those who had been redeemed out of the earth. 4b These are those who follow the Lamb wherever he goes. These were redeemed by Jesus from among men, the first fruits to God and to the Lamb. 5 In their mouth was found no lie, for they are blameless.

Responsorial Psalm: Psalms 24: 1bc-6

1 The earth is Yahweh's, with its fullness;
the world, and those who dwell in it.
2 For he has founded it on the seas,
and established it on the floods.
3 Who may ascend to Yahweh's hill?
Who may stand in his holy place?
4 He who has clean hands and a pure heart;
who has not lifted up his soul to falsehood,
and has not sworn deceitfully.
5 He shall receive a blessing from Yahweh,
righteousness from the God of his salvation.
6 This is the generation of those who seek Him,
who seek your face—even Jacob.

Gospel: Luke 21: 1-4

1 He looked up and saw the rich people who were putting their gifts into the treasury. 2 He saw a certain poor widow casting in two small brass coins.† 3 He said, "Truly I tell you, this poor widow put in more than all of them, 4 for all these put in gifts for God from their abundance, but she, out of her poverty, put in all that she had to live on."

1. Invite the Holy Spirit into this reading, asking the Author of Scripture to speak to you through His Word
2. Read today's passage as many times as you need, take your time
3. Write down (below) what the Lord is saying to you today
4. Live with this Word in your heart through the day

Tuesday, November 26, 2024

First Reading: Revelation 14: 14-19

14 I looked, and saw a white cloud, and on the cloud one sitting like a son of man,* having on his head a golden crown, and in his hand a sharp sickle. 15 Another angel came out of the temple, crying with a loud voice to him who sat on the cloud, "Send your sickle and reap, for the hour to reap has come; for the harvest of the earth is ripe!" 16 He who sat on the cloud thrust his sickle on the earth, and the earth was reaped.

17 Another angel came out of the temple which is in heaven. He also had a sharp sickle. 18 Another angel came out from the altar, he who has power over fire, and he called with a great voice to him who had the sharp sickle, saying, "Send your sharp sickle and gather the clusters of the vine of the earth, for the earth's grapes are fully ripe!" 19 The angel thrust his sickle into the earth, and gathered the vintage of the earth and threw it into the great wine press of the wrath of God.

Responsorial Psalm: Psalms 96: 10-13

10 Say among the nations, "Yahweh reigns."
The world is also established.
It can't be moved.
He will judge the peoples with equity.
11 Let the heavens be glad, and let the earth rejoice.
Let the sea roar, and its fullness!
12 Let the field and all that is in it exult!
Then all the trees of the woods shall sing for joy
13 before Yahweh; for he comes,
for he comes to judge the earth.
He will judge the world with righteousness,
the peoples with his truth.

Gospel: Luke 21: 5-11

5 As some were talking about the temple and how it was decorated with beautiful stones and gifts, he said, 6 "As for these things which you see, the days will come in which there will not be left here one stone on another that will not be thrown down."

7 They asked him, "Teacher, so when will these things be? What is the sign that these things are about to happen?"

8 He said, "Watch out that you don't get led astray, for many will come in my name, saying, 'I am he‡,' and, 'The time is at hand.' Therefore don't follow them. 9 When you hear of wars and disturbances, don't be terrified, for these things must happen first, but the end won't come immediately."

10 Then he said to them, "Nation will rise against nation, and kingdom against kingdom. 11 There will be great earthquakes, famines, and plagues in various places. There will be terrors and great signs from heaven.

_____

_____

Wednesday, November 27, 2024

First Reading: Revelation 15: 1-4

1 I saw another great and marvelous sign in the sky: seven angels having the seven last plagues, for in them God's wrath is finished.
2 I saw something like a sea of glass mixed with fire, and those who overcame the beast, his image,† and the number of his name, standing on the sea of glass, having harps of God. 3 They sang the song of Moses, the servant of God, and the song of the Lamb, saying,
"Great and marvelous are your works, Lord God, the Almighty!
Righteous and true are your ways, you King of the nations.
4 Who wouldn't fear you, Lord,
and glorify your name?
For you only are holy.
For all the nations will come and worship before you.
For your righteous acts have been revealed."
Responsorial Psalm: Psalms 98: 1-3ab, 7-9

1 Sing to Yahweh a new song,
for he has done marvelous things!
His right hand and his holy arm have worked salvation for him.
2 Yahweh has made known his salvation.
He has openly shown his righteousness in the sight of the nations.
3 He has remembered his loving kindness and his faithfulness toward the house of Israel.
All the ends of the earth have seen the salvation of our God.
7 Let the sea roar with its fullness;
the world, and those who dwell therein.

8 Let the rivers clap their hands.
Let the mountains sing for joy together.
9 Let them sing before Yahweh,
for he comes to judge the earth.
He will judge the world with righteousness,
and the peoples with equity.

Gospel: Luke 21: 12-19

12 But before all these things, they will lay their hands on you and will persecute you, delivering you up to synagogues and prisons, bringing you before kings and governors for my name's sake. 13 It will turn out as a testimony for you. 14 Settle it therefore in your hearts not to meditate beforehand how to answer, 15 for I will give you a mouth and wisdom which all your adversaries will not be able to withstand or to contradict. 16 You will be handed over even by parents, brothers, relatives, and friends. They will cause some of you to be put to death. 17 You will be hated by all men for my name's sake. 18 And not a hair of your head will perish.
19 "By your endurance you will win your lives.

1. Invite the Holy Spirit into this reading, asking the Author of Scripture to speak to you through His Word
2. Read today's passage as many times as you need, take your time
3. Write down (below) what the Lord is saying to you today
4. Live with this Word in your heart through the day

_____

_____

Thursday, November 28, 2024
Thanksgiving Day
First Reading: Revelation 18: 1-2, 21-23; 19: 1-3, 9a

1 After these things, I saw another angel coming down out of the sky, having great authority. The earth was illuminated with his glory. 2 He cried with a mighty voice, saying, "Fallen, fallen is Babylon the great, and she has become a habitation of demons, a prison of every unclean spirit, and a prison of every unclean and hated bird!
21 A mighty angel took up a stone like a great millstone and cast it into the sea, saying, "Thus with violence will Babylon, the great city, be thrown down, and will be found no more at all. 22 The voice of harpists, minstrels, flute players, and trumpeters will be heard no more at all in you. No craftsman of whatever craft will be found any more at all in you. The sound of a mill will be heard no more at all in you. 23 The light of a lamp will shine no more at all in you.

The voice of the bridegroom and of the bride will be heard no more at all in you, for your merchants were the princes of the earth; for with your sorcery all the nations were deceived.

1 After these things I heard something like a loud voice of a great multitude in heaven, saying, "Hallelujah! Salvation, power, and glory belong to our God; 2 for his judgments are true and righteous. For he has judged the great prostitute who corrupted the earth with her sexual immorality, and he has avenged the blood of his servants at her hand."

3 A second said, "Hallelujah! Her smoke goes up forever and ever."

9a He said to me, "Write, 'Blessed are those who are invited to the wedding supper of the Lamb.'

Responsorial Psalm: Psalms 100: 2- 5

2 Serve Yahweh with gladness.
Come before his presence with singing.
3 Know that Yahweh, he is God.
It is he who has made us, and we are his.
We are his people, and the sheep of his pasture.
4 Enter into his gates with thanksgiving,
and into his courts with praise.
Give thanks to him, and bless his name.
5 For Yahweh is good.
His loving kindness endures forever,
his faithfulness to all generations.

Gospel: Luke 21: 20-28

20 "But when you see Jerusalem surrounded by armies, then know that its desolation is at hand. 21 Then let those who are in Judea flee to the mountains. Let those who are in the middle of her depart. Let those who are in the country not enter therein. 22 For these are days of vengeance, that all things which are written may be fulfilled. 23 Woe to those who are pregnant and to those who nurse infants in those days! For there will be great distress in the land and wrath to this people. 24 They will fall by the edge of the sword, and will be led captive into all the nations. Jerusalem will be trampled down by the Gentiles until the times of the Gentiles are fulfilled.

25 "There will be signs in the sun, moon, and stars; and on the earth anxiety of nations, in perplexity for the roaring of the sea and the waves; 26 men fainting for fear and for expectation of the things which are coming on the world, for the powers of the heavens will be shaken. 27 Then they will see the Son of Man coming in a cloud with power and great glory. 28 But when these things begin to happen, look up and lift up your heads, because your redemption is near."

1. Invite the Holy Spirit into this reading, asking the Author of Scripture to speak to you through His Word

2. Read today's passage as many times as you need, take your time
3. Write down (below) what the Lord is saying to you today
4. Live with this Word in your heart through the day

Friday, November 29, 2024

First Reading: Revelation 20: 1-4, 11-21: 2

1 I saw an angel coming down out of heaven, having the key of the abyss and a great chain in his hand. 2 He seized the dragon, the old serpent, who is the devil and Satan, who deceives the whole inhabited earth,† and bound him for a thousand years, 3 and cast him into the abyss, and shut it and sealed it over him, that he should deceive the nations no more until the thousand years were finished. After this, he must be freed for a short time.

4 I saw thrones, and they sat on them, and judgment was given to them. I saw the souls of those who had been beheaded for the testimony of Jesus and for the word of God, and such as didn't worship the beast nor his image, and didn't receive the mark on their forehead and on their hand. They lived and reigned with Christ for a thousand years.

11 I saw a great white throne and him who sat on it, from whose face the earth and the heaven fled away. There was found no place for them. 12 I saw the dead, the great and the small, standing before the throne, and they opened books. Another book was opened, which is the book of life. The dead were judged out of the things which were written in the books, according to their works. 13 The sea gave up the dead who were in it. Death and Hades‡ gave up the dead who were in them. They were judged, each one according to his works. 14 Death and Hades§ were thrown into the lake of fire. This is the second death, the lake of fire. 15 If anyone was not found written in the book of life, he was cast into the lake of fire.

I saw a new heaven and a new earth, for the first heaven and the first earth have passed away, and the sea is no more. 2 I saw the holy city, New Jerusalem, coming down out of heaven from God, prepared like a bride adorned for her husband.

Responsorial Psalm: Psalms 84: 3-6a and 8a

3 Yes, the sparrow has found a home,
and the swallow a nest for herself, where she may have her young,
near your altars, Yahweh of Armies, my King, and my God.
4 Blessed are those who dwell in your house.
They are always praising you.
5 Blessed are those whose strength is in you,

who have set their hearts on a pilgrimage.
6 Passing through the valley of Weeping, they make it a place of springs.
8 Yahweh, God of Armies, hear my prayer.

Gospel: Luke 21: 29-33

29 He told them a parable. "See the fig tree and all the trees. 30 When they are already budding, you see it and know by your own selves that the summer is already near. 31 Even so you also, when you see these things happening, know that God's Kingdom is near. 32 Most certainly I tell you, this generation will not pass away until all things are accomplished. 33 Heaven and earth will pass away, but my words will by no means pass away.

1. Invite the Holy Spirit into this reading, asking the Author of Scripture to speak to you through His Word
2. Read today's passage as many times as you need, take your time
3. Write down (below) what the Lord is saying to you today
4. Live with this Word in your heart through the day

———————————————————————————————————————

———————————————————————————————————————

Saturday, November 30, 2024
Saint Andrew, Apostle

First Reading: Romans 10: 9-18

9 that if you will confess with your mouth that Jesus is Lord and believe in your heart that God raised him from the dead, you will be saved. 10 For with the heart one believes resulting in righteousness; and with the mouth confession is made resulting in salvation. 11 For the Scripture says, "Whoever believes in him will not be disappointed."*
12 For there is no distinction between Jew and Greek; for the same Lord is Lord of all, and is rich to all who call on him. 13 For, "Whoever will call on the name of the Lord will be saved."*
14 How then will they call on him in whom they have not believed? How will they believe in him whom they have not heard? How will they hear without a preacher? 15 And how will they preach unless they are sent? As it is written:
"How beautiful are the feet of those who preach the Good News of peace,
who bring glad tidings of good things!"*
16 But they didn't all listen to the glad news. For Isaiah says, "Lord, who has believed our report?"* 17 So faith comes by hearing, and hearing by the word of God. 18 But I say, didn't they hear? Yes, most certainly,
"Their sound went out into all the earth,
their words to the ends of the world."

Responsorial Psalm: Psalms 19: 8- 11

8 Yahweh's precepts are right, rejoicing the heart.
Yahweh's commandment is pure, enlightening the eyes.
9 The fear of Yahweh is clean, enduring forever.
Yahweh's ordinances are true, and righteous altogether.
10 They are more to be desired than gold, yes, than much fine gold,
sweeter also than honey and the extract of the honeycomb.
11 Moreover your servant is warned by them.
In keeping them there is great reward.

Gospel: Matthew 4: 18-22

18 Walking by the sea of Galilee, he‡ saw two brothers: Simon, who is called Peter, and Andrew, his brother, casting a net into the sea; for they were fishermen. 19 He said to them, "Come after me, and I will make you fishers for men."
20 They immediately left their nets and followed him. 21 Going on from there, he saw two other brothers, James the son of Zebedee, and John his brother, in the boat with Zebedee their father, mending their nets. He called them. 22 They immediately left the boat and their father, and followed him.

1. Invite the Holy Spirit into this reading, asking the Author of Scripture to speak to you through His Word
2. Read today's passage as many times as you need, take your time
3. Write down (below) what the Lord is saying to you today
4. Live with this Word in your heart through the day

_____

_____

Sunday, December 1, 2024
FIRST SUNDAY OF ADVENT

First Reading: Jeremiah 33: 14-16

14 "Behold, the days come," says Yahweh, "that I will perform that good word which I have spoken concerning the house of Israel and concerning the house of Judah.
15 "In those days and at that time,
I will cause a Branch of righteousness to grow up to David.

He will execute justice and righteousness in the land.
16 In those days Judah will be saved,
and Jerusalem will dwell safely.
This is the name by which she will be called:
Yahweh our righteousness."

Responsorial Psalm: Psalms 25: 4-5, 8-10, 14

4 Show me your ways, Yahweh.
Teach me your paths.
5 Guide me in your truth, and teach me,
for you are the God of my salvation.
I wait for you all day long.
8 Good and upright is Yahweh,
therefore he will instruct sinners in the way.
9 He will guide the humble in justice.
He will teach the humble his way.
10 All the paths of Yahweh are loving kindness and truth
to such as keep his covenant and his testimonies.
14 The friendship of Yahweh is with those who fear him.
He will show them his covenant.

Second Reading: First Thessalonians 3: 12 – 4: 2

12 May the Lord make you to increase and abound in love toward one another and toward all men, even as we also do toward you, 13 to the end he may establish your hearts blameless in holiness before our God and Father at the coming of our Lord Jesus with all his saints.
1 Finally then, brothers, we beg and exhort you in the Lord Jesus, that as you received from us how you ought to walk and to please God, that you abound more and more. 2 For you know what instructions we gave you through the Lord Jesus.

Gospel: Luke 21: 25-28, 34-36

25 "There will be signs in the sun, moon, and stars; and on the earth anxiety of nations, in perplexity for the roaring of the sea and the waves; 26 men fainting for fear and for expectation of the things which are coming on the world, for the powers of the heavens will be shaken. 27 Then they will see the Son of Man coming in a cloud with power and great glory. 28 But when these things begin to happen, look up and lift up your heads, because your redemption is near."
34 "So be careful, or your hearts will be loaded down with carousing, drunkenness, and cares of this life, and that day will come on you suddenly. 35 For it will come like a snare on all those who dwell on the surface of all the earth. 36 Therefore be watchful all the time, praying

that you may be counted worthy to escape all these things that will happen, and to stand before the Son of Man."

Monday, December 2, 2024

First Reading: Isaiah 2: 1-5

1 This is what Isaiah the son of Amoz saw concerning Judah and Jerusalem.
2 It shall happen in the latter days, that the mountain of Yahweh's house shall be established on the top of the mountains,
and shall be raised above the hills;
and all nations shall flow to it.
3 Many peoples shall go and say,
"Come, let's go up to the mountain of Yahweh,
to the house of the God of Jacob;
and he will teach us of his ways,
and we will walk in his paths."
For the law shall go out of Zion,
and Yahweh's word from Jerusalem.
4 He will judge between the nations,
and will decide concerning many peoples.
They shall beat their swords into plowshares,
and their spears into pruning hooks.
Nation shall not lift up sword against nation,
neither shall they learn war any more.
5 House of Jacob, come, and let's walk in the light of Yahweh.

Responsorial Psalm: Psalms 122: 1-9

1 I was glad when they said to me,
"Let's go to Yahweh's house!"

2 Our feet are standing within your gates, Jerusalem!
3 Jerusalem is built as a city that is compact together,
4 where the tribes go up, even Yah's tribes,
according to an ordinance for Israel,
to give thanks to Yahweh's name.
5 For there are set thrones for judgment,
the thrones of David's house.
6 Pray for the peace of Jerusalem.
Those who love you will prosper.
7 Peace be within your walls,
and prosperity within your palaces.
8 For my brothers' and companions' sakes,
I will now say, "Peace be within you."
9 For the sake of the house of Yahweh our God,
I will seek your good.

Gospel: Matthew 8: 5-11

5 When he came into Capernaum, a centurion came to him, asking him for help, 6 saying, "Lord, my servant lies in the house paralyzed, grievously tormented."
7 Jesus said to him, "I will come and heal him."
8 The centurion answered, "Lord, I'm not worthy for you to come under my roof. Just say the word, and my servant will be healed. 9 For I am also a man under authority, having under myself soldiers. I tell this one, 'Go,' and he goes; and tell another, 'Come,' and he comes; and tell my servant, 'Do this,' and he does it."
10 When Jesus heard it, he marveled and said to those who followed, "Most certainly I tell you, I haven't found so great a faith, not even in Israel. 11 I tell you that many will come from the east and the west, and will sit down with Abraham, Isaac, and Jacob in the Kingdom of Heaven

1. Invite the Holy Spirit into this reading, asking the Author of Scripture to speak to you through His Word
2. Read today's passage as many times as you need, take your time
3. Write down (below) what the Lord is saying to you today
4. Live with this Word in your heart through the day

Tuesday, December 3, 2024
Saint Francis Xavier, Priest

First Reading: Isaiah 11: 1-10

1 A shoot will come out of the stock of Jesse,
and a branch out of his roots will bear fruit.
2 Yahweh's Spirit will rest on him:
the spirit of wisdom and understanding,
the spirit of counsel and might,
the spirit of knowledge and of the fear of Yahweh.
3 His delight will be in the fear of Yahweh.
He will not judge by the sight of his eyes,
neither decide by the hearing of his ears;
4 but he will judge the poor with righteousness,
and decide with equity for the humble of the earth.
He will strike the earth with the rod of his mouth;
and with the breath of his lips he will kill the wicked.
5 Righteousness will be the belt around his waist,
and faithfulness the belt around his waist.
6 The wolf will live with the lamb,
and the leopard will lie down with the young goat,
the calf, the young lion, and the fattened calf together;
and a little child will lead them.
7 The cow and the bear will graze.
Their young ones will lie down together.
The lion will eat straw like the ox.
8 The nursing child will play near a cobra's hole,
and the weaned child will put his hand on the viper's den.
9 They will not hurt nor destroy in all my holy mountain;
for the earth will be full of the knowledge of Yahweh,
as the waters cover the sea.
10 It will happen in that day that the nations will seek the root of Jesse, who stands as a banner
of the peoples; and his resting place will be glorious.

Responsorial Psalm: Psalms 72: 1-2, 7-8, 12-13, 17

1 God, give the king your justice;
your righteousness to the royal son.
2 He will judge your people with righteousness,
and your poor with justice.
7 In his days, the righteous shall flourish,
and abundance of peace, until the moon is no more.
8 He shall have dominion also from sea to sea,

from the River to the ends of the earth.
12 For he will deliver the needy when he cries;
the poor, who has no helper.
13 He will have pity on the poor and needy.
He will save the souls of the needy.
17 His name endures forever.
His name continues as long as the sun.
Men shall be blessed by him.
All nations will call him blessed.

Gospel: Luke 10: 21-24

21 In that same hour, Jesus rejoiced in the Holy Spirit, and said, "I thank you, O Father, Lord of heaven and earth, that you have hidden these things from the wise and understanding, and revealed them to little children. Yes, Father, for so it was well-pleasing in your sight."
22 Turning to the disciples, he said, "All things have been delivered to me by my Father. No one knows who the Son is, except the Father, and who the Father is, except the Son, and he to whomever the Son desires to reveal him."
23 Turning to the disciples, he said privately, "Blessed are the eyes which see the things that you see, 24 for I tell you that many prophets and kings desired to see the things which you see, and didn't see them, and to hear the things which you hear, and didn't hear them."

1. Invite the Holy Spirit into this reading, asking the Author of Scripture to speak to you through His Word
2. Read today's passage as many times as you need, take your time
3. Write down (below) what the Lord is saying to you today
4. Live with this Word in your heart through the day

_____

_____

Wednesday, December 4, 2024
Saint John Damascene, Priest and Doctor of the Church

First Reading: Isaiah 25: 6-10a

6 In this mountain, Yahweh of Armies will make all peoples a feast of choice meat,† a feast of choice wines, of choice meat full of marrow, of well refined choice wines. 7 He will destroy in this mountain the surface of the covering that covers all peoples, and the veil that is spread over all nations. 8 He has swallowed up death forever! The Lord Yahweh will wipe away tears

from off all faces. He will take the reproach of his people away from off all the earth, for Yahweh has spoken it.

9 It shall be said in that day, "Behold, this is our God! We have waited for him, and he will save us! This is Yahweh! We have waited for him. We will be glad and rejoice in his salvation!"

10 For Yahweh's hand will rest in this mountain.

Responsorial Psalm: Psalms 23: 1-6

1 Yahweh is my shepherd;
I shall lack nothing.
2 He makes me lie down in green pastures.
He leads me beside still waters.
3 He restores my soul.
He guides me in the paths of righteousness for his name's sake.
4 Even though I walk through the valley of the shadow of death,
I will fear no evil, for you are with me.
Your rod and your staff,
they comfort me.
5 You prepare a table before me
in the presence of my enemies.
You anoint my head with oil.
My cup runs over.
6 Surely goodness and loving kindness shall follow me all the days of my life,
and I will dwell in Yahweh's house forever.

Gospel: Matthew 15: 29-37

29 Jesus departed from there and came near to the sea of Galilee; and he went up on the mountain and sat there. 30 Great multitudes came to him, having with them the lame, blind, mute, maimed, and many others, and they put them down at his feet. He healed them, 31 so that the multitude wondered when they saw the mute speaking, the injured healed, the lame walking, and the blind seeing—and they glorified the God of Israel.

32 Jesus summoned his disciples and said, "I have compassion on the multitude, because they have continued with me now three days and have nothing to eat. I don't want to send them away fasting, or they might faint on the way."

33 The disciples said to him, "Where could we get so many loaves in a deserted place as to satisfy so great a multitude?"

34 Jesus said to them, "How many loaves do you have?"
They said, "Seven, and a few small fish."

35 He commanded the multitude to sit down on the ground; 36 and he took the seven loaves and the fish. He gave thanks and broke them, and gave to the disciples, and the disciples to the multitudes. 37 They all ate and were filled. They took up seven baskets full of the broken pieces that were left over.

1. Invite the Holy Spirit into this reading, asking the Author of Scripture to speak to you through His Word
2. Read today's passage as many times as you need, take your time
3. Write down (below) what the Lord is saying to you today
4. Live with this Word in your heart through the day

_____

_____

Thursday, December 5, 2024

First Reading: Isaiah 26: 1-6

1 In that day, this song will be sung in the land of Judah:
"We have a strong city.
God appoints salvation for walls and bulwarks.
2 Open the gates, that the righteous nation may enter:
the one which keeps faith.
3 You will keep whoever's mind is steadfast in perfect peace,
because he trusts in you.
4 Trust in Yahweh forever;
for in Yah, Yahweh, is an everlasting Rock.
5 For he has brought down those who dwell on high, the lofty city.
He lays it low.
He lays it low even to the ground.
He brings it even to the dust.
6 The foot shall tread it down,
even the feet of the poor
and the steps of the needy."

Responsorial Psalm: Psalms 118: 1 and 8-9, 19-21, 25-27a

1 Give thanks to Yahweh, for he is good,
for his loving kindness endures forever.
8 It is better to take refuge in Yahweh,
than to put confidence in man.
9 It is better to take refuge in Yahweh,
than to put confidence in princes.

19 Open to me the gates of righteousness.

I will enter into them.

I will give thanks to Yah.

20 This is the gate of Yahweh;

the righteous will enter into it.

21 I will give thanks to you, for you have answered me,

and have become my salvation.

25 Save us now, we beg you, Yahweh!

Yahweh, we beg you, send prosperity now.

26 Blessed is he who comes in Yahweh's name!

We have blessed you out of Yahweh's house.

27 Yahweh is God, and he has given us light.

Gospel: Matthew 7: 21, 24-27

21 "Not everyone who says to me, 'Lord, Lord,' will enter into the Kingdom of Heaven, but he who does the will of my Father who is in heaven.

24 "Everyone therefore who hears these words of mine and does them, I will liken him to a wise man who built his house on a rock. 25 The rain came down, the floods came, and the winds blew and beat on that house; and it didn't fall, for it was founded on the rock. 26 Everyone who hears these words of mine and doesn't do them will be like a foolish man who built his house on the sand. 27 The rain came down, the floods came, and the winds blew and beat on that house; and it fell—and its fall was great."

1. Invite the Holy Spirit into this reading, asking the Author of Scripture to speak to you through His Word
2. Read today's passage as many times as you need, take your time
3. Write down (below) what the Lord is saying to you today
4. Live with this Word in your heart through the day

_____

_____

Friday, December 6, 2024
Saint Nicholas, Bishop

First Reading: Isaiah 29: 17-24

17 Isn't it yet a very little while, and Lebanon will be turned into a fruitful field, and the fruitful field will be regarded as a forest? 18 In that day, the deaf will hear the words of the book, and the eyes of the blind will see out of obscurity and out of darkness. 19 The humble also will

increase their joy in Yahweh, and the poor among men will rejoice in the Holy One of Israel. 20 For the ruthless is brought to nothing, and the scoffer ceases, and all those who are alert to do evil are cut off— 21 who cause a person to be indicted by a word, and lay a snare for one who reproves in the gate, and who deprive the innocent of justice with false testimony.

22 Therefore Yahweh, who redeemed Abraham, says concerning the house of Jacob: "Jacob shall no longer be ashamed, neither shall his face grow pale. 23 But when he sees his children, the work of my hands, in the middle of him, they will sanctify my name. Yes, they will sanctify the Holy One of Jacob, and will stand in awe of the God of Israel. 24 They also who err in spirit will come to understanding, and those who grumble will receive instruction."

Responsorial Psalm: Psalms 27: 1, 4, 13-14

1 Yahweh is my light and my salvation.
Whom shall I fear?
Yahweh is the strength of my life.
Of whom shall I be afraid?
4 One thing I have asked of Yahweh, that I will seek after:
that I may dwell in Yahweh's house all the days of my life,
to see Yahweh's beauty,
and to inquire in his temple.
13 I am still confident of this:
I will see the goodness of Yahweh in the land of the living.
14 Wait for Yahweh.
Be strong, and let your heart take courage.
Yes, wait for Yahweh.

Gospel: Matthew 9: 27-31

27 As Jesus passed by from there, two blind men followed him, calling out and saying, "Have mercy on us, son of David!" 28 When he had come into the house, the blind men came to him. Jesus said to them, "Do you believe that I am able to do this?"
They told him, "Yes, Lord."
29 Then he touched their eyes, saying, "According to your faith be it done to you." 30 Then their eyes were opened. Jesus strictly commanded them, saying, "See that no one knows about this." 31 But they went out and spread abroad his fame in all that land.

1. Invite the Holy Spirit into this reading, asking the Author of Scripture to speak to you through His Word
2. Read today's passage as many times as you need, take your time
3. Write down (below) what the Lord is saying to you today
4. Live with this Word in your heart through the day

First Reading: Isaiah 30: 19-21, 23-26

19 For the people will dwell in Zion at Jerusalem. You will weep no more. He will surely be gracious to you at the voice of your cry. When he hears you, he will answer you. 20 Though the Lord may give you the bread of adversity and the water of affliction, yet your teachers won't be hidden any more, but your eyes will see your teachers; 21 and when you turn to the right hand, and when you turn to the left, your ears will hear a voice behind you, saying, "This is the way. Walk in it."
23 He will give the rain for your seed, with which you will sow the ground; and bread of the increase of the ground will be rich and plentiful. In that day, your livestock will feed in large pastures. 24 The oxen likewise and the young donkeys that till the ground will eat savory feed, which has been winnowed with the shovel and with the fork. 25 There will be brooks and streams of water on every lofty mountain and on every high hill in the day of the great slaughter, when the towers fall. 26 Moreover the light of the moon will be like the light of the sun, and the light of the sun will be seven times brighter, like the light of seven days, in the day that Yahweh binds up the fracture of his people, and heals the wound they were struck with.

Responsorial Psalm: Psalms 147: 1-6

1 Praise Yah,
for it is good to sing praises to our God;
for it is pleasant and fitting to praise him.
2 Yahweh builds up Jerusalem.
He gathers together the outcasts of Israel.
3 He heals the broken in heart,
and binds up their wounds.
4 He counts the number of the stars.
He calls them all by their names.
5 Great is our Lord, and mighty in power.
His understanding is infinite.
6 Yahweh upholds the humble.
He brings the wicked down to the ground.

Gospel: Matthew 9: 35 – 10: 1, 5a, 6-8

35 Jesus went about all the cities and the villages, teaching in their synagogues and preaching the Good News of the Kingdom, and healing every disease and every sickness among the people. 36 But when he saw the multitudes, he was moved with compassion for them because

they were harassed§ and scattered, like sheep without a shepherd. 37 Then he said to his disciples, "The harvest indeed is plentiful, but the laborers are few. 38 Pray therefore that the Lord of the harvest will send out laborers into his harvest."

1 He called to himself his twelve disciples, and gave them authority over unclean spirits, to cast them out, and to heal every disease and every sickness.

5 Jesus sent these twelve out and commanded them, saying, "Don't go among the Gentiles, and don't enter into any city of the Samaritans. 6 Rather, go to the lost sheep of the house of Israel. 7 As you go, preach, saying, 'The Kingdom of Heaven is at hand!' 8 Heal the sick, cleanse the lepers,‡ and cast out demons. Freely you received, so freely give.

1. Invite the Holy Spirit into this reading, asking the Author of Scripture to speak to you through His Word
2. Read today's passage as many times as you need, take your time
3. Write down (below) what the Lord is saying to you today
4. Live with this Word in your heart through the day

_____

_____

Sunday, December 8, 2024
SECOND SUNDAY OF ADVENT

First Reading: Baruch 5: 1-9

1 Take off the garment of your mourning and affliction, O Jerusalem, and put on forever the beauty of the glory from God. 2 Put on the robe of the righteousness from God. Set on your head a diadem of the glory of the Everlasting. 3 For God will show your splendor everywhere under heaven. 4 For your name will be called by God forever "Righteous Peace, Godly Glory". 5 Arise, O Jerusalem, and stand upon the height. Look around you toward the east and see your children gathered from the going down of the sun to its rising at the word of the Holy One, rejoicing that God has remembered them. 6 For they went from you on foot, being led away by their enemies, but God brings them in to you carried on high with glory, on a royal throne. 7 For God has appointed that every high mountain and the everlasting hills should be made low, and the valleys filled up to make the ground level, that Israel may go safely in the glory of God. 8 Moreover the woods and every sweet smelling tree have shaded Israel by the commandment of God. 9 For God will lead Israel with joy in the light of his glory with the mercy and righteousness that come from him.

Responsorial Psalm: Psalms 126: 1-6

1 When Yahweh brought back those who returned to Zion,
we were like those who dream.
2 Then our mouth was filled with laughter,
and our tongue with singing.
Then they said among the nations,
"Yahweh has done great things for them."
3 Yahweh has done great things for us,
and we are glad.
4 Restore our fortunes again, Yahweh,
like the streams in the Negev.
5 Those who sow in tears will reap in joy.
6 He who goes out weeping, carrying seed for sowing,
will certainly come again with joy, carrying his sheaves.

Second Reading: Philippians 1: 4-6, 8-11

4 always in every request of mine on behalf of you all, making my requests with joy, 5 for your partnership† in furtherance of the Good News from the first day until now; 6 being confident of this very thing, that he who began a good work in you will complete it until the day of Jesus Christ.
8 For God is my witness, how I long after all of you in the tender mercies of Christ Jesus.
9 This I pray, that your love may abound yet more and more in knowledge and all discernment, 10 so that you may approve the things that are excellent, that you may be sincere and without offense to the day of Christ, 11 being filled with the fruits of righteousness which are through Jesus Christ, to the glory and praise of God.

Gospel: Luke 3: 1-6

1 Now in the fifteenth year of the reign of Tiberius Caesar, Pontius Pilate being governor of Judea, and Herod being tetrarch of Galilee, and his brother Philip tetrarch of the region of Ituraea and Trachonitis, and Lysanias tetrarch of Abilene, 2 during the high priesthood of Annas and Caiaphas, the word of God came to John, the son of Zacharias, in the wilderness. 3 He came into all the region around the Jordan, preaching the baptism of repentance for remission of sins. 4 As it is written in the book of the words of Isaiah the prophet,
"The voice of one crying in the wilderness,
'Make ready the way of the Lord.
Make his paths straight.
5 Every valley will be filled.
Every mountain and hill will be brought low.
The crooked will become straight,
and the rough ways smooth.
6 All flesh will see God's salvation.' "

1. Invite the Holy Spirit into this reading, asking the Author of Scripture to speak to you through His Word
2. Read today's passage as many times as you need, take your time
3. Write down (below) what the Lord is saying to you today
4. Live with this Word in your heart through the day

_____

_____

Monday, December 9, 2024
THE IMMACULATE CONCEPTION OF THE BLESSED VIRGIN MARY
(Patronal Feastday of the United States of America)

First Reading: Genesis 3: 9-15, 20

9 Yahweh God called to the man, and said to him, "Where are you?"

10 The man said, "I heard your voice in the garden, and I was afraid, because I was naked; so I hid myself."

11 God said, "Who told you that you were naked? Have you eaten from the tree that I commanded you not to eat from?"

12 The man said, "The woman whom you gave to be with me, she gave me fruit from the tree, and I ate it."

13 Yahweh God said to the woman, "What have you done?"

The woman said, "The serpent deceived me, and I ate."

14 Yahweh God said to the serpent,

"Because you have done this,

you are cursed above all livestock,

and above every animal of the field.

You shall go on your belly

and you shall eat dust all the days of your life.

15 I will put hostility between you and the woman,

and between your offspring and her offspring.

He will bruise your head,

and you will bruise his heel."

20 The man called his wife Eve because she would be the mother of all the living.

Responsorial Psalm: Psalms 98: 1-4

1 Sing to Yahweh a new song,

for he has done marvelous things!

His right hand and his holy arm have worked salvation for him.

2 Yahweh has made known his salvation.

He has openly shown his righteousness in the sight of the nations.

3 He has remembered his loving kindness and his faithfulness toward the house of Israel.

All the ends of the earth have seen the salvation of our God.

4 Make a joyful noise to Yahweh, all the earth!

Burst out and sing for joy, yes, sing praises!

Second Reading: Ephesians 1: 3-6, 11-12

3 Blessed be the God and Father of our Lord Jesus Christ, who has blessed us with every spiritual blessing in the heavenly places in Christ, 4 even as he chose us in him before the foundation of the world, that we would be holy and without defect before him in love, 5 having predestined us for adoption as children through Jesus Christ to himself, according to the good pleasure of his desire, 6 to the praise of the glory of his grace, by which he freely gave us favor in the Beloved.

11 We were also assigned an inheritance in him, having been foreordained according to the purpose of him who does all things after the counsel of his will, 12 to the end that we should be to the praise of his glory, we who had before hoped in Christ.

Gospel: Luke 1: 26-38

26 Now in the sixth month, the angel Gabriel was sent from God to a city of Galilee named Nazareth, 27 to a virgin pledged to be married to a man whose name was Joseph, of David's house. The virgin's name was Mary. 28 Having come in, the angel said to her, "Rejoice, you highly favored one! The Lord is with you. Blessed are you among women!"

29 But when she saw him, she was greatly troubled at the saying, and considered what kind of salutation this might be. 30 The angel said to her, "Don't be afraid, Mary, for you have found favor with God. 31 Behold, you will conceive in your womb and give birth to a son, and shall name him 'Jesus.' 32 He will be great and will be called the Son of the Most High. The Lord God will give him the throne of his father David, 33 and he will reign over the house of Jacob forever. There will be no end to his Kingdom."

34 Mary said to the angel, "How can this be, seeing I am a virgin?"

35 The angel answered her, "The Holy Spirit will come on you, and the power of the Most High will overshadow you. Therefore also the holy one who is born from you will be called the Son of God. 36 Behold, Elizabeth your relative also has conceived a son in her old age; and this is the sixth month with her who was called barren. 37 For nothing spoken by God is impossible."‡

38 Mary said, "Behold, the servant of the Lord; let it be done to me according to your word." Then the angel departed from her.

1. Invite the Holy Spirit into this reading, asking the Author of Scripture to speak to you through His Word

2. Read today's passage as many times as you need, take your time
3. Write down (below) what the Lord is saying to you today
4. Live with this Word in your heart through the day

_____

_____

Tuesday, December 10, 2024
Our Lady of Loreto

First Reading: Isaiah 40: 1-11

1 "Comfort, comfort my people," says your God. 2 "Speak comfortably to Jerusalem, and call out to her that her warfare is accomplished, that her iniquity is pardoned, that she has received of Yahweh's hand double for all her sins."
3 The voice of one who calls out,
"Prepare the way of Yahweh in the wilderness!
Make a level highway in the desert for our God.
4 Every valley shall be exalted,
and every mountain and hill shall be made low.
The uneven shall be made level,
and the rough places a plain.
5 Yahweh's glory shall be revealed,
and all flesh shall see it together;
for the mouth of Yahweh has spoken it."
6 The voice of one saying, "Cry out!"
One said, "What shall I cry?"
"All flesh is like grass,
and all its glory is like the flower of the field.
7 The grass withers,
the flower fades,
because Yahweh's breath blows on it.
Surely the people are like grass.
8 The grass withers,
the flower fades;
but the word of our God stands forever."
9 You who tell good news to Zion, go up on a high mountain.
You who tell good news to Jerusalem, lift up your voice with strength!
Lift it up! Don't be afraid!
Say to the cities of Judah, "Behold, your God!"

10 Behold, the Lord Yahweh will come as a mighty one,
and his arm will rule for him.
Behold, his reward is with him,
and his recompense before him.
11 He will feed his flock like a shepherd.
He will gather the lambs in his arm,
and carry them in his bosom.
He will gently lead those who have their young.

Responsorial Psalm: Psalms 96: 1-3 and 10-13

1 Sing to Yahweh a new song!
Sing to Yahweh, all the earth.
2 Sing to Yahweh!
Bless his name!
Proclaim his salvation from day to day!
3 Declare his glory among the nations,
his marvelous works among all the peoples.
10 Say among the nations, "Yahweh reigns."
The world is also established.
It can't be moved.
He will judge the peoples with equity.
11 Let the heavens be glad, and let the earth rejoice.
Let the sea roar, and its fullness!
12 Let the field and all that is in it exult!
Then all the trees of the woods shall sing for joy
13 before Yahweh; for he comes,
for he comes to judge the earth.
He will judge the world with righteousness,
the peoples with his truth.

Gospel: Matthew 18: 12-14

12 "What do you think? If a man has one hundred sheep, and one of them goes astray, doesn't he leave the ninety-nine, go to the mountains, and seek that which has gone astray? 13 If he finds it, most certainly I tell you, he rejoices over it more than over the ninety-nine which have not gone astray. 14 Even so it is not the will of your Father who is in heaven that one of these little ones should perish.

1. Invite the Holy Spirit into this reading, asking the Author of Scripture to speak to you through His Word
2. Read today's passage as many times as you need, take your time
3. Write down (below) what the Lord is saying to you today

Wednesday, December 11, 2024
Saint Damasus I, Pope

First Reading: Isaiah 40: 25-31

25 "To whom then will you liken me?
Who is my equal?" says the Holy One.
26 Lift up your eyes on high,
and see who has created these,
who brings out their army by number.
He calls them all by name.
By the greatness of his might,
and because he is strong in power,
not one is lacking.

27 Why do you say, Jacob,
and speak, Israel,
"My way is hidden from Yahweh,
and the justice due me is disregarded by my God"?
28 Haven't you known?
Haven't you heard?
The everlasting God, Yahweh,
the Creator of the ends of the earth, doesn't faint.
He isn't weary.
His understanding is unsearchable.
29 He gives power to the weak.
He increases the strength of him who has no might.
30 Even the youths faint and get weary,
and the young men utterly fall;
31 but those who wait for Yahweh will renew their strength.
They will mount up with wings like eagles.
They will run, and not be weary.
They will walk, and not faint.

Responsorial Psalm: Psalms 103: 1-4, 8 and 10

1 Praise Yahweh, my soul!
All that is within me, praise his holy name!
2 Praise Yahweh, my soul,
and don't forget all his benefits,
3 who forgives all your sins,
who heals all your diseases,
4 who redeems your life from destruction,
who crowns you with loving kindness and tender mercies,
8 Yahweh is merciful and gracious,
slow to anger, and abundant in loving kindness.
10 He has not dealt with us according to our sins,
nor repaid us for our iniquities.

Gospel: Matthew 11: 28-30

28 "Come to me, all you who labor and are heavily burdened, and I will give you rest. 29 Take my yoke upon you and learn from me, for I am gentle and humble in heart; and you will find rest for your souls. 30 For my yoke is easy, and my burden is light."

1. Invite the Holy Spirit into this reading, asking the Author of Scripture to speak to you through His Word
2. Read today's passage as many times as you need, take your time
3. Write down (below) what the Lord is saying to you today
4. Live with this Word in your heart through the day

_____

_____

Thursday, December 12, 2024
Our Lady of Guadalupe

First Reading: Revelation 11: 19a; 12: 1-6a, 10ab

19a God's temple that is in heaven was opened, and the ark of the Lord's covenant was seen in his temple.
1 A great sign was seen in heaven: a woman clothed with the sun, and the moon under her feet, and on her head a crown of twelve stars. 2 She was with child. She cried out in pain, laboring to give birth.

3 Another sign was seen in heaven. Behold, a great red dragon, having seven heads and ten horns, and on his heads seven crowns. 4 His tail drew one third of the stars of the sky, and threw them to the earth. The dragon stood before the woman who was about to give birth, so that when she gave birth he might devour her child. 5 She gave birth to a son, a male child, who is to rule all the nations with a rod of iron. Her child was caught up to God and to his throne. 6a The woman fled into the wilderness, where she has a place prepared by God.

10ab I heard a loud voice in heaven, saying, "Now the salvation, the power, and the Kingdom of our God, and the authority of his Christ has come;

Responsorial Psalm: Judith 13: 18bcde, 19

18 Ozias said to her, "Blessed are you, daughter, in the sight of the Most High God, above all the women upon the earth; and blessed is the Lord God, who created the heavens and the earth, who directed you to cut off the head of the prince of our enemies. 19 For your hope will not depart from the heart of men that remember the strength of God forever.

Gospel: Luke 1: 26-38

26 Now in the sixth month, the angel Gabriel was sent from God to a city of Galilee named Nazareth, 27 to a virgin pledged to be married to a man whose name was Joseph, of David's house. The virgin's name was Mary. 28 Having come in, the angel said to her, "Rejoice, you highly favored one! The Lord is with you. Blessed are you among women!"

29 But when she saw him, she was greatly troubled at the saying, and considered what kind of salutation this might be. 30 The angel said to her, "Don't be afraid, Mary, for you have found favor with God. 31 Behold, you will conceive in your womb and give birth to a son, and shall name him 'Jesus.' 32 He will be great and will be called the Son of the Most High. The Lord God will give him the throne of his father David, 33 and he will reign over the house of Jacob forever. There will be no end to his Kingdom."

34 Mary said to the angel, "How can this be, seeing I am a virgin?"

35 The angel answered her, "The Holy Spirit will come on you, and the power of the Most High will overshadow you. Therefore also the holy one who is born from you will be called the Son of God. 36 Behold, Elizabeth your relative also has conceived a son in her old age; and this is the sixth month with her who was called barren. 37 For nothing spoken by God is impossible."‡

38 Mary said, "Behold, the servant of the Lord; let it be done to me according to your word." Then the angel departed from her.

1. Invite the Holy Spirit into this reading, asking the Author of Scripture to speak to you through His Word
2. Read today's passage as many times as you need, take your time
3. Write down (below) what the Lord is saying to you today
4. Live with this Word in your heart through the day

Friday, December 13, 2024
Saint Lucy, Virgin and Martyr

First Reading: Isaiah 48: 17-19

17 Yahweh,
your Redeemer,
the Holy One of Israel, says:
"I am Yahweh your God,
who teaches you to profit,
who leads you by the way that you should go.
18 Oh that you had listened to my commandments!
Then your peace would have been like a river
and your righteousness like the waves of the sea.
19 Your offspring also would have been as the sand
and the descendants of your body like its grains.
His name would not be cut off nor destroyed from before me."

Responsorial Psalm: Psalms 1: 1-4 and 6

1 Blessed is the man who doesn't walk in the counsel of the wicked,
nor stand on the path of sinners,
nor sit in the seat of scoffers;
2 but his delight is in Yahweh's† law.
On his law he meditates day and night.
3 He will be like a tree planted by the streams of water,
that produces its fruit in its season,
whose leaf also does not wither.
Whatever he does shall prosper.
4 The wicked are not so,
but are like the chaff which the wind drives away.
6 For Yahweh knows the way of the righteous,
but the way of the wicked shall perish.

Gospel: Matthew 11: 16-19

16 "But to what shall I compare this generation? It is like children sitting in the marketplaces, who call to their companions 17 and say, 'We played the flute for you, and you didn't dance. We mourned for you, and you didn't lament.' 18 For John came neither eating nor drinking, and they say, 'He has a demon.' 19 The Son of Man came eating and drinking, and they say, 'Behold, a gluttonous man and a drunkard, a friend of tax collectors and sinners!' But wisdom is justified by her children."

1. Invite the Holy Spirit into this reading, asking the Author of Scripture to speak to you through His Word
2. Read today's passage as many times as you need, take your time
3. Write down (below) what the Lord is saying to you today
4. Live with this Word in your heart through the day

_____

_____

Saturday, December 14, 2024
Saint John of the Cross, Priest and Doctor of the Church

First Reading: Sirach 48: 1-4, 9-11

1 Then Elijah arose, the prophet like fire.
His word burned like a torch.
2 He brought a famine upon them,
and by his zeal made them few in number.
3 By the word of the Lord he shut up the heavens.
He brought down fire three times.
4 How you were glorified, O Elijah, in your wondrous deeds!
Whose glory is like yours?
9 You were taken up in a tempest of fire,
in a chariot of fiery horses.
10 You were recorded for reproofs in their seasons,
to pacify anger, before it broke out into wrath,
to turn the heart of the father to the son,
and to restore the tribes of Jacob.
11 Blessed are those who saw you,
and those who have been beautified with love;
for we also shall surely live.

Responsorial Psalm: Psalms 80: 2ac and 3b, 15-16, 18-19

2 Before Ephraim, Benjamin, and Manasseh, stir up your might!
Come to save us!
3 Turn us again, God.
Cause your face to shine,
and we will be saved.
15 the stock which your right hand planted,
the branch that you made strong for yourself.
16 It's burned with fire.
It's cut down.
They perish at your rebuke.
18 So we will not turn away from you.
Revive us, and we will call on your name.
19 Turn us again, Yahweh God of Armies.
Cause your face to shine, and we will be saved.

Gospel: Matthew 17: 9a, 10-13

9 As they were coming down from the mountain, Jesus commanded them, saying, "Don't tell anyone what you saw, until the Son of Man has risen from the dead."
10 His disciples asked him, saying, "Then why do the scribes say that Elijah must come first?"
11 Jesus answered them, "Elijah indeed comes first, and will restore all things; 12 but I tell you that Elijah has come already, and they didn't recognize him, but did to him whatever they wanted to. Even so the Son of Man will also suffer by them." 13 Then the disciples understood that he spoke to them of John the Baptizer.

1. Invite the Holy Spirit into this reading, asking the Author of Scripture to speak to you through His Word
2. Read today's passage as many times as you need, take your time
3. Write down (below) what the Lord is saying to you today
4. Live with this Word in your heart through the day

_____

_____

Sunday, December 15, 2024
THIRD SUNDAY OF ADVENT

First Reading: Zephaniah 3: 14-18a

14 Sing, daughter of Zion! Shout, Israel! Be glad and rejoice with all your heart, daughter of Jerusalem. 15 Yahweh has taken away your judgments. He has thrown out your enemy. The King of Israel, Yahweh, is among you. You will not be afraid of evil any more. 16 In that day, it will be said to Jerusalem, "Don't be afraid, Zion. Don't let your hands be weak." 17 Yahweh, your God, is among you, a mighty one who will save. He will rejoice over you with joy. He will calm you in his love. He will rejoice over you with singing. 18 I will remove those who grieve about the appointed feasts from you. They are a burden and a reproach to you.

Responsorial Psalm: Isaiah 12: 2-6

2 Behold, God is my salvation. I will trust, and will not be afraid; for Yah, Yahweh, is my strength and song; and he has become my salvation." 3 Therefore with joy you will draw water out of the wells of salvation. 4 In that day you will say, "Give thanks to Yahweh! Call on his name! Declare his doings among the peoples! Proclaim that his name is exalted! 5 Sing to Yahweh, for he has done excellent things! Let this be known in all the earth! 6 Cry aloud and shout, you inhabitant of Zion, for the Holy One of Israel is great among you!"

Second Reading: Philippians 4: 4-7

4 Rejoice in the Lord always! Again I will say, "Rejoice!" 5 Let your gentleness be known to all men. The Lord is at hand. 6 In nothing be anxious, but in everything, by prayer and petition with thanksgiving, let your requests be made known to God. 7 And the peace of God, which surpasses all understanding, will guard your hearts and your thoughts in Christ Jesus.

Gospel: Luke 3: 10-18

10 The multitudes asked him, "What then must we do?"
11 He answered them, "He who has two coats, let him give to him who has none. He who has food, let him do likewise."
12 Tax collectors also came to be baptized, and they said to him, "Teacher, what must we do?"
13 He said to them, "Collect no more than that which is appointed to you."
14 Soldiers also asked him, saying, "What about us? What must we do?"
He said to them, "Extort from no one by violence, neither accuse anyone wrongfully. Be content with your wages."
15 As the people were in expectation, and all men reasoned in their hearts concerning John, whether perhaps he was the Christ, 16 John answered them all, "I indeed baptize you with water, but he comes who is mightier than I, the strap of whose sandals I am not worthy to loosen. He will baptize you in the Holy Spirit and fire. 17 His winnowing fan is in his hand, and he will thoroughly cleanse his threshing floor, and will gather the wheat into his barn; but he will burn up the chaff with unquenchable fire."
18 Then with many other exhortations he preached good news to the people

1. Invite the Holy Spirit into this reading, asking the Author of Scripture to speak to you through His Word
2. Read today's passage as many times as you need, take your time
3. Write down (below) what the Lord is saying to you today
4. Live with this Word in your heart through the day

_____

_____

Monday, December 16, 2024

First Reading: Numbers 24: 2-7, 15-17

2 Balaam lifted up his eyes, and he saw Israel dwelling according to their tribes; and the Spirit of God came on him. 3 He took up his parable, and said,
"Balaam the son of Beor says,
the man whose eyes are open says;
4 he says, who hears the words of God,
who sees the vision of the Almighty,
falling down, and having his eyes open:
5 How goodly are your tents, Jacob,
and your dwellings, Israel!
6 As valleys they are spread out,
as gardens by the riverside,
as aloes which Yahweh has planted,
as cedar trees beside the waters.
7 Water shall flow from his buckets.
His seed shall be in many waters.
His king shall be higher than Agag.
His kingdom shall be exalted.
15 He took up his parable, and said,
"Balaam the son of Beor says,
the man whose eyes are open says;
16 he says, who hears the words of God,
knows the knowledge of the Most High,
and who sees the vision of the Almighty,
falling down, and having his eyes open:
17 I see him, but not now.
I see him, but not near.
A star will come out of Jacob.
A scepter will rise out of Israel,

and shall strike through the corners of Moab,
and crush all the sons of Sheth.

Responsorial Psalm: Psalms 25: 4-9

4 Show me your ways, Yahweh.
Teach me your paths.
5 Guide me in your truth, and teach me,
for you are the God of my salvation.
I wait for you all day long.
6 Yahweh, remember your tender mercies and your loving kindness,
for they are from old times.
7 Don't remember the sins of my youth, nor my transgressions.
Remember me according to your loving kindness,
for your goodness' sake, Yahweh.
8 Good and upright is Yahweh,
therefore he will instruct sinners in the way.
9 He will guide the humble in justice.
He will teach the humble his way.

Gospel: Matthew 21: 23-27

23 When he had come into the temple, the chief priests and the elders of the people came to him as he was teaching, and said, "By what authority do you do these things? Who gave you this authority?"
24 Jesus answered them, "I also will ask you one question, which if you tell me, I likewise will tell you by what authority I do these things. 25 The baptism of John, where was it from? From heaven or from men?"
They reasoned with themselves, saying, "If we say, 'From heaven,' he will ask us, 'Why then did you not believe him?' 26 But if we say, 'From men,' we fear the multitude, for all hold John as a prophet." 27 They answered Jesus, and said, "We don't know."
He also said to them, "Neither will I tell you by what authority I do these things.

1. Invite the Holy Spirit into this reading, asking the Author of Scripture to speak to you through His Word
2. Read today's passage as many times as you need, take your time
3. Write down (below) what the Lord is saying to you today
4. Live with this Word in your heart through the day

_____

_____

Tuesday, December 17, 2024

First Reading: Genesis 49: 2, 8-10

2 Assemble yourselves, and hear, you sons of Jacob.
Listen to Israel, your father.
8 "Judah, your brothers will praise you.
Your hand will be on the neck of your enemies.
Your father's sons will bow down before you.
9 Judah is a lion's cub.
From the prey, my son, you have gone up.
He stooped down, he crouched as a lion,
as a lioness.
Who will rouse him up?
10 The scepter will not depart from Judah,
nor the ruler's staff from between his feet,
until he comes to whom it belongs.
The obedience of the peoples will be to him.

Responsorial Psalm: Psalms 72: 1-4ab, 7-8, 17

1 God, give the king your justice;
your righteousness to the royal son.
2 He will judge your people with righteousness,
and your poor with justice.
3 The mountains shall bring prosperity to the people.
The hills bring the fruit of righteousness.
4 He will judge the poor of the people.
He will save the children of the needy,
and will break the oppressor in pieces.
7 In his days, the righteous shall flourish,
and abundance of peace, until the moon is no more.
8 He shall have dominion also from sea to sea,
from the River to the ends of the earth.
17 His name endures forever.
His name continues as long as the sun.
Men shall be blessed by him.
All nations will call him blessed.

Gospel: Matthew 1: 1-17

1 The book of the genealogy of Jesus Christ,† the son of David, the son of Abraham.

2 Abraham became the father of Isaac. Isaac became the father of Jacob. Jacob became the father of Judah and his brothers. 3 Judah became the father of Perez and Zerah by Tamar. Perez became the father of Hezron. Hezron became the father of Ram. 4 Ram became the father of Amminadab. Amminadab became the father of Nahshon. Nahshon became the father of Salmon. 5 Salmon became the father of Boaz by Rahab. Boaz became the father of Obed by Ruth. Obed became the father of Jesse. 6 Jesse became the father of King David. David the king‡ became the father of Solomon by her who had been Uriah's wife. 7 Solomon became the father of Rehoboam. Rehoboam became the father of Abijah. Abijah became the father of Asa. 8 Asa became the father of Jehoshaphat. Jehoshaphat became the father of Joram. Joram became the father of Uzziah. 9 Uzziah became the father of Jotham. Jotham became the father of Ahaz. Ahaz became the father of Hezekiah. 10 Hezekiah became the father of Manasseh. Manasseh became the father of Amon. Amon became the father of Josiah. 11 Josiah became the father of Jechoniah and his brothers at the time of the exile to Babylon.

12 After the exile to Babylon, Jechoniah became the father of Shealtiel. Shealtiel became the father of Zerubbabel. 13 Zerubbabel became the father of Abiud. Abiud became the father of Eliakim. Eliakim became the father of Azor. 14 Azor became the father of Zadok. Zadok became the father of Achim. Achim became the father of Eliud. 15 Eliud became the father of Eleazar. Eleazar became the father of Matthan. Matthan became the father of Jacob. 16 Jacob became the father of Joseph, the husband of Mary, from whom was born Jesus,§ who is called Christ.

17 So all the generations from Abraham to David are fourteen generations; from David to the exile to Babylon fourteen generations; and from the carrying away to Babylon to the Christ, fourteen generations.

1. Invite the Holy Spirit into this reading, asking the Author of Scripture to speak to you through His Word
2. Read today's passage as many times as you need, take your time
3. Write down (below) what the Lord is saying to you today
4. Live with this Word in your heart through the day

_____

_____

Wednesday, December 18, 2024

First Reading: Jeremiah 23: 5-8

5 "Behold, the days come," says Yahweh,
"that I will raise to David a righteous Branch;
and he will reign as king and deal wisely,

and will execute justice and righteousness in the land.
6 In his days Judah will be saved,
and Israel will dwell safely.
This is his name by which he will be called:
Yahweh our righteousness.
7 "Therefore, behold, the days come," says Yahweh, "that they will no more say, 'As Yahweh lives, who brought up the children of Israel out of the land of Egypt;' 8 but, 'As Yahweh lives, who brought up and who led the offspring of the house of Israel out of the north country, and from all the countries where I had driven them.' Then they will dwell in their own land."

Responsorial Psalm: Psalms 72: 1-2, 12-13, 18-19

1 God, give the king your justice;
your righteousness to the royal son.
2 He will judge your people with righteousness,
and your poor with justice.
12 For he will deliver the needy when he cries;
the poor, who has no helper.
13 He will have pity on the poor and needy.
He will save the souls of the needy.
18 Praise be to Yahweh God, the God of Israel,
who alone does marvelous deeds.
19 Blessed be his glorious name forever!
Let the whole earth be filled with his glory!
Amen and amen.

Gospel: Matthew 1: 18-25

18 Now the birth of Jesus Christ was like this: After his mother, Mary, was engaged to Joseph, before they came together, she was found pregnant by the Holy Spirit. 19 Joseph, her husband, being a righteous man, and not willing to make her a public example, intended to put her away secretly. 20 But when he thought about these things, behold,† an angel of the Lord appeared to him in a dream, saying, "Joseph, son of David, don't be afraid to take to yourself Mary as your wife, for that which is conceived in her is of the Holy Spirit. 21 She shall give birth to a son. You shall name him Jesus,‡ for it is he who shall save his people from their sins."
22 Now all this has happened that it might be fulfilled which was spoken by the Lord through the prophet, saying,
23 "Behold, the virgin shall be with child,
and shall give birth to a son.
They shall call his name Immanuel,"
which is, being interpreted, "God with us."*

24 Joseph arose from his sleep, and did as the angel of the Lord commanded him, and took his wife to himself; 25 and didn't know her sexually until she had given birth to her firstborn son. He named him Jesus.

1. Invite the Holy Spirit into this reading, asking the Author of Scripture to speak to you through His Word
2. Read today's passage as many times as you need, take your time
3. Write down (below) what the Lord is saying to you today
4. Live with this Word in your heart through the day

Thursday, December 19, 2024

First Reading: Judges 13: 2-7, 24-25a

2 There was a certain man of Zorah, of the family of the Danites, whose name was Manoah; and his wife was barren, and childless. 3 Yahweh's angel appeared to the woman, and said to her, "See now, you are barren and childless; but you shall conceive and bear a son. 4 Now therefore please beware and drink no wine nor strong drink, and don't eat any unclean thing; 5 for, behold, you shall conceive and give birth to a son. No razor shall come on his head, for the child shall be a Nazirite to God from the womb. He shall begin to save Israel out of the hand of the Philistines."
6 Then the woman came and told her husband, saying, "A man of God came to me, and his face was like the face of the angel of God, very awesome. I didn't ask him where he was from, neither did he tell me his name; 7 but he said to me, 'Behold, you shall conceive and bear a son; and now drink no wine nor strong drink. Don't eat any unclean thing, for the child shall be a Nazirite to God from the womb to the day of his death.' "
24 The woman bore a son and named him Samson. The child grew, and Yahweh blessed him. 25 Yahweh's Spirit began to move him

Responsorial Psalm: Psalms 71: 3-6ab, 16-17

3 Be to me a rock of refuge to which I may always go.
Give the command to save me,
for you are my rock and my fortress.
4 Rescue me, my God, from the hand of the wicked,
from the hand of the unrighteous and cruel man.
5 For you are my hope, Lord Yahweh,
my confidence from my youth.

6 I have relied on you from the womb.
You are he who took me out of my mother's womb.
I will always praise you.
16 I will come with the mighty acts of the Lord Yahweh.
I will make mention of your righteousness, even of yours alone.
17 God, you have taught me from my youth.
Until now, I have declared your wondrous works.

Gospel: Luke 1: 5-25

5 There was in the days of Herod, the king of Judea, a certain priest named Zacharias, of the priestly division of Abijah. He had a wife of the daughters of Aaron, and her name was Elizabeth. 6 They were both righteous before God, walking blamelessly in all the commandments and ordinances of the Lord. 7 But they had no child, because Elizabeth was barren, and they both were well advanced in years.

8 Now while he executed the priest's office before God in the order of his division 9 according to the custom of the priest's office, his lot was to enter into the temple of the Lord and burn incense. 10 The whole multitude of the people were praying outside at the hour of incense.

11 An angel of the Lord appeared to him, standing on the right side of the altar of incense. 12 Zacharias was troubled when he saw him, and fear fell upon him. 13 But the angel said to him, "Don't be afraid, Zacharias, because your request has been heard. Your wife, Elizabeth, will bear you a son, and you shall call his name John. 14 You will have joy and gladness, and many will rejoice at his birth. 15 For he will be great in the sight of the Lord, and he will drink no wine nor strong drink. He will be filled with the Holy Spirit, even from his mother's womb. 16 He will turn many of the children of Israel to the Lord their God. 17 He will go before him in the spirit and power of Elijah, 'to turn the hearts of the fathers to the children,'* and the disobedient to the wisdom of the just; to prepare a people prepared for the Lord."

18 Zacharias said to the angel, "How can I be sure of this? For I am an old man, and my wife is well advanced in years."

19 The angel answered him, "I am Gabriel, who stands in the presence of God. I was sent to speak to you and to bring you this good news. 20 Behold,† you will be silent and not able to speak until the day that these things will happen, because you didn't believe my words, which will be fulfilled in their proper time."

21 The people were waiting for Zacharias, and they marveled that he delayed in the temple. 22 When he came out, he could not speak to them. They perceived that he had seen a vision in the temple. He continued making signs to them, and remained mute. 23 When the days of his service were fulfilled, he departed to his house. 24 After these days Elizabeth his wife conceived, and she hid herself five months, saying, 25 "Thus has the Lord done to me in the days in which he looked at me, to take away my reproach among men."

1. Invite the Holy Spirit into this reading, asking the Author of Scripture to speak to you through His Word
2. Read today's passage as many times as you need, take your time

3. Write down (below) what the Lord is saying to you today
4. Live with this Word in your heart through the day

_____

_____

Friday, December 20, 2024

First Reading: Isaiah 7: 10-14

10 Yahweh spoke again to Ahaz, saying, 11 "Ask a sign of Yahweh your God; ask it either in the depth, or in the height above."
12 But Ahaz said, "I won't ask. I won't tempt Yahweh."
13 He said, "Listen now, house of David. Is it not enough for you to try the patience of men, that you will try the patience of my God also? 14 Therefore the Lord himself will give you a sign. Behold, the virgin will conceive, and bear a son, and shall call his name Immanuel.

Responsorial Psalm: Psalms 24: 1-6

1 The earth is Yahweh's, with its fullness;
the world, and those who dwell in it.
2 For he has founded it on the seas,
and established it on the floods.
3 Who may ascend to Yahweh's hill?
Who may stand in his holy place?
4 He who has clean hands and a pure heart;
who has not lifted up his soul to falsehood,
and has not sworn deceitfully.
5 He shall receive a blessing from Yahweh,
righteousness from the God of his salvation.
6 This is the generation of those who seek Him,
who seek your face—even Jacob.

Gospel: Luke 1: 26-38

26 Now in the sixth month, the angel Gabriel was sent from God to a city of Galilee named Nazareth, 27 to a virgin pledged to be married to a man whose name was Joseph, of David's house. The virgin's name was Mary. 28 Having come in, the angel said to her, "Rejoice, you highly favored one! The Lord is with you. Blessed are you among women!"

29 But when she saw him, she was greatly troubled at the saying, and considered what kind of salutation this might be. 30 The angel said to her, "Don't be afraid, Mary, for you have found favor with God. 31 Behold, you will conceive in your womb and give birth to a son, and shall name him 'Jesus.' 32 He will be great and will be called the Son of the Most High. The Lord God will give him the throne of his father David, 33 and he will reign over the house of Jacob forever. There will be no end to his Kingdom."

34 Mary said to the angel, "How can this be, seeing I am a virgin?"

35 The angel answered her, "The Holy Spirit will come on you, and the power of the Most High will overshadow you. Therefore also the holy one who is born from you will be called the Son of God. 36 Behold, Elizabeth your relative also has conceived a son in her old age; and this is the sixth month with her who was called barren. 37 For nothing spoken by God is impossible."‡

38 Mary said, "Behold, the servant of the Lord; let it be done to me according to your word." Then the angel departed from her.

1. Invite the Holy Spirit into this reading, asking the Author of Scripture to speak to you through His Word
2. Read today's passage as many times as you need, take your time
3. Write down (below) what the Lord is saying to you today
4. Live with this Word in your heart through the day

Saturday, December 21, 2024
Saint Peter Canisius, Priest and Doctor of the Church

First Reading: Zephaniah 3: 14-18a

14 Sing, daughter of Zion! Shout, Israel! Be glad and rejoice with all your heart, daughter of Jerusalem. 15 Yahweh has taken away your judgments. He has thrown out your enemy. The King of Israel, Yahweh, is among you. You will not be afraid of evil any more. 16 In that day, it will be said to Jerusalem, "Don't be afraid, Zion. Don't let your hands be weak." 17 Yahweh, your God, is among you, a mighty one who will save. He will rejoice over you with joy. He will calm you in his love. He will rejoice over you with singing. 18a I will remove those who grieve about the appointed feasts from you.

Responsorial Psalm: Psalms 33: 2-3, 11-12, 20-21

2 Give thanks to Yahweh with the lyre.

Sing praises to him with the harp of ten strings.
3 Sing to him a new song.
Play skillfully with a shout of joy!
11 The counsel of Yahweh stands fast forever,
the thoughts of his heart to all generations.
12 Blessed is the nation whose God is Yahweh,
the people whom he has chosen for his own inheritance.
20 Our soul has waited for Yahweh.
He is our help and our shield.
21 For our heart rejoices in him,
because we have trusted in his holy name.

Gospel: Luke 1: 39-45

39 Mary arose in those days and went into the hill country with haste, into a city of Judah, 40 and entered into the house of Zacharias and greeted Elizabeth. 41 When Elizabeth heard Mary's greeting, the baby leaped in her womb; and Elizabeth was filled with the Holy Spirit. 42 She called out with a loud voice and said, "Blessed are you among women, and blessed is the fruit of your womb! 43 Why am I so favored, that the mother of my Lord should come to me? 44 For behold, when the voice of your greeting came into my ears, the baby leaped in my womb for joy! 45 Blessed is she who believed, for there will be a fulfillment of the things which have been spoken to her from the Lord!"

1. Invite the Holy Spirit into this reading, asking the Author of Scripture to speak to you through His Word
2. Read today's passage as many times as you need, take your time
3. Write down (below) what the Lord is saying to you today
4. Live with this Word in your heart through the day

_____

_____

Sunday, December 22, 2024
FOURTH SUNDAY OF ADVENT

First Reading: Micah 5: 1-4a

1 Now you shall gather yourself in troops,
daughter of troops.
He has laid siege against us.

They will strike the judge of Israel with a rod on the cheek.
2 But you, Bethlehem Ephrathah,
being small among the clans of Judah,
out of you one will come out to me who is to be ruler in Israel;
whose goings out are from of old, from ancient times.
3 Therefore he will abandon them until the time that she who is in labor gives birth.
Then the rest of his brothers will return to the children of Israel.
4 He shall stand, and shall shepherd in the strength of Yahweh,
in the majesty of the name of Yahweh his God.
They will live, for then he will be great to the ends of the earth.

Responsorial Psalm: Psalms 80: 2-3, 15-16, 18-19

2 Before Ephraim, Benjamin, and Manasseh, stir up your might!
Come to save us!
3 Turn us again, God.
Cause your face to shine,
and we will be saved.
15 the stock which your right hand planted,
the branch that you made strong for yourself.
16 It's burned with fire.
It's cut down.
They perish at your rebuke.
18 So we will not turn away from you.
Revive us, and we will call on your name.
19 Turn us again, Yahweh God of Armies.
Cause your face to shine, and we will be saved.

Second Reading: Hebrews 10: 5-10

5 Therefore when he comes into the world, he says,
"You didn't desire sacrifice and offering,
but you prepared a body for me.
6 You had no pleasure in whole burnt offerings and sacrifices for sin.
7 Then I said, 'Behold, I have come (in the scroll of the book it is written of me)
to do your will, O God.' "*
8 Previously saying, "Sacrifices and offerings and whole burnt offerings and sacrifices for sin
you didn't desire, neither had pleasure in them" (those which are offered according to the law),
9 then he has said, "Behold, I have come to do your will." He takes away the first, that he may
establish the second, 10 by which will we have been sanctified through the offering of the body
of Jesus Christ once for all.

Gospel: Luke 1: 39-45

39 Mary arose in those days and went into the hill country with haste, into a city of Judah, 40 and entered into the house of Zacharias and greeted Elizabeth. 41 When Elizabeth heard Mary's greeting, the baby leaped in her womb; and Elizabeth was filled with the Holy Spirit. 42 She called out with a loud voice and said, "Blessed are you among women, and blessed is the fruit of your womb! 43 Why am I so favored, that the mother of my Lord should come to me? 44 For behold, when the voice of your greeting came into my ears, the baby leaped in my womb for joy! 45 Blessed is she who believed, for there will be a fulfillment of the things which have been spoken to her from the Lord!"

1. Invite the Holy Spirit into this reading, asking the Author of Scripture to speak to you through His Word
2. Read today's passage as many times as you need, take your time
3. Write down (below) what the Lord is saying to you today
4. Live with this Word in your heart through the day

_____

_____

Monday, December 23, 2024
Saint John of Kanty, Priest

First Reading: Malachi 3: 1-4
1 "Behold, I send my messenger, and he will prepare the way before me! The Lord, whom you seek, will suddenly come to his temple. Behold, the messenger of the covenant, whom you desire, is coming!" says Yahweh of Armies. 2 "But who can endure the day of his coming? And who will stand when he appears? For he is like a refiner's fire, and like launderers' soap; 3 and he will sit as a refiner and purifier of silver, and he will purify the sons of Levi, and refine them as gold and silver; and they shall offer to Yahweh offerings in righteousness. 4 Then the offering of Judah and Jerusalem will be pleasant to Yahweh as in the days of old and as in ancient years.

Responsorial Psalm: Psalms 25: 4-5ab, 8-9, 10 and 14

4 Show me your ways, Yahweh.
Teach me your paths.
5 Guide me in your truth, and teach me,
for you are the God of my salvation.
I wait for you all day long.
8 Good and upright is Yahweh,

therefore he will instruct sinners in the way.

9 He will guide the humble in justice.

He will teach the humble his way.

10 All the paths of Yahweh are loving kindness and truth

to such as keep his covenant and his testimonies.

14 The friendship of Yahweh is with those who fear him.

He will show them his covenant.

Gospel: Luke 1: 57-66

57 Now the time that Elizabeth should give birth was fulfilled, and she gave birth to a son. 58 Her neighbors and her relatives heard that the Lord had magnified his mercy toward her, and they rejoiced with her. 59 On the eighth day, they came to circumcise the child; and they would have called him Zacharias, after the name of his father. 60 His mother answered, "Not so; but he will be called John."

61 They said to her, "There is no one among your relatives who is called by this name." 62 They made signs to his father, what he would have him called.

63 He asked for a writing tablet, and wrote, "His name is John."

They all marveled. 64 His mouth was opened immediately and his tongue freed, and he spoke, blessing God. 65 Fear came on all who lived around them, and all these sayings were talked about throughout all the hill country of Judea. 66 All who heard them laid them up in their heart, saying, "What then will this child be?" The hand of the Lord was with him.

1. Invite the Holy Spirit into this reading, asking the Author of Scripture to speak to you through His Word
2. Read today's passage as many times as you need, take your time
3. Write down (below) what the Lord is saying to you today
4. Live with this Word in your heart through the day

Tuesday, December 24, 2024

First Reading: Second Samuel 7: 1-5, 8b-12, 14a, 16

1 When the king lived in his house, and Yahweh had given him rest from all his enemies all around, 2 the king said to Nathan the prophet, "See now, I dwell in a house of cedar, but God's ark dwells within curtains."

3 Nathan said to the king, "Go, do all that is in your heart, for Yahweh is with you."

4 That same night, Yahweh's word came to Nathan, saying, 5 "Go and tell my servant David, 'Yahweh says, "Should you build me a house for me to dwell in?

8 Now therefore tell my servant David this: 'Yahweh of Armies says, "I took you from the sheep pen, from following the sheep, to be prince over my people, over Israel. 9 I have been with you wherever you went, and have cut off all your enemies from before you. I will make you a great name, like the name of the great ones who are in the earth. 10 I will appoint a place for my people Israel, and will plant them, that they may dwell in their own place and be moved no more. The children of wickedness will not afflict them any more, as at the first, 11 and as from the day that I commanded judges to be over my people Israel. I will cause you to rest from all your enemies. Moreover Yahweh tells you that Yahweh will make you a house. 12 When your days are fulfilled and you sleep with your fathers, I will set up your offspring after you, who will proceed out of your body, and I will establish his kingdom.

14a I will be his father, and he will be my son. 15 but my loving kindness will not depart from him, as I took it from Saul, whom I put away before you. 16 Your house and your kingdom will be made sure forever before you. Your throne will be established forever."'

Responsorial Psalm: Psalms 89: 2-5, 27 and 29

2 I indeed declare, "Love stands firm forever.
You established the heavens.
Your faithfulness is in them."
3 "I have made a covenant with my chosen one,
I have sworn to David, my servant,
4 'I will establish your offspring forever,
and build up your throne to all generations.'"
5 The heavens will praise your wonders, Yahweh,
your faithfulness also in the assembly of the holy ones.
27 I will also appoint him my firstborn,
the highest of the kings of the earth.
29 I will also make his offspring endure forever,
and his throne as the days of heaven.

Gospel: Luke 1: 67-79

67 His father Zacharias was filled with the Holy Spirit, and prophesied, saying,
68 "Blessed be the Lord, the God of Israel,
for he has visited and redeemed his people;
69 and has raised up a horn of salvation for us in the house of his servant David
70 (as he spoke by the mouth of his holy prophets who have been from of old),
71 salvation from our enemies and from the hand of all who hate us;
72 to show mercy toward our fathers,
to remember his holy covenant,
73 the oath which he swore to Abraham our father,

74 to grant to us that we, being delivered out of the hand of our enemies,
should serve him without fear,
75 in holiness and righteousness before him all the days of our life.
76 And you, child, will be called a prophet of the Most High;
for you will go before the face of the Lord to prepare his ways,
77 to give knowledge of salvation to his people by the remission of their sins,
78 because of the tender mercy of our God,
by which the dawn from on high will visit us,
79 to shine on those who sit in darkness and the shadow of death;
to guide our feet into the way of peace."

1. Invite the Holy Spirit into this reading, asking the Author of Scripture to speak to you through His Word
2. Read today's passage as many times as you need, take your time
3. Write down (below) what the Lord is saying to you today
4. Live with this Word in your heart through the day

Wednesday, December 25, 2024
THE NATIVITY OF THE LORD (Christmas)

First Reading: Isaiah 52: 7-10

7 How beautiful on the mountains are the feet of him who brings good news,
who publishes peace,
who brings good news,
who proclaims salvation,
who says to Zion, "Your God reigns!"
8 Your watchmen lift up their voice.
Together they sing;
for they shall see eye to eye when Yahweh returns to Zion.
9 Break out into joy!
Sing together, you waste places of Jerusalem;
for Yahweh has comforted his people.
He has redeemed Jerusalem.
10 Yahweh has made his holy arm bare in the eyes of all the nations.
All the ends of the earth have seen the salvation of our God.

Responsorial Psalm: Psalms 98: 1-6

1 Sing to Yahweh a new song,

for he has done marvelous things!

His right hand and his holy arm have worked salvation for him.

2 Yahweh has made known his salvation.

He has openly shown his righteousness in the sight of the nations.

3 He has remembered his loving kindness and his faithfulness toward the house of Israel.

All the ends of the earth have seen the salvation of our God.

4 Make a joyful noise to Yahweh, all the earth!

Burst out and sing for joy, yes, sing praises!

5 Sing praises to Yahweh with the harp,

with the harp and the voice of melody.

6 With trumpets and sound of the ram's horn,

make a joyful noise before the King, Yahweh.

Second Reading: Hebrews 1: 1-6

1 God, having in the past spoken to the fathers through the prophets at many times and in various ways, 2 has at the end of these days spoken to us by his Son, whom he appointed heir of all things, through whom also he made the worlds. 3 His Son is the radiance of his glory, the very image of his substance, and upholding all things by the word of his power, who, when he had by himself purified us of our sins, sat down on the right hand of the Majesty on high, 4 having become as much better than the angels as the more excellent name he has inherited is better than theirs. 5 For to which of the angels did he say at any time,

"You are my Son.

Today I have become your father?"*

and again,

"I will be to him a Father,

and he will be to me a Son?"*

6 When he again brings in the firstborn into the world he says, "Let all the angels of God worship him."

Gospel: John 1: 1-18

1 In the beginning was the Word, and the Word was with God, and the Word was God. 2 The same was in the beginning with God. 3 All things were made through him. Without him, nothing was made that has been made. 4 In him was life, and the life was the light of men. 5 The light shines in the darkness, and the darkness hasn't overcome† it.

6 There came a man sent from God, whose name was John. 7 The same came as a witness, that he might testify about the light, that all might believe through him. 8 He was not the light, but was sent that he might testify about the light. 9 The true light that enlightens everyone was coming into the world.

10 He was in the world, and the world was made through him, and the world didn't recognize him. 11 He came to his own, and those who were his own didn't receive him. 12 But as many as received him, to them he gave the right to become God's children, to those who believe in his name: 13 who were born, not of blood, nor of the will of the flesh, nor of the will of man, but of God.

14 The Word became flesh and lived among us. We saw his glory, such glory as of the only born‡ Son of the Father, full of grace and truth. 15 John testified about him. He cried out, saying, "This was he of whom I said, 'He who comes after me has surpassed me, for he was before me.' " 16 From his fullness we all received grace upon grace. 17 For the law was given through Moses. Grace and truth were realized through Jesus Christ.§ 18 No one has seen God at any time. The only born† Son,‡ who is in the bosom of the Father, has declared him.

1. Invite the Holy Spirit into this reading, asking the Author of Scripture to speak to you through His Word
2. Read today's passage as many times as you need, take your time
3. Write down (below) what the Lord is saying to you today
4. Live with this Word in your heart through the day

_____

_____

Thursday, December 26, 2024
Saint Stephen, The First Martyr

First Reading: Acts 6: 8-10; 7: 54-59

8 Stephen, full of faith and power, performed great wonders and signs among the people. 9 But some of those who were of the synagogue called "The Libertines", and of the Cyrenians, of the Alexandrians, and of those of Cilicia and Asia arose, disputing with Stephen. 10 They weren't able to withstand the wisdom and the Spirit by which he spoke.

54 Now when they heard these things, they were cut to the heart, and they gnashed at him with their teeth. 55 But he, being full of the Holy Spirit, looked up steadfastly into heaven and saw the glory of God, and Jesus standing on the right hand of God, 56 and said, "Behold, I see the heavens opened and the Son of Man standing at the right hand of God!"

57 But they cried out with a loud voice and stopped their ears, then rushed at him with one accord. 58 They threw him out of the city and stoned him. The witnesses placed their garments at the feet of a young man named Saul. 59 They stoned Stephen as he called out, saying, "Lord Jesus, receive my spirit!"

Responsorial Psalm: Psalms 31: 3cd-4, 6 and 8ab, 16bc and 17

3 For you are my rock and my fortress,
therefore for your name's sake lead me and guide me.
4 Pluck me out of the net that they have laid secretly for me,
for you are my stronghold.
6 I hate those who regard lying vanities,
but I trust in Yahweh.
8 You have not shut me up into the hand of the enemy.
You have set my feet in a large place.
16 Make your face to shine on your servant.
Save me in your loving kindness.
17 Let me not be disappointed, Yahweh, for I have called on you.
Let the wicked be disappointed.

Gospel: Matthew 10: 17-22

17 But beware of men, for they will deliver you up to councils, and in their synagogues they will scourge you. 18 Yes, and you will be brought before governors and kings for my sake, for a testimony to them and to the nations. 19 But when they deliver you up, don't be anxious how or what you will say, for it will be given you in that hour what you will say. 20 For it is not you who speak, but the Spirit of your Father who speaks in you.
21 "Brother will deliver up brother to death, and the father his child. Children will rise up against parents and cause them to be put to death. 22 You will be hated by all men for my name's sake, but he who endures to the end will be saved.

1. Invite the Holy Spirit into this reading, asking the Author of Scripture to speak to you through His Word
2. Read today's passage as many times as you need, take your time
3. Write down (below) what the Lord is saying to you today
4. Live with this Word in your heart through the day

_____

_____

Friday, December 27, 2024
Saint John, Apostle and Evangelist

First Reading: First John 1: 1-4

1 That which was from the beginning, that which we have heard, that which we have seen with our eyes, that which we saw, and our hands touched, concerning the Word of life 2 (and the life was revealed, and we have seen, and testify, and declare to you the life, the eternal life, which was with the Father, and was revealed to us); 3 that which we have seen and heard we declare to you, that you also may have fellowship with us. Yes, and our fellowship is with the Father and with his Son, Jesus Christ.† 4 And we write these things to you, that our joy may be fulfilled.

Responsorial Psalm: Psalms 97: 1-2, 5-6, 11-12

1 Yahweh reigns!
Let the earth rejoice!
Let the multitude of islands be glad!
2 Clouds and darkness are around him.
Righteousness and justice are the foundation of his throne.
5 The mountains melt like wax at the presence of Yahweh,
at the presence of the Lord of the whole earth.
6 The heavens declare his righteousness.
All the peoples have seen his glory.
11 Light is sown for the righteous,
and gladness for the upright in heart.
12 Be glad in Yahweh, you righteous people!
Give thanks to his holy Name.

Gospel: John 20: 1a and 2-8

1 Now on the first day of the week, Mary Magdalene went early, while it was still dark, to the tomb, and saw that the stone had been taken away from the tomb. 2 Therefore she ran and came to Simon Peter and to the other disciple whom Jesus loved, and said to them, "They have taken away the Lord out of the tomb, and we don't know where they have laid him!"
3 Therefore Peter and the other disciple went out, and they went toward the tomb. 4 They both ran together. The other disciple outran Peter and came to the tomb first. 5 Stooping and looking in, he saw the linen cloths lying there; yet he didn't enter in. 6 Then Simon Peter came, following him, and entered into the tomb. He saw the linen cloths lying, 7 and the cloth that had been on his head, not lying with the linen cloths, but rolled up in a place by itself. 8 So then the other disciple who came first to the tomb also entered in, and he saw and believed.

1. Invite the Holy Spirit into this reading, asking the Author of Scripture to speak to you through His Word
2. Read today's passage as many times as you need, take your time
3. Write down (below) what the Lord is saying to you today
4. Live with this Word in your heart through the day

Saturday, December 28, 2024
The Holy Innocents, Martyrs

First Reading: First John 1: 5 – 2: 2

5 This is the message which we have heard from him and announce to you, that God is light, and in him is no darkness at all. 6 If we say that we have fellowship with him and walk in the darkness, we lie and don't tell the truth. 7 But if we walk in the light as he is in the light, we have fellowship with one another, and the blood of Jesus Christ his Son, cleanses us from all sin. 8 If we say that we have no sin, we deceive ourselves, and the truth is not in us. 9 If we confess our sins, he is faithful and righteous to forgive us the sins and to cleanse us from all unrighteousness. 10 If we say that we haven't sinned, we make him a liar, and his word is not in us.
1 My little children, I write these things to you so that you may not sin. If anyone sins, we have a Counselor† with the Father, Jesus Christ, the righteous. 2 And he is the atoning sacrifice‡ for our sins, and not for ours only, but also for the whole world.

Responsorial Psalm: Psalms 124: 2-5, 7b-8

2 if it had not been Yahweh who was on our side,
when men rose up against us,
3 then they would have swallowed us up alive,
when their wrath was kindled against us,
4 then the waters would have overwhelmed us,
the stream would have gone over our soul.
5 Then the proud waters would have gone over our soul.
7b The snare is broken, and we have escaped.
8 Our help is in Yahweh's name,
who made heaven and earth.

Gospel: Matthew 2: 13-18

13 Now when they had departed, behold, an angel of the Lord appeared to Joseph in a dream, saying, "Arise and take the young child and his mother, and flee into Egypt, and stay there until I tell you, for Herod will seek the young child to destroy him."

14 He arose and took the young child and his mother by night and departed into Egypt, 15 and was there until the death of Herod, that it might be fulfilled which was spoken by the Lord through the prophet, saying, "Out of Egypt I called my son."*

16 Then Herod, when he saw that he was mocked by the wise men, was exceedingly angry, and sent out and killed all the male children who were in Bethlehem and in all the surrounding countryside, from two years old and under, according to the exact time which he had learned from the wise men. 17 Then that which was spoken by Jeremiah the prophet was fulfilled, saying,

18 "A voice was heard in Ramah,

lamentation, weeping and great mourning,

Rachel weeping for her children;

she wouldn't be comforted,

because they are no more."

1. Invite the Holy Spirit into this reading, asking the Author of Scripture to speak to you through His Word
2. Read today's passage as many times as you need, take your time
3. Write down (below) what the Lord is saying to you today
4. Live with this Word in your heart through the day

Sunday, December 29, 2024
THE HOLY FAMILY OF JESUS, MARY AND JOSEPH

First Reading: First Samuel 1: 20-22, 24-28

20 When the time had come, Hannah conceived, and bore a son; and she named him Samuel,§ saying, "Because I have asked him of Yahweh."

21 The man Elkanah, and all his house, went up to offer to Yahweh the yearly sacrifice and his vow. 22 But Hannah didn't go up, for she said to her husband, "Not until the child is weaned; then I will bring him, that he may appear before Yahweh, and stay there forever."

24 When she had weaned him, she took him up with her, with three bulls, and one ephah† of meal, and a container of wine, and brought him to Yahweh's house in Shiloh. The child was young. 25 They killed the bull, and brought the child to Eli. 26 She said, "Oh, my lord, as your soul lives, my lord, I am the woman who stood by you here, praying to Yahweh. 27 I prayed for this child, and Yahweh has given me my petition which I asked of him. 28 Therefore I have also given him to Yahweh. As long as he lives he is given to Yahweh." He worshiped Yahweh there.

Responsorial Psalm: Psalms 84: 2-3, 5-6, 9-10

2 My soul longs, and even faints for the courts of Yahweh.
My heart and my flesh cry out for the living God.
3 Yes, the sparrow has found a home,
and the swallow a nest for herself, where she may have her young,
near your altars, Yahweh of Armies, my King, and my God.
5 Blessed are those whose strength is in you,
who have set their hearts on a pilgrimage.
6 Passing through the valley of Weeping, they make it a place of springs.
Yes, the autumn rain covers it with blessings.
9 Behold, God our shield,
look at the face of your anointed.
10 For a day in your courts is better than a thousand.
I would rather be a doorkeeper in the house of my God,
than to dwell in the tents of wickedness.

Second Reading: First John 3: 1-2, 21-24

1 See how great a love the Father has given to us, that we should be called children of God! For this cause the world doesn't know us, because it didn't know him. 2 Beloved, now we are children of God. It is not yet revealed what we will be; but we know that when he is revealed, we will be like him, for we will see him just as he is.
21 Beloved, if our hearts don't condemn us, we have boldness toward God; 22 so whatever we ask, we receive from him, because we keep his commandments and do the things that are pleasing in his sight. 23 This is his commandment, that we should believe in the name of his Son, Jesus Christ, and love one another, even as he commanded. 24 He who keeps his commandments remains in him, and he in him. By this we know that he remains in us, by the Spirit which he gave us.

Gospel: Luke 2: 41-52

41 His parents went every year to Jerusalem at the feast of the Passover. 42 When he was twelve years old, they went up to Jerusalem according to the custom of the feast; 43 and when they had fulfilled the days, as they were returning, the boy Jesus stayed behind in Jerusalem. Joseph and his mother didn't know it, 44 but supposing him to be in the company, they went a day's journey; and they looked for him among their relatives and acquaintances. 45 When they didn't find him, they returned to Jerusalem, looking for him. 46 After three days they found him in the temple, sitting in the middle of the teachers, both listening to them and asking them questions. 47 All who heard him were amazed at his understanding and his answers. 48 When they saw him, they were astonished; and his mother said to him, "Son, why have you treated us this way? Behold, your father and I were anxiously looking for you."

49 He said to them, "Why were you looking for me? Didn't you know that I must be in my Father's house?" 50 They didn't understand the saying which he spoke to them. 51 And he went down with them and came to Nazareth. He was subject to them, and his mother kept all these sayings in her heart. 52 And Jesus increased in wisdom and stature, and in favor with God and men.

1. Invite the Holy Spirit into this reading, asking the Author of Scripture to speak to you through His Word
2. Read today's passage as many times as you need, take your time
3. Write down (below) what the Lord is saying to you today
4. Live with this Word in your heart through the day

Monday, December 30, 2024
Sixth Day within the Octave of the Nativity of the Lord

First Reading: First John 2: 12-17

12 I write to you, little children, because your sins are forgiven you for his name's sake.
13 I write to you, fathers, because you know him who is from the beginning.
I write to you, young men, because you have overcome the evil one.
I write to you, little children, because you know the Father.
14 I have written to you, fathers, because you know him who is from the beginning.
I have written to you, young men, because you are strong, and the word of God remains in you, and you have overcome the evil one.
15 Don't love the world or the things that are in the world. If anyone loves the world, the Father's love isn't in him. 16 For all that is in the world—the lust of the flesh, the lust of the eyes, and the pride of life—isn't the Father's, but is the world's. 17 The world is passing away with its lusts, but he who does God's will remains forever.

Responsorial Psalm: Psalms 96: 7-10

7 Ascribe to Yahweh, you families of nations,
ascribe to Yahweh glory and strength.
8 Ascribe to Yahweh the glory due to his name.
Bring an offering, and come into his courts.
9 Worship Yahweh in holy array.
Tremble before him, all the earth.
10 Say among the nations, "Yahweh reigns."

The world is also established.
It can't be moved.
He will judge the peoples with equity.

Gospel: Luke 2: 36-40

36 There was one Anna, a prophetess, the daughter of Phanuel, of the tribe of Asher (she was of a great age, having lived with a husband seven years from her virginity, 37 and she had been a widow for about eighty-four years), who didn't depart from the temple, worshiping with fastings and petitions night and day. 38 Coming up at that very hour, she gave thanks to the Lord, and spoke of him to all those who were looking for redemption in Jerusalem.
39 When they had accomplished all things that were according to the law of the Lord, they returned into Galilee, to their own city, Nazareth. 40 The child was growing, and was becoming strong in spirit, being filled with wisdom, and the grace of God was upon him.

1. Invite the Holy Spirit into this reading, asking the Author of Scripture to speak to you through His Word
2. Read today's passage as many times as you need, take your time
3. Write down (below) what the Lord is saying to you today
4. Live with this Word in your heart through the day

_____

_____

Tuesday, December 31, 2024
Seventh Day within the Octave of the Nativity of the Lord
Saint Sylvester I, Pope

First Reading: First John 2: 18-21

18 Little children, these are the end times, and as you heard that the Antichrist is coming, even now many antichrists have arisen. By this we know that it is the final hour. 19 They went out from us, but they didn't belong to us; for if they had belonged to us, they would have continued with us. But they left, that they might be revealed that none of them belong to us. 20 You have an anointing from the Holy One, and you all have knowledge.§ 21 I have not written to you because you don't know the truth, but because you know it, and because no lie is of the truth.

Responsorial Psalm: Psalms 96: 1-2, 11-13

1 Sing to Yahweh a new song!
Sing to Yahweh, all the earth.
2 Sing to Yahweh!
Bless his name!
Proclaim his salvation from day to day!
11 Let the heavens be glad, and let the earth rejoice.
Let the sea roar, and its fullness!
12 Let the field and all that is in it exult!
Then all the trees of the woods shall sing for joy
13 before Yahweh; for he comes,
for he comes to judge the earth.
He will judge the world with righteousness,
the peoples with his truth.

Gospel: John 1: 1-18

1 In the beginning was the Word, and the Word was with God, and the Word was God. 2 The same was in the beginning with God. 3 All things were made through him. Without him, nothing was made that has been made. 4 In him was life, and the life was the light of men. 5 The light shines in the darkness, and the darkness hasn't overcome† it.
6 There came a man sent from God, whose name was John. 7 The same came as a witness, that he might testify about the light, that all might believe through him. 8 He was not the light, but was sent that he might testify about the light. 9 The true light that enlightens everyone was coming into the world.
10 He was in the world, and the world was made through him, and the world didn't recognize him. 11 He came to his own, and those who were his own didn't receive him. 12 But as many as received him, to them he gave the right to become God's children, to those who believe in his name: 13 who were born, not of blood, nor of the will of the flesh, nor of the will of man, but of God.
14 The Word became flesh and lived among us. We saw his glory, such glory as of the only born‡ Son of the Father, full of grace and truth. 15 John testified about him. He cried out, saying, "This was he of whom I said, 'He who comes after me has surpassed me, for he was before me.' " 16 From his fullness we all received grace upon grace. 17 For the law was given through Moses. Grace and truth were realized through Jesus Christ.§ 18 No one has seen God at any time. The only born† Son,‡ who is in the bosom of the Father, has declared him.

1. Invite the Holy Spirit into this reading, asking the Author of Scripture to speak to you through His Word
2. Read today's passage as many times as you need, take your time
3. Write down (below) what the Lord is saying to you today
4. Live with this Word in your heart through the day

_____

_____

Made in the USA
Middletown, DE
11 December 2023

45278929R00329